Doing the Ethnography of Schooling

Educational Anthropology in Action

Doing the Ethnography of Schooling

Educational Anthropology
in Action

edited by George Spindler
Stanford University

WAVELAND
PRESS, INC.
Prospect Heights, Illinois

For information about this book, write or call:

Waveland Press, Inc.
P.O. Box 400
Prospect Heights, Illinois 60070
(312) 634-0081

This book is dedicated to
Professor Robert Nelson Bush,
Stanford School of Education.
A man ahead of his time.

Contributors

Paul Epstein
Frederick Erickson
Christine Robinson Finnan
Frederick Gearing
Judith Lynne Hanna
Sylvia Hart
Shirley Brice Heath
Gerald Mohatt
Alan Peshkin
Susan Urmston Philips
Walter Precourt
George Spindler
Louise Spindler
Hervé Varenne
Richard L. Warren
Kathleen Wilcox
Harry F. Wolcott

Preface

This book is about schooling in the United States of America. It is about schooling from the particular point of view of ethnography. It tries to show how ethnography, as the field arm of anthropology, can give fresh insights into perplexing educational problems. In this sense it is a book for educators. But it is also a book for anthropologists, for it shows how what anthropologists know and what they can do can be useful to our own society and to other complex modern societies. And it contributes new theory, new models for research, and new research techniques to anthropology, as well as to the other social sciences.

We intend, therefore, that this book shall be read and used by a wide and varied audience. Educators and anthropologists clearly have a vested interest in its content and procedures of discovery. It should be of interest to sociologists and psychologists, for they, too, are much concerned with both educational processes and strategies for research on them. Sociologists, particularly, have their own useful models for ethnographic as well as correlational research. Nevertheless, they should find some challenging ideas and research strategies in this book, for their research models and conceptual frameworks are quite different. Psychologists also have some models for ethnographic types of research, though these models have not achieved even remotely equal status with their traditional experimental and correlational approaches. In fact, psychological research designs have been so constrained by these traditional models that important contextual and qualitative factors have been overlooked. Therefore, psychologists, too, should find some challenges in this book.

The research procedures demonstrated in this collection do not replace correlational and experimental designs. There is no either/or proposition in ethnographic strategies, though a few commentators have implied that there is. Ethnographic research can accomplish certain ends better than other methods, and vice versa. Ethnography should concentrate on the study of patterns—repetitive patterns of behavior and patterns in cultural knowledge. These patterns should be elicited from informants from the vantage point of long-term intimacy with the field site and the people being studied. When it is pursued in this way, ethnography can produce valid results. It extends knowledge of human behavior in depth, wherever it is properly used. Sometimes it shows the way to a more quantitative correlational or even experimental research design that can test hypotheses formulated and honed by an in-depth ethnographic probe. Ethnography can then be merged with other research strategies.

The work described in this book is not only methodological but substantive. Each chapter is data-based and produces important insights. Some analyses are, inevitably, more productive than others, but each one makes a contribution to the understanding of educational process. The authors deal with the resistance to change shown by educational institutions, problems in the diffusion of understandings derived from ethnographic studies into education, and the nature of the role of the ethnographer in the school and in evaluation. They reveal deep cultural differences in patterns of social interaction, perception, and style in such areas as kinds of questioning in classrooms and kinds of answers expected—differences that interfere grossly with teaching and learning. They describe the stability and functions of social cliques and social strata in the school, socialization in the schools for working-class roles versus managerial and professional work roles, the consequences of desegregation, the ingredients for success in bicultural programs, the nature of spontaneous play groups in the school environment, learning to read and not learning to read, and school and community history.

A reader who approaches this book with an open mind will find many fresh and significant insights into these processes and will be informed about a wide range of ethnographic techniques, as well as their common features. The reader will also, no doubt, find enough to criticize. The anthropological ethnography of schooling is in its formative stages, and some of its attempts exhibit greater precision and coherence than others. But even the less precise and less coherent attempts to study the processes of schooling point to new directions for further development.

G.S.

Preface, 1988

Since 1982, when DEOS (as students and colleagues refer to this volume) was first published, Louise Spindler and I have taught our seminar in ethnographic methods for the study of schooling four times at the University of Wisconsin at Madison, six times at Stanford, and once at the University of California at Santa Barbara. We have also published two more volumes (1987) on the subject and there has been no slackening of the pace of publication of related works on the part of others.

And yet, DEOS stands as an important contribution to the continuing development of the ethnography of education. The foundations of an ethnographic approach to the study of education are clear. The products of this approach represented by each chapter have lost none of their significance. And the book raises questions about ethnography, and about education, that will stand as markers of an enlarging view of educational process for a long time.

This would all sound like self-congratulatory chest-pounding by an egotistical author were it not for the fact that DEOS is mainly written by 15 people whose names are not Spindler. These fifteen colleagues are all pioneers whose research and interpretations have stood the test of time. Their chapters are much more than simply examples of "doing ethnography." They are original explorations of significant educational processes from a sociocultural point of view. The volume contributes to the sociocultural foundations of education and to the anthropology of education. Since the chapters were all written for the volume, they are available nowhere else. Together they constitute an indispensable assemblage of analyses of process and issues in education as well as a consistently high-level demonstration of the utility of ethnography in the study of these processes.

This volume should continue to find wide acceptance as a text for qualitative methods courses and as a reference for a wide variety of sociocultural foundations courses in education.

G.S.

References

Spindler, George, ed. 1987. *Education and Cultural Process: Anthropological Approaches, Second Edition.* Prospect Heights, IL: Waveland Press, Inc.

Spindler, George and Louise, eds. 1987. *Interpretive Ethnography of Education at Home and Abroad.* Hillsdale, NJ: Lawrence Erlbaum Associates, Inc.

Acknowledgments

No collected volume of original papers by a group of colleagues is easily born. This book, however, made its way from conception to parturition without major difficulties. The people who wrote the chapters are responsible for this relative ease. Without exception they were patient, enduring, open to criticism, and undemanding. Perhaps it was because they are all anthropologists. (This explanation seems unlikely, though it is an entertaining one.) As an editor I can only say that we were lucky. My first acknowledgment, therefore, goes to them.

One is always indebted to one's students in any publication venture. As editor and as a contributor to this volume I am deeply indebted to mine, particularly those in my advanced education course, "Cultural Transmission." I also recently offered this course, now finishing its third decade at Stanford, at the University of Wisconsin, Madison, in the Department of Educational Policy Studies. Students at both Stanford and Wisconsin have raised questions, challenged positions, and contributed ideas, as well as substantive materials, in discussions and papers. I am particularly indebted as well to the students, nearly all of them in the dissertation phase, who took Louise Spindler's and my experimental training seminar in ethnographic methodology at Wisconsin and at Stanford. We shared with them an exhilarating experience and came to feel that there is more to ethnography than any of us know about yet.

I am grateful to many of my colleagues at Stanford and elsewhere for their support and encouragement when the idea for this book was discussed with them. They are too numerous to mention but will recognize themselves in my expression of gratitude to them. I must, however, name Ray McDermott, whose suggestions were particularly influential, and Pertti Pelto, whose critical reading of the manuscript was very useful.

I would be remiss if I did not acknowledge the direct help and influence of Louise Spindler, my wife and collaborator. She read all the papers in their various drafts and made many suggestions to me, most of which were transmitted in some form to the authors, to their benefit and to the benefit of the book. We have also discussed together in depth the overall strategy of the volume, both in its intellectual orientation and in its specific format.

We are all deeply indebted to the Institute for Research on Educational Finance and Governance, School of Education, Stanford University. Professor Henry Levin of the Institute secured support for an extensive review of the literature in the ethnography of education (Chapter 15) and lent his office staff for the distribution of memos, correspondence, and significant manuscript typing for the book. We are also deeply indebted to Dorothy Ester Madden and Sharon Carter for their consistent and extensive help in manuscript preparation. One is always indebted to one's publisher, and in this instance particularly to David P. Boynton, anthropology as well as education editor at Holt, Rinehart and Winston, who has been consistently encouraging, helpful, and critical, and to Pamela Forcey, special projects editor, whose work substantially improved this book.

G.S.

Contents

George Spindler

GENERAL INTRODUCTION

Anything anyone wants to do that has no clear problem, no methodology, and no theory is likely to be called "ethnography" around here.
    —A state department of education official

This book has two purposes. The first is to define and describe a field of inquiry—educational ethnography—that has had a meteoric rise in the past decade, particularly during the past few years. The second purpose is to clarify the potential of this field for contributing to the solution of vexing educational problems and generally to the development of anthropological theory and method that relate to education.

Educational ethnography draws practitioners from sociology, psychology, and anthropology. It also attracts many who do ethnography but have no major professional disciplinary affiliation in the social sciences. In fact, "ethnography" has become virtually a household word in professional education, and it is the rare research project today that does not have somewhere in the table of operations at least one ethnographer and somewhere in the research design some ethnographic procedures. To those of us who have long struggled to persuade educators that ethnographic studies would help illuminate the educational process and fellow scientists that they should undertake ethnographic studies of this process, the sudden wave of popularity is exhilarating. It is also alarming. Inevitably, any movement that rapidly acquires many followers has some of the qualities of a fad, and this is true of ed-

1

ucational ethnography. It is not surprising that some work called "ethnography" is marked by obscurity of purpose, lax relationships between concepts and observation, indifferent or absent conceptual structure and theory, weak implementation of research method, confusion about whether there should be hypotheses and, if so, how they should be tested, confusion about whether quantitative methods can be relevant, unrealistic expectations about the virtues of "ethnographic" evaluation, and so forth. Order must be brought into the effort to make use of ethnography in and about educational institutions.

This book does not attempt either to review or to represent all the types of "ethnographic studies" or ethnographically inspired interpretations of educational phenomena that now exist. Rather, the book focuses on the anthropological ethnography of schooling.[1] It explores anthropological ethnography as applied to the study of educational process and searches for unifying features in these applications. We, the contributors to this volume, do not claim that ethnography can only be done by anthropologists, nor even that it is always done best by anthropologists. Nor do we perceive disciplinary boundaries as of great significance. However, we do claim historical priority, because the use of ethnography as a recognized part of the research procedures of contemporary social science began when the first anthropologists left their armchairs and went to the field around the turn of the century.

Ethnography is the field arm of anthropology. An anthropologist without ethnographic field experience is like a surgeon without experience in surgery or a clinical psychologist without experience in clinics. Therefore when anthropologists first turned serious attention to schooling in our own society, they quite naturally did so in the ethnographic style. Anthropologists Solon Kimball, Jules Henry, George Spindler, and a few others were already doing the ethnography of schooling in the late 1940s and early 1950s. Many other anthropologists have entered the field since then.

Thus we anthropologists do have a certain proprietary interest in ethnography. But we certainly do not mean to imply that professionally trained people from disciplines other than anthropology

---

[1] The terms "ethnography of schooling" and "educational ethnography" mean nearly the same thing but are not exactly synonymous. At least in my usage, "educational ethnography" refers to the study of any or all educational processes, whether related to a "school" or not. "Ethnography of schooling" is therefore a little narrower in that it refers to educational and enculturative processes that are related to schools and intentional schooling, though this concept leaves room for studies of playgrounds, play groups, peer groups, patterns of violence in schools, and other aspects of school-related life.

should deny themselves the benefits of doing ethnography. In fact, many of us feel that ethnographic training can be very valuable for nonanthropologists and for people who do not expect to be professional researchers but who are directly involved in education. For guidance counselors, curriculum developers, administrators, and classroom teachers, ethnography can provide a sensitizing experience of great significance; under certain conditions these professional people should "do ethnography." More will be said about this in the Concluding Remarks.

Nevertheless, because we anthropologists do have a proprietary interest in ethnography and because of our prior claims to its use, we should clarify what it is we are about — what methods of study we use and for what purposes. This book attempts to do this.

This clarification of the central features of an anthropological ethnography[2] of schooling will interest both educators and anthropologists. Educators, particularly, are concerned because the tried-and-true methodologies and research designs used most widely in educational research have failed to answer pressing questions. These experimental and correlational approaches that isolate variables from context and overlook the all-important dimensions of meaning in human behavior have been overworked. As Lee Cronbach said in his Distinguished Scientific Contribution Award address to the American Psychological Association in 1974:

> The experimental strategy dominant in psychology since 1950 has only limited ability to detect interactions. . . . [And further] The two scientific disciplines, experimental control and systematic correlation, answer formal questions stated in advance. Intensive local observation goes beyond discipline to an open-eyed, open-minded appreciation of the surprises nature deposits in the investigative net. . . . [And in conclusion] Social scientists are rightly proud of the discipline we draw from the natural science side of our ancestry. Scientific discipline is what we uniquely add to the time-honored ways of studying men. Too narrow an identification with science, however, has fixed our eyes upon an inappropriate goal. The goal of our work, I have argued here, is not to amass generalizations atop which a theoretical tower can someday be erected (cf. Criven, 1959b, p. 471).* The special task of the social

___

[2] Henceforth we will refer to anthropological ethnography as *anthroethnography* and to our sibling field disciplines as *socioethnography* and *psychoethnography*. It is also proper to refer to the collection of data in the field through observation and interviews as *ethnography* and to its interpretation as *ethnology*, as Dell Hymes suggests in his Presidential address to the Council on Anthropology and Education (*Anthropology and Education Quarterly*, 1980, 11:3-8).

* M. Criven, "Truisms as the Grounds for Historical Explanations," in P. L. Gardiner, ed., *Theories of History* (Glencoe, Ill.: Free Press, 1959).

scientist in each generation is to pin down the contemporary facts. Beyond that, he shares with the humanistic scholar and the artist in the effort to gain insight into contemporary relationships and to realign the culture's view of man with present realities. To know man as he is is no mean aspiration.[3]

Ethnography can shed new light on old problems and ask new questions that will make some of the old problems obsolete. Ethnography cannot do this, however, if it is prematurely killed by the hostility inevitably directed at such more qualitative and more descriptive research methods — methods most professional educators and social scientists have been taught to believe are not acceptable. But ethnography must not invite justifiable hostility. Its real potential as a source of new knowledge and understanding for educators will not be realized if its practitioners tolerate ambiguous, loose, and conceptually and methodologically inadequate research. Such inferior research is more likely in the absence of specific criteria for excellence. This book does not give the final word on what ethnography is or what it can and cannot do. It does furnish models for excellence and explicitly defines criteria for the appropriate use of ethnography in the study of education.

This book must also serve the interests of anthropologists. Our discipline emerged as a by-product of a colonialized world where exotic "have-nots" were studied by scholars from the "haves." That we fostered receptivity for cultural differences and argued for cultural self-determination, encouraged respect for the integrity of other cultures, and worked against ethnocide is not to be denied. And our contributions to the development of social, cultural, and psychological theory and research methodology are significant. Nor do I, for one, see the anthropologists of this earlier period as simply servants of the colonial enterprise. After all, anthropologists have always tended to see things from the bottom up rather than from the top down. But the fact remains that we collected knowledge, facts, and insights from politically powerless peoples largely outside the benefit structure of modern economic and political systems. In doing so we gained a better understanding of the world and we built a discipline.

Now it is time to apply the tools and insights of this discipline to problems that plague people everywhere, particularly people in our own complex, conflict-ridden, multicultural, dynamic society. We must study the poor *and* the rich, the mainstreamers as well as the minorities, and their interaction. (We have done better on

---

[3] Lee J. Cronbach, "Beyond the Two Disciplines of Scientific Psychology," *American Psychologist,* 1975, 30(2):116–127.

the poor and the minorities than on the rich and the mainstreamers, so far.)

We can turn our attention and energy to questions such as these: Why do bright children distinguished from the mainstream by ethnicity and/or social class not learn to read? How does socialization for the mainstream take place in the schools? Why do desegregated schools often become storm centers for violence and the disruption of schooling? Why do primeval forms of instruction, subject matter, and classroom management persist despite repeated attempts at reform? Why don't bicultural education programs work (when they don't)? How do schools perpetuate and reinforce unequal distribution of access, success, and reward in our society? Not merely *why* but *how* do failures in communication occur between teachers and students when there is either a social class or ethnic difference between the two?

These are problems of crucial significance that anthroethnographers can sink their teeth into. In so doing they can help implement the democratic ideals that are held to be paramount in our society and simultaneously feed back into their own discipline the energy and decisiveness that are generated when complex, compelling, significant, and relevant phenomena are studied. The chapters in this book center on problems such as those just stated. You will recognize them as you read it.

Questions of the kind already mentioned can always be asked at two levels. The first is the level at which we have just been operating—the level of public concern, the level of questions and problems of significance to the well-being of a society or group within it. But there is another level that more immediately guides our research. We must translate our ethical concerns, our frustration at failure to reform, our anger over injustice, into disciplined questions and ways to pursue them. What is sociocultural knowledge?[4] How does it make it possible for people to interact sensibly and productively or, conversely, insensibly and nonproductively? What is the difference between general sociocultural knowledge and situationally specific knowledge, and how does each influence

[4] By "sociocultural knowledge" we mean the knowledge participants (students, teachers, principals, mothers, fathers, friends, et al.) use to guide their behavior in the various social settings they participate in. Such knowledge is complex and subtle; it includes specific knowledge of social roles and rules and generalized, usually only dimly conscious, knowledge of categories and management skills that makes it possible, for instance, to detect shifts in conversational contexts. "Cultural knowledge" is often used rather than "sociocultural," but I wish to call attention to the inclusiveness of this knowledge held by participants in social interactions. More will be said about such knowledge as we go on.

behavior? How are the different kinds of sociocultural knowledge generated and acquired? Are symbols and behavior coterminous? How is social organization created, and how does it constrain behavior? How do differing perceptions of the realities of life in the classroom develop, and how do they act as barriers to effective teaching/learning? How do models drawn from descriptive linguistics help to explain "hidden curricula" and implicit cultural knowledge that may defeat the intention of schooling? How far does the context of a social event have to be explored to make the event understandable? These and similar questions will be encountered in various forms in the chapters of this book.

The Criteria for a Good Ethnography of Schooling

We have not defined the criteria by which you will recognize anthroethnography as you read this book. This volume is in itself a definition of anthroethnography, though not a final or complete one. Its contents exhibit the qualities of good anthroethnography, though not in equal degree and never perfectly. However, all of the researches reported in this book hold some of these attributes in common. Though their full meaning can only be grasped by reading the articles reporting the researches, stating them succinctly now will help orient us to what will be encountered in the rest of the book. These criteria may be taken together as an operational definition of anthroethnography as applied to the study of education.

- Observations are contextualized. The significance of events is seen in the framework of relationships of the immediate setting being studied but is pursued, as necessary, into contexts beyond.
- Hypotheses and questions for study emerge as the study proceeds in the setting selected for observation. Judgment on what is significant to study is deferred until the orienting phase of the field study has been completed.
- Observation is prolonged and repetitive. Chains of events are observed more than once.
- The native (any participant in a social setting) view of reality is brought out by inferences from observation and by various forms of ethnographic inquiry: interviews, other eliciting procedures (including some instruments), even, at times and only cautiously, questionnaires.

- Sociocultural knowledge held by social participants makes social behavior and communication sensible to oneself and to others. Therefore a major part of the ethnographic task is to understand what sociocultural knowledge participants bring to and generate in the social setting being studied.
- Instruments, codes, schedules, questionnaires, agenda for interviews, and so forth, are generated in the field as a result of observation and ethnographic inquiry.
- A transcultural perspective is present, though frequently as an unstated assumption. That is, cultural variation over time and space is considered as a natural human condition. All cultures are adaptations to the exigencies of life and exhibit common as well as distinguishing features.
- Some of the sociocultural knowledge affecting behavior and communication in any particular setting being studied is implicit or tacit, not known to some participants and known only ambiguously to others. A significant task of ethnography is therefore to make explicit what is implicit and tacit to informants and participants in the social settings being studied.
- Inquiry and observation must disturb as little as possible the process of interaction and communication in the setting being studied.
- Since the informant (any person being interviewed) is the one who has the emic,[5] native cultural knowledge (in varying degrees of self-conscious articulation), the ethnographic interviewer must not predetermine responses by the kinds of questions asked. The conversational management of the interview or eliciting interaction must be so carried out as to promote the unfolding of emic cultural knowledge in its most heuristic, "natural" form.
- Any form of technical device that will enable the ethnographer to collect more live data—immediate, natural, detailed behavior—will be used, such as cameras, audiotapes, and videotapes.

There is no single one of these attributes of anthropological ethnography that is equally or uniformly represented in all the reports of research in this book. Nor is there any single attribute that is represented in only one report. All of the attributes are represented in some degree in most of the reports, and each of them is expressed in full form in several.

---

[5] By "emic" is meant the view from within the culture, the folk view, in terms of native categories.

Limitations and Capabilities

These attributes are not those of a loose, ambiguous, undisciplined research field. They call for a discipline that is as demanding as that required by any experimental design or correlational research strategy. Yet ethnographic inquiry by its nature focuses on single cases or at most on a limited setting of action. Thus there are searching questions about using ethnographic data for scientific generalization, as well as for policy formation and decision-making. There are answers, of course. For example, ethnographers feel that an in-depth study that gives accurate knowledge of one setting not markedly dissimilar from other relevant settings is likely to be generalizable in substantial degree to these other settings. Ethnographers also usually feel that it is better to have in-depth, accurate knowledge of one setting than superficial and possibly skewed or misleading information about isolated relationships in many settings. In other words, the results obtained by survey methods that educational decision-making has often been based on are ethnographically suspect because they may have been distorted by the fractionalization of inquiry and by ignoring meanings shared by informants.

Another answer is that in-depth ethnographic study should enable instruments to be constructed that can collect information that is subject to quantification and the application of inferential statistics. There is no argument between qualification and quantification, even though some people who should know better maintain that there is. Many anthroethnographers use quantification and inferential statistical data treatments. Most field research done by graduate students in modern departments of anthropology uses quantified data at some point and many students use inferential statistics of a high degree of sophistication in their analysis of data. Actually, quantitative and qualitative data and methods should be interdependent. Qualitative data obtained from ethnography can tell us what may be significant on a wider scale. The two strategies may often simply be phases of a larger research project, and ethnography may or may not come first. In some cases, the analysis of survey results indicates where an ethnographic probe in depth should then be carried out.

A final answer to questions about generalizability is that correlational and experimental research designs are also subject to severe strictures. They also sample universes. And if these designs fail to take context and meaning into adequate consideration, their results may be significantly less generalizable than the results from a good ethnographic study.

Though the papers comprising this book exhibit the attributes of good ethnography, they are separable into groups on the basis of differences in research strategies, theoretical background and concept formation, and focus. The criteria for separation cannot be applied with entire consistency since the researches have much in common and at the same time express so much variety. The separation, however, makes this volume easier to digest and contributes to the definition of an emerging ethnographic character structure.[6]

Plan of the Book

Part I, "Self-Appraisals: Concerns and Strategies," sets the stage for what is to follow. Its three chapters share some features with those in the rest of the book, but they also differ sharply from them. They are like the other chapters in that they are research-centered; they contain information about completed field research and some of its results. They differ in that they are ruminative and reflective. They are in varying degrees personal documents, more concerned with what the fieldwork was like, what motivations lay behind it, and what doubts the authors have about it. Alan Peshkin's goes farther than the other two in the personal dimension. He reflects on what there was about his own socialization that led him to do ethnography and to value doing it in a small Middle Western community with a tight nexus with its schools. The Spindlers describe fieldwork in two research sites, one in the elementary school in a California community, the other in an urbanizing German village. The teachers in both of these schools resisted change, in different ways and for different reasons, and the authors discuss this. Their emphasis, however, is on a different problem—that reflected in the title, "Roger Harker and Schönhausen: From the Familiar to the Strange and Back Again." This title is clarified in the

---

[6] This Introduction was written after some months of extensive reading in the field and editorial work with the contributed papers. It is difficult to single out the reading that has particularly influenced me, but I select the following as especially important: Dell Hymes, "What Is Ethnography?", a paper delivered to the Ethnography and Education Conference, Philadelphia, April 8, 1978; Shirley Brice Heath, "Ethnography in Education: Toward Defining the Essentials," to be published by the University of Pennsylvania Press in *Ethnography and Education: Children in and out of School,* edited by Perry Gilmore and Allan A. Glatthorn; Harry F. Wolcott, "Confessions of a 'Trained' Observer," an unpublished paper prepared for a seminar on Field-Based Methodology in Educational Research; Frederick Erickson, "Some Approaches to Inquiry in School-Community Ethnography," 1977, *Council on Anthropology and Education Newsletter,* 8(2):58–69.

editorial commentary on Part I and, of course, in the chapter itself. Harry Wolcott provides a corrective to any over-optimism we may feel as we ride the crest of the new wave of enthusiasm for ethnography. He describes what can, and often does, happen to ethnographic models and results as they are assimilated to educators' concerns.

It is no accident that the authors of these first three chapters are all veterans of the ethnographic campaigns. Only they could write essays like these.

The studies reported in Part II, "Communication and Interaction," are shaped by three major influences. The first stems from descriptive linguistics and sociolinguistics, language in culture, and a developing ethnography of communication. Both the patterning of speech behavior and the functions of speech in social interaction are considered significant. None of the researches reported are linguistic studies as such, but all show the influence of speech and communication models. Sociological and symbolic interactionist influences are also apparent. The third influence appears to be in part derived from the first two—a focus on the implicit, covert, or tacit aspects of communication and interaction. This concern appears in various forms in most of the papers in this volume.

Some of the most sophisticated and productive engagements with schooling are contained within this section. The chapters within it not only demonstrate a variety of research strategies and concepts but make specific substantive gains. Heath demonstrates how styles of questioning and answering are so different for black children and white teachers in one school that communication and teaching/learning are grossly interfered with. Erickson and Mohatt show how Odawa and Ojibwa (American Indian) and white styles of interaction differ to the extent that they affect classroom behavior and learning environments. Philips shows how language socialization, through advanced schooling, defines boundaries for professional groups and acts to exclude outsiders because a special way of talking is learned and employed. And, lastly, Varenne shows how the social organization of a school is much more flexible and ambiguous than previous studies of social cliques and stratification have indicated.

Part III, "Cultural Transmission and the 'Hidden Curriculum,'" consists of only two chapters. The first, by Gearing and Epstein, is a contextualized microanalytic study of a reading group consisting of four children and one teacher. The other is an intensive study by Wilcox of one classroom each in two elementary schools on the West Coast, one serving a lower-middle-class neighborhood, the other an upper-middle-class one. The first paper is concerned with how an attitude of "learning to wait," of cutting one's losses by hanging back, a cultural pattern the children bring with them to school from their community, is projected into the classroom and into the activities and behaviors involved in learning to read. The second paper details how socialization for work roles at the opposite ends of the scale of prestige in our society takes place in the schools studied.

These two chapters, though dealing with quite different topics, have much in common. They both show how the cultural context and community background are projected into, in fact determine, the educational process. Their authors take a cultural transmission position. Most of the ethnographers in this volume do, but it is particularly explicit in these two instances. They are both centered on showing how a "hidden curriculum"—a pattern of expectation and relevant behaviors that is implicit and tacit—operates to defeat declared educational intentions.

Neither of these chapters draws its inspiration directly from linguistically shaped models, though both utilize verbal behavior as the most important source of data. These two papers report researches that are among the most rigorous discussed in this volume, and both are thoroughly ethnographic, as measured by the orienting criteria already set forth.

Each of the chapters in Part IV, "Five Diverse Ethnographic Analyses," discusses research that was conducted with and results interpreted with different models and persuasions. The diversity of ethnographic research is well illustrated, and yet beneath this diversity there are commonalities such as direct observation, deferred judgment, selective holism and broad contextualization, and the elicitation of emic data—the natives' view and knowledge.

Readers will be upset and discouraged by the data in Hanna's chapter on the consequences of desegregation in a "magnet" school. It is important that readers understand that the analysis is not simply disguised racism appearing as ethnography. The situation and interactions described are precisely those we should expect and be prepared to cope with constructively. We are committed to desegregation and must face the problems inherent in the process squarely. Readers will find Finnan's ethnography of children's spontaneous play more relaxing and will see in it both the separation of sex roles and the contemporary confusion and ambiguity about them reflected from the larger society. They will find hope in Warren's ethnography of a bicultural program in southern California that such programs can work to achieve their ends, under certain conditions (described by the ethnographer). Hart's essay on the social organization of reading will raise questions in the reader's mind about how best to apply standard anthropological constructs to the analysis of educational process. And the concluding chapter, by Precourt, raises the possibility of an ethnohistorical, in contrast to a synchronic, approach to the study of schools.

Part V, "Methods and Issues: A Review," consists of a single chapter, a review by Wilcox of selected literature on ethnographic method with emphasis on adaptation and resistance to change in educational institutions. Though I was principal investigator for the project of which this review is a product, the review is entirely the author's. The reader will find it indispensable for a balanced overview of the field. It is placed near the end of the volume rather than at the beginning because readers who did not already know the field to some extent would find the review difficult to assimilate. For these readers it will serve more as a consolidation and extension of experience now accumulated than as an introduction to the concerns of the volume. Other readers who are already knowledgeable about the ethnography of schooling may want to begin with this review, then go to the various chapters in which anthroethnographers discuss their work.

My Concluding Remarks outline the ethnographic world view and propose that ethnographic training should be part of the professional preparation of a wide range of professional education personnel.

Editing and Format

The role of the editor has been to solicit, critique, and encourage (and sometimes discourage) the potential and actual contributors from the time when the chapters were first conceived as possibilities until they became final drafts. As editor I was also responsible for creating some kind of unity for the volume. In order to do this it was necessary to put the contributions of my colleagues in their best light, make the overall organization and strategy of the book sensible and effective, and raise issues. Of course, any editor is only partly successful in any complex endeavor of this sort.

With these purposes in mind I have: furnished this General Introduction; grouped the chapters into parts on the basis of features held in common; provided editorial commentary on each of the parts; written an editorial introduction to each chapter, highlighting certain features; added the Concluding Remarks.

My General Introduction and editorial commentaries as related to the parts of the book are not designed to be reviews of the literature or to provide extensive citations of relevant works. This important task is accomplished by Wilcox's review, Part V. They are fairly free-wheeling and suggest ways that the common as well as distinctive features of the works in this book, from both a methodological and a substantive viewpoint (but more the former than the latter), may be significant to the development of an ethnography of schooling. That I have made mistakes in interpretation, misplaced emphases, and not always given due credit is inevitable — but, I hope, forgivable.

PART I

Self-Appraisals: Concerns and Strategies

Editorial Commentary

The chapters in Part I have been chosen to introduce some of the character-defining concerns of anthroethnographers and some of the most significant features of their research strategies. These essays cannot introduce all of the relevant concerns and strategies, since they are written from certain vantage points. The authors are senior ethnographers, each of whom has done several field studies of schooling in the U.S.A. and abroad; and all have made the ethnography of schooling a dominating focus of their work from the beginning of their relatively long professional careers. These chapters, as noted in the General Introduction, are ruminative and retrospective. The Spindlers, Alan Peshkin, and Harry Wolcott reflect on their work and its consequences. In doing so they encounter and present matters of imperative concern to an emerging anthroethnography of schooling.

The Spindlers discuss a problem that *every* native-born ethnographer of schooling in the U.S.A. encounters, though often without full recognition — getting enough perspective on the cultural processes and social interaction in an all-too-familiar setting to make significant discovery possible. They have described the problem, as have Frederick Erickson, Victor Turner, M. N. Srinivas, and probably others, as "making the familiar strange."[1] This problem, though stated a little flippantly, is one of the most important that must be dealt with in producing ethnographic research in our own schools in our own society that is both penetrating and useful.

In their struggle with this problem the Spindlers produce other insights into the ethnographic strategy concerning such matters as audiovisual recording and the analysis of this material, use of two observers of opposite sex in the classroom, the complementarity of qualitative and quantitative data and methods, the development of research instruments out of ethnographic observation, and the need for broad contextualization.

Alan Peshkin reflects on the personal factors that led him to do ethnographic research in a school in a small Middle-Western community and may have predisposed him to value especially the stability and coherence of this community and its relationships with its schools. These kinds of factors are important in all professional ca-

---

[1] Though various anthropologists (and the German poet Goethe) have described the problem (in various ways), Erickson is the first, to my knowledge, to apply this phrase specifically to the problems encountered in doing the ethnography of schooling. See F. Erickson, "What Makes School Ethnography Ethnographic?" 1973, *Council on Anthropology and Education Newsletter*, 2:10-19.

reers and in all research on human behavior. They are critically important in ethnographic work, for such work involves the whole person in ways that more distanced study of human behavior does not.

His essay also calls attention to the dilemma of an anthropological construction of school-community relations. In the anthropological view, schooling is cultural transmission. Schooling exists, in this view, to recruit new members into the community (usually its own offspring) and maintain the cultural system. Mansfield schools exist to maintain Mansfield, in the narrow sense, and to maintain a culture and world view appropriate to the small, stable community, in the broader sense. We will find that a cultural transmission view of schooling appears in various forms in most of the chapters of this volume. Kathleen Wilcox's review at the end of this book suggests that this view is held by most anthroethnographers of schooling.

This is not the view of schooling shared by most educators, administrators, and politicians, or by large sectors of the public. At least at the ideological level, most Americans seem to regard the schools as instruments of change and improvement. The belief in the school as an instrument of change is in fact a central value orientation in the dominant American culture. It has rationalized intervention in ethnic, regional, local, and community schooling since the public school system began in this country. This intervention, as a part of the melting pot ideology in action, has often resulted in the destruction or corrosion of ethnic or other differences that in another part of the American ideology are regarded as attributes of a multicultural, democratic society. Peshkin's essay affords us telling insights into these relationships and dilemmas.

Harry Wolcott, in a case study of his own classic ethnography of an elementary school principal, *The Man in the Principal's Office,* calls our attention to dissonance in the diffusion of what anthropologists think is important in our work to our intended educationist receivers. What remains of Wolcott's complex ethnography of the principal's role, after it is assimilated by educators, is a method of study, not the content resulting from the application of it. And this method is further converted to a framework alien to the ethnographic stance but essential to educators— that of evaluation. Though many, perhaps most, anthroethnographers doing the ethnography of schooling in contemporary settings will accept "evaluation" as an *ultimate* purpose of doing school ethnography, the role conflicts involved in doing ethnography and evaluation simultaneously in the field will continue to plague the profession. (We suggest later that evaluation should be deferred and de-emphasized.) Wolcott's case study of the reception and use of his ethnography helps to illuminate this underlying problem.

Of equal importance is the problem of a stripped-down concept of ethnography that sometimes appears in the educationist adaptation of ethnographic models. Though Wolcott's study was done with the greatest care and attention to detail, the model of "ethnography" that appears to be diffused to educators is often that of mere description, and superficial description at that. This is particularly vexing to the careful ethnographer because ethnographic validity depends upon prolonged, intimate contact with, observation of, and inquiry about repetitive patterns of behavior and interaction.

The purpose of these introductory remarks is certainly not to denigrate educators because they may have different concepts of the purposes of schooling, or of the study of it, than do anthroethnographers, or even because they may tend to strip ethnographic models down to what anthropologists perceive to be the lowest common denominator. Rather, my purpose is to underline the critically important message in Wolcott's case study of the reception of his own pioneering work. That message is that those doing the ethnography of schooling, or about to do it, must not expect either their methods or the results of their work to be received exactly or even approximately as they were intended. Our ethnographic studies may have unanticipated consequences in educationist thinking and practice that are shockingly different than we envision. The process has just begun, but given the tidal wave of popularity ethnography is enjoying (though it may be short-lived) we may soon begin to see those unanticipated consequences more clearly, and not all of the view will be pleasing.

Anthropologists, particularly young ones, desperate for employment in a shrinking academic market, may be tempted to forgo and forget the principles of good ethnography. These principles require dedication to a validity of results that can only be obtained through enduring attention to the microfacts of everyday behavior in context, with a broadened and relatively objective perspective that issues from cross-cultural experience and from commitment to a cultural view of reality. The "quick and dirty" pseudo-ethnographic style that is likely to emerge when the emphasis is altogether on evaluation and on getting this evaluation done quickly, as in some contract research, is antithetical to the basic strategies of anthroethnography. It will eventually have destructive consequences for both educators and anthropologists interested in understanding educational processes in depth.

We anthroethnographers of schooling have a sobering challenge set squarely before us: to understand the needs and purposes of teachers, administrators, professors of education, contract researchers, and funding agencies and to maintain the core principles of our ethnographic model and world view while producing data and understandings relevant to those purposes. Anthropologists and educators have two quite different cultures. They are now in intimate and possibly prolonged contact with each other. If this contact is to be productive, there will have to be adaptation from both sides. If educators assimilate ethnography and in so doing erase its identity, ethnography will not be capable of challenging educationist assumptions and suggesting innovations in educational practice. If anthropologists blindly pursue only their more detached and theory-relevant ends in doing the ethnography of schooling, their tenure in educational enterprises will be of short duration.

Wolcott's essay helps us to understand what some of the important problems are in this culture contact relationship.

1

George Spindler and Louise Spindler

Roger Harker and Schönhausen: From Familiar to Strange and Back Again

George and Louise Spindler

The Authors

George and Louise Spindler have been a working research team since the beginning of their Menominee fieldwork in 1948. Out of this experience came George's dissertation in 1952 and Louise's in 1956. Various publications followed, written together and separately. The Spindlers' work in the psychology of culture change and urbanization is reviewed by L. Spindler in chapter 5 of *The Making of Psychological Anthropology*, edited by G. Spindler (University of California Press, 1978). Louise was one of the pioneers in the study of women's roles in culture change.

George's interest in the application of anthropological concepts and methods to the analysis of educational process began before World War II. He incorporated certain aspects of anthropology into the general science and biology courses he taught at Park Falls High School in Wisconsin in 1941-1942, following a summer of graduate work at the University of Wisconsin at Madison. After he returned from World War II to continue his graduate work at Wisconsin, this interest was reinforced by a year-long fellowship, 1947-1948, awarded by John Guy Fowlkes, then dean of the School of Education. The interest has continued. When George went to Stanford in 1950, he received an active joint appointment in the Department of Anthropology and the School of Education, which he still holds.

George and Louise have collaborated in continuing ethnographic field research with the Menominee, the Kanai, and the Cree since 1948, and in studies of urbanization in Germany since 1959. Some of their work is summarized in L. Spindler's *Culture Change and Modernization: Mini Models and Case Studies* (A Basic Anthropology Unit: Holt, Rinehart and Winston, 1977). Louise joined George in ethnographic studies in German education in the 1977 restudy of the Schönhausen elementary school. They recently developed an experimental training seminar in the ethnography of schooling, first given at the University of Wisconsin at Madison for the Department of Educational Policy Studies in the fall semester of 1979-1980.

George Spindler, sometimes credited with being a father, or grandfather, of educational anthropology, has edited and contributed to three collected volumes on the subject. The first, *Education and Anthropology*, published by Stanford University Press in 1955, resulted from a seminar-conference on the relations, mostly potential at that time, between anthropology and education. The conference was organized by G. and L. Spindler and supported by the Carnegie Foundation. Notable anthropologists such as Alfred

Kroeber, Cora DuBois, Margaret Mead, C. W. M. Hart, Bernard Siegel, Jules Henry, Solon T. Kimball, Felix Keesing, and Dorothy Lee participated, with a like number of educators, including I. James Quillen, Lawrence K. Frank, Robert Bush, William Cowley, Lawrence Thomas, Hilda Taba, Theodore Brameld, Paul Hanna, Francis Shaftel, Arthur Coladarci, and William Martin. This was the first major volume published on the subject. Since then G. Spindler has edited and contributed to *Education and Culture: Anthropological Approaches* (Holt, Rinehart and Winston, 1963) and *Education and Cultural Process: Toward an Anthropology of Education* (Holt, 1974). In 1957 he gave the Third Burton Lecture in Elementary Education at Harvard University, published in 1959 by that university's press under the title, *The Transmission of American Culture* (abridged version reprinted in *Education and Culture,* 1963).

The Spindlers are joint editors for several series published by Holt, Rinehart and Winston, including the Case Studies in Cultural Anthropology and Case Studies in Education and Culture. They were editors of the *American Anthropologist* from 1962 to 1966. Louise Spindler is lecturer in the Department of Anthropology at Stanford University and George Spindler is emeritus professor of anthropology and education, having taken early retirement in 1978 to pursue a career in field research, writing, editing, and occasional visiting professorships. He continues to take an active role in teaching and advising at Stanford.

George and Louise Spindler are both teachers, as well as researchers and editors. Between them they have taught every grade from kindergarten to advanced graduate studies. They met in 1941 at Park Falls High School in northern Wisconsin, where they were both teaching. George recently received the Lloyd H. Dinkelspiel award for outstanding contributions to undergraduate education at Stanford University.

Louise Spindler received the first Ph.D. conferred by the Department of Anthropology at Stanford University, in 1956. George Spindler received his Ph.D. in anthropology, sociology, and psychology from UCLA in 1952.

This Chapter

In this chapter the authors attempt to move beyond the formal presentation of data, interpretation, and conclusion to a dimension of reflection that is uncommon in scholarly publications. In doing so they reveal something of the backstage aspects of ethnographic fieldwork and cultural translation. The two projects described — the studies of Roger Harker and his fifth-grade classroom in a West

Coast elementary school and the Schönhausen elementary school in West Germany — were carried out in two different countries and separated by nearly three decades. And yet there are certain factors that make them similar. Much of what was learned both substantively and methodologically in the first study, begun in January, 1951, is still being learned today in current ethnographic studies of schooling. This can be construed as a vote of confidence in ethnography and its methodology. It also raises the question: why did it take so long for anthroethnography to become popular, if not universally accepted? This chapter may shed some light on that question.

Introduction

Doing the ethnography of schooling is nearly as interesting as doing the ethnography of the Menominee, the Kanai (the Blood Indians of Alberta, Canada), or the Mistassini Cree hunters (near James Bay, Quebec). We have "done ethnography" with the first two intermittently for several decades (and intend to do more) and with the last one for a season. Our task in all these studies was complicated by the necessity of making the strange familiar. We observed and tried to understand behavior that seemed unusual, different, exotic, and at first inexplicable. We tried to make the strange familiar to our readers, as we translated our observations into logic and expressions understandable to them. We did a cultural translation. In the process, we did some violence to the cultural knowledge we had gained in our fieldwork.[1] That is, we used our cultural categories, such as "religion," "ritual," "social organization," "kin terms," "acculturation,"

"psychological adaptation," and so forth, in translating our informants' cultural knowledge as they expressed it and practiced it into the language and cognitive categories of: (1) anthropology, (2) the English language; (3) the Euro-American culture. If we had used their language and their categories of thought and interpretation, no one would have understood us except those Menominee, Kanai, or Cree who spoke their own language and lived the traditional way of life. Making the strange familiar is the usual task of ethnography.

Making the strange familiar was not the problem in doing ethnography in schools in the U.S.A. When I (George Spindler) started fieldwork in 1950 in West Coast elementary schools, what I observed was indeed strange enough, but since it was a mirror of my own cultural strangeness I could not see it—at first. I came very near to quitting fieldwork on my first research assignment for the team I had been hired to participate in, working out of Stanford University under the direction of Robert Bush, Professor of Education.[2] I sat in classes for days wondering what there was to "observe." Teachers taught, reprimanded, rewarded, while pupils sat at desks, squirming, whispering, reading, writing, staring into space, as they had in my own grade-school experience, in my practice teaching in a teacher training program, and in the two years of public school teaching I had done before World War II. What should I write down in my empty notebook? In the fieldwork with the Menominee, with whom we had already spent three seasons, I couldn't write fast enough or long enough, and I spent hours each night working on my field notes. And when I could take pictures I took hundreds. It never occurred to me to take a picture in any of the classrooms I worked in during the 1950s, and for several weeks in the first classrooms my notebook remained virtually empty, except for some generalized comments such as "79.1 T [we used codes for everybody] seems nervous today" or "3 girls whisper together until teacher glances in their direction and says 'Must you do that?'" The familiar was all too familiar.

As Margaret Mead (I believe) once said (approximately), "If a fish were to become an anthropologist, the last thing it would discover would be water." I was an American fish in my own element. The last thing I would discover would be the intricacies of communication and reinforcement of cultural values and class position that were the key to the classroom and what was happening there. But eventually I began to see the teacher and the pupils

as "natives," engaging in rituals, interaction, role-playing, selective perception, cultural conflict, sociometric networks, defensive strategies, and so on. I began the cultural translation from familiar to strange and back to familiar.

Doing the ethnography of schooling in the U.S.A. is, indeed, nearly as interesting as doing the ethnography of the Menominee, the Kanai, and the Cree— and a lot more difficult.

This chapter is devoted to a discussion of doing ethnography in two elementary schools, one in 1951 on the West Coast, the other in a village we called "Schönhausen" in Southern Germany. George Spindler did the first work without the field collaboration of Louise Spindler, though one of the major research techniques utilized, the Expressive Autobiographical Interview, had been developed by her in the Menominee fieldwork and in her analysis of the data on Menominee women adapting to cultural change.[3] The field research in Germany was done in two phases, one in 1967–1968, the other in 1977. During the first phase George and Louise were working in the villages of the Rems Valley near Stuttgart, including Schönhausen, on a project on urbanization. In the 1977 study Louise Spindler was a full collaborator in the fieldwork in the school and in the data analysis and cultural translation phases following.

Each of the studies will be outlined briefly, then discussed. Each discussion will cover some points that the other does not, but both will include consideration of making the familiar strange, and vice versa.

Roger Harker and His Fifth-Grade Classroom

I worked in depth with Roger Harker for six months. Although I did an ethnography of his classroom and the interaction between him and his pupils, I say I worked with him, because much of our study was collaborative, particularly during its later phases. This young man had taught for three years in the elementary school. He regarded his teaching as a kind of apprenticeship for an administrative role, which he shortly achieved with the enthusiastic support of his supervisors and principal. He volunteered for the study in order, he said, "to improve my professional competence." Only volunteers were accepted as subjects by the Stanford Consultation Service, but Professor Bush and other team members were so persuasive in the faculty meetings where the project was introduced that nearly all of the teachers and administrators present volunteered.

My collection of data fell into the following categories: (1) personal, autobiographical, and psychological data on the teacher; (2) ratings of him by his principal and other superiors in the superintendent's office; (3) his own self-estimates on the same points; (4) observations of his classroom, emphasizing interaction with children; (5) interviews with each child and the elicitation of ratings of the teacher in many different dimensions, both formally and informally; (6) his ratings and estimates for each child in his classroom, including estimates of popularity with peers, academic performance and capacity, personal adjustment, home background, and liking for him; (7) sociometric data from the children about each other; and (8) interviews with each person (superintendent, principal, supervisors, children) who supplied ratings of him.

I also participated in the life of the school to the extent possible, accompanying the teacher where I could and "melting" into the classroom as much as feasible. I was always there, but I had no authority and assumed none. I became a friend and confidant to the children. These are anthropological habits.

This teacher was regarded by his superiors as most promising—"clear and well-organized," "sensitive to children's needs," "fair and just to all of the children," "knowing his subject areas well." I was not able to elicit either with rating scales or in interviews any criticisms or negative evaluations. There were very few suggestions for change—and these were all in the area of subject matter and curriculum.

Roger Harker described himself as "fair and just to all my pupils," as making "fair decisions," and as "playing no favorites." This was a particular point of pride with him.

His classroom was made up of children from a broad social stratum—upper-middle, middle, and lower classes—and the children represented Mexican-American, Anglo-European, and Japanese-American ethnic groups. I was particularly attentive to the relationships between the teacher and children from these various groups.

One could go into much detail, but a few items will suffice since they all point in the same direction, and that direction challenges both his perceptions of his own behavior and those of his superiors. He ranked highest on all dimensions, including personal and academic factors, those children who were most like himself—Anglo, middle to upper-middle social class, and, like him, ambitious (achievement-oriented). He also estimated that these children were the most popular with their peers, and were the leaders of the classroom group. His knowledge about the individual children, elicited without recourse to files or notes, was distributed in the same way. He knew significantly more about the children culturally like himself (on items concerned with home background as well as academic performance), and least about those culturally most different.

The children had quite different views of the situation. Some children described him as not always so "fair and just," as "having special pets," as not being easy to go to with their problems. On sociometric "maps" of the classroom showing which children wanted to spend time with other specific children, or work with them, sit near them, invite them to a party or a show, etc., the most popular children were not at all those the teacher rated highest. And his negative ratings proved to be equally inaccurate. Children he rated as isolated or badly adjusted socially, most of whom were non-Anglo and non-middle-class, more often than not turned out to be "stars of attraction" from the point of view of the children.

Observations of his classroom behavior supported the data collected by other means. He most frequently called on, touched, helped, and looked directly at the children culturally like himself.

He was never mean or cruel to the other children. It was almost as though they weren't there. His interaction with the children of Anglo-European ethnicity and middle and upper-middle social class background was more frequent than with the other children, and the quality of the interaction appeared to be differentiated in the same way.

This young man, with the best of intentions, was confirming the negative hypotheses and predictions (as well as the positive ones) already made within the social system. He was informing Anglo middle-class children that they were capable, had bright futures, were socially acceptable, and were worth a lot of trouble. He was also informing lower-class and non-Anglo children that they were less capable, less socially acceptable, less worth the trouble. He was defeating his own declared educational goals.

This young teacher did not know that he was discriminating. He was rated very positively by his superiors on all counts, including being "fair and just to all the children." Apparently they were as blind to his discrimination as he was. The school system supported him and his classroom behavior without questioning or criticizing him. And, of course, the dominant social structure of the community supported the school.

Discussion of Roger Harker

Dissemination

One of the problems we face as anthroethnographers is how to disseminate our findings in such a way that they penetrate the complex subculture of professional education. This "case study" (as I prefer to term what we usually do as ethnographers) of Roger Harker has been presented and interpreted before my classes at Stanford every year since 1952. It has also appeared, but only in partial form, in various publications, the most widely known of which is probably *The Transmission of American Culture* (G. Spindler 1959). Many of the people influential in the development of an anthropology of education took these classes (Harry Wolcott, Richard King, John Singleton, Richard Warren, earlier, and, more recently, Ray McDermott, Stephen Arvizu, David Fetterman, Jose Maceas, Christine Finnan, Patricia Phelan, Pat Hishiki, and others). From 1952 to the present more than 2,700 graduate students in education and a smaller number of graduate students in anthropology have taken courses or seminars in which Roger Harker was presented. Through these channels Harker and his fifth-grade classroom have become a part of the lore, if not the scientific corpus, of educational anthropology.

It is probable that the teaching of the Roger Harker case has been more effective as a mechanism for diffusion into the culture of professional education than its publication. In our efforts to disseminate the results of anthroethnography we should not overlook the teaching channel. In some ways the classroom or seminar is the most salubrious setting for the transmission and diffusion of ethnographic case study material and the lessons to be learned from it. The classroom is more flexible and less permanent than the printed page. One can be wrong, find out, and

correct oneself. Nuances can be better communicated, and there is less chance of damage to the object of study. I have never published the details of Roger Harker's autobiographic interview, for example, for I fear that without my being there to correct misunderstandings or warped interpretations, he might seem other than he is (or was).

My first point in this discussion is that the results of the ethnography we do should be taught as much as or more than published. My teaching career is based on case materials, from the Menominee, the Kanai, the Cree, Roger Harker, Miss Mildew, Burgbach, and Schönhausen. I have published, and will publish, only a small portion of the material. Somehow this relationship between fieldwork and teaching is rarely made explicit, and yet most of our colleagues exploit their fieldwork in their teaching.

Models and Interdisciplinary Translations

I did not have a singularly anthropological theoretical model to guide my collection of data and interpretation in the study of Roger Harker and his classroom. My graduate training at Wisconsin and at UCLA was equally distributed in psychology, sociology, and anthropology. Not so strangely, the fieldwork and interpretation of the Harker case study were guided about equally by concepts and theory from each of these three fields. I conceived of Roger as engaged in three dimensions of action: projecting in his behavior a personality formed out of past experience and particularly from familiar socialization; acting out a role as teacher that he had developed from professional training, experience, and prior observation; and converting a culture that he had learned at home, in school, and from the peer group into action in the classroom. That these three dimensions are artifacts, what we usually term "constructs," is clear enough. They are cultural translations as well. One takes the "raw" data of observation and the emic data of interviews and biographies and translates it into categories that "make sense" of it.

The translation of Roger Harker has changed over the three decades that I have used this case study to demonstrate some of what seemed important in the anthropology of education as it developed through time. In 1952–1960 I saw personality factors as more important than role and cultural factors. The fact that Roger identified with his mother and older sister and was hostile to his father was indisputably demonstrated by his autobiographic interview, his thematic apperception test (TAT), and the Rorschach projective technique (the "inkblot test"). This seemed to help explain why he became an elementary school teacher, why he got along so well with an all-female faculty and school administration, why he rated girls in his class higher on all counts than boys, and why he was a little passive about his own goals and ambitions. The socialization-personality factor still seems to help explain these matters, but they don't seem as important now.

Since about 1958 I have been shifting toward greater emphasis on the social role and cultural transmitter dimensions. What loomed as more and more important—though it had been there and recognized from the start—was the selectivity with which Harker's culture, which was thoroughly Anglo middle class, achievement-oriented, and respectable, was projected into his interactions with the children of various backgrounds in his classes and the positive sanction for this selectivity afforded by the school and school system.

More recently I have shifted further yet in a cultural direction and am more concerned with the kinds and specifics of cultural knowledge brought into the setting and acted out in the various scenes by the children, by Roger Harker, and by others who appear in the scenario. This development is essentially an extension of the second phase of translation I engaged in over the years.

It could be that these phases of cultural translation noted above are just different ways of talking about things. Sometimes, in my darker moments, I am sure of it. But almost certainly they are more than that. Roger Harker's case has grown and become more clear and more subtle as new constructions have been placed upon the data in the process of translation.

But what if the data for these multiple translations were not there? I spent six months, at least two days each school week, working with Roger. My file on him is about two feet long, but I have never used all the data in that file. The data I do use are detailed and comprehensive enough so that I can answer, at least well enough for my purposes, the new questions that the new constructs pose for me as I retranslate. This is an argument for the ethnographic stance. More observation, more interviews, more contextualization, more photos are collected on more kinds of events and circumstances than one sees a use for within the focus of a sharply delimited problem. I think there is also an argument, in the range of translations we are discussing, for an interdisciplinary orientation. It seems to me that Roger Harker, viewed as a socialized personality, a role-player, and a cultural transmitter, was well contextualized in theory as well as in the school system and community. Perhaps ethnography should be a part of a broad clinical approach as well as a procedure for doing highly focused microanalyses of sharply delimited event chains and interactions.

The techniques of data elicitation and collection used in the study of Roger Harker were marshaled, of course, by the three disciplines I drew upon. Psychology gave me the projective techniques (I had studied for two years under Bruno Klopfer in his advanced seminar at UCLA). Sociology gave me rating scales, Likert intervals, questionnaires, status reputation tests and sociograms, and a Warner-type rating procedure for a house-to-house survey of the school district as background information. Anthropology, especially the then-emergent psychological anthropology, gave me interviewing techniques, ethnographic observation of interaction in the classroom with special attention to nonverbal communication, the concept of culture and especially of covert or tacit culture, and Louise Spindler's Expressive Autobiographic Interview technique (the E.A.I.). The E.A.I. technique allows one to selectively elicit attitudes about and expressions of culture from respondents, but with a flexible, broadly chronological self-centered framework. It proved particularly

crucial in Roger Harker's case study, because it was largely from the E.A.I. that I was able to place Roger with respect to sociocultural origins and specific cultural patterns identifying him as upper-middle class and achievement-oriented.

Locked into the System

My last major point in the discussion of the Harker case study is that he was locked into a self-reinforcing, self-maintaining sociocultural system of action, perception, and reward, and that in my interaction with him as a consultant (my role was both to do research and to consult with the teacher being studied) I had to make the familiar strange to him in order to have any effect. He was rated by administrators and by all supervisory personnel, on forms that our research team had prepared for this purpose, at or near the top of the five-point Likert-type scale. On all items they were unanimous in rating him as fair and just, not playing favorites, and fair in all decisions concerning students. He was perceived as an alert, dedicated, unprejudiced teacher, fair in all respects. He was rated as one who had the best interests of his students at heart and made every effort to understand their problems and bring out the best in them. He perceived himself in exactly the same terms and with the same degree of approval, and he even predicted, on a form that we converted to this purpose, that his superiors and supervisors would perceive him this way. This pattern of self-reinforcing estimates is clearly established in the case material, both through responses on rating forms and in followup interviews with each respondent.

Just as unimpeachable is the evidence for his pattern of perceptions and estimates that show something very different operating in the classroom. Roger Harker, with the best of intentions, was highly biased and very selective in his interactions with and knowledge about the children in his classes. He was never cruel or overtly racist. But he matched, albeit unconsciously, the children like himself— middle class, achievement-oriented, and "respectable"—to all that was good and desirable. The children perceived this, but not even those whom he disadvantaged could hate him for it, because he was such a nice, kind person.

There were three cultural dimensions operative in the classroom. Roger Harker had his version of this culture— who was liked or disliked and by whom, who was "respected," who was maladjusted, who was succeeding and who wasn't, who was known for being fun, hard-working, or mean, etc. The children had quite another version, encompassing the same items, though differently phrased. And there was a third cultural dimension—the tacit culture of the children to the effect that the teacher was selective and prejudiced in his interaction with children. This was reflected in such phrases as "he has pets and favorites," "doesn't talk to me," "can't go to him with my personal problems," produced by children in interviews and a teacher rating form.

Roger could not see the strangeness of his selective perceptions, interactions, and approval because this pattern was customary and familiar, not only to him, but to his superiors, and probably

to all the teachers and other professional school personnel with whom he came in contact. His "normal" environment was assimilationist, racist, and mainstream. This environment was "normal" at that time for the American school system as a whole. A great accumulation of studies indicates that the situation has not changed much. Roger Harker's case study could be replicated many times over today.

There was no way Roger Harker by himself could see and change what he was doing. If it had not been for intervention that came quite unexpectedly from the outside to challenge the interlocking and self-sustaining system of perceptions, beliefs, and rewards of which he was a part, it is most unlikely he would have changed.

Cultural Therapy

Part of my role was to do what came later to be called "cultural therapy." It consisted of feeding back to Roger what I had collected, collated, and translated about him. He saw where and how his perceptions and understandings were skewed, and quite out of line with both reality as I perceived it and the realities of classroom life as the children perceived them. At first he was disbelieving and hostile. Eventually he assimilated what was being presented. The process was one of cultural translation for him as well as for myself. I was collating data and translating observations into a cultural framework called "social science." By doing this I objectified the relationships in his field of action. He could accept this objectification where he would have rejected translations in his own idiom. I also translated into the children's perceptions—so he could understand the tacit culture of his own classroom.

In these ways I made the familiar culture of Roger Harker's classroom, the school, and his interactions with children strange. As he said in one of our "therapy" sessions, "It seems so strange to me now that I could be doing that [selectively interacting with the children as described]. Why couldn't I see it for myself?"

Schönhausen Grundschule: Study and Restudy

Introduction

We now turn to quite a different study, with different concepts, methods, and results. However, the case study of Roger Harker and his classroom and the study of Schönhausen Grundschule have something in common. They are both studies, in different ways, of resistance to change. In Roger Harker's case he was a part of a self-reinforcing system that selected children out for the class and caste roles they would play in society. In the Schönhausen school this was true as well, but an educational reform had been phrased less in terms of equal opportunity than in terms of modernization. Germany is not as multicultural and multiethnic as is our society, though there are more differences than one might at first suspect.

Schönhausen is an urbanizing German village of about 3000 population in the Rems Valley, near Stuttgart.[4] It has one elementary school (Grundschule) with six full-time teachers, a Rektor (similar to a principal) and two others

who teach music and religion on a part-time basis, and about 150 students in grades 1 through 4. Our purposes in the original study in the winter and spring of 1967–1968 were to observe cultural transmission as it occurred in the school and relate it to children's perceptions of instrumental alternatives (such as occupations, habitat, religion, recreation, and sex roles) available in their environment and leading to lifestyles of greater and less urbanization. We were also concerned with the assimilation of children whose parents had migrated during the massive relocation after World War II from culturally and linguistically quite different areas of Germany.

The 1967–1968 Study [5]

In the first study, I (George Spindler) participated in as many of the school activities as possible, including nature hikes, trips to local historical centers, excursions, staff and parent meetings, and so forth, and observed in all of the classrooms of the six teachers then at the school. This enabled me to write an ethnography of the educative process focusing on the transmission of culture and particularly on the transmission of values. To study the perceptions of instrumental alternatives related to urban versus traditional lifestyles, I adapted a research technique called the Instrumental Activities Inventory (I.A.I.), which we had developed in our studies of acculturation among American Indians (G. & L. Spindler 1965). The "inventory" consists of 37 line drawings of activities, such as working in the vineyard, living in a traditional Bauernhaus (farmer's house), baking bread in the communal oven, working in a factory, working as an independent shopkeeper or craftsman, a chemist, a lawyer, or a doctor, etc. The "instrumental activities" also include avocations, hobbies, and even choices of "activities" such as having an intimate dinner at home for friends or throwing a party at a tavern or other public place. This series of 37 line drawings was first administered individually to 30 children representing the age range I anticipated working with (9 to 18 years). On the basis of this pilot study, 17 drawings were selected, which were then converted to 35mm slides that could be shown with projectors to groups of approximately 30 each, beginning with the third grade. In this group administration of the Instrumental Activities Inventory most of the 17 drawings were shown in contrastive pairs, forcing choices between urban-oriented and tradition-oriented activities—for example: living in a traditional Fachwerkhaus (exposed beam construction) versus living in a modern single-family row house; working in a factory versus working in the vineyard; being a big farmer (Grossbauer) versus being a chemist; going to a newly built, very modern church versus attending an ancient, very traditional church. Drawings of a Grundschule, a modern Bauernhaus, and the Weinlese (wine-grape harvest) were shown by themselves and respondents indicated whether they liked the school, wanted to live in the house, or wished to participate in the Weinlese, and why. Each respondent also wrote a short essay commenting on two statements, one favorable to urban life and one favorable to village life.

The essay statements and the I.A.I. line drawings were administered to all children in the third and fourth grades in the Grundschule, to children in the fifth, sixth, seventh, and ninth classes in the Hauptschule that most Schönhausen graduates attended (and to 15 Gymnasium students on an individual basis), to 31 parents of children in the Schönhausen Grundschule, and to the teachers in that school.[6] The data thus obtained were treated statistically for differences in distributions of responses between class groups, and for relationship to sex, age, occupation of father, geographical origin of each parent, educational level of parents, and a host of other background variables. Age and sex proved to be the most powerful.

The results of the I.A.I. administration showed an interesting mix of idealization of rural village life—being a vintner or farmer and working in and with nature—and pragmatism about occupational choices and lifestyles. Certain values evoked as support for given instrumental choices appeared consistently in support of the rural village lifestyle ("fresh air," "less traffic," "more person-to-person contact," etc.) and dominated alternative values supporting more urban lifestyles ("live closer to work," "more shops," "more to do"). There appeared to be an idealized identification with the small village and land-related activities. This identification, however, did not interfere with the making of pragmatic instrumental choices. It did seem to serve some useful stabilizing functions during the urbanization process.

The results obtained with the I.A.I. were related to the ethnography of the school and its classrooms. Though the cultural transmission process in the school was tilted toward village-land-tradition it was also pragmatically oriented and gave children a wide range of skills and understandings that were very effectively transmitted. I concluded that part of the effectiveness of cultural transmission in the school was the emphasis on excursions and visits to local historical sites and the attention to the local environment and geographical area (its present state as well as its history) in the Heimatkunde (study of the homeland) and Naturkunde (study of nature) classes.

A content analysis of textbooks and other teaching materials used in the Grundschule indicated that they were consistent with these and other emphases in cultural transmission as detected in the ethnographic study of the classroom and related activities (G. Spindler 1974).

The 1977 Field Study

In March, 1977, we returned to Schönhausen to repeat the study described briefly above, though with some changes in research design. The purpose was to study the effects of the elimination of Heimatkunde and Naturkunde programs from the Grundschule curriculum, the total replacement of village and land-oriented texts with urban-oriented ones, and other extensive changes resulting from sweeping federal and provincial educational reforms initiated by the ministries of education. We wished to find out whether these had resulted in: (1) changes in the cultural transmission process in the classroom and other teacher-managed learning situations (e.g., excursions); (2)

changes in perceptions of instrumental alternatives related, as before, to urban versus village-land traditional lifestyles.

We both participated extensively in the life of the school and observed for many hours in each of the classrooms in the Schönhausen Grundschule. The I.A.I. was again administered, to all children in the third- and fourth-grade classes in the school, to all teachers in the school, to 60 parents of children in the school, and to graduates of the Schönhausen Grundschule attending secondary schools in the area. In addition, 65 children attending an urban Grundschule nearby were administered the I.A.I. as a comparative control group.

The protocols collected from these 296 respondents were coded and computerized. Statistical tests of difference were applied to the 1968 and 1977 samples. The results were: (1) The children attending the Schönhausen Grundschule produced a profile of I.A.I. responses exhibiting strong continuity with that produced by the children nearly a decade before. Again, they idealized the village-land tradition but made pragmatic choices of occupational alternatives that often appeared to violate this romanticized identity. (2) The children attending the more urban Grundschule (80 percent lived in high-rise apartments in a very densely populated urban area) exhibited more urban-oriented choices and perceived the advantages of urban living significantly more frequently than did the children in the Schönhausen sample. Nevertheless, a majority of the children attending the urban school engaged in the same romantic idealization of village-land-traditional life as did the

Schönhausen children. (3) Age and sex again overrode any other background factors in relationship to choices of instrumental alternatives. (4) Older children attending the advanced schools (Realschule, Hauptschule, or Gymnasium) made urban-oriented choices more frequently, but retained the pattern of values idealizing the traditional village-land complex. (5) Television viewing was included as a variable, with respect to both program choice and number of hours of viewing per week, for every child in the sample. Television viewing, insofar as it varied within our sample, was not a significant factor influencing I.A.I. choices. (6) Most important in the framework of our purposes was the surprising finding that children in the 1977 sample made significantly *more* tradition-oriented land-village instrumental choices than did the children in 1968. This was true picture-by-picture of the I.A.I. and also by statistical comparison of a combined modernization score for each protocol. No significant differences between 1968 and 1977 samples of teachers appeared. Teachers, however, tended to be more oriented towards traditional instrumental choices and values than either children or parents in both the original and restudy samples. The 1977 parents' sample showed significantly more land-village choices than the parents' sample in 1968. The educational reform apparently had no effect on children's perceptions of instrumental choices available to them in their changing environment, unless the swing towards traditional values exhibited by both parents and children is a reflection of resistance to the declared policy directed at change.

The 1977 classroom observations were similar in nature to those carried on in 1968, but this time we included certain observational techniques that were not used the first time. For example, we charted the movements of teachers about the classroom. The "travel maps" resulting from this activity showed that teachers had characteristic paths and rest stations in their classrooms, from which they only occasionally deviated. This in turn influenced which children they attended to the most frequently.

We also taped most of the classes that we observed. It was not our purpose to collect the content of all verbalizations in this way, but rather to collect data on the ebb and flow of classroom activity—noise level, degree of teacher dominance, distribution of student response, etc. These tapes, when correlated with our written notes and travel maps, produce a fairly complete nonvisual record of the classroom activity.

In order to supplement this nonvisual record, we took several hundred still photos, using a 35mm compact camera with a 40mm semiwide lens and high-speed (400 ASA) color film. We have found that a series of 25 slides from an hour of classroom instruction adds a vital dimension to our observations. Of particular interest is the styling that becomes more obvious with the visual material. Teachers assume characteristic postures, use characteristic gestures, project varying degrees of intensity, travel about the classroom differently, and so on.

Another dimension was added to our classroom observations in the 1977 study through the use of movie film. We shot over 2000 feet of sound-color film, covering all classrooms in the Schönhausen Grundschule, but particularly the three teachers we were concentrating on—the teachers of the third and fourth grades. We also filmed playground activity, excursions, and community scenes. We used a simple fixed-focus super-8mm existing light sound and color camera to avoid technical complications that would have distracted from our observations in other media, which we were carrying on simultaneously (this is where two observers were essential). The filming was done in the last two weeks of our observational period. This permitted us to film behavioral sequences that we felt sampled critical areas of teacher-student behavior. We tried to collect key behavioral episodes that would show variations in individual teaching styles. We were at least partly successful. The film sequences provide support for our inferences about style drawn from the nonvisual data and from the 35mm timed shots. For example, the film, together with the 35mm still shots and our notes, shows how teachers act when they retire to their "stations," such as a seat in a certain part of the room or a certain window ledge against which they lean, when temporarily turning over the class to student activity. One teacher tries to retain active command, albeit unintentionally, as bespoken by head and body posture and gestures. Another withdraws so completely, with only changes in facial expression as the children proceed, that she seems to disappear. Or the visual material shows how teachers behave when they invade student territory, out of their usual travel route. One teacher leans into the territory as though there were an invisible electric fence marking the boundary; another crouches down, making herself smaller and less distinguishable; and so forth.

Discussion of the Schönhausen Study

Cultural Conservatism and the Grundschule

Despite sweeping curricular reforms, an almost complete turnover of teachers, and increasing urbanization of the environment, there is strong continuity, and in fact a marked conservative swing, in instrumental perceptions and supporting values exhibited by the Schönhausen children over almost a decade. Antecedent factors, such as the diverse geographic and cultural origins of parents, religious affiliation, and degree of urbanization of family of origin, exert little differential influence on instrumental choices and supporting values. There appears to be a regional culture complex that can be called "Remstal" or "Schwäbisch" that is persistent through time and that tends to homogenize, with the aid of the school, the perceptions and evaluations by children. This regional culture is land and small community oriented. Despite sweeping urbanization and industrialization, the Rems valley remains a major wine-producing area. And the Schwäbisch are famous for their stubborn conservatism.

The precise role of the school in the process is still difficult for us to define. On the one hand the fact that the curriculum, textbooks, and personnel were radically changed between our 1968 and 1977 studies, without any discernible effect on children's I.A.I. choices or supporting values, suggests that the influence of the school is unimportant. On the other hand, the diversity of cultural background represented by the families (about 40 percent are from other parts of Germany, including the former East Zone, now the D.D.R., and the outlying settlements, such as Sudetenland and Bessarabia) in the face of the homogeneity of instrumental perceptions and values exhibited in their children's responses suggests that *some* institution or experience setting is having an effect on these children.

Culture must be transmitted and acquired. We think that the teachers are transmitting a conservative cultural orientation and encouraging its acquisition in their classrooms and in their management of extra-classroom activities and relationships with children, irrespective of formal structural changes and educational reforms, and irrespective of individual differences in teaching styles. The school, of course, is a part of a larger, mutually reinforcing cultural whole.

The relative cultural conservatism in I.A.I. choices displayed by the teachers in both 1968 and 1977 samples (even though the overall profile is balanced between urban and village-land preferences) suggests that the school has been a steady influence in the direction of traditional values.[7]

Contextualization

Fieldwork in the Rems Valley has been a major preoccupation for us since 1967, though we began in the fall of 1959 when we were appointed faculty for Gruppe III at Stanford in Germany. We did not return to this undergradu-ate study center until the winter of 1967, but then spent at least one academic quarter each year there until it was closed, for financial reasons, in 1976. The 1977 restudy of the Schönhausen school was carried out independently of any Stanford program, as was the 1968 study, but in all of the other years we had the benefit of the fieldwork of our students who were learning anthropology by doing it. *Burgbach: Urbanization and Identity in a German Village* (G. Spindler 1973) is a product of this fieldwork. These undergraduate students did excellent ethnography, and in doing so were sensitized to German culture and, reflexively, to their own, in a way that is not possible by any other means. For us as professional research anthropologists this arrangement had great benefits, in that we had a more thorough contextualization for our own more focused work than would have been possible otherwise. We had a team, for almost a decade, of over 400 field ethnographers.

When we presented our research at a University of Wisconsin Symposium recently, a sociological colleague asked—somewhat tartly, we thought—how far we thought we had to go to contextualize adequately. The only response we could think of was "as far as time and resources permit."

Substitute Change Versus Change in Principle

There cannot be too much context information, as we see it. One keeps finding surprises. For example, we discovered that one of the most important forces for continuity in the traditional way of life in the Remstal villages was substitute change (as against change in principle).

Tractors were substituted for dray-age animals, electric power was substituted for human muscle to turn turnip and hay choppers, rototillers were substituted for the hoe, and so on. These changes of apparent significance technologically were actually forces for conservatism. They made doing the old tasks easier and more efficient and therefore kept traditional patterns of land use and residence associated with them intact long past the time this complex would have disappeared without this help. It was not until a sweeping consolidation of land ownership and a total physical recontouring of the vineyards—a change in principle—was implemented that the traditional pattern was broken. This occurred during our residence in Germany and we were able to record the consequences (G. Spindler 1973).

The function of substitute change in stabilizing traditional cultural complexes was something we first discovered in the context outside of the school. As we proceeded with our study, this discovery became the base for a hypothesis relevant to schooling. Of course, we did not have the results of our application of the I.A.I. indicating a conservative swing until we returned from the field, but our ethnographic work told us that despite a new curriculum, new textbooks and readings, new state directives, and new personnel (six teachers had been replaced) not much had really changed.

We will mention only one example. Heimatkunde had been eliminated by the reform. It had been the object of scathing criticisms by professional ed-ucators, sociologists, and folklorists. *Das Bild der Heimat im Schullesebuch* by Jörg Ehni, for example, analyzed many of the readings used in elementary school to show how a "false" sentimentality and distorted romanticism were presented to children in the established curriculum, and particularly by Heimatkunde. This was regarded as inappropriate in an age of transformative modernization. Some analysts went further to argue that the sentimental attachment to the home, village, and local area fostered a kind of amoral localism that had been one of the factors permitting the rise of Hitler and the Nazis.

A subject called *Sachskunde* had been substituted for Heimatkunde in the new curriculum. Sachskunde was to emphasize urban life, civic affairs, Germany and Europe, governmental processes, and an objective view of social life. The curriculum for Sachskunde is quite specific. We observed Sachskunde lessons and interviewed teachers about them. We accompanied classes on local excursions. We watched children role-playing the presentation of a petition for a public playground-park to the Bürgermeister and Town Council. The conclusion we drew was that the substitution of Sachskunde for Heimatkunde and those aspects of Naturkunde that were concerned with nature and the local area was not at all a change in principle. Though it was so intended, it was converted to a substitute change in the process of instruction and classroom management. The examples used during Sachskunde sessions, the excursions, the role-playing, were heavily in favor of the local community. There was much lost. The richness of local history and folklore and the appreciation of the manifestations of nature literally outside of the school windows were reduced and made diffuse. In essence, however, Sachskunde became a kind of Heimatkunde. As one teacher said when we asked her what happened to Heimatkunde, "Oh, we do most of that now, but we call it Sachskunde."

No change in principle had occurred. A new subject matter category had been implemented as a curriculum change appropriate to the new age, but it served largely as a mechanism of stabilization and continuity. It was a substitution, not a transformation.

Another kind of continuity was revealed in our ethnographic work, but we did not fully understand it until we returned home and analyzed our films of classroom behavior. In fact, for a while we were fairly confused about some observations we had made of teachers in their classrooms. It had to do with making the strange familiar—quite the opposite of what G. Spindler had to do in the study of Roger Harker.

Teaching Styles and Central Questions

Our classroom observation and recording techniques were described in the summary of the Schönhausen study. At the end of the first two weeks of observation we had decided that each of the six teachers whose classrooms we visited had a very distinctive teaching style but that the three on whom we were concentrating represented the whole range. One, the Rektor, a middle-aged male and a very experienced teacher, orchestrated his classroom every mo-

ment. He spent most of the time in the front of the room lecturing and demonstrating. He aroused interest, called on students, most of whom were trying to get his attention so he would call on them, paced back and forth, and used vigorous gestures and bodily movements to make points. When he was not lecturing or demonstrating, the class was working on assigned projects while he moved among them examining their work, correcting, and urging them on. He never relinquished overt control and virtually never rested. We began to call him the "Conductor" (as of an orchestra).

Another teacher, young, female, and with four years of teaching experience, seemed totally different in her classroom behavior. She rarely lectured; her arm and head gestures were subtle and close to the body. She never paced about in or orchestrated from the front of the room. Her rest stations, where she stopped in repose, observing but not overtly controlling, were window-side-front (to the left of the students) or in the back of the room in either corner. She turned the class over to the children, or seemed to, for group work and particularly for role-playing, her favorite technique for getting the children involved and teaching them to think through the workings of everyday situations—working in a newspaper office, learning etiquette, petitioning the mayor, reenacting history, and so forth. We began to think of her as the "Fader," because she literally seemed to fade from the scene. One had to look for her in the classroom at times.

The style of the third teacher, also young and female and less experienced, was somewhere between the two just described. She spent most of her time in front of the classroom, lectured and demonstrated with more emphasis and gesturing than the other female teacher but much less than the Rektor, and moved among the children occasionally when they were working, but more often remained in the front of the room while children came up to her with their work. She never used role-playing as a teaching technique during our periods of observation.

All three teachers seemed highly effective. Children were eager to learn and on the whole cooperative and involved. The work they did, much of which we examined, seemed substantially above grade level for American elementary school children in substance and competence, though not as diverse and individualistic.

We were so impressed with the differences in teaching styles among these three teachers whom we had observed and recorded with field notes, travel maps, audio recording, and 35mm shots that we began to wonder how we could ever pose our central question: How is culture transmitted in the school and how does this transmission relate to the perceptions and choice of instrumental alternatives leading to more urban or more traditional lifestyles? If there were such great differences in transmitting styles, we could hardly use our observations as an argument for some relatively uniform influence of the school.

Making the Strange Familiar Through Film

When we began filming in classrooms during the last two weeks of our field-

work, we concentrated on behavioral episodes that would document the observed differences in teaching styles. We succeeded, for when the films are shown everyone immediately sees the differences and describes them approximately as we have. We know this because we have shown the films to 209 graduate students in education, nearly all of them experienced teachers, in three different classes at Stanford and at Wisconsin, to a seminar in ethnography, and to individual colleagues. The students in our classes wrote out their observations. They saw something we did not, however, and this something turned us around in our interpretations.

We had been so impressed with the diversity in styles that we could not see the commonalities. We began to form our perception of the differences during the first days of fieldwork, and everything we observed and recorded seemed to confirm these perceptions. When we started filming, we filmed in order to record the differences. It was not until more than a year after our return home, following repeated reviewings of the films and finally the observations by our students and colleagues who had not been in the field with us, that we began to see the commonalities.

The features that the three teachers have in common in their classroom management are perceived as follows:

- There is strong task orientation. A clear instructional goal is laid out, worked on, and completed. Work is immediately turned in to the teacher at completion.
- The materials used, as well as the task definition, are uniform. All

children do the same lesson at the same time.

- There are clear definitions of limits in tolerated behavior at all times, even when teachers appear to relinquish control.
- The classrooms are clearly teacher-centered, teacher-controlled, teacher-directed, and teacher-disciplined.
- There is little fostering of self-responsibility or autonomy.
- The relationship to authority is fixed and constant, even when it appears superficially not to be.
- Teacher approval rather than peer approval is sought by children, and given; it is the major sanction.
- All three teachers appear to assume that if they do not control the classroom, disorder will result.

All of these commonalities were detected and recorded by most of the people who observed the films, with no previous suggestions or information about the classrooms viewed except for general statements about when and where the work was done, general background on the Rems Valley area, and an overall statement of the purpose of the project as a whole.

The differences in style impressed us so strongly that we could not see the commonalities, but why? As we reconstruct the situation, we think we were so overwhelmingly impressed because we were in an exotic setting. "Exotic" is too strong a word, but it conveys our meaning. German culture, language, and social behavior are much more like our own than, say, traditional Kanai culture, but they are still different enough so that despite regular visits lasting months for many years we never lost our sense of being in a "foreign" country. In ways we do not fully understand, this directed our attention to the differences rather than the commonalities—in fact, to the exclusion of the commonalities. We acquired a "mind-set" early in the fieldwork and used our recording techniques to record what our mind-set told us was there.

We had to make the strange familiar back home, in our own setting, by reviewing our recorded data and the films of classroom behavior and showing the films to others, to make this possible.

This episode in our field experience convinced us that one of our common professional problems in ethnographic cultural translation may be that we are prone to making the strange even stranger than it really is. Perhaps it is this occupational hazard that has made cultural anthropology as a discipline more oriented toward differences in humankind than toward basic commonalities.

Of more direct importance to the anthroethnography of schooling was the fact that without our films and, of course, our slides, audiotapes, field notes, etc., to review again and again and display to others, we would not have been able to correct the deficiencies in interpretation produced by our fieldwork mind-set. Anthroethnographers must be collectors of more than they know uses for at the time.

Further, this episode underlines the unique importance of films (and videotapes). There is no parallel to the capturing of experience on sound-color film. The gestalt of movement, gesture, voice level, pitch, pause, facial expressions, and interactions with children is there to review again and again.

To be sure, the camera is selective. One of our frustrations is that we would be pointed in one direction while something was happening in six other sectors. We tried to pan and move from event to event quickly. Our films have a great deal of information in them. They are also the world's worst cinema. They are jerky and spasmodic and make one dizzy. They also miss much and highlight selectively. Nevertheless, they are indispensable.

Our use of the camera in the field, incidentally, was quite different from the kind of use often advocated and practiced by many careful ethnographers. The work done by Frederick Erickson using videotape (see Chapter 5 by Erickson and Mohatt) depends on a continuous, unmanned, and less selective record of classroom activity. The videotape is the primary source of data in this and some similar studies and is microanalyzed. In our usage, the camera is an extension of the fieldworker's eye, after enough fieldwork has been done to sensitize one to what is happening and what is important. We carried the super-8mm camera and compact 35mm camera everywhere we went for two weeks, and when we saw something we thought should be filmed, we filmed it. That our mind-set caused us to film classroom episodes that make the stylistic differences loom large in our film record is not to be gainsaid. It is a tribute to the value of the relatively complete record film makes possible, even when shot selectively, that we could recover the commonalities underlying differences that we did. We have

also found a source of renewed inspiration and a continued flow of new information in the film shots of playground activity, street scenes in the village, vineyard operations, panned shots of the whole valley from vantage points high above it, Sunday walkers, sports contests, and much more. We are still doing fieldwork years later as we view the films.

Qualitative Versus Quantitative Methods: Strange Bedfellows?

It has been said by some colleagues, in papers at professional meetings and in print, that quantitative and qualitative methods are incompatible. We reject this notion. In all of our nonschooling ethnographic fieldwork we have used quantitative methods and statistical analyses extensively. In both the original and the restudy phases of the Schönhausen study such methods and analytic procedures are a central part of the methodology.

Confining our remarks to the Schönhausen study, we make the point that the major instrument, the Instrumental Activities Inventory, elicits *emic* understandings with *emic* stimuli, and yet the responses can be treated quantitatively. It is the native's view and his or her cultural knowledge that we are eliciting with an instrument composed of stimuli that are formulated in native terms. The translation into social science occurs after the native responses are elicited, and is facilitated by the fact that the instrument is etically organized as well. That is, the conceptual structure that lies behind the I.A.I. model is drawn from theories and research on culture change and cognitive control.

This conceptual structure remains constant. It remained essentially the same in our application of the instrument with the Kanai and the Cree, and in Germany. But the emic stimuli, the line drawings themselves, are made relevant to the local culture, and to the local version of modernization.[8] The line drawings of which the I.A.I. consists are accurate representations, taken directly from 35mm shots and modified by stripping out background "noise," of activities and settings in the immediate environment of the respondent. Further, these drawings were critiqued during their development, by natives, on native terms, both for selectivity and for realistic accuracy. The instrument elicits qualitative data (choices of instrumental activities and statements of supporting values) that can be coded and treated nonparametrically.

The statistical treatment of the I.A.I. data provides a framework within which certain phases of the ethnographic study proceed, but the ethnographic study determines what will be in the instrument. Without the I.A.I. data we would not have known any of the things we listed as major conclusions of the study. Without the ethnography we would never know how these results could have come about. Qualitative and quantitative techniques are in no way incompatible. They provide information on different dimensions of the same phenomena, *if* the instruments used for quantification are heuristic to the setting and are formed out of field experience.

Fieldwork and Sex

As a last point in the discussion of the Schönhausen study we wish to take up the matter of sex in the classroom. It is usually the case that there are two sexes present, and yet most classroom ethnographies have been done by either a man or a woman or two persons of the same sex. In our experience in the Schönhausen school we found that as a man-woman team we had access to many more aspects of school life than did G. Spindler alone in the 1968 study. Since most of the teachers were then, and are now, female, there were some awkwardnesses for a lone male. It was not possible, for instance, for George alone to enter and feel comfortable in the teachers' room where all teachers assembled before, in between, and after classes. The Rektor never entered the room himself. As a man-woman team, and particularly as a married team, we found that most of the awkwardness in research evaporated and an easy give-and-take developed that was invaluable as a source of insight and information regarding the operation of the school and the attitudes of individual teachers.

In the classroom, and on excursions, it was very useful to have both sexes represented on the team. Louise Spindler saw behavior that George did not see the first time and did not record. For example, the Rektor tended to favor girls in his classroom interaction. This is probably quite usual for male teachers, but though George had perceived it in the study of Roger Harker it did not appear in his observations in either 1968 or 1977. This was noted and recorded extensively by Louise.

There were many other instances where the presence of both sexes was important. In general, George Spindler had relatively low direct contact with the girls, but they clustered around Louise Spindler at every opportunity, allowing for free interviewing and exchange.

Even if both sexes are not doing ethnography in the same situation at the same time, it does seem important that at least two persons be present. Observers on both sides of the room see and record many events and interactions that one would miss. Two people can also do different things at the same time. One can photograph while the other writes notes. One can interview a teacher while the other observes and records the interaction, even filming it. There were many situations in and around the Schönhausen school where the presence of two fieldworkers seemed indispensable.

In the social life outside the school, with teachers and townspeople alike, the married couple relationship was very important, since most of the parents and teachers were married. We formed friendships and made contacts that would have been difficult for a single person.

Conclusion to This Chapter

It seems useful to summarize the major methodological points that we have made in the discussion of Roger Harker and of the Schönhausen school.

1. Teaching should be considered (more than it is) as a means of diffusing ethnographic innovations into professional education.

2. Collecting enough data in scope and depth so that it can be used in different cultural translations is highly desirable.

3. Ethnographers may profitably draw from an interdisciplinary corpus of concepts and research techniques.

4. Contextualization can usefully extend as far as time and resources permit and often provides the base from which relevant hypotheses can be drawn.

5. Securing as complete an audiovisual record as possible is important, because this record can be analyzed and interpreted in different ways again and again.

6. Qualitative and quantitative methods and data are not opposed, but on the contrary are complementary.

7. Instruments, when used, should be emically relevant, oriented to the views and cultural knowledge of the natives.

8. It is desirable to have both sexes or at least two observers on the ethnographic team.

9. Making the strange familiar will remain a basic task in transcultural ethnography. Making the familiar strange will continue to be a basic problem in the anthroethnography of schooling in our own society.

Notes

[1] The Menominee fieldwork is described in the chapter by George and Louise Spindler in G. Spindler, ed. 1970a.

[2] The team was called the "Stanford Consultation Service." Its purposes were to offer in-service, individualized consultation and at the same time to do basic, case-study-oriented research in classrooms, schools, and school systems. It was supported by the Rosenberg Foundation during its initial phases. On the team were a sociologist, a psychiatrist, Professor Bush, and various graduate students working on dissertations in education and sociology.

[3] See L. Spindler, *Menomini Women and Culture Change*, 1962.

[4] "Schönhausen" is a fictitious name. Though the Rektor and other participants in the study have no objection to our using the real name of the community, we feel it is best to cloak its identity.

[5] The results of this study are published in one paper (G. Spindler 1970b), a chapter in a collected volume on education and cultural process (G. Spindler 1974), another chapter in a monograph on urbanization and identity in a German village (G. Spindler 1973), and in an analysis of long-term research on the psychology of culture change and urbanization (L. Spindler 1978). Our purposes in the restudy of 1977 were focused on studying the effects of sweeping educational reform that had been instituted since our first study. Louise Spindler did not work in the school in the 1967–1968 study, though she was active in its community phases. She was a full partner in the 1977 restudy.

[6] There are several kinds of secondary schools in Germany. The Hauptschule is not university-preparatory; the Gymnasium is.

[7] We wish to extend our special thanks to the teaching staff in the Schönhausen Grundschule, particularly its Rektor. The parents, the graduates of the Grundschule attending other schools, the children themselves, and the personnel of the urban control school also deserve our warm gratitude. Doubtless we were extended special privileges and courtesies, because we were foreigners, that might not have been as enthusiastically rendered to a native researcher. We are in deep debt to all of the people who so generously helped us and we only regret that the anonymity that we hope to preserve for the school and community makes it impossible to thank them publicly by name. We should also like to express our gratitude to the National Institute of Mental Health, the Wenner-Gren Foundation for Anthropological Research, the Human Factors Programme of NATO, and the Spencer Foundation for the support of the

1977 study. The 1968 study was supported by the National Science Foundation and by the School of Education at Stanford University.

[8] See G. Spindler 1974b for a statement of the model and G. and L. Spindler 1965 for the application to the Kanai study.

References

Ehni, Jorg. 1967. *Das Bild der Heimat im Schullesebuch.* Volksleben, Vol. 16. Tübingen: Tübinger Vereinigung für Volkskunde.

Spindler, George. 1959. *The Transmission of American Culture.* The Third Burton Lecture in Elementary Education, Harvard University. Cambridge, MA: Harvard University Press. Abridged version in G. Spindler, ed., *Education and Culture: Anthropological Approaches.* New York: Holt, Rinehart and Winston, 1963, 148–172.

———. 1970 (reissued 1986)a. *Being an Anthropologist: Fieldwork in Eleven Cultures.* Prospect Heights, IL: Waveland Press, Inc.

———. 1970b. "Studying Schooling in Schönhausen," *Council on Anthropology and Education Newsletter,* 1:1–6.

———. 1973. *Burgbach: Urbanization and Identity in a German Village.* New York: Holt, Rinehart and Winston.

———. 1987. "Schooling in Schönhausen: A Study of Cultural Transmission and Instrumental Adaptation in an Urbanizing German Village." In G. Spindler, ed., *Education and Cultural Process: Anthropological Approaches,* 2/e. Prospect Heights, IL: Waveland Press, Inc.

———. 1974b "From Omnibus to Linkages: Models for the Study of Cultural Transmission." *Council on Anthropology and Education Newsletter,* 1(4).

Spindler, George, and Louise Spindler. 1965. "The Instrumental Activities Inventory: A Technique for the Study of the Psychology of Acculturation." *Southwestern Journal of Anthropology,* 21:1–23.

———. 1978. "Schooling in Schönhausen Revisited." *Anthropology and Education Quarterly,* 9:181–182.

———. 1978. "Die Vermittlung von Kulturellen Werten and Spezifischen Anpassungmechanismus in einen Dorf mit zunehmend städtischen Gepräge." In M. Matter, ed., *Rheinisches Jarhbuch für Volkskunde.* Universität Bonn, 85–96.

Spindler, Louise. 1962. *Menomini Women and Culture Change.* American Anthropological Association, vol. 64, no. 1, memoir 91. See also her doctoral dissertation, *Women and Culture Change: A Case Study of the Menomini Indians,* 1956, and her M.A. thesis, *The Autobiographical Approach to the Study of*

Acculturation of Menomini Indian Women, 1952, Stanford University, for further information on the development and use of the expressive autobiographic interview.

———. 1978. "The Psychology of Culture Change and Urbanization." In G. Spindler, ed., *The Making of Psychological Anthropology*. Berkeley: University of California Press, 174–200.

2

Alan Peshkin

The Researcher and Subjectivity: Reflections on an Ethnography of School and Community

Alan Peshkin

The Author

Alan Peshkin, professor of comparative education at the University of Illinois, Urbana, has done fieldwork in Pakistan ("A Case Study of Planned Change in East Pakistan," 1962, University of Chicago, unpublished dissertation) and in Nigeria (*Kanuri Schoolchildren,* Holt, Rinehart and Winston, 1972). Since 1972, he has been working in the American Middle West, beginning with an ethnographic study of school and community in "Mansfield" (*Growing Up American,* University of Chicago Press, 1978), followed by an investigation of a consolidated school district that decided to close the only school in one of its five villages ("The Imperfect Union: School Consolidation and Community Conflict," in preparation). With Spencer Foundation support, he will continue his work on the communal function of schooling in a study of a fundamentalist Christian day school and its host church.

This Chapter

In this chapter Alan Peshkin honestly and tellingly considers the factors that brought him to study the relationship of school and community in "Mansfield," a small town in Illinois, and to use as his method what he has come to regard as ethnography. He identifies the singular qualities of the ethnographic style, but claims that he has followed it more by inclination than by rational choice—it "suits me." Personal taste in the selection and carrying through of research procedures in the social sciences is of great significance. Possibly what ethnographic methods have in common are actually the predispositions of people who do a wide range of studies characterized as ethnography. Peshkin proceeds further to provide us with certain facts of his youthful experience in a Chicago neighborhood and in a Michigan village during long summers, which could predispose him to the study of a small community, and toward the personality characteristics that make it possible to do fieldwork in a small community. So both the choice of research methods and the selection of field site, Peshkin's preamble tells us, are decisively affected by nonrational personal predispositions. Only too often discussions and criticisms of research methods, samples, and field sites proceed as though these predisposing factors were irrelevant.

The central focus of the analysis of Mansfield and its school is one that is identifiable in many small communities throughout the United States, and has parallels in any culturally distinctive group in relationship to its school. The movement to school consolidations has left many of America's smaller communities without schools, particularly high schools, and without the identity and self-extension that the school-community relationship affords. This is a dimension of an accelerating trend in American life away from localism, continuity, and identity, and towards conglomerate impersonalization. Mansfield, the Hutterites, the Amish, hinterland Wisconsin (and other) communities, and alternative cultures and communities, carried forward mostly by the young, exist as obstacles to or self-conscious protests against this trend.

The immediate question of relevance to us as professionals interested in school-community relations is to what degree a community, an ethnic or religious group, or a social class has the right to determine how its offspring shall be educated. Is a private school for upper-class elites all right but a Mansfield school wrong? Is a parochial school acceptable but a Mansfield school wrong? An anthropological view of schooling inclines us towards the concept of education as cultural transmission, functioning to maintain communities, social structures, and values. This is, of course, a very different view than one that regards educational institutions, including even elementary schools and kindergartens, as mediators of change or as innovators. The mandate for public education in the United States has, from the beginning, been to produce "Americanized" products as well as to produce persons with the capabilities that fit the needs of an expanding industrial-urban economy. Peshkin's analysis makes the problems attendant upon local and cultural influence on schooling in our kind of society painfully clear. This kind of discussion has immediate relevance to the formulation of educational policy

Introduction

Why does one scholar study the metabolism of toads? Why does another pursue research topics that require the use of experimental methods or observation in naturalistic settings? As at least a partial answer to this type of question, it is my thesis that a close association exists among the four Rs of research: (1) researcher (who, in terms of personal qualities and background, is doing the study); (2) research (what is studied); (3) researching (how the study is conducted); (4) results (what is found in the data). This association may be merely an interesting speculation to the many scholars who consider their work to be essentially objective. However, for those of us who are doing ethnographic research—those of us who are committed to objectivity but still acknowledge the subjective nature of our work—understanding the association is essential. Investigators of social phenomena, which we are, always run the risk of finding in their data not what is there but what is in their beholding eye. Though the risk never can be reduced to zero, it can be minimized by the effort to "know thyself."[1] Accordingly, this paper attempts to illuminate the relationship among the four Rs by analyzing how they join together in my study *Growing Up American: Schooling and the Survival of Community* (1978).

Growing Up American resulted from two years of fieldwork in the Midwestern community of "Mansfield," the site of my examination of school and community in a rural area. The Mansfield school district contains almost 2500 persons and includes the village of Mansfield, with its population of about 1500. Agriculture is the area's dominant occupation, though most villagers commute to factory jobs in several nearby towns. Locally, jobs are available in shops, village maintenance, and the school system. Mansfield has no industry or tourist attractions and is set off from major roads which could facilitate outsiders' coming to town. Newcomers trickle in as housing becomes available, but growth has been slow—an increase of 100 between 1960 and 1970. Like many small towns, Mansfield has a high proportion of older persons, especially elderly widows who live alone in village homes.

In my first year in Mansfield I spent three full days a week in the school district and employed four research assistants; in the second year, I lived full time in Mansfield, for all practical purposes, and employed two research assistants. Although I planned to organize a complete community study, we began our work in Mansfield's high school (my educational focal point), having obtained the necessary consent of the school board and the superintendent. Word travels fast in small towns, and Mansfielders soon knew something unusual was happening in their school. Nonetheless, we ventured cautiously beyond the school, establishing ourselves first as acceptable persons who came, as we claimed, to learn about small towns and their schools rather than to evaluate or to present a blueprint for change. (An "acceptable" person is one who is so reassuring to Mansfielders that they talk and behave just as they do in his absence. At this time I can do no more than suggest that such a presence, critical to successful fieldwork, is the product of several factors, including personality, timing, luck, and experience.)

Mr. Tate, Mansfield's beloved and charismatic superintendent of schools, arranged our transition from the high school to the community. He would introduce me to the mayor, for example, or to Mansfield High School's oldest living graduate and venerable ex-newspaper editor. Such people couldn't refuse Tate's request that they meet me; moreover, they were very curious to learn who I was and what I was doing. Further prevailing upon Mr. Tate, I joined him at church and at Kiwanis meetings. By attending all local football games, other social events, and as many community activities as I thought would welcome me, I meant to become visible and known, and thereby to facilitate my access to other activities and the many people I planned to interview.

Since I intended to acquire the most comprehensive picture possible of both high school and community, there was no limit, beyond those provided by the constraints of my imagination, to what I endeavored to learn. Thus we operated simultaneously on three levels: that of the present, by means of participant observation, with the emphasis on observation; that of the past, by means of newspapers, photographs, minutes, reports, yearbooks, membership lists, and records; and that of the generally indefinite past, present, and future, by means of interview schedules and mailed questionnaires (directed, for example, at perceptions and values concerning what it is like to live in a small town or what kind of future Mansfield will have). In general, questionnaire data were used to confirm the impressions derived from the interviews.

Of course, it is impossible to learn everything about a school and village, however small they are. Over two years we did manage to attend each extracurricular activity several times and all classes many times. Nonetheless, one always samples, if only unconsciously. Without being explicit about it, English and social studies classes seemed more valuable to us as samples of local sentiment and social exchange than algebra and industrial arts; accordingly, we saw more of the former than of the latter. There were five churches in town, but two of them, in terms of size of membership and scale of activity, dominated Mansfield's religious life; though we interviewed all five ministers, we spent more time in the two dominant churches. By means of a questionnaire we elicited opinions from a stratified sample of all school district residents, but followed other criteria to select interviewees. If we wanted to learn about an organization, we saw officers or long-standing members. If we wanted an historical perspective, we went to the oldest nonsenile natives. The point is that we selected persons to be interviewed in terms of a particular purpose; mere accessibility was not a sufficient reason.

The issue of accessibility highlights an association among the four Rs. Is it not the case that each of us pleases some persons more than others? What the researcher is allowed to see and whom the researcher is allowed to meet depends on who the researcher is perceived to be. Given this perception, one may obtain, therefore, no, limited, fair, or excellent cooperation and access. Corollary to this is the fact that throughout one's fieldwork numerous decisions are made about what to see and whom to meet. Because of the researcher's priorities and unavoidable omissions, these decisions result in data stamped with the researcher's imprint. As a result, the data base from which a study is reconstructed bears the singular limitations and strengths inherent in the researcher's decisions.

Twenty-four months of fieldwork, abetted by six research assistants and the tape recorder, produced a mass of data—more, clearly, than could be crammed into one volume. Though guided by my avowed purpose to study the relationship between school and community in a rural area, I was never certain what that one volume would contain. At no particular point, until the book was written, could I have articulated its contents; yet the book was being written all the time. I see now that some events, some facts, some associations struck home with me and found their way into my anecdotal accounts of what I was experiencing and was motived to relate to family and friends during weekend visits at home. It sounds too mysterious (and unacademic) to say the evolving experience of fieldwork "led" me, for this characterization suggests I was caught up in an inexplicable process over which I had no control.[2] However, my full comprehension of what I was doing and finding occurred after I had completed the fieldwork and could enjoy the luxury of reflective introspection. This paper contains the results of my introspection; it focuses on the four Rs and their association in the next two sections and on my major finding regarding the communal function of schooling in the final section.

Researchers and How and What They Study

The methodologically orthodox might be more reassured if I had chosen an ethnographic approach to the study of schooling after careful, calculated deliberation—if, indeed, in best Ben Franklin style I had listed and weighed the pros and cons of alternative approaches and, finally, ethnography had won out. Many researchers choose their methods as a result of formal training—adopting the ethnographic mode, for example, if they have been inducted into the tribe of anthropologists. Confession, good for the soul, does not make the most felicitous commentary on an ethnography of schooling, but the

fact is I chose my data-collecting techniques neither by calculation nor by training. I set out to investigate school and community in a rural area;[3] I announced this intention as frequently as I needed to in Mansfield and in fund-seeking proposals; and I ended up conducting what *I think* is an ethnographic study.

I believe I can reconstruct how I chose my research procedures. To begin with, I am not comfortable with quantitative analysis, though I do not reject statistics and join those who claim numbers dehumanize or "If you can measure it, that ain't it" (Kaplan 1964:206). I try to avoid the mystiques of both quantity and quality that Kaplan so aptly describes (1964:172, 206–214). However, what choice of methodology comes down to for many of us, I suspect, is personal taste: the sense of adventure which I like in research is present for me under the circumstances of the ethnographic approach. Moreover, I like the literary style that ethnographies permit. Finally, I am attracted to the particular way good ethnographies powerfully portray and illuminate concepts and relationships. In light of this acknowledgment, perhaps it is not too far-fetched to hypothesize that some researchers have methodological commitments in search of a study.

Of course, I could rationalize my preference by identifying the ethnographic style's singular qualities of intimacy, of access to the actor's perspective, of holistic compass. I could extend the case by reference to its hypothesis-generating potential and its peculiar strengths for exploring phenomena for which an extensive literature does not exist or for which other methodologies have not developed promising variables. And I could cite the quantitative versus qualitative literature to bolster the case for avoiding a priori commitments to one methodological orthodoxy or another (for example, see Wilson 1977, Cronbach 1975, and Rist 1977). I know these things; I teach them every spring. The fact remains that for now I like and prefer to work in a certain way. This way suits me (hopefully, it suits the problems I have been pursuing) and I just naturally follow it.

In addition to following the dictates of taste, I also believe (rationalization after the fact?) that my research purpose required an ethnographic approach. How else could I explore the whole life of a village and the place of a school in that village? Such research requires the type of association that ethnographies exemplify: long-term, in-depth, personal, intensive, and encompassing. Moreover, while the ethnographic mode implies an approach, it does not dictate particular research techniques. This, too, suited me, even though the longer I was in the field, the more the details of data collection took shape. And the more I knew what I needed to know, the more I understood what means I must use and in what order.

But if we call an approach or a product "ethnographic," are we just using jargon, a time-honored label to obfuscate potential readers? That is, does the label actually do more than legitimate what we do when we want to study a multidimensional phenomenon and are unable to articulate precise ends and means? Wolcott refers to muddling about and pursuing hunches, observing

that traditional anthropology is satisfying because "one is free to discover what the problem is" (1975:113). While reasonably exact definitions of ethnography exist, they do not necessarily absolve the claim of "jargon." For example, Conklin writes:

> An ethnographer is an anthropologist who attempts . . . to record and describe the culturally significant behaviors of a particular society. Ideally, this description, an ethnography, requires a long period of intimate study and residence in a small, well-defined community, knowledge of observational techniques, including prolonged face-to-face contacts with members of the local group, direct participation in some of that group's activities, and a greater emphasis on intensive work with informants than on the use of documentary or survey data. [1968:172][4]

If we think of Conklin's specifications as a set of conditions, then which are the necessary and which are the sufficient ones to verify the presence of ethnographic behavior and ethnographic description? I confess to not knowing the answer, to believing that an "answer" does not exist, and to feeling that it is inconsequential that no answer exists. I tried to identify the critical part or parts of Conklin's definition by framing sentences such as "If one does X (or X and Y), then one is an ethnographer" or "If an account contains X (or X and Y), then it is an ethnography or, more particularly, an ethnography of schooling." I found no such critical Xs, Ys, or combinations of Xs and Ys, although I am aware that persons called ethnographers, more than other researchers, are prone to use the practices Conklin describes.

Of course, people need an identity and enjoy the company of like-minded, like-trained, and like-named persons. Issues of identity and fellowship aside, I fail to see how Conklin's definition establishes distinctive boundaries for either ethnographer or ethnography. However, if it is useful,—whether or not necessary—to have terminology that has proved valuable for communicating one's intentions to persons who must be assured about one's plans (persons like colleagues, funders, and editors), then one makes warranted use of that terminology. In short, while the wide variety of approaches and outcomes labeled "ethnographic" belies the precision of the label, it does signal behavioral dispositions which suggest the general character of an approach, if not a product, and thus it is beneficial.

Retrospection may help to illuminate both the ends and the means of the researcher. For, once the experience in Mansfield was past, I became aware of a more predictable link between personal taste and choice of research topic than I had sensed and than scholars usually acknowledge. To be sure, the point can be pressed to absurdity, but researchers seeking to understand shyness, friendship, failure, communication, the handicapped, or contemporary fascism often may be engaged in the satisfaction of very personal needs or concerns which long preceded their scholarly work or even their intent to become scholars.[5] So it is with me and community, just as it was with Redfield's and Lewis' study and restudy, since I am persuaded that the harmony Redfield found in his Mexican village (1930) and the discord that Lewis described in the same village (1951) resulted not only from variant times of study and theoretical starting points, but also from personal commitments and concerns of which neither may have been at all conscious.

To illustrate this point, I know now that my path to the geographical, if not the psychological, community of Mansfield began at Chicago's west side in a era when the city was an amalgam of relatively stable ethnic neighborhoods. Such a neighborhood often constituted a community: if I was in, or causing, trouble, I knew and was known by hundreds of people who could point out where I lived and to whom I belonged; I had a proprietary sense about "our" territory, though not the degree of possessiveness that demands battle with transgressors of one's turf; and I felt at home in this area where one group's ethos dominated all the stores and services and local activities. I didn't understand much about the word until I was older, but I believe that "ghetto" aptly describes the neighborhood of my youth.

This feeling of community was dramatically reinforced in the six summers I spent in a tiny unincorporated village in southern Michigan, where the same families returned year after year and where, even more than in Chicago, I had an overwhelming feeling of belonging, of being cared for, of being known and important. It was my home ghetto extended to the shores of Lake Michigan. Belonging came easily: you arrived the day after school was out, you left the day before school began, you had dry, brown skin for three months, and throughout the intervening nine months you looked forward to returning and hoped the same persons would return to join you on the sand, summer after summer after summer.

Midway through my undergraduate years, the city of Chicago in general and my neighborhood in particular shifted population. My family moved, after living more than 20 years on the same corner of the same block. The combination of war-related job opportunities, post-World War II affluence, and pressure for housing produced the waves of internal and external migration that transformed the city. That stability which made my old neighborhood mine was shattered. I could not go home again. Old-time Chicagoans lamented "For Rent" signs on apartment buildings whose owners previously had transacted all changes of renters exclusively by word of mouth. Chicagoans and other urbanites experienced dramatic changes, though for many the changes represented occasions for upward mobility. They departed their old neighborhoods with alacrity tinged, at most, with a trace of nostalgia.

After graduating from college, I moved to a town of about 6000 and then to Madison, Wisconsin. I returned frequently to friends and family in Chicago and vicinity, loving the sight of my city even as seen from the new Edens and Kennedy expressways which themselves abetted the destruction of old neighborhoods. On one of these homebound trips I hit on the right word to describe what I had sensed and had been unable to articulate about the places I'd moved to after leaving Chicago. The word is "antiseptic." These post-Chicago places were not dirt clean; they were disturbingly people clean. Where was the street life? Didn't people

allow their children out except to go to and return from school? Weren't there attractive corners to hang around? Walls and street signs off which to bounce balls?

Scores of sad and dreary newspaper stories of urbanites displaced by the wrecker's swinging steel ball reinforced this post-Chicago sentiment. The claims of progress, of the right of eminent domain, and of transportation exigencies converged to create a class of urban evacuees and, for their shelter, those new, instantly old towers of public housing. If the migrations of the 1950s and 1960s included the urban middle and upper classes, they nonetheless brought greater grief to the dispossessed poor, who were powerless to decide where they would live and for how long. Personally, urban decline and its attendant disasters were peripheral to my life. I had moved to university towns, and my sense of community, having losts its geographic base, was grounded in persons widely dispersed among several cities. It did exist, however, since strong feelings about community survival eventually surfaced in the midst of my research.[6]

I spent part of the summer of 1970 in the Indian city of Visakhapatnam, setting up interviews to pilot test a questionnaire designed to study schooling and modern value orientations. These interviews took me to Jalaripet, a village of caste fishermen, anomalously located within the municipal limits of Visakhapatnam. While waiting for my interviews to be arranged, I visited the village's five-grade primary school, observed that the school had the too typical pyramidal age distribution (many children in grade 1, few in grade 5), and learned that noncaste fishermen from the city working in motorized vessels jeopardized the livelihoods of Jalaripet's canoe-borne fishermen. In short, I perceived that Jalaripet, apparently adopting neither economic nor educational means of the sort that would redress their troubled situation, was a village in decline. I resolved to explore its plight: I would complete my modernization research and then return to India to mount a full-scale village study.

Meanwhile, Pakistan and Bangladesh went to war, the United States "tilted" toward Pakistan, and India punished American scholars by restricting their entry for research. So much for Jalaripet. Unable to go to India, I decided to stay home and investigate the same issue—the relationship between schooling and community well-being. Although I did not seek an American setting which seemed as endangered as Jalaripet, I was conscious of the issue of economic viability in the choice of American sites. Considering the possible influence of other studies, I see West's description of Plainville as similar to Mansfield, although I had read *Plainville, U.S.A.* long before coming to Mansfield and was not aware of any direct influence. West writes that "no town was considered if its inhabitants drew any important portion of their income from mines, factories, summer resorts, or any other industrial or urbanizing activity that would confuse the economics of a traditional farming community" (1945:vii). The choice of Mansfield meant that I had located such a community, at least in a geographic sense; Mansfield's future, while not necessarily in peril, was by no means secure. Notwithstanding the demand that I articulate my research goals, it was only after my fieldwork was complete that the notions of community (in a psychological sense), survival, and schooling converged into a single theme, the product of fieldwork which I believe is conventionally termed "ethnographic." (The next section describes how this convergence occurred.)

Given that I planned to explore the life of an entire village, I needed access to a place of manageable size. Mansfield suited my purpose, and I ended up being there in the anthropologist's special (albeit not exclusive) way. In short, I found my village, located a residence, met people, learned about the power structure, established rapport, acquired informants, participated, and observed. For the most part, I could forgo mastering a new language; I did need to do some genealogies. By doing what anthropologists did, I believe I acquired that holistic sense, that grasp, that feeling of the ambience of a place which anthropologists claim as their hallmark.

The Researcher and the Reconstruction of Results

However much an ethnographic approach may provide a license to muddle about and pursue hunches, formal plans still are a likely prelude to embarking on an ethnographic project. Yet there is the abiding reality of each day's field experience, where possibilities, if not imperatives, for the next day's work are set in motion. In time, the fine sense of adventure and the discoveries which enliven the early days of fieldwork lead to impressions that compound and eventually evolve into promising ideas and patterns. In my case, a number of ideas emerged as a series of patterns which together suggested where I was going.

Whether one studies a factory, village, park, or school, some persons come forth readily to the researcher. They are easy to meet, like being met, enjoy talking, love being listened to; they may reach out to you before you have extended your best, most practiced efforts to tell your story—who you are, why you're wherever you are, and how your needs and their cooperation just naturally intersect. Such good folks abounded in Mansfield; they made and kept appointments; tape recorders did not disconcert them. I may not have known where I was headed, but I soon sensed I was getting somewhere. That somewhere was into the snare set for unwitting fieldworkers who, unless jerked back to reality, may conclude that they are truly grasping their factory or school, uncovering its essence, when, in fact, they are being led only where the most friendly, hale, and generally middle-class citizens (and also often the older and lonelier citizens of the chosen setting) are able to lead them—where those citizens are.

My friendly folk I called the "mainstream Mansfielder." Perhaps elevating necessity to a virtue, I was convinced they constituted the majority in the village, judged from questionnaire survey results that they were a reasonably congruent group, and determined that *Growing Up American* would be about them. The point is that there is a book

I did not write; it would be about the people from Mansfield's "underside." They are statistically less consequential (perhaps no more than 12 percent, according to survey data) but, obviously, no less human and important. They are, however, clearly less integrally incorporated in Mansfield's community than the Mrs. Brightwoods of whom I did write and whose dominating presence suggested the thrust I meant my book to reflect.

During the fall of my first year in Mansfield I met Mrs. Brightwood, a knowledgeable 85-year-old resident who could inform me of Mansfield's past. Midway through my set of first-visit questions Mrs. Brightwood told me a story to clarify what it's like for her to live in a small town. Her friend Adah, about Mrs. Brightwood's age, lived in a city. Adah decided that while she was still of sound mind she would select a desirable nursing home and voluntarily admit herself. Finding institutional life too formal and cold, she soon regretted her decision. Distressed by her friend's grief, Mrs. Brightwood declared that she herself didn't need a nursing home, because she was looked after. If she ever missed a Sunday school class, she could expect a telephone call as soon as services were over. Her groceries were delivered. The children next door, who called her "Grandma," picked up her mail at the post office. Neighbors took out her garbage when she was ill or the sidewalks were too icy. And she laughed as she remembered the lady across the street who "keeps an eye on me. One day she called up to ask after my health, thinking I might not be OK because I'd opened my drapes later than usual."

I was impressed by Mrs. Bright-wood's story and set out to ascertain whether she was an aberration or if in fact Mansfielders looked after their elderly. The reality was that not all ill or aged persons received attentions of that kind, but that many did—the churchgoers, the organization members, the old timers, and others. In pursuit of the generality of the point, I heard repeatedly about garbage taken out, mail collected, groceries delivered, and shades observed. Mrs. Brightwood alerted me to my first point: the pattern of Mansfield's nurturant network.

"You must remember," I would remind my interviewees, "that I'm a city boy and I depend on you to tell me what life is like in Mansfield." This query elicited one predictable response: "Well," I'd be told, "take care who you tell your insults to because in Mansfield we're all related to each other." I heard this often enough to begin a genealogical probing which revealed that residents have many kin outside of their immediate family living within the school district boundaries (approximately 40 percent have 11 or more relatives outside their nuclear family living in the school district), and that many families have resided in Mansfield over three, four, and even five generations. Beginning with impressions obtained from open-ended inquiry, which later were verified by responses to a questionnaire administered throughout the school district, I established a second point: the pattern of Mansfield's substantial kin network.

Mansfield's students often expressed views of their community at variance with their elders'. Yet both groups agreed on the fact, though not on its meaning, that in Mansfield you knew and were known to everyone. Adolescents objected to their fishbowl existence and to the excessively successful communication channels which propelled the events of their life throughout the village—even, they complained only half-jokingly, before they occurred. Their parents, however, referred to the friendliness of village life, to the concern people have for each other. When widow Velma Hodgkins, a long-time Mansfield resident, sits in her living room, she peers out the window at every passing car and person. "Just a habit," she explains, but with variations it is a common habit in Mansfield. Notwithstanding different motivations for doing so, the villagers monitor each other, attend to their neighbors' behavior, keep track of what goes on. Such habits, pursued within the context of Mansfield's social stability, high nurturance, and small physical scale, suggested my third point—the pattern of intimacy, which perturbs adolescents and enhances the comfort of their parents.

While attending the junior-senior prom, I noticed that the dates of many students were outsiders who lived in other towns and attended other school districts. I wondered if an exogamous disposition operated here. Preliminary inquiries uncovered the sentiment that outsiders often were more attractive than one's too-well-known, almost sibling-like classmates. In fact, over the ten-year period for which data are available, approximately two-thirds of the seniors had been classmates since first grade. This verified the point of general social stability and encouraged me to inquire about who Mansfielders married. Accordingly, I tracked down students in over 20 different graduating classes.

At first I asked, "Did so-and-so marry a local person?," forgetting to clarify what "local" meant. Though this lack of clarity did not prevent anyone from responding, I eventually realized my mistake and began to ask what area "local" included. The answer was that while local boundaries were more extensive for shopping, recreation, or medical services, one was said to have married a local person only if he or she lived within the school district.

This insight into the meaning of "local" connected with an earlier experience I'd had with a Mansfield native. He responded emotionally to what I thought was a casual question about the prospects for a new high school building. He thought that a building project could succeed with the support of the right people, but said there was considerable reluctance to raise money because of the prospects of consolidation. As for him, he concluded, "Mansfield High School will consolidate with the other county schools over my dead body."

Surprised by his intensity, I further explored this point by incorporating appropriate questions into my continually changing interview schedule. Two salient orientations soon emerged: (1) Inquiry about school purpose elicited responses about individual student success in getting good jobs or entry to college. (2) However, inquiry about consolidation evoked an entirely different perspective. Despite their obvious interest in individual student success, Mansfielders rejected a countywide school even though it could offer an expanded program and thus more curricular depth and breadth. To the contrary, the possible loss of their high school produced concerns for the community. "What will happen to Mansfield if the high school closes?" "The town will dry up and blow away." "It'll be awful dark in town if that school ever shuts down."

Informed by these understandings, I saw that the school not only set boundaries of feeling, but also integrated Mansfield's citizens. All other community organizations or institutions were limited in their capacity or intent to embrace all Mansfielders. Churches, social groups, and service clubs do contribute to social integration, but they are sectarian and exclusive and thus do not have the impact of the school. Its centripetal activities suffuse young and old alike with a territorial "our" spirit. Thus, while Mansfielders hoped their school would serve the occupational and educational ends of individual students, they clearly perceived that it had a community maintenance function.

These four patterns—a nurturant network, a kin network, intimacy, and the school as a boundary-setting, integrating factor—created a firm impression that a sense of community prevailed in Mansfield. And they provided context and meaning for otherwise discrete facts and one opinion I had acquired during the first year of study. First, I had criticized its instructional standards, believing that teachers in Mansfield fell short of ideal because they did not press students to be critical and analytical, to cast doubt on cherished beliefs, or to be intellectually independent. Second, most teachers grew up and were educated in the small towns and countryside within 50 miles of Mansfield. Even more recently, when applicants were abundant, the school board hired teachers with a rural background. Third, when board members hired their first new superintendent in 15 years, they picked a candidate they agreed was "country" and therefore the right man for the job.

Now, given an awareness of Mansfield's sense of community and of its conviction that Mansfield High School contributed to the maintenance of its community, each of these three points assumed a particular meaning. (1) The teachers, possibly deficient by my uninvited outsider's standards, did not mean to serve me or others like me. The level of discourse prevailing in their classrooms was acceptable to those persons to whom the school needed to be responsive. I was not included in this group. (2) Moreover, by selecting teachers with rural origins the school district could be confident that its educators already were socialized to work and live in a small-town school and community. (3) And hiring a man the school board perceived as "country" meant they selected one who would fit Mansfield and thus perpetuate the particular school-community relationship Mansfielders favored.

Although inarticulate about their general operating principles under direct questioning, the school board unerringly made decisions that would tend to promote a high school shaped in Mansfield's image. Its members seem to be chosen for this capacity. Since the school board's inception, farmers and natives have dominated it. The president and at least five of the seven members are always farmers, even though nonfarmers are the school district ma-

jority. Their decisions do not reflect some abstraction called "the best education," but, rather, their views as stable, rooted Mansfielders of who and what is best for the school district they serve as elected guardians.

To summarize the preceding discussion, I concluded that a sense of community existed in Mansfield and that Mansfield High School functioned to sustain this sentiment. For the mainstream social group, the school was an integrative agent. This unplanned function did not originate in written school board policies or in teacher curriculum goals. That teachers respected small-town norms was attributable not to school board regulations but to the process of teacher recruitment and self-selection.

My notion of the school-community relationship in Mansfield might have been left in the terms stated above, save for a chance experience that extended the case beyond Mansfield. In the year following my fieldwork I served on a university committee involved with bilingual-bicultural studies. Attempting to clarify my own feelings about such studies and the commitment a university should make to their development, I met with several colleagues who had attended schools for black youth in the pre-integration South. I learned that their schools' relationship to the black communities they served seemed just like Mansfield's. Both types of schools, those for black and those for white children, were controlled by their respective communities in such a way that the schools looked, felt, and sounded as if they were meant to fit a particular constituency. Though educational disasters, the black schools were comfortable places both for children and for their parents; in social and political terms, they were appropriate institutions.

Once I understood that the school-community relationship observed in Mansfield extended beyond the white, rural Midwest, I understood more than just the issues which had perplexed me about bilingual-bicultural education. To begin with, I could see that the type of relationship prevailing in Mansfield (which desegregation undermined in the South in the course of redressing the grievances of segregation) was the type that bilingual-bicultural schools were supposed to promote. Moreover, I then saw the post-1954 opening of private schools for white children as an attempt to restore the milieu created by the particular interplay of prejudice, schooling, and community that prevailed in pre-integration days. Further, I perceived the resistance to busing in 1975 by citizens of South Boston and Louisville as stemming *at least in part* from a desire to maintain a relationship which, when threatened, seemed critical to them. In contrast to the mostly beneficent school-community tie in Mansfield, the controversial nature of the latter two relationships, in terms of national ideals, points to the complexity of the issue: while school-community congruence may foster cultural pluralism and community well-being, it may also support undesirable ideals and fragmentation in American society.

At the risk of overextending the generalization drawn from Mansfield, I claim that the school function of maintaining a certain group may be identified in an array of ostensibly different cases. This function may be jeopardized by particular types of textbooks in Kanawha County, West Virginia; consolidation in small, rural towns; and busing in essentially homogeneous urban neighborhoods. In each case, a school, *operating in a certain way*, enhances a locally valued sense of community. If events threaten to modify an extant school-community congruence, then, as in Boston, violence may occur. Barring the failure of other means to sustain the relationship, an "offended" group may establish special institutions, such as the white-flight schools in the North and South; and if a group's children attend "alien" schools, it may attempt to establish congruence, as in the bilingual-bicultural movement. The point for educational policy is clear: since American education serves more than national political goals and individual vocational goals, decision-makers must not ignore those often covert communal goals which relate to a community's concern for survival.[7]

In terms of this paper's intent, the significance of this section is that the aforementioned series of patterns, their meaning, and their eventual reconstruction into results emerged from the subjective researcher. Nevertheless, each element in the series, as well as my reconstruction, is verifiable, or, in Kaplan's term, "intersubjective." That is,

> A scientific observation could have been made by any other observer so situated . . . I ask [Kaplan continues] "Do you see what I see?" to help decide whether what I see is to be explained by self-knowledge or by knowledge of the presumed object. [1964:128]

Any number of observers could have joined me in Mansfield and shared my "scientific observation." To be sure, they might have seen something else, something I overlooked or valued less and therefore ignored in my reconstruction. Indeed, they could have overlooked what I was seeing, by fastening upon some dimension of the phenomena before us that was central to them. But I believe that if I pointed to what I was seeing, the overlookers would then be able to say, "Yes, I see what you see," and thereby establish that agreement among observers which Kaplan calls "intersubjectivity."

Of course, it is insufficient to note that I was not the only observer in Mansfield, that I had six research assistants and we all saw the same thing. For the sake of discussion only, we can agree that because of continuous discussion our seven sets of eyes saw as one. This leaves the conclusions drawn from my case study, which is basically a sample of one, where they generally are left—in the public domain, open to the reactions of other persons, scholars and laymen alike, who can affirm or deny by virtue of their own data and experience. In a sense, each reader may evaluate my reconstruction and conclude with a confirming "Yes, this is the way it is" or a denying "No, this is all in the writer's head. His idiosyncracies prevailed." In sum, my observations and what I made of them result from the interaction of what is out there and what is in me. Notwithstanding the subjectivity of this process, its elements (the series of patterns) and their organization (my reconstruction) need to be verifiable. I believe they are.[8] The same setting—Mansfield and its high school—permits an indefinite number of patterns and reconstructions. Each,

potentially, is subject to the same public domain and each may or may not prove to be equally valid and interesting compared with the one that seemed right to me.

The Communal Function of Schooling

In 1972, anthropologists Conrad Arensberg and Solon Kimball published the papers they had written on community, in their book *Culture and Community*. In the first chapter, Arensberg makes a useful distinction between community "as object and as sample of study":

> . . . one must first recognize and mark off one community among the many. Only later . . . must one next ask: In what way is what I find here representative? In what way is this community and the place of my problem data in it capable of standing for, and leading me to explanation of, the universal occurrence of the problem and its place and reasons in the whole culture or society of its occurrence? [1972.8]

For most of my fieldwork, and for an uncomfortably long time thereafter, Arensberg's view plagued me. I thought I had conceptualized a perspective of Mansfield and its school that transcended description. I hoped, however, to explicate some reality that was not merely confined to other places just like Mansfield, though I was ready to settle for this degree of generalization. Ths possibility of identifying a more nearly universal "universal occurrence" followed the previously mentioned excursion into the world of bilingual-bicultural education; as the title of this section suggests, this universal occurrence relates to the communal function of schooling.

In exploring social phenomena as complex as schools and communities, a host of researchers may reach diverse conclusions. Clearly, schools serve a multitude of ends. The poor may pray that schools serve their children for status reversal purposes; the rich for status maintenance. Parents of awkward children ardently hope their child's school will promote social skills. Sociologists acknowledge the school's allocative function; many emphasize its contribution to social control. Schools in a democracy are urged to educate their masters—all the children of all the people. Goals proliferate, ad infinitum, as do the actual functions of schooling. I completed my study in Mansfield with a heightened sense of the communal nature of education—which, of course, includes schooling. To be sure, education and schools serve both glorious and mundane ends. However, my questions repeatedly evoked strong sentiments about the consequences of Mansfield High School not only for the comfort but also for the survival of Mansfield.

Confronted with this conclusion, I eventually experienced a sense of *déjà vu*. As it happens, I had been reading anthropological accounts of the communal function long before I prepared for fieldwork in Mansfield. The Poro of West Africa's Kpelle came to mind as a notable instance of a group's recourse to formal schooling to insure its survival (Watkins 1963). And recollection of the Poro recalled Herskovitz' idea that "In its widest sense, education . . . [is] that part of the enculturative expe-

rience that, through the learning process, equips an individual to take his place as an adult member of his society" (1948:310). It also recalled other studies which reinforce the same point—Hugh Ashton, *The Basuto* (1967); Henri Junod, *The Life of a South African Tribe* (1912); S. F. Nadel, *Black Byzantium* (1969); and Dorothy Eggan, "Instruction and Affect in Hopi Society" (1963). The list could be extended, but the point remains the same: using a wide variety of means, human groups in all societies "seek," as Kneller asserts, "to maintain an unbroken continuity between the generations" (1965:75). They desire this continuity in order to survive in physical terms and, of course, in cultural terms, i.e., to perpetuate particular behavior and norms.

In premodern societies, the association between group survival and education or schooling, as the case may be, is reasonably direct. Sufficient homogeneity prevailed among group members to insure reasonable harmony between communal ends and educational means. Since the extraordinary complexity and scale of modern mass society often masks (and even precludes) education's communal function, individualistic functions ordinarily dominate our attention. The exception occurs on those increasingly common occasions when a group feels jeopardized by the decisions and practices of the public schools. Such contemporary groups constitute a mixed lot: suburbanites, anxious to insure their youngsters' Ivy League credentials; fundamentalists, anxious to avoid the godlessness of P.S. 84; urbanites, compromised by "outsiders" bused in to their children's school; and villagers, threatened by plans to close their local school. While the list of illustrative cases could be extended, the point is that schools are expected to help perpetuate the values of those persons who together form the school's host community.

If we acknowledge education's primordial communal function, demonstrated so graphically in its premodern perspective, we can appreciate the antagonism many parents feel toward their children's schools, their fierce resistance to acts which threaten to close their schools, or their attraction to alternative schools. It is not a long way from the Basuto and Poro of Africa to Mansfield. Along the way to comprehending the communal function of schooling, I came to realize the close association between my idiosyncratic past and personality and (1) what I study, (2) by what means, and (3) the conclusions I reach. Subjective factors operate continually to shape the four Rs—researcher, research, researching, and results. I was an aching, joyful human being prior to going to India or Mansfield; I do not cease to be this human being either when I'm away or after I return home. These observations do not suggest to me a hopeless, anything-goes subjectivity so much as they underscore an especially enduring dimension of the problem of verification and generalization in all social research.

Notes

[1] In this regard, note Erickson's "test questions," e.g., "How did you arrive at your overall point of view? What details did you leave out and what did you leave in? . . . From the universe of behavior available to you, how much did you monitor?" (1973:14).

[2] Nonetheless, my feeling of being led resulted, I hypothesize, from immersion in an experience whereby for long, unbroken periods of time I was mostly aware of only that experience. In this state, impressions may become facts and then data in a process of which the researcher is seemingly unconscious.

[3] The results are presented in the full study (see Peshkin 1978).

[4] Wolcott (1975:113) writes more particularly about the conjunction of ethnography and schooling. He indicates that an ethnography is a "cultural" description" which "conveys how it is to 'walk in someone else's shoes,'" as well as representing the actor's perspective. He adds that research in schools must attend to what is learned inside and outside the school, "what is taught formally" and "learned informally," and what are the latent and the manifest consequences of instruction.

[5] Not that shy people necessarily study shyness; the connection is more complex. I suggest that the issue of shyness may intersect with the researcher's personal concerns and needs which originated long before his or her shyness research began.

[6] Not only did *Growing Up American* concentrate on schooling and community survival, but so did my next study (concerned with a village whose school board closed its only school), which is currently being written up, and my present study (relating to a Christian day school and the community it serves). My methodological commitment appears to be attached to a personally significant topic.

[7] The issue is complicated by the controversial nature of some groups which may seek to shape a school on behalf of their survival, notably if the school is public.

[8] To date, reactions from the "public domain" largely confirm the authenticity of the mainstream's Mansfield. That is, there are places whose sense of community is closely linked to their high schools. Thus, what I observed in Mansfield is most likely not attributable to what, unconsciously, I may have hoped to find there.

References

Arensberg, Conrad M., and Solon T. Kimball. 1972. *Culture and Community*. Gloucester, MA: Peter Smith.

Ashton, Hugh. 1967. *The Basuto*. New York: Oxford University Press.

Conklin, Harold. 1968. "Ethnography." In David L. Sims, ed., *International Encyclopedia of the Social Sciences*. New York: Macmillan Company, 172–178.

Cronbach, Lee J. 1974. "Beyond the Two Disciplines of Scientific Psychology." *American Psychologist*, 30:116–127.

Eggan, Dorothy. 1963. "Instruction and Affect in Hopi Cultural Continuity." In George Spindler, ed., *Education and Culture*. New York: Holt, Rinehart and Winston, 321–350.

Erickson, Frederick. 1973. "What Makes School Ethnography Ethnographic?" *Council on Anthropology and Education Newsletter*, 4:10–19.

Herskovitz, Melville. 1948. *Man and His Works*. New York: Alfred A. Knopf, Inc.

Junod, Henri A. 1912. *The Life of a South African Tribe*. London: David Nutt.

Kaplan, Abraham. 1964. *The Conduct of Inquiry*. Scranton, PA: Chandler Publishing Company.

Kneller, George F. 1965. *Educational Anthropology*. New York: John Wiley and Sons, Inc.

Lewis, Oscar. 1951. *Life in a Mexican Village: Tepotzlan Restudied*. Urbana, IL: University of Illinois Press.

Nadel, S. F. 1969. *A Black Byzantium*. London: Oxford University Press.

Peshkin, Alan. 1978. *Growing Up American: Schooling and the Survival of Community*. Chicago: University of Chicago Press.

Redfield, Robert. 1930. *Tepotzlan: A Mexican Village*. Chicago: University of Chicago Press.

Rist, Ray C. 1977. "On the Relations Among Educational Research Paradigms: From Disdain to Detente." *Anthropology and Education Quarterly*, 8:42–49.

Stayt, Hugh A. 1931. *The Bavenda*. London: Oxford University Press.

Watkins, Mark Hanna. 1963. "The West African 'Bush' School." In George Spindler, ed., *Education and Culture*. New York: Holt, Rinehart and Winston, 426–443.

West, James. 1945. *Plainville, U.S.A*. New York: Columbia University Press.

Wilson, Stephen. 1977. "The Use of Ethnographic Techniques in Educational Research." *Review of Educational Research*, 47:245–265.

Wolcott, Harry. 1975. "Criteria for an Ethnographic Approach to Research in Schools." *Human Organization*, 34:111–128.

3

Harry F. Wolcott

Mirrors, Models, and Monitors: Educator Adaptations of the Ethnographic Innovation

Harry F. Wolcott

The Author

Harry Wolcott is professor of anthropology and education at the University of Oregon. He completed the requirements for a Ph.D. at Stanford in the spring of 1964, with a major in education and a minor in cultural anthropology. His dissertation research, under the guidance of George Spindler, had focused on teaching and learning among the Kwakiutl Indians of British Columbia, Canada. During that same spring the federal government funded the start-up of a number of educational research and development centers at universities throughout the country. Reflecting the strong interest in interdisciplinary approaches to educational research at that time, the new "R & D Centers" actively recruited staff among social scientists interested in education and, perhaps more successfully, among educational researchers conversant with the social sciences. Wolcott accepted a faculty position at the University of Oregon that included an appointment as a Research Associate in its new R & D Center.

Each of the newly established R & D Centers had its special focus in the educational arena; Oregon's Center took educational administration for its special purview. And that is how Wolcott's broad interest in ethnographic approaches to educational research came to be focused specifically on an ethnographic study of the elementary school principalship, the study which he describes and analyzes in this volume. In addition to fieldwork on the Northwest Coast and extensive writing about education and educational research from an anthropological perspective, Wolcott has conducted fieldwork in southern Africa and in Southeast Asia. He is a past president of The Council on Anthropology and Education.

This Chapter

In this chapter Harry Wolcott grapples with the problem of consequences. On the basis of many months' diligent fieldwork focused on the role behaviors of one individual, an elementary school principal, he wrote a definitive educational ethnography, *The Man in the Principal's Office*. Wolcott traces the diffusion of what he describes as an "ethnographic innovation" into the complex culture of education. His analysis serves as a warning to those of us who are doing or want to do ethnographic studies of schooling. We must not expect too much. The great maw of professional education scoops up anything and everything, but the digestive system of the organism often fails to derive much nourishment and instead leaves important qualities undigested. What is digested is often what seems least important to the innovator. Even those aspects of the potential innovation that are selected for incorporation may, from the innovator's perspective, become quite distorted. As Wolcott points out, the process of assimilation is more adaptive than adoptive. In the case of *The Man in the Principal's Office*, it was more the notion of doing ethnography than the content of the principal's role as perceived ethnographically that educators seized upon as creative and useful. But what is applied as "ethnographic" in education often violates basic principles of anthropological ethnography. Wolcott raises, moreover, essential questions about the "new" educational ethnography: What happened to culture? Is a "quick and dirty" ethnography an ethnography? Can ethnographers evaluate and still do ethnography? How thick does an ethnographic description have to be to be thick enough, or too thick?

Wolcott's chapter raises issues central to the future of the ethnography of schooling.

Introduction

In May, 1966, I began fieldwork on a research project officially titled "An Ethnography of the Principalship." The fieldwork continued through two years. During the second year I began organizing my notes and thoughts toward the intended outcome of the project, a publishable monograph. Analyzing and writing the material took longer than expected, and those tasks had to be sandwiched between the on-going teaching and committee assignments of a university position. But eventually—at about draft number five—the manuscript was completed to my satisfaction and to the satisfaction of critic readers, editors, and a publisher. Like the monograph itself, its title went through a number of revisions; some earlier possibilities (*The Abiding Principals of Education, The Superdedi-*

cated) were set aside in favor of a rather straightforward description, *The Man in the Principal's Office.* In abbreviated form the book is often referred to as "MIPO."

The monograph was published in April, 1973, one of the "Case Studies in Education and Culture" edited by George and Louise Spindler and published by Holt, Rinehart and Winston. It was my second book, and that is not so many books that I did not feel a keen sense of accomplishment in seeing years of work finally come to fruition. Though I doubted that I had written a best seller or that the movie moguls would be beating at my door for film rights, I was satisfied that the book was "solid." I waited eagerly to watch its impact on educational practice, particularly among school administrators.

Many years have gone by since publication of the monograph. In terms of accumulating evidence of any visible impact on the practice of educational administration, however, I think my wait has just begun. To the extent that *The Man in the Principal's Office* has had an impact on education, both by itself and as part of the genre of monograph-length descriptive case studies that began to appear in the 1960s, that impact certainly has not been what I anticipated. The nature of the monograph's influence is suggested by the title of this paper, "Mirrors, Models, and Monitors." The title serves both to outline this essay and to summarize its message.

Like myself, a number of colleagues in my cohort of doctoral students in the early 1960s were intrigued with the possibilities of ethnographic research in schools. Encouraged and supervised by such luminaries as George Spindler at Stanford and Solon Kimball at Columbia, we were attracted to the barely tapped anthropological potential of providing educators with richly descriptive accounts about the human experience of schooling. Following the imagery suggested by anthropologist Clyde Kluckhohn, who had taken the title *Mirror for Man* for his eminently readable and popular book first published in 1949, we took the challenge provided by our mentors to provide a *mirror for educators*. Our intent was to help educators look at themselves in their "infinite variety," to turn their attention to what *actually* goes on in schools rather than to be so singularly preoccupied with what *ought to* go on in them. We became the self-appointed silverers of education's mirrors. If there was a conscious anthropological tilt (mirrors do, after all, have to be placed or held) it was to catch more of the educational context, to help educators see themselves in "holistic" perspective.

Considering the slight interest in descriptive approaches to educational research in the 1950s, our determination and efforts to develop and expand the basis for a solid "ethnography of schooling" in the 1960s and 1970s now seem remarkable. Our efforts were augmented by those of a small number of other researchers in education who are not of anthropological persuasion but who have made substantial contributions to the descriptive literature. One might accuse us collectively of having tried to turn education into a hall of mirrors.

But, if the account I will provide here about the impact of *The Man in the Principal's Office* accurately portrays what has happened to the ethnography of schooling more generally, our educator colleagues have fooled us. The educators who looked in our mirrors saw things all too familiar. A quick glance satisfied them that closer inspection would not reveal what they felt they most needed to find—a clear image of what they should do about problems and shortcomings. Most of our would-be viewers turned away from us. A few educators were fascinated by the mirror effect, but instead of looking at themselves as we had hoped they would, they hastened to join us in turning mirrors on other educators in other educational settings; they began doing studies of their own. Our techniques were acclaimed not for the utility of our findings, but for the novelty and seeming simplicity of our approach.

Important canons of our anthropological approach—describing rather than judging, attending carefully to context, spending adequate time in the field setting to know it thoroughly— were neither clearly understood nor zealously followed by those who eagerly began "doing" ethnography. This became increasingly apparent as educators with particular responsibility for one of education's pervasive problems—the issue of evaluation—became interested in adopting the ethnographic approach within their own special domain. For them, ethnographic techniques provided an alternative way to meet their assignment in monitoring educational programs. A research style born in a tradition of deferred judgment was quickly adapted to the problems of that influential group of educators whose specialty is rendering judgments.

What follows is a case study of a case study. I will review what I saw as the potential contribution of *The Man in the Principal's Office* and compare that with its actual use as a model rather than as a mirror. Of course, one case cannot singlehandedly illustrate the whole story of ethnography in education, any more than a detailed study of one principal can address all the concerns and all the styles of all the people who administer schools. But I view the case as representative of a class of events that can instructively be examined by detailed attention to one instance. In the ethnographic tradition, my sample is small but my perspective is wide. The intent here is to locate my own ethnographic study of a principal within the broader framework of the role of ethnography in educational research in the past two decades.

An Ethnographic Mirror

The Man in the Principal's Office was intended to give an accurate portrayal of the "real world" of one elementary school principal and, by extension, to identify those behaviors, beliefs, and circumstances shared by many, if not most, other elementary school principals. The emphasis of the study was on social rather than psychological dimensions of behavior. The portrayal unfolds in a progression from the moment-to-moment behavior of one particular principal during one particular day at work (chapter 2, "A Day in the Life") to some overarching concerns of all who occupy the role (chapter 11, "Prudence and Patience").

Neither the focus of the research effort—a study of the professional life of a school administrator—nor the ethnographic approach I took can be viewed as happenstance. I was at the time a Research Associate at the University of Oregon's educational research and development center, then called CASEA, the Center for the Advanced Study of Educational Administration. I had come to that position upon completion of my doctoral studies in education and anthropology at Stanford University. I had been hired specifically because I was an experienced educator who had been trained in anthropology and had completed fieldwork in a cross-cultural setting. Though my interests were (and continue to be) related more to the processes of enculturation than to the practice of school administration, an ethnographic study of the work of a principal promised ample opportunity for me to pursue matters of interest common to me and to the sponsoring agency.

I can hardly lay claim to discovering the principalship as a subject for research. There must be hundreds, perhaps thousands, of studies—especially doctoral dissertations—dealing with aspects of the principal's role. But three features of my proposed study made it uncommon, if not unique, at the time. First, the study was not a doctoral study. (How severely I rebuked anyone with the temerity to suggest that it was!) Second, funding for the research was projected through adequate time for an extended case study. From the outset I allowed one entire year for basic fieldwork and a second year for continued but less intensive fieldwork, accompanied by a heavier commitment to writing. Although I did not continue the fieldwork beyond the second year, preparing several shorter articles and a book-length manuscript took two additional years. Revising and editing the manuscript continued through two years beyond that. Clearly, the research project allowed time to pursue the task thoroughly to its completion. Third, I promised a new twist by heralding the study as "ethnographic." To reassure myself and the rest of the world on that score, I appended a subtitle to the monograph: *The Man in the Principal's Office: An Ethnography.*

In those days I was inclined to think of ethnography as the inevitable end product of traditional fieldwork practices. Explanations about my ethnographic approach tended to emphasize how I was behaving like an anthropologist more than how I was thinking like one. My self-confidence that I was following a genuinely "anthropological" approach may have been bolstered by the fact that I had recently completed fieldwork among the Kwakiutl Indians of British Columbia, was then maintaining close contact with them through regular summer visits, and had just finished rewriting my doctoral research for publication (Wolcott 1967). When asked about my intended study of the principalship, I felt able to satisfy virtually any inquiry simply by explaining that I was viewing the principal as though he were the chief of a small tribe and I intended to accompany him and to see him in as many different settings as possible to learn what he had to do and know in order to be chief. Many listeners nodded understandingly and volunteered on their own, "Oh, sorta like Margaret Mead!"

Any individual who directs a research project is identified in research protocol as the "principal investigator." The potential for a play on words was too strong a temptation; chapter 1 of the monograph, a detailed description of my fieldwork procedures, was titled, "A Principal Investigator in Search of a Principal." The decision to put the methodological section "up front," rather than relegate it to an appendix or omit it entirely, was a tactical one. I wanted to explain to readers how I had set out to understand the principalship through an in-depth study of one principal before they became preoccupied with customary harangues about sample size, replicability, and hypothesis testing.

In that opening chapter I discussed the traditional ways that ethnographers conduct their studies, with the anthropologist serving as the "research instrument" and with heavy reliance on variations of the two major fieldwork techniques: participant-observation and interviewing. I detailed the variety of ways that I gathered information, the variety of sources I had contacted, the extended period devoted to fieldwork, and the extent to which my prior experience as a teacher had helped me understand and appreciate both the language and the traditions of educators.

I intended the study to be rich with insights helpful to any educator interested in understanding how educator subculture functions. Chapters dealt, in order, with some of the routes and reasons which bring people to careers in education and to the principalship, the interaction between school personnel and adults in the immediate neighborhood, the kinds of encounters a principal has, how the different reckoning of what constitutes a "year" creates some stress between teachers who have a work year of about $9\frac{1}{2}$ months and principals who must be "thinking about next year" almost from the time school opens, and differences between what one does to become a principal and what one does to hold the position once attained. I also identified some paradoxes about educational administrators, such as the low esteem many of them have for their own formal education (especially their graduate professional training) contrasted with the importance they assign to education for others, the everyday realities for principals contrasted with their idealized image of a "leadership role," and the apprehension with which many of them approach the critical task of teacher evaluation because they feel they are inadequately prepared to do it well.

My editors pressed for additional commentary that would help the intended educator audience not only to recognize their problems but to see some possible remedies. Eventually I squeezed out an "Epilogue" of ten additional pages, carefully warning the reader that I felt caught between my ethnographic commitment to describe rather than to judge and my responsibility as a fellow educator to offer any help or suggestions that seemed warranted. Following a perspective offered by anthropologist A. F. C. Wallace (1970: chapter 3), I suggested that blaming problems related to the administrative structure of schools on the fact that they are bureaucracies seems to lead nowhere; as Wallace suggests, we can more wisely attend to how to make our bureaucracies more effective (i.e., responsive) than lament that we allowed them to become bureaucracies in the first place. I also questioned whether principals, who in the 1960s even more than today were entreated to be agents of change, might better be recognized and appreciated as agents of continuity, helping to maintain stable systems in the face of turmoil.

Trusting that my study would also be read by professors responsible for training future cadres of principals, I directed several suggestions to them. I echoed the criticism that educational administration programs train for the superintendency and ignore issues at the level at which school principals deal with them. Following a suggestion offered by Sarason (1971), I posed that principals whose training helped them to understand the systems in which they worked might be in a better position to play active rather than passive roles within those systems. I also wondered if administrative training or in-service programs might deal more effectively with two problem areas I had identified: teacher evaluation and the administration of justice. In conclusion, I suggested that the (anthropological) study of mainstream society and of some of its major subgroups might be useful for principals, noting further how the role of principal itself reflects idealized statements about American "culture" but often puts principals at odds with the realities of that culture by asking them to be "too good to be true."

Only reluctantly did I add that "so what" chapter to the monograph. Yet I realized that if my study became widely known among principals I might be invited to speak at their professional meetings, and while they might be willing to hear me describe my research approach and summarize my observations, they most assuredly would insist that I share whatever insight I had for helping them create a more effective role. If the years I had spent observing and analyzing the principalship had led to any conclusions or recommendations, I could not plead an ethnographic cop-out. In fact, I felt that I should be especially prepared to discuss the principalship in a reflective way and from a perspective that busy principals virtually never achieve. When the call came, I wanted to be ready to help.

I started a file in which I collected ideas, recommendations, and observations that might be of interest or help to principals or to those interested in problems of the principalship. I recalled seeing such tips from management specialists like Peter F. Drucker. I combed his words for suggestions and pithy observations relevant to school administration, such as his maxims

"One can either meet or work; one cannot do both" or "Focus on results, not on work." I contrasted his recommendation on taking adequate time to make personnel decisions with the hasty decisions principals usually have to make. Drucker places great value on the effective use of time. I wondered what his reaction would have been to my discovery that the case study principal spent an average of one-quarter of his day in formal meetings, another quarter in what I called "deliberate but not prearranged" encounters, and another quarter in casual encounters or in telephoning.

I did not turn to the counsel of management specialists like Peter Drucker (or, subsequently, Henry Mintzberg) for insights into cultural processes; I looked to them because they speak directly to ways of getting things done in our society. They do not ask whether we need to be preoccupied with time; rather, they tell us how to use time effectively. I assumed that principals wanted to hear that kind of "straight talk."

Similarly I thought principals might reflect upon the paradox of success in their work, what Veblen once described as the penalty of taking the lead: the more outstanding a school's program, the more that success will probably result in draining away resources as the principal and staff are called upon to help or host others. I also thought principals might consider how their preoccupation with salary could be interpreted as an indicator of status uncertainty. Or they might probe a certain tendency to *not* deal with problems rather than to confront them boldly, as seen in such behaviors as "trading" weak teachers instead of either seeking their dismissal or helping them improve.

In addition to being able to speak to immediate administrative concerns, however, I also wanted to be able to suggest the excitement—and possibly the utility—of insights of a more anthropological nature. For example, I was fascinated to realize that what one needs to know to be a principal is transmitted essentially as an oral literature rather than a written one. Once away from their formal programs of study, principals do not consult their texts, they consult each other, a mode of cultural transmission well suited to an occupational group whose members appear not to engage extensively in professional reading or writing but do spend most of their working day in dialogue.

Anthropological interest in proxemics, the cultural use of space, offered another perspective. Assuming principals really want to be more actively involved in instructional matters, what would happen if they were surrounded by the instructional resources of the school (e.g., the library, the media center) instead of its management resources (the receptionist, the secretary, the nurse, the counseler)?

In a separate article which I prepared at the time for George Spindler's then forthcoming *Education and Cultural Process* (Spindler 1974), I described a series of meetings in which several principals in the school system—including the case study principal—met to screen and make final recommendation on the applicants for three new appointments to the principalship to be made the following year.

The result of their deliberations was that, although they interviewed and ostensibly considered a wide range of applicants, in fact they narrowed the range of "recommended" individuals to a slate of candidates strikingly similar to themselves in background, experience, and orientation. In helping me interpret that behavior, anthropologist Alfred G. Smith drew upon his interest in communication and in cybernetic systems models to suggest a contrast between "variety-generating" and "variety-reducing" behaviors as a way of examining administrative strategies. Smith observed how, in spite of their seeming advocacy of change, the principals actually engaged in variety-reducing behavior that served to minimize potential disruption in one of the few arenas over which they could effectively exercise control.[1]

In the face of constant pupil and teacher "turnover" and a constant call for program changes, the behavior of those principals showed an understandable concern for stability and continuity. I thought that posing the contrast between wanting to be perceived as variety-generators and needing to act as variety-reducers might help principals understand some of their role stress. I incorporated that perspective into the article (Wolcott 1974) and was prepared to elaborate upon it, should it prove of interest to audiences of principals.

That I readied myself with an arsenal of tips, ideas, and perspectives may seem a bit presumptuous. To the extent that I entertained any delusions of grandeur or believed that I had some spectacular contribution to the practice of school administration, I suppose it was. However, there were other motives beyond pure self-aggrandizement. The R & D Center was under pressure from its federal sponsor in Washington, D.C., to make its work immediately relevant and available to practitioners. After enjoying the luxury of engaging in basic descriptive research, I was willing to lend whatever help I could to our mandate to be of service to the educator community. Further, I recalled a conversation years earlier when anthropologist Dorothy Lee explained that although the attention she gave to the teaching and teachers of home economics in high schools was rather critical in nature (cf. Lee 1955), she quickly became popular with "home ec" teachers because no social scientist had ever paid them any attention. I thought that principals might be feeling that same kind of loneliness. Might they, perchance, enlist me to help champion their cause?

A Model for Ethnography

As you may well have guessed, the "call" for which I had been preparing never came.

This is not to say that *The Man in the Principal's Office* was either rejected or totally ignored by principals. Rather, following a brief fanfare and some routine courtesies, both author and monograph were quietly shelved in the administrative archives, permanently accessible but conveniently out of the way.

The earliest review to come to my attention appeared in the *American School Board Journal* in December,

1973. I was delighted to see the monograph specially cited for "Recommended Reading" but was dismayed to learn that I had written what the anonymous reviewer called an "astonishingly juicy slice of real elementary school life." The monograph was also the subject of a favorable seven-page essay review in *The Elementary Principal* (Keller 1974), but I do not recall seeing any mention of it in that journal thereafter.

Brief reviews appeared the same year in *Educational Administration Quarterly* and in *Urban Education*, one reviewer commending the study as unique, the second dismissing it as banal. I saw a ray of hope in the words of the first reviewer, a career principal and past president of the National Association of Elementary School Principals:

> A close look in the mirror can be a sobering experience and usually we have trouble seeing our own face. Although the image is at times less than complimentary, the elementary school principal will find the text a stimulus for analyzing his own role and behavior as a principal. [Forsberg 1974:99]

The anticipation of a "sobering experience" may not have proven much inducement to get one's colleagues to read a new book about their chosen vocation. I doubt that many principals took the challenge. The reviewer also raised the spectre that haunts every case study and serves as a convenient rationale for dismissing them all: "How different would the conclusions and recommendations be if another person in another setting were chosen as the subject of the study?" (p. 101).

Invitations to seminars with administrators or students in educational administration programs were few in number. I looked forward to one all-day session at a summer "workshop" for elementary school principals in the Midwest and was able to arrange for the case study principal to join me, but what I thought might be the first of such events proved instead to be the last. The organizer of the workshop wrote later that the reaction of the participants—all elementary school principals—was not one of having been fascinated and stimulated; it was more like having one's toes stepped on. He noted, "Many people did not like the idea that they had as little flexibility and elbow room in their elementary principalship positions as your study indicated."

I fared no better in reaching practicing administrators as a guest speaker. The study actually provoked more local interest when it was first conceived than after it had been "delivered"; I was occasionally asked to speak at administrative seminars about the research when I was beginning the fieldwork, but later, when I had something to report, my study was no longer viewed as "new." During a sabbatical year spent overseas, and still prior to publication, I received an inquiry from the office of the National Association of Elementary School Principals in Washington, D.C., asking whether I would like to present my research findings at their next annual meeting. That opportunity was planned for a session when 20 similar presentations were to be scheduled simultaneously. I replied that by the time I returned from my leave I expected the book to be published and I felt ready to give a major

talk rather than play again in the "little leagues" of concurrent sessions as I had once done in the past. Apparently my reply sounded arrogant. In the final letter of a brief correspondence, I was mildly castigated for "holding out for mass exposure" instead of being willing to help in a more modest way. That took care of my opportunity to address principals nationally.

I fared slightly better in Canada, where I received an invitation to teach a course called "The Principalship" at McGill University in Montreal during the summer of 1976 and to address the Leadership Course sponsored by the Canadian Education Association at Banff, Alberta, in May, 1980. By 1980, however, my thoughts had turned to the issues I am considering in this paper; 14 years had elapsed since I began the study.

In the locale where the fieldwork was done I learned that I was once considered as a possible speaker for the annual meeting of elementary principals, but the final choice that year was to invite an address about high school "graduation competencies" instead. At the time I felt somewhat vindicated, since I had suggested in my analysis that it was the constant preoccupation with the immediate that kept principals from ever being able to achieve a deeper understanding of their role. Professor Paul Hanna at Stanford University used to describe that as the problem of "letting the urgencies get ahead of the essentials." The sense of urgency comes through repeatedly in the concerns expressed by principals.

I did receive a handful of complimentary letters from practicing administrators and professors of educational administration, but five years went by before I received a request for permission to reprint passages for a book specifically addressed to an audience of principals and would-be principals (Blumberg and Greenfield 1980). A detailed summary and synthesis of principal behavior, distilled almost exclusively from the case study, appeared two years earlier in *Survival in the Classroom* (House and Lapan 1978). However, the audience of that book was not those who occupy the principal's office but beginning teachers whose professional survival depended in part on their success in what the authors described as "dealing with bosses."

As far as I know, that about exhausts the account of the book's direct impact—and my own—in providing a *mirror* for educators. That influence has been limited largely to students and professors in education courses rather than the intended audience, practicing administrators. But the story does not end here. Along with other case studies of its genre, *The Man in the Principal's Office* has become something different to a different audience. It has become a *model* for a "new" approach among educational researchers: ethnography.

By commercial standards, sales of *The Man in the Principal's Office* have been modest, but each year since its publication an average of almost 1,000 copies have been sold. (Royalties are retained by the Center and the federal sponsoring agency, but at least I do see the annual reports.) Although the book's "market" ranges from undergraduate students taking Foundations of Education courses to graduate students in Educational Administration, its primary audience is among students enrolled in classes in "Anthropology and Education." Those students are learning to look at educational processes from an anthropological perspective. And they are interested more in the anthropological approach than in the specific descriptive details of any particular study.

For that growing audience of students in Anthropology and Education, chapters from *The Man in the Principal's Office* have been taken verbatim for inclusion in one collection of readings dealing with *Schooling in the Cultural Context* (Roberts and Akinsanya 1976) and another addressed to *Anthropology and Educational Administration* (Barnhardt, et al. 1979). The article I prepared especially for Spindler's *Education and Cultural Process* enjoyed the wide readership of that volume and was reprinted in two collections of articles dealing with perspectives on educational administration (Barnhardt, et al. 1979; D. Erickson 1977). An article dealing exclusively with the research techniques of the study appeared in *Human Organization* (Wolcott 1970) and was subsequently published in the "Methods and Problems" section of a collection on *Social Interaction in Educational Settings* (Yee 1971). The result of these various appearances and reappearances is that, more because of its *approach* than its *focus*, the study achieved something of a "mass exposure" after all.

I have no way to assess the relative size of these various audiences. Judging by correspondence and conversations through the years, the study seems to have "inspired" or served as a model for a number of parallel case studies of individuals in specific educator roles. I feel this is the area in which the monograph has had its most significant impact. Though the variety and number of such studies undoubtedly exceeds the following list, I know for certain of studies modeled after *The Man in the Principal's Office* concerning a high school principal in Texas, eight urban principals in Chicago (studied by a team of four researchers), a school superintendent in northern California, a series of "shadow" studies of administrators of early childhood education programs in southern California, a special education director in Minnesota, a state-level social studies director in Georgia, a sixth-grade teacher's "classroom perspective" in Michigan, a junior high school art teacher in Oregon, a male first year first-grade teacher in Washington, and a master coach and swim team in Alberta.

Conspicuous by its absence from that list of "restudies," contrary to my hopes, is an in-depth study of another elementary principal. I seem inadvertently to have staked out "territory," making the ethnographic study of the elementary school principal my exclusive domain. The most nearly comparable ethnographic study (although a study of an entire elementary school faculty rather than of the principal) was conducted quite independently from my work by Richard Warren, a colleague from the "Anthropology and Education" program at Stanford who, like me, had turned his research attention to the contemporary American educational scene (Warren 1973, 1975) after a preliminary immersion in cross-cultural fieldwork (1967). The research that led eventually to the publication of another important descriptive study in which an elementary school principal was a key actor, *Anatomy of Educational Innovation*, was completed while my fieldwork was still in progress (cf. Smith and Keith 1967, 1971). Missing the point of how reliability is best attained in ethnographic research, students have often asked me when I intend to conduct my own replication study (and, since the advent of affirmative action, they chide me about researching *The Woman in the Principal's Office*), but to the best of my knowledge no one has taken up the task that must be done by someone else.

To summarize to this point: *The Man in the Principal's Office* did not serve in any major way as a mirror for its intended audience, those immediately involved in the work of educational administration. It did, however, serve as the model or archetype for other studies in education. As a validating footnote for a whole research "style" it continues to be widely cited. That raises a different and critical question: How good is it as a *model* of ethnography? Before turning to that issue, however, let me diverge briefly to note another arena where ethnography has recently "caught on" in education: the work of educational evaluation.

Ethnographic Monitoring

Just as "ethnography" refers both to the completed product (usually a research monograph or series of articles, sometimes a novel or film) and to the research process that leads to that final product, so educators have come to know and to use the term ethnography both as product and as process. Educator interest in the ethnographic pro-

cess—in method *per se*—blossomed in the 1970s and may have been a consequence of anthropologists' own self-consciousness about and explication of their fieldwork techniques beginning in the mid 1960s.

Not surprisingly from an educator point of view, ethnographic method has proven of considerable interest to those charged with education's vexing problems of evaluation. Educators with responsibilities for program "monitoring" or "evaluation" at virtually every level, from school systems large enough to have research departments to the National Institute of Education, have increasingly drawn upon ethnographic techniques and ethnographic talent to augment traditional evaluation procedures in meeting the growing demands for evidence of education's effects and accountability. Published just as this recognition of the evaluative potential of ethnography was awakening in the early 1970s, *The Man in the Principal's Office* could not help but get linked with the efforts of education's new "ethnographic evaluators."

At the national level ethnographers were employed during the 1970s to help assess the consequences of ambitious programs to create educational change (e.g., the Office of Education and National Institute of Education's "Experimental Schools" project of the early 1970s as reported in Herriott and Gross [1979] and Knapp [1979]), to describe and help expedite the diffusion of innovative ideas from one school system to the next (e.g., the Center for New Schools' "Documentation and Technical Assistance in Urban Schools" project carried out for NIE in the mid 1970s), and to conduct wide-ranging status studies to determine national ed-

ucational "needs" (e.g., the Case Studies in Science Education funded by the National Science Foundation and conducted by the University of Illinois' Center for Instructional Research and Curriculum Evaluation in the late 1970s). I have been professionally associated with ethnographers doing program evaluations for such seemingly unlikely employers as Educational Testing Service (an evaluation of experience-based career education programs), regional educational laboratories (projects in multi-ethnic education and in basic literacy), and even the Research, Development, and Evaluation unit of the local school system where I reside (looking at alternative schools and at the school district's reading program).

During those same years a new committee within the Council on Anthropology and Education, the Committee on Ethnographic Approaches to Evaluation, grew and prospered. A Conference on Educational Evaluation sponsored by that committee in 1978 included topics that reflected a remarkable transformation from traditional ethnography to ethnographic evaluation: "Ethnographic Evaluation of Classroom Processes," "Clinical Anthropology in the Evaluation Process," "Data Crunching," "Use of Short Ethnographies in Curriculum Evaluation," and "Writing Evaluative Reports and Recommendations, or, You Don't Give Them an Ethnography."

In large, long-term projects like the five-year federally funded Experimental Schools study, fieldwork and analysis were sufficiently divorced from the thrust of the project that the ethnographic dimension was evaluative only in the sense of trying to obtain a complete and contextualized account of what happened. Educators have come to describe this form of program evaluation as "summative evaluation." But most projects utilizing ethnographic talent have been of smaller scale and shorter duration; they are (unabashedly) designed to provide immediate feedback on which decisions can be made concerning the course (or fate) of a project. Educators refer to this type of evaluation as "formative evaluation." Formative evaluation is clearly of more immediate utility than summative evaluation for those faced with impending decisions about budgets and programs. Even the descriptive assessment of the status of science, mathematics, and social studies programs summarized in the Case Studies in Science Education (cf. Stake and Easley 1978) was tied in ultimately to evaluative concerns—though this was a project that (1) self-consciously opted for an ethnographic approach, (2) placed qualified, experienced, relatively autonomous field-workers in an intentionally small number of sites instead of relying more heavily on survey research, and (3) set out to "see" rather than to "measure." By the late 1970s the term "ethnography" was closely linked and had even become synonymous with "evaluation" in the minds of many educators.

From an educator's perspective, the growing interest in ethnographic approaches to evaluation, paralleling the demand for educational accountability, is hardly surprising. From an anthropological point of view, on the other hand, this is all rather shocking: "ethnographic evaluation" seems a contradiction in terms! Accustomed to a perspective of cultural relativism, anthropologists have customarily followed a tradition of deferred judgment (cf. Herskovits 1973). Their concern—and their message—has been to understand what things mean to those involved rather than to pronounce judgment in terms of some external set of values or preferences (e.g., the anthropologist's).

This is not the forum in which to debate such issues as whether anthropologists should render evaluative judgments, whether they in fact make them anyway, or whether ethnographic method is appropriately used when applied to problems in evaluation. Perhaps too secure in my "ivory tower," I have long held and frequently stated a preference for exploiting the descriptive rather than the evaluative potential of ethnography in educational research (Wolcott 1971, 1975), but there are convincing arguments on either side of that complex issue. For anthropologists, the issue extends to "evaluation research" in many areas of applied anthropology in addition to education. Although the issue of ethnographic evaluation as broadly defined in contemporary circumstances (e.g., federally funded projects calling for an ethnographic component as an integral part of the evaluation process) appears both current and vogue, the dialogue between anthropologists and educators on the question of value judgments goes back at least a quarter of a century.[2]

Further, and consistent with my position, *The Man in the Principal's Office* was not intended to be and has not been perceived to be an evaluative study. A review by John Singleton specifically commends the "distinct attempt to avoid evaluative statements based on some professional assumptions of 'correct' standards and practices" (Singleton 1974). Though one could be disheartened by so intimate a view of a principal at work or by the frustrations of principals who would like the role to be something more than it is, the study does not attempt to inventory the pluses and minuses of the position or render a global judgment on it. Nevertheless, the study is frequently cited by evaluators, even though their references are restricted to its educational focus and to its fieldwork style.

The critical point is that educators have borrowed ethnographic techniques—and borrowed ethnographers as well—to help with the problem of evaluation. In so doing, they have separated ethnographic process from ethnographic product. Where ethnography could well serve as an *alternative to* evaluation, it has instead been perceived by evaluators as an alternative *form of* evaluation.

"Ethnographic evaluation" is the phrase most often heard in referring to the use of fieldwork techniques for educational evaluation. "Ethnographic monitoring" is another way that anthropologists have labeled efforts at focused descriptive research intended to provide a basis for program evaluation.[3] By whatever label it is identified, the evaluative use of fieldwork techniques represents a significant adaptation of ethnography in education.

How Adequate Is the Monograph as a Model of Ethnography?

The Man in the Principal's Office, intended to provide a mirror for educators, has instead been used in two other ways in education: as a model for those who want to produce ethnographic accounts of their own and, to a lesser extent, as an alternative research approach that can be applied to problems of evaluation.

In terms of techniques, the chapter on fieldwork, "A Principal Investigator in Search of a Principal," though certainly not intended as a research guide, ought to serve as a cautionary note to otherwise hasty adopters of the ethnographic approach. That chapter provides a reminder about traditional ethnographic concerns for description and interpretation rather than for rendering judgments. It also emphasizes a traditional approach presupposing the ethnographer as research instrument, an adequate period of time in the field, and a commitment to gathering information through multiple research techniques.

Had I fully anticipated the growing interest in evaluation studies, I would have placed even more emphasis on these ethnographic prerequisites. My intent would have been to raise the question whether borrowing a research technique or two is an adequate basis for claiming that a descriptive or evaluative study is perforce an ethnographic one. In terms of field techniques *per se*, however, I think the study is strong and the chapter describing the research approach reflects that strength. Though I did not intend the chapter as a general treatise on fieldwork in educational settings, fieldworkers who avail themselves of sufficient time and of sources of information that are comparable in variety to those described and illustrated in the monograph ought to have few anxieties about validity.

A more important question, I think,

is whether the study is adequate as a model for ethnography. Here I must express ambivalence. I have been inclined to see it as ethnographic-in-approach more than as ethnography, or, to be a bit less rigorous, to say that it is ethnography but it could have been "even more so." When I offer my graduate seminar on "Ethnographic Method in Educational Research," my students and I tear the monograph apart to examine its "ethnographicness" in search of the critical attributes of ethnography.

In order to keep the issue of "ethnographicness" from becoming an obstacle for readers of *The Man in the Principal's Office*, I stated the purpose of ethnography in the first sentence of the Preface ("to provide description and analysis regarding human social behavior") and offered a test of adequacy before I reached the bottom of that same page. No words I have ever written have haunted me more than the sentence about "purpose" just quoted or this related sentence about criteria:

> The test of ethnography is whether it enables one to anticipate and interpret what goes on in a society or social group as appropriately as one of its members. [Wolcott 1973:xi]

These words have been quoted time and time again as authoritative, accurate, and adequate. Though I selected and compiled them from the words of others with utmost care, I never for a moment considered that I might be furnishing a definition that others would cite and attribute to me. Nonetheless, in addition to the verbatim repetition of my words in papers submitted by each wave of graduate students in my

classes, I have found numerous occasions on which some part either of those two sentences or of a third sentence on the same page ("The ethnographer selectively records certain aspects of human behavior in cultural terms") is presented as gospel and apparently assumed to be all that needs to be said about ethnography.

The longer I have been interested in "doing" ethnography, the more difficulty I have had attempting to define it with greater precision than statements like "a description of the way of life of some (other) group of people." Part of the problem is that one's definition of ethnography rests upon assumptions about a definition of culture, and I have difficulty with too-precise definitions of that concept as well. I was heartened to find anthropologist Ward Goodenough taking the view that the culture of any society is attributed to that group *by an ethnographer* when he wrote:

> The culture of any society is made up of the concepts, beliefs, and principles of action and organization that an ethnographer has found could be attributed successfully to the members of that society in the context of his dealings with them. [Goodenough 1976:5]

Though "successful attribution" is hardly the rigorous criterion we seek for separating thick description from thin, Goodenough does remind us that the locus of culture lies within ethnographic concerns: it is a construct of the social scientist, not a directly observable phenomenon. The definitions I originally supplied had also been influenced by Goodenough's (earlier) writings (and the writings of others as well—particularly Berreman

1968:338). Unfortunately, if pushed to logical extremes, those definitions imply that unless one is an insider to educator subculture—and actually takes the role of principal and fills it appropriately—one could never really know whether my account is adequate. Further, as David Kaplan and Robert Manners have noted, discovering what one would have to know in order to get around in a particular culture may be *one* aim of ethnography, but that does not mean it is *the* aim (Kaplan and Manners 1972:22). My method chapter was not intended as a guide to fieldwork, and the rest of the monograph was not intended as a manual for principals. What I intended with my brief discussion on the nature of ethnography was simply to provide a working definition so that I could proceed with the descriptive narrative. For my purposes in providing a "mirror," I felt I had said enough.

For use as a model, however, my words were too few and too glib. Those for whom my work served as inspiration for conducting other "ethnographics" or ethnographically oriented case studies, role studies, or "shadow" studies should have felt it necessary to agonize a bit in their proposals or introductory statements about how best to define ethnography or to state its purposes. Instead, they dismissed the problem or, as often, saw none. Without such agonizing, there is a good likelihood of failing to realize that how we view culture cannot help but influence and guide what we look at and how we subsequently describe it (cf. Keesing 1974). We need to hear how each ethnographer has grappled with the problems of distinguishing what was observed from what was reported secondhand, of differentiating between words and deeds, and of sorting his or her own meanings from those of informants. Of course, these were not issues I expected my intended audience of principals to find of much concern. They could assess the adequacy of my study for themselves; they would know better than I whether I had quite gotten it right.

Beyond matters of definition, I also feel ambivalence about the emphasis the study places on role behavior, on man as principal rather than on principal as man. In early descriptions about the project I made the claim that I was studying a human who happened to be a principal rather than a principal who happened to be a human. That nicely turned phrase eventually disappeared from my accounts as I began to wonder whether it was true. Though I have no personal misgivings on this point, I think the study would have been "more ethnographic" if I had given more attention to the principal as a human who happened to be an administrator. Had I conducted the study in another society, I know I would have looked less at role behavior on the job and more at the individual in society, looking for links between the broader context in which the administrator lived and the type of institutional environment she or he sought to create for others. More of that emphasis on my part would have given more of the personality-in-culture emphasis to the completed account, helping to keep its anthropological dimensions more central, its concern for an occupational role more peripheral.

The period of fieldwork for one educational researcher who admitted to carrying out a "modest" study of a school administrator, but who nonetheless described the study as ethnographic, was limited to at-the-office hours of one administrator during only *one day!* I was dumbfounded to read that my work had served as the "research touchstone" for that study. On the other hand, the argument might be made that the difference between our studies was only one of degree (i.e., I simply extended my fieldwork over many more working days). However, I did accompany the principal in numerous settings outside the school and school district, and I interviewed family members, attended a family wedding, and worked at getting a "sense" of his home and personal life. Given the immediate project concern for a study of the principalship, the R & D auspices under which the research was funded, and the other university commitments I was meeting, it did not seem thinkable at the time to become more intimately involved in the principal's personal life. It was thinkable to become immersed in the professional concerns of his conveniently compatible 8:00 A.M.–5:00 P.M. Monday to Friday job, with allowances for sampling among his numerous school-related evening and weekend commitments. Yet I certainly could have done more; in a less familiar cultural milieu, I am sure I would have.

How would the completed account have differed had I become more of a participant-observer in the principal's total life, even if for a brief period? Quite likely it would have attended more to out-of-school contexts and less to immediate and obvious settings like office, school, and school system. Educational researchers themselves now cover such scenes quite adequately. Though I have not heard the complaint from educators, anthropologist colleagues have suggested that the monograph is too detailed on matters of little consequence. I find that to be an intriguing criticism—and a telling reminder that ethnography does not require the ability to describe everything; rather, it requires the sense (partly intuitive, partly trained) to know what does and does not need to be described and in what level of detail.

If for some unanticipated reason my time immediately after the period of fieldwork had been preempted by other duties and only now was I able to turn to the task of completing the monograph, I think I could expect my friendly critics to express reservations on exactly the opposite account. That is, today I might be inclined to give too much attention to the context of the larger society and to concepts like "ethos" or "ideational system," and too little attention to minute-by-minute transactions. Most asuredly I would give the monograph such a focus if I knew in advance that it was going to serve more as model than as mirror, for in so doing I could stress what I feel is one of the unique contributions of anthropology to education: how "culture" pervades the lives of educators and is, in turn, so thoroughly reflected in the practice of schooling. But I was not ready to take that approach in the mid 1960s, and in spite of subsequent opportunities for new cross-cultural experience I still think it is difficult to "do" anthropology in one's own society, especially among one's own professional subgroup. For all the difficulty in gaining adequate perspective, however, the task is well worth pursuing.

Since I did not take that broad cultural sweep in the original writing, it is easier now for me to see the monograph as a piece of something rather than the "total" ethnography I once thought I was preparing. I must confess my surprise at finding my work cited in one reference as an example of "macrostudy." In that reference a contrast was made with other ethnographers of school settings (e.g., Ray McDermott, Frederick Erickson), who give concerted attention to far smaller units of interaction than I do (e.g., a classroom reading group, counseling interviews). On the other hand, while the term "micro-ethnography" has been used in descriptive educational research for over a decade (cf. Burnett 1968, Smith 1967), I did not particularly care for it. But when reviewers in *American Anthropologist* cited *The Man in the Principal's Office* as an example of "urban micro-ethnography at its best" (Basham and DeGroot 1977:428), I decided to reconsider. "Flattery," as an old saying goes, "will get you everywhere." Reviewers Basham and DeGroot also assuaged my concern that the book had been taken as a model instead of used as a mirror. They liked the model.

> Wolcott's research demonstrates the value which exhaustive analysis of any occupation can have in highlighting the assumptions of a society as a whole.... [It] stands as a model for the heretofore under-used technique of approaching the study of urban society through careful analysis of the fusion of individual goals and identity with the behavioral expectations appropriate to their occupations. [Basham and DeGroot 1977:428]

To return to the question: Is *The Man in the Principal's Office* ethnography? By the unintentionally vague criteria I set forth in my Preface, we may never know, for it is not clear just who is to "anticipate and interpret" what goes on and to what degree of appropriateness. Yet I did "selectively record certain aspects of human behavior," and I did "construct explanations of that behavior in cultural terms."

According to Goodenough's (1976) mandate, my task as ethnographer was not to *describe* a culture as it was revealed to me but to *construct* a culture out of what I observed. The "culture" I constructed was drawn cautiously, emphasizing role behavior in a highly structured system more than broad, overarching values of the mainstream society. The account was "cultural"; it might have been more so. Reactions to the book by people familiar with schools and with the principalship have generally been approving, though more than one principal has insisted, "If you wanted to learn about schools, you should have followed *me* around." I think it safe to say that I more or less successfully "attributed" a culture to the members of the group I was studying. More accurately, I described some part of the culture of a special subgroup of a society. Even the disappointed (and non-anthropologist) reviewer who dismissed the study as "banal" unwittingly acknowledged my effort to describe the commonplace.

Working in one's own society, the ethnographer always risks the accusation of having done no more than make the obvious obvious.

Educator Adaptation of the Ethnographic Innovation

Though I have tied my remarks closely to the fate of one particular monograph, my thesis is a broader one: educational ethnography generated over the past two decades and intended to provide *mirrors* for educators has largely been delegated to two other functions instead—to serve as *models* for further research and to provide an alternative way to meet the demand for monitoring educational programs. In this concluding section I discuss four issues related to the thesis.

My first point is that ethnography has become something of an innovation in educational research. Those of us in "my" generation of graduate students—perhaps the first big wave of educators whole-heartedly committed to the anthropological perspective and approach—were warned by our mentors that the anthropological potential would probably remain unnoticed by educators. Instead, some of us have come to view with alarm the crushing embrace of educator enthusiasm. Though not everybody is "doing it," a lot of educational researchers talk about ethnography, often in a nonchalant manner implying that all one needs is a notebook, a little extra time, and a capacity for endless detail. Pleased as we may have been to see anthropology

"catch on," we have also watched our efforts go slightly awry. Our books and articles—the crowning achievements of our descriptive and interpretive efforts—are largely ignored by our intended audiences, while our "ethnographic approach" has been eagerly added to the repertoire of the educational researcher. Yet our approach, intentionally nonjudgmental by design, has often been usurped for the purposes of "quick and dirty" program evaluation instead of careful, contextual description.

Curiously, I think we "ethnographers of education" have failed to look in our own mirrors. For years we have patiently observed and reported on the fate of other innovations in education, but we have forgotten that ethnography itself might become an educational innovation and undergo that same fate. By "fate" I refer to the frequently reported sequence in which new ideas in education, though faced with strong initial opposition, occasionally burst forth upon the educational scene, only to have their impact quickly dissipated by smothering enthusiasm coupled with incomplete understanding, so that in the end the establishment itself remains largely (though not entirely) unchanged. Two colleagues at the R & D Center where I conducted my research once characterized the innovative process in education as one of "adaptation" rather than "adoption" (Charters and Pellegrin 1972). The process by which intended "mirrors" have instead become "models" and "monitors" is a splendid example of the adaptation of an innovation within educator subculture. What caught us by surprise is that this time it was ethnography itself that was adapted.

A second, related point is that if educational researchers are going to turn ethnography to their own purposes, then those among us who have a professional investment in anthropology (and probably a deep personal commitment as well) should take whatever opportunity we can to applaud the new interest and to help it become an informed one. If we recognize that our monographs are more likely to be read by novice educational researchers than by seasoned educational practitioners, we should elaborate our statements on the perspective and approach of our studies. In that way any subsequent use as models will necessitate solid descriptive work and increasing concern for the meaning that observed behavior has to those involved. And while we're at it, why not stress the anthropologist's preference for good description and interpretation rather than a preoccupation with method *per se?*

If our techniques are to be applied in settings where evaluation is of major concern, why not impress education's own breed of "new ethnographers" with the importance of looking at broader contexts? Why not take the opportunity to remind them that the ways human beings devise for resolving their problems or attaining their goals are often self-defeating, and thus attention to the unanticipated and unintended consequences of evaluation might be in order? Even though educators seem to be adapting rather than adopting the ethnographic innovation, there is opportunity for an infusion of anthropological perspective and ethnographic

practice. As so often happens, these opportunities have come neither at the time nor in the manner we expected, but they are here nonetheless.

My next point, perhaps in contradiction to the previous one, may reveal either a reactionary bias—coupled with the inherent conservatism of anthropology—or at least the effects of all these decades slipping by. I suggest that those of us who have a commitment to doing "traditional" (i.e., pre-adaptation) ethnography in educational research should continue our work in that vein, maintaining clearly identifiable links not only to traditional fieldwork practice but to the traditional literature as well. The "anthropology of education" presents both an opportunity and an obligation to treat education anthropologically. An overriding concern for culture, for context, and for comparison ought to be evident in every genuine piece of educational ethnography.

Such preoccupation with anthropological underpinnings may prove distracting to educator audiences, but I think we should, at times, risk seeming to be irrelevant; educators are too caught up in a field in which too many things are entirely too relevant. In a case study of the implementation (and subsequent de-implementation) of an educational innovation, I made a concerted effort to ground my analysis in the traditional anthropological literature on social organization and to use that literature as a basis for examining a contemporary case (1977). Reviews were mixed; some critics took me to task for seeming to introduce extraneous concepts from the study of small preliterate groups in the examination of complex modern settings. Be that as it may, the subtitle of the monograph promised "An Educational Innovation in Anthropological Perspective" and that is what the reader got.

I do not mean to take the position "ethnography for ethnography's sake," though it is certainly hope more than experience that makes me feel that educators might eventually come around in front of our mirrors in greater numbers than they have. I feel more concern that educators using ethnography—particularly for monitoring—may inadvertently miss or even deliberately ignore the important concern for culture and for context that is the very essence of the anthropological approach.

Evaluation itself, for example, is part of a cultural ethos. When educators start doing participant-observer studies in order to evaluate their colleagues, it is time for some anthropologists of education to begin questioning how it is that certain educators become the evaluators of others, to look at the various interests evaluation may serve (e.g., in enhancing the power and influence of evaluators, in bolstering or intimidating), and to look comparatively at other ways humans have devised to accomplish what formal evaluation accomplishes for educators.

The fourth and final point deals with the nature of ethnography and the question of whether ethnography itself changes over time. Anthropologists Basham and DeGroot placed *The Man in the Principal's Office* at one end of an ethnographic continuum, contrasting it with the polar opposite of a "macro-study" and identifying community study as a "middle level" of analysis

(1977: 428–429). I can live quite well with their locating *The Man in the Principal's Office* at the micro-ethnographic extreme, "focusing upon a single occupation among the thousands upon which American society is based" (Basham and DeGroot 1977:428). What a challenge for the ethnographer whose efforts are in macro-study and who takes responsibility for depicting the thousands rather than the one! To keep the concept of culture viable, we seem to be developing more complex ways to differentiate the micro-cultures of individuals and the "official" or "macro-cultures" of their nation-states (cf. Basham and DeGroot, p. 431; see also Goodenough 1976). One could do worse than be accused of doing micro-ethnography in contemporary American society.

How was it in the ethnographic "good old days"? When earlier generations of ethnographers returned from their exotic excursions, had they gathered sufficient information to produce total and complete descriptions of those whom they had studied? Was it ever quite so simple? Perhaps the notion of ethnography has been elusive in that regard. I know of no account that purports to be the complete ethnography of any human group. At best, in any given time, certain studies are recognized as definitive ones. (For some right reasons and some wrong ones, *The Man in the Principal's Office* has enjoyed its moment as a definitive work in its class.) True, there are some generally recognized "classics," but it is difficult to get consensus in identifying more than a handful of them.

Thus the idea of the ethnography of any human group must remain just that: an idea. Malinowski's venerable classic, *Argonauts of the Western Pacific*, so often cited or quoted by educational researchers, is a very good example of a very inadequate ethnography, if one takes ethnography to mean the description of a *total* life way of a group of people, for that study deals essentially with only one institution among the Trobrianders, the Kula exchange, and Malinowski's work was confined largely to one particular village in one particular district. Virtually any ethnographic statement can be similarly faulted; the more adequate its attention to some aspects of human behavior, the more surely it can be found wanting in attention to others.

Were I writing *The Man in the Principal's Office* today, I would subtitle it *A Micro-ethnography*. Such modesty would have been becoming at the time and might have served as a caution for others who modeled their research after it and labeled it ethnography. I do not mean to suggest that micro-ethnography is something less than ethnography or is only partial ethnography. Rather, I think micro-ethnography properly identifies an attempt to de-scribe a particular micro-cultural system. The "tricky part" will continue to be in relating the micro-culture to the macro-culture.

Writing *The Man in the Principal's Office* now, rather than a decade ago, I would attempt a stronger "cultural" interpretation, giving more attention to micro-macro links. That shift in emphasis would surely cause me to agonize over the writing and over the finished product, and I would probably be torn trying to make the study speak to both "micro" and "macro" concerns at the same time. In that regard Clifford Geertz writes unsettling but nonetheless consoling words concerning the challenge of the genuine ethnographic venture:

> Cultural analysis is intrinsically incomplete. And, worse than that, the more deeply it goes the less complete it is. It is a strange science whose most telling assertions are its most tremulously based, in which to get somewhere with the matter at hand is to intensify the suspicion, both your own and that of others, that you are not quite getting it right. [1973:29]

Notes

[1] Subsequently Smith has extended the variety-reducing, variety-generating contrast suggested by the cyberneticists to an examination of contrasting styles of information processing which he identifies as monopathic and polypathic (Smith 1979).

[2] See, for example, the proceedings of the Stanford-sponsored Conference on Education and Anthropology held in 1954, especially the section, "Should the Anthropologist Make Value Judgments?" (Spindler 1955:185–187).

[3] Frederick Erickson (1977) and Dell Hymes (1976) were among the first to relate the term "ethnographic monitoring" to educational research, although when used in the sense of the on-going nature of ethnography, the phrase goes back at least to Wallace's use of it in the first edition of *Culture and Personality:* "The ethnographic inventory will never be complete and will ever have to be supplemented by ethnographic monitoring" (1961:2).

References

Barnhardt, Ray, John H. Chilcott, and Harry F. Wolcott, eds. 1979. *Anthropology and Educational Administration.* Tucson, AZ: Impresora Sahuaro Press.

Basham, Richard, and David DeGroot. 1977. "Current Approaches to the Anthropology of Urban and Complex Societies" [an essay review]. *American Anthropologist* 79:414–440.

Berreman, Gerald D. 1968. "Ethnography: Method and Product." In James A. Clifton, ed., *Introduction to Cultural Anthropology.* Boston: Houghton Mifflin.

Blumberg, Arthur, and William Greenfield. 1980. *The Effective Principal: Perspectives on School Leadership.* Boston: Allyn and Bacon.

Burnett, Jacquetta Hill. 1968. "Event Description and Analysis in the Microethnography of Urban Classrooms." Paper presented at the American Anthropological Association, Seattle. Subsequently revised and printed in Francis A. J. Ianni and Edward Storey, eds., *Cultural Relevance and Educational Issues.* Boston: Little, Brown and Company, 1973.

Charters, W. W., Jr., and Roland J. Pellegrin. 1972. "Barriers to the Innovation Process: Four Case Studies of Differentiated Staffing." *Educational Administration Quarterly* 9(1):3–14.

Drucker, Peter F. 1967. "The Effective Administrator." In *Report on the First Annual Conference of the School of Community Service and Public Affairs.* Eugene: University of Oregon.

Erickson, Donald A., ed. 1977. *Educational Organization and Administration.* Berkeley, CA: McCutchan Publishing Corporation.

Erickson, Frederick. 1977. "Some Approaches to Inquiry in School-Community Ethnography." *Anthropology and Education Quarterly* 7:58–69.

Forsberg, William H. 1974. Review of *The Man in the Principal's Office: An Ethnography. Educational Administration Quarterly* 10(2):98–101.

Geertz, Clifford. 1973. *The Interpretation of Cultures.* New York. Basic Books.

Goodenough, Ward H. 1976. "Multiculturalism as the Normal Human Experience." *Anthropology and Education Quarterly* VIII(4):4–7. Also reprinted in Elizabeth Eddy and William L. Partridge, eds., *Applied Anthropology in America.* New York: Columbia University Press, 1978.

Herriott, Robert E., and Neal Gross, eds. 1979. *The Dynamics of Planned Educational Change.* Berkeley, CA: McCutchan Publishing Corporation.

Herskovits, Melville J. 1973. *Cultural Relativism.* New York: Vintage Books.

House, Ernest R., and Stephen D. Lapan. 1978. *Survival in the Classroom: Negotiating with Kids, Colleagues, and Bosses.* Boston: Allyn and Bacon.

Hymes, Dell. 1976. "Ethnographic Monitoring." Paper prepared for a symposium on "Language Development in a Bilingual Setting," California State Polytechnic University, Pomona, California, March 19–21.

Kaplan, David, and Robert A. Manners. 1972 (reissued 1986). *Culture Theory.* Prospect Heights, IL: Waveland Press, Inc.

Keesing, Roger M. 1974. "Theories of Culture." *Annual Review of Anthropology* 3:73–97.

Keller, Arnold J. 1974. "Inside the Man in the Principal's Office." *The Elementary Principal* 53(3):20–26.

Kluckhohn, Clyde. 1949. *Mirror for Man.* New York: McGraw-Hill Book Company.

Knapp, Michael S. 1979. "Ethnographic Contributions to Evaluation Research: The Experimental Schools Program Evaluation and Some Alternatives." In Thomas D. Cook and Charles S. Reichardt, eds., *Qualitative and Quantitative Methods in Evaluation Research.* Beverly Hills, CA: Sage Publications.

Lee, Dorothy. 1955. "Discrepancies in the Teaching of American Culture." In George D. Spindler, ed., *Education and Anthropology.* Stanford University Press.

Malinowski, Bronislaw. 1922 (reissued 1984). *Argonauts of the Western Pacific.* Prospect Heights, IL: Waveland Press, Inc.

Mintzberg, Henry. 1973. *The Nature of Managerial Work.* New York: Harper and Row.

Roberts, Joan I., and Sherrie K. Akinsanya. 1976. *Schooling in the Cultural Context: Anthropological Studies of Education.* New York: David McKay Company.

Sarason, Seymour B. 1971. *The Culture of the School and the Problem of Change.* Boston: Allyn and Bacon.

Smith, Alfred G. 1979. *Cognitive Styles in Law Schools.* Austin: University of Texas Press.

Smith, Louis M. 1967. "The Micro-ethnography of the Classroom." *Psychology in the Schools* 4:216–221.

Smith, Louis M., and Pat M. Keith. 1967. *Social Psychological Aspects of School Building Design.* U.S. Office of Education, Bureau of Research, Final Report, Project No. S-223.

————. 1971. *Anatomy of Educational Innovation.* New York: John Wiley and Sons.

Singleton, John. 1974. "Education as a Cultural Process" [an essay review]. *Reviews in Anthropology* 1(1):145–151.

Spindler, George D., ed. 1955. *Education and Anthropology.* Stanford University Press.

————. 1987. *Education and Cultural Process: Anthropological Approaches,* Second Edition. Prospect Heights, IL: Waveland Press, Inc.

Stake, Robert E., and Jack A. Easley, Jr., eds. 1978. *Case Studies in Science Education.* Urbana-Champaign: University of Illinois, Center for Instructional Research and Curriculum Evaluation.

Wallace, Anthony F. C. 1961. *Culture and Personality.* New York: Random House.

————. 1970. *Culture and Personality.* Second edition. New York: Random House.

Warren, Richard L. 1967. *Education in Rebhausen, A German Village.* New York: Holt, Rinehart and Winston.

————. 1973 *The Teaching Experience in an Elementary School: A Case Study.* Stanford University: Stanford Center for Research and Development in Teaching, Technical Report No. 35.

————. 1975 "Context and Isolation: The Teaching Experience in an Elementary School." *Human Organization* 34(2):139–148.

Wolcott, Harry F. 1967 (reissued 1984). *A Kwakiutl Village and School.* Prospect Heights, IL: Waveland Press, Inc.

————. 1970. "An Ethnographic Approach to the Study of School Administrators." *Human Organization* 29(2):115–122.

————. 1971. "Handle with Care: Necessary Precautions in the Anthropology of Schools." In *Anthropological Perspectives on Education.* Murray L. Wax, Stanley Diamond, and Fred O. Gearing, eds. New York: Basic Books.

————. 1973 (reissued 1984). *The Man in the Principal's Office: An Ethnography.* Prospect Heights, IL: Waveland Press, Inc.

————. 1987. "The Elementary School Principal: Notes from a Field Study." In George D. Spindler, ed., *Education and Cultural Process: Anthropological Approaches,* 2/e. Prospect Heights, IL: Waveland Press, Inc.

————. 1975. "Fieldwork in Schools: Where the Tradition of Deferred Judgment Meets a Subculture Obsessed with Evaluation." *Anthropology and Education Quarterly* 6(1):17–20.

————. 1977. *Teachers Versus Technocrats: An Educational Innovation in Anthropological Perspective.* Eugene, OR: Center for Educational Policy and Management, University of Oregon.

Yee, Albert H., ed. 1971. *Social Interaction in Educational Settings.* Englewood Cliffs, NJ: Prentice-Hall, Inc.

PART II

Communi-cation and Interaction

Editorial Commentary

Ethnography as a research strategy, a method of study, does not in itself determine what shall be observed and recorded or how it shall be interpreted. It is essential to have a model of relationships among phenomena in order to do sensible ethnography. Even if the object of the "ethnography" is to produce a "straightforward," nontheoretical, nontechnical description of events and behavior in some setting, there will inevitably be many models of how the events relate to each other that will influence what is observed and recorded and how it is interpreted. If those models are not drawn from a body of more or less coherent theory or from constructs based on diversified observation and study, they may, by default, be based on constructs and models of relationships that are drawn from personal experience and prejudice; or at best they may be an inchoate mix of ideas picked up here and there.

The papers in this section are far from the latter type. They are based on definite models. As noted in the General Introduction, they are all formulated in ways influenced by theoretical models that developed out of descriptive linguistics and sociolinguistics, language and culture interests, and the ethnography of speaking. Nevertheless, as might be expected, the researches and the papers reporting them differ in the degree to which they focus on speech behavior or language as such.

Shirley Heath, in her chapter on styles of questioning and speech interaction between black parents and their children and white teacher-parents and their own children and black pupils in their classrooms, draws directly from socio-linguistic constructs and research to formulate her inquiry and interpretation. Her data are not collected by using videotapes, records of movements about the classrooms, or sociometric schedules. Her data are largely collected through records of verbal interactions that occur *in situ*—at home, in the classroom, or anywhere else she is with a child, parent, or teacher. She contextualizes her audio-observations by attention to social context in both the larger community and the more limited settings of home and classroom. Her inquiry and analysis of data are different from those employed by Erickson and Mohatt and others of their persuasion. The data used in the microanalysis of the classroom in Erickson and Mohatt's study fall into categories such as duration, tempo, and movement. The data themselves are usually observations of activity rather than units of meaning. Even speech behavior is analyzed in terms of pauses, stress, and pitch by which a rhythmic cadence is maintained or disrupted as people interact face to face. Inferences are then drawn about styles of leadership or social control as well as about interaction styles. These inferences, in turn, are related to a general hypothesis drawn from background literature. This style of inquiry does not depend upon the emic content and cultural knowledge of the native speakers as elicited by verbal interaction between ethnographer and informant — as is the case in ethnographic interviewing or recording of verbal exchanges. Nor is it dependent on the semantic content of situated verbal interaction. Rather it depends on recording, audiovisually, the interactions among natives and between natives and others and interpreting them in as many dimensions as possible given time and technical competence. With adequate videotaping it is not even necessary for the analyst to be on the scene.

Erickson and Mohatt explicitly acknowledge their intellectual debt to theoretical models that have emerged out of linguistics and the ethnography of speaking. Their data consist of detailed observations of interaction in the classroom. This fine-grained observation of interaction in a limited setting they term microethnography, in contrast to general or macroethnography. One of the important developments in the ethnography of schooling has been attention to the minutiae of everyday behavior in the classroom and in even more limited settings such as counseling sessions and reading groups, as carried forward in Erickson's work and in the studies by McDermott, Florio, Darnell, and others, many of them cited in the Erickson-Mohatt paper. This development is interdisciplinary and cannot be claimed by anthroethnography as its sole property.

Though Erickson and Mohatt are inspired and directed by a model that has emerged from studies of speech behavior, they attend more to social interactions, in all their expressed forms, than to speech as such, though the reader will find an analysis, in their chapter, of categories of speech as well as of pauses, stress, and pitch. Their use of videotape in the classroom also permitted an analysis of movement about the room and the duration and tempo of interaction between students and teachers. The model is therefore not exclusively a language- or speech-focused model. Analysis of acts of speech in earlier work in the ethnography of communication called attention to the necessity of carrying out detailed studies of all phenomena involved in communication in specific social contexts. The model that Erickson and Mohatt draw from is by no means narrow, though the methods are microanalytic.

Also derived from the paralinguistic model is attention to covert, implicit, tacit, or "hidden" cultural patterns that affect behavior and communication, particularly in face-to-face social interaction, but that are largely outside the consciousness of the actor. This is strong in Erickson's work in general and in this paper by Erickson and Mohatt. It is also present in much of the other work reported in this book.

As a veteran of the early culture and personality period in anthropology, however, I would enlarge the background from which the concern with the hidden dimension and its study was derived. Its antecedents are not solely in sociolinguistic, speech behavior, or social interactionist theory. Covert culture, hidden postulates, dynamic themes, and the like were a primary preoccupation on the part of many anthropologists of the 1940s, such as Clyde Kluckhohn and Morris Opler, Adamson Hoebel, and Scudder McKeel. All of these people had been exposed to linguistic theory and practice as part of their anthropological education, but much of the inspiration to attend to the dimension of the implicit and covert came from psychodynamic models (though linguist Edward Sapir's early influence is also especially significant).

This focus on the hidden but influential dimension in behavior also stemmed in quite a different way from the sociological models of Robert K. Merton, Talcott Parsons, and many others who had been influenced by the much earlier work of Pareto, Simmel, and, of course, Max Weber. The "implicit" or "latent" functions of social action were a major aspect of their systematic sociological analyses.

Various models that call attention to the hidden dimension were developed in the early work in educational anthropology, as in various papers (particularly those by Jules Henry, Dorothy Lee, and George Spindler) in two previously cited books on schooling as cultural transmission that I edited, published in 1955 and 1963. The formulations were not the same as those developed by Erickson and others, but they clearly point in the same direction. In fact, the importance of the covert, unintended, inexplicit aspects of education-related behavior was a cornerstone of the theoretical positions emerging during that formative period in educational anthropology.

I call attention here to these historical matters because it is important to realize that most of what we do methodologically and most of what we use in theory have antecedents that have antecedents that have antecedents. What Erickson and Mohatt have done, and what McDermott, Mehan, and a score of others, including those represented in this volume, have done is to bring the concept of the hidden dimension into a new and clearer focus by microanalytic techniques of data collection and analysis. A concept of the hidden dimension itself has been given its most recent shape through the work of linguists, kinesiologists, ethnoscientists, and cognitive anthropologists. Microanalysis made it come into a new and useful focus of great significance in modern educational anthropology and of real importance to practitioners who want to understand why educational programs are not working and why educational goals are not being attained.

There are more problems, it seems to me, in the analytic processes involved in the style of the Erickson-Mohatt study than in the instance of Heath's study. The relationship between observation and inference to a hidden cultural mode, hypothesized as due to an extended time-space culture, as in the case of the Odawa, is somewhat more indirect than that between an examination of the content of questions asked in various contexts and inferences about styles of questioning characteristically used between different adults and children. But both styles of study have brought ethnographic inquiry into focus as the rigorous examination of highly specific and detailed elements of behavior and communication in settings directly relevant to educational problems.

Susan Philips' emphasis is on the "cant" used in the legal profession that distinguishes lawyers in their professional subcultural behavior from the rest of us. She shows how cant is acquired as well as what it is and how it distinguishes the legal profession from other professions and excludes all others from participation in the inner circle of communication. Sociolinguistic models have clearly guided her ethnographic research and her interpretations. There are many other phenomena she could have studied — clique formations in law schools, for example. The theoretical model she carried with her into her fieldwork strongly influenced her choice of subject.

Hervé Varenne's chapter stands by itself in Part II and in the book as a whole. It is grouped with the others in this section because in it Varenne treats language mainly as a source of data, though, as an ethnographer must, he gives his language data social and environmental context. Like Heath and Philips, he exploits the utterances (the "rhetoric") of native speakers for relevant data. He is more interested in what people say than in how they say it or with what pauses or rhythm of exchange. And he uses data elicited in interviews and collected from school papers as well as data collected in everyday social interaction. He employs these data differently than Philips and Heath. He pursues symbols of self and self-other references contained in the statements by the natives as a point of entry for the discovery of cliques. He consequently sees cliques, in fact the whole "social organization" of the school, as much less concrete, much more fluid and ambiguous, much more situational, than previous workers armed with more standard concepts of social organization.

The question that remains is whether self-other reference symbols, or behavioral grouping based on them, are the best index to social organization. He carries the situationist tendencies of contemporary social science to a logical extreme by giving significance to symbols that float around depending on who is talking to whom about whom. Given this orientation, any attempt to judge what is "real" social organization is spurious. Social organization in its complete functional sense must be cognitive (a model, though never complete, in the mind), symbolic (representations defining boundaries and we/they relationships), and interactional (who goes with or conflicts with or avoids whom, when).

Varenne has chosen a symbolic approach. His analysis is refreshing because it challenges conventional notions about the "reality" and fixity of social organization. Though the immediate impact of his analysis may be greater on anthropologists and other social scientists, the information and insights to be gained from this approach should be of use to administrators and counselors in educational institutions. Judgments one might make about school policy could be directly influenced by one's conception of cliques, leadership, prestige hierarchies, and the channels of communication within the school.

4

Shirley Brice Heath

Questioning at Home and at School: A Comparative Study

Shirley Brice Heath with Trackton children

The Author

Shirley Brice Heath began her career in education in elementary classrooms, teaching reading, composition, and English as a second language. Helping students learn to use written and spoken language depended not only on the teacher's knowledge of language structures and processes, but also on an understanding of the uses and valuations of language in students' communities. This led her to graduate work in anthropology at Columbia University. Her anthropological fieldwork in Mexico, Guatemala, and communities of the Southeastern United States focused on the language and culture of minorities placed in schools in which success depended on knowledge of a standard language. She has served as consultant for curriculum projects and educational policy-making, and has written curriculum materials for language arts and social studies. She is author of *Telling Tongues: Language Policy in Mexico, Colony to a Nation* (1972) and articles on language planning in the United States. Her forthcoming study, *Ways with Words: Ethnography of Communication—Communities and Classrooms*, describes language learning and use in two communities of the Southeastern United States. She is currently professor of education and anthropology at Stanford University and was formerly associate professor of anthropology and educational linguistics in the Graduate School of Education of the University of Pennsylvania.

This Chapter

In this chapter Shirley Heath engages with a problem that in one form or another has vexed most classroom teachers where there is a difference between the cultural background of the teacher and that of some or all of the children in the classroom. In the instances with which Heath is concerned, the lack of cultural congruence is between black children and white teachers, where the teachers assumed that the children in their classes would respond to language routines and the uses of language in building knowledge, skills, and dispositions just as other children, including their own, did. The object of her research was to discover why the particular black children in those classrooms she studied in a specific community did not respond "just as the other children did." The focus became the role of questioning in language and socialization. "We don't talk to our children like you folks do" was the response of some Trackton parents to questions put to them about their children's behaviors.

Trackton children are not regarded as information givers or as appropriate conversational partners for adults. But they are by no means excluded from language participation—in a language that is rich in styles, speakers, and topics. The predominant characteristic of teacher questions was to pull attributes of things out of context, particularly out of the context of books, and name them— queens, elves, police, red apples. Trackton parents did not ask the children these kinds of questions, and Trackton children had different techniques for responding to any questions—including deflection of the question itself.

This research required going well beyond the classroom to the interactions in the homes of teachers and of Trackton children. This is a kind of selective holism that we have come to feel is one of the important criteria for a good ethnography of schooling. The ethnographer identifies and moves into whatever context is necessary for an understanding of the phenomena taking place in the classroom.

This research demonstrates the desirability of long-term research. Heath was engaged intermittently in this study for about five years. Much of what she knows could only be learned through long-term exposure. Much of the validity of a good ethnography comes from this kind of exposure.

The study also demonstrates the utility of having a clear frame of reference from and within which to work. In this case the frame of reference is language socialization and the ethnography of communication, both of which are relatively recent developments in cultural anthropology and, by nature, interdisciplinary.

Lastly, it is noteworthy that this research has direct potential for application to the classroom for the improvement of education. Heath discusses this application at the end of the chapter. She stresses interaction of the school and the community and states an important position—that it is a two-way path. She makes the point that the success of such an effort depends on participation on the part of all parties involved. It is not a matter of outside experts telling teachers what to do nor of teachers telling parents how they should talk, but rather a mutual and collaborative effort to discover what the problems are and what can be done about them. This is in the emerging tradition of an applied social science appropriate to a democratic society.

Introduction

"Ain't nobody can talk about things being about theirselves."

A third-grade boy in a community in the Southeastern part of the United States directed this statement to his teacher when she persisted in asking questions about the story just completed in reading circle.

> TEACHER   What is the story about?
>
> CHILDREN   *(silence)*
>
> T   Uh ... Let's see ... Who is it the story talks about?
>
> C   *(silence)*
>
> T   Who is the main character? Um ... What kind of story is it?
>
> CHILD   Ain't nobody can talk about things being about theirselves!

The boy was saying: "There's no way anybody can talk (and ask) about things being about themselves." As an ethnographer who had worked in the boy's community and school for more than five years, I was able to place his summative statement about the kinds of questions asked in school into the context of knowledge about those asked of him in his own community.

The boy was reacting to the fact that teachers' questions were so often about things being about themselves; that is, they asked for labels, attributes, and discrete features of objects and events in isolation from the context. Someone—most often the teacher and the brightest kids in class—always had answers for school questions. These answers could usually be given in one word. In the boy's community, people asked questions about whole events or objects and their uses, causes, and effects. Often no one had an answer which was the "right answer." Community members accepted many answers and ways of answering, and their answers almost always involved telling a story, describing a situation, or making comparisons between the event or object being described and another known to the audience.

This paper presents some data on uses of questions in three different situations in a moderate-sized city of the Southeastern United States: a working-class community of black residents, the classrooms attended by children of this community in 1970–1975, and the homes of teachers from these classrooms. We will attempt to show how questions varied in proportion to other types of utterances across the three situations, and we shall look at different uses of questions and the assumptions made by the questioners about the functions of questions. Our aim is to indicate how ethnographic data on verbal strategies in community and home settings can be useful for comparison with data collected in studies of the functions of language in the classroom.

Ethnography in the Community and Classroom

The goal of ethnography is to describe the ways of living of a social group, usually one in which there is in-group recognition by the members that they indeed must live and work together to retain group identity. Traditionally, ethnographers have taken up residence in communities made up of one or more of these social groups to record and describe the behaviors, values, and tangible aspects of their culture. More recently, ethnographers have also become participant-observers in settings which do not necessarily have a cross-generational on-going sense of social identity. Anthropologists have studied institutions, such as schools, hospitals, and factories, or short-lived but repetitive group interactions, such as court sessions, conversations, and service encounters. Some anthropologists have made their data available for decision-making by political leadership and institutional management. Anthropologists studying communities in complex societies have also begun to make their studies available to these communities and have offered to provide data about the operations of political/economic institutions through which community members must move in daily interactions outside their own social group.

The fieldwork reported in this paper was carried out over a period of five years in both community and institutional settings. Results of the work were shared with both community and institutional members. One phase of the fieldwork was done in an all-black residential group whose members identified themselves as a community both spatially and in terms of group membership. To distinguish this group from the public community at large, we will hereafter refer to it as Trackton. Over the period of time in which I worked there, its membership declined from 150 to 40, as families moved from the neighborhood into public housing or purchased new homes. Most Trackton households contained one or more members, ages 21 to 45, who worked in

jobs providing salaries equal to or above those of beginning public school teachers in the region; however, jobs were seasonal, and work was not always steady. Trackton was located in a Southeastern city with a population of approximately 40,000; in the period from 1970 to 1975, children from the community attended either of two public elementary-level schools. As a volunteer neighborhood service aide, I worked in these schools and with city personnel in a variety of agencies, collecting data on interactions of Trackton residents in institutions with which they came in frequent, if not daily, contact. As a professor at a state teacher-training institution for which the region's citizens had a longstanding respect, I had many of the teachers, their spouses, or other family members in classes, and I worked informally with others on local civic or church-related projects. Over the years, I became colleague, co-author, aide, and associate to many of the classroom teachers, and I had access to not only their classrooms, but also their homes and their activities in the public domain.

I began working in Trackton at the request of some of the older residents who had known me for several years. My initial task, in their view, was to read and talk with the children and explain to adults why their children were not doing better in school. Gradually, I was called on to be a source of information about available services and opportunities for them and their children in public institutions, and I was asked to explain the systems of entry and maintenance which made for success in these institutions. In the late 1960s, numerous policy changes in schools and public systems regulating housing, employment, and preschool educational and medical experiences brought the children of all-black communities into many new situations. Desegregation rulings put black students into formerly all-white classrooms, usually with white teachers. There were many complaints in the first years, but particularly disturbing to older residents was the hatred of their young for school.

> The teachers won't listen.
> My kid, he too scared to talk, 'cause nobody play by the rules he know. At home, I can't shut 'im up.
> Miss Davis, she complain 'bout Ned not answerin' back. He say she asks dumb questions she already know 'bout.

It seemed clear that parents felt there was little meaningful communication going on between teachers and their children in the classroom. When I talked over this view with classroom teachers, they agreed there was relatively little "real" exchange of information, feeling, or imagination between them and many of the black students, especially those in the primary grades.

During this period, much research on language pointed out differences between the structures of Black English and those of standard English, and the effects of these differences on academic performance (Labov 1968, Baratz and Shuy 1969, Wolfram 1969). Many local teachers knew of this research (especially Labov 1970, 1972), and some suggested that perhaps differences between the structures of their language and those of their black students were major reasons for communication breakdowns. Other teachers did not agree; they reasoned that almost daily

for many years they had lived and worked with Black English speakers in nearly all institutions except schools and churches. Therefore, the structures of the languages used by teachers and their Black English-speaking students were probably not so different as to cause the almost-total lack of communication which seemed to exist in some classrooms. Their view was that reasons for the breakdown lay in the nature of interactions called for in school. The interactional tasks between teacher and child called for particular kinds of responses from students. These responses depended primarily on two kinds of knowledge: first, the rituals and routines of classroom life, and second, the information and skills acquired in the classroom. It was difficult, however, for teachers to pin down exactly what was called for in these interactions; thus they felt they could not help their students achieve success in these tasks. To be sure, the entry of black students into the schools had caused negative attitudes and bitter prejudices to surface, but there were many well-intentioned teachers who, having accepted the desegregation decision as final, wanted to get on with teaching. They felt a strong need to know more about ways in which they could effectively communicate with all their students.

Of the students with whom they had communication problems, teachers said:

> They don't seem to be able to answer even the simplest questions.
> I would almost think some of them have a hearing problem; it is as though they don't hear me ask a question. I get blank stares to my questions. Yet when

I am making statements or telling stories which interest them, they always seem to hear me.

The simplest questions are the ones they can't answer in the classroom; yet on the playground, they can explain a rule for a ballgame or describe a particular kind of bait with no problem. Therefore, I know they can't be as dumb as they seem in my class.

I sometimes feel that when I look at them and ask a question, I'm staring at a wall I can't break through. There's something there; yet in spite of all the questions I ask, I'm never sure I've gotten through to what's inside that wall.

Many teachers and administrators felt they were "not asking the right questions" of either the children or their own teaching strategies, and I was asked to help them find ways of helping themselves. As an aide, tutor, traveling librarian, and "visiting fireman" occasionally asked to talk about archaeology or show slides of other countries in which I had done fieldwork, I served numerous functions in classrooms across a wide range of grade levels and subject areas for five years. I participated and observed, shared data, and acted as change agent at the request of the institution's members. During this period, some of the teachers enrolled in graduate courses of study which included some anthropology and linguistics courses I taught. They then used techniques of ethnographic fieldwork and data interpretation in their own classes and schools and incorporated into their teaching some of the observation skills associated with anthropology. Some teachers collected data on their own practices in guiding language learning for their preschool children at

home; others agreed to allow me to participate and observe in their homes, recording uses of language and language input for their children. Particularly critical to these teachers' understanding and acceptance of ethnography in familiar educational settings—both their classrooms and their homes—was their view that the ethnographic/linguistic research was in response to their felt needs, and they were themselves involved.

During the period of participating and observing in classrooms and some teachers' homes, I continued work in Trackton. A major focus of fieldwork there was the acquisition of uses of language, ways in which children learned to use language to satisfy their needs, ask questions, transmit information, and convince those around them they were competent communicators. Participating and observing with the children and their families and friends intensively over a period of five years, I was able to collect data across a wide range of situations and to follow some children longitudinally as they acquired communicative competence in Trackton and then attempted to take this competence into school settings.[1] Likewise, at various periods during these years, I observed Trackton adults in public service encounters and on their jobs, and I was able to compare their communicative competence in these situations with those inside Trackton. The context of language use, including setting, topic, and participants (both those directly involved in the talk and those who only listened), determined in large part how community members, teachers, public service personnel, and fellow workers judged the communicative competence of Trackton residents. Proper handling of questioning was especially critical, because outsiders often judged the intelligence and general competence of individuals by their responses to questions and by the questions they asked.

In settings outside Trackton, questions had several functions relatively rarely used by residents there. The first situation in which this difference became important for Trackton children came when they entered school. There they had to learn that teachers did not always make the same assumptions about the uses of questions they did. What follows here provides an indication of the interrogatives teachers used with their own preschoolers at home, questions Trackton adults asked their preschool children, and the conflict and congruence between these differing approaches to questioning as they evolved in classrooms.

Questions and Language Learning

Questions and their uses by children's caretakers have received relatively little attention in studies of language input and acquisition. In general, what emerges from the literature is the view that questions are used for training children to interact verbally with their caretakers and for directing their attention to what it is they should learn (Holzman 1972, 1974; Snow, et al. 1976; Goody 1977). Several studies point out that a large percentage of utterances middle-class mothers direct to their preschool children is made up of ques-

tions (Newport, et al. 1977; Snow 1977), and some studies indicate that questions become successively more complex in correspondence with the child's increased language skill (Levelt 1975). Most of these studies consider questions only as they may relate to the child's acquisition of grammatical competence or the structures of his speech community's language system (Ervin-Tripp 1970).

Some attention has also been given to the role of questions in children's acquisition of communicative competence, i.e., how they learn conversational skills (Snow 1977, Ervin-Tripp and Miller 1977) and determine appropriate language uses for different listeners, settings, and topics (Hymes 1962, Blount 1977). Cross-cultural research in child language acquisition has pointed out that the linguistic environment and the language socialization of children vary across cultures. Uses of questions vary in numerous respects. For example, in one society, it may not be the mother or even members of the immediate family who direct the highest proportion of questions to young children, because the language socialization network includes a wide range of participants (Harkness 1977). In another society, questions are not considered highly relevant to learning how to accomplish tasks (Goody 1977); in another, children have very little exposure to *why* or *how* questions (Blank 1975). Among other groups, questions may be intimately linked to imperatives, explaining the reasons for commands or the consequences of not obeying orders (Cook-Gumperz 1973; Sachs, et al. 1976).

The specific characteristics of questions and their uses in socializing young children are highly dependent on the network of those who ask questions. A preschool child who has frequent contacts with individuals of both sexes, different ages, and varying degrees of familiarity with his world will learn very different uses of questions from the child accustomed to a small network of family and close associates. In particular, the assumptions made by questioners about the functions of their questions in the socialization of the child will be very different. The wide variation possible in child language socialization, and especially in the uses of questions, is exemplified in the community of Trackton and the homes of its classroom teachers.

Classroom Teachers and Their Own Children

Within their homes, children of the classroom teachers involved in this study[2] were socialized into a fairly small network of language users: mother, father, siblings, and maids or grandparents. Children below the age of four rarely communicated with anyone on an extended basis except these primary associates. Visits to Sunday School, the grocery store, shopping centers, and so on provided very limited opportunities for questions addressed to the children by nonintimates. Within the homes, talk to preschool children emphasized questions. In their questioning routines with preverbal as well as verbal children, adults supplied the entire context, giving questions and answering them (cf. Gleason 1973)[3] or giving questions and then pausing to hold conversational space for a hypothetical

answer before moving on to the next statement, which assumed information from the hypothetical answer (cf. Snow 1977).

> MOTHER *(addressing an 8-week-old infant)* You want your teddy bear?
> MOTHER Yes, you want your bear.
>
> . . .
>
> MOTHER *(addressing her 2-month-old infant)* You don't know what to make of all those lights, do you?
> *Pause (3 seconds)*
> MOTHER That's right, I know you don't like them. Let's move over here. *(picks up infant and moves away from lights)*
>
> . . .
>
> MOTHER *(addressing her child age 2;9)* Didja forget your coat?
> MOTHER Yes, you did. Let's go back 'n get it.

When parents wanted to teach a politeness formula, such as *thank you* or *please*, they used interrogatives: "Can you say 'thank you'?" "What do you say?" (cf. Gleason and Weintraub 1976). Questions served a wide variety of functions in adult-child interactions. They allowed adults to hold pseudo-conversations with children, to direct their attention to specific events or objects in the array of stimuli about them, and to link formulaic responses to appropriate occasions. Perhaps most important, adults' uses of questions trained children to act as question-answerers, as experts on knowledge about the world, especially the names and attributes of items in their environment and those introduced to them through books.

> MOTHER *(looking at a family photograph album with Missy, age 2;3)* Who's that, Missy?

(The mother has pointed to the family dog in one of the pictures.)

MISSY   That's Toby.

MOTHER   What does Toby say?

MISSY   Woof, woof, *(child imitates a whine)* grrrrrr, yip.

MOTHER   Where does Toby live?

MISSY   *My* house.

The children seemed to feel compelled to give answers to adults' questions. When they did not know answers (or were bored with the usual routine of expected answers), they sometimes invented fantastic answers.

Adults addressed questions to their children in great numbers and variety. During a period of 48 hours, Missy (age 2;3) was asked 103 questions; 47.9 percent of all utterances (215) directed to her during this period were questions (cf. Sachs et al. 1976).[4] Table 1 contains a description of these questions. Questions designated Q–I are those in which the questioner has the information being requested of the addressee; A–I questions are those in which the addressee has the information being requested. Unanswerable questions (U–I) are those for which neither questioner nor addressee has the information. Of the A–I questions, 25 percent were clarification requests (Corsaro 1977), in which questioners asked the child to clarify, confirm, or repeat a previous utterance. Q–I questions were often

used in game-playing, especially games of hide-and-seek or peek-a-boo. These two types, Q–I and A–I, fit the simplicity of syntax expected in utterances directed to children of this age (cf. Newport, et al. 1977), but the U–I questions do not. These were both Why–questions and "I wonder" questions which asked for information neither the child nor the adult was expected to have. The syntax of these and the answers they called for was far more complex than that of other types addressed to the child. For example, a father walking the child outside before putting her to bed would look up at the sky and ask: "I wonder what's up there?" These questions seemed to be self-talk, an out-loud sort of reverie. For these questions, the child was expected to be a passive listener, but a listener nevertheless, thus giving the adult an "excuse" for talking to himself.

Interrogative forms predominated in types of utterances directed to preschoolers. Over a six-month period, a teacher arranged for her child (age 2;8–3;2) and the child (age 3;2–3;8) of another teacher to play in one or the other of the two homes each afternoon from 3 to 5. Adult-children interactions were taped one afternoon each week for six months. Adults who interacted with the children usually included either or both of the teachers (mothers), one grand-

TABLE 1   **Percentages and Types of Questions (Missy 2;3)**

Types	Examples	Total	Percentage
Q–I	What color is that?	46	44.7
A–I	What do you want?	24	23.3
U–I	Why is it things can't be simpler than they are?	18	17.5
Others	(directives, etc.)	15	14.5

parent, and two older siblings. In the first month (four sessions), interrogatives made up 58.6 percent of the total utterances (640) directed to the children, imperatives 28.1 percent, exclamations 6.7 percent, declaratives 6.6 percent. In the sixth month (four sessions), interrogatives made up 52.4 percent of the total utterances (770) directed to the children, imperatives 30.3 percent, exclamations 4.4 percent, and declaratives 12.9 percent. Lumping all interrogative forms together in the data masks the uses of questions in behavior correction and accusations of wrong-doing. Many of the interrogatives were, in fact, directives or condemnations of the children's behavior. For example, tag questions attached directly to statements were counted here as interrogatives because of their form, but the speakers usually meant these as declarative or directive. For example, in the utterance "That's a top. You've never seen one of those, have you?" the adult was not calling for a response from the child, but making a declarative statement for the child: "No, I've never seen one of those." In the statement, "You wouldn't do that, would you?" the speaker provides a somewhat softened directive which means "Don't do that." Questions similar in type to tag questions were directives in intent and followed immediately after imperatives in form, extending their force: "Stop it, Jamie. Why can't you behave?" The latter part of this utterance extends the scolding power of the imperative and calls upon the child to *think* about a response to the question, but not to respond verbally to the condemnation.

Adults and older siblings seemed compelled to communicate to the pre-

schoolers in questions. At the end of the third month, when the strong patterning of questioning was definitive in the data, the teachers agreed to make a conscious effort for one month to reduce their questions and use statements instead. This change evolved out of discussions surrounding analysis of the past three months' tapes. One teacher believed (though she admitted perhaps ideally so) that statements transmitted more information than questions did. Therefore, since she also believed her purpose in holding conversations with her preschoolers was to pass on information, she should make statements, not ask questions. The other teacher was skeptical, believing questions necessary to check on information-transmission. However, both agreed to try to reduce their level of questioning (and that of adults around them) directed to the children for one month to see if their feelings about statements and questions could be borne out in the data in any concrete way. During this period, the percentage of questions dropped to 50.6 percent and the percentage of statements increased to 11.9 percent. However, both teachers reported they were not satisfied with what was happening. They felt they gave more orders, the questions they did ask were scolding in nature, and they were not getting the behavior modifications they expected from their children. They reported they felt they did not involve their children when they used statements. They received no sense of interaction and felt they were "preaching" to a third party; they could not be sure they were being heard. They viewed questions as a way to "share talk" with children of this age.

Just "talking *to* them" (interpreted now by both teachers as using statements only) seemed to have no impact; questions allowed adults to "talk *with* children."

Without being aware of any change in their behavior, in the last month of data collected from these adult-children interactions, adults seemed to focus on teaching the children to ask the right questions in the right places and not to ask questions which seemed to challenge the authority of adults. The children were told:

> Don't ask why people are sick.
> Don't ask that kind of question.
> Don't ask so many questions.
> Don't ask why.

These corrections seemed to increase dramatically when someone from outside the family circle entered the home. Adults seemed to use correctives to questions to announce they were training their children in the right way. If a child asked an "impertinent" question of a visitor, the adult would reprimand the child and offer an explanatory aside to the visitor. "What do you say?" as a request for politeness formulas such as "please" and "thank you" was an especially favorite question when outsiders were present.

In summary, teachers socializing their own preschoolers to language depended heavily on questions. They used questions to teach their children what they should attend to when looking at a book ("What's that?" "Where's the puppy?" "What does he have in his hand?"). The children were taught to label (Ninio and Bruner 1978), to search out pieces of pictures, to name parts of the whole, and to talk about these out of

context. As the children grew older, adults used questions to add power to their directives ("Stop that! Did you hear me?") and to call particular attention to the infraction committed ("Put that back. Don't you know that's not yours?"). Adults saw questions as necessary to train children, to cause them to respond verbally, and to be trained as conversational partners.

Language Learning in Trackton

In the past decade, linguists have described the structure of Black English, its history, and its particular systems of usage in appropriate contexts. Numerous myths about the language of the black child have been exploded by research, which has shown this language to be rule-governed and as capable of providing an adequate basis for thinking as any other language. Speech acts given particular labels in Black English, such as "signifying," "playing the dozens," and "jiving," have been described in their uses by adolescent and adult members of black communities (Labov, et al. 1968; Mitchell Kernan 1971; Kochman 1972).

Nevertheless, many stereotypes still exist about language learning in black communities. Studies of black communities provide only bits and pieces of evidence on adults interacting with young children for language socialization. Ward (1971) describes a community in Louisiana in which the children have numerous language difficulties in school, but little systematic attention is given to the acquisition of communicative competence by young children in the community. Adult-child interactions described in Young 1970 and

Stack 1976 provide few data directly relevant to language socialization. Teachers who participated in the study reported here initially held a variety of stereotypes about how black children learned language: black parents don't care about how their children talk; black children don't have adequate exposure to language, because their parents are probably as nonverbal as the kids are at school; black parents don't spend enough time with their children to train them to talk right. All of these views show that teachers thought black children's language socialization was somehow different from that of other children. Yet in their interactions with black children in the classroom, teachers invariably assumed they would respond to language routines and uses of language in building knowledge, skills, and dispositions just as other children did. Some teachers were aware of this paradox, but felt that since they did not know how language was taught in black communities and how it was used to make children aware of the world around them, they had no basis on which to rethink their views of the language socialization of black children. The teachers could only assume these children were taught language and cognitive skills in the same ways they used to teach their own children.

That was not the case for children in Trackton, as examination of the role of questions in their language socialization indicates. Questions addressed by adults to children occurred far less frequently in Trackton than in the homes of teachers. In Trackton, adults were not observed playing peek-a-boo games with young children; thus, a major source of Q–I questions was eliminated.

Adults and siblings also did not direct questions to preverbal infants; instead, they made statements about them to someone else which conveyed the same information as questions directed by teachers to their children. Trackton adults would say of a crying preverbal infant: "Sump'n's the matter with that child." The equivalent in the teacher's home would be to direct a question or series of questions to the child: "What's the matter?" "Does something hurt you?" "Are you hungry?" Trackton adults did not attempt to engage children as conversational partners until they were seen as realistic sources of information and competent partners in talk.

It has been suggested that the language used by adults, especially mothers, in speaking to young children has numerous special properties; some of these develop because of the limited range of topics which can be discussed with young children (Shatz and Gelman 1977). In addition, most of the research on mother-child interaction has been done in homes where a single child and a single parent were recorded in their interactions (Brown 1973). In this situation, mothers have no one other than their children to talk to or with, and language interactions with their children may thus be intensified over those which would occur if other conversational partners were consistently present. In Trackton, adults almost always had someone else around to talk to; rarely were mothers or other adults left alone in the home with young children (cf. Young 1970, Ward 1971, Stack 1976). The children did not have to be used as conversational partners; others more knowledgeable and more competent as conversants were available. Children were not excluded from activities of adults or from listening to their conversations on any topic. Trackton parents, unlike teachers with their preschoolers, never mentioned the fact that something should not be talked about in the presence of children or that particular words were inappropriate. However, if children used taboo words, they were scolded (cf. Mitchell Kernan's comments in Slobin 1968:15). Young children would often sit on the laps of conversants, at their feet or between them on the sofa, listening. They were rarely addressed directly, however, in an effort to bring them into the conversation. Sometimes they were fondled, their faces and mouths touched, and food offered by community members as well as older siblings. In these cases, the person offering the food would address a comment such as "Hey, he really goes for these!" to someone else in the room. Questions directed by a teacher to her child in similar situations were: "Does that taste good, huh!" "You like that, don't you?"

When weather permitted, the children played on the porch of their home or in the yard within close range of the porch. When intimate associates were present, approximately 10 percent of the utterances conceivably directed to the nearby preschoolers were questions, 75 percent imperatives, 10 percent exclamations, and 5 percent statements (cf. Mitchell Kernan's comments in Slobin 1968:12)[4]. However, Trackton children were exposed to a wide variety of individuals other than their family and neighborhood associates. Friends and kin from other areas of the county came and went often, sometimes tem-

porarily taking up residence in Trackton. These frequent visitors to the community would tease the children, challenging them to particular feats or making statements of fact about the children.

> You ever gonna learn to ride 'at tractor?
> Can you lemme see you go, boy?
> Your momma better come change your pants.
> I betcha momma don't know you got dat.

Children were not expected to respond verbally, but to do what any command clearly addressed to them called for. Children were more talked "at" than "with."

A wide variety of strangers—utility servicemen, taxi drivers, bill collectors, and the like—came to the community. They usually acknowledged preschoolers, addressing questions such as "What's your name?" "Anybody home?" "Are you out here by yourself?" to the children. Most of the time these were met with no verbal responses. Occasionally when older preschoolers answered these questions, they would later be chastised by adults of the community. Children learned very early that it was not appropriate to report on the behavior of their intimates to strangers whose purposes in the community were not known. Likewise, outside the community, when nonintimates asked information about the children's family or living arrangements, they usually got no answer. Thus when school or community service personnel asked questions such as "How many people live in your house?" or "Doesn't James live on your street?"

the children would often not respond and would be judged uncooperative, "stupid," or "pathetic."

In Trackton, children did not hold high positions as information-givers or question-answerers, especially in response to questions for which adults already knew the answer. When children were asked questions, they were primarily of five types. Table 2 provides a description of the types of questions used with preschoolers in Trackton. The various uses noted here do not include all those evidenced in Trackton, but they constitute the major types used by adults to young children. Crucial to the flexibility in the uses of interrogative forms is their embeddedness in particular communication and interpersonal contexts. In the analysis of types, it should be evident that there is a distinction between what some of these interrogatives mean and what the

speaker means in uttering them. Another way of stating this is to say that the questioner using each of the types has a conception, perhaps unique to this particular communication context, of what the appropriate response by a preschooler to the question asked will be. In other cultures and in other contexts where different age and status relationships might prevail, these question types might not call for the response noted here as appropriate for preschool children. For example, in a classroom, a teacher asking questions similar to "What's that like?" very often has in mind as the answer a specific piece of information assumed to be known to both questioner and addressee.

TEACHER *(pointing to a small circle used on a map to depict a city of a certain size)* What does that remind you of?

TABLE 2 **Types of Questions Asked of Children in Trackton**

Types	Responses Called For	Examples
Analogy	Nonspecific comparison of one item, event, or person with another	What's that like? (referring to a flat tire on a neighbor's car) Doug's car, never fixed.
Story-starter	Question asking for explanation of events leading to first questioner's question	Question 1: Did you see Maggie's dog yesterday? Question 2: What happened to Maggie's dog?
Accusatory	Either nonverbal response and a lowered head or a story creative enough to take the questioner's attention away from the original infraction	What's that all over your face? Do you know 'bout that big mud-puddle . . .
A–I	Specific information known to addressee, but not to questioner	What do you want? Juice.
Q–I	Specific piece of information known to both questioner and addressee	What's your name, huh? Teeg.

EXPECTED RESPONSE   That set of circles in our book. *(the set of circles talked about in the social studies book in the section on reading maps)*

Teachers often "answer" questions to themselves as they ask them, and they expect answers from students to conform to those preconceived in the questioner's mind.

It is important to compare these questions with those which called for analogies from Trackton children. These were the closest thing to "training questions" Trackton adults had for young children. Children were not asked "What's that?" but "What's that like?" "Who's he acting like?" Requests that children name objects or list discrete features of objects or events, which appeared in teachers' talk to their preschoolers, were replaced in Trackton by questions asking for analogical comparisons. Adults seemed to assume children knew how to compare events, objects, and persons. Adults' use of these questions, as well as their frequent use of metaphors in conversations in the presence of children, seem to underscore their assumption that listeners understood similarities and differences.

You know, he's the one who's got a car like the one Doug useta have.
She's got eyes like a hawk.
You jump just like a toadfrog.
Sue sound like some cat got its tail caught in the screen door.

Young children noticed likenesses between objects, and even preverbal but mobile children would, on seeing a new object, often go and get another that was similar. Older children also gave great attention to details of objects; this attention was, however, not expressed as questions but as statements: "That thing on your belt look like that flower in your blouse." In parallel situations in teachers' homes, their preschoolers would say "Is that flower like that thing on your blouse?" At early ages, Trackton children recognized situations, scenes, personalities, and items which were similar. However, they never volunteered, nor were they asked by adults, to name the attributes which were similar and added up to one thing's being like another. A grandmother playing with her grandson age 2;4 asked him as he fingered crayons in a box: "Whatcha gonna do with those, huh?" "Ain't dat [color] like your pants?" She then volunteered to me: "We don't talk to our chil'un like you folks do; we don't ask 'em 'bout colors, names, 'n things."

What these speakers meant in asking questions calling for analogical comparisons was very different from what teachers meant in classrooms when they used the same interrogative forms. At home, Trackton children could provide nonspecific comparisons without explanation. Thus, in the classroom, they were likely to respond to questions of "What's that like?" with answers which seemed to teachers too broad or totally unrelated to the lesson at hand.

TEACHER *(pointing to a new sign to be used in arithmetic)*   What was it we said earlier this sign is like?
EXPECTED RESPONSE   The mouth of an alligator. *(an explanation used earlier in the day by the teacher)*
TRACKTON STUDENT'S RESPONSE   Dat thing up on da board. *(The student looks at a bulletin board for social studies*

which has yarn linking various cities; the yarn forms a shape like the sign)

Though the gross outlines of the sign's shape have been recognized by the student, he has made the comparison to a temporary and highly specific representation in the room. He has not envisioned the similarity between the open mouth of an alligator (presumably a permanent symbol in the minds of children familiar with this picture from books) and the mathematical symbol. The comparison is valid, but the teacher's response ("Huh? Uh . . . , I guess that's okay") indicated she considered the answer neither as useful nor as relevant as the one proposed in the lesson.

Another type of question used by Trackton residents was a *story-starter*. These questions were addressed to the oldest preschool children as well as to older children and adults. In situations which called for these, a person knew a story, but wanted an audience to ask for the story. However, there had to be some way of letting the audience know the story was there for the telling. A frequent technique was to ask what was ostensibly an A–I question: "Didja hear Miss Sally this morning?" The appropriate response to this question was "Uh-oh, what happened to Miss Sally?" If the respondent (especially an adult) heard the question as an A–I question and replied "No," the questioner would say, "Well, I ain't gonna tell you nut'n."

Accusatory questions were also used by Trackton residents. Similar in form to story-starters, they occurred more frequently than story-starters with children. In these questions, the adult or older child asked a question which was

known by all to be a statement of accusation; the addressee, if guilty, had only two appropriate responses. One of these was to bow the head, say nothing, and wait for the verbal diatribe which was sure to follow. The other was to create a story or word play which would so entertain the questioner that the infraction would be forgotten. In these responses, the child was allowed to shift roles, to step out of a submissive role, to exhibit behavior which for older children would be judged as "uppity." One mother exasperated with her son 3;9 years of age, said "Whadja do with that shoe? You wan me ta tie you up, put you on da railroad track?" The child responded:

> Railroad track
> Train all big 'n black
> On dat track, on dat track, on dat track.
> Ain't no way I can't get back.
> Back from dat track,
> Back from dat train,
> Big'n black, I be back.

All the listeners laughed uproariously at this response, and his mother forgot about the accusation. Older children could use these playful responses to other children or to certain low-status adults in the community, but they dared not do so with high-status adults, either kin or nonkin.

A–I questions were fairly straightforward, asking the child to express a preference or desire or to give a specific piece of information he was known to have which the questioner either could not or did not have. Q–I questions, so frequent in the homes of teachers, occurred rarely in Trackton. When they occurred, they usually did not have the purpose which dominated teachers' Q–I questions to their own children at home, i.e., requests for confirmation that the children had an objective piece of knowledge (the name of an object, its color, size, use, etc.). In Trackton, Q–I questions were used to confirm subjective knowledge held between the questioner and the addressee. For example, an adult or older child would accost a preschooler with "Whatcha name, huh?" The preschooler would be expected to give as an answer the nickname developed in relations between the questioner and the child, not his given name. In providing the appropriate nickname, the child confirmed the special relationship between him and the questioner.

The creativity of children in language use and their awareness of differences in language use were often displayed in situations where they engaged in self-talk. For example, Mandy, a child 4;1 years of age, was observed playing with a mirror and talking into the mirror. She seemed to run through a sequence of actors, exemplifying ways in which each used questions:

> How ya doin, Miss Sally?
> Ain't so good, how you?
> Got no 'plaints. Ben home?
>
> .   .   .
>
> What's *your* name, little girl?
> You a pretty little girl.
> You talk to me.
> Where's yo' momma?
> You give her this for me, okay?

When Mandy realized she had been overheard, she said, "I like to play talk. Sometimes I be me, sometimes somebody else." I asked who she was this time; she giggled and said, "You know Miss Sally, but dat other one Mr. Griffin talk." Mr. Griffin was the insurance salesman who came to the community each week to collect on insurance premiums. Mandy had learned that he used questions in ways different from members of her community, and she could imitate his questions. However, in imitation as in reality, she would not answer his questions or give any indication of reception of the messages Mr. Griffin hoped to leave with her.

In summary, children in Trackton were not viewed as information-givers in their interactions with adults, nor were they considered appropriate conversation partners, and thus they did not learn to act as such. They were not excluded from language participation; their linguistic environment was rich with a variety of styles, speakers, and topics. Language input was, however, not especially constructed for them; in particular, they were not engaged as conversationalists through special types of questions addressed to them. Occurrences of Q–I questions were very rare, and frequently involved a focus by an adult on speech etiquette when individuals outside the intimate circle of regulars were present. For example, preschoolers running through the room where a guest was preparing to leave might cause an adult to ask: "Didja say 'goodbye' to Miss Bessie?" Other question types addressed to preschoolers were also used by adults in conversation with other adults and were in no way especially formed for preschoolers. The intent and/or expected response to some of the question types, especially analogy, was sometimes special for preschoolers. (When analogy questions were addressed to adults, they were generally A–I, and the answerer was expected to provide information the questioner did not have, e.g., "What's his new car like?") In general, children were expected to learn to respond to questions which asked them to relate to the whole of incidents and composites of characteristics of persons, objects, and events. Preschoolers were judged as competent communicators if they learned when and how to use the various responses, both verbal and nonverbal, appropriate for the various question types.

Interrogatives in the Classroom

Questions teachers used in their homes with their own preschoolers were very similar to those they and their colleagues used in school with their students. Both of these were different from those used in Trackton. Therefore, children enculturated into competence in responding to adults' questions in Trackton had to acquire new uses in the school. The early nursery-school experiences of Lem, a Trackton 4-year-old, provide one example of the kind of shift which the acquisition of school questioning strategies required.

Before Lem began attending nursery school, he was a very talkative child by community standards. He was the baby of the family and, for several years, the youngest child in the community, and he was on every possible occasion challenged to respond verbally and nonverbally to others in the community. Lem was particularly fascinated by fire

trucks, and in the car he would keep up a chain of questions whenever we passed the fire station.

> Dere go a fire truck.
> Where dat fire truck go?
> What dat fire truck do?
> What dat dog do at da fire?
> Whose dog dat is?

As soon as answers were given to this series of questions, he began asking others about the sources of information which the participants had.

> How da firemen know where dey going?
> How come dat dog know to stay on dat truck?

At age 4;3, Lem began attending nursery school. It was his first experience in an institutional setting away from family and primary associates of the community. The nursery school was a cooperative run by middle-class parents and taught by a woman from a local church. During the first few weeks in school, Lem said almost nothing except when cookies and juice were passed out and he felt he was not getting a fair share. At other times, he watched and listened, showed strong preference for manipulative toys, and had little patience for talk-centered tasks directed by adults. At the end of the first 19 days of nursery school, in the car on the way home, he saw a fire truck. His sequence of questions ran as follows:

> What color dat truck?
> What dat truck?
> What color dat truck?
> What color dat coat?
> What color dat car?
> What color . . .

My response was: "What do you mean, 'What color is that truck'? You know what color that truck is. What's the matter with you?" Lem broke into laughter in the back seat, realizing his game had been discovered. During the first weeks of school, he had internalized the kinds of questions which occurred in teacher-talk centered tasks, and he was playing "teacher" with me. In the next few weeks, Lem's game in the car was to ask me the same kinds of questions he had been asked that day in school: "What color dat?" "Dat a square?" "What's dat?"

During those school activities which focused on giving labels to things and naming items and discussing their attributes, Lem did not participate. He listened and often tried to escape these structured sessions to play with trucks, puzzles, and so forth. He had no interest in looking at books and being asked questions about them, and he preferred to be involved in some kind of activity during story-reading time. He enjoyed activities taught to music, and when new activities were taught, he was the first to learn and always showed irritation with the repetitions required for other children to learn. In those learning tasks in which the teacher showed the children how to do things, rather than talked about the things themselves and what one did with them, Lem was enthusiastic and attentive. It is significant that in these tasks, teachers did not ask questions about the things or events themselves, but said instead: "Can you do that?" "Let's try it together. Remember the rope goes this way." (Compare Goody 1977, which discusses cognitive skills in the learning of manipulative tasks and the role of questions in this

learning among the Gonja of Africa.) Once Lem began going to school, he had acquired information and had had experiences of which Trackton adults had no knowledge, and many of their questions became information-seeking ones.

> Whadja do today?
> Didja go anywhere?
> Didja have juice?

Lem rarely answered these questions directly, but he volunteered other information he judged relevant.

> Mike got dirty pants.
> Joey go over de swing, and fall off de top. She cried, and her mamma had to come. Mrs. Mason tol us not to go on dat swing like dat anymore.

If questions were directed to Lem about this incident, he would answer; however, if other unrelated questions were continued, he would act as though he had not heard the questions. Adults did not pursue their questioning, and they soon turned their attention to other matters.

The types of questions Lem faced in nursery school were very similar to those used in the first grades of elementary school. At this level, teachers asked questions of children to become acquainted with their students and to assess their level of knowledge of the world.

> What's your name?
> Where do you live?
> Have you ever seen one of these?
> What color's this?
> Can you find the apple in the picture?

These are common and seemingly harmless approaches to acquaintance and judgments of ability. However, children from Trackton either did not respond or gave minimal answers. Increasingly after the first few days of school, when most of the questions were centered around teachers' getting to know their students, the questioning shifted to other topics. Colors, numbers, letters, and elements of pictures in books became the foci of questions. A predominant characteristic of these questions was their requirement that students pull the attributes of objects out of context and name them. The stimuli for such questions were often books or picture cards which represented the item in flat line drawings with no contextual background. Among these items, many of the characters (queens, elves, uniformed policemen) and objects (walnuts, sleds, and wands) were unknown in Trackton. Indeed, to Trackton children, their teachers asked foreign questions about foreign objects.

Research on teacher questions has delineated numerous features of their use in the classroom (for surveys of this literature, see Gall 1970 and Hargie 1978). In studies of classroom language the percentage of questions in comparison to other types of utterances is uniformly shown to be high. Moreover, there are special properties of classroom questions and their use in sequences of units of language arranged to produce interaction (cf. Mehan 1978). In extended interactions, questions consume nearly 60 percent of the classroom talk (Resnick 1972).

Questioning in the classrooms by teachers involved in the study reported here fit the general patterns revealed in research in other classrooms. Questions dominated classroom talk; the predominant type of question used in class-

room lessons called for feedback of information included in the lesson; questions which asked for analysis, synthesis, or evaluation of lesson data occurred much less frequently and were used predominantly with top-level reading groups. Of particular importance in this study is attention to types of question used in the classroom as compared with the homes of teachers and students.

In the research literature which attempts to classify question types, little attention is given to questions which do not have directly evident educational objectives, i.e., are not recall, analytic, synthetic, or evaluative questions (Bloom 1956, Gall 1970). In the classrooms of this study, questions which regulated behavior, especially with respect to classroom routines and attention to learning skills, emerged as particularly important (Heath 1978). Many questions asked by teachers were interrogative in form but were imperative or declarative in intent. "Why don't you hang your coat up, Tim?" was intended to be interpreted as "Hang your coat up, Tim." "What's going on here?" was intended to be interpreted as a declarative ("Someone is misbehaving") and a directive ("Stop misbehaving"). The question "Didja forget again?" was to be interpreted as "You forgot again." Teachers used questions with these meanings with their preschoolers at home and continued their use at school. Trackton students had relatively little experience with these indirect directives, viewed by teachers as the "polite way" of controlling the behavior of others. Of the types of questions used in Trackton, the accusatory were closest to these, and neither of the responses used in Trackton (bowing the head or offering a creative answer) was appropriate in the classroom. Trackton students generally ignored these questions and did not alter their behavior until given explicit directives ("Hang your coat up").

In lessons, teachers often asked questions which required confirmation of certain skills necessary to exhibit knowledge. Attention to appropriate stimuli—the person reading, a letter chart, or a specific page of a book—was tested by questions. Teachers used these in extended interactions with single students, small groups, and the entire class. If directed to a specific student, this question type demanded a response, either by display of the skill or by verbal confirmation. If directed to a group of students or the class, these questions were not to be answered, for they were merely forerunners to questions which would require answers.

> Can you point to the short *a?* How do we say it?
> Do you see the silent *e?* What does that make the vowel?

As might be expected, most of the questions used in lessons were Q–I questions, in which teachers asked for information which both they and often many students in class had. Trackton students were unfamiliar with questions which asked for labels ("What's the name of . . . ?") or called for an account of attributes ("How do we know that's a . . . ?") They usually did not respond or would parrot the answer given immediately preceding the question directed to them. Their communicative competence in responding to questions in their own community had

very little positive transfer value to these classrooms.

The learning of language uses in Trackton had not prepared children to cope with three major characteristics of the many questions used in classrooms. First, they had not learned how to respond to utterances which were interrogative in form, but directive in pragmatic function (e.g., "Why don't you use the one on the back shelf?" = "Get the one on the back shelf"). Second, Q–I questions which expected students to feed back information already known to the teacher were outside the general experience of Trackton students. Third, they had little or no experience with questions which asked for display of specific skills and content information acquired primarily from a familiarity with books and ways of talking about books (e.g., "Can you find Tim's name?" "Who will come help Tim find his way home?"). In short, school questions were unfamiliar in their frequency, purposes, and types, and in the domains of content knowledge and skills display they assumed on the part of students.

Intervention: A Two-Way Path

The task of schools is to transmit certain kinds of content and skills, but much of this transmission depends on classroom questions. For Trackton students to succeed academically, therefore, they had to learn to use questions according to the rules of classroom usage. However, intervention did not have to be one-way; teachers could also learn about the rules for community uses of questions. The choice in intervention was therefore not only to change Trackton students, but also to provide an opportunity for alterations in teachers' behaviors and knowledge.

Teachers were dissatisfied with the lack of involvement and the minimal progress of students from Trackton and similar communities. Teachers felt that questions were important to check on pupil learning and students' memory of skills and lessons, and to discover gaps in their knowledge. Yet questions were obviously not working to help teachers achieve these goals. Several agreed to look at the kinds of questions used in Trackton and to incorporate these, when appropriate, into classroom activities. They found that several types of questions used in Trackton could be considered what education textbooks called "probing questions" (cf. Rosenshine 1971). These were questions which followed questions, and questions designed to compare the knowledge questioner and addressee had about situations. Interrogatives modeled on some of the types used in Trackton were therefore justifiable in terms of good pedagogy. If used in classrooms, they would not only benefit students of low achievement; education research had shown these kinds of questions could benefit students across ability levels.

For some portions of the curriculum, teachers adapted some teaching materials and techniques in accordance with what they had learned about questions in Trackton. For example, in early units on social studies, which taught about "our community," teachers began to use photographs of sections of different local communities, public buildings of the town, and scenes from the nearby countryside. Teachers then asked not questions about the identification of specific objects or attributes of the objects in these photographs, but questions such as:

> What's happening here?
> Have you ever been here?
> Tell me what you did when you were there.
> What's this like? (pointing to a scene, or an item in a scene)

Responses of children were far different from those given in usual social studies lessons. Trackton children talked, actively and aggressively became involved in the lesson, and offered useful information about their past experiences. For specific lessons, responses of children were taped; after class, teachers then added to the tapes specific questions and statements identifying objects, attributes, and so on. Answers to these questions were provided by children adept at responding to these types of questions. Class members then used these tapes in learning centers. Trackton students were particularly drawn to these, presumably because they could hear themselves in responses similar in type to those used in their own community. In addition, they benefitted from hearing the kinds of questions and answers teachers used when talking about things. On the tapes, they heard appropriate classroom discourse strategies. Learning these strategies from tapes was less threatening than acquiring them in actual classroom activities, where the facility of other students with recall questions enabled them to dominate teacher-student interactions. Gradually, teachers asked specific Trackton students to work with them in preparing recall questions and answers to add to the tapes. Trackton students then began to hear *themselves* in successful classroom responses to questions such as "What is that?" "What kind of community helper works there?"

In addition to using the tapes, teachers openly discussed different types of questions with students, and the class talked about the kinds of answers called for by certain questions. For example, *who*, *when*, and *what* questions could often be answered orally by single words; other kinds of questions were often answered with many words which made up sentences and paragraphs when put in writing.[5]

Tapes and discussions of types of questions were supplemented by photographed scene sequences showing action in progress. *Why* questions were often the focus of these sequences, because both Trackton students and other students were especially tentative about answering these. Inferencing strategies in reading comprehension depended on the ability to answer *why* questions, making them particularly critical to reading success. The photographed scene sequences depicted a series of events, and students would arrange them in order and explain why they had chosen a particular order. For example, in picture A, a girl was riding a bicycle; in picture B, the bicycle was on the ground, the girl nearby frowning and inspecting her knee; in picture C, the only details different from those in A were a bandage on the knee and a broad smile on the girl's face.[6] Because workbook exercises in the primary

grades frequently called on the children to arrange pictures and later sentences in the proper sequence, children had to be taught to verbalize the characteristics of phenomena in and of themselves and in their relations with other things in the environment in order to complete workbook tasks. Teachers and students came to talk openly about school being a place where people "talked a lot about things being about themselves." Students caught onto the idea that this was a somewhat strange custom, but one which, if learned, led to success in school activities and, perhaps most important, did not threaten their ways of talking about things at home.

The primary rationale behind the research reported here was simple: if change agents (teachers and parents) were willing and involved, knowledge about language use could proceed along a two-way path, from the school to the community, and from the community to the school. Traditionally, education research has emphasized the need to train parents of children who are not successful in school achievement to conform to school practices. Knowledge had proceeded along a one-way path from school to "culturally different" communities. In this research the movement of ideas along that path was made two-way, so that a we-they dichotomy did not develop. In the past decade, research has identified standard English structures and patterns of discourse as "school talk" and non-standard English as "at-home" talk. Prescriptions derived from this dichotomy have found their way into parent education programs, encouraging early home initiation of children to "school talk" and school tasks and ways of thinking. There has been a decided we-they dichotomy, emphasizing how "we" of the school can enrich the background of the "they" of culturally different communities.

Moreover, remediation of language skills in classrooms traditionally followed the pattern of slowing down the process used for teaching "average" children, breaking the pieces of work into smaller and smaller units, presenting them repeatedly, and insisting upon mastery of the skills prescribed for each stage before moving on to the next stages. This breakdown of skills, stages, and units emphasized the use of recall questions, Q–I types for those of low achievement and analytic, evaluative, and synthetic questions with the academically successful. Elaboration and analysis of classroom language, habits leading to academic success, and ways of categorizing knowledge about things often led educators to believe these patterns of behaving had to be transferred to home settings of low-achievers before they could succeed in school. No one, either in teacher training programs or in the daily practice of education, seemed able to tap the uses of language and ways of "talking about things" of the culturally different and to bring these skills into the classroom.

To do so, at least two components were necessary: first, teachers as inquirers and second, credible data from both the classroom and the students' communities. For teachers to be involved in the inquiring process, they had to want to know what and how they and their students learned in language socialization, and they had to

take part in collecting the data to answer these questions. In carrying out research on their own families and in their own classrooms—voluntarily and in situations where their job performance was not being evaluated—they acted from their own felt needs. They learned that their own behavior exemplified patterns which were sometimes contrary to their ideals and principles, or, at the very least, unexpected. Taking part in data collection and analysis gave them opportunity to consider how and why data on everyday behavior—their own and that of others—can be useful in bringing about attitude and behavior changes.

Teacher-training activities, whether workshops, graduate courses, or inservice programs, often involve teachers in the inquiry process. Equally necessary, however, in order to bring about change in response to their felt needs, are ethnographic data from their students' communities. Ethnographic data on communities and institutions of the United States can be used in a wide variety of teacher training and curriculum preparation programs. However, such data are rarely available, and of those studies which do exist, many do not provide either the degree or kind of detail and focus on language and learning needed to inform decisions about formal education changes. It is hoped that as anthropologists increasingly turn their attention to the United States, its communities and institutional settings, the ethnographic data needed will become available in formats appropriate for consideration by educators.

Such ethnographic data from communities and schools shared across participants should insure the exchange of information and skills along a two-way path. Ethnographic data which contributed to changes in teaching materials and methods in the classrooms reported here were not collected with the purpose of proving the ways of one group right and another wrong. They were not used to evaluate the practices of teachers. They were not used to prove to school authorities that they should change the ways in which Trackton residents interacted with their children. Data collected by teachers in their own homes and in their classrooms, combined with data from Trackton, led them to ask questions of their own practices and to admit other practices into their interactions which would not necessarily have emerged otherwise. The long period of time over which these data were collected, the large number of people involved, and the openness of communication among groups insured that the ethnographic research was not pressuring change. Innovations and adaptations emerged in the educational process in accordance with felt needs of the teachers.

Notes

[1] The materials reported here on Trackton, teachers' homes, and classrooms are based on research conducted between 1970 and 1975 by myself and by my graduate students at Winthrop College. A full ethnography of communication study, containing data on Trackton and a Southern Appalachian-oriented community comparable in socioeconomic class, and schools attended by the young of both communities, is in preparation (Heath, forthcoming).

[2] The teachers whose children are cited in the study of questioning at home were all primary-level teachers; all either were teaching in local public schools at the time of the study or had taught in the academic year preceding the study.

[3] The questions and answers quoted from adults and children in this paper are represented in standard orthography rather than in phonetic transcription, since our focus is not on pronunciation. Some contractions and other indications of relaxed casual speech are used for the sake of realism, but they are not intended as exact portrayals of speech.

[4] Tape recordings were never made in Trackton; all field notes were written either on the scene or immediately after extended stays in the community. Percentages given here are averages based on analysis of field notes recording language use in play periods approximately two hours in length one day a week for eight months of each year, 1973 to 1975.

[5] The teachers whose classroom data are reported here include those involved in the study of questioning at home plus the teacher in the nursery school and three additional teachers at the upper primary grades who were familiar with the results of the home-questioning study.

[6] Based on reading materials prepared by Shirley B. Faile, Rock Hill, South Carolina.

References

Baratz, Joan, and Roger Shuy, eds. 1969. *Teaching Black Children to Read*. Washington, D.C.: Center for Applied Linguistics.

Blank, Marion, 1975. "Mastering the Intangible Through Language." In Doris Aaronson and Robert W. Rieber, eds., *Developmental Psycholinguistics and Communication Disorders*. New York: New York Academy of Sciences, 44–58.

Bloom, B. S., ed. 1956. *Taxonomy of Educational Objectives: Handbook I: Cognitive Domain*. New York: David McKay Co.

Blount, Ben G. 1977. "Ethnography and Caretaker-child Interaction." In Catherine E. Snow and Charles A. Ferguson, eds.,

Talking to Children: Language Input and Acquisition. London: Cambridge University Press, 297–308.

Brown, Roger. 1973. *A First Language: The Early Stages.* London: George Allen and Unwin.

Cook-Gumperz, Jenny. 1973. *Social Control and Socialization: A Study of Class Difference in the Language of Maternal Control.* London: Routledge & Kegan Paul.

Corsaro, William A. 1977. "The Clarification Request as a Feature of Adult Interactive Styles with Young Children." *Language and Society* 6:183–207.

Ervin-Tripp, Susan. 1970. "Discourse Agreement: How Children Answer Questions." In R. Hayes, ed., *Cognition and Language Learning.* New York: John Wiley and Sons, 79–107.

Ervin-Tripp, Susan, and Wick Miller. 1977. "Early Discourse: Some Questions about Questions." In Michael Lewis and Leonard A. Rosenblum, eds., *Interaction, Conversation, and the Development of Language.* New York: John Wiley and Sons, 9–25.

Gall, Meredith D. 1970. "The Use of Questions in Teaching." *Review of Educational Research* 40:707–720.

Gleason, J. Berko. 1973. "Code Switching in Children's Language." In T. E. More, ed., *Cognitive Development and the Acquisition of Language.* New York: Academic Press, 159–167.

Gleason, Jean B., and Sandra Weintraub. 1976. "The Acquisition of Routines in Child Language." *Language in Society* 5:129–136.

Goody, Esther. 1977. "Towards a Theory of Questions." In Esther N. Goody, ed., *Questions and Politeness: Strategies in Social Interaction.* London: Cambridge University Press, 17–43.

Hargie, Owen. 1978. "The Importance of Teacher Questions in the Classroom." *Educational Research* 20:99–102.

Harkness, Sara. 1977. "Aspects of Social Environment and First Language Acquisition in Rural Africa." In Catherine E. Snow and Charles A. Ferguson, eds., *Talking to Children: Language Input and Acquisition.* London: Cambridge University Press, 309–318.

Heath, Shirley Brice. 1978. *Teacher Talk: Language in the Classroom.* No. 9, Language in Education Series. Washington, D.C.: Center for Applied Linguistics.

———. *Ethnography of Communication: Communities and Classrooms.*

Holzman, M. 1972. "The Use of Interrogative Forms in the Verbal Interaction of Three Mothers and Their Children." *Journal of Psycholinguistic Research* 1:311–336.

———. 1974. "The Verbal Environment Provided by Mothers for Their Very Young Children." *Merrill-Palmer Quarterly* 20:31–42.

Hymes, Dell H. 1962. "The Ethnography of Speaking." In T. Gladwin and W. C. Sturtevant, eds., *Anthropology and Human Behavior*. Washington, D.C.: Anthropological Society of Washington, 13–53.

Kochman, Thomas, ed. 1972. *Rappin' and Stylin' Out*. Urbana: University of Illinois Press.

Labov, William. 1970. *The Study of Non-Standard English*. Champaign, Ill.: National Council of Teachers of English.

———. 1972. "The Logic of Nonstandard English." In *Language in the Inner City*. Philadelphia: University of Pennsylvania, 201–240. (First published 1969.)

Labov, William, et al. 1968. *A Study of the Non-Standard English of Negro and Puerto Rican Speakers in New York City*. Report on Cooperative Research Project 3288. New York: Columbia University.

Levelt, W. J. M. 1975. *What Became of LAD?* Peter de Ridder Publications in Cognition I. Lisse, Netherlands: Peter de Ridder Press.

Mehan, Hugh. 1978. "Structuring School Structure." *Harvard Educational Review* 48:32–65.

Mitchell Kernan, Claudia. 1971. *Language Behavior in a Black Urban Community*. Monograph No. 2 of the Language-Behavior Research Laboratory, Berkeley, CA.

Newport, Elissa, Henry Gleitman, and Lila R. Gleitman. 1977. "Mother, I'd Rather Do It Myself: Some Effects and Non-Effects of Maternal Speech Style." In Catherine E. Snow and Charles A. Ferguson, eds., *Talking to Children: Language Input and Acquisition*. London: Cambridge University Press, 109–150.

Ninio, Anat, and Jerome Bruner. 1978. "The Achievement and Antecedents of Labelling." *Journal of Child Language* 5:1–15.

Resnick, L. 1972. "Teacher Behavior in an Informal British Infant School." *School Review* 81:63–83.

Rosenshine, B. 1971. *Teaching Behaviors and Student Achievement*. Sloughi National Foundation for Education Research.

Sachs, Jacqueline, Robert Brown, and Raffaela Ann Solerno. 1976. "Adults' Speech to Children." In W. von Raffler Engel and Y. Lebrun, eds., *Baby Talk and Infant Speech*. The Netherlands: Sevets and Zeitlinger, 246–252.

Shatz, Marilyn, and Rochel Gelman. 1977. "Beyond Syntax: The Influence of Conversational Constraints on Speech Modifications." In Catherine E. Snow and Charles A. Ferguson, eds., *Talking to Children: Language Input and Acquisition*. London: Cambridge University Press, 189–198.

Slobin, Don J., 1968. "Questions of Language Development in Cross-Cultural Perspective." In *The Structure of Linguistic Input to Children*. Working Paper No. 14. Berkeley, CA: Language-Behavior Research Laboratory, 1–25.

Snow, Catherine E. 1977. "The Development of Conversation Between Mothers and Babies." *Journal of Child Language* 4:1–22.

Snow, C., A. Arlman-Rupp, Y. Hassing, J. Jobse, J. Joosten, and J. Vorster. 1976. "Mothers' Speech in Three Social Classes." *Journal of Psycholinguistic Research* 5:1–20.

Stack, Carol. 1976. *All Our Kin*. New York: Harper and Row.

Ward, Martha C. 1971 (reissued 1986). *Them Children: A Study in Language Learning*. Prospect Heights, IL: Waveland Press, Inc.

Wolfram, Walt. 1969. *A Sociolinguistic Description of Detroit Negro Speech*. Urban Language Series, No. 5. Washington, D.C.: Center for Applied Linguistics.

Young, Virginia Heyer. 1970. "Family and Childhood in a Southern Negro Community." *American Anthropologist* 72:269–288.

5

*Frederick Erickson and
Gerald Mohatt*

Cultural Organization of Participation Structures in Two Classrooms of Indian Students

Frederick Erickson   Gerald Mohatt

The Authors

Frederick Erickson is currently professor of education and medicine at Michigan State University and has taught at the University of Illinois, Chicago Circle, and at the Harvard Graduate School of Education. He was president of the Council on Anthropology and Education for the 1976 term. He says of himself:

"My involvement with the ethnography of schooling happened as something of an accident. After completing a master's degree in musicology (which involved some work in anthropology and ethnomusicology) I spent two years during the early 1960s doing youth work in Lawndale, a black neighborhood in Chicago. My involvement with schools from outside them, seeing the kinds of recurring intercultural and interracial misunderstandings that went on within them, prompted me to do doctoral work in anthropology and education rather than continue on in ethnomusicology or in academic anthropology. I enrolled in a doctoral program at Northwestern University; Edward T. Hall, Ethel Albert, and Paul Bohannon all happened to be there at the same time, all interested in the study of face-to-face interaction and all interested in the study of educational settings. Through the influence of Hall I came in contact with the film microanalysis of Birdwhistell and his followers. Through Albert, I was introduced to ethnosemantics and to the 'ethnography of communication' of Gumperz and Hymes. Bohannan advised me to read Simmel and a volume edited by George Spindler.

"Through all of this I became interested in the situation-specific analysis of people's use of sociocultural knowledge in the conduct of face-to-face interaction. I have tried to do this by combining participant observation with detailed analysis of audiovisual records of naturally occurring interaction in key scenes in people's lives — often scenes in which people from differing speech communities meet to do business that is important to them. I have called this approach microethnography, or focused ethnography, as distinct from general ethnography.

"Much of the work has involved studying schools as gate-keeping institutions which are intercultural meeting grounds. In addition to the research described in the article in this book, I have done studies of children at school and at home in an Italian-American neighborhood and of bilingual Mexican-American children in early-grade classrooms, some taught by Anglo teachers and some by Latino teachers. I also have studied job interviewers and junior college counselors conducting interviews with people of varying ethnic and racial backgrounds. A book on that work is forthcoming. Co-

133

authored with Jeffrey Shultz, it is titled *Talking to the Man: Social and Cultural Organization of Communication in School Counseling Interviews."*

Gerald Mohatt says of himself:

"I was raised in rural western Iowa, where I went to Catholic schools and graduated from high school in Vail, Iowa. I attended a Jesuit college and entered the Jesuits to study for the priesthood. I remained in the Jesuits for nine years. During this time I finished classical, asectical, and philosophical training and also an M.S. in psychology from St. Louis University.

"In 1968, I went to teach in the Jesuit Mission School on the Rosebud reservation (Sicangu Lakota) and taught and was school psychologist for 2½ years. Although I discontinued my Jesuit training, I remained on the reservation and worked in community mental health. In 1970, I and a number of Lakota people initiated an effort to form a college. We succeeded, and I served as president for 2½ years. After working to form the college, I went to Harvard to complete a doctorate in Learning Environments, specializing in Clinical and Community Psychology. I returned to the reservation in 1975 to work in the Sinte Gleska College's Human Services department in order to develop primary prevention and treatment services for local people.

"Throughout my work on the reservation I have been struck by the fact that educational endeavors have typically been ineffective. Research on education has often been either naive or irrelevant to the actual learning of Indian children. The variable of culture was often discussed as if it were a past or decayed phenomenon. I was greatly impressed by the power of culture seen in a sociolinguistic framework. The research related in this paper is an attempt to examine sociolinguistic factors in the teaching of native children in Ontario. I used videotapes, research reports, and articles from the project to teach native and nonnative teachers of native children in Ontario during the last four summers. The response has been excellent and has provided the necessary connection between research and practice.

"Currently I live on a ranch on the reservation with my wife and two children."

This Chapter

Frederick Erickson and Gerald Mohatt are interested in the similarities and differences in the cultural organization of social relationships in two classrooms of culturally similar children (Odawa and Ojibwa, Northern Ontario) taught by teachers whose cultural backgrounds differ. They are testing a hypothesis drawn from work by Susan Philips on the Warm Springs Reservation in Oregon: "In everyday life on the reservation, Philips noted an absence of participation structures in which one person overtly controls or attempts to control a great deal of activity of other people in the interacting group." They use direct observation, videotaping, and interviews as research techniques in a style that we have come to term "microethnography."

Unlike many ethnographic observers in classrooms, Erickson and Mohatt thus began with a hypothesis, in this case one drawn from previous work by someone else in another area. The proposition that they are attempting to generalize is one that has solid ethnographic support from a very wide area of native North America. A. Irving Hallowell, Victor Barnouw, Ernestine Friedl, G. and L. Spindler, and many other workers in the Northeastern culture area have noted that overt authority that would interfere with the autonomy of the individual is rarely or never exercised. Hallowell, in particular, has marshaled evidence to indicate that this is a long-standing psychocultural trait, probably extending even into the period before contact. Though this chronological hypothesis is contestable, the muted character of authority relationships in this area and others in North America is not.

This is a kind of contextualization that goes beyond attention to the larger framework of the community as such. In this instance a vast geographic-cultural area is the relevant context.

The evidence marshaled by Erickson and Mohatt is convincing. Interactional etiquette is clearly a factor both in everyday life and in the classroom, and does differ from one cultural context to another. The Indian and white teachers do appear to interact differently with the children in their classrooms in several relevant dimensions. This finding has implications for educational policy in considering the "cultural congruence" of teaching styles in relationship to children's cultures. At the same time the study has another implication — that indeed teachers can adapt, and under propitious circumstances do so. A style of interpersonal relationship that might be culturally incongruent can be modified appropriately. Policy, then, should be based not only on the concept of cultural congruence but also on the concept of modification of behavior through appropriate, culturally oriented training for teachers.

Introduction

When people experience what is called "culture shock" on going from one society to another, it is probably not the obvious differences which cause the greatest sense of personal disorganization. In other words, it is probably not the differences in physical landscape, climate, religion, dress, or even food which bring about the strongest sense of confusion. More often, it is in the assumptions underlying everyday life, shared by members of a society by virtue of constant interaction from birth, assumptions which are so much a part of the culture that they are not even consciously held. [Watson 1974: 29]

It is only within the last 25 years that anthropologists have begun systematic study of specific aspects of everyday social life that are culturally patterned in ways that are outside the conscious awareness of the people who act out the patterns. This patterning has been called "invisible culture," "implicit" rather than "explicit," a "silent language." Such research, initially inspired by the theory and methods of descriptive linguistics, has evolved rapidly, both criticizing and accommodating to theoretical shifts in linguistics and developing a theoretical stance of its own (see Watson 1974 for an excellent brief review of these issues, and also Hall 1959, Frake 1964, Goodenough 1971, Goffman 1967, Hymes 1974, Bauman and Sherzer 1975, and Gumperz 1968, 1976, 1977, and 1979b).

Until recently there has been little application of these perspectives to the study of teaching in classrooms. Some of the basic issues in such work were articulated by Hymes in an introduction to a collection of studies of social functions of language use in classrooms that was edited by Cazden, Hymes, and John (1972). More recent work in the field is reviewed in Erickson 1977. Others working along these lines include Griffin and Shuy 1978, McDermott, et al. 1978, and McDermott and Gospodinoff 1979, Mehan 1979, Gumperz and Cook-Gumperz 1979, Michaels and Cook-Gumperz 1979, Scollon 1979, Van Ness 1977, Bremme (see Bremme and Erickson 1977), Shultz and Florio (see Shultz, Florio, and Erickson, in press), and Darnell 1979—and this list is by no means exhaustive.

This paper reports data on implicit culture in the classroom. It begins with a section on theoretical rationale, which is followed by a brief discussion of research methods and procedures. That is followed by a section reporting classroom interaction data and a discussion of the implications of the data.

The site of the study is an Odawa Indian Reserve in Northern Ontario, Canada. It is a community of 2000 persons with two schools, a lower primary and an upper primary school. They are operated by the Ontario Department of Indian Affairs and Northern Development. All the students in the schools are Indian (with the exception of a few children of non-Indian teachers). In the lower primary school some of the teachers are non-Indian. Others are Indian, as is the principal, and the Indian staff are all members of the local reserve community.

The Odawa are an Algonkian people whose traditional culture was similar to that of the Ojibwa. Both the Odawa and the Ojibwa have lived in the region since at least as long ago as the time of their first contact with French Jesuit missionaries, who met them in the mid-seventeenth century. Some general features of traditional Odawa and Algonkian social structure and social etiquette will be discussed briefly later in the paper.

We were interested in the similarities and differences in the cultural organization of social relationships in these two classrooms of culturally similar children who were taught by teachers whose cultural backgrounds differed. We were interested especially in how the teachers exercised their authority over their students.

Our evidence comes from three sources: limited firsthand observation, videotaping in the two classrooms and in some of the children's homes, and interviews and collaborative research with school staff. Indian members of the school staff became involved in studying communicational etiquette in everyday life outside school through summer courses that involved field observation and reflection on their own experience as teachers and as members of the reserve community. Projects and final papers from these courses have become a valuable source of insights and data for us. Teaching teachers is a valuable kind of "fieldwork" in the anthropological study of education.

The research approach we used has been described elsewhere (Erickson 1976, Gumperz 1979a) as *microethnographic*. It differs in a number of respects from the more usual approach of *general ethnography*.

One major difference is in the scope of investigation. While general ethnography attempts to describe the whole way of life of a naturally bounded social group, microethnography focuses

on particular cultural scenes within key institutional settings. These settings and scenes are selected because of their salience to people in the community as occasions in which activities occur whose "outcomes" are crucial in shaping the character of individual and group life. This selection is made on the basis of participant observation in the community.

Another difference from general ethnography is in the analytic focus of investigation. While general ethnography reports overall narrative descriptions of events, microethnography attempts to specify the processes of face-to-face interaction in the events by which the "outcomes" of those events are produced (cf. Mehan 1978). Detailed analysis of audiovisual records of events is the means by which the interaction processes are studied intensively. The more usual fieldwork methods of participant observation, interviewing, and study of written public records in the setting and community provide broader contextual information which is also employed in the interpretive analysis of the audiovisual records.

Microethnography shares with general ethnography a concern for taking into account in analysis of everyday community life the perspectives of the community members whose actions constitute everyday life there (cf. Hymes 1977 and Erickson 1977). Detailed study of people's actions and of the concrete circumstances of those actions sheds light on the underlying principles according to which the actions are organized socially and culturally. It is assumed that what researchers call variously *points of view, values, attitudes, social structure,* or *culture pat-*

terns are revealed by people, explicitly and implicitly, in and through the specific actions they take in the conduct of everyday social life (cf. McDermott 1978, McDermott and Gospodinoff 1979). Careful analysis of the *how* of face-to-face interaction—the ways people accomplish their everyday doings—helps reveal the *what* of interaction—what they are about in their customary doings. General ethnography provides summary accounts of what people customarily do; microethnography investigates how the doings get done. Each approach needs the other. Microethnographic specificity becomes meaningless if it is cut off from the contextual scope provided by general ethnography. Broad-gauge general ethnography can be analytically shallow and underspecified without the careful attention to detail and nuance that microethnography provides as it focuses closely on actual instances of everyday happenings.

Research Focus and Rationale

As a result of participant observation and interviewing in the community and through reading related research, we paid attention to particular aspects of classroom interaction that seemed to vary cross-culturally:

   a. the overall tempo of teaching—how fast the teacher and the students interact, how quickly classroom "scenes" change from one activity to the next
   b. the overall directiveness of teaching—how much and what kinds

of "control" the teacher can appropriately exercise over student behavior in the classroom, how much "leeway" or "elbow room" is provided for students
   b-1. the teacher's pedagogical use of public scrutiny or "singling out," calling attention to individual children's behavior in front of an audience of other children, the "teacher searchlight" phenomenon—to what extent the teacher, by questioning, commanding, praising, smiling, looking pointedly, and other means of directing attention to a specific child, focuses on what the child is doing in the presence of an "audience" of other children; at issue here is not the positive or negative emotional content of the teacher's attention to an individual child (i.e., the function of such attention as "positive" or "negative" reinforcement) but the public, "audienced" nature of such attention

Psychologists studying schools have often assumed that differences among teachers in the pacing and directiveness of their teaching and differences among students in doing work on their own are caused by individual differences among teachers and among students in personality factors such as temperament, intelligence, motivation, and developmental level. It seems reasonable to assume that individual differences do influence the social behavior of teachers and students in classroom learning environments. Anthropologists assume *group differences* also influence social behavior in classrooms and in learning environments such as families in the wider community outside school. It is assumed that these group differences are cultural in origin and are due in part to conventionally shared definitions and expectations of what is appropriate in the conduct of everyday social interaction—definitions that are partially learned at an early age and held and acted on outside conscious awareness by both children and adults.

Relevant here is Goodenough's definition of culture in cognitive, ideational terms as "a system of standards for perceiving, believing, evaluating, and acting." This definition is distinctive in that it encompasses both patterns for one's own social action and patterns for interpreting the meaning of the social actions of others. That is, it asserts that what one has to know in order to act appropriately as a member of a given group includes not only knowing what to do oneself, but how to anticipate and judge the actions of others (cf. Goodenough 1971: 41ff).

Operating from this theoretical orientation, the anthropologist Philips (1972, 1975) investigated the cultural organization of social relationships in classrooms and homes on the Warm Springs Indian reservation in central Oregon. Philips identified a number of features of *cultural incongruity* or cultural conflict between non-Indian adults on the one hand and Warm Springs Indian adults and children on the other. Differences exist in the expectations the two groups have for how social interaction should take place.

Through careful firsthand observation, Philips identified models for the organization of persons' reciprocal rights and obligations in social interaction— models of the most common *participation structures* at home and at school (Philips 1972). These models of interactional etiquette account for what all parties to an interactional occasion are doing, e.g., not only for how the teacher or parent talks to children but how children listen as the adult talks, how people get a turn to speak or allocate turns at speaking to others, how people hold the floor once they have a turn at speaking, how people ask questions in appropriate ways and provide relevant answers in appropriate ways.

In the contrasting learning environments of the Indian community and the school Philips found different kinds of participation structures that were customarily appropriate and expected. A major difference between the participation structures most commonly found in the Indian home and those most commonly found in the school classroom involved the role of the adult (or other leader, such as an older brother or sister) in the interaction. At school the leader (the non-Indian teacher) attempted to control all activity, communicative and otherwise. In terms of the social organization of children's appropriate talk in school, the teacher functioned as a "switchboard operator," to whom much talk was addressed and by whom all allocations of legitimate turns at speaking were granted. In such a participation structure, the Indian students performed much more situationally inappropriate behavior inside the classroom (silence, failure to answer questions, nervous giggling) than did white students in the classroom. The school was a public rural school attended by non-Indian and Indian children and staffed almost entirely by non-Indians. The teacher's way of organizing interaction in the classroom seemed culturally congruent with the white students' expectations for how things should happen, but culturally incongruent with the expectations of Indian students.

Evidence for attributing the Indian children's confusion and inappropriate behavior to cultural incongruity rather than to personality characteristics of individual Indian children came from Philips' observation of the Indian children's everyday life outside school. In everyday life on the reservation, Philips noted an absence of participation structures in which one person overtly controls or attempts to control a great deal of the activity of other people in the interacting group. It was not that such participation occurred less frequently on the Indian reservation than in the non-Indian farming communities around it, but that such participation structures simply *did not occur* in everyday life on the reservation. From this Philips concludes, "The notion of a single individual being structurally set apart from all others, in anything other than an observer role, and yet still a part of the group organization, is one that Indian children probably encounter for the first time in school" (Philips 1972: 391).

If the findings and interpretations reported by Philips and others generalize beyond the Warm Springs community in Oregon to other North American Indian communities and the schools they attend, this could explain the often reported phenomenon of the "silent In-

dian child" in the classroom—the child reacting to the cultural inappropriateness of non-Indian teachers' questioning and directing strategies by "dropping out" from interaction with the teacher (cf. Dumont 1972). Other factors besides cross-cultural differences in communication style are no doubt also involved, but Philips' research provides at least a partial explanation for the generally low school achievement and high drop-out rates among Indian school students that are apparent in both Canada and the United States.

Research Procedures

In attempting to determine if Philips' findings could be generalized to another reservation setting in a different geographic region and different Indian culture area, we worked in a Northern Ontario reserve and videotaped two teachers. One was an experienced Indian first-grade teacher who was a member of the local reserve community and who had taught in a one-room school for 14 years and in a self-contained primary classroom for about seven years. The other was non-Indian and was an experienced teacher who had just come to the school and was teaching Indian children for the first time.

In planning this work we took care to find two competent teachers to observe and compare. According to their colleagues both teachers were experienced and skilled. They were effective as judged by outcome measures. This point cannot be overemphasized: in comparing the teachers we do not mean to do so invidiously or even "evaluatively," as that term is commonly used in educational practice. Readers should keep in mind that the differences between the teachers that we report and interpret are not differences in their good intent or in their technical ability as professionals. The differences consist in the relative "cultural congruence" of the two teaching styles with the children's experience of social life outside school.

Both first-grade teachers were videotaped across one school year—in the early fall, in the late fall, in the winter, and in the late spring. The videotaping was done by a member of the reservation community. He knew the community culture intimately as a member of it, and knew the individual children and their families, and the teachers. He was trained in our methods of videotaping. Usually taping began as the class entered the room and ended as they left the room for some reason. The teacher in Classroom I (Indian) was videotaped for 11 hours across nine different days. The teacher in Classroom II (non-Indian) was taped for 13 hours across ten different days.

Videotaping was done continuously for the duration of each hour-long tape cassette. There was a minimum of "camera editing" by the camera operator ("zooming" in and out and "panning" around the room). This was to provide a record which was as comprehensive and undistorted as possible of the naturally occurring flow of interaction across sizeable "chunks" of the school day. In 16 of the tapes, sound was recorded by a microphone suspended from the ceiling, and in six of the tapes a wireless lavaliere microphone was worn by the teacher and by a few students.

A few of the tapes in the whole *corpus* were of spotty technical quality.

The data reported here came from repeated viewing of 18 tapes: ten hours from Classroom I, and eight hours from Classroom II.

Synoptic analytic charts were made for each tape. The chart served as an index for the tape, indicating the occurrence and duration of major social occasions and activities and their constituent subactivities or episodes.[1] Since taping had been done continuously, the tape indexes gave us an overview of the naturally occurring succession of social occasions across the classroom day. Since taping was done on a number of days, the indexes identified multiple instances of the same sort of recurring occasion. We focused on mornings, from the time children entered before school began to the time they left the room for some reason. We were interested in determining the overall shape of a typical morning and the relative amounts of time spent on typical activities in the two rooms. We were also interested in going beyond general statements of typical patterns (whether those summary accounts were in the form of narratives or of statistical tables), to describe the particular features of organization employed by the teachers and students as they conducted instances of the various social occasions which typically occurred. It was at this level of analysis that specific cultural differences would or would not be most clearly revealed in the participation structures the two teachers employed in doing what ostensibly might seem to be the "same" events.

It is worthwhile to describe briefly the logic of choice-making by which we proceeded through summary analysis of large amounts of material to the selection of representative instances for fine-grained analysis. The instances we were looking for were not examples of a bounded "speech event" or "interactional event"—those segments of the continuous flow of interaction for which members of a cultural group have discrete labeling terms, such as *speech, prayer, argument, tea ceremony, contract negotiation session,* or, in the case of the classroom, *story time, show and tell time,* or *lesson.* This sort of unit of analysis has been used profitably in the "ethnography of communication" tradition in anthropological linguistics (cf. the review in Bauman and Sherzer 1975) and in classroom microethnography by McDermott (1978, 1979) and Mehan (1978, 1979), who studied the organization of interaction in small-group reading lessons and in whole-group lessons, respectively. But folk-labeled event units such as the lesson were not appropriate for our investigation, because our purpose was to determine whether particular kinds of social relationships—patterns of participation structure—were pervasively present across many sorts of events in classroom life. We were especially interested in the kinds of leadership employed by the teachers, and the kinds of student followership which were congruent with the teachers' ways of leading.

Consequently, we searched our limited field notes and our extensive videotape indexes, looking for recurring "times" or occasions of classroom life in which a teacher's *ways of leading* were saliently displayed. The most striking examples proved to be the openings and closings of interactional activity. These occurred at the beginnings and endings of events with discrete folk names, such as *lessons* and

seatwork time. Openings and closings also occurred at times of transition between sequences of activity which were of longer duration than named events, e.g., the transition time beginning the school day, which occurs between the sequence *before school* and the sequence *after school has started.* (Such sequences and transitions are so obvious to people engaged in them daily that these sequences are usually not given discrete names.) Opening and closing activity also occurs at the transitions between episodes or phases within a named event, e.g., the transition between one topically related set of questions and the next in a whole group lesson (cf. Mehan 1979) or between one child's turn at reading and the next child's turn in a reading lesson (cf. McDermott 1978, 1979).

We viewed tapes with the teachers in open-ended "viewing sessions" to get a general sense of their perspectives on teaching, and of what was important to them about classroom management, especially at times of transitions between and within events and occasions. Then as we examined the tape indexes and reviewed the tapes themselves, taking into account what the teachers had said in viewing sessions, we found that the beginnings of school days and the times of getting organized to leave the room appeared to be useful occasions on which to focus. We identified all instances of these occasions in the *corpus* of tapes and took various kinds of closer looks at them. Data from those analyses are presented in the next section of the paper. A few instances were selected for especially fine-grained analysis.

The criteria used in selecting instances for detailed study were: *tape quality*—there was continuous tape with good sound across the whole duration of the occasion, and *typicality*—the instance selected contained all the constituent subsections most usually found in the other instances of that occasion contained in the whole *corpus* of tapes. Typicality is defined in such a way as to insure that the instance selected is one in which the teacher and student faced a normally recurring set of organizational problems or issues in coordinating leadership and followership in reciprocal and complementary ways. We were not interested in the "typicality" of particular discrete behaviors found in the instance—in ways of speaking or ways of gesturing *per se*. Rather, we were interested in the "typicality" of the social ecology of face-to-face interaction found in the instance—the typicality of ways in which, through their actions, the children and the teacher presented each other with environmental constraints within the social occasion in which they were engaged, in the sense McDermott means when he says, "people in interaction are environments for each other" (McDermott 1976).

Data Analysis: Major Findings

When one first looks at and listens to the tapes of the two classrooms they seem intuitively different. Some of these differences are global. They are apparent in the relative amounts of time spent by the teachers and children in main classroom activities, such as be-

ginning the school day, recitation, small group instruction, individual seatwork and instruction, and leaving the room to go to recess. More subtle are such things as the overall pacing in each of these classroom scenes and in the sequencing between scenes. In this section we will first report the most global data on the two classrooms and then proceed to more fine-grained data.

Overall Indicators of Teaching Style and Participation Structure

When one summarizes the amounts of time spent in main activities in the two classrooms, some similarities as well as differences are immediately apparent (see Table 1). Both teachers spend the largest amounts of time circulating among the students and giving individual attention (Activity 6), with relatively little time spent at the blackboard in teacher-focused instruction (Activity 4). For this the percentages of time spent are almost the same.[2]

Some differences between the classrooms are also significant. Looking at the percentages for Activity 12, "class leaving," it is apparent that a considerably greater proportion of time is spent on this in Classroom II, taught by the non-Indian teacher, than in Classroom I, taught by the Indian teacher. In Classroom I the teacher spends time waiting for students to finish their work (Activity 10), and this does not occur in Classroom II. More small group work (Activity 8) occurs in Classroom I than in Classroom II. In Classroom II there are two instances of free time for play (Activity 11); in Classroom I there are none.

TABLE 1. **Relative Amounts of Time Spent in Major Classroom Social Situations**

Activity	Classroom I			Classroom II		
	Minutes	*Percentage*	*Number of instances*	*Minutes*	*Percentage*	*Number of instances*
1. Entering and settling	43.7	7.3	(7)	28.7	5.9	(7)
2. Prayer	1.7	.2	(2)	0	0	(0)
3. Finding the day's date	1.3	.2	(2)	0	0	(0)
4. Teacher at blackboard, class reading aloud	10.4	1.7	(2)	8.9	1.9	(2)
5. Teacher passing out paper	5.3	.8	(2)	1.2	.3	(2)
6. Teacher circulating, giving individual attention	225.0	37.5	(11)	177.5	36.9	(6)
7. Teacher sitting, giving individual attention	58.7	9.7	(4)	50.3	10.0	(1)
8. Small-group work	66.6	10.1	(3)	15.8	3.3	(1)
9. Teacher waiting for class	36.2	6.0	(4)	0	0	(0)
10. Finishing work	15.1	2.5	(1)	15.5	3.2	(3)
11. Free time playing in class	0	0	(0)	26.3	5.5	(2)
12. Class leaving	18.7	3.1	(7)	39.1	8.1	(7)
13. Other	212.3	29.9		116.7	33.9	
Total	600.0	100.0		480.0	100.0	
	(N of tapes: 10 hrs.)			(N of tapes: 8 hrs.)		

When these relatively small differences are considered in the light of Philips' model and in the context of other data we will present, the following interpretations of the significance of those differences seem justified.

In terms of Philips' model, the differences between the two classrooms for Activity 11, "free time," are especially significant. *Free time,* as distinct from *work time,* presupposes a discrete boundary between two loci of social control: activity "belonging" to the students, and activity "belonging" to the teacher. This is the case for Classroom II, taught by the non-Indian teacher, which can be characterized overall as a place where one thing is supposed to be happening at a time. It is the teacher's time, then the students'—work time or free time, time for everybody to pay attention (or for an individual to pay attention immediately) or for nobody to pay attention. The teacher exercises social control overtly to make clear whose time it is now. When the time "belongs" to the teacher, the teacher "monitors" the attention of the children: "John, pay attention," or (looking at a particular child) "Sit still."

In Classroom I, taught by the Indian teacher, the distinction between two separate loci of social control is not made so sharply or monitored so overtly. Social control is distributed in Classroom I as a *shared quantity*—leadership by teacher and by students interpenetrates rather than being divided into separate compartments. The teacher clearly has "control" of the students, but achieves this partly by paying much attention to the rhythms of student activity and judging when the students are ready for things to change. This is our interpretation of the frequencies for Activity 9 (Teacher waiting) and Activity 1 (Entering and settling). The teacher in Classroom I is accommodating to the children's rates of beginning, doing, and finishing work at the same time as they accommodate to her. Over the year the teacher in Classroom II also began to accommodate more to student time and share it, e.g., Activity 7 typically increased during the second part of the year. Interestingly, though, while things start much more slowly in Classroom I (Entering and settling—Activity 1), they end more quickly than in Classroom II during the process of getting organized to leave and leaving the room (Activity 12). (We will return to this point after presenting the next table.)

Watching the tapes of Classroom I, one has the impression of slowness and smoothness as classroom events unfold. The sense of pacing—of doing the right things at the right time—has been noted by Smith and Geoffrey (1968) and by Kounin (1970) as a key feature of successful teaching performance. We will argue that a shared sense of pacing between teacher and students (part of their mutually congruent interactional competence—their shared *culture* as it is defined by Goodenough) is manifested behaviorally in an interactional smoothness whose presence or absence is empirically observable. This observable smoothness in getting through an event and in getting from one event to the next can be taken as an indicator of shared expectations and interpretive

strategies on the part of the participants in the interactional scene (cf. Erickson 1976; Bennet, Erickson, and Gumperz 1976; Gumperz 1979; and Shultz, Florio, and Erickson in press).

The overall impression of slowness and interactional smoothness in Classroom I is borne out when one considers more closely the *durations of activities* summarized in Table 1. This can be done by dividing the total time alloted for various activities by the number of instances each activity occurs, showing the average length of each episode for a given activity (see Table 2).

In Table 2 it is clear that things happen somewhat more slowly in Classroom I than in Classroom II. Entering the classroom at the beginning of the day (and coming back into the room after leaving it during the day) occurs at a slower rate (see Activity 1). Teacher I passes out paper twice as slowly as Teacher II. Students were given 15 minutes to finish work in Classroom I, and an average of 5 minutes in Classroom II (see Activity 10).

At first glance one might infer that Teacher I just moves more slowly than Teacher II, because of her age, temperament, or sex. Consideration of further evidence shows clearly this is not the case. Despite the more gradual pace of starting up activities in Classroom I, children there spend just as much time engaging academic subject matter as those in Classroom II—perhaps more. Also, in Classroom I it takes the children and the teacher much less time to get organized to leave the room than it does in Classroom II (an average of 2.7 minutes, contrasted with 5.6 minutes).

There are also differences in the time the teachers spend in giving individual

TABLE 2. **Mean Episode Duration for Selected Classroom Activities**

	Classroom I			Classroom II		
	Mean duration (minutes)	*Number of instances*	*Total minutes*	*Mean duration (minutes)*	*Number of instances*	*Total minutes*
1. Entering and settling	6.2	(7)	43.7	4.1	(7)	28.7
5. Teacher passing out paper	2.7	(2)	5.3	.6	(2)	1.2
6. Teacher circulating, giving individual attention	20.5	(11)	225.0	28.8	(6)	177.5
7. Teacher sitting, giving individual attention	14.7	(4)	58.7	50.3	(1)	50.3
9. Teacher waiting for class	9.1	(4)	36.2	0	0	0
10. Students finishing work	15.1	(1)	15.1	5.2	(3)	15.5
12. Leaving	2.7	(7)	18.7	5.6	(7)	39.1

attention to students, either by circulating around the room (Activity 6) or by sitting at a desk with the student (Activity 7). The durations for giving attention are shorter for Teacher I than for Teacher II because, for Teacher I, giving attention to individual students is interspersed with other activities of formal instruction and classroom management, e.g., passing out paper and working with children in small groups. Teacher I handles issues of classroom logistics and works individually with students while she circulates around the room. She does this often in response to the silent request of a student, who will look up from seatwork to ask nonverbally for help from the teacher. Teacher II gives individual attention in larger chunks to each student, stays in one place longer while working with students individually, and then moves more rapidly around the room. During the latter he will do classroom social management and logistical work. He will then return to working with one student at a time.

In the next section we will consider differences in the ways the teachers exercise social control in moving around the room. This is one area which did remain constant over the year.

A Closer Look at Classroom Processes

The characteristic slowness and smoothness with which social occasions are enacted in Classroom I and the faster pace and relatively irregular quality of interaction in Classroom II are apparent not only in the general tables for the overall timing of classroom activity but in the way each teacher starts and concludes particular classroom activities. We examined a number of instances of the beginnings of activities, looking for indicators of overall smoothness and pacing. Two of these activities are described below: beginning a lesson, and leaving a room.

Setting Up a Lesson: Teacher Movement Our first example comes from an analysis of one instance for each teacher of getting a small group organized for a reading lesson, while the rest of the class begins seatwork. What we focused on in this analysis was the movement of the teacher around the room in the course of setting up the lesson. Figures 1 and 2 show the pathways of movements for the two teachers. Table 3, which appears just after the second chart, presents the total number of times each teacher moved around the room ("passages"), the number of places or stations arrived at ("destinations"), and the mean times of all passages and all destinations for the teacher.

What the floor diagrams and Table 3 show is that although it actually takes Teacher I less time to get the lesson started than Teacher II, it appears as if Teacher I is teaching more slowly as well as more smoothly. This is because of the interaction of four factors: (1) Teacher I moves across a much smaller area of the classroom than Teacher II (see Figures 1 and 2); (2) Teacher I makes only half as many moves from table to table as does Teacher II (5 *passages* as compared to 11; see Table 3); (3) the total time (31 seconds) spent by Teacher I in passage moves within a smaller area is less than half that spent by Teacher II (66.0 seconds) within a larger area; (4) Teacher I has just over

half as many *destinations* as Teacher II (6 to 11) and stays on the average almost twice as long at each *destination* (24.7 seconds to 13.1 seconds).

From watching the tapes one could characterize Teacher I's movement pattern as slow and smooth and that of Teacher II as more disjunct, a "stop-and-go" pattern. Work by Ruiz (1971) and by Florio (1977) suggests that the way a teacher moves around the room is one of the methods by which social control is exercised and an ongoing flow of classroom events is maintained.

Relationships Between Teacher Movement and Giving Directives Another means of exerting social control is through speech. A *directive* is a use of speech not so much to communicate referential content as to get other persons to do what the speaker wants them to do. (The term *directive* is used by students of classroom interaction whose work is informed by *speech act theory* in sociolinguistics and ordinary language philosophy; see Sinclair and Coulthard 1974, Olson and Hildyard in press, and Griffin and Shuy 1978.)

A *teacher directive* can be defined as any utterance or nonverbal act by the teacher whose function is to get a student to change his/her behavior in compliance with the teacher's wishes. In speech, the directive function can be realized by a variety of linguistic forms: (1) the imperative declarative statement, such as "Sam, sit down"; (2) a "wh-question," such as "Why don't you sit down?"; (3) an indirect declarative sentence, such as "It's time for people to stop running around" or "Now we're going to get started." As one can see

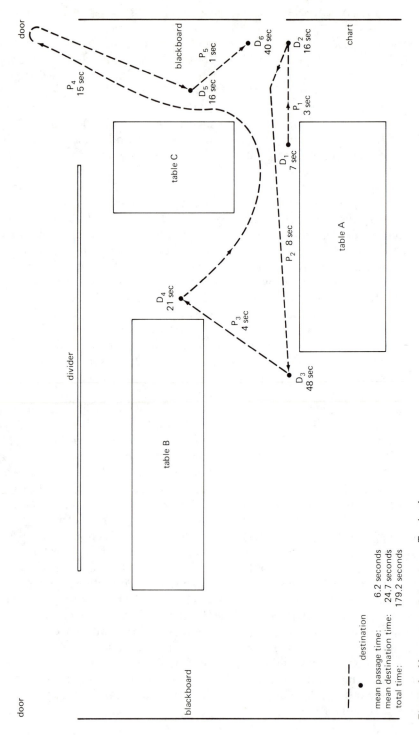

Figure 1 Movement pattern: set up—Teacher I.

door

blackboard

chart

table A

table C

table B

divider

blackboard

door

D_2 16 sec
P_1 3 sec
D_1 7 sec
P_2 8 sec
D_6 40 sec
P_5 1 sec
D_5 16 sec
P_4 15 sec
D_4 21 sec
P_3 4 sec
D_3 48 sec

destination

mean passage time: 6.2 seconds
mean destination time: 24.7 seconds
total time: 179.2 seconds

148

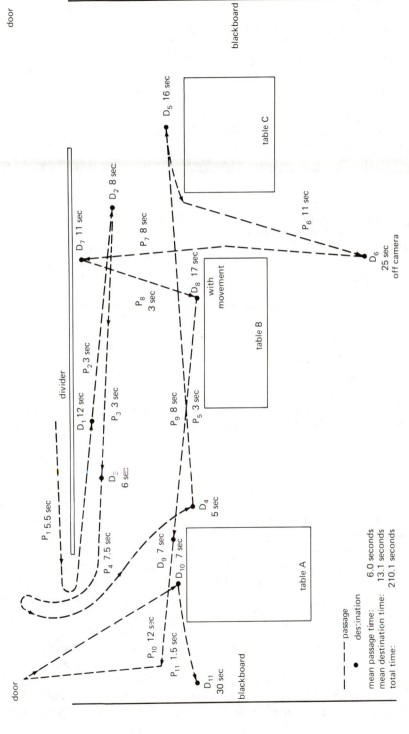

Figure 2 Movement pattern: setup—Teacher II.

door

blackboard

D_5 16 sec

table C

D_2 8 sec

P_6 11 sec

divider

D_7 11 sec

P_7 8 sec

P_1 5.5 sec

P_2 3 sec

D_1 12 sec

P_8 3 sec

D_8 17 sec

P_3 3 sec

with movement

table B

D_6 25 sec off camera

D_3 6 sec

P_9 8 sec

P_5 3 sec

P_4 7.5 sec

D_4 5 sec

D_9 7 sec

D_{10} 7 sec

table A

door

P_{10} 12 sec

P_{11} 1.5 sec

D_{11} 30 sec

blackboard

— — — passage
● destination

mean passage time: 6.0 seconds
mean destination time: 13.1 seconds
total time: 210.1 seconds

149

TABLE 3. **Teacher Movement During Lesson Setup**

	Teacher I	Teacher II
Number of passages	5.0	11.0
Mean passage time (seconds)	6.2	6.0
Number of destinations	6.0	11.0
Mean destination time (seconds)	24.7	13.1
Total passage time (seconds)	31.0	66.0
Total destination time (seconds)	148.2	144.1
Total passage-destination time	179.2	210.1

from the previous examples, directives can be issued to named individuals, putting the spotlight of public attention on them in front of an audience of other children, or directives can be accomplished in a more masked, indirect way that does not single out individual children for public scrutiny. Part of the "spotlight effect" of issuing a directive comes from using the name of the individual child to whom the directive is addressed. Another part of the spotlight effect can come from an aspect of what Hall (1966) terms a *proxemic relationship:* interpersonal distance that carries social meaning. If the teacher calls out a directive to a single individual from all the way across the room, the spotlight effect is heightened, giving the directive the force of a command rather than a suggestion about what behavior is appropriate at the moment. Calling out across the room, no matter how indirect the linguistic structure of the utterance, usually carries the social meaning of an imperative and rebuke mixed together.

Thus the frequency of directives and their spatial placement as the teacher moves around the room, "casting" them like a fisherman, provide an index of the teacher's social control. This shows not only how overtly the control is being exercised but how large the span of control is—whether the teacher is trying to control the behavior of many of the children at once, the class as an aggregate, or separate individuals. That is, teachers can differ in the frequency of overt exercise of control, and also in the generality or specificity of targeting the recipients of directive moves.

Accordingly we looked through the videotapes to see how teacher movement, proxemic relationship to students, and the issuance of directives were related in each classroom.

Considering the movement pattern of Teacher I (see Figure 1), we see that she begins to set up the reading lesson by giving directions to Table A while at D_2. She then moves to D_3 and asks Alice, Mark, and Henry, who are seated at D_3 (Table A), to come to reading. Her next destination is D_4 (Table B), where she asks Grace and others at the table to come with their readers. After directing the children to the reading table she closes the door and goes to D_5 (in front of Table C), where she stands with her hands on her hips, waiting for the children to assemble for reading (16 seconds). When they are ready she moves to the blackboard to begin the lesson with "OK, this list."

Teacher I's movement and directives are highly intercorrelated. She does not call across the room to named individuals. She generally is in face-to-face contact with the child or children she is addressing. She follows a clear path to the reading table.

Teacher II, on the other hand, moves in and out around the tables and creates a pattern that appears to be less symmetric. His movements and directives are not as highly intercorrelated. He calls across the room to named individuals. He begins by asking the children with the new readers to come to the table at which he is pointing. He has not established the same intimate contact with the children in the reading group either by using their names or by being in closer proximity to them, both of which Teacher I did. (Later in the year, when he has established more intimate contact, we see greater economy in his organization. Students seem by then to have a better grasp of the contexts and his expectations for them.) From off camera he calls to Joe and Frank to get their readers and "come over here." But "here" is the reading table across the room from where he is standing. Later he again talks across the room to tell the class in general to be quiet, then finally tries quieting Julia, who is off camera.

Most of Teacher II's commands are quite direct and often repeated, and addressed to named individuals. For example, before he beings to work with the small reading group he talks to the class as a whole, speaking over their voices: "Remember, no noise while I am talk ... reading here," "Shhh," "Julia, work to do."

The economy of Teacher I's way of giving directions is illustrated by her three words and one gesture which indicate to the children in the reading group to begin oral reading of the work list on the blackboard: "OK, this list." For Teacher II the analogous situation is longer. He repeats "Look up here" twice and frames the task with a rationale: "In order to read the first story there are some new words you have to know. Here they are up here." He then repeats "Look up here" again and elaborates "There are the boys' names up here."

Both teachers have completed the setup when they are standing at the blackboard going over a word list. Accomplishing the setup has involved seven destination points for Teacher II and six for Teacher I.

Summary

The strategies for accomplishing the very ordinary classroom management work, "getting a small group started," were quite different for the two teachers. Teacher I's strategies involved proceeding fairly slowly and deliberately, exerting control over the whole class at once, not singling out individuals in the total classroom group, yet singling out and calling by name those children in the more intimate, more "private" reading group. Teacher II moved more rapidly and moved around the whole room, gave directions to the total classroom group and the small reading group at the same time, and kept control of the public arena of the whole classroom scene, calling out directions to individual children across the room and over the other children's heads.

Leaving the Room: Teacher Movement and Directives Winding up a classroom event is another of the points at which it is appropriate to study how a teacher accomplishes social control. During a school day leaving the room is perhaps the most complete process of finishing things. In our tapes of the two teachers across the school year, there are a number of instances of the teachers' organizing the class to leave the room—to go to recess, to the washroom, to lunch, to the library, or home. This happens seven times in our tapes of Teacher I and seven times in our tapes of Teacher II. Most instances did not involve the children's putting on clothes for going outside.

In the general overview of amounts of time spent in different classroom activities (Tables 1 and 2) it was apparent that leaving the room took longer in Classroom II than in Classroom I— twice as long, on the average. Those tables account for all 14 instances of leaving for both classrooms in our *corpus* of tapes. Nine of these instances were examined in greater detail: four instances in Classroom I and five instances in Classroom II. These nine were chosen on the basis of the quality of picture and sound on the videotape.

As it happens, these technically "best" tapes do not include the two slowest instances of leaving in Classroom II, and so the mean duration for this subsample of instances of leaving the room is almost the same for each classroom (see Table 4). While leaving still takes slightly longer in Classroom II, the most striking differences between the rooms are apparent in how leaving is socially organized and interactionally accomplished.

Table 4 shows that it takes both teachers about the same amount of time to get the class to leave the room. However, the pattern of interaction by which leaving is accomplished and authority is exercised (as indicated by the frequency and timing of the teachers' issuing of directives) is quite different in each classroom. Teacher II uses three times as many directives as Teacher I, and issues them at a rate more than twice as fast as Teacher I (13 per minute as contrasted with 5 per minute). The linguistic form of the di-

TABLE 4.   **Duration of Leaving the Room and Pacing of Directives**

	Classroom I	Classroom II
	4 instances	*5 instances*
Total time (in minutes) for all instances of leaving the room	7.5	10.7
Mean time (in minutes) for leaving the room	1.9	2.2
Total teacher directives while leaving the room	37.0	126.0
Pacing of directives (number per minute)	5.0	13.0

rectives and the way they are addressed—to individuals on the one hand and to the total group on the other—also show marked variation between the two teachers' modes of social control (see Table 5).

From Table 5 it is apparent that Teacher II uses directives more frequently than Teacher I. He also differs from Teacher I in his use of directives to a particular child, both in total frequency as compared with Teacher I (who uses 10 directives to individual children, while Teacher II uses 39) and in the proportion of directives addressed to individuals and to the general class (10:8 for Teacher I, 39:24 for Teacher II). Thus in Classroom II individual children are singled out for attention in classroom management instructions far more frequently than in Classroom I. Moreover, Teacher II uses the direct linguistic form of issuing a command, the imperative form, proportionally more than the less direct linguistic form, the syntactic question. Teacher I also uses more imperative forms than question forms, but the difference is not nearly so great proportionally (for Teacher I, 7 imperatives to 4 questions; for Teacher II, 36 imperatives to 3 questions).

Finally, we can turn to the relationship between the teacher's location in the classroom and the giving of procedural instructions as the children are leaving the room. Teacher I goes to few *destinations* and makes fewer *passages* between destinations in leading the children out of the room. She also issues more directives at the first two destinations, but then she issues as many directives in the subsequent passages as in the destinations. Throughout the exit period Teacher II gives directives. After the first two destinations, Teacher I issues almost no directives (see Table 6). Relatively more time is spent by Teacher II at the last destinations and passages in the process of leaving than is spent by Teacher I (see Table 7).

Examples of Classroom Discourse

To illustrate even more specifically some of the differences in the cultural organization of social relationships in

TABLE 5.   **Form and Address of Directives While Leaving the Room**

Linguistic form of directives	Classroom I			Classroom II		
	Directives to individual auditor	Directives to general audience	Row totals	Directives to individual auditor	Directives to general audience	Row totals
Question	1	3	(4)	3	0	(3)
Imperative	6	1	(7)	21	15	(36)
Nonimperative statement	3	4	(7)	15	9	(24)
Column totals	(10)	(8)		(39)	(24)	

TABLE 6.   **Directives and the Location of the Teacher While Leaving the Room**

	D_1	P_1	D_2	P_2	D_3	P_3	D_4
Teacher I	5	1	6	1	2	0	0
Teacher II	13	1	18	4	4	7	1

(D = Destination, P = Passage)

TABLE 7.   **Timing of Destinations and Passages While Leaving the Room**

	D_1	P_1	D_2	P_2	D_3	P_3
Teacher I	51	32	170	39	22	0
Teacher II	138	40	92	53	198	55

(Time in seconds)

the two classrooms, two texts are presented. They come from two beginnings of the school day: one from Classroom I, the other from Classroom II. A few notes are necessary to explain the notation conventions employed.

Usually each line of text represents a "tone group" in speech. These groups are divided by a half pause, indicated by a single diagonal stroke (/), analogous to a comma, or by a full sentence-terminal pause, analogous to a period, which is indicated by a double diagonal stroke (//). Stress (increased loudness) is indicated in two ways: (1) if the stressed syllable does not contain a pitch shift, stress is indicated by a vertical stroke just above or below the line of text, depending upon whether the pitch is relatively high or low, e.g., ʹgood, or ₗgood; (2) if stress is accompanied by a rising or falling pitch shift, this is indicated by a diagonal stroke preceding the stressed syllable. Four different pitch contours can be shown: good (low rising), good (high rising),

good (low falling), and good (high falling).

Pauses, stress, and pitch are indicated in such detail in the text examples because in English these features of prosody in speech are means by which a regular rhythmic cadence is maintained as people interact face to face. Nonverbal behavior occurs in synchrony with the rhythmic cadence of speech (cf. Byers 1972). It appears that this rhythmic organization of talk and body motion is a means by which people coordinate their activity in discourse and signal to one another strategically important *next moments* in their interaction (Bennet, Erickson, and Gumperz 1976, and Shultz, Florio, and Erickson, in press).

Usually the stress marks and pauses occur evenly spaced in time. One of the places the rhythmic cadence is most apparent is in question-answer sequences. Read the following example aloud, keeping a metronomically even spacing between each of the stressed syllables and reading each "pause" aloud as well:

(pause)	on our	ˈcalendar	*(pause)*
ˌwhat's the next		ˈnumber?	*(pause)*
ˋTen!		*(pause)*	ˋRight
(pause)		ˈMarch	ˌtenth
ˈnineteen		ˌseventy	ˌsix
(pause)	in your	ˌprinting	*(pause)*
ˌthis word		*(pause)*	ˈHockey!

This is an artificially regularized example, but it serves to illustrate the cadence-like organization of the exchange of speaking turns in discourse. The control of turn-exchange is one of the essential aspects of classroom management for teachers. By displaying the rhythmic organization of turn exchange a text sheds light on the teachers' ways of exercising social control in engaging children with curriculum.

Portions of the following text examples should be read aloud, especially those in which the stress marks show the cadential rhythm clearly and those in which hesitation and arhythmically overlapping speech indicate that speakers have altered the rhythmically regular flow of discourse, coming in "too late" or "too soon." Overlapping speech is indicated in the text by a vertical

stroke with two "flags" going in the same direction ([). Speech or nonverbal action which begins immediately after the prior action ended is indicated by a vertical or horizontal stroke with two "flags" going in opposite directions: (⌐) or (⌐). Elongation of a vowel is indicated by successive double dots (te::n).

Classroom I   The first example, from Classroom I, begins before the official opening of the school day. From points 1 to 14 in the text the teacher issues directives in a soft "off the record" voice to children close to her as she walks around the room. Then at point 15 the school day begins. The teacher's voice is slightly louder, and she speaks "on the record" to the whole class. This continues until point 52. After that, talk by the teacher becomes "off the record" again. Notice the relationships between what the teacher and children say and their relative positions in space as the teacher moves around the room. All the comments addressed by the teacher are "off the record"; they are "privatized" by the teacher's near proximity to the child addressed and by the low volume.

CLASSROOM I

Scene: Children are at their tables. It is just before school begins. The teacher stands at the long room-dividing counter, taking attendance (see floor plan in Figure 1).

(1)		(T starts to walk toward children.)
(2)	T: Take this to the office	(said quietly to one child T was standing next to)
(3)		(T turns and walks toward door.)
(4)	T: Okay?	(to child just entering room)
(5)		(As T walks back from near door to front rightmost table a girl takes upside-down chair off table and sets it on floor.)
(6)	T: ˈPut the chair down now// before ˈsomebody gets hurt	(As she says this quietly, T puts down chair that she refers to.)

(7)

(Girl on other side of table puts down her own chair.)

(8) A: Teacher/ we're gonna watch ourselves in the 'TV at lunch time 'ain't we?

(Child next to where T stands addresses T in quiet voice.)

      T: ⌊Maybe//

You people don't 'wanna watch yourselves 'sometimes

("because what you would see would be yourselves not acting right")

(9)

(T walks away from table.)

(10)

(B, seated, holds up money in right hand.)

(11)

(T walks back to table, reaches out for money, which had been left on table overnight.)

      T: (sigh)// Who's ‚sitting here/ ‚Roland?//

(Child B hands T money.)

(12) B: Yup

(13) T: Must be ‚his/   I'll ‚give it to him

(14)   //   //

(T turns and walks toward center of front of classroom.)

(15) T: Okay we'll stand up / Let's say our ‚prayers now

(T arrives at destination and stops. She speaks louder than before.)

(16) T: / In the name of the ‚Father/   and of the ‚Son/   and of the ‚Holy/ ‚Spirit A-‚men//

(All recite prayer together; the children have stood, facing forward, with hands folded in prayer position, by the time T begins to speak.)

Hail Mary full of grace/the Lord is with thee/ Blessed art thou amongst women/   and blessed is the fruit of Thy womb Jesus/ ‚Holy Mary ‚Mother of God/ ‚pray for us sinners ‚now and at the ‚hour of our ‚death/ A-‚men /   In the name of the ‚Father/   and of the ‚Son/   and of the ‚Holy/ 'Spirit   A-‚men//

(17)   //   // (step)   (step)   (step) (step)

(T walks from center of front of room to side front by the windows. As she does this, the children all sit.)

(18) T: (sigh)
     //   On our
     'calendar/
     /   what's the next
     ₗnumber//

(T has reached calendar easel—her destination—and now stands stationary.)

(19) C: Te::ːn
     G:⌊ten/

(Whole class (C) answers, in appropriate rhythmic "slot" for answer, and a few children repeat answer a moment later.)

(20) T: Ten/
(21) D: Ten/   (One child repeats answer.)
(22) T: And
     ₗthis is/
(23) C: Ma::rch
     G: March//
(24) T: ₗMarch ₗtenth/ soˌmebody's
(25)   E: ₗnineteen-

(One child initiates "next" answer in the formulaic series, "Naming today's date," and then whole class repeats the answer.)

(26) C: ₗNineteen-
(27) T: ₗSomebody's got these all
     ₗmixed/

(There are interchangeable number and letter cards on calendar board and the numbers 1976 are out of order.)

(28) F: 'Wednesday

(As T adjusts misplaced letters a child initiates "next" answer to question not yet asked.)

(29) T: To-
     ₗday is/
(30) C: ₗWednesday//   (whole class)
(31)   F:⌊ₗWednesday/   (Child F)
(32) TC: ₗWednesday   (T and whole class)
(33)   (T turns and starts to walk across front of room in front of blackboard.)

     T: ₗHow many in the grade   (Walking continues.)
     ₗones/are ₗputting the date in their
     books?
     //   //

(Children do not answer. T has stopped walking. She touches board, pointing to place where date is written on it.)

     I notice some books you for-
     ₗget to put it and I
     ₗput down/
     ₗMarch//

(34) C: Te::n   (chorus of voices)
     ⌊ten⌋   (individual speakers)
        ⌊ten//
(35) T: //   And this is/
     ₗnineteen ₗseventy ₗsix//

(Some children recite in unison with T.)

'Now we don't have this on the
,calendar but we 'put it in our
,books/   This is the year/
'nineteen 'seventy ,six

(36) T: /   In your
          printing/   ,this word

          /   you re-
          ,member what this is from
          ,yesterday?

          /   You made a
          'picture of 'people 'playing?
(37)   //

(38) T: ,What's that first ,letter?//

(39) T: "H"/   / 'n
(40) T: ,here?   //

(41)   //   //

(42) T: ,Anybody remember the
          ,picture they made?
(43)   //
(44) C: / ,Hock-ey
          //
(45) T: ,Ri::ght   //
(46) C: Hockey
(47) T: This is //
(48) C: HOCK|EY
          T: H|ockey/   /   the

          ,one with a ,big letter and the
          ,one with the ,small letter//
          ,hockey//

          (step 1)   (step 2)
(49) T: //   //
(50) F: When we made this
          (lean over table)
          T: //   //
          F: this/   //
          (step 3)   (step 4)
          T: //   //
          F: yesterday eh?//

(Only a few children recite in unison with T.)

(In brief pause before "in your" T steps back once, moving to location on board of yesterday's *printing word*.)

(In brief pause before "you re-" T takes one more step back, simultaneously pointing to *printing word* on the board, "hockey.")

(No response from children in brief pause before "you made a.")

(No response in this pause, which is twice as long as previous one.)

(T points to first of two *printing words;* the one with a capital H.)

(voiceless aspirate as cue to letter sound)

(Points to second "hockey" with small letter "h.")

(T places hands on hips, turns from orientation toward board to full frontal orientation toward class.)

(not very loudly)

(slightly louder)
(louder)
(slightly louder than normal volume)
(loudly)
(slightly louder than normal speaking volume)

(Volume drops to normal level for addressing whole class.)

(T takes two steps forward and picks up stack of workbooks from small table in front of board. As she does this a child begins to speak "off record" to her.)

(Having picked up books, T turns and walks to table of children nearest her. It

```
        (step 5)    (step 6)
    T: //          //
        (lift bk,    (drop bk,
        step 7)      step 8)
(51) T: //          //
        (drop bk,   (step 10)
        step 9)
    T: Charles      //
```

(T lifts and drops first book in stack on table in front of student to whom it belongs.)
(Having given Charles his book—he sits next to the child who was given the first book   T moves next to Roland, who came into classroom late.)

```
        (drop bk)    (stand still)
(52) T: Roland did you have a dollar?
        (step 11)   (drop bk)
(53) T: //          No?
                    (drop bk,
        (step 12)   step 13)
    T: Somebody else's then

        (drop bk)
        (drop bk)   (drop bk)   (drop bk)
    T: //          //          /Did
        (drop bk)   (stand still)
(54) T: anybody bring some money to
        school today?
        (stand still)
    T: //
(55) H: No

(56) G: No
(57) T: (step 14)   (step 15)
        //          //
```

was a child at that table who addressed her.)

(T has come to some books of children who are absent. She stands still and drops them in a pile on table. She does not resume walking until children have answered her next question.)

(T looks up and around, and speaks louder.)

(An individual child answers. This is followed by chorus answer from small group of children.)
(T walks off to back of room to set up small reading group and assign individual seatwork to a few children. All the children who had received workbooks so far had begun to work in them within four or five seconds after book was dropped in front of them.)

Discussion   Notice that the directives issued by the teacher to the children at points 2 and 6 during the initial "off the record" phase are imperatives, but are "privatized" by the close proximity and low voice volume of the teacher. This avoids putting the recipient of the directive in the spotlight of public attention. After the "on the record" phase begins at point 15, the teacher addresses no comment to an individual child. All the questions about academic content, as in points 18, 29, 36, 38, 40, and 42, are questions appropriate for "choral" answers from the whole classroom group. The teacher persists in asking questions only of the total group even after the group has trouble answering at point 36. At no time does the teacher employ the "fallback strategy" of calling on an individual child who is likely to know the correct answer. After point 49, when an "off the record" phase begins again, however, the teacher addresses comments to individual children, and one child (point 50) addresses a comment to the teacher.

The teacher also avoids explicit evaluation of the correctness of student answers, in the classic "lesson discourse" sequence characteristic of culturally mainstream teachers in Canada and the United States. That sequence, *teacher question-student response-teacher evaluation*, has been described as ubiquitous among North American teachers by Bellack et al. (1966) and by Mehan (1979). The teacher in Classroom I, however, usually does not correct wrong responses explicitly, nor does she praise right responses explicitly. A right response is communicated implicitly, by going on to the next question in the elicitation routine, e.g., points 18 to 24, during which the teacher first asks what day of the month it is and then asks for the name of the month. The only exception to this occurs at point 45, where, after the children have had unusual difficulty in producing the correct answer, the teacher says "Ri::ght" after the class finally produces the answer, "Hockey!"

Rhythm is present as an implicit organizing device permitting coordination of activity among teacher and students. This is especially apparent in the question-answer sequences. See, for example, points 18 to 32, in which the elicitation routine is culminated by the metronomically rhythmic repetition of the answer "Wednesday" by the teacher and students together. (Note that this repetition of the student answer by the teacher is another implicit way of telling the students their answer was correct.) The social coordination function of nonverbal and verbal rhythmic cadencing is also apparent at points 50 to 52. In that instance, the student addressing the teacher adjusts the pacing of his speech to the rhythm of the teacher's steps. The teacher intersperses her speech to children with rhythmically regular steps and droppings of the workbooks in front of the various children. (On another tape the teacher passes out pieces of drawing paper one by one to children at exact five-second intervals over one and a half minutes.)

The overall tempo of the cadence established by the teacher is relatively slow. There is also much silence in the room. The teacher does not call out to students, nor do they call out across the room to her or each other. The teacher initiates some of the major transitions between activities silently, by beginning to walk in a new direction. Note this at points 14, 17, and 49. Silence also occurs when the students are having trouble producing the right answer to the question about the "printing word." At point 40 the students are given three full pauses (about three seconds) in which to answer. This contrasts with the culturally mainstream North American teacher's pattern of providing, on the average, one-half second as the usual response time for students. The combination of slow tempo, points of silence, and highly regular rhythm all contribute to giving one an overall impression of deliberateness and calm in the classroom.

The teacher initiates each next stage in a sequence of activities without waiting for all the children to be ready to comply. At point 16 as the prayer begins not all the children have stood up yet, but the teacher goes ahead with only a half pause before saying the first words of the prayer. Similarly at point 17 the teacher takes the first step toward the calendar stand without waiting for the class to "get ready for calendar time." At point 36 the teacher asks the "printing word" question immediately after the calendar episode has been brought to a close. At point 49 the teacher moves directly into the next sequence, passing out the workbooks, and "off the record" time has begun again.

Not only does the teacher initiate activity without waiting for the students, but the students do so without waiting for the teacher. Interaction is organized throughout so that the teacher and the children can initiate and follow without either holding up the other. Notice that as the books were passed out children opened them and began to work in them without having to be ordered explicitly to do so. Notice, too, that at points 25 and 28, children answer the next questions in the elicitation routine—"This is: 1976" and "Today is:

Wednesday"—before the teacher asks the questions. The teacher does not reprimand the children for taking such initiative. There is no such principle operating as "The next moment in the rhythmic cadence is the moment in which you children must comply with my directives as the teacher."

Classroom II The second example, from Classroom II, begins as did the first, before the official opening of the school day. The official opening comes at point 4 in this text. Immediately after that (point 6) the teacher makes one "off the record" comment to a child. All other comments made to children are "on the record." They are made public by the (usually) far distance of the teacher from the child addressed, and by the relative loudness of the teacher's voice. As with the first teacher, the *academic content* of talk between teacher and pupils is closely related to the teacher's positioning in space from moment to moment. In contrast to that of the first teacher, however, the *social content* of talk by the teacher changes very little as his distance from the child addressed changes. He does not make the nonverbally defined distinction between "on the record" and "off the record" talk to the children which the teacher in Classroom I is so careful to maintain.

CLASSROOM II

(T stands near middle of front of room, checking off on an attendance list the names of those present and absent, saying the children's names softly to himself as he comes to them on the list. As he does this, the children call out to one another from one set of tables to the next, where most of them are seated, writing in workbooks. Each set of tables has about six children seated around it.)

(1) T: Cynthia// //
Marie // //

(2) //

(T hands attendance sheet to Child A to take to the office. The child is seated near front and center of the room, where the T has been standing.)

(3)

(T walks rapidly over to side counter, pauses a moment and then picks up piece of chalk.)

(4) T: Okay guys/
let's look at the ⌈words//

(loudly)

(5) B: ⌊I'm an
Indian girl⌋

(Girl sitting at front table, right side of room addresses T.)

(6) T: ⌈You sure are⌋

(said approvingly, touching girl on head)

(7) G: ⌈Pa:t// ⌈Ma:t//

(8) T:⌊Put the books away
G: 'Sa:t//

(One table group begins to recite the left-most column of words on the black-board, reciting in an even rhythm.)

(9) T: ⌊Nelson//

(to one boy, "Put your book away.")

(10) G: PAT/ SAT/ MAT/
(11) T: ⌊SH::/ wait for me now/
(12) G: 'PA⌊T// 'SA:T//
(13) T: ⌊Louis put the pencil down//
(14) 'Nelson// //
(15) Gabriel/ ⌈put that away
(16) Nelson/ ⌊put that away
⌊PAT (one child)

(More children recite, louder and faster. T raises finger to lips as he says, "SH::")
(Only one table group speaks, but does so loudly. T paces back and forth, call-ing out directives.)

(As the T leaves the left front blackboard area, Child B gets up and goes to board.)

(17) B: I know ⌈what this one is//

(Apparently spoken to Child B's table group. Child B points to third column of words.)

(18) T: ⌊put it away
B: 'be:d// ⌊'fe:d// //no/

(addressed to Nelson)

(19) T:⌊put it away/ we'll make the
Christmas decorations after//
(20) G: 'BE:D// 'FE:D// 'TE:D//
(21) B: be:d// bed// 'fed// 'ted// //
(22) T: ⌈Natalie// // // //
C: ⌊bed

(T is walking to front left corner of room—destination is leftmost column of words on board. Here each // indicates one step by T.)

(23) //

(On this step T reaches destination and turns to face class.)

(24) T: 'Okay/ I'm 'sure everybody 'knows these 'easy 'words?//

(25) C: 'PA::T// 'SA::T// /MAT//

                SG: 'ba::t//

(T points to each word on board in series, in rhythm which controls timing of class responses. All children respond in unison.)

(Children at John's table begin to call out wrong word—T is now pointing to "mat"—and rest of class says correct answer a split second later.)

(26) T: John/ what is that?
(27) C: MAT//
(28) T: ‚M:at/ like 'M:ommy o-kay?/
         'Bobby's table ‚stand
         //   //
         'Bobby's table O-kay?/

(A girl who has entered takes her chair down from her table.)

(29) G: 'Pa:t// 'm/
                   ⌊m⌈a:t// 'sa:t/
              D: ⌊mat
(30)   T:⌈Very
         'good // 'a::h //   ⌊
(31) 'Louis' table put 'that away
      Louis
      // // // //

(Bobby's table group responds.)
(A smaller subset of the table responds after the whole group hesitates, and one child comes in later and louder than all the rest. T in pointing to the words has altered the order of their presentation from that in which they appeared in the column. This may account for the hesitations over the second word of the three.)

(32)   // / O-kay watch 'here then
          let's get 'tricky// // //

(T points to second word of series, the word "pat," after the pause.)
(individual child at Louis' table)
(Louis' table group)

(33) E: 'Ma:/⌉
           G:⌊'ma:[:t
(34)   T: ⌊No::/⌉
(35)   E:⌈Pa⌊t
               G: ⌊Pa:[:t
                     Pa:t//
      'Ma:t // `Sa:t/⌉
(36)   T:⌊o-
      'kay //

(In the pause after "Pat" T points to the word "Mat," and in the pause after "Mat" T points to the word "Sat.")
(In the pause after "kay" T takes one step forward to a position where he can point to words in the next column to the right of the one to which he was previously pointing. From this new position at the board he will ask a new series of questions to another table group.)

Discussion Perhaps the most striking thing about the second example is the frequency with which the teacher issues directives across relatively long distances, e.g., points 9, 13, 14, and 22. This occurs as part of the teacher's overall strategy of framing major transitions between and within classroom activities by gathering up the actions of all the children to a single focal point, after which the new activity will begin. The teacher attempts this at point 4, the activity of the whole group is finally focused at point 23, the activity of the first table group to be called on is focused at point 28, and the activity of the second table is focused by the teacher at points 31 and 32. The teacher exercises overt control according to some such principle as "When everyone is *ready* (focused by my directives), we can begin."

Attempts to operate according to such a principle are repeatedly interfered with by the children's tendency to initiate action at points in time they themselves choose. After the teacher's first focusing move at point 4, children in various parts of the room begin to read aloud the columns of words. They have done this for two of the columns by the time the teacher gets the activity of the total group focused at point 23. Before point 23, however, according to the teacher's agenda the children's reading aloud was "off the record." It only becomes "on the record" after the teacher directs that at point 24. In the context of the teacher's ways of organizing, the children's initiations are "too soon." Notice the teacher's comment at point 11, "SH::/wait for me now."

In the social ecology of Classroom I, because the teacher goes ahead from one transition to the next without waiting for children to catch up or stopping them from anticipating what will happen next, the same kinds of initiating moves that children in Classroom II make do not interfere. Those moves do interfere in Classroom II because the second teacher's classroom management strategies produce a different social ecology from that of Classroom I.

While the teacher in Classroom II frequently calls out "management" directives to named individual children in the whole group lesson—something the teacher in Classroom I never does—he avoids asking academic content questions of individual children by directing the questions to the whole class and to individually named table groups. The strategy of calling on the named table group lies partway between the Classroom I teacher's way of teaching, and that of culturally "mainstream" teaching, in which named individuals are frequently called on to answer academic content questions. The importance of this point will be discussed further in the concluding section of this chapter.

In Classroom II as in Classroom I, the teacher's positioning in space and orientation to objects and people in space is a fundamental organizing device for focusing the curricular attention of students from moment to moment. And, as in Classroom I, there is in Classroom II a distinct rhythmic patterning to verbal and nonverbal behavior across successive "next moments." This seems to enable the activity of all to be coordinated.

Since the tempo of the cadence established by the second teacher is faster than that established by the first teacher, sensitive coordination of activity is essential if the lesson is not to fall apart. Notice the extremely regular rhythmic organization of the question-answer pair at points 24 to 25, in which the first answer appears exactly one full pause-length after the end of the teacher's question. Notice also that the small group's "wrong" answer, "ba::t/" begins exactly in the "right" time for an answer, and the whole class's correcting response, "MAT//" occurs a split second late. Just after that, the teacher's evaluative confirmation of the informational correctness of the class's response at point 27 is underscored rhythmically as the teacher repeats the answer and then adds another "m-word" at the next rhythmic interval: "ₗM:at/ like ₗM:ommy," elongating the /m/ sound, as well as stressing it by added loudness. All this "reinforcement" occurs for the right answer which had been given at point 27, even though the answerers (whole class) were not the one designated (John). That they were the wrong people is overlooked; they gave the right answer in the right time. Notice the temporal fine tuning in the rhythmic intercalation between teacher question, student answer, and evaluative teacher response, and subsequent answer correction at points 33, 34, and 35.

The tempo of interaction is faster than that in Classroom I. There is not much silence in the room—the teacher calls out to children, and they do so to him and to each other. Clearly, students in Classroom II have become adept at this kind of rapid alternation of turns at speaking. But the very trickiness of timing involved, together with the teacher's tendency to evaluate student responses and single out individuals as responders, produces social control patterns fundamentally different from those in Classroom I. Both teachers succeed in engaging their students directly with academic tasks; both are able to use face-to-face interaction as a me-

dium for focusing student attention on the curriculum. But they do this in qualitatively differing ways.

Traditional Cultural Patterns of Social Control

An extensive discussion of everyday life on the reserve is not possible here, nor is it appropriate, given the special focus of this microethnographic study. However, our interviews with the Indian teacher we videotaped, our observations, and the reported observations and recollections of the Indian teachers we have worked with in summer session courses all point to a key feature of interactional etiquette in the life of children and adults in the community—the avoidance of direct and overt social control in situations where such exercise of control over others would be regarded as entirely appropriate and "natural" by non-Indians. This feature of etiquette is mentioned frequently in the general ethnographic literature. It is related to fundamental assumptions of social relations in many North American Indian cultural groups.

Notions held by non-Indians of what is proper in the exercise of social control derive from Western European cultural assumptions about the nature of authority relationships. Notions of and sensitivity to the exercise of social control that are held and acted upon by people from the Odawa community where we have been working seem to be consonant with traditional Algonkian patterns of defining authority relationships—patterns that seem to have survived more than 300 years of contact with Western Europeans. These are patterns that seem to have persisted at the level of implicit, informal culture despite much acculturative change at the explicit, formal level—changes in language, dress, technology, participation in a money economy, and the like.

The traditional Algonkian patterns have been well documented from the seventeenth century to the present. At the general level of political organization there was great decentralization within the various Algonkian societies that occupied the Eastern Woodlands region of North America, extending from the Atlantic Coast inland through the Great Lakes as far west as what is now called Manitoba and Minnesota. (See Hallowell 1955: 120.)

At the level of daily life, the virtual absence of central political authority (except on a temporary basis) was reflected in face-to-face social relations. Work groups and hunting groups were not organized around fixed positions of leadership to be permanently occupied by particular individuals, as were analogous groups among Europeans. This cultural difference was extremely salient for the European missionaries and explorers. They mentioned it again and again in their reports to Europe. Selecting from such accounts, Hallowell (1955: 135) cites the following sources, among others:

> They held it as a maxim that each one is free: that one can do whatever he wishes: and that it is not sensible to put constraint upon men.
> —Le Clercq, French Jesuit missionary, 17th century, writing of the Micmac of the Gaspé Peninsula

> Every word that looks like a command is immediately rejected with contempt by an Indian, proud of his liberty. The chief must endeavour to rule over his people merely by calm reasoning and friendly exhortation.
> —Loskiel, German United Brethren missionary, 18th century, writing of the Delaware

> Our Generals and Presidents of the Council have not more power than any other Huron ... everyone is his own Master ... without being accountable to another, or censur'd by his Neighbor.
> —Adaric, Huron chief, quoted by de Lahontan, French explorer, 17th century

Hallowell notes that the pattern of a social structure in which no one was in a position to order anyone else around had as its interactional concomitant the avoidance of levels and kinds of social pressure that to non-Indians would seem very trivial. He found this pattern persisting in the 1930s and 1940s among both relatively traditional and relatively acculturated Ojibwa in Eastern Manitoba (1955: 378ff). Since the Ojibwa, the Huron, and the Odawa were neighbors in Ontario in the seventeenth century (and still are today) and since similar traditional patterns of political decentralization and everyday conduct have been reported for the Odawa (Kinietz 1972: 226, 1st ed. 1940), it seems reasonable to infer that the patterns we find in community life on the reserve today represent the persistence of traditional patterns of interactional etiquette—in modern dress, as it were.

But it is precisely because of the presence in everyday life on the reserve of modern dress, cars, outboard motors, television sets, and fluency in English, that these relatively subtle aspects of interactional etiquette are likely to go unrecognized by non-Indian teachers as they meet Odawa children at school. Ways of avoiding direct commands and not putting people in the spotlight are not seen as a part of culture. Apparently, "culture" is traditional art, beadwork, foods, language, tales, from the point of view of school authorities, curriculum developers, and teachers, non-Indian and Indian. In teacher education courses, Indian as well as non-Indian students learn that "culture" is formal, explicit patterning, primarily producing artifacts and languages. The idea that implicit, informal culture shapes people's ways of acting in everyday life does not seem to be generally taught to teachers, whether Indian or non-Indian.

This is not to excoriate "The Authorities." As we noted in our introduction, it is only recently that social scientists (including anthropologists) have begun to take really seriously (and to study really systematically) those subtle differences in people's ways of acting which, while they may seem trivial at first thinking, turn out to have profound effects on people's reactions during face-to-face interaction—on feelings and on inferences of intent—especially in encounters between people of differing ethnic and cultural backgrounds.

Culturally Responsive Pedagogy: Some Implications of "Mixed Forms"

There is considerable ethnographic evidence that between communities of North American Indians generally and communities of people of European ancestry generally there are differences in

fundamental principles of social organization—differences which have consequences for the conduct of face-to-face interaction. G. and L. Spindler (1971) report patterns of interaction among the native-oriented Menomini of North Central Wisconsin which are similar to the Odawa patterns we have described. General similarities to these patterns are found widely across North America. Evidence from the Eastern Woodlands, and Philips' work on a Northwest Coast reservation, have already been mentioned. Basso (1970) discusses the important role of silence in speaking among the Western Apache. Darnell (1979) and Urion (1978) report similar patterns among the Cree of Manitoba, as do Scollon and Scollon (1979) for the Central Athabaskan communities in Alaska. Van Ness (1977), in a microethnographic analysis of an Alaskan Athabaskan teacher's conduct of reading instruction, shows the same careful distinction between public and private arenas of discourse—the "on the record"/"off the record" distinction—which has been shown here for an Odawa teacher. It is reasonable to assume that these kinds of cultural differences between Indian and non-Indian social organization of interaction obtain widely in North America.

But a *caveat* is in order. It does not seem that the teaching of Native American teachers differs totally from that of non-Native Americans. What one sees in Classroom I in this study and in other classrooms taught by Native American teachers is not an ideal cultural type of purely "Indian" interactional etiquette—nor, as Urion points out (1978), does one see only purely "Indian" ways of interacting in Native American speech communities currently. Those speech communities are in interethnic contact situations. What one finds today are *mixed forms* in everyday life outside schools, and in everyday life inside them.

The Indian teacher in Classroom I had developed adaptive ways of teaching culturally "mainstream" English-American curriculum. Much of what she did is what many other North American teachers do. But within the standard curriculum and within the overall constraints of standard "teacherly" ways of engaging children with curriculum content the Indian teacher had intuitively found ways of accommodating to Odawa principles of communicative etiquette. Her classroom was truly multicultural.

Mixed forms were also found in the teaching of the non-Indian teacher, who was teaching Indian children for the first time. He had taught non-Indian children before. At the beginning of the school year his teaching style was much more "standard" than it was by the end of the year. He had the children arranged in rows of individual seats and spent much of each day in whole-group lessons, during which he asked academic content questions of named individual children.

As the year progressed the non-Indian teacher adopted some of the ways of teaching of the Indian teacher next door. This happened partly because of clinical supervisory suggestions made by the principal of the school, who was a member of the reserve community. That principal seems intuitively to have understood the underlying logic of the Indian first-grade teacher's ways of

teaching. Another reason the non-Indian teacher's ways of teaching changed somewhat was that the new ways of teaching *worked*. We think that his "teacher radar" told him that his adaptations were making sense. His adaptations were made without an explicit theory of Odawa communicative etiquette. Whatever the reasons for the changes, they did occur. The children were seated in table groups instead of sitting individually in rows. During whole group lessons the teacher began to call on table groups rather than on individual children. He also decreased the total amount of time spent each day in whole group lessons. He began to teach reading by individually tutoring each child in the room and increasing the amount of time he spent with children in small groups. In doing so, he created "privatized" arenas for interacting with children. In the public arena of large group instruction he still tended to "spotlight" individual children, in the ways considered by European and North American pedagogical standards to be "good teaching." But by changing overall patterns of classroom organization, he introduced "privatized" arenas for contact with students, and as the year progressed these became the predominant arenas for academic skill instruction. He too had developed culturally mixed forms of classroom participation structures.

Both teachers had made adaptations in the direction of greater cultural congruence with community principles of interactional etiquette. What they did, apparently mostly because of good teacher intuitions, resembles what happened in another intercultural school setting in which adaptations in ways of teaching were made intuitively by teachers. That school is the Kamehameha Early Education Project in Hawaii (K.E.E.P.).

In the speech community to which Hawaiian children belong, principles of interactional etiquette obtain which are very different from those found on the Odawa reserve. Among Hawaiian children and adults, overlapping speech is common in ordinary conversation and in the stylized version of ordinary conversation termed "talk story," a speech event which has been studied by Boggs (1976) and by Watson-Gegeo and Boggs (1977). In "talk story" a narrative is told overlappingly by more than one narrator, and the speech of the narrators is overlapped by responses from the audience to which the story is being told.

In the K.E.E.P. school an attempt was made to improve the academic performance of Hawaiian children in the early grades. A phonics-based method of teaching reading was used for the first two years of the program. The children's reading performance was at the 8th percentile according to national norms during the program's first year and at the 27th percentile during the program's second year (Au and Jordan 1980).

In the program's third year a new approach to reading instruction was tried. The new program was chosen because its pedagogical model was the opposite of the previously unsuccessful program. In the new program greater emphasis was placed on reading *comprehension* than on decoding skills, which had received most emphasis in the program used formerly. This choice of a way of teaching reading, made on technical grounds, had unanticipated

social consequences. In the new approach, the means by which comprehension was stressed was small group discussion of the reading stories by the children and teachers. These discussions took on an overlapping turn format similar in some ways to "talk story," the speech event whose participation structure children were familiar with in life outside school (cf. the microethnographic analysis of reading lesson discourse by Au 1980). By the end of the third year this participation structure was used, the children's reading scores had increased to the 67th percentile, and in the two subsequent years achievement has been maintained slightly above the 50th percentile. This dramatic increase in reading scores is attributed by Au and Jordan to the children's familiarity with the social organization of discourse in the new way of conducting the reading lessons.

Still, the K.E.E.P. reading lessons look like school talk; they only partially resemble the ways of speaking apparent in the "talk story" speech event as it is found in the more folk-culturally "pure" form in everyday life in the community. The reading lesson was a culturally mixed form, a small change in social relations inside school which seems to have had large consequences for pedagogical effectiveness.

Both in the K.E.E.P. reading lessons and in the ways of teaching used by the Indian and the non-Indian teacher in the Odawa classrooms, cultural congruence between home and school participation structures was adaptively arrived at, apparently by intuitive happenstance. Microethnographic analysis reveals the specific features of the cultural organization of social relationships in communication which differ, albeit only slightly, from "mainstream" ways of teaching. The findings of general ethnography help place the microethnographic analysis in the broader context of community life outside school.

These findings have implications for pedagogy in the education of Native American and Hawaiian children and, more generally, for the education of minority ethnic children in complex polyethnic societies. It may well be that by discovering the small differences in social relations which make a big difference in the interactional ways children engage the content of the school curriculum, anthropologists of education can make practical contributions to the improvement of minority children's school achievement and to the improvement of the quality of everyday school life for such children and their teachers. Making small changes in everyday classroom participation structures may be one of the means by which more culturally responsive pedagogy can be developed.

We hope that the line of inquiry which has been begun can provide insights for educators and anthropologists, both as basic research on the cultural organization of social relations in community and school socialization and as application of these perspectives and findings in teacher education both at the college level and in continuing education for teachers in local schools.

Notes

The work reported here was supported by the Ontario Department of Indian Affairs and Northern Development, whose assistance is gratefully acknowledged. To preserve confidentiality we cannot thank by name the local tribal officials, the principal of the school, and the teachers who cooperated with us, but their support is deeply appreciated. The following helped in the work, and we thank them: Alex Fox, Anne Medicine, Linda Belarde, Joseph Logan, Zina Steinberg, Matthew King, Kathryn Hu-Pei Au, and Donna Fox.

[1] Duration was first judged by noting the revolution counter number that was displayed on the videotape playback deck at the approximate beginning of a new activity. The counter numbers were later converted into equal units of real time. This conversion is necessary because the intervals between counter numbers at the beginning of a reel or cassette are not equivalent to the numbers at the end of the reel, as indicators of real time.

[2] Percentages are more useful for comparing the two rooms than are the actual amounts of real time, since they adjust for the differences in the total amount of time the rooms were taped—ten hours for Classroom I and eight hours for Classroom II.

References

Au, Kathryn Hu-Pei. 1980. "Participation Structures in a Reading Lesson with Hawaiian Children: Analysis of a Culturally Appropriate Instructional Event." *Anthropology and Education Quarterly*, 11:2:91–115.

———, and Catherine Jordan. 1980. "Teaching Reading to Hawaiian Children: Finding a Culturally Appropriate Solution." In H. Trueba, G. P. Guthrie, and K. H. Au, eds., *Culture in the Bilingual Classroom*. Rowley, MA: Newbury House.

Basso, K. 1970. "To Give Up on Words: Silence in Western Apache Culture." *Southwestern Journal of Anthropology*, 26: 213–230.

Bauman, R., and J. Sherzer. 1975. "The Ethnography of Speaking." *Annual Review of Anthropology*, 4:95–119.

Bellack, A. A., et al. 1966. *The Language of the Classroom*. New York: Teachers College Press.

Bennet, A., F. Erickson, and J. Gumperz. 1976. *Coordination of Verbal and Nonverbal Cues in Conversation*. MS report on workshop held at the University of California Language-Behavior Research Laboratory, Berkeley, California.

Boggs, Steven T. 1976. "The Meaning of Questions and Narrations to Hawaiian Children." In C. Cazden, V. John, and D. Hymes, eds., *Functions of Language in the Classroom*. New York: Teachers College Press.

Bremme, Donald, and Frederick Erickson. 1977. "Behaving and Making Sense: Some Relationships Among Verbal and Non-verbal Ways of Acting in a Classroom." *Theory into Practice.* School of Education, Ohio State University.

Byers, Paul, and Happy Byers. 1972. "Nonverbal Communication and the Education of Children." In C. Cazden, D. Hymes, and V. John, eds., *Functions of Language in the Classroom.* New York: Teachers College Press.

Cazden, Courtney B., Vera P. John, and Dell Hymes, eds. 1972 (reissued 1985). *Functions of Language in the Classroom.* Prospect Heights, IL: Waveland Press, Inc.

Darnell, R. 1979. "Reflections on Cree Interactional Etiquette: Educational Implications." In *Working Papers in Sociolinguistics.* Austin, TX: Southwest Educational Development Laboratory.

Dumont, R. V. 1972. "Learning English and How to be Silent: Studies in Sioux and Cherokee Classrooms." In C. Cazden, V. John, and D. Hymes, eds., *Functions of Language in the Classroom.* New York: Teachers College Press.

Erickson, Frederick. 1976. "Gatekeeping Encounters: A Social Selection Process." In P. R. Sanday, ed., *Anthropology and the Public Interest.* New York: Academic Press.

———. 1977. "Some Approaches to Inquiry in School/Community Ethnography." In *Anthropology and Education Quarterly*, 8:1.

Florio, Susan. 1977. *Learning How to Go to School: An Ethnography of Interaction in a Kindergarten/First Grade Classroom.* Unpublished dissertation. Harvard University, Graduate School of Education.

Frake, C. O. 1964. "A Structural Description of Subanun 'Religious Behavior.'" In W. Goodenough, ed., *Explorations in Cultural Anthropology.* New York: McGraw-Hill Book Co.

Goffman, Erving. 1967. *Interaction Ritual: Essays on Face to Face Behavior.* Garden City, NY: Doubleday and Co.

Goodenough, Ward. 1971. *Culture, Language and Society.* Addison-Wesley module. Reading, MA: Addison-Wesley Publishing Co.

Griffin, P., and R. Shuy. 1978. *Children's Functional Language and Education in the Early Years.* Final report to Carnegie Corporation of New York. Arlington, VA: Center for Applied Linguistics.

Gumperz, John J. 1968. "The Speech Community." In *International Encyclopedia of the Social Sciences.* New York: Crowell, Collier, and Macmillan.

———. 1976. "Language, Communication and Public Negotiation." In P. R. Sanday, ed., *Anthropology and the Public Interest.* New York: Academic Press.

———. 1977. "Sociocultural Knowledge in Conversational Inference." In M. Saville-Troike, ed., *Linguistics and Anthro-*

pology. Georgetown University Roundtable on Language and Linguistics, 191–211.

———. 1979a. *The Retrieval of Sociocultural Knowledge in Conversation.* Working paper, Language-Behavior Research Laboratory, University of California at Berkeley.

———. 1979b. "The Sociolinguistic Basis of Speech Act Theory." In J. Boyd and S. Ferrar, eds., *Speech Act Ten Years After.* Milan, Italy: Versus Press.

———. 1980. "Conversational Inference and Classroom Learning." In J. Green and C. Wallat, eds., *Ethnographic Approaches to Face to Face Interaction in Educational Settings.* Norwood, NJ: Ablex.

Gumperz, John, and Jenny Cook-Gumperz. 1979. *Beyond Ethnography: Some Uses of Sociolinguistics for Understanding Classroom Environments.* Paper presented at the annual meeting of the American Educational Research Association, San Francisco.

Hall, E. T. 1959. *The Silent Language.* New York: Fawcett Books.

———. 1966. *The Hidden Dimension.* Garden City, NY: Doubleday and Co.

Hallowell, A. I. 1955. *Culture and Experience.* Philadelphia: University of Pennsylvania Press.

Hymes, Dell. 1974. *Foundations in Sociolinguistics: An Ethnographic Approach.* Philadelphia: University of Pennsylvania Press.

———. 1977. "Qualitative/Quantitative Research Methodologies in Education: A Linguistic Perspective." In *Anthropology and Education Quarterly,* 8:3:165–176.

Kinietz, W. V. 1972. *The Indians of the Western Great Lakes: 1615–1760.* Ann Arbor: University of Michigan Press (1st ed., 1940).

Kounin, J. J. 1970. *Discipline and Group Management in Classrooms.* New York: Holt, Rinehart and Winston.

McDermott, R. P. 1976. *Kids Make Sense: An Ethnographic Account of the Interactional Management of Success and Failure in One First-Grade Classroom.* Unpublished dissertation. Stanford University, Anthropology Department.

———, et al. 1978. "Criteria for an Ethnographically Adequate Description of Concerted Activities and Their Contexts." *Semiotica* 24:3–4:245–275.

McDermott, R. P., and K. Gospodinoff. 1979. "Social Contexts for Ethnic Borders and School Failure." In A. Wolfgang, ed., *Nonverbal Behavior.* New York: Academic Press.

Mehan, H. 1978. "Structuring School Structure." *Harvard Educational Review,* 48:1:32–64.

———. 1979. *Learning Lessons: Social Organization in the Classroom.* Cambridge: Harvard University Press.

Michaels, Sara, and Jenny Cook-Gumperz. 1979. *A Study of Sharing Time with First-Grade Students: Discourse Narratives in the Classroom.* Working paper, Language-Behavior Research Laboratory, University of California at Berkeley.

Olson, D. R., and A. Hildyard. In press. "Assent and Compliance in Children's Language Comprehension: Knowing and Doing." In R. P. Dickson, ed., *Children's Oral Communication Skills.* New York: Academic Press.

Philips, S. 1972. "Participant Structures and Communicative Competence: Warm Springs Children in Community and Classroom." In C. Cazden, D. Hymes, and V. John, eds., *Functions of Language in the Classroom.* New York: Teachers College Press.

———. 1975. *The Invisible Culture: Communication in Classroom and Community in the Warm Springs Reservation.* Unpublished dissertation. Philadelphia: University of Pennsylvania Press.

Ruiz, S. 1971. *Use of Space in the Classroom,* research report #11, Center for Urban Affairs, Michigan State University.

Scollon, R., and S. B. K. Scollon. 1979. *Literacy as Interethnic Communication: An Athabaskan Case.* Sociolinguistic working paper #59, Austin, TX: Southwest Educational Development Laboratory.

Shultz, Jeffrey, Susan Florio, and Frederick Erickson. In press. "Where's the Floor?: Aspects of the Cultural Organization of Social Relationships in Communication at Home and at School." In P. Gilmore and A. Glatthorn, eds., *Ethnography and Education: Children In and Out of School.* Washington: Center for Applied Linguistics.

Sinclair, J., and R. Coulthard. 1975. *Toward an Analysis of Discourse.* Oxford: Oxford University Press.

Smith, L., and W. Geoffrey. 1968. *The Complexities of an Urban Classroom.* New York: Holt, Rinehart and Winston.

Spindler, G., and L. Spindler. 1971 (reissued 1984). *Dreamers With Power: The Menominee.* Prospect Heights, IL: Waveland Press.

Urion, C. 1978. *Control of Topic in a Bilingual (Cree-English) Speech Event.* Unpublished dissertation. Edmonton, Alberta: University of Alberta.

Van Ness, H. 1977. *Social Control and Social Organization in an Alaskan Athabaskan Classroom: A Microethnography of "Getting Ready" for Reading.* Qualifying paper, Harvard Graduate School of Education.

Watson, Karen Ann. 1974. "Understanding Human Interaction." *Topics in Cultural Learning,* 2:57–66. (Available from the Culture Learning Institute, East-West Center, Honolulu, Hawaii.)

Watson-Gegeo, K. A., and S. T. Boggs. 1977. "From Verbal Play to Talk Story: The Role of Routines in Speech Events Among Hawaiian Children." In C. Mitchell-Kernan and S. Ervin-Tripp, eds., *Child Discourse.* New York: Academic Press.

6

Susan Urmston Philips

The Language Socialization of Lawyers: Acquiring the "Cant"

Susan Urmston Philips

The Author

Susan Urmston Philips is an assistant professor of anthropology at the University of Arizona. Her area of specialization is linguistics, and more particularly language and culture. She is properly called a sociolinguist, because her work reflects the influence of the several disciplines that contribute to sociolinguistics. She did her graduate work at the University of Pennsylvania, receiving the Ph.D. in anthropology in 1974. She says of herself:

"I became involved in classroom research when I did my Ph.D. dissertation research. My dissertation fieldwork was concerned with ways that Indian use of English on the Warm Springs Indian Reservation was culturally distinctive. I wanted my research to be of use to the tribe. It was clear to them that their children were having difficulty in school, and the potential utility of a sociolinguistic perspective for the solution of minority educational problems had been made clear to me by Dell Hymes. So I designed my research to determine whether Indian ways of using language were involved in the Indian children's classroom difficulties. I observed and tape recorded in both Indian and Anglo classrooms at the first- and sixth-grade levels. Then, through participation in Warm Springs community activities, I sought to identify the sources of the differences I saw in the behavior of Anglo and Indian students. A book entitled *The Invisible Culture* is my analysis of the data gathered in that research.

"My initial involvement in classroom research, then, was motivated in part by the needs of the people I was interested in studying.

"Now I am involved in research on language use in American courtrooms. In both the courtroom and the classroom, question-and-answer sequences are pervasive. And those sequences are of great consequence for the parties being processed through both institutional complexes. Such comparisons of language use in different American institutional settings show me that my classroom research experiences are still very much with me in my current research."

This Chapter

Most of us, at one time or another, have encountered the "cant" of the legal profession that Susan Philips discusses in this paper. The encounter is almost always a vexing one for the layperson, for even though he or she may be articulate and generally well-read, the jargon used by lawyers will be obscure at best and opaque at worst.

In this chapter Philips describes legal cant as a special form of communication. She places the emphasis on how it is acquired. The language socialization of law students is different in some respects from those occurring in other professional training programs, but everyone who has had advanced professional training in any field will note some similarities.

All professional training serves as an initiation into a special status in society. In the non-Western societies that anthropologists have traditionally studied, initiation ceremonies are often the single most important formal educational institution. Though initiation rites for females are found in many societies, the emphasis is usually on males. They are invariably inducted into the special non-domestic areas of male privilege, as in politics and religion. These rituals also serve to separate males from female-dominated groups and relationships and from the household of origin.

There are parallels to professional education of any kind in these initiation rituals, and particularly to professional education involving esoteric language and behavior patterns, such as in the legal profession. In any society it is the nature of nearly all formal education beyond the first years to specialize, select, and exclude. These features are increasingly questioned in modern society as we become more egalitarian and the social structure of our society more open. Traditional hierarchies and special statuses are challenged, as well as the special initiation rites leading to membership in them. The relationship between education and exclusiveness is so basic, however, that the problem may never be resolved.

Philips' analysis makes clear the dilemma we face in a complex modern society, where educational initiations proliferate and harden as governmental bureaucracies, industrial systems, professions, and trades each require their own initiations and maintain their boundaries with their specialized "cant."

This chapter also furnishes us with a helpful commentary on ethnographic methods and how they were applied in the author's study of the law school classrooms. This demonstration further reinforces an emerging model of ethnography as applicable to any situation, anywhere. It is apparent, however, that the demonstration is successful because the ethnographer is trained in more than methodology. Philips had an established language and culture framework within which to observe and interpret.

Introduction

My purpose here is to provide an ethnographic description and analysis of the processes through which lawyers learn how to use legal jargon.

The analysis is based on knowledge I acquired as a participant observer in the College of Law of a large Southwestern university. For one academic year I took courses in that law school as a special student, supported by a Russell Sage Residency in Law and Social Sciences.

In the discussion to follow, I will first consider how legal jargon is acquired through the process of face-to-face interaction and what we can learn about language socialization through a look at the acquisition of legal jargon.

The next section of the paper is devoted to what lawyers' language socialization can tell us about the allocation of special terminologies that embody and are a key to areas of knowledge. This concern is particularly relevant to ethnic minorities, women, and individuals who view access to certain areas of knowledge as a necessary part of their increase of control over their own lives. Legal jargon is characterized by its inaccessibility to outsiders. Thus, in addressing the issue of what makes legal language inaccessible, we will address the larger issue of what more generally causes languages and their associated areas of knowledge to be accessible to some and not to others.

The final section of the paper is devoted to consideration of the relationship between ethnographic methods of data collection and the type of analysis of language socialization provided in the rest of the paper. Here the concern is to explicate the three-way relationship between methods of data collection, the kind of data that can and cannot be obtained through particular methods, and the sort of analysis that is and is not possible with a given body of data.

Acquiring the Cant

Legal Jargon as "Cant"

The term "cant" has been used to refer to expressions peculiar to, and generally understood only by members of, a particular sect, class, or occupation. "Cant" also conveys something more than just a special vocabulary. In addition, it has the connotation of depreciation of some aspect of the cant, its use, or its users, as in the sense one has of the phrases "thieves' cant" and "beggars' cant."

Legal jargon is generally fully understood only by lawyers and judges, so it can be said to be associated with an occupation group.[1] Lawyers are distrusted in part because it is difficult to understand their language, so users of that special language are sometimes disparaged. For these reasons, it seems appropriate to speak of the use of legal jargon as lawyers' cant.

Linguistic anthropologists have given little attention to special vocabularies that are associated with particular occupational or professional categories. Spradley's (1970) book on skid row bums and Agar's (1973) on heroin users come close, although those subjects are not associated with activities we think of as occupations. Still less attention has focused on the use of special terminological systems, or on how people learn to use special vocabularies.

At the same time, linguistic anthropologists have been strongly influenced by Hymes' (1962) arguments for looking at language in its social context, and by the efforts of Gumperz and Hymes (1964, 1972) and Goffman (1964) to encourage anthropological attention to sociological approaches to the study of language in its social context. More specifically, sociological modes of analysis of face-to-face interaction (Goffman 1963, 1972; Garfinkel 1967; Sacks, Schegloff, and Jefferson 1974) have been taken up by anthropologists (McDermott 1974, Philips 1976, Erickson 1979, Keenan and Schieffelin 1976).[2] Recently, Goodenough (1976) has focused attention on the way in which socialization occurs through the process of interaction.

Clearly sociological approaches to interaction fit well with some of the most fundamental anthropological views on language. Anthropologists see language as the key vehicle for transmission of cultural knowledge. Culture in turn is viewed as the distinctively human element in the adaptational flexibility of the human species. Communication, or the transmission of cultural information, occurs in the context of face-to-face interaction. Thus the examination of that process of communication in face-to-face interaction should tell us more about the role of language in the socialization or enculturation process.

The Nature of the Cant

Law students often say that getting through law school, particularly the first year, is chiefly a matter of learning a new language. By that the students suggest the scale on which unknown terms must be mastered, but they do not convey the nature of the language learned. Legal cant, as encountered in law school, consists of both new words and new oral and written activities in which the language is used. I will say a little about each of these in turn.

The new words consist of familiar terms with new or specialized meanings and new terms (some of them from languages other than English). In addition, there are new rules (collocation rules) for combining those terms with other already known terms.

Two examples of old terms with new meanings and uses are the words "construction" and "depose." Most of us have heard and use the word "construction" in the phrase "construction worker." The *legal* use of that term is as a noun form or nominalization of the verb "to construe" rather than the verb "to construct." Thus when one asks what construction was given to a statute one is asking how that statute was interpreted.

At some point in our classroom contact with European history, we learn that rulers can be "deposed," or taken out of their positions of authority. For legal purposes, however, the term "depose" refers to taking a deposition or oral testimony recorded by a court reporter from a witness outside the courtroom, and usually before a trial takes place. Thus new homonyms emerge as legal cant is acquired.

The new meanings of most legal terms that already have old familiar meanings are not usually so different from the old meanings. More often a general term comes to stand for a more specialized and focused concept. That is the case, for example, with the phrase "selective incorporation." One may readily infer that selective incorporation refers to a process through which some but not all of some set of things are taken in. But for legal purposes "selective incorporation" refers specifically to the position taken by some U.S. Supreme Court justices that only some, not all, of the rights in the Bill of Rights should be considered "fundamental." And only those that are considered fundamental are to be included in applying the Fourteenth Amendment of the Constitution to the states. Terms like "jurisdiction," "probable cause," "contract," and "exclusionary rule" all function in a similar manner. This source of terminology may be the one from which the greatest number of legal terms are drawn.

However, completely unfamiliar terms, not heard in daily conversation, are also numerous. Terms like "tort," "collateral estoppel," "plaintiff's intestate," "bailor," "pursuant to," and others fall into this category.

The rules for combining the new terms with other parts of speech, or in other words for contextualizing the new terms, are part of the meaning of the terms themselves.[3] Law school professors may be quite explicit about the proper syntactic context for certain terms. For example, when law school students begin to speak and write about Supreme Court decisions, they must discuss actions "the Court" has taken.

Most of us have heard the term "court" used or used it ourselves as an object in utterance such as, "You can take me to court," or "I have to appear in court because of a traffic ticket." But in law school the term is used to refer to one or more justices or judges, and it appears as the subject of many utterances.

Students may be explicitly instructed that "the Court" be used with some verbs, but not others. Thus one may say that "the Court decided to restrict application of the exclusionary rule" or "the Court upheld the lower court's decision," but one must not say "the Court felt" or "the Court believed." Lawyers who eventually engage in actual courtroom practice will find "the Court" being used in still other ways there, as when a judge refers to himself as a third person subject in saying, "The Court finds that a plea of guilty has been knowingly and voluntarily made."

As I indicated at the beginning of this section, acquisition of the cant entails learning not only appropriate vocabulary and syntax, but also new forms of speech and writing that go beyond the sentence level. A brief and general characterization of law school education should convey some initial general sense of the nature of those new verbal and written forms.

Most law schools still rely on what is referred to as "the case method" for teaching the core of their curriculum. The chief or only textbook for a course is a casebook, made up of partial or whole "opinions," otherwise known as past and present "decisions" of the U.S. Supreme Court and State Supreme Courts.

Students are assigned "cases" to read and to "brief" in preparation for class. To "brief" a case, the students extract from each opinion the key facts of the case, the legal issues in the case, the Court's holding, or main decisions, and the arguments for and against the decision.

In the law school classes that I attended, seating was fixed, in that once a student had chosen a place and committed his or her last name to that position on the professor's seating chart, that seat was taken each time. The students regularly brought to class their casebooks and their briefs, as well as their notebooks.

Where the classic law school format for teaching appears in the *classroom*, it is referred to as "the Socratic method." In my own experience, the application of that method was consistent: the teacher would call on a student, by title and last name (e.g., Ms. Smith), whether or not she or he had volunteered to speak, and ask that student a series of questions. Each question was structurally and topically dependent on the student's last answer or response, rather than having been planned out beforehand as part of predetermined sequence. Anthropologists will recognize that law school professors used "open-ended" questioning. The teacher might ask one student one or several questions before moving on to the next student.

When the teachers took up new cases, the first student asked to speak on such a case was often required to present information quite directly from the brief. Thus that student might be asked to present the facts of the case or the reasons for the Court's holding. As the questioning proceeded, it was more likely to depart from the focus of the

brief. This is a very normative view, of course, and variations in this process will be discussed further on.

The *specialized forms of speech and writing* in the law school student's training are closely associated with appellate (case) law and practice. The students become familiar with written Supreme Court "opinions" and one form of the "brief." Their briefs are both like and unlike the briefs used in appealing lower court decisions to a higher court, as will be discussed in further detail later on.

Through classroom interaction, the students are given the opportunity to hear the words they first encountered in their casebooks used by the teacher in new utterances, new constructions. They are also required to use the terms themselves in responding to the professor's questions, and to hear one another's uses responded to by the teacher as meaningful or not.

The students also become familiar with an *interactional format* used often in open court, where the judge has the opportunity to question lawyers in a manner similar to the way that law professors question students.[4] The interactional analogy between the law school classroom and the courtroom will also be discussed in further detail later on. For now, let it suffice to point out that where speaking rather than writing is involved, training does not focus on learning how to handle specific verbal formats, such as how to give an opening or closing statement at a trial, or how to handle a divorce case. Instead, for the most part, verbal training involves preparation for a verbal role differentiation that is generally relevant for most courtroom interaction—namely, the differentiation between lawyer and judge.

In sum, legal jargon is itself constrained by syntactic rules, by specialized forms of writing, and by specialized verbal role differentiations. And, as we shall see in the sections to follow, the acquisition of legal cant basically involves learning how to speak and write in specific ways that require the use of legal terms, but that go considerably beyond knowledge of the dictionary meaning of the terms themselves.

Here I have described some linguistic and sociolinguistic characteristics of legal cant. The terms and phrases linked together by collocation rules are embedded in written and spoken forms of speech. The students learn to take part in verbal interaction using the legal language. And through that interaction they organize their language in a role-differentiated manner. The most crucial aspect of that socializing process is probably the great amount of talk by students in the law school classroom.

From this brief characterization of the cant and the process through which use of the cant is acquired, we will turn to a closer examination of the processes through which law school students learn *verbal* usage of the cant.

The Structural Segregation of Law School Students: Talking to One Another

Although I have suggested in general that it is through the talk by students in the *classroom* that they learn to use the cant, such classroom learning is supported by an external environment in which students talk to one another, using legal terminology.

It may seem commonplace to say that the students talk to one another, and hardly less so that they sometimes talk law. But unlike college students, law students are initiating that process whereby they eventually become unintelligible to the rest of us when they speak to one another. Unlike the graduate students or professors of any given academic discipline, law students or lawyers are numerous in our society. Lawyers run an entire set of legal institutions that are by definition supposed to be responsible and responsive to the public. Those institutions are not in fact accessible to the public, however, in part because the language used in the interaction that maintains them is impenetrable. We ask here how that process begins.

In the university where I was a law school student, and probably at others as well, structural segregation of the law school contributed to the creation of an environment in which students talked to each other and not to people who were not law students. Law schools often have autonomous bureaucracies and their own buildings, so that they are organizationally and physically distinct. This means there is also spatial and interactional segregation of people involved with the law school. My law school ran on a slighly different academic calendar than the rest of the university, as well. Classes began sooner in the fall and ended sooner than in the other colleges. Final exams came sooner and there was, of course, a separate exam schedule for the law school. Spring break was held at a different time than the break for the rest of the university. Individual teachers rescheduled their classes without regard to activities outside the law school.

For all these reasons, few students from outside the law school were taking law school courses. And some of these features also limited the law student's ability to take courses outside the law school. Thus law school students encountered mainly one another in their courses.

The law school student body political organizations were also structurally autonomous, or separated from those of the rest of the university. At the law school's fall orientation meetings for first-year students, representatives from a number of law student organizations described their activities. There was a student body organization with elected officers, the law review, a law school newspaper, law school versions of chapters of the American Bar Association and the Lawyers Guild, legal fraternities, a women's organization, and an organization for spouses of law students.

In such ways law students are provided with ample opportunity to engage in the structured interactions with one another that sustain these voluntary associations. Such associations reflect the structures and functions of some of the "real" professional associations the students will later become involved with as practicing attorneys. Accordingly, the law school organizations give the students ways of relating to one another that they will draw upon again and again later in professional life.

In sum, the structural segregation of the law school, which is manifested in its autonomous bureaucracy, its autonomous student social organization, and its physical autonomy, contributes sig-

nificantly to a situation where law students see no one but other law students and, if they seek them out, law faculty. Accordingly, they talk primarily to one another. This interactional segregation is probably especially great in private universities that draw a number of out-of-state students lacking the community ties that in-state students sometimes have.

It does not follow from this structural segregation that the law school students, who literally cannot avoid one another, will talk about law to one another. Indeed, some faculty members in my law school believed that students do not talk about law much and that when they do they misinform one another. But there is a second set of factors beyond those contributing to structural segregation that encourage the students to talk law to one another, and those factors are part of or present in the nature of the educational process itself.

First, the curriculum for the law students at most law schools is organized in such a way that they have a high degree of shared knowledge, which in itself fosters and eases talk on the topics for which there is such a sharedness. All of the first-year students take exactly the same courses and are in all of the same teachers' classes with some of their class members. Where I was a student, the classes were organized so that all of the first-year students had to be at the law school for a large portion of each day, yet were free from classtime during some of the middle hours. While most of the classes had over 100 students in them, and were held in the traditional law school arenas, there were some small classes that indirectly fostered students' talking to one another.

Each first-year student had one

small class of less than 30 during the first semester which was linked to the research methods course taught by the head law school librarian. Thus those who had a small class for Civil Procedure would work on research assignments on Civil Procedure topics. It was my experience that a great deal of talk went on around the research assignments handled through that small class, throughout the semester. Students looking up cases in the library invariably ran into other students in the course looking up the exact same cases, and they puzzled together over the relevance of the cases to the assignment at hand. It was my impression that the Moot Court course of the spring semester fostered similar dialogue among the students.

Moreover, there was a tradition of forming study groups to prepare for the sole exam in each course at the end of the semester. Those study groups also provided a basis for much talk about law among the students.

Through all of the processes just described, the students acquire a great deal of shared knowledge that allows them to develop a very contextualized way of speaking to one another. That is, in conversation they are able to draw upon or refer cryptically to both shared information and the shared meaning of legal terminology. It is perhaps the sharing of the terminology and the syntactic and conversational rules associated with the terminology that distinguishes this process among law students from the same process among any set of persons in a relatively closed and overlapping network of persons and contexts.

But while the students may in fact benefit in many ways from exchanging information about their assigned coursework, they also benefit greatly from the exchange of more practical information that can best be characterized as "survival" information. It is exchanged among students constantly on all university campuses, and is to some extent concealed from faculty members, particularly when it is about the faculty. In general, such information consists of course and professor reputations—what courses are good or bad and why, and what professors are good and bad and why.

In the law school, there are several other specific sorts of information that are regularly exchanged. First and foremost is information about study aids. As I indicated earlier, the main textbook used in law classes is a casebook, made up of edited opinions from the U.S. and state Supreme Courts. Sometimes Horn books are recommended as sources, although readings from them are not assigned. Horn books are treatises on the essential law of a given subject written by highly regarded legal scholars whose specialties are the topics they write on. The Horn books provide the general principles that the students are supposed to learn to abstract from the individual cases they are assigned to read.

But law professors rarely recommend other sources of information to their students. Thus while a law dictionary is a necessity for first encounters with the new terminology, teachers do not urge its use on students. And some professors explicitly direct their students not to use some other sorts of written sources. The two most often forbidden sources are published outlines that briefly summarize the contents of courses like those the students are taking, and published "canned briefs," or briefs of the cases students are most likely to be reading for their courses.

Yet in practice virtually all of the students use these study aids, and the further on they are in a semester, the more they rely on them. The students learn from their fellow students that these aids exist, and they also learn from their peers which aids are thought to be the best ones for particular courses. While the outlines and canned briefs just described are published sources sold by the book store, student-produced outlines of courses in the law school are also circulated among the students.

A second type of necessary information obtained primarily from other students in the particular law school I attended, which may not be necessary in all law schools, was information about class scheduling. Classes were much more often cancelled and rescheduled in the law school than in college and graduate school courses. Law school professors may find it easier to accomplish such rescheduling than those who teach courses in the rest of the university, because they are obliged to avoid only the other courses that their colleagues are teaching. In other words, whereas teachers of college-level courses encounter quite diverse student schedules, and feel they must reschedule classes only for times when all or almost all of the students in the class may come, the orientation of the law professors is somewhat different. They feel obliged to avoid only the other law school courses that students in their courses might be taking.

Moreover the teachers in law school

courses did not feel obliged to inform the students of class cancellations and reschedulings directly, during an earlier class. Often notices of such changes were simply posted on a bulletin board outside the largest law school classroom, where each day the greatest numbers of students passed. The fact that such a posting was considered adequate notice of class changes indicated the extent to which an effective informal network of student information exchange was assumed by the faculty.

In general, then, law school students have both the shared knowledge that facilitates contextualized conversation and the need to acquire the knowledge that can be gotten only from other students. Those conditions lead to their talking about law in a variety of styles or ways of speaking. The legal jargon that they encounter first in their casebooks and then in the classroom is also used in their encounters with one another, although given terms will appear with different frequencies and in different syntactic combinations in each of these learning environments.

Furthermore, the conditions in law school that give rise to students' talking to one another about the law in structurally segregated contexts will continue to exist throughout their professional careers, allowing for the further elaboration of talk that is mutually intelligible only to members and unintelligible to those outside the profession.

The sort of peer interaction that I have been discussing continues through lawyers' careers in much the same fashion that one sees among students: lawyers who work in the same office or who meet in the halls and offices of court buildings will pause to talk shop and exchange information with one another in their pursuit of individual tasks, even though such information and the ways of speaking about it may be little valued or subject to conscious control or evaluation.

The organization of such peer talk and the attitudes surrounding it differ markedly from the organization of and attitudes toward talk in the more formal setting of the courtroom, in which the work of lawyers is most available to the public. For a better understanding of how students learn to use the cant *in the courtroom*, it is necessary to look more closely at the organization of interaction in the law school classroom.

The Organization of Interaction in the Law School Classroom: The Appellate Courtroom as a Model

In the law school classroom, legal cant is embedded in verbal interaction between the instructor and individual students. Through that interaction the law students learn how to use the language in relating to judges in the courtroom. In other words, the role differentiation of teacher and student parallels the role differentiation between judge and lawyer in the courtroom, particularly the appellate courtroom.

When cases from lower trial courts are appealed to higher courts, there are two basic stages in the review process that lawyers must go through. The first is the submission of a written brief to the Court. In this type of brief, the lawyer lays out the facts of the case, the points of law which he or she wishes to establish, the legal arguments and legal authorities for those points, and rebut-tals to the arguments in the brief of the opposing counsel.

The second stage of the appellate review is the "oral argument" in the presence of the justices who comprise the appellate court. In this stage, both lawyers appear before the court so that they may each give time-limited oral presentations of the legal arguments laid out in their written briefs, and rebut the arguments of the opposing counsel. There the lawyers focus on what they consider to be the crucial points they wish the Court to give greatest attention to, and on any new authorities (decisions that may be cited as precedents) or arguments that have become relevant since the briefs were submitted. The lawyers try to present their crispest points in the clearest fashion.

At the same time, the lawyers must anticipate that their presentations may be interrupted at any time by questions from the Court on points raised in either the written brief or the oral argument. Thus a lawyer may be questioned repeatedly by a judge, and then be allowed to pick up the ordered presentation again, only to be questioned again by that same judge or another judge on the bench. All of the time allotted to the lawyer may be consumed by this impromptu questioning by the judges.

For a lawyer to be effective in this context of verbal interaction, she or he must be able to bring forth immediately the relevant legal arguments and citations of the earlier appellate opinions that constitute the legal precedents or authorities, in response to the justices' questioning. At the same time, the lawyer should be able to return readily to a planned discussion of the arguments in the written brief, and even to omit material covered by the justices' questioning, without allowing the presentation to lose coherence. It is also desirable that this be done in clear English with as few incomplete, rephrased, or awkward utterances as possible.

As can be imagined, keeping one's verbal "cool" in this context is difficult, and those who are able to do so are highly regarded. At the same time, it is never clear how much difference an effective verbal performance will make to the Court as it arrives at a decision. Nevertheless, since an effective verbal performance might make a difference in getting across the relevant arguments, the lawyers who give verbal performances before appellate Courts make an effort to be coherent and fluent in their use of language.

The particular relationship between the lawyer and the judge that I have just described for the appellate courtroom also exists in the trial courtroom in some proceedings. In other words, it is often the case in the trial courtroom that each of two opposing lawyers will present arguments for her or his position to the judge. The judge is free to interrupt at any point with questions to the lawyer that will provide information of use in deciding how to rule on the issue.

For example, in the Initial Appearance, when defendants are brought before a judge for the first time and told what they are charged with, the judge must decide whether those who have been arrested and held in custody at the local county jail should be let out of jail, and under what conditions such a release should occur.

This process is referred to as "determining the conditions of release." For this purpose the defendant's lawyer may give the judge reasons why the defendant should be released with little or no bond money put up to insure that he or she will show up for later proceedings, and with few or no restrictions on activities while out of jail. The attorney for the state, on the other hand, may give the judge reasons why the defendant should be kept in jail, given a high bond to meet, or given certain restrictive conditions of release that dictate where the defendant must live or with whom she or he may or may not associate. It is up to the judge to decide how much of any of this to listen to and what further information to elicit from the lawyers, before deciding on the conditions of release.

One observes the same process of arguments from lawyers and questions from the judge when pretrial motions are presented before the judge. In a criminal trial, the attorney for the state may wish to introduce evidence that the defense attorney feels is irrelevant, or so inflammatory or prejudicial that it will unfairly bias any jury against the defendant. In such an instance, the defense attorney will give reasons why the evidence *should not* be allowed to be presented to the jury and the attorney for the state will give reasons why the information *should* be allowed to be presented. Once again the judge may interrupt either lawyer at any time with questions, or cut the lawyer off, having decided that she or he has heard enough on which to base a decision regarding whether to allow the evidence to be presented to the jury.

There are repeatedly situations

where this pattern occurs at the trial level in courtroom interaction. However, it is important to bear in mind that a good deal which goes on in a trial courtroom is *not* represented in the appellate courtroom. Specifically, the trial court interactional relationships that the lawyer has with witnesses, with plaintiffs and defendants, and with the jury have no counterpart in the appellate courtroom. As we will see, those relationships between lawyer and courtroom personnel other than the judge are not a focus of socialization in the law school classroom.[5]

Although law students learn to use legal jargon in a particular role relationship that has characteristics of the relationship between the appellate judge and the individual lawyer, it is important to bear in mind that this role socialization takes place within the broader context of a general emphasis on appellate law in law school socialization. Accordingly, before going on to specify some of the ways in which the teacher-student relationship in the law classroom is like that of the judge-lawyer relationship in the appellate courtroom, it may be useful to describe the ways in which law schools focus on appellate law, and why this is done.

First, the focus on appellate law should already be apparent from the earlier characterization of the case method through which law students are introduced to legal terminology. Casebooks are edited collections of the "opinions" or decisions appellate courts produce in response to the briefs and oral arguments of attorneys, presented in the matter described earlier. Often those opinions draw very heavily on the briefs provided by the lawyers, or more

precisely on the arguments presented in those briefs. Often, too, the written opinions of both the federal and state supreme courts address those arguments without explaining them or identifying them. This is done as if the lawyers' briefs had been read by every reader of the opinion and provided a context for that opinion, when in fact that obviously does not occur.

While law students may not initially recognize the contribution of the lawyers to the Courts' written opinions, they very soon become aware of those contributions through their Moot Court course. This is a required course taken by first-year students in their second semester, in which students are required to go through the same process lawyers do when taking a case to a court of highest appeal. They are given a case that has gone through a trial court and are asked to appeal the lower court's decision by doing library research on cases that may provide precedents or authorities for their positions, writing a brief laying out those arguments, and presenting oral arguments to a mock appellate court made up of second- or third-year law students. That court then decides which side has the more convincing arguments.

There is also an annual Moot Court competition, in which law school students compete with one another in the presentation of oral argument. In addition, the State Supreme Court holds court at the law school twice a year, so the students have the opportunity to see the process of oral argument as it normally occurs.

Before the case method was introduced at Harvard in 1870 by Christopher Langdell and disseminated from there (Dente 1974), law school courses followed the format used in the Horn books: the general principles underlying or reflected in myriad individual court opinions were laid out for the students, while cases were used to illustrate those principles, rather than being used to derive the principles as they are today.

There are at least two reasons why the case method was thought to be preferable to the approach the Horn books use. Langdell believed the case method would enable law students to see how the law undergoes change through the decision-making process of the appellate courts. One can thus see, in the opinions the students must read, how notions of the nature of courts' "jurisdiction over the person" have changed over the past 100 years, or how rapidly the U.S. Supreme Court extended the Fourteenth Amendment's requirement of due process to the States during the 1960s. And it is probably no accident that Langdell was arguing for the importance of knowledge of legal change just at the time that change through case law was beginning to occur at a more rapid pace, while the stability of precedent gave way.

More importantly, many law professors believe the cases and the classroom dialogue about them teach the students how to *think* like lawyers. Ultimately the students should be able to envision how they as lawyers can play an important role in bringing about legal change, through their anticipation of the ways in which matters being handled at the trial level may entail a basis for appeal at a later date.

The fact that the law school teachers are concerned with conveying a mode of thinking through their classroom activities does not necessarily mean that they are all consciously trying to get their students to act like lawyers in the courtroom, except insofar as acting like lawyers involves demonstrating through talk that one can think like a lawyer. Nevertheless, some teachers do deliberately try to generate a courtroom atmosphere, and there are basic similarities between the way the teachers relate to their students and the way appellate judges relate to the lawyers who appear before them.

I have already described those similarities in my initial characterization of the case method, but a brief recapitulation may be useful here. First, lawyers often enter the appellate courtroom assuming that the judges have read their briefs, and present their arguments in a manner that uses those briefs as a context for their remarks. Similarly, students enter the classroom assuming that they and the professor share the cases assigned as readings as background knowledge that can provide a context to refer to during the classroom discussion.

Second, just as lawyers must come into the appellate courtroom with "briefs" of their own briefs, from which they must be prepared to give a presentation to the Court, so law students come to class with a brief of each judicial opinion assigned as class reading, from which they are prepared to present information to the teacher.

Third, while lawyers begin their presentations by speaking from a brief, they may expect to be interrupted repeatedly by questions from any of the judges on the bench. And these questions often take the form of extended dialogues with each individual judge. Similarly, in the law school classroom, while teachers may begin by asking a student to deliver some information from a brief, they will usually then depart from the formal order of the brief, to ask a series of related questions about the case. Again, it is common to engage in a series of exchanges with a single student before moving on to another student.

Finally, in both the appellate courtroom and the law school classroom, the abilities to think quickly and clearly about issues raised at the moment and to deliver a coherent opinion on those issues are highly valued.

While the parallels between courtroom and classroom may appear fortuitous, a comparison between the law school class and the usual college lecture class reveals the ways in which classroom interaction in the law school is distinctive. First, in the usual college lecture course, the student is not expected to use knowledge shared with the teacher as the basis for contextualized discussion in the classroom. The teacher is expected to deliver *new* information in the classroom. Often (to the students' dismay) the lecture is not even closely related to the material the students have been reading.

Second, students do not usually come to their college lecture classes prepared to deliver information to their teachers. New information is not imparted through dialogue between student and teacher, but rather through the teacher's delivery of a lecture.

Third, teachers in regular college lecture courses do not typically question their students, although this sometimes does occur. Instead, the students

are occasionally given the opportunity to question their teachers. Whenever questioning does occur in the usual college classroom, it is unusual for a dialogue between an individual student and the teacher to involve more than one or two exchanges, the way it so often does in the law school classroom.

In sum, the student's role in the average college lecture class is verbally a relatively passive one, when compared with that of the law school student.

Nevertheless, it would not be appropriate to suggest that law school classes are like higher-level seminars for graduate students in other fields. Seminars may provide the students with the opportunity to assume a role similar to the teacher's position in the lecture course, by allowing them turns at giving formal lecture presentations. Seminars may also involve a relaxation of the teacher's control over turns at talk and the general classroom pattern of students addressing the teacher, so that students talk more spontaneously and address one another rather than just the teacher. Such courses are for higher-level students, who are assumed to know something about what they are discussing, and law schools have such courses for their higher-level students also.

In general, then, it should be evident that the classic format for law school classes is quite distinctive in ways that parallel the organization of interaction in the courtroom.

There is one crucial way in which the organization of interaction in the law school classroom does share a great deal with the organization of interaction in most classrooms that reflect the Western mode of formal education.

Classroom interaction prepares people for the assumption of bureaucratic roles in our society (Sieber 1978). The law school classroom may be seen as a variant of the general classroom model of role differentiation that prepares people for the courtroom rather than for some other bureaucratic setting.

The law school classroom accordingly shares certain characteristics with other classrooms:

1. There is always one person, namely the teacher, in a structural position of control over the interaction of all present. The teacher determines who will talk when about what.

2. The remaining people, the students, are structurally undifferentiated in that they all have basically the same relationship with the teacher. Any differentiation among students is created by the teacher or emerges through the process of interaction that causes some students to be perceived as smarter, more aggressive, or more favored than others.

3. Verbal exchange is between the teacher and the individual student. As a rule, students do not respond to one another, but to the teacher. Where students are allowed to address one another directly, as we all do in conversation, such address is usually mediated through the teacher, who determines who may speak next.

The teacher's control, the lack of differentiation among students, and the restriction of the exchange of talk to that between teacher and individual student are often reflected in the pattern of spatial organization of the classroom, where the teacher faces the students and the students face the teacher, but the students do not face one another.

The many years that students spend engaged in classroom interaction, where the format just described predominates, prepare them for the assumption of bureaucratically organized positions in the occupational sphere. More specifically, those years prepare them for the positionally based status-differentiated relationships of superior and inferior, in which the superior controls the interaction. But those years most particularly train students to function effectively in focused interactions involving many people where a single person controls the talk of others. Most often that format is used in what we refer to as "meetings."

The *law school* classroom is distinctive in that it socializes students for the courtroom, where one key characteristic of the status differentiation is that the person in control, namely the judge, asks repeated questions of the person under control, who must answer those questions in a highly specialized language.

What I have provided up to this point is a very normative view of the law school classroom. There is, in fact, considerable variation in the extent to which the classic format that I have described is used.

In all of the law classes that I have observed, the teachers have used cases as the basic reading material. They have presupposed the cases have been read and briefed, so that the teacher's talk cannot really be comprehended without having read the cases. And one does not regularly encounter lectures based on material that is not in the case-books.

In addition, all law professors ask their students more questions than professors in the other academic disciplines, even though some ask more questions than others. All the law professors I have observed return to the same student repeatedly in questioning, so that extended dialogues take place in the presence of the rest of the class. However, teachers vary in the extent to which they engage in such dialogues, and the individual teacher varies in which students this is done with, and the purposes for which such dialogues are used.

Finally, there are no law professors who do nothing but ask their students questions. All of the teachers take some questions from students, but they differ in the amount of time they devote to answering questions.

All of the law school professors that I observed spend some time lecturing, although much less than in college and graduate lecture courses. Towards the end of the semester it is not unusual for a professor to switch from the Socratic method to lecturing, as a way of cramming in material before time runs out. Younger law school teachers may have a tendency to lecture more, and in other ways to teach in a manner more like that of college and graduate school teachers. This may be a result of their critical view of the dialogic process. The younger teachers may also have had more exposure to college and graduate school courses than the older teachers.

One key source of variation that affects the students a great deal is the extent to which the teacher calls on students without their volunteering. When we enter school as first graders, we are often *required* to participate. One sees compulsory participation, for example, in reading circles, where each child in turn is required to read aloud from a story. Over the years, compulsory participation is used less and less by teachers, and students increasingly are given the choice between volunteering and not volunteering to participate. The return to compulsory participation in the law school classroom is viewed as a hardship and a humiliation by many law school students.

Compulsory participation is probably required less often than it used to be generally, and younger law professors are probably less likely than older law professors to call on students who have not volunteered to participate. Decreased use of compulsory participation is due to its being viewed as part of an authoritarian teaching style that was criticized by students in the late 1960s and early 1970s.[6]

Compulsory participation is used more in the first-year courses than it is in second- and third-year courses. One common pattern is for the instructor to let the students know that they will be called on whether or not they raise their hands, but to require compulsory response with any frequency only at the beginning of the course. Then only when voluntary participation lags will the teacher require individuals to speak.

If we say that law school teachers are authoritarian in their teaching style, then we will most surely say that judges are authoritarian in the courtroom, because clearly lawyers are compelled to answer judges' questions. Thus, regardless of one's attitude toward the law school style, it is still true that it prepares lawyers for what they will encounter in the courtroom.

From this discussion of the parallels between the law school classroom and the courtroom, it should be apparent that students learn a social organizational format of language use, or part of one, as they learn the legal cant. They can then apply that knowledge by mapping it onto a variety of procedural and substantive contexts where there is interaction between judge and lawyer. Other relational aspects of the trial courtroom (e.g., the relationship between lawyer and client, or lawyer and witness) are acquired at a later time. The language forms specific to particular procedures, for example initial appearances, preliminary hearings, the taking of a deposition, or the questioning of a witness, are also acquired at a later time.

A Summary of Basic Features of the Language Socialization of Lawyers

Legal cant involves an interaction between written and spoken communication that sends students cycling through first one and then the other repeatedly in the acquisition of legal terminology.

Students learn the *verbal* use of the cant by talking about law in contexts where they can hear others use terms correctly and hear others use them incorrectly and be corrected, and by experiencing both of those processes themselves. They also hear the terms being used in a variety of syntactic combinations and find themselves struggling to produce sentences in which the terms occur in acceptable combinations.

It is probably generally true that one does not typically learn the *verbal* use of special terminologies from reading alone. One must have access to contexts in which the terms are *verbally used*, and participate in those contexts. It is the peculiar segregatedness of the learning contexts the law students have access to that causes us to describe the jargon as cant, and thus to convey the sense that it is mutually intelligible only among the initiated, and not to outsiders. Of this more will be said in the next section.

It is probably also generally true that the acquisition of language, whether we refer to language in general or to special languages or terminologies, cannot be separated from the acquisition of social roles, so that all language use and training for language use is to some degree role differentiated as it is in the classroom.

Yet we cannot assume that special language socialization will reflect the common denominator in the users' experience with the cant. Law school focuses on appellate law, and on the interactional format associated with that tradition, yet few lawyers will ever spend very much of their time in an appellate court. Thus we see in legal instruction not the most common activities, but rather the most influential activities of the profession.

Practical Implications

The ways in which law school students learn to use legal cant can tell us a good deal about the factors that generally determine how cultural knowledge is distributed among members of a given society.

Interest in this issue is motivated here by the very practical educational concern that some segments of our society are barred from access to areas of knowledge which are associated with control over positions of power and authority. Thus both minorities and women feel barred from access to power, in part because they do not acquire the same kinds of knowledge that white males do; they are, in other words, socialized differently. In addition, many individuals see the specialized knowledge of certain professions, particularly the medical and legal professions, as controlled by the professionals. The lawyer's control over knowledge makes it difficult for a person who is not a member of the profession to acquire that knowledge and the control over certain spheres of activity in one's life associated with the knowledge.

To gain access to legal knowledge, one must learn the legal cant, for by acquiring the cant, one acquires the concepts that are conveyed through this special language. Legal language is viewed by many as more difficult to penetrate, or to acquire, than other special occupational languages. In this section, attention will be given to some of the factors contributing to its impenetrability, and to the features of the language socialization process that cause the code to be intelligible only to members of the legal profession. The purpose of the discussion will be to identify processes that create barriers to the wider dissemination of knowledge, with the long-range goal of eliminating such barriers.

When legal cant is characterized as impenetrable, we may be dealing with the perception of the casual eavesdropper at a cocktail party, the observer in the courtroom, the policeman, bailiff, or reporter who knows some of the jargon, or the client who is doling out money for legal services without fully understanding what the attorney is doing or why.

There are a number of reasons why legal talk is difficult to comprehend. The knowledge brought to bear by those engaged in legal talk is often highly specialized and complex. The legal cant itself may also be more complex and extensive than other special occupational or technical languages. There may be a larger special vocabulary. More of the terms (like *res judicata*, and "plaintiff's intestate") may have primary legal meanings, rather than drawing in part from meanings known by the general populace, the way terms like "target population" and "cultural adaptation" do. Legal terminology may range across a greater number of word classes than other occupational jargons. Thus, in addition to numerous special nouns, there may also be either numerous special verbs and adverbs or verbal forms of the nouns, with associated rules for combining them with words from other classes. And legal language may also be associated with a greater range of special written and spoken procedures than other occupational languages in our society—for example, with written contracts, deeds, licenses, plea agreements, briefs, and statutes, each with its own special rules of format, order, and phrasing.

The legal socialization process also contributes to the impenetrability of legal cant. Most generally, the structural segregatedness of that socialization process creates an environment where it is possible to use an unusually complex special language and still be understood by those with whom one speaks. We will now consider that structural segregation in greater detail.

One characteristic of the acquisition of legal cant is that it is almost necessary to go to law school to learn how to use the language. As was indicated earlier, it is difficult for students from outside the law school to take law courses and get credit for them, because of the bureaucratic autonomy of the law school and the specific policies that discourage outsiders from taking the law school courses. When students *are* able to take the law school courses, they may have difficulty understanding the content of those courses because of the extent to which the courses build on one another, so that comprehension in one course depends on having taken other courses.

One who desires simply to acquire some working knowledge of the vocabulary associated with a particular area of law, like tax law or contract law, will acquire little simply by "sitting in" on the classes, because the class discussion is highly contextualized; the shared knowledge of the case readings may simply be referred to rather than explicated during the class discussion.

Finally, the person who aspires to learning the law on his or her own through the study of written materials will find a fragmented literature held together only by the verbal interaction of the classroom. In other words, the basic text, the casebook, tells one very little if it is used by itself, and the reader has no feedback regarding the extent to which the identification of key issues or key word meanings is accurate. The Horn books, probably the most likely source for the independent learner, lack what the case method was designed to convey—that crucial sense of the way in which change in the legal system comes about, and the ability to identify key issues, as one must later on as an individual practitioner, seeking precedents and ways of framing issues that will be immediately useful to the client at hand. An effort to approach the literature without the classroom verbal interaction that enlightens that literature heightens our awareness of the continued importance of the transmission of cultural knowledge through the direct process of face-to-face interaction.

Because law school students are so segregated from others in their socialization, and encounter so few students from other disciplines in their courses, they have less opportunity and less need than they would otherwise have to attempt to speak about the law in an intelligible manner to those who have not been trained to be lawyers. In their classroom interaction and in their peer interactions outside the classroom, those they must talk to are overwhelmingly lawyers or law students like themselves. Law students have no need to alter or change their mode of discourse from one that is heavily laced with jargon so that others can understand them, because there are no others that they are compelled to talk to about law.

In addition, the method of teaching encourages the students to learn how to apply the terms and the analytical distinctions underlying those terms, but not how to explain them to others. Thus in the classroom a teacher might ask, "What was the 'cause of action' in this case?" rather than asking a student to explain what is meant by the phrase "cause of action."

The mode of testing at the end of each semester or school year uses a similar approach. The standard exam relies almost exclusively on the presentation of hypothetical factual situations to which legal principles are applied. Thus for example, a Criminal Procedure exam may describe the commission of a crime and the arrest of a criminal, and ask the student to explain what evidence is admissible and what evidence must be excluded under "the exclusionary rule," which forbids use in court of evidence obtained in violation of the defendant's Constitutional rights. One is not asked, "What is the exclusionary rule?" The same exam process may be illustrated by the Legal Profession course, where lawyers' professional ethical obligations under the American Bar Association's Code of Professional Responsibility are reviewed. In the exam, various actions by lawyers may be described, and the students will be asked whether such actions are deemed ethical. While both the mode of teaching and the mode of testing are compatible with practicing lawyers' need to identify legal issues in their own clients' factual circumstances, those modes will not enable lawyers to explain to clients what they are doing.

Nor are members of the legal profession encouraged to believe that it is necessary or desirable to explain to outsiders what they are doing. Many of the American Bar Association's policies are motivated by the belief that the professional activities of lawyers are too complex to be understood by the average layman. Thus, for example, there is nothing outside our regular criminal statutes to assure that lawyers will behave in an ethical manner towards their clients, other than the aforementioned Code of Professional Responsibility. Enforcement of the code is in the hands of the local State Bar Associations, and ultimately the Supreme Court of each state. Members of the American Bar Association acknowledge that many infringements of the Code are not acted upon in any way (ABA 1970), and that more effective means for enforcing the code are needed. However, the ABA is reluctant to seek public tax funds for that purpose, because this might lead to *public* involvement in assuring ethical behavior on the part of lawyers. Lawyers generally assume that the public cannot understand legal matters well enough to be able to judge lawyers' behavior in a satisfactory manner.

The American Bar Association resistance to advertising by lawyers has similarly been based in part on the view that laymen are incapable of evaluating the relative skills of those who advertise, or of picking a good product. And the ABA's advocacy of a "merit" selection system for the recruitment of judges, through which judges are initially selected by governor-appointed commissions rather than by voters, is in part similarly motivated.

Lawyers obviously have a vested interest in believing that what they do cannot be transmitted to others, because if it could, they might be out of a job. But the point here is that their own abilities and experiences also encourage them to believe their knowledge is too difficult to transmit. Not only have they themselves come by the knowledge in a somewhat agonized manner by struggling over the casebooks, but they also have not been taught how to explain the material to others. It is little wonder, then, that lawyers find it so difficult to explain to others what they do.

Discussion

If we consider the features of law school socialization that contribute to the impenetrability of legal cant, it is possible to identify some processes that may be generally relevant to our efforts to understand what aspects of socialization create barriers to general access to particular areas of cultural knowledge.

Cultural knowledge is acquired through the process of communication in face-to-face interaction. Yet until recently little attention has been given to that process by anthropologists interested in socialization. Such lack of attention may be due to our preoccupation with socialization in reading and writing. We tend to view reading and writing as communicative skills which transcend the interactional limits of space and time. In other words, we of the literate society are inclined to see writing as freeing us from the need for face-to-face interaction in acquiring cultural knowledge.

In fact, however, *all* of our formal educational processes involve some face-to-face interaction between teacher and students as a crucial part of the learning experience. Moreover, most of the things we teach through the

process of interaction are rarely learned without that process. In other words, just as it is rare to learn law without experiencing the classroom interaction of law school courses, so too is it rare to learn grade school social studies, college algebra, or graduate school research methodology simply by reading books.

The law school socialization experience I have described demonstrates the importance of interaction with the teacher in the classroom and with peers outside the classroom in acquiring the crucial ability to use the legal cant. The special organization of law school classroom interaction further demonstrates the shaping effect of face-to-face interaction organized in a particular fashion.

Most importantly for our concern with the causes of barriers to the dissemination of knowledge, we see that *the transmission of knowledge follows the lines of interaction*. Those who are cut off from the interactional contexts through which information is disseminated will have little access to that information in other contexts.

We are talking, then, about segregation—about the inclusion of *some* in the crucial learning environments (which are not just limited to the classroom) and the exclusion of *others*.

As anthropologists are well aware, segregation is a common tool of socialization. There are numerous cross-cultural examples of the segregation of particular segments of a society for the purpose of focused and concentrated socialization of those segments. The best known examples in the anthropological literature are probably those from African societies where the members of a given male adolescent age grade are isolated from their village, instructed in knowledge associated with manhood, and declared to be men at the end of the period of socialization.

The segregation intensifies the learning experience, so that the attention of the learners is not distracted by other activities and is focused on the material to be learned. Segregated learning also heightens awareness of the aspect of one's social identity that is associated with the knowledge being acquired. Thus our African adolescent males will have a surer sense of their manhood by being the only ones who have the knowledge associated with the social identity of "man." The knowledge may also be associated with exclusive access to positions of power and authority within the social system.

Where there is a concern to allow persons other than those segregated for socialization to have access to the knowledge, so that they may have access to the power, the social organization of face-to-face interaction must be altered to change the pattern of segregation.

At the same time, it is important to keep in mind that such reorganization is also likely to change the patterns of social identification within the society. Thus while some members of ethnic minority groups would like their children to acquire the knowledge necessary for upward social mobility, they also fear that the new knowledge may replace ethnic knowledge and weaken the students' sense of identity with the minority group. And in the women's movement there is a tension between the goal of acquiring knowledge that males have in order to acquire some of the same sorts of power men have, and the goal of elaborating the knowledge that women have as a way of strengthening women's sense of self worth and identity as women.

Yet the law school experience should tell us that the reorganization of face-to-face interaction would not be enough to change who has access to what information. The belief of lawyers that their knowledge is too complex to be transmitted to others otherwise than through a law school curriculum is only a slightly clearer and stronger version of similar beliefs among other professional groups in this country. Notably, educators believe that the issues they face are so complex that they cannot be explained at the local community level to the parents of ethnic minority children. That complexity is then taken as a reason for failing to involve local communities in educational decisions which affect their children.

From another point of view, we must say that educators are skilled only in certain modes of transmission of knowledge in certain contexts, and have come to consider those modes and contexts as the only ones possible. Thus educators' belief that minority parents cannot understand is, when taken in another light, an admission of their own failure to develop new teaching techniques.

Finally, to the degree that a body of knowledge is transmitted in part through a special language, and the complexity of the language is facilitated by the structural segregation of those being socialized, the language itself should change if the organization of face-to-face interaction is changed.

In sum, we see that the transmission

of cultural knowledge is dependent upon and shaped by the organization of communication in face-to-face interaction. Reorganization of interaction can alter the pattern of allocation of knowledge, but the attitudes towards who can learn what and the language used to transmit knowledge must also undergo modification, if knowledge is to be redistributed.

Lacking ethnographic methodology, it would not have been possible to articulate this organization of the transmission of culture through communication in face-to-face interaction. The final section of this paper considers the contribution of ethnography to the research process.

Methodology

Introduction

In this section I want to consider the relation between data collection methods and the type of analysis of the data that is carried out. More specifically, attention will focus on the relation between the use of ethnographic research techniques and the analysis of the role of face-to-face interaction in language socialization. My purpose here is to contribute to our understanding of the role of ethnography in the study of classroom interaction.

This section is divided into two parts. The first part reviews the changes in the meaning of the term "ethnography," as that term has been used by anthropologists, and identifies some key research techniques associated with ethnography as a research methodol-

ogy. The second part discusses the use of various ethnographic techniques in the study of classroom interaction, including my own use of participant observation as the basis for the analysis offered in this paper.

Ethnography

Since the turn of the century and the professionalization of anthropology under the influence of Franz Boas, ethnography has basically referred to the description of activities in a single society. From that time to the present, ethnography and ethnology have been contrasted as two conceptually rather different aspects of anthropological inquiry. Ethnology is the process of comparing and contrasting societies on the basis of ethnographic descriptions of each individual society. Viewed in this way, ethnography is the more workmanlike and less intellectually challenging or theoretically sophisticated activity.

The work of Goodenough (1956a, 1956b, 1957) altered the view of ethnography. Goodenough made the crucial point that ethnographic descriptions themselves are always accomplished through the employment of some sort of analytical and comparative framework developed by the anthropologist. He argued that we should take as our initial descriptive goal the characterization of culture from the natives' point of view, with greatest attention to the cognitive distinctions made by the members of the culture being studied. Those distinctions would be added to the pool of distinctions made by the social scientists, and later comparisons could be made among the cognitive distinctions used by members of different societies. Thus, while priority was given to the point of view of the members of societies over the point of view of the anthropologist, Goodenough's fundamental notion that a description always entails a selective focus and an implicit theoretical framework altered the anthropological view of ethnography.

Recently, ethnography has been discussed less as a theoretical construct and more as a methodology for gathering data. This is in part due to the introduction of ethnographic field techniques into contexts of study where they have not been used on a large scale before, most notably the context of the American classroom.

There are several general ways in which "ethnography" as a research methodology differs from other major traditions of research methodology. First, and most notably for the study described here, ethnography involves the direct and face-to-face encountering of the social processes being studied. Anthropologists go to the societies they are interested in studying and directly perceive the people and their activities that are the focus of research. That direct approach contrasts markedly with research based on what others have written, and with research based on questionnaires mailed to the subjects to be studied or to someone who has known them.

A second characteristic of ethnography is the concern to avoid altering or disrupting the social system being studied, particularly while the study is going on. That key aspect of ethnographic method contrasts most mark-

edly with the experimental approach, which involves arranging or setting up social activities so that those activities may be studied.

A third methodological feature of ethnography is the concern to obtain what might best be called in-depth knowledge of the situation being studied (Geertz 1973, Schieffelin 1979). At the most general level, that priority is reflected in the expectation that field studies in other societies be given a minimum of a full year's full-time data collection. On a more concrete level, the typical ethnographic approach to any activity is to find out about it from a number of points of view. Thus a ritual that is the focus of study will not merely be observed. It will be repeatedly observed, and both those involved in the ritual and those who observed it may be interviewed about why activities were carried out in the way they were, and how and why particular individuals were involved in the ways they were. Nor will this information simply be allowed to pass through the anthropologist's head as background information. Instead, the information is recorded in detail in field notes taken on a regular basis before it fades from mind.

A fourth feature of ethnographic methodology is the evolving nature of the methodology (Hymes 1978). Thus whereas some disciplines have their research format laid out precisely before they begin their data collection, and do not deviate from it during the process of data collection, it is understood that various approaches may be tried and abandoned in the quest for the one most appropriate to ethnographic data collection. An evolving methodology has been most necessary in cross-cultural research where anthropologists could not readily determine in advance what they would be able to do among people in a society they knew very little about.

There are several specific methods associated with ethnography that are particularly compatible with the concern to have direct contact with the phenomenon being studied and the concern to avoid disrupting the processes being studied. The method most closely associated with anthropological inquiry is "participant observation."

In the strictest sense of its meaning, participant observation refers to the simultaneous occupation of a structural position within a social system and study of that system. Anthropologists, for example, sometimes are assigned positions within the kinship systems of the local communities they live in. We speak of participating and observing what we participate in at the same time.

While that is the central conceptualization of "participant observation," in practice the term is used to refer loosely to a variety of activities, ranging from living among the people studied, as Malinowski did, to engaging in the same activities as the people studied are engaged in.

"Observation" is distinguished from participant observation by the fact that interactionally the observer's role is more one of reception of communicative behavior than the participant observer's role. Therein lies its chief virtue: it is possible to receive more information when one is not obliged to produce it. It is, of course, necessary that an observer's role be culturally permissible and socially appropriate for that mode of data collection to be used.

Recordings of various sorts, including audiotapes, videotapes, and films, can be seen as tools of observation of face-to-face interaction. Although some people assume recorders cause those recorded to alter their behavior, in fact those observed can't do what they are there for if they change much. Recording as a method of data collection is consequently very compatible with the anthropological emphasis on the need to disrupt the social process as little as possible while studying it.

Those who focus on classroom interaction as a phenomenon (e.g., Mehan 1979; Cazden 1970; Cazden, et al. 1977; Erickson and Mohatt MS; McDermott 1976; Philips 1979) do so because they believe that the educational process is located in face-to-face interaction. They also believe that an understanding of educational "problems" is to be derived from the study of classroom interaction. Both of those beliefs suggest that sociologists have succeeded in convincing people interested in the educational process that what goes on in face-to-face interaction somehow matters.

The Present Study

The data on which this paper is based are primarily from a gathering of information through participant observation. In the rest of this section, I will discuss my experiences as a participant observer, focusing on the relation between the mode of data collection I used and the kind of analysis of interaction that was possible with that data. I will also consider the sort of analysis that would have been possible had I relied more heavily on other modes of data collection.

My primary purpose in attending law school was to acquire enough knowledge of the law to do research on language use in courtrooms. I wanted to do research that I felt could not be done without such knowledge.

Much of what I had seen and heard during my first exploratory courtroom observations in the fall of 1975 was incomprehensible to varying degrees. I couldn't tell how much of my noncomprehension was due to my not knowing what law schools teach. My efforts to question lawyers about what I had seen led them repeatedly into explanations *they* had gotten in law school. It seemed more efficient to get such information from law school itself.

I had already decided I wanted to study judges' use of language in the courtroom. I expected to acquire knowledge in law school that would have bearing on that research. For example, I was interested in the relationship between judges' behavior in the courtroom and the way they are perceived and evaluated by lawyers. Accordingly, I hoped to learn what sorts of attitudes towards judges are conveyed through law school socialization.

Once I began to attend first-year law school classes, mainly in first-year courses, I found myself thinking more generally about the socialization of lawyers and about the contribution of the organization of classroom interaction to that process. Such a focus was stimulated in part by my earlier research on the organization of interaction in North American Indian classrooms (Philips 1979).

I envisioned myself as a participant observer, in the sense of being one who occupied a position in the structure of the social process I was studying from the beginning of my year (1977–78) as a law student. Mehan (1979) and Cazden (1977) had just completed a year-long study of a classroom in which Mehan and his students had functioned as observers and Cazden had functioned as a participant observer in the role of the classroom teacher, so it was natural for me to think of myself in this light. Accordingly, I tried to act like a student as much as possible.

At the same time, there were some limits to my functioning as a student. Although I took the courses for credit and grades as a way of making myself do the work, I had not applied to be a law student through the regular selection process, but rather received permission to take courses as a special student. I did not receive the mailed information from the law school bureaucracy that the regular students did and was not included in class rank calculations. I chose my courses and instructors rather than being required to take particular courses from particular teachers.

Almost invariably my status as a special student came out when first-year students assumed, by virtue of my status as a first-year student, that I shared information with them which I did not in fact have, because my experience was different from theirs. This might come out through as simple a question as "Who do you have for Property?" when I wasn't taking the Property course.

By virtue of my conscious efforts to be a participant observer, my behavior was different from what it would otherwise have been, but only in a limited number of ways. I attended the orientation sessions for first-year students at the beginning of the school year to see more of the first-year students' experience than I would have otherwise. I went to the first meetings of student organizations in which I would have had an interest or did have an interest as a student. And I continued to participate in the activities of the Law Women's organization through the first semester, because I enjoyed it.

For a few months I kept a journal in which I wrote down both descriptive material and analysis of the socialization process in which I was involved. During class time, I wrote down as many verbatim question and answer sequences as I could without losing the substance or content of what was being said. But after the first half of the semester, this activity was carried out only in fits and starts rather than with any systematicity.

I frequented the coffee room and law library in the law school building and talked to law students. But I participated very little in the off-campus social life of the law school students. I did not know how to do that with ease. Moreover, my need to sustain my own social and professional networks in the community left me without strong motivation to become involved in student social life.

Yet, as a student, I became less of an observer and more of a participant as the year went on. I experienced the feelings of inadequacy as a law student that many students talked about. I expressed privately to other students my dissatisfaction that there was so little

room in the classroom for the expression of simple moral outrage where the direction of the law was in conflict with one's own political ideology. Like many law students, I came to have a favorite U.S. Supreme Court Justice (Harlan), whose written opinions I relished for their elegance and clarity. I did *not* devote mental energy to trying to decide whether I really wanted to be a lawyer, as some students did. I knew I didn't want to be a lawyer. However, I recognized the process as one I had gone through as a graduate student.

As the pressure mounted to devote more time to getting the actual daily school work for my courses done, I felt I had to make a choice between my primary and secondary purposes in going to law school. I had to choose between absorbing whatever the teachers thought I should absorb and analyzing what was going on from a sociolinguistic perspective. I chose to give priority to that primary concern with making myself into as much of a lawyer as I could in one year.

Thus, after one semester, data collection that I would have pursued, had I given priority to my role as a researcher and observer, was not pursued. For example, I wished to explore further, but did not, the nature of the variation in the process of questioning and answering in the classroom. I wanted to try to determine what could account for or explain that variation. I would have liked to explain variation from one teacher to another and variation in the ways the teachers interacted with different students.

Examination of such variation would have required some systematic tape-recording and transcription of classroom interaction. That process would have required time which I wanted to use for acquiring the substance of the materials in the law school courses. More research on the law school classroom would also have deterred me from my initial commitment to a study of judges' use of language in the courtroom. Accordingly, I did not undertake the further research on the smaller-scale level of classroom organization.

It may be useful at this point to compare the advantages and disadvantages of participant observation as against observation and recording in the analysis of classroom interaction, assuming that in any classroom research greater or lesser time will be spent in one form of data gathering than in another.

It is clear that participant observation does enable the investigator to see things from at least one structural position of membership in the system being studied and to acquire in-depth knowledge of whatever persons in that position must know to maintain the position.

In my own research, I was not concerned to function in the interpretive mode of the Geertzian tradition of anthropology, through which the anthropologist conveys to anthropologists and others how the culturally distinctive population studied manages and views daily life. Nor was I focused on the sociological and phenomenological concern to identify the interpretive procedures used by members of the social category I occupied, to make sense out of the actions of others.

However, I did benefit considerably from the in-depth access to the socialization process that my position as a student allowed. There were certain fea-

tures of the socialization process that would not have been available to me or present in my analysis of that process, had I not labored diligently as a student. I would not have been able to understand how the different ways in which students are exposed to the legal cant mesh together. The relation between the written and spoken sources of knowledge would not have been as readily available to me. I would not have understood the briefing process used in courses to cover case materials, or the role of that process in the replication of courtroom interaction. If I hadn't been a student in the classrooms I observed, I would not have had the contextualized shared knowledge that made verbal interaction intelligible and comprehensible.

At the same time, I was limited in my inquiry as a participant observer by my need to fulfill my role as a *participant*. I was unable to analyze interactional structure at its more microcosmic levels because I did not carry out recording and spend time examining the record and questioning participants about it.

On the other hand, I was able to carry out analysis of a higher or more general level of the structure of socialization for language use through interaction than would have been available by examination of audio and video tapes alone.

In the use of recordings for the analysis of the structure of interaction, it is important to be sure that one is not trying to analyze a phenomenon of which there is only one instance recorded or analyzed. Harvey Sacks (1967) was able to use a single therapy session between a therapist and several adolescent males to illustrate certain properties of conversation because those properties were evident over and over again in a single encounter. Had he tried instead to delineate the nature of group therapy sessions from a single session, he would have faced a much higher probability of mistaking features of limited occurrence for features of more general occurrence.

One of the ways in which that problem of too limited a data base can be overcome is to combine firsthand participant observation and observation with the analysis of recordings. The investigator who mixes data collection methods has the advantage of the diverse perspectives they offer. Yet each researcher will give priority to some data sources over others on the basis of the level of structure focused upon and the type of analysis to be carried out.

In the present instance, the heavy reliance on participant observation facilitated a broader and more integrated view of the language socialization process, but limited the opportunity for close scrutiny of the structure of the interaction, which would have been afforded greater scope by more observation and by recording.

Summary

The sociological tradition of the study of social interaction focuses on the naturalistic description of interaction and the interpretive procedures used to make sense of interaction. Ethnographic research procedures are compatible with those concerns because the procedures are oriented toward non-manipulative direct perception of the processes being studied. And the ethnographic study of face-to-face interaction enables us to learn more about how language socialization and, more generally, the transmission of culture are accomplished through interaction.

Notes

[1] Legal cant is partially known to clerks, bailiffs, court reporters, legal secretaries, and police officers. Those legal co-workers, however, also find large portions of legal cant inaccessible.

[2] Cicourel (1970) in turn has conveyed the anthropological orientation of Goodenough, Hymes, and Gumperz to sociologists.

[3] This information can be represented in a grammar by the lexical entry of each lexical item, but only in part.

[4] The format entails both verbal and nonverbal role-differentiated behavior.

[5] Note that the *pairing* of adversaries which pervades the courts is also lacking in the law school classroom, except in the Moot Court course.

[6] One law school professor has suggested that the younger teachers may not in fact differ that much from the older teachers, because they must follow *some* model of teaching, and they follow their own older teachers.

References

Agar, M. 1973. *Ripping and Running: A Formal Ethnography of Urban Heroin Addicts.* New York: Seminar Press.

American Bar Association. 1970. *Problems and Recommendations in Disciplinary Enforcement.* ABA Special Committee on Evaluation of Disciplinary Enforcement (also known as *The Clark Report*).

Cazden, C. 1970. "The Situation: A Neglected Source of Difference in Language Use." *The Journal of Social Issues,* 26:2, 35–60.

Cazden, C., M. Cox, D. Dickenson, Z. Steinberg, and C. Stone. In press. "'You All Gonna Hafta Listen': Peer Teaching in a Primary Classroom." To appear in W. A. Collins, ed., *Children's Language and Communication.* Hillsboro: L. Eilbarn.

Cicourel, A. 1970. "The Acquisition of Social Structure: Toward a Developmental Sociology of Language and Meaning." In J. Douglas, ed., *Understanding Everyday Life.* Chicago: Aldine, 136–168.

Dente, J. 1974. "A Century of Case Method: An Apologia." *Washington Law Review,* 50:93–107.

Erickson, F. 1979. "Talking Down: Some Cultural Sources of Miscommunication in Interracial Interviews." In A. Wolfgang, ed., *Nonverbal Behavior.* New York: Academic Press, 99–126.

————, and G. Mohatt. MS. *Participant Structures at School and at Home on an Odawa Indian Reservation.* Final Technical Report to the Canadian Ministry of Education.

Garfinkel, H. 1967. *Studies in Ethnomethodology.* Englewood Cliffs, NJ: Prentice-Hall, Inc.

Geertz, C. 1973. *The Interpretation of Cultures.* New York: Basic Books.

Goffman, E. 1963. *Behavior in Public Places.* New York: Macmillan Company.

————. 1964. "The Neglected Situation." In J. Gumperz and D. Hymes, eds., "The Ethnography of Communication." *American Anthropologist,* 66:6 (Part 2, special issue), 133–136.

————. 1972. *Relations in Public.* New York: Harper & Row.

Goodenough, W. 1956a. "Residence Rules." *Southwestern Journal of Anthropology,* 12:22–37.

————. 1956b. "Componential Analysis and the Study of Meaning." *Language,* 32:195–216.

————. 1957. "Cultural Anthropology and Linguistics." In P. Garvin, ed., *Report of the Seventh Annual Round Table Meeting on Linguistics and Language Study* (Monograph Series on Languages and Linguistics, No. 9). Washington: Georgetown University Press.

————. 1976. "Multi-Culturalism as the Normal Human Experience." In M. A. Gibson, ed., "Anthropological Perspectives on Multi-Cultural Education," *Anthropology and Education Quarterly,* 7:4:4–7.

Gumperz, J., and D. Hymes, eds., 1964. "The Ethnography of Communication." *American Anthropologist,* 66:6 (Part 2).

Gumperz, J., and D. Hymes. 1972. *Directions in Sociolinguistics.* New York: Holt, Rinehart and Winston.

Hymes, D. 1962. "The Ethnography of Speaking." In T. Gladwin and W. C. Sturtevant, eds., *Anthropology and Human Behavior.* Washington: Anthropological Society of Washington.

————. 1978. *What Is Ethnography?* Sociolinguistic Working Paper Number 45. Austin, TX: Southwest Educational Development Laboratory.

Keenan, E. D., and B. Schieffelin. 1976. "Topic as a Discourse Notion: A Study of Topic in the Conversations of Children and Adults." In C. Li, ed., *Subject and Topic.* New York: Academic Press, 337–385.

McDermott, R. P. 1974. "Achieving School Failure." In G. Spindler, ed., *Education and Cultural Process.* New York: Holt, Rinehart and Winston.

————. 1976. *Kids Make Sense: An Ethnographic Account of the Interactional Management of Success and Failure in One First Grade Classroom.* Unpublished Ph.D. dissertation, Department of Anthropology, Stanford University.

Mehan, H. 1979. *Learning Lessons.* Cambridge: Harvard University Press.

Philips, S. 1976. "Some Sources of Cultural Variability in the Regulation of Talk." *Language in Society,* 5:1:89–95.

———. 1979. *The Invisible Culture: Communication in Classroom and Community on the Warm Springs Indian Reservation.* In press.

Sacks, H. 1967. *Lecture Notes.* UCLA.

———, E. Schegloff, and G. Jefferson. 1974. "A Simplest Systematics for the Organization of Turn-taking for Conversation." *Language,* 50:696–735.

Schieffelin, B. 1979. "Getting It Together: An Ethnographic Approach to the Study of the Development of Communicative Competence." In E. Ochs and B. Schieffelin, eds., *Developmental Pragmatics.* New York: Academic Press.

Sieber, R. T. 1978. "Schooling, Socialization, and Group Boundaries: A Study of Informal Social Relations in the Public Domain." *Urban Anthropology,* 7(1): 67–98.

Spradley, James. 1970. *You Owe Yourself a Drunk: An Ethnography of Urban Nomads.* Boston: Little, Brown and Co.

7

Hervé Varenne

Jocks and Freaks: The Symbolic Structure of the Expression of Social Interaction Among American Senior High School Students

Hervé Varenne

The Author

Hervé Varenne, born and raised in France, is associate professor of education at Teachers College, Columbia University. He received his doctorate from the Department of Anthropology at the University of Chicago in 1972. There he was strongly encouraged by Milton Singer and David Schneider to follow his inclination and do extensive field work in the United States on those groups and situations where one might expect to see American culture realized.

Varenne has done field work in a Midwestern town, in a suburban high school, and on a middle-class urban family. The results of his first investigation have been published in *Americans Together: Structured Diversity in a Midwestern Town* (Teachers College Press, 1977) and in several articles. He has published articles on his work in the high school and he is now completing a full-length monograph on it. More recently he has been working with Clifford Hill, a sociolinguist, on a book in which they analyze a familial conversation. Varenne says of himself:

"Friends with whom I was initiated into professional anthropology at the University of Chicago told me later that I was then in total culture shock. Indeed I should have been, since I was living for the first time in the United States by myself. For the first time I was outside my family's fold. I could barely speak English and my writing was not much better. But I did not quite know yet that there was such a thing as culture shock and, to this day, I am not certain that it is an appropriate term to describe what happened to me then. One thing that did happen was that I got hooked into cultural anthropology (I had come to Chicago for its archaeology program) and I found 'symbolic' approaches most congenial, particularly those where the Durkheimian/Saussurian/structuralist tradition dominated, as against the Weberian/phenomenological tradition. Another thing that happened that first year in Chicago was that, in my search for real-life material which I could use to confront the theories I was learning to discuss, I turned regularly to details of the American life I was also discovering. Milton Singer encouraged this curiosity. He convinced some of the more reticent of his colleagues that it was time for 'foreign' anthropologists to do to Americans what Americans had been doing to others and that there might be validity to my contention that there was such a thing as 'American culture' (and that such a thing could be found in downstate Illinois, an even more controversial assumption of mine!).

"How this work, eventually published in my first book, *Ameri-*

cans Together, led me to the ethnography of schooling is a matter for which I cannot claim much more responsibility than I can claim for having become a cultural anthropologist (I still find it hard to adopt the voluntaristic stance so common in American biographies). I happened to be looking for a job when the Department of Family and Community Education at Teachers College was looking for an anthropologist. I was invited to teach in the department and to participate in the project on the social organization of schools for which Professors Francis Ianni and Hope Leichter had received a grant.

"Quite a lot could have happened that would have taken me upon different roads. But, in my years at Teachers College, I have come to realize that schools are in fact good places to check and refine the therories that were developed after encounters with the very alien. They are very good places because they are environments relatively limited in size which can still be explored holistically. More important, they are 'focused' institutions and as such can help the anthropologists to concentrate on and deal more systematically with a set of data, since many sources of variation are controlled. But mostly schools can provide anthropologists with situations where they can test the generalizations they have been making about human beings. Fifty years ago Margaret Mead went to Samoa to test psychological generalizations. In these years we have done much more than test other disciplines' theories. We have developed our own, and are very willing to phrase them in general, universalistic terms. We must now come back home and see how the shoe fits—for the good of the discipline and for the good also of the people to whom we belong, our own."

This Chapter

Cliques are the building blocks in the literature on informal social organization in schools. Previous writings of note have described cliques as concrete entities with members and identifiable boundary markers such as dress, grooming, and mannerisms. In this chapter Hervé Varenne provides quite a different analysis. He acknowledges that if he had proceeded to the analysis armed with the concepts of social organization other researchers have used he would probably have come out about where they have. The kind of evidence they used to establish cliques is, Varennes believes, present among and exhibited by the Sheffield High School students he and his coworkers observed and interviewed.

But Varenne does not use the concepts other workers have used. He follows a line of inquiry and interpretation that connects to Lévi-Strauss and symbolic analysis. Though he "sees" differences in dress and casual groupings about the school, he attends to what students *say* about each other, that is, the symbols, particularly in self-other references using personal pronouns. This kind of attention produces for him, and for us, his readers, quite a different picture of school social "organization"—a fluid and ambiguous one in which social assignments of oneself or others are treated with considerable ambivalence and ambiguity.

I leave it to the reader to discover what Varenne is saying and how he says it. Of greatest importance to us is that the theoretical model used by Varenne leads him to a very different interpretation of social "reality" than he would have evolved, reacting to the same phenomena, if he had utilized conventional concepts of social structure and organization. This demonstrates a point that is essential to the whole ethnographic enterprise as it is presented in this volume. "Ethnography" does not stand by itself as an independent data-producing procedure. What the ethnographer discovers is determined not only by how he or she proceeds to observe and interrogate, but also by what is observed and interrogated about. The *what* more than the *how* is determined by the model of relationships and meanings held by the investigator in his or her brain. Without this model of meanings and relationships the ethnographer is a mindless machine going nowhere.

Introduction

One of the few matters on which there seems to be an essential consensus in the sociology of American high schools concerns the organization of the student body into cliques. The "discovery" can be traced at least as far back as the first ethnographics of high schools (Hollingshead 1949, Gordon 1957, Coleman 1961). They made much of the fact that students in these schools did not socialize randomly with each other but that there were definite patterns which the students themselves somehow perceived in that they could talk about them. Student bodies were found to be divided into "cliques" which seemed rather easy to describe in their sociological substance. These cliques could be labeled. Students could be assigned to them on the basis of supposedly objective tests. And the groups made up from these tests could then serve as stable variables on which complex statistical procedures could rest.

Since the pioneering studies, a clique analysis has been a common-sense matter that has ceased to be considered problematic (Henry 1963, Cusik 1973, Palonsky 1975, Clement and Harding 1978). There is evidence of some historical and geographical variation in the labels of the cliques, the ensemble of symbols which are used to mark the distinctiveness of the clique, or the exact placement of the boundaries. People also mention the possibility of variation in the "strength" of the cliques in a particular school. But many matters have remained stable over the past 30 years for which we have somewhat comparable information: everywhere, it seems, students who are active in sports are identified as a separate category of some sort. So are the students who are good scholars, the students who protest the system in a publicly defiant manner, the students whose parents are prominent in the town, and those who are the children of the poorest people. In multiethnic or multiracial districts the situation can become even more complicated, but the main lines are still there.

The initial work was produced under the influence of theories of social structure which have greatly evolved since. This evolution, and new thinking about the organization of human relationships, has not yet been systematically represented in the literature. It is time for a new look. I do not believe, however, in the utility of radical reinterpretations. Coleman and the others did not manufacture their original experiences. They certainly saw something, and I can say immediately that I had experiences in Sheffield High School that I believe to be essentially the same ones as those which Hollingshead, Gordon, Coleman, et al., and their teams lived through when they conducted their own fieldwork. The students performed something in front of them, they told them certain things, and, later, when

the original experiences were solidified into survey questions, the students could still answer questions about who were their best friends, whom they admired, whom they in fact spent time with, and so on. Given all the evidence of the difficulties anthropologists confront when they try to give questionnaires devised *a priori* to people who have a different culture from those who drafted the questionnaire, the very fact that students could answer suggests that the questionnaires were tapping something that had validity in the students' own experience.

My discussion will be based on fieldwork which two students and I conducted in a surburban high school in 1972–1973. Very soon we did discover the cliques which we fully expected we would find. But as the year passed the fluidity and fuzziness of the phenomenon imposed itself as something which could not be dismissed. This led me to question the process of discovery and to look more carefully at the experiences we had in the field which led us sometimes to see and sometimes not to see the cliques. I am talking here, not simply of a return to the data, but of a return to the ever more fundamental moments when the data were generated.

What was happening at these moments? Students were *talking*. Almost never did we "purely" observe. We always listened, and we conducted extensive interviews. Thus, all of our data were mediated by symbolic processes. And even when we "just observed," our data collection method was field notes, that is, *written* reports. In all this we followed the sociological and anthropological tradition. The data we generated were of the same type as those

---

---

used by all researchers in schools from Hollingshead onward. Indeed, there is no reason why we should not collect such data, since talk was a fundamental part of the total experience our informants had of themselves. There never were "pure" encounters between social groups in the school; all encounters possessed a symbolic element which participated in constituting the situation. Someone interested in purely social organizational processes might thus have been led to heed Harris' advice (1964) and move away altogether from talk. Such a purely ethnological study might in fact be extremely interesting and yield new insights. My goal here is different. What I want to understand is the exact source of the perception that observers (including the participants) have that cliques sometimes are there and sometimes are not there. What is it, in the symbolic encounters, that suggests the presence of cliques and then dissipates the image as the wind sweeps away a fog?

Sheffield and Its High School

First, a few ethnographic details must be set down. They form the immediate situation of the students, their environment—what is often called their "context," though I would like to reserve this word for a more technical use. It is within this environment that they operate. This environment also offers the props which they need to stage their dramatic performances.

The town of Sheffield has only one high school, the one I studied. It is a geographically small suburb (2.3 square miles) in the massive Northeastern suburban belt. In 1972–1973, when the fieldwork was conducted, about 10,000 people lived there. Only three of these were black. The average family income was close to $18,000. Only 2 percent of all families had incomes lower than the poverty level. Sheffield was built as a suburb in the 1920s and 1930s and thus had lost the raw quality of more recent suburbs. In terms of class and ethnicity, at least, it is certain that Sheffield stands at an extreme of homogeneity rather rare in the United States. But this, in fact, makes all the evidence of the presence of group segmentation even more fascinating. There were five major religious denominations: Presbyterian, Methodist, Congregational, Episcopal, and Roman Catholic. There were many clubs. There were Republicans and Democrats.

These groupings did not have a direct role in the students' life in the school, to the extent, at least, that little mention was made of them. In school other things were mentioned. To understand these, a few more things need be said. There were about 700 students in the school, a fourth of these seniors. The overall organization of their daily routine was directed by the adults who determined the classes they had to take, the periods during which they could have lunch, and so on. The adults also directed the students in less explicit ways through their own lifestyle choices. There were teachers who were conservative and others who were liberal. There were teachers who were glad to talk about sports at length and others who refused to discuss the topic. Finally, the adults gave the students a complex building which, surprisingly for a modern construction, offered various types of spaces that various groups could call their own. For example, there were the many tables in the cafeteria, there were nearly a dozen small and only intermittently occupied offices in the library, there were the guidance office and the nurses' office. There were the bathrooms, isolated stairway landings, the backstage area in the auditorium. There were hidden spots on the grounds—behind bushes, in a drainage ditch. All these spaces had "formal" functions, but their character and the frequency of their intended uses were such that they could be put to alternative uses.

I do not have to stress that there is much variation in the force of the inherent constraints in any of these situations on the ability of the students to manipulate them. Students could try to shift lunch period, to drop a class in favor of another one. But their range was severely limited in these matters. They could do more with the variation in the adults' lifestyle choices. But they were still limited here, both by the need for reciprocity on the part of the teacher and by the fact that the teacher remained a teacher in a structurally different position from theirs. The building, on the other hand, was a shell that allowed an extended range of symbolic discriminations.

This is worth developing. What I have just said about the building also applies to the social organization of any space within the building. Take the cafeteria, a large hall that could seat about 200 students around tables of 10. These tables could be arranged in two basic ways, either as islands or in rows. In both cases the effective range for easy face-to-face communication was severely limited. Beyond the 10 students who could sit around a single table, relaxed conversation became difficult, if only because one had to raise one's voice beyond propriety or even physical feasibility because of the noise level during lunch periods. This is important since, as we shall see, the easiest rule of thumb for recognizing the existence of a clique is: "The people who sit together regularly for lunch are a clique." I suspect that this is indeed the rule which the students themselves followed. Outside of the lunch periods the same students might also congregate, though they were less restricted. Little groups could be found in various nooks and corners of the building, and soon the space they regularly occupied became somehow identified with them. In the same manner there was a strong tendency for the same groups to sit at the same tables each lunch.

During the times when they were not required to be in a class, the students thus continually had to make decisions about where to go or where to sit. By ordinary right they could be in only three places: the "commons" (outside of lunch periods the cafeteria room was available under this name for students who did not want to study during the free periods in their daily schedule), the library, or a study hall. By extraordinary right, most often by virtue of membership in some special "club," students could be found in the private offices in the back of the library, in the coordinators' office, in the room where the audiovisual equipment was kept, in the guidance office, in the central office, in the nurses' office, or even in certain classrooms as teachers' aides. By self-proclaimed right, students might also be found in the bathrooms for very long periods of time not solely dedicated to the satisfaction of biological functions or on the stairway landing from which the roof could be reached, in the band room or the auditorium, on outside steps at the most remote back door of the building, in the bushes further away from the school, and even not in school at all.

The Discovery of the Cliques

One member of my team was a Jewish woman who attended Protestant schools in New York City. Another was a WASP-ish man raised in central Pennsylvania, where he attended the public schools. All of us saw the movie *American Graffiti* while conducting the fieldwork. As for me, a Frenchman who had only been in the States for five years, I had just finished writing a dissertation on my experiences in clique-like groups in a Midwestern town. It did not take us more than a few days to "discover" that there were indeed cliques in Sheffield, to identify the main members of the various cliques, and to adopt, in our field notes, the labels which then seemed totally appropriate. We talked of the "jocks" and the "freaks" with great ease. There was no culture shock. It was only later, as we started interviewing and as we began to know the school better, that we realized that things were in fact more complicated.

In field notes written by one of us, the initial process can be followed in a very revealing way. The first day, he simply reports that he sat with several groups of "seniors"—as he put it—some of whom told him that they were on the football or hockey teams. Over the course of the day he talked with four groups of students. Given that presence in the cafeteria was predicated on scheduling, it couldn't be ascertained whether these groups were more than ad hoc transient phenomena. The following day things became "clearer." The fieldworker recognized students and named them in his notes. Of the first group, he writes, "These boys were the freaks." While talking of another group, he writes that "they" (no reference to a name) "had seen Patricia [the other fieldworker] in the area for the lungs." These notes were written at the end of the day after several hours of interaction with the students and particularly after a long conversation with a student who

> introduced me to the idea of the lungs, namely, a group referred to as the long hair or freaks. They got their nickname from a Jethro Tull album called "Aqualung" where a freak appears with an aqualung on the front cover. I was informed that the lungs were responsible for wrecking the school lounge and that you could tell a lung, not only by their long hair, but by the fact that they wore flannel shirts and jeans. I noticed that Chris Borden, a first-string football player, was wearing a flannel shirt and jeans, but he was not sitting with the lungs. [T1]

When he wrote of the first group of students he met that day, he said that they were "freaks." There is in fact no evidence that this observation was a logical deduction from his observation of a pattern of behavior. Later, in fact, he is careful to note that at least one football player was dressed the way the freaks are supposed to dress. Nor is there any evidence that it is the "freaks" who suggested to him their own identification. What seems to have happened that day was that many students told him that another group of students, those with whom he and the other field worker had been seen earlier, were freaks. Later in the field notes, the other groups was labeled "jock." But it is a label *which they too do not seem to have volunteered*. What they had volunteered was the name of the other groups.

This is a general point. All the students we talked to could and generally were also willing to talk about cliques in the school. They could disagree among themselves about certain aspects of the actual organization. They could discuss whether a person was or was not a member of a clique, and whether cliques were stronger or weaker than they used to be or than they were in other schools they knew. But they did understand each other enough to continue such conversations and to be able to answer our inquiries. It would be easy for me to accumulate examples. "Jocks and freaks" was one of the subjects which students were most willing to talk to us about. We have many pages of interview transcript on the topic. However, this predominance was partially a fabrication of our interest and of the essential safeness of the topic. There was little emotional involvement and no reluctance. The other two topics that interested us and about which we got less and less were the relationship of the students with their teachers and male-female relationships. We tried to make all interviewees talk about the latter topic. Almost all refused, more or less directly.

I would thus not try to evaluate how "important" cliques were in the school. Various students had various opinions on this topic; the same individual sometimes told us different things at different points in the interview. It remains that the clique experience *was* a favorite topic. All students could provide broad sketches. Some—perhaps more observant or more imaginative—could describe very complex and slightly fantastic pictures. There was much disagreement about the details of these pictures. The membership lists varied from student to student. But there was enough agreement for the broad sweep of the pictures to be recognizable as somehow representing Sheffield.

I mentioned earlier that there is no evidence, in our field notes, that students ever volunteered *their own* identification.[1] They identified other students. These other students eventually identified them, and it is only through this process of triangulation that we, as observers, could come to a conclusion as to "who" the first students were. It is not that students did not know how they were identified by other students. Most of the students we talked to were very sophisticated, and they would discuss in great detail their own situation. Let us listen to Maureen Travers:

Maureen Travers said that people have certain interests and so they hang around with each other. She said therefore people with similar interests hang around together. She said, however, that this does not really divide people. She said that when she sees jocks and freaks drinking and smoking together at parties, she knows that the so-called division is a fallacy. In school, she said the jocks and freaks segregate themselves because they are pursuing different interests and therefore would not tend to be in the same place at the same time. Outside of school, however, the jocks and freaks are together. She then noted that all of the people in Sheffield have a lot in common because they are all from the same type of families and the same background. [T2]

In another situation she specifically denied that she and her "loose group of friends" labeled themselves anything. She then told George Singer, one of these friends, that other people knew him as jock (probably because of his habit of wearing a suit and tie to school and because he had applied to West Point). On another occasion *he* had told us that he was "nothing." He was also seen regularly with the student government president and his friends, who were known by some as "freaks" and who regularly expressed ultraliberal political sentiments. As least one student did in fact list him with the freaks.

Things were actually even more complex. There were students who were so universally known that they could not escape the label. Students in the corridor would whisper "jock" when they walked by. They would read graffiti in the bathrooms about how they should cut their hair and get clean. The star of the basketball team, Paul Taft, was in this position. He was undoubtedly a gifted athlete. He was the first student in the high school's history to have scored more than 1000 points during his career. Also in this position was Abe Stevenson, whose hair fell below his shoulders, who came to school only in dubiously clean jeans, and who constantly talked of bucking the authorities. Paul Taft was *the* jock for anybody but himself and his closest friends. Abe Stevenson was *the* freak

for anybody but, again, himself and his closest friends. Abe Stevenson told us that he was "a loner" who stayed mostly "by himself" and that he was in fact "a jock at heart." Paul Taft told us the same things, in reverse:

> But those people that want to get away from it, those that are, you know, use *the system with a derogatory tone in their* voice, are the ones that are the freaks, the radicals, the outsiders. I don't look at them as outsiders because I am part of that myself. I think a lot of the freaks ... [T3]

All this indicates that several things are going on at the same time. All the students act. All of them have friends (except for a very few true loners). All can talk about cliques. It is these phenomena that lead observers to talk about cliques and then reify them for analytic manipulation. My question is: Do these phenomena justify that step?

The Social Function of Clique Identification

Before we move on, I would like to provide other types of ethnographic detail to illustrate how clique identification was used in actual interaction. What I have talked about until now has been based essentially on *reflections* of the informants on their situation. What do they in fact do? I mentioned earlier the definite tendency of students not to interact randomly. Some students *were* always seen together, certain spaces *were* known as the private turf of a particular clique. For a few months in the fall, for example, the guidance office became an informal "jock" lounge until the adults intervened after complaints by other students that they could not get to talk to the guidance personnel. A few girls continually complained that they could not use the bathroom because of the atmosphere certain students created there. Even though we did not, in fact, chart networks as Coleman might have done, I have a sense that similar methods would have yielded comparable results.

Other aspects of the situation must also be mentioned, for they will mitigate the impression of rigidity which the summary picture I just presented might suggest. A clique was never an immediately apprehensible reality. Cliques never walked down corridors like phalanxes. They did not have a sanctioned distinctiveness. All the diacritic marks which students did use to differentiate between the cliques (the length of the hair, dress, bodily stance, speech style, expressed attitudes, etc.) could be used by people who did not belong to the clique which was normally symbolized by a particular pattern of these markers. They might sometimes even be used by members of the opposite cliques: all male students, for example, whatever their clique affiliation, were photographed in a suit and tie for the pictures that appeared in the yearbook. This means that mistakes could be made about the identification of certain students (Jack Saario, who saw himself as "the last freak," was seen as a member of the "brain trust" by Roy Carter, and was not seen often with either of the two friendship groups with a highly freakish appearance). It also means that students could deny their most obvious clique identification by emphasizing the fact that particular markers generally associated with an-

other clique in fact applied to them. Thus Taft could justify his self-identification with the freaks on the basis of the facts that he liked the hardest, most advanced rock music and had very liberal political views.

Cliques did have a certain political reality. The distribution of the turf was not a mechanical affair. Certain spaces were preferred, and conflicts could develop over the control of such spaces. I will now present a particularly vivid case in which certain students (students who would have been identified by others as the female counterparts of the jocks, "the most cliquish group in the school" as many other students told us, a "nice, open informal group of friends" as the girls themselves told us) struggled for the creation of something which they labeled, very significantly, a *senior* lounge.

When we first arrived in the school, one of the first things we were told (see T1) was that the "lungs" had destroyed the "senior lounge" that had been set up the year before in a hallway with a few second-hand couches and chairs from the teachers' lounge, which had been renovated. At the end of the year things were in a state of disarray, the furniture was "destroyed," and the administration cleared the space; the following year "the seniors had no place to go," as some of them complained. The people who complained were not numerous but were very visible. They raised the issue at most of the student council meetings and at the "senior luncheons" (when the principal talked informally over lunch with a group of seniors). The administration was noncommittal. The girls who were at the forefront of the protest were the same girls who said that it would be "bad news" if freaks lingered in the guidance office, which, during the first part of the year, was used by them as an informal gathering place (until they were ejected by the guidance staff). By implication they had stated that they were *not freaks*. But what was it that they presented themselves as, positively?

Let us look at extracts from a very controlled text (an article in the school paper by a student named Morrison) where stylistic stereotypification could be maintained to the highest degree:

> ... For three years the seniors had a lounge of their own.... In the three years since its inception, the senior lounge has been a tremendous catastrophe. Many will disagree ... less than ten percent of the seniors have used the lounge.... [T4]

To talk about jocks and freaks in such a setting would have been totally unacceptable. Morrison had to elevate his style in certain systemic ways. How did he do this? What he did was to construct two groups: "the seniors" and "ten percent of the seniors." The first group is a total universe where no further divisions are suggested except for one, the "ten percent" who have seceded by adopting a mode of behavior antithetical to the mass's interest, something which justifies an attempt at rejection and punitive control on the part of the policing authorities.

Given what everybody knew about the school, this constructed social structure might appear totally fantastic. This particular way of dealing with the incident hid as much of the reality of the school as it made manifest. The article,

like most statements by the proponents of the lounge, was politically manipulative, and we could talk of "false consciousness" in a quasi-Marxist sense. The jock girls were not really interested in a "senior" lounge, as they would always put it, using the universalistic label as their positive identity, but a *jock* lounge which, as we were once told, freaks would be forbidden to enter. I also suspect that what happened the year before was not that the freaks "destroyed" the lounge but that they appropriated it to themselves and made it freak-like, which made it unacceptable for the jocks (and also for the school administration, since the lounge was located in a place where it was the first thing seen by parents—the most vocal of whom were rather conservative—when visiting the school). However, and this is a major theme of my whole study, the socio-psychological "reality" of the senior lounge as it was raised by the jocks did not determine the way jock speakers expressed their political needs. They did not say, "We want a jock lounge!"

The Reality of the Cliques

The picture I just painted is almost stereotypical. Sheffield might be considered a somewhat atypical town because of its suburban homogeneity, and it is not impossible that the ambivalence of the students towards cliquish behavior may have been the result of their perception of the relative arbitrariness of their groupings. In a multiethnic setting cliques might be seen as more directly reflecting broader social realities, and one might expect the students to be less ambivalent. But most of the literature on high school cliques was built from observations made in small and suburban towns. Furthermore, there is indication that people like Coleman or Henry did have evidence of ambivalence. Of the two students Henry quotes at length (1963:185–190, 249–257), one does talk of "our gang," while the other one systematically distances himself. Henry sees the difference as a difference in personality structure and adaptation to an alienating world, but there is little data on which to base a decision. As for Coleman, in the two examples he gives of students talking about cliques, there is explicit denial of the *personal* relevance of the cliques:

> To be sure, when students were asked [what does it take to be in the leading crowd in the school], some, particularly in the smallest school, did object to the idea that there was a leading crowd. Yet this kind of objection is in large part answered by [a boy] . . . in a group interview. A friend of his denied that there was any leading crowd at all in the school, and he responded: "You don't see it because you're in it." [1961:34]

And the student he quotes as giving a "vivid picture of how such crowds function" began with the following:

> You mean like cliques? Well there are about two cliques. There's me. . . . I'm in it, but as far as I am concerned, I'm not concerned about being in it. . . . I just go along with them. [1961:36]

The researchers until now have discounted this ambivalence and chalked it up to ignorance, psychological resistance, or various forms of false consciousness, i.e., to a "myth" against which they offered a picture of a "reality." They talked of "informal" structures not recognized by the school but still quite real. And since this form of social structural analysis demanded that groups be actual events of some persistence, they constructed the lists which the school did not keep. They counted the cliques, determined their size, and compared them in terms of a whole set of variables, from father's occupation to amount of drinking or college plans (Coleman 1961: chap. VII). All evidence of overlap, fuzziness of boundaries, or ties between cliques was considered a matter suggesting caution in the process of ascribing membership. But it remained a secondary methodological issue.

In fact it is an issue of central theoretical importance, particularly given the data base utilized. As I mentioned earlier, these data were essentially made up of *talk* with the students in various settings and in response to different types of questions. Only a very small number of the observations made were produced independently of the students' symbolic performances. All of this suggests that it is time to look back at what the informants actually do say with little *a priori* notion of what is relevant, to see whether there is an organization to these statements as statements, that is, as the *symbolic* productions which they inevitably are. The matter of social structural constraints should remain open until the structuring processes of the symbolic productions through which social structure is known are fully understood.

The Symbolic Production of Cliques

For various reasons, I will mainly look at statements in interviews to outline the symbolic structure of clique and personal identification. The interview situation itself probably led the students to overemphasize the expression of diffidence towards cliques, and I would certainly not rely on the statements we collected in such situations to evaluate the overall "importance" of cliques in the school. Other situations might also require different types of performances from the students, and the following is not intended to be an overall account of all the possible types. The advantage of interviews is that they could be tape recorded and thus provide us with data which have been only minimally translated by the field-worker.[2] This is of paramount importance for me, since I need the detail[3] of the student performance in order to produce a convincing analysis.

Let us look at Roy Carter's overall account of the cliques in Sheffield High School:

It shouldn't be too difficult [to classify students into groups]. Cliques are some of the most obvious things in the school. There's the, well, let's see. . . .

[Follows a consideration of various cliques and various students who "transcend the line drawn by cliques."]

Some other people might classify say, William Gregory, myself, Jack Saario, and a few others as Miss Kennedy says the "brain trust," which I prefer not to think of because whether it's true or not I like to think of myself as getting along

well with most other groups in the school.

Q: Who belongs to that?

C: Well, in other people's eyes . . . [T5]

Carter at the same time affirms and denies the existence of cliques and helps us to specify a basic opposition in the rhetoric he uses:

I like to think of myself . . .
In other people's eyes . . .

A distinction has been made: "I" "get along" "with most other groups." "/Some others/" might classify "/list of names/"[4] as "the 'brain trust'." *I*, *friendship*, and *most* go together, as against *some others*, *clique label*. The distinction is not accompanied, in this instance, with a definite statement of evaluation of the fact that "some" saw Carter as a member of a clique. We did collect statements which implied much more directly that to talk of cliques is to talk of something that is bad and reflects negatively either on the school or on those who behave in terms of clique membership. But this value judgment is not what is of interest to us directly. Whether they liked cliques or not (in fact, nobody ever told us that cliques were a good thing), all students could talk about cliques. Carter did not hesitate to assert that there were cliques in the school. What is important is that, in his speech and, as we shall see, in the speech of all students, cliques are associated with "others" or "they," and never with "I."

It would be an error, however, to think that "they" forms are only used in relation to people who are objectively not the members of one's group of friends. "They" can be people who both the student and the interviewer know very well are the best friends of that student. To talk of "them" is a symbolic resource with which speakers can do whatever they wish. Their social situation does not determine them. Let us look at another text.

In T6 Paul Taft had been asked by the fieldworker to talk about "cliques" (the word was suggested by the fieldworker), "what the different groups are like," "the names people apply." Taft, in the way I have documented, agrees to talk about the subject ("the most obvious cliques are the athletes and the freaks"), rejects the initiation of the division of the outsiders ("there are certain rules that are set up for [the athletes] by, most likely, the freaks"), when pushed starts describing the "stereotype" (sic) of the freak and then starts insisting that he himself does or has done what freaks only are supposed to do (wear dirty jeans, smoke pot, like hard rock, etc.)—"many of the things they do are things I do, you know." Until then, all the "they's," like the one in the last sentence, refer to "the freaks," or so it seems. This remark is followed by a request for clarification, "Like what? Can you give me an example?" Taft answers:

> You know, going to parties. Although myself, I'm not really involved with narcotics of that type. Even though my view on marijuana is one where it really doesn't bother me. People that do it, I could care less. But some kids in the high school, the guys that are involved in athletics, think a kid does pot—he's a real screwball. It doesn't bother me. My feeling of pot really, you know, is liberal. I'd like to see it legalized, because the penalties that are put on it are really severe to the kids and it really screws them up. So if anyone wants to get high on that, let them. I myself, we go to a party, we drink beer, you know, wine. You know, you go to a concert or something like that, you're going to drink. I shouldn't always be like that, but that's one of the characteristics of it. [T6a]

This is a verbatim, nonedited statement. What is fascinating is the variety of ways Taft has at his disposal to talk about people in a general way. He can talk of "I," "my view," "my feeling," "people," "some kids," "the guys," "a kid," "anyone," In other words, Taft is modulating the system of personal reference that is available to him, and we can ask ourselves whether all these forms are functionally equivalent.[5]

It must be noted first that the variation is not solely grounded in syntactic or referential necessity. Taft is not describing to the fieldworker an event that is occurring concurrently with his speech. The "event" is in fact a sequence of events that have taken place sometime in the past and are irretrievable. Thus there is no "reality testing" of the utterance, no feedback from the situation pointing out the selective nature of Taft's speech. He is not even talking in terms of a specific action to be performed. All this means that we must be very skeptical about the extent to which Taft is *referring* to historical events. Let us look at the progression "some kids in the high school, the guys that are involved in athletics." The purely referential interpretation of this passage could run something like this: Taft knows that some students (a subgroup of the total student population) disapprove of pot smoking; he also knows who these students are and thus specifies that they are "the guys in athletics." If this were all there was to this statement, there would be no justification for going further. However, all evidence outside of this passage shows that this interpretation is wrong.

Obviously, Taft is differentiating himself from both "the guys . . . in athletics" and "people that do it." He is neither one of those who "do" pot, nor one of those who disapprove. Nor is he even one of "the guys . . . in athletics," until the last sentence, when he shifts to "we." Later in the interview he makes it clear that the people he includes in "we" are a subset of those involved in "the guys . . . in athletics."

> The guys that I hack around with are really close. We've been together a really long time. About four or five guys are really close even though I think the clique encompasses a lot of guys. . . . No one is hung up on any problems. But there are a lot of guys in the cliques who are. . . . They follow everything that was followed before. [T6b]

The element of evaluation is unmistakable: "they" becomes "we" only when "friendship" can be assumed, and friendship has to do with the agreement between the people under consideration on a particular point. Taft disagrees with "a lot of guys," those guys who, in the earlier text, were "the guys . . . in athletics." There has been a shift. After having assumed a distanced stance where he stood outside and described the overall situation, Taft shifts to a description of his personal involvement: from an *I/they* opposition he moves to a *we/a lot* opposition.

Throughout, then, Taft uses different forms to refer to the *same* people—

the athletes. At the time of the interview he stands towards them all in the same relationship: they are the absent (from the setting) persons with whom he regularly socializes. And yet these people are successively "we," "they," and "some" or "a lot," depending on the points of reference Taft adopts. They are at the same time:

- clearly marked as a subgroup within the school and as a totality in relation to a certain activity;
- a fuzzy set of subgroups.

Taft can also either put himself out or put himself in.

What all this suggests is that the social situation of Taft (either his overall place in the school or the interview) does not directly motivate his speech. It is probable that the overall situation is, in fact, quite complex, more complex than traditional clique analyses made it, and that he has a certain leeway. Thus, at the end we may still not know whether the athletes are a clique, whether Taft is a member, who disapproves of pot smoking, and what form this disapproval takes. We could not directly reconstruct these things from what Taft said. The forms he used do not have an inherent referential meaning. *What is expressed is the attitude or stance the speaker adopts towards the object of his statement.* This stance is expressed by the actual form used, and we can distinguish between the forms as to the stance implied.[6]

Bobby Christian, the speaker, was, it will be remembered, Taft's best friend.

> It was such a war almost going on between the two groups. This year it's in football. I didn't hardly associate with

anyone because we were always busy at football. Now in basketball we see kids in the school and everything. It seems there's an interest rising now because we're doing well and the hockey team is doing well. So people are concerned. Karl Cousin and Gerard Dillon, they were never really interested, but we're friends with them now and they're interested. Like today, for instance, Karl asked me, "When is your next game?" I told him. He said, "Oh, yeah? Congratulations." Last night, Gerard said, "You played a good game." I think it's general, you know, everyone's kind of concerned now. [T7]

There is no collective "they" in this text. Indeed, Christian did not use many of them in the interview we taped with him. What he uses again and again is "we," and in that "we" he includes the football, basketball, and hockey teams. Conversely, when he shifts to the present he does not talk of "the freaks" becoming concerned. He also shifts to using first names, "Karl" and "Gerard," whom everybody would know as the most prominent members of the hard core freaks. Christian knows that they could be so labeled too. But at this moment he treats them as separate individuals. A few exchanges later, the interviewer asked for clarification: "You mean the freak kids rather than the jock kids." Christian agreed but rephrased the statement: "Yes, these were jock kids," i.e., *some* jocks, in the *past*. And still later he explained, "There are still some kids [who don't appreciate sports]."

As a total statement, this text is different from Taft's. Christian seems much more involved in the jock world and less aware of this world as a special, separate world. But the instru-

ments he uses are the same as those Taft uses. Indeed if we examine the exact source of the assumption we might make that Christian is more involved and less introspective, it will be seen that it is not because he says so in so many words but because of the relative predominance of certain rhetorical forms over others (especially /I/, /first names/, and /we/).

I want to stress this to re-emphasize that I am not trying to interpret what Taft or Christian as individual informants "meant" in an abstract, general sense. It is enough for me that they *appear* to mean something different *because they use differently the same meanful forms.*

Let us pursue our analysis of these forms. I have suggested the broad lines of the distributions to be made. What do they in fact do? I have suggested that the emic unit I will refer to as /they/ is always used to refer to something in which *I* is not made to participate. There are apparent exceptions. In T7 Christian comes very close to saying "the jocks, we . . ." But in fact he does not. He says, "Last year the big thing was Jock and Freak. . . . It was such a war." Cliques were real then, in temporal distance. Walt Mason and Bill Silvestri (the core members of the political freak clique) once had an argument in our presence that illustrates even more clearly this process of distanciation. The discussion was about whom they were friends with. It meandered in the usual fashion between "I am a loner," "I am friendly with so many kids," and "So-and-so is my best friend." At some point Mason said, "There are no cliques in the school." Silvestri disagreed: "I have been in a lot of them."

"I *have been*," in the past. He didn't

say "But *we* are a clique," which they were according to any outsider (whether participant in the school or social anthropologist). Structurally this movement is equivalent to Taft's distinguishing between "my four friends" (we) and the other "guys" who are encompassed by the clique (they). The statement is in the present, but some distance has been established, a discontinuity.[7]

The issue, then, is not really one of evaluation. Taft, to focus again on him, may have wished to evaluate fellow athletes and criticize them for being too cliquish, but this is not the source of his ability to make the statement. What he has at his disposal is the ability to establish discontinuities or to assume continuities through the use of syntactic means (pronouns, first names, labels, or the tense system). And it is only because there are no rules prescribing where the discontinuities must be placed in the social world about which he is talking that Taft can then manipulate them to express his evaluation of his acquaintances.

Structurally speaking, the principle at work is that of the extension of identification and the placing of a signifying discontinuity, all *from the point of view of an "I," and from the point of view of the present exchange.* For not only is there variation as to the placing of the discontinuity between two speakers—however close they may be from an organizational point of view—and the rest of the student body, there is also variation from context to context *within* the speech of the same speaker.

It was common, for example, for speakers to shift to an all-encompassing "we" when talking about certain topics. Jack Saario, for example, after giving

us the most personalized statements about cliques, volunteered to talk to us about the bomb threats which had plagued the school the year before.

> We never had any trouble like this before, but last year. . . . OK, last year they started with bomb threats. There was a couple of bomb threats. They just phoned in bomb threats and everybody had to go outside and it was a big joke and we had locker searches, etc. etc. [T8]

"*We* never had any trouble . . . *they* started with bomb threats." No specific referent is marked in the immediate context. The preceding exchanges in the interview had been about Saario's taking an advanced physics course at the local university, and then he volunteered "Maybe I should get into the bomb threats we have had?" Like the author of the newspaper article, he encompasses the whole student body, indeed the whole school, in his statement and subtracts the few responsible. Later in the text, he starts labeling the reaction of "the board of education" to the bomb threats, and all subsequent "they's" refer to it. In both cases Saario does the same thing: he subtracts an ad hoc group from an undifferentiated whole and does not make any specific personal reference within the subtracted group: they are just people on the other side of a symbolically created chasm. It is not that Saario doesn't know that there are actual persons on the other side of the chasm but that, to make explicit this knowledge, he would have to shift his rhetoric and would lose the intended effect.

The broad use of "we" is an interesting phenomenon, well worth spending some time on. "We" could refer to a very large universalized group of students versus a small minority, or versus people in a formally defined position other than the one "we" occupy, particularly the administration. "We" could also refer to the whole school, including the administration, versus the outside world, the parents, and the community. But it would again be a mistake to say that the broad meaning of "we" is determined by such social structural matters. Let us look at another interesting instance of manipulation of the we/they segmentation. The speaker is Pat Goldberg, a junior who was running for election as vice-president of the student council. He was being interviewed as to his reasons for running ("It looks good for college and I want to do something for the school") and what he thought could be done:

> ... I think that this year, we only have like two student council classes ... we have representatives who conduct a class and in the class you'll have a group of students who chose this person to be their representative.... It's really a good way for the student council to know what all the students think. You have to know what the people that you're governing—what they think, how they feel, and what their opinions are. So the student council itself can govern and keep the students happy.... I think it's really important that students know what's going on. [T9]

The situation is again an artificial one from the point of view of the activities being discussed. There are no cues in the immediate environment to give direct referential meaning to Goldberg's speech. The whole meaning must be generated within the text by signifying cues that can help suggest a "real"

world to the audience. It is a process that is myth-bound rather than reality-bound. How did Goldberg conjure this mythical world? The means are the usual ones: "we have representatives"; "a group of students"; "what all the students think"; "the student council"; tell the students "what we're doing." All these essentially pronominal phrases refer to the same sort of "real" people: students. However, Goldberg is allowed to make several distinctions that will evidently reveal themselves to be, on a larger scale, the same as those which were made by the students when they talked about the people nearest to them.

There is first "we," the students as a whole (as in "we have representatives"), and the symmetrical "they" (as in "and keep the students happy"), which refers to the same persons from which *one* person has been subtracted, "I."[8] Somewhere between these two extremes Goldberg placed two boundaries. At one point he talks of "a group of students" (who elect a representative) and of "the student council." The reference is personalized and specified. The student council is also referred to as "we" ("they don't know what *we*'re doing"), signifying that Goldberg is already identifying with the council (as he well may have, since he was running unopposed).

Goldberg's "we" in reference to the student council is not an expression of his being friendly with the people in the council. Goldberg was involved in several clubs that year, but not in the council. As for the council the following year, it did not yet exist. For Goldberg, the council was an abstract entity which he had never experienced. His "we" did not reflect a social experience.

It was a product of Goldberg's symbolic competence: he knew that it was an appropriate construction of a future social reality to place a boundary around an otherwise defined group in which he would sometimes participate.

A complete specification of this symbolic competence would demand much more space than I have at my disposal here. I have published elsewhere a slightly more technical preliminary statement (1978) and I am preparing a full scale analysis (MS). What I have done here should be sufficient, however, to suggest concretely both the process of a symbolic analysis and its product in terms of this particular set of texts.

Symbolic Structure and Social Reality

One of the fundamental powers of language lies in the ability it gives us to manipulate people, events, and situations which are not present at the moment of the utterance or which, even, do not quite "exist" except as symbolic creations. Language can also be used to describe people, events, and situations which are extremely real in social, political, or economic terms. But it is the same language that does both, and there is no way to mark in an incontrovertible fashion the exact status of an utterance: one is never obliged to state "I made the following up" before telling a tall tale. Indeed, the speaker may not be quite conscious of the fact that it is a tall tale. It would not have been beyond some of our informants to play with the fieldworker when answering questions about cliques. Some descrip-

tions were so long and so detailed in comparison with the other descriptions we got that they may have been a pure invention or simply an artifact of the interview situation. But perhaps these texts were so long and complex because the speakers were playing the game more seriously than other students.

What makes all this even more delicate is the fact that I am myself using language to "describe" a set of situations which are already lost in the rather distant past. To what extent I am indeed "describing" and to what extent I am "creating" is something which, in the social sciences, is extremely difficult to ascertain. All that remains of the fieldwork that has not been retranslated by my own writing processes is the transcription of a few interviews. This very text is a constructed symbolic performance on which I have worked for a very long time. I cannot be quite sure that it works, but whether it does or not depends on my ability to manipulate symbolic means (in this case mostly linguistic) to suggest a world which is not now present.

I brought to you fragments of this world, transcripts from interviews through which we might be able to increase intersubjectivity. While the interviews were certainly generated by the fieldworker's interest, each student did participate. And we can check the extent of this participation by looking at similar data published by other researchers about similar situations. Few social scientists, in fact, do quote at any length the people they observe. But in the few cases when it does happen I believe I recognize my informants. In a study of the process of initiation into a high school sorority, Schwartz and

Merten quote one of their informants (whom they do not identify in terms of membership or nonmembership in the sorority) talking about a girl who "hung around" but didn't belong to the sorority:

... I can think of one girl that was just like that, Barbara; you know she hung around with ABCs.
Q: Who else?
A: Ah, a couple of kids, they were real close ... but anyway Barbara hung around with them, and they were all ABCs, and they were real close and always had lunch together and everything, and when it came to being ABCs everybody still knew that Barbara wasn't one. And I think she wanted to be one. She always wanted to be one and I think she tried to convince herself that she was an informal one, but still I don't think anyone else was convinced. [1968:1122]

The situation is different in this high school from what it was in Sheffield, since the dominant female cliques had become formalized as sororities. One could have expected this to lead to the maintenance of absolute boundaries. And yet it seems that a gray area did exist. More importantly, the informant is talking, very regularly from my point of view, of "I," "Barbara," "they." The boundary has been set at the very edge of the "I"; the sorority is "they." Indeed, in the eight passages Schwartz and Merten quoted, only one "we" is used (by a girl recalling how she and, apparently, some of her friends had been recruited). The sorority is *always* "they," even when the speaker is obviously a member of it. Even when the question seems to have included a di-

rect attempt at personalization, the answer could be distanced:

Q: Well, when one becomes inducted into the sorority, are you leaving one category of people and entering another?
A: I think the members of the sorority and the pledges think of it that way. [1968:1122]

Such evidence suggests that the interviews I have analyzed are not purely *my* artifacts. Investigators can collect such statements, and I would expect that they could have been collected in many different American high schools and can still be collected there. But this argument does not quite deal with the fundamental issue. I am still writing about something that is not present, in a way that must evoke this reality in a conventional manner. Were I writing a novel, I would probably use some of the same linguistic tools as I have been using here. Look how Updike described Tarbox's "society" in *Couples:*

The people who did throw parties were a decade older and seemed rather coarse and blatant—Dan Mills, the bronzed, limping, and alcoholic owner of the abortive Tarbox boat yard; Eddie Warner, the supervisor of a Mather paint plant, a bullet-headed ex-athlete who could still at beery beach picnics float the ball a mile in the gull-gray dusk; Doc Allen.... To Janet they seemed desperate people, ignorant and provincial and loud. Their rumored infidelities struck her as pathetic; their evident heavy drinking disgusted her.... The boatyard crowd, a postwar squirearchy of combat veterans, locally employed and uncollegiate, knew that it was patronized by these younger cooler people and suffered no regrets when they chose to form a separate set and to leave them alone with their liquor and bridge games and noisy reminiscences of Anzio and Guadalcanal. [1968:115-116]

Updike could be treated as an informant manipulating his own ethno-sociology. But he could also be treated as an extremely perceptive observer of suburban life, an outsider looking in, a sociologist describing. Whether it is Gans (1967) or Vidich and Bensman (1968) describing contemporary towns or Wallace (1978) describing a nineteenth-century manufacturing district, the technique is the same: "I" think this is the way "they" think about it.

This poses a very interesting problem. All sociologists—even those who want to ground their analyses in the "participants' meanings"—write of the people they observed as "they." What we have seen here is that American naive participants (the "natives") use the same term to perform the same descriptive function. However, we have also seen that in everyday speech /they/ does not simply connote "objective description" in any simple sense. /They/ connotes distance, rigidity, lack of personal involvement. It might not be wrong to say that it does connote object-ivity, i.e., a stance where human actors are made, or treated as, *objects*. When this stance is taken, cliques appear and are overwhelmingly "present."

But our naive participants can adopt—because the pragmatic grammar of their language allows them to—another stance, where they appear as subjects and treat the people they refer to as subjects too, as /I/. At such moments, cliques disappear. Fluidity and ambiguity are brought to the fore and distant forms that seemed so solid in the other mode evaporate in a mist of hedges and exceptions.

Sociologists, when they have recognized such processes, have generally considered them irrelevant to their purposes, with the argument that the personal feelings of participants were not a matter of sociological interest. What I would like to say is that this fundamental theoretical stance is methodologically misapplied when, in a setting like American schools, it leads the researcher to consider only certain statements as relevant and then to generalize these statements to the full sociological experience of the observed participants. In two ways, in fact, the /I/ of participants is a matter of sociological interest. First, the very presence of this /I/ is predicated on the unfolding of a sociological process: the development of a set of rules for the social use of linguistic forms, a pragmatic grammar that is specific to a particular social group. Second, there is no way to distinguish within the actual social experience of the students what is motivated by social structural constraints such as informal clique structures and what is motivated by psychological or emotional responses. Students have to interact with each other in terms of both, and both are elements in their social experience.

That we must say that, from the point of view of this experience, cliques are *at the same time* there and not there in a school such as Sheffield is a paradox which we should not resolve too hastily. At the beginning of this paper, I made a point of emphasizing that from Hollingshead to Clement and Harding, two or three generations of sociologists have undoubtedly "seen" something and that their descriptions are not "in error." What they are is partial, for no good theoretical reason. What has been lacking in the previous research is a focused gaze on the detail of the actual interactions before theoretical operations are performed. We do know now that such a gaze is not an easy or natural process. It must be informed by a creative critique of earlier ethnographic and theoretical work. The work of Coleman, et al., was a necessary step in our journey toward more disciplined understanding of social life in schools and elsewhere. And now, to paraphrase Lévi-Strauss, "the orders are to keep marching."

Notes

I would like to acknowledge the financial help I received from the Ford Foundation, The National Institute of Education, and the Horace Mann-Lincoln Institute at Teachers College. I want to thank those who helped me with data collection, particularly Patricia Caesar, Fritz Ianni, and Rodney Riffle. I also gained much from the comments of Ray McDermott and George Spindler, who read drafts of this paper.

[1] I can, in fact, conceive of many situations when students might symbolically act out the label imposed on them by their social environment. In jokes, horseplay, and perhaps unfocused anger, self-identification in clique terms might be found. Our field notes were not detailed enough about such matters to settle this issue. What we did record were "serious" statements when emotional involvement was relatively low and formal or public statements when rhetorical pressures were quite strong.

[2] In a recent paper, Keenan made a fundamental point which no social scientist should ever forget: never do we work on the actual phenomenon which we are studying. We always work on a transcript of this phenomenon, a linear statement that is the product of rewrite rules, more or less standardized transcription conventions, which produce the text on which we work.

[3] The rewrite rules which transform a field experience into a working text can take many forms and produce many different texts useful for various types of analysis. In this case, I have found it sufficient to transcribe recorded speech at a rather gross level in comparison with recent sociolinguistic standards (e.g., Labov & Fanshel 1977). I did not try to incorporate any paraverbal or nonverbal cues, for example. However, I do not believe I need them to do what I am doing here.

[4] To refer to a paradigm of functionally equivalent surface symbolic forms, I shall employ the / / symbol used in structural linguistics to refer to emic units. (See also note 5.)

[5] The underlying question is an old and difficult one in all the social sciences. It concerns the mechanisms that can be used to ascertain whether two events which share some surface features but do not share others should be considered "the same" or "different" from a certain point of view. In classical structural linguistics, a test of functional significance was evolved: two forms were considered equivalent if it could be shown that, from the point of view of the system studied, the differences between them had no effect; the unit was not changed. It performed the same functions. This functional unit was the original emic unit (as in phoneme) and it is in this sense that I will talk of such units (as against the popular understanding of Pike's emic/etic distinction, which cannot be used in any productive analytic and systematic manner).

⁶ To pursue the discussion in more technical terms, what all this means is that the speaker is made the point of reference: when Taft talks of "the guys" we cannot assume whom he is referring to. What we know is how he stands in relation to them on the particular issue. In other words, "the guys" does not mean anything except as it is used by a speaker. This makes the form and equivalent ones a subset of what linguists have called "shifters" (Jakobson 1957, Silverstein 1976). The prototype of such forms is the first-person pronoun "I," which can only be interpreted if we know who is talking but as such only indicates the stance of the speaker. I have argued elsewhere (Varenne 1978) why I believe that certain third-person and nominal forms (e.g., "the guys") should also be considered shifters in American usage, in spite of Benveniste's argument (1966) that they should not be so considered.

⁷ From a broad cross-cultural point of view this process could be perceived as another example of what Lévi-Strauss has seen as a fundamental capacity of human "wild" thinking: the mythological transition from continuity to discreteness, of which he gives three examples in his analysis of Myths 1, 2, and 3 in *The Raw and the Cooked* [1969:53–54].

⁸ Given what happens later in the text, this "we" is in fact ambiguous: Goldberg may already be thinking of the student council, as he obviously does later.

References

Benveniste, Emile. 1966. *Problèmes de Linguistique générale.* Paris: Gallimard.

Clement, Dorothy, and Joe Harding. 1978. "Social Distinctions and Emergent Student Groups in a Desegregated School." *Anthropology and Education Quarterly*, 9 (4): 272–282.

Coleman, James S. 1961. *The Adolescent Society.* New York: The Free Press.

Cusik, Philip. 1973. *Inside High School.* New York: Holt, Rinehart and Winston.

Gans, Herbert J. 1967. *The Levittowners: Ways of Life and Politics in a New Suburban Community.* New York: Random House, Vintage Books.

Gordon, C. Wayne. 1957. *The Social System of the High School: A Study in the Sociology of Adolescence.* Glencoe, IL: The Free Press.

Harris, Marvin. 1964. *The Nature of Cultural Things.* New York: Random House.

Henry, Jules. 1963. *Culture Against Man.* New York: Random House.

Hollingshead, A. B. 1949. *Elmtown's Youth*. New York: John Wiley and Sons.

Jakobson, Roman. 1957. *Shifters, Verbal Categories, and the Russian Verb*. Cambridge: MA.: Russian Language Project, Department of Slavic Languages and Literature, Harvard University.

Keenan, E. Forthcoming. "Transcription as Theory." In E. Keenan, ed., *Studies in Developmental Pragmatics*. New York: Academic Press.

Labov, William, and D. Fanshel. 1977. *Therapeutic Discourse. Psychotherapy as Conversation*. New York: Academic Press.

Lévi-Strauss, Claude. 1969. *The Raw and the Cooked: Introduction to a Science of Mythology*, Vol. 1. New York: Harper & Row.

Palonsky, Stuart B. 1975. "Hempies and Squeaks, Truckers and Cruisers: A Participant Observer Study in a City High School." *Educational Administration Quarterly*, 11(2):86–103.

Schwartz, Gary, and Don Merten. 1968. "Social Identity and Expressive Symbols: The Meaning of an Initiation Ritual." *American Anthropologist*, 70:1117–1131.

Silverstein, Michael. 1976. "Shifters, Linguistic Categories and Cultural Description." In K. Basso and H. Selby, eds., *Meaning in Anthropology*. Albuquerque: University of New Mexico Press, 11–55.

Updike, John. 1970. *Couples*. New York: Fawcett World Library.

Varenne, Hervé. 1978. "Culture as Rhetoric: Patterning in the Verbal Interpretation of Interaction Between Teachers and Administrators in an American High School." *American Ethnologist*, 5(4):635–650.

Vidich, Arthur J., and Joseph Bensman. 1968. *Small Town in Mass Society: Class, Power and Religion in a Rural Community*. Princeton: Princeton University Press.

Wallace, Anthony F. C. 1978. *Rockdale: The Growth of an American Village in the Early Industrial Revolution*. New York: Alfred A. Knopf.

PART III

Cultural Transmission and the "Hidden Curriculum"

Editorial Commentary

There are only two chapters in Part III. One is a contextualized microanalytic study of a reading group consisting of four children and one teacher. The other is an intensive study of one classroom in each of two elementary schools on the West Coast, one serving a lower-middle-class neighborhood, the other an upper-middle-class one. The first paper is concerned with how a culturally patterned attitude, "learning to wait," cutting one's losses by hanging back, is projected into the classroom and specifically the reading activity by the children who come from a community where they have been socialized to this attitude. The second paper details how socialization for work roles at the opposite ends of the scale of prestige and reward in our society takes place in the schools studied. These two chapters, among the most rigorous in research design and implementation in the book, both deal with educational problems of great significance.

Though dealing with quite different topics, these two chapters have much in common. They both show how the cultural context and community background are projected into, in fact determine, the educational process. They take a cultural transmission stance. Most of the ethnographers in this volume do, but it is particularly explicit in these two instances. Further, they are both centered on showing how a "hidden curriculum," a pattern of expectations and relevant behaviors, operates to defeat declared educational intentions. Neither one draws its interpretations directly from linguistically shaped models, though both utilize verbal behavior as a most important source of data. These two papers report researches that are both rigorous and thoroughly ethnographic, as measured by the orienting criteria already set forth in the General Introduction.

These chapters are set apart, rather than being grouped with the papers in Part II, because their theoretical positions are not as directly influenced by linguistic and speech behavior models, though it would not be correct to say that these influences are entirely lacking. They both draw from structural-functional theory and see the classroom in a reflexive relationship to the broader community.

These two chapters, in different ways, call attention to the fact that ethnographic inquiry proceeds in stages. Each stage is derived out of the one preceding and, of course, they overlap. The first is what may be called *reconnaissance*. Gearing and Epstein refer to it as an orienting phase and Wilcox does not label it, but she does it. In this phase the ethnographer explores, as the term "reconnaissance" suggests, the relevant literature, the broader community, and the more limited settings within which the research is to be done. The ethnographer acquires a general outline of "what's out there."

The first step in the reconnaissance stage is to find relevant facts and sometimes ideas from the literature about the research site or surrounding area (if available), and from topical literature concerned with the kinds of relationships one wishes to study. Frequently some orienting hypothesis will emerge from the initial reconnaissance. This was the case with Kathleen Wilcox. By the time she had read the literature on social class and social organization for work roles, she had begun to form the hypothesis that would guide her ethnographic research. This was true in several other studies reported in this volume. It is probably more often true than most anthroethnographers will admit. Gearing and Epstein do not make this phase explicit, though we know from familiarity with Gearing's previously published work that he researches the literature carefully and that it feeds into his own theoretical formulations.

The next step is to actually reconnoiter the environment surrounding the field site, and the field site itself. One interviews as wide a variety of personnel as possible, sometimes formally (making appointments, etc.), more often informally (friendly conversations, chance contacts, etc.). One visits the area, the school, the classroom (assuming one has already acquired entrée) and records impressions and personal reactions as well as observed behavior. By now, various "hunches" about not only what is "out there" but "what is going on" have begun to form. Some become researchable.

The second stage involves determining, in Gearing-Epstein terminology, the "event structure." In more general terms this stage can be described as "locating critical relationships." It is the stage when one has spent a fair amount of time on the research site, knows "who's who," and has begun to decide that some things are more important than others. Readers should have no trouble identifying this stage in the two papers in this section. Decisions that some things are more important than others are made, to be sure, as a product of what one knows from stage one interacting with what one finds out is actually there where the research is to be done in stage two. Frequently one finds out about critical relationships that were not anticipated by any of the phases of stage one

Many ethnographers stop essentially somewhere in stage two. This stage may take months or years before the outlines of the whole setting or situation have been sufficiently observed and recorded. At this point the ethnographer knows or thinks that he or she knows the critical relationships pertaining to a general "problem" and has answered some specific self-generated questions. Any ethnographer who stays on the site long enough will see questions answered again and again and again. New questions that round out the description of the action and the setting may be generated, but the focus will not be narrowed to some very particular set of relationships in any one setting unless stage three is entered.

Most modern ethnographers enter stage three at some point in their careers. Few carry the definition of focus as far as Gearing and Epstein and Wilcox do. In stage three there are very focused and—from the viewpoint of the general or macroethnographer—rather narrowly defined relationships that must now be scrutinized close up and in the greatest detail. Various kinds of data may be collected, and various kinds of analytic schemes may be used to collate and interpret these data. This is where video taping in the Erickson mode furnishes unparalleled information that can be scrutinized repeatedly. It is also the time when codes, rankings and ratings, and schedules are likely to be generated and emphasized. Gearing and Epstein use a schedule for recording finite observations of a small reading group to detail essentially dyadic interactions. Wilcox uses an elaborate coding and classifying schema to record observations in the three dimensions she has defined as important to socialization for work roles.

In both studies, data are produced that answer questions and test hypotheses in a manner not wholly dissimilar to the way they would be tested by many psychologists, sociologists, and ethnographically oriented educators. The difference lies in the fact that the questions or hypotheses specify a focus embedded in concentric circles of relevant context. And the "instruments" that are used emerge from the reconnaissance of stage one and the observations collected in stage two. They are heuristic to the setting and to a problem that, though staged by "reading the literature" and acquiring background information, is given its operational shape by direct field experience.

8

*Frederick Gearing
and Paul Epstein*

Learning to Wait:
An Ethnographic Probe
into the Operations of
an Item of
Hidden Curriculum

Frederick Gearing

Paul Epstein

The Authors

Frederick Gearing is professor of anthropology and a Fellow of the Center for Studies of Cultural Transmission at the State University of New York at Buffalo. His anthropological fieldwork includes studies in American Indian communities and in rural Greece, and his principal current interest is urban anthropology, specifically the development of ethnographic method and theory appropriate for work in culturally complex and heterogeneous settings such as contemporary American cities. His works include *Priests and Warriors: Structures for Cherokee Politics in the 18th Century* (American Anthropological Association), *The Face of the Fox* (Aldine), and *Toward a Cultural Theory of Education and Schooling* (Mouton). He says of himself:

"I became an ethnographer of schools in a circuitous manner. First (in 1964–1965) Malcolm Collier brought me into the American Anthropological Association's Anthropology Curriculum Study Project, principally to draw on my knowledge of Indians and Greece in that curriculum development effort. As a result of that work, I was appointed to the State of California's Statewide Social Sciences Study Committee and its very intensive curriculum-design efforts (1966–1968). As a further result of both, I was made director of the AAA's Program in Anthropology and Education in Washington, D.C., the salient outcome of which was the formation of a professional association, the Council on Anthropology and Education. Throughout these five years (1964–1969) my interests shifted steadily, from initial concerns with curriculum to increasingly greater curiosity about the cultures of schools and classrooms, by virtue of which these curricula come off or do not. This last, in turn, has led to my current virtually total preoccupation with the methodological and theoretical foundations which will allow us to see and understand those cultures of schools and the culturally heterogeneous societies in which schools operate."

Paul Epstein is a doctoral candidate in cultural anthropology and a Fellow of the Center for Studies of Cultural Transmission at the State University of New York at Buffalo. His anthropological studies include the development of ethnographic methodologies, contributions to theories of cultural transmission, and exploration of synchrony in face-to-face interaction. He has special interests in China as a cultural area. He holds a B.A. from Dartmouth College in psychology and education and is certified as a public elementary school teacher and as a Montessori teacher. He is currently a Montessori classroom teacher and an instructor in ethnographic methods at the A.E.R.C.O. Philadelphia Montessori Teacher Training Program.

This Chapter

In this chapter Frederick Gearing and Paul Epstein analyze the influence of a hidden agenda on the performance of students and teachers in an elementary school in a depressed "white ghetto" area in an urban context. Their approach can be described as microanalytic, in contrast to macroanalytic. They progressively narrow the focus of their concerns and data as they proceed through the chapter. The result is "an emically phased structural-functional description." But this phrase does not describe the precision with which data are presented and analysis proceeds.

The starting point of their analysis is one that is entirely understandable to anthropologists and phrased in more or less traditional terms: "we describe the group and its features from the inside — through the eyes of the actors, as it were — as in our judgment, ethnography must; and we describe the group and its affairs as a single whole, as in our judgment ethnography must." Attention to the native view of reality and an assumption of holism are a part of our anthropological heritage.

The three stages of ethnographic inquiry, however, that Gearing and Epstein lay out in this chapter go beyond the point most anthropologists reach in the traditional format. The first stage can be described as general orientation; the second as definition of the event structure; and the third as a focus on the internal structure of selected parts of the event structure. The procedure is therefore progressively microanalytic.

Gearing and Epstein are taking a kind of "cultural knowledge" approach. They are interested in the perceptions and phrasings of the natives — the actors in their scenes. But they rest their case largely on observed behavior, using relatively fewer, in this paper, other procedures such as casual ethnographic conversations and the more formal ethnographic interview. They use the observed behavior to infer the operation of a tacit assumption — a kind of "hidden agenda" that influences how children and teachers behave in reading scenes. This is an important point, for a part of the cultural knowledge we must uncover in ethnography consists of tacit assumptions which are difficult, if not impossible, for natives to talk about directly. Nevertheless they are among the most important influences on behavior. We must, therefore, infer them. We go from casual observation of behavior and listening to wisecracks and off-the-cuff comments to the observation of behavior with precisely formulated foci and some hypotheses. The movement from general participation and observation to focused participation and inquiry and back again to observation is a particularly salient feature of a valid ethnographic approach as it must be practiced in the ethnography of schooling.

Introduction

Universally, as it appears, the members of any well-established group of humankind are guided in their group affairs by various tacit assumptions which they have come to share about the underlying nature of the commonplace things entailed in their group affairs. Members of the group never verbalize these assumptions in any well-formulated way, but they enact them, and newcomers to the group learn them. The phrase "hidden curriculum" points to the fact that, in school contexts specifically, side-by-side with the manifest curriculum, a set of such tacit assumptions is being enacted and thereby being taught and learned.

We report the results of an ethnographic probe into the structured interactions through which one bit of hidden curriculum unfolds. The setting of this study is a small remedial reading group (one teacher and four students) in an elementary school which serves a neighborhood in a city in upper New York State. The behaviors of members of this reading group are patterned in ways such that they seem shaped by certain unstated assumptions about what, beyond "learning to read," the members are up to when they meet. Critically, but in hindsight not surpris-

ingly, these assumptions seem to be the same as those shared tacitly by their parents and fellows of their parents about what these adults are up to when they meet.

This last lends credence to our intuitive sense that this and other empirical studies of schools and classrooms are usefully oriented if the notion of hidden curriculum is given slightly narrowed meaning: *an item of hidden curriculum is any set of unspoken but acted-out assumptions which is about the underlying nature of a classroom or school and which is simultaneously about the underlying nature of some saliently germane sector of the wider community.* The notion of hidden curriculum, so narrowed, helps point inquiry toward matters of unusual interest and, as it would appear, matters of quite ramified practical and humane importance.

An item of hidden curriculum in this small reading group becomes visible to the observer insofar as, through observation and analytic description, the reading group's own small culture becomes visible. This group coexists, in this modern urban setting, with a near-infinity of other well-established organized groups, small and large. Each of these groups has, in the course of becoming well established, necessarily created a cultural system which in some nontrivial respect is unique. In such culturally heterogeneous settings, the study of all things cultural must be circumspect. This study is about an item of hidden curriculum which unfolds in this one place, one classroom in one school in one neighborhood in one metropolitan area. It is, in full empirical seriousness, about that alone. We confess, however, to strong intuitions which suggest that very similar items of hidden curriculum can be found to be operating quite generally in closely analogous situations throughout the United States. We have, then, the conceit that the study is also about certain more general features of contemporary American culture; but that is a confession, not a claim.

The populations involved in this study are two: the members, young and old, of one economically depressed neighborhood which is surrounded by more affluent residential and commercial areas; and persons from outside the neighborhood who relate to it. Both populations are found in the neighborhood elementary school: the students and the school staff, respectively. The school serves only this neighborhood, and the neighborhood is served by only this one elementary school. We report on a "white ghetto" and its school.

One set of unstated assumptions which members of these two populations appear regularly to act out whenever they come together can be verbally formulated as follows:

> People are not equal; by virtue of accidents of birth and experience, some have more ability than others. We, the adult members of this neighborhood school, have been losing, and we are losing now, some of us more than others.

However, if we are patient and deliberate, we can cut our losses; before acting it is necessary to pause, to reconsider and thereby more probably to be correct, and then to act.

The phrasing from the vantage point of those from outside the neighborhood would be, "You have been losing.... You can cut your losses...."

We shall be mapping how these tacit assumptions are jointly acted-out by one teacher and four fourth-grade students who make up the remedial reading group. In this school context, the acting-out of these tacit assumptions becomes an item of hidden curriculum which, through enactments, is being taught and learned. Put more precisely, that formulation of this item of hidden curriculum (which *we* devised) *describes* the patterns of interaction which regularly unfold among those five persons in that setting. This item of hidden curriculum, we will more tersely say henceforth, is "learning to wait."

The product of this study is an ethnography. We describe the reading group and its affairs as a small cultural system. This is to say, we describe the group and its affairs from the inside—through the eyes of the actors, as it were—as in our judgment ethnography must; and we describe the group and its affairs as a single whole, as in our judgment ethnography must. We describe, we said, "from the inside." Whenever, among all humankind, the same people come frequently together in the same place for the same purposes, the small world of that scene gets rather elaborately classified by them, principally into classes and subclasses of activity and classes and subclasses of person.

Thus what one member of the group sees when another acts is a recognized and familiar *kind* of act by a recognized and familiar *kind* of person. To describe the group and its affairs from the inside is to describe its members' behaviors in terms of the classes of activity and of person already established by them. That is, the observer, like those who make up the group, must identify each public behavior as a member of some pre-established class of acts performed by a member of some pre-established class of persons. We describe, we also said, "as a whole." Those classes of activity have structural relationships one with the other, and those classes of persons have structural relationships similarly; the two together constitute one inclusive structure. And, through joint actions by members of the group, which are given form and regularity by that structure, certain businesses-at-hand, both manifest and tacit, get done. To describe the group as a whole is to describe that functioning structure. In the jargon of anthropology, the product of this study is an emically phrased structural-functional description of the behaviors of members of this reading group; we describe the group as a small culture being enacted in the actual behaviors of the group's members.

This portrait will be reported in the approximate sequence of the ethnographic work through which it was revealed. The purposes thereby served are two: to report the results of this ethnographic inquiry and, at the same time, to outline tersely a generally applicable method of ethnographic inquiry. The method is designed to permit the analytic description of established groups as operating cultural systems, and to enable such description to proceed with some precision and efficiency in the culturally heterogeneous settings which are found throughout the modern world.

The Neighborhood, the School, the Remedial Reading Class

The first stage in ethnographic inquiry in culturally heterogeneous settings must proceed unhurriedly. Early inquiry proceeds in part through repeated sessions of rather loose looking-on. The observer "hangs around" as permitted and as seems reasonably comfortable to all, takes developments much as they come, and watches and listens, allowing naturally occurring everyday activities to wash over him or her. Early inquiry proceeds as well through quite unstructured, conversation-like interviews as occasions permit. The general purpose is to get oriented. This means acquiring a reasonably clear sense of the general arena, of the variety of scenes found there wherein the same persons come together regularly for the same purposes, of the kinds of events which regularly unfold in some of those scenes, and of some of the connections between and among those scenes.

The neighborhood of interest is a part of a large metropolitan area, a pair of industrial cities and their environs in upper New York State. Between the two cities there is a politically autonomous township dating back to the previous century, which is today fairly densely populated and only moderately affluent. Within this town are found the neighborhood and its school.

The neighborhood is economically depressed; it numbers some 1200 families and a few small shops and is quite clearly set off from the more affluent areas that surround it. The neighborhood was originally constructed during World War II as temporary two- and three-family housing units for military personnel. Though it has another name, it is usually referred to, by residents and outsiders, as "the projects" or "the proj."

In objective economic and social fact, this is a community of people who have been losing and who still are, and both the residents and outsiders often refer to the neighborhood in such terms. The neighborhood is described by the wider community as a "haven for the poor, delinquent and transient" (a metropolitan newspaper, December 11, 1977). Foremost among the problems of "the proj," according to the residents, are living conditions. Of the 1200 housing units, as many as 1000 are owned by absentee landlords. Streets have many potholes, homes are in need of repair. Residents refer to one particular area as the "back end," where most of the worst units are found; some are said to have wooden sinks and wooden plumbing. Said one resident, "Some are so bad, I wouldn't want to raise my dog in them." Residents throughout the neighborhood complain about "redlining" by insurance companies and banks when they seek loans for home rehabilitation.

Within the last year, community members have organized a "Community Improvement Association" (CIA, quite possibly a joke) consisting of three committees: Housing, Utilities, and Parks and Recreation. The Association is run by volunteers. It sends representatives to sit in on the meetings of the local government bodies and the school board. Its major goal is to secure an appropriation from the U.S. Department of Housing and Urban Development for community renewal and development. The Association has, more specifically, called for demolishing certain homes that fall far below the standards set forth in housing codes, for resurfacing streets, and for providing new water and sewage lines, fire hydrants, improved lighting, curbs, parking space, and trees to line streets. The Association also seeks to reverse the attitudes of residents and outsiders about the neighborhood.

The Association continually urges residents to attend Association meetings and other meetings with officialdom, with mixed success. Residents recount similar efforts by similar associations, and they express at best only cautious optimism. Yet it appears that patience and timely action are bearing fruit. HUD is giving the neighborhood considerable attention, the town appears slated to receive $2.8 million for work in the neighborhood, and some $350,000 in federal funds is already being channeled into improvements (repaving, burial of electric and telephone wires) in one of the better areas within the neighborhood.

The neighborhood has its own public elementary school. The school is located on the neighborhood's main street; this is also the street in best repair. Children walk to and from the school.

The school is part of a school district which consists of 15 elementary schools, three junior high schools, and two senior high schools. Among educators throughout the district, this neighborhood school is reputed to be a difficult and undesirable place to work. "Proj kids" are seen as "socially unruly," poorly clothed and fed, and tough. Some of the educators ask rhetorically, "Why try to teach them?" The school is sometimes vandalized; over several recent years some 400 windows have had to be replaced because of rocks thrown at them. The students in the school do not perform well on academic achievement tests compared to other district school children. Toward the end of the 1976–1977 year about one-fourth of the first-grade children enrolled throughout the district read below grade level; 85 percent of these children attended the neighborhood school. Children from the neighborhood are bused out for junior high beginning at grade 7, and they are said to be ill-prepared for the academic work they then must do.

The neighborhood has been federally identified as a "culturally-economically deprived area", thus the school receives funds for lunch programs, and 65 percent of the enrolled students receive those lunches. The school receives Title I funds to hire remedial teachers in reading and mathematics. The school's principal earlier insisted on, and has recently received, funding for an "early-childhood program" through which preschool children from the age of 3 years and 9 months attend school for half the day in order to "catch them up" to children in other areas. Finally, the school provides summer programs for neighborhood parents; these programs are intended to educate the par-

ents in practices which would improve the quality of life for the children before they enter school and afterwards.

Throughout the district, teachers are hired by the central office and assigned by them to schools; teachers have tenure in the district after five years. These facts restrict what a school principal can do, but during the past three years the principal of the neighborhood school has obtained nine teacher transfers, seeking to bring in "guidance-oriented" teachers who "accept children" in place of teachers who "tear down children" or "put the squeeze on children." Some of the teachers who have been in the school many years are referred to by parents and others as "dead wood," and some of these teachers do seem to think of the neighborhood children as unteachable. Said one, "You can't change those who have done it for a long time"—"it" meaning old ways, old habits. A parent said, "You can always tell which children had that [dead wood] teacher; they're so far behind the others." Children, on their part, think of each teacher as being either "nice" or "mean." A mean teacher is "sort of old, and she can't keep her patience," and mean teachers "never let you do anything that's fun." Nice teachers are less impatient and "let you play games." Usually these are games with academic content; thus a teacher may be something of a taskmaster and still be "nice."

The school principal sees himself living with a dilemma. On the one hand, he is fully aware of the community's economic plight, and he sees his school as of necessity a "social agency"; but, on the other hand, he is concerned that too much school time is spent dealing with family-based and community-based problems and that too little time is being spent on curriculum planning and other academic development activities. He serves on the Community Improvement Association's Board. At least once a week, he reports, his office becomes a "family court"—a child's father accuses the mother of child neglect, the mother accuses the father of physical abuse, and each claims sole custody of the child. Thereupon the principal often spends the morning talking to county court officials; often, by early afternoon, the parents are ordered to court; then the father calls the school from the court, asking for the mother, who never appeared; then case workers are assigned to the case; and so on. Similarly, the secretarial staff spend hours on the phone or talking in person with parents about problems. The school's assistant principal has formal responsibility as the "Elementary Program Supervisor," but she spends over two-thirds of her day dealing with "outside" problems.

Curriculum-improving efforts have nevertheless resulted in several developments, among them special remedial programs in math and reading. Besides the math programs, there is a remedial reading program for the early grades and a second program, which concerns us, for grades 4, 5, and 6. This latter program is run by a teacher with 16 years of teaching experience in this school; we will call her Mrs. Clark. She was originally hired at a time of increasing student enrollment and therefore was permitted to choose her assignment; she chose this school because it was on a convenient bus route. Three years ago she was selected to teach re-medial reading, replacing a teacher going on maternity leave. In the eyes of the children we know, she is one of the "nice" teachers.

Mrs. Clark's program consists of six classes. Of these we have closely observed one. At the beginning of the 1977–1978 year, this class has five fourth-grade children; in January two children moved from the school district, and one new child joined the class. These four children, two boys and two girls, come to the reading room from two different fourth-grade classrooms; we will call them Jack, Will, Leya, and Karen. The class meets five days a week for one-half hour. Each day the children enter the reading room, usually one at a time, and silently take seats around a small rectangular table which comfortably accommodates the four children and the teacher. "Greeting conversations" are rare; when they occur they are usually initiated by Mrs. Clark, and the topics are limited—a query about a child yet to arrive or a comment or query about other school events. Occasionally one child, Jack, asks whether this is to be "game day." The children then wait a minute or two in silence while Mrs. Clark assembles materials for the day's business at hand, and then the lesson begins.

Mrs. Clark is fully sensitive to neighborhood conditions, and in response to these she has developed what she calls her "educational philosophy." These are children, she says, who, because of those conditions, often fail, and who have come to expect failure—children who, by her reports, turn in work sheets with "I bet I got it all wrong," and who answer questions with "That's not right, is it?" In her words, she has to identify and isolate those "skills" a child lacks and she has to "slide right down on those skills and build those skills up." Her goal is to insure their success in this classwork and thereby to "develop their self-confidence."

In keeping with that philosophy, she has devised a teaching strategy. Instruction unfolds in two forms: she introduces a new skill (e.g., synonyms, nouns, vowel sounds); then on subsequent days the children practice the skill and practice it again until the slowest child knows it. That is, the remedy for low self-confidence in Mrs. Clark's eyes is repeated practice and the successes that result. During most of these activities Mrs. Clark watches for "frustration cues" and tries to cause the child to slow down whenever these are evident. Through this she hopes to insure that when a child answers a question he or she is correct. Besides such instruction and drill, at least once a week there are games, seen as vehicles for further practice and to help insure motivation. All these games are structured so that each child waits for his or her individual turn, all involve reading skills, but a child wins or loses through chance, the roll of the dice or the draw of the cards.

On one day, Mrs. Clark may introduce a new reading skill to the children—for example, synonyms. She defines "synonym," discusses the idea, and gives several examples of synonyms and their use. Then she asks a question and the first child who can calls out an answer; other children usually echo the answer; then a second question, and so on. During lessons of this kind the children do not raise their hands and she almost never calls on a

specific child. The next day may be devoted to practicing the same skill. For example, Mrs. Clark spreads some cards on the table; each has a word and they are placed so that the children are able to read the words. She defines the rules of the drill, then says, "I am thinking of a synonym for ——." Children raise their hands to be called on and one child is selected; that child points to a card and reads it, with help from Mrs. Clark if necessary, which often includes using the pretense that a wrong answer (for example, reaching toward the wrong card) was not really an answer; having answered correctly, the child may then take the card from the table and keep it. This continues—question, raising hands, calling on a child, response, removal of a card—until there are no longer any cards on the table.

Friday is usually "game day." On these days, the winners get points which are accumulated over time and earn small prizes. On a game day the children come in a bit excited, but as before they sit down and wait silently while their teacher gets the game set up. A favorite game is "bundles." Mrs. Clark shuffles a deck of cards (almost every card has a word on it; a few have only a picture of a sack tied closed with a rope, called a "bundle"). The deck is placed face down in the center of the table. A child is selected to start the game, draws the card on top, and places it on the table so that everyone else can see the word. With help if necessary, the child reads the card and keeps it; then the next child on the left, who has been waiting more than participating, can take a turn; and so on. A child who draws a "bundle" card gets to take all of the cards the child to the right has accumulated. When the last card has been played, the child who holds the most cards wins, and this means points added to his or her total.

Mrs. Clark's philosophy and teaching strategy are expressed in a variety of ways partly suggested by the above examples. In general, the efforts seem to work. The children seem to be learning to read, and they seem to enjoy their sessions.

One impression which emerged for us out of this first orienting stage of the inquiry was the sense of similarity of pattern, on the one hand, in affairs which unfolded in the adult community—for example, the negotiations between the neighborhood Association and outside governmental officials—and, on the other, the "echoing" patterns in the daily meetings of the remedial reading group. Later we formulated this in the form of the tacit assumptions put down at the outset of this report. The echoing patterns in the classroom suggested an item of hidden curriculum, "learning to wait," which, although never verbalized in any systematic way by teacher or student, was somehow being taught and being learned in the course of the meetings of this small group.

Classes of Activity, Classes of Person

In the first stage of ethnographic inquiry the observer seeks a general orientation; the results of the first stage of this inquiry we have now sketchily reported. In the second stage of ethnographic inquiry, one seeks to identify the salient elements in the structured array of classes of activity and of person which, in this instance, the members of this remedial reading group have settled upon.

Presumably, these agreed-upon classes of things screen the selective-perceptions of group members in such a way that, when any member acts, fellow members "see" selectively. What they see they assign to those classes, and, thereby, they recognize a familiar *kind* of act by a familiar *kind* of person. What the observer can in fact see, however, is never perceptions as such, but regularities in the ways the members of the group talk and otherwise act with each other. Common sense suggests, and for partly mysterious reasons may virtually demand, that at frequent junctures the observer "think perception," but in full analytic seriousness this has no status and is only a metaphor, sometimes helpful as an expedient. It should therefore be especially noted: ethnographic description, as we here conceive it, starts from observations of talk and action, analytically describes regularities of talk and action, and on that basis predicts how talk and action will regularly unfold.

This paper reports an ethnographic probe, not a full-blown ethnographic study. It is well to suggest now, abstractly, the extremely select nature of this probe. Urban places do admit, as we hope, description as cultural systems. The "skeletal structure" of such a large and heterogeneous cultural system, that which gives the cultural system its form and holds it together, is made evident if one describes that urban place by describing a judicious sampling of *scenes*, of *connections* between and among those scenes, and of the *events* which regularly unfold within each of those scenes.

A scene is that kind of human encounter wherein (to overstate slightly) the same people or the same sets of people come frequently together in the same places and times for the same purposes. Thus every scene is a little cultural system, similar to some other scenes but still different in nontrivial ways from any other, and, in cultural studies of modern, culturally heterogeneous settings especially, scenes must be examined one at a time. Scenes are variously connected, as suggested, at least, by the phrases, division of labor, life career, political structure, and so forth. Scenes, of this kind of human encounter, are made up of events—those interactional affairs, large and small, which the people so brought together regularly conduct.

Of all this, this probe makes only casual allusion to scenes (Mrs. Clark's reading program, consisting of six classes, is one), and to connections among scenes. This probe into the operations of an item of hidden curriculum closely examines only one recurring event, the meetings of one remedial reading class.

In this close examination there are three tasks. First, in the course of occasions of this event, as of any event, there unfolds a stream of activity which is seen by the actors to be made up of familiar segments and subsegments; that is, to the actors the concrete acts which concretely occur are members of pre-established *classes of activity*, often named or otherwise labeled by them. The task of the observer is to identify these classes of activity, and to discover

and schematically to map structural relations among the classes of activity. Similarly, the actors sort and resort each other into *classes of person*, also often named; the second task is to identify these classes of person and to discover and map the structural relations among them. Through these two tasks one describes and redescribes the event, the comings-together of this reading group, first as an "activity system" and then as a "role system."

The third task is to join the two. In the unfolding of occasions of an event, as the behaviors which constitute one class of activity shift to those behaviors which constitute a second, so, often, does one set of classes of person shift to a second set. The result is a description of meetings of this reading group as a single structure, the "event structure" of this group. This description lays a claim: that any particular meeting of the reading group, past and future, is well described by this underlying structure.

The ethnographic work in this second stage of the inquiry proceeds through the creation and subsequent analysis of two kinds of documents. The first consists of transcriptions derived from eliciting sessions with individual members of the group, in the first of which sessions a member is asked to describe "what will happen" during some selected forthcoming occasion of the event, beginning to end. The second comprises narrative accounts derived from intensive observations of the same occasion of the event as it in fact unfolds, beginning to end. The first kind of documentation is then employed again, in the transcription of an eliciting session wherein the member is asked to describe "what happened" during the same occasion of the event. Through analysis of documents of the first kind one finds verbal allusions and other clues to the structural relations among the classes. Through analysis of documents of the second kind one finds recorded enactments of many of the same classes of activity and classes of person and enactments of many of the same structural relations among the classes. Where discrepancies arise and cannot be resolved, it is the acted-out classes, not the talked-about classes, which are deemed "real."

The results of the first task are shown in Figure 1. The event, the recurring meetings of this group, is selectively described as activity system, in schematic outline. Words or phrases in quotation marks are their labelings of the segments in question; the rest are not labeled by them and the phrasings are ours. The system unfolds left to right, as shown. Where two or more segments are parallel and spatially separated, these are alternates; one or another must occur, but only one can occur, at a given time. Segments drawn with dotted lines may or may not occur; they are optional.

The second task, redescribing the

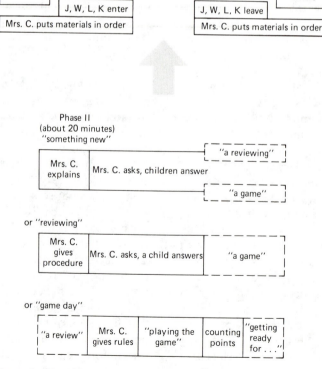

Figure 1 The reading group described as an activity system.

event as role system, is closely parallel. These five people are five autonomous individuals—Mrs. Clark, Leya, Karen, Jack, and Will—and they of course see themselves as such. They also see themselves, however, as kinds of persons: they sort and resort themselves as classes of person. One member is, of course, "teacher" and four are "students." Among the students, two are "boys" and two "girls"; two (the boys) are "lows" in terms of academic reputation; two (the girls) are "highs." All this the observer can learn from their uses of these labeling nouns and phrases in elicited interviews and, at appropriate junctures, by observing them. Further, one girl (Leya) is in the group by mistake (not really needing remedial work) and one boy (Will) is virtually a dropout; these are not merely attributes by which these children contrast with each other and with the remaining boy and girl but kinds of person which, though only dimly evident through eliciting (for these kinds of persons have no established verbal labels), are evident through observing and noting contrasting patterns in interactional behaviors. Finally, one salient fact would not be clearly evident through eliciting, indeed in interviews would probably be stoutly denied, though it is rather dramatically evident to observation: there is almost incessant interchange between Mrs. Clark and one or another of the four children but virtually no direct interchange between and among the children. This means that, although among five persons there are in principle ten dyads $(4 + 3 + 2 + 1)$, in this group only four are to be found in empirical fact.

As any occasion of the event unfolds, these five people sort and resort themselves in these terms. To describe all this is to describe the event as a role system, specifically in this case as three sets of classes of persons. The event described as role system is schematically shown in Figure 2. The names in quotation marks are used during group meetings by all five members, but for purposes of reference only; in addressing one another proper names (Mrs. Clark, Jack, Will, etc.) are used.

The third task is to draw the two descriptions, the event as activity system and as role system, together. One asks how the group is sorting itself at that time in respect to one segment of activity, then a second segment, and so on. To so articulate the two descriptions is to describe the event as an underlying

1. Four dyads of one kind

2. Four dyads of two kinds

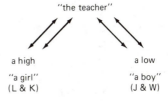

3. Four dyads of three kinds

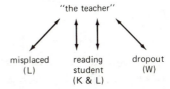

Figure 2 The reading group described as a role system.

"event structure." The event, so described, is schematically shown in Figure 3.

The observer draws all these inferences from analysis of the two kinds of documents named, transcripts derived from eliciting sessions and narrative accounts derived from direct observation. The conclusions as drawn mean that, in bringing off the activity "something new," one pattern of interactional behavior regularly unfolds between Mrs. Clark and both Leya and Karen, while a second pattern regularly unfolds between Mrs. Clark and both Jack and Will. During this activity, Leya and Karen are one kind of person (a high), interchangeably, and Jack and Will are a second kind (a low), interchangeably. The conclusions also mean that, when the group turns to bring off the activity "reviewing" or "a review," highs and lows disappear and the group resorts itself as teacher, misplaced, dropout, and reading student—four dyads of three kinds—in the manner shown.

Routines

In the preceding stage of ethnographic inquiry, the event was described as an event structure. Now the event structure is to be redescribed in some of its parts, but at a level of greater and more precise detail.

In this third stage of ethnographic inquiry the observer seeks to describe the internal structure of selected parts of the event structure—for example, of that part of the event structure when the group, sorted as "four dyads of two kinds," is bringing off the activity, "something new." The internal structure of any such part is made up of a small repertory of "routines," and each of these routines is made up in turn of a chain of "moves and answering moves," which chain, once started, predictably runs its course. The acts now to be identified and mapped are small subclasses of those classes of activity described earlier; the classes of person earlier identified remain the same.

This is to say that when, in the specific context of any such part of the event structure, a member of the group behaves toward another, that action is usually seen by fellow members as a kind of act by a kind of person. Now, at this level of smaller detail, the action is a recognizably familiar "move" which frequently occurs in that specific context. And where a second member

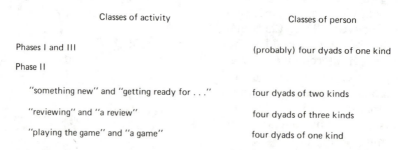

Classes of activity	Classes of person
Phases I and III	(probably) four dyads of one kind
Phase II	
"something new" and "getting ready for . . ."	four dyads of two kinds
"reviewing" and "a review"	four dyads of three kinds
"playing the game" and "a game"	four dyads of one kind

Figure 3 The reading group described as an event structure.

reacts, that is also usually seen as a kind of act by a kind of person, as a recognizably familiar answering move which frequently follows in that context. The very strong regularities which are always to be found in recurring human encounters are embodied in routines.

Inquiry proceeds in this stage through designing and using in observation a small battery of ethnographic schedules. An ethnographic schedule is an observational tool which is designed for the observational task in its specifics; it is so designed that the observer can systematically record those small subclasses of activity and those classes of person which are being specifically enacted in some specific context. One must, through earlier observation, know with some certainty and in some detail that a particular routine is "there," and one designs the schedule so as to try to capture that routine specifically. Even so, some trial-and-error is irreduceably necessary; the records which will follow are from the third or fourth, not the first, attempts to capture the routines in question.

There follows (Figure 4) an excerpt from a record of interaction, so captured, which reveals a repertory of three routines which together are the internal structure of that specific part of the event structure when these five people sort themselves as "four dyads of two kinds" and, so organized, bring off "something new."

The particular lesson was briefly and anecdotally described earlier (page 249). Mrs. Clark is introducing the idea of "synonyms"; principally, she is asking the children to provide synonyms for words she names. With only one exception, she does not call on specific children; as quickly as they can, they simply call out answers, and she responds to their answers.

This particular ethnographic schedule was designed so as to capture who acts as a kind of person, given the way the group sorts itself to bring off "something new." That is, the actor at any moment is "the teacher" or "a high" (Leya or Karen, interchangeably) or "a low" (Jack or Will, interchangeably). Similarly, as earlier found, the familiar activity "something new" has familiar subsegments, among them the subsegment we labeled, "Mrs. Clark asks, children answer." Within this last, in turn, of the virtual infinity of specific acts which can and do occur, virtually all are seen by the actors as members of one or another of a remarkably few classes of acts, and each act thereby becomes, to them, a familiar move or a familiar answering move. Specifically, the sundry acts by Mrs. Clark, as captured in the schedule, are assigned to membership in classes according to those differences in her behaviors which made a difference to the children as seen in their consequent acts. That is, in their perceptions (note the metaphor), either she is talking or not talking, and if talking, she is talking in a way which seems to them to require only listening behaviors ("talking" on the schedule), or she is talking in a way which seems to require verbal response of them ("asking for answers" on the schedule), or she is talking in some third way that is neither—for example, about things unconnected with the business at hand (the residual "other" on the schedule). Conversely, the acts by the children, as assigned to classes and captured by the schedule, are those differences in their behaviors which made a difference *to Mrs. Clark*, as seen in her consequent acts (thus: "answering correctly" or "answering incorrectly" and the residual "other"). Each vertical column in the schedule represents about one second of clock time. Figure 4 shows a brief excerpt from such a record.

The numbered arrows entered on the record indicate the beginning points of two routines and of a possible third routine, which together are the internal structure of the group's joint behaviors during the subsegment of "something new" under examination. That is, the record begins with the latter part of the subsegment earlier named "Mrs. C. explains," and at the first arrow (Mrs. Clark says, "Who can tell me a word for ——?") the group shifts to the subsegment earlier named, "Mrs. C. asks, children answer," and a routine, "a," begins to unfold, a pingpong-like interchange between Mrs. Clark, as teacher, who asks questions and Karen and Leya interchangeably, as highs, who answer. A few moments later, this routine is interrupted by an action by Mrs. Clark which the schedule, as designed, does not capture (in particular she directs her eyes fixedly toward Jack, a low), an act that may function to switch from routine "a" to some other involving the lows. This effort appears, however, to abort; a high takes over, as it would appear, and the highs hold the floor for some while. The second arrow points to the brief reintroduction of the "a" routine. The third arrow marks the onset of routine "b," which, in terms of duration, seems to dominate occasions of this subsegment of "something new" generally; here the teacher asks for an answer, a high answers, and a low echoes the answer (typically using the identical word or phrase). After a series of these interchanges, this routine is terminated by an action by Mrs. Clark (for the first time she calls on a child by name, a low) with unclear consequence. Then the "a" routine reappears briefly, followed by a string of talk by Mrs. Clark, only partially shown, which closes this subsegment of activity "Mrs. C asks . . . ," and opens an activity of another kind, "a game," which is an optional subsegment of "something new."

On a later day, Mrs. Clark establishes a drill in synonyms; this particular lesson was briefly described earlier (page 249). Mrs. Clark has written words on cards which are now spread face up on the table, and she explains the rules. Then Mrs. Clark says, "I am thinking of a synonym for ——"; the children try to find the card with the right word and raise their hands; Mrs. Clark waits and at intervals repeats and gives hints, usually until two or more hands are up; then one child is called on, and that child points to the card, reads it, and takes the card. This is an occasion of that part of the event structure wherein the activity called by them "reviewing" unfolds, specifically that subsegment called "Mrs. C. asks, a child answers." Now the group sorts itself as "four dyads of three kinds"; that is, of the four children one (Leya) is "misplaced," one (Will) is "dropout," and two (Jack and Karen, interchangeably) are "reading students" proper, the labels being ours.

The internal structure of this subsegment of "reviewing" consists of one routine plus certain licenses with the

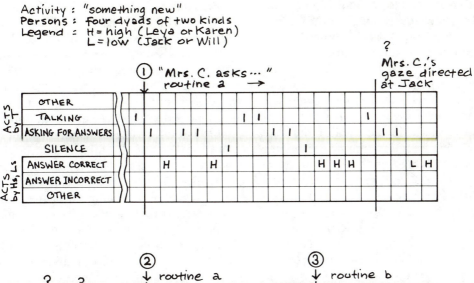

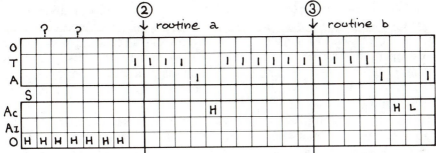

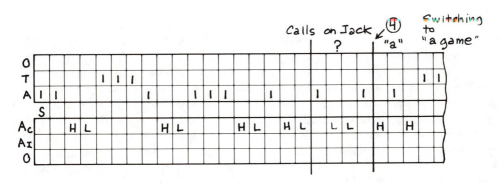

Figure 4   Excerpt from a record of interaction.

routine granted to "dropout" and a special form of involvement in the routine by "misplaced." This is captured by observation, using an ethnographic schedule designed according to the specifics of this specific context. In this context, in contrast with the earlier-treated segment "something new," the sundry acts of Mrs. Clark, in the eyes of the children, are seen as members of the classes "talking" or "calling on" (verbally or by a gesture) or the residual "other." Exactly, as it happens, as in that earlier context, acts by the children, in the eyes of Mrs. Clark, are seen as members of the classes "answering correctly" or "answering incorrectly," or "other." The record of the class session, so captured, is shown in Figure 5.

The record opens during the latter part of "Mrs. Clark explains" (i.e., showing the cards, saying she will be asking for synonyms, that they should raise their hands, etc.). The number "1" indicates the beginning of the subsegment "Mrs. Clark asks, a child answers" and the onset of the first occurrence of the routine (in particular, Mrs. Clark says, "I am thinking of a synonym for ——"); then silence; then various repetitions and hints by Mrs. Clark while children tentatively point and hands are going up, and down, and up again; then she calls on one of the two "reading students" (R); that student correctly points to a card and takes it; and Mrs. Clark confirms (the "other" talk) the correctness of the answer. The number "2" indicates the beginning of a repetition of the same routine (again Mrs. Clark says, "I am thinking of a synonym for ——"), and the routine unfolds. Similarly, the number "3." The fourth occurrence of the routine in-

volves dropout (D) and is special in two respects. First, there is the unusually long period of silence which precedes Mrs. Clark's calling on D; and second, D's answer is wrong, and another child (R) is called on. (The record reflects, but as designed does not show, that during that period of silence, although three other hands are up, Mrs. Clark fixes her gaze on D, virtually forcing him, as it would seem, to put his hand up.) Occurrence "5" of the routine is again normal. With "6" D is allowed license: he answers correctly, but without being called on, and this is permitted. There follows a series, "7" through "11," in which the routine repeatedly unfolds normally (in "10" R mispronounces a word, Mrs. Clark repeats, R repeats correctly). With "12" D answers again without being called on. With "13" a deterioration sets in; Mrs. Clark gives an ambiguous signal, and three children (two R's and D) answer simultaneously, and there follows a series of exchanges among those three children which, in this routinized context, is disorderly. Throughout, to this point, the "misplaced" child (M) has had her hand up only infrequently and has participated only once. The affair has now deteriorated; and now M participates, correctly according to the routine, in "14" and again in "15." The record does not show, except for the cryptic notation "M as 'shill'" that at the outset of "14," the "talking" by Mrs. Clark included side comments to M (in effect, "Karen has her hand up, why don't you?"). That is, M's participation in this context appears to be as Mrs. Clark's right arm, indirectly assisting her in the drill of the other students. With "16" the routine, now reestablished, is normal. In

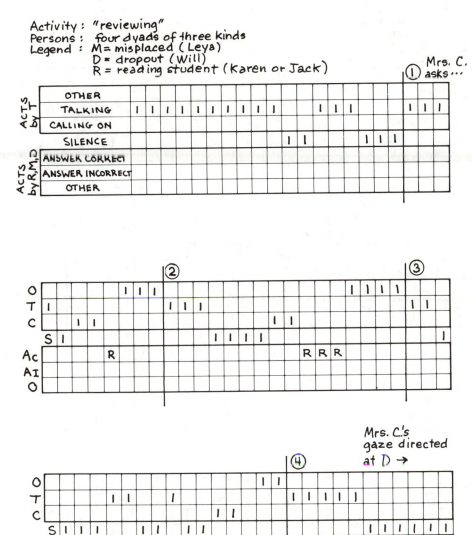

Figure 5   A day's record of interaction (about 25 minutes).

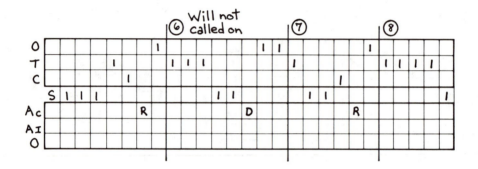

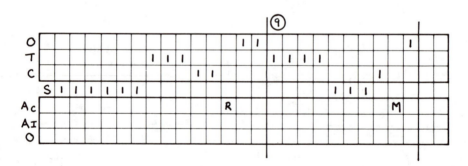

Figure 5 (continued) A day's record of interaction (about 25 minutes).

"17" D answers without being called on, but on this occasion is reminded to raise his hand, and he promises to remember. "18" is normal. "19" is a rather massive stumble involving everyone, including Mrs. Clark, with no evi- dent cause or consequence. "20" is nor- mal again, and with "21" D finally gets everything, the answer and the routine, right. After "21" there are only two cards left on the table, on both of which are written words which are new to the

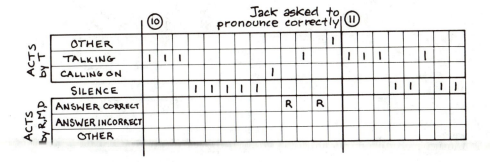

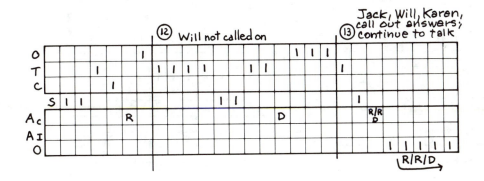

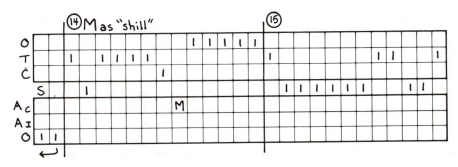

Figure 5 (continued)   A day's record of interaction (about 25 minutes).

children and Mrs. Clark says they are "new," and "hard," but "we'll have to get used to them," and so on. Rather amazingly, perhaps, the children seem almost to snap into "something new," that is, into "four dyads of two kinds,"

and possibly into "highs answer, lows echo," that is, routine "b" in Figure 4. The transition is abrupt, and almost certainly not recognized as such by Mrs. Clark or the students. Of course, the schedule was designed for "review-

⑯ ⑰ Mrs.C. reminds Will to raise hand

							⑯					⑰				
ACTS by T OTHER		I	I	I						I						
TALKING					I	I					I		I	I		
CALLING ON	I								I							
SILENCE						I	I				I	I			I	I
ACTS by R,M,D ANSWER CORRECT	M								R			D				
ANSWER INCORRECT																
OTHER													D			

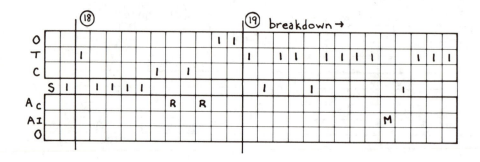

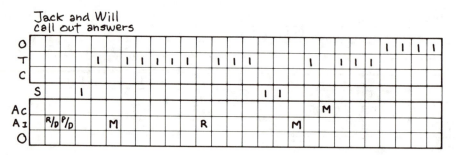

Figure 5 (continued)   A day's record of interaction (about 25 minutes).

ing," not "something new," and it describes poorly the interchanges that follow.[1] The schedule, therefore, is only selectively reproduced from this point. This, whatever "this" is, continues another two or three minutes to the end of the class period.

To recapitulate, this third stage of inquiry reveals that that part of the event structure wherein the subsegment of "something new" is brought off is internally structured as a repertory of two routines, either one of which, but only one, may occur at any time.

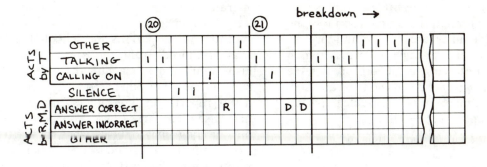

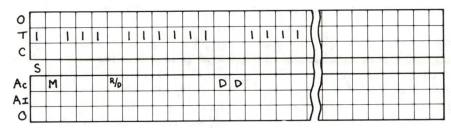

Figure 5 (continued) A day's record of interaction (about 25 minutes).

TTT → H,   TTT → H, etc.

TTT → H → L,   TTT → H → L, etc.

Similarly, that part of the event structure wherein "reviewing" is brought off is internally structured by repeated occurrences of a single routine, with variations.

TTT (silence) T → R, TTT (silence) T → R, etc.

By virtue of the strongly hierarchical organization of this classroom, like most others, choices as to the occurrence of one routine or one of its variants probably lie with Mrs. Clark almost solely. Such choices, consciously or otherwise, are brought off through switching behaviors by her, which we have only casually alluded to.

In the third kind of segment of the event structure, "playing a game," the group sorts itself as "four dyads of one kind," that is, actors are "teacher" or "student" (Leya, Karen, Jack, Will, interchangeably). Here Mrs. Clark's regulatory role is taken over by the rules of the game itself, and she monitors and at junctures enforces those rules. We will skip past the details. The internal structure is again a chain of moves and answering moves which constitute a single routine.

(await turn) → S, (await turn) → S, (await turn) → S, etc.

Through mapping routines internal to selected segments of an event, one adds detailed precision to the earlier description of the event as event structure. Through mapping routines one also identifies the nature and precise locus of the strong regularities which make unfolding behaviors predictable and which make occasions of any segment of an event recognizable to participant and observer alike.

Functions: the Manifest Curriculum

In any structural-functional description these two ideas, structure and function, are always present, variously filtering observation and shaping thought in ways that can be made only partly self-conscious. Some control is gained by drawing first the one and then the other to the foreground of thought. Through the stages of inquiry now behind us, clearly structure was foreground and function, though present in many difficult-to-recognize ways, was background. Now, in this fourth and final stage of inquiry, we reverse that: structure is now "done," and we ask how that structure functions. For the limited purposes of this ethnographic probe, this involves only interpretation of data already in hand.

This reading group meets five days a week. The central and fully explicit business at hand, in Mrs. Clark's eyes, is to insure each child's success with one, then another, reading skill and thereby to raise each child's self-confidence. Related to that primary business as means to end are two secondary businesses that are also explicit: to introduce—that is, to identify and demonstrate—one skill, then another, and to create motivation.

In the eyes of parents and school officials removed from the scene, the business at hand is "teaching these children to read." For our narrow purpose in this report, this is germane only in the sense that Mrs. Clark's purposes must be congruent to theirs, since she is accountable to them, and of course her purposes are. The business at hand, in the eyes of the children, is more saliently germane to us, though not well known to us at this juncture; probably it is something like "having fun learning to read." Since power in this hierarchically organized group is concentrated, and since the affairs of the group are regularly brought off quite smoothly, the children's perception, whatever it might more precisely be, will surely be found to be different from but congruent with their teacher's.

The event, the recurring meetings of this reading group, has been described as an event structure. That structure now reveals that the different segments of activity differently serve Mrs. Clark's three businesses at hand. Obviously, in "something new" the main purpose served is her secondary business, introducing a skill, and in "playing a game" the main purpose is another secondary business, creating motivation. However, her principal business at hand is insuring success and (as Mrs. Clark imagines, perhaps correctly) thereby building self-confidence. This principal business is served in all three segments, but differently in each, as follows.

During occasions of the segment "something new," successes and the presumptive increases in self-confidences do seem to occur for the two children who are highs, but for lows probably the opposite occurs. During occasions of the segment "reviewing," successes and the presumptive increases in self-confidence would occur for the two children called by us "reading students" and would occur doubly, because of her special "teacher's right hand" role, for the child we call misplaced, but the opposite would seem to occur for the child called by us dropout. Finally, during occasions of the segments "playing the game" or "a game," insuring success and the presumptive increases in self-confidence would probably occur for all four children alike.

On the average, week in and week out, the time spent in the three kinds of activity is approximately in this proportion: for one hour spent in "something new," three are spent in "reviewing" and two in "playing the game" or "a game."

Recapitulating: the estimated results for the individual children—insuring their successes and building their self-confidence—as derived from the three activities, given the relative time spent in those activities, are cumulatively about as follows:

	1	2	3	
Leya (H,M,S)	+	+++(+)	++	6 plus
Karen (H,R,S)	+	+++	++	6
Jack (L,R,S)	−	+++	++	4
Will (L,D,S)	−	−−−	++	−2

Ethnographic description, we parenthetically infer from this, might well provide an additional tool to be brought to bear in the diagnosis and evaluation of the operations of manifest curriculums.

Functions: Hidden Curriculum

We began by defining this study as a probe into the operations of one item of hidden curriculum, and to this we finally return. What remains is simply to show how the description of meetings of this reading group as a small cultural system, the "event structure," actually is a description of an item of hidden curriculum in operation.

The item of hidden curriculum, as we initially phrased it, was two propositions: (1) "People are not equal . . ." and (2) "We . . . are losing . . . [and] if we are patient and deliberate, we can cut our losses. . . ." Or, more tersely, for those who are less equal than others, "learning to wait." It need only be noted that as occasions of this event unfold, one of these two propositions is highlighted, then the other, but *throughout both are being enacted and throughout neither is contradicted.*

As we saw, in the course of occasions of this event the manifest curriculum is spottily served. As we can now see, the hidden curriculum is served incessantly and with much consistency.

This is to say, during the segments called "something new" the inequality of the children, as highs and lows, is foregrounded; but at the same time the lows, by waiting, by not answering at all, or by hanging back and echoing, are exercising (and perfecting?) one device by which it is possible to be right; quite possibly, if paradoxically, this serves as a lesson—a demonstration—for the highs as well, to be used by them in other contexts. During the segments called "reviewing," inequality is again celebrated in the special elevated role played by the misplaced child and the special depressed and "tolerated" role of the dropout. The foreground, however, is occupied by the requirements of waiting to be called on (quite arbitrarily, one surmises, in such a small group) and is very regularly practiced by all the children but one, the dropout; there are also "waiting for" cues from Mrs. Clark, which frequently are sought and as frequently given. And during the segments called "playing the game" and "a game" waiting is again foreground, now entailed by the turn-taking structure of the game itself. Here inequality is not paraded, but by making the games turn on luck, the rewards which usually go differentially to students according to their abilities are suspended, and perhaps that in itself is one way of enacting inequality.

The consistence of the operations of this item of hidden curriculum is revealed in detail if one slowly and thoughtfully "reads through" in the mind's eye the event structure as it unfolds, beginning to end, in the three principal forms any occasion of this event can take.

This study is a probe, not a rounded and complete inquiry. But even as probe, there is one major flaw. If the reading group had been observed beginning in September and ending in June, possibly we would have seen changes; that is, the children in September would surely have been seen en-

acting the tacit assumptions in some form (they are fourth graders and presumably have been practicing since infancy), but at that early date, in all probability, they would have been doing this somewhat ineptly. In fact we observed this class closely for only a few weeks, intermittently during March and April. Leya, Karen, and Jack seemed to have mastered the hidden curriculum already; Will, the dropout, had not, but neither was he learning it, so far as we could see. Will, be it noted, is working at being a real "loser." In a word, we do not in these data see teaching and learning, only their end products.

In some more ambitious ethnographic study of this neighborhood and its school, the close examination of at least two additional scenes should follow. In this school there are surely pockets of children, drawn from the neighborhood, who are regularly winning, relative to their fellow students. We would be most interested to learn what form this same hidden curriculum takes in contexts where such children interact among themselves and with others. Second and most pivotally, the study requires the close examination of adult affairs in some scene, as regular occasions of interchange between the neighborhood Association and governmental officialdom. We would have to ask how, in behavioral detail, the set of tacit assumptions is acted out in that context, if indeed it is, as we strongly but only impressionistically believe.

At issue, in this and other culturally oriented studies of hidden curriculum, is an often-noted and little understood phenomenon, pattern replication. In any modern setting wherein there is an array of scenes which are closely interconnected by systems overlapping kinds of linkages, whatever the variety of businesses at hand and contrary to surface appearances, the scenes often come to resemble each other in their underlying structures. Thus U.S. schools resemble U.S. jails and both resemble U.S. asylums, and so on. Thus, more narrowly, school classrooms tend strongly to replicate in microcosm the wider community, but selectively. One gets the sense that, in part through the operations of hidden curriculums, the society at large is busily replicating itself across the generations, "warts and all." Good ethnographic descriptions, in sufficient number and in an appropriate array of selected places, promise to map, in social space, the areas wherein pattern replication in one form normally occurs and other spaces wherein it occurs in a second or third form, and ethnography promises to reveal the cultural processes by which all this is normally brought about. So armed, educators might be able to interrupt those processes and forestall their results, where it seems to them good to do so.

Note

[1] "M" on this schedule is unambiguously Leya, a "high," and "D" is Will, a "low"; but "R" on this schedule is either Karen or Jack, a "high" and "low" respectively; translation from the one record to the other is thus impossible.

9

Kathleen Wilcox

Differential Socialization in the Classroom: Implications for Equal Opportunity

Kathleen Wilcox

The Author

Kathleen Wilcox is devoting her time to research and writing. She was a member of the faculty of the Department of Human Development at California State University, Hayward, for three years. She also spent a year as a Visiting Scholar at the Center for Educational Research at Stanford University. Although she has done fieldwork in Czechoslovakia and Kenya, her major interest is in the anthropology of education in the United States. This interest developed during her graduate training in social anthropology at Harvard University, where she received the Ph.D. degree. At Harvard she spent several years investigating the role of major social institutions in the processes of cultural transmission and change in China.

As she completed her graduate work, Wilcox became increasingly convinced of the value of a cross-cultural perspective in attempting to understand the workings of one's own culture. Persuaded that the anthropological perspective could shed great light on problems of continuity and change in social institutions in the United States, she became particularly interested in the institution of education. She has done fieldwork in both classrooms and work places in order to explore the linkage between schooling and work. Her publications have focused on socialization for adult work roles in the classroom and on policy implications of the ethnography of schooling.

Wilcox is the author also of Chapter 15 in this book.

This Chapter

In this chapter Kathleen Wilcox analyzes certain features of teacher behavior in two classes in two elementary schools on the West Coast, one drawing children from a working-class neighborhood, the other from a professional, executive-level neighborhood. The research design is one with an established history in anthropology—the controlled comparison. Both neighborhoods are "mainstream." Social class is the independent variable. The focus is on the dimensions of teacher behavior in interaction with children in the classroom: external versus internal direction; anticipation of the future, particularly with respect to work role; and fostering skills in self-presentation. In the literature on work roles in the United States, dimensions of this kind are regarded as differentiating features in the work and social class hierarchy.

Wilcox's study draws constructs from the background literature and reconstitutes them on the basis of classroom observation. She formulates hypotheses that she then tests in the classrooms. The study is therefore contextualized in the broadest possible framework—social class and work hierarchies in the United States, as well as in the respective communities selected to represent this framework.

Wilcox's research design holds true to the anthropological ideal of holism, an ideal that is all too easily laid aside in the microethnography of the classroom or one of its segments. Her design departs from ethnographic tradition in that she tests specific hypotheses, but is true to form in that the hypotheses, though inspired by the background literature on social class and work roles, are, in their final form, the product of an orienting phase of ethnographic inquiry. Also a product of this phase of inquiry are the highly specific codings she and a coworker use to gather data. For some ethnographers such codings are anathema, and indeed they are more widely used by socioethnographers and psychoethnographers. Wilcox's study demonstrates how precoded categories of observation can be useful to an anthropological ethnographer when the codes are developed from observations on the site.

This chapter is more explicitly concerned with educational policy than most. The self-fulfilling prophecies that work to socialize children for the hierarchy of work roles go unchallenged unless there is significant intervention from the outside, for teachers and administrators are as enculturated to the status quo as anyone. The forms, intensity, and even direction of this intervention process remain moot. This chapter raises the issues to consciousness in clear form.

Introduction

This chapter suggests ways in which the use of an anthropological frame-

I would like to express my deep appreciation for the contribution made by Pia Moriarty to all phases of the work reported here. Her creativity, intelligence, and insight have been of inestimable value. I would also like to thank Henry Levin for reviewing and commenting on the manuscript throughout several stages of its development and to acknowledge gratefully the support of the Center for Economic Studies, Harvard University, and National Institute of Education Grant #G-00-3-0205.

work can throw new light on our thinking about the possibility of attaining equal opportunity through education and our thinking about methods appropriate to reaching this goal. The chapter presents results obtained in an ethnographic study of equal opportunity in the classroom, along with the underlying assumptions, methodology, research design, and techniques used in the study. In particular, it explores ways in which children are socialized for adult work roles by teachers in the classroom. The study asks whether children are given equal opportunity to learn skills and attitudes appropriate to a wide variety of work roles, or if instead only a small segment of work-related skills and attitudes is transmitted to particular groups of children. It focuses especially on the effect of student social class on patterns of socialization for work roles in the classroom, and investigates whether or not children are socialized differently according to their social class background.

The design of the study emerged from a conviction that much of the writing about education and equal opportunity in the U.S. is grounded in some serious misconceptions about the role of schools in society and about the role of the teacher in the classroom.

Speaking within an anthropological framework, it is crucial to keep in mind that schooling is a social institution with a key role in socializing children for *available* adult roles. Schools are not set up to socialize children for membership in some ideal society; they are set up to socialize children for membership in their own society as it currently exists and as it is likely to exist in the near future. This is not to say that there is no room at all for change, for innovation, or for ideals in education, but that to expect an institution responsible for child socialization to depart radically from the needs of the culture as currently constituted is to expect a culture to commit suicide.

The conception of schools as primary *transmitters* of culture is very different from the conception common in the United States of schools as *reformers* of culture. A view of the school as transmitter of culture has interesting implications for the issue of equal opportunity in education.

As transmitters of culture, schools need to ensure that children are satisfactorily prepared to assume adult work roles. Imagine the fate of the culture if students graduated from schools, wandered into work places, and started tearing up concrete floors with jackhammers because they wanted to be farmers instead! Or imagine what would happen if students felt they could only take orders from their mothers, fathers, and other relatives, not from some stranger called the "boss" whom they had never met before in their lives. In countless ways which are taken for granted, children emerge from the institutions of socialization ready to step into the work place in a minimally disruptive manner.

One fundamental characteristic of adult work roles in the culture of the United States is that these roles are highly differentiated and stratified. Horatio Alger myths aside, it is a rare person in this day and age who spends substantial portions of his or her work life at drastically different levels of the stratified work place. To be a properly socialized person in this culture, one has to be willing at least to tolerate one's place at a particular level in the work hierarchy, and to have the skills and capabilities appropriate to that level. The school becomes an institution which is crucial in differentiating students, in allocating them to one level or another, and in socializing them to perform adequately in and at least minimally accept their place.

In short, the school is a social institution upon which the culture places highly contradictory expectations. Receiving most obvious attention is the expectation that schools will maximize social equality by promoting equal opportunity; less obvious is the expectation that schools will maximize social differentiation by allocating persons to positions in a differentiated and stratified work force (Brookover and Erickson 1975:105).

Given that, from a structural-functional perspective, the school is heavily involved in differentiating students, on what basis is this differentiation likely to take place? Much of the educational literature proposes or assumes that schools are able to sort out individual differences in an equitable and neutral fashion (*Harvard Educational Review* 1968, Special Issue on Equal Educational Opportunity; McMurrin 1971). The indigenous image of this process is that the child is born with an innate academic potential which can be "divined" by watchful parents and teachers (Fischer 1963) and which is expected to be indicative of all future skills, abilities, and successes. An elaborate ritual procedure of testing, grading, and ranking accompanies this belief, and is conducted in such a way as to emphasize the neutrality and objectivity of the process.

In fact, the person most intimately involved with this testing and grading process, the teacher, is a cultural being who is operating in a cultural context— a swirling constellation of forces in which it is humanly and culturally impossible to be "neutral." There is considerable evidence that teachers label and form expectations of children with regard to their individual ability on the basis of the child's membership in particular groups, the most obvious of which are social class, sex, and ethnicity (Rist 1970, Leacock 1969, Brophy and Good 1970).

This chapter suggests that teachers socialize children differentially for work roles based on the teacher's perception of these roles and the social class of the children's parents. This does not appear to happen intentionally or consciously, but rather virtually without plot or plan, in a series of actions woven throughout the fabric of day-to-day life in the classroom.

What teacher behavior can be seen to constitute socialization for adult work roles? Background reading and research about the economic structure and organization of the United States, including characteristics of work roles at various levels of the occupational hierarchy, provided a series of concepts and constructs to be drawn upon in operationalizing the concept of socialization for work roles in the classroom. They did not provide a ready-made set of characteristics which could be taken to the classroom and simply checked off as absent or present. A great effort was made in the research I will report shortly to build a picture of behavior constituting socialization for work roles out of the teachers' own construction of the work process in the classroom. However, the knowledge gained through background reading and research was extremely helpful in interpreting the significance of the teachers' activity.

Three general dimensions for analyzing classroom interaction emerged as a result of the combined process of background research and on-site observation. The dimensions consisted of (1) cognitive or skill requirements for different jobs, including self-presentation skills; (2) the relationship to authority at different levels of the work hierarchy; and (3) self-image and general level of work-related expectations suitable for different positions.

The most common view of the way in which schools prepare and sort students for work roles is through the teaching and testing of cognitive skills. This view is grounded in a conception of the work place known as the "human capital model" (Becker 1967, Mincer 1970). According to this model, employers are willing to pay more for people with greater amounts of "human capital," "human capital" being a rather vague term referring to cognitive skills, the "capacity to learn," and certain technical skills as well. It is seen to be acquired through investment in education as well as on-the-job training. Consistent with this view, the role of the school is seen as teaching cognitive skills and evaluating and differentiating pupils according to how well they have learned these skills, or according to their general ability. Parsons' (1959) statement that the primary factor underlying the child's opportunity for achievement is his or her individual ability also exemplifies the "human capital" perspective on the role which schools play with respect to the work place.

Skills in self-presentation can also be thought of as acquired in the classroom and related to work role characteristics at various levels of the work hierarchy. A person's work role has been linked to the presentation of self in both the popular and the scholarly domain (Goffman 1959). A mention of the roles of used car salesman, hard hat, lawyer, or doctor, for example, brings to mind images of particular styles of self-presentation. As Bowles and Gintis point out:

[Individuals who have attained a certain educational level tend to] ... acquire manners of speech and demeanor more or less socially acceptable and appropriate to their level. As such, they are correspondingly valuable to employers interested in preserving and reproducing the status differences on which the legitimacy and stability of the hierarchical division of labor is based. [1976:141]

Appropriate manners of speech and demeanor vary according to the level of the job hierarchy at which one is placed. For example, at the professional and managerial level there is a need to participate in discussions in a culturally defined "articulate" and "confident" manner to a much greater degree than at the lower levels. Production and service workers are far less likely to find themselves called upon to become involved in extended discourse in the upper-middle-class style as a criterion for adequate job performance.

There is substantial evidence that the cognitive aspect of job performance and therefore of schooling has been greatly overemphasized. Bowles and Gintis (1976) summarize a body of literature which suggests that cognitive ability, as measured by IQ, is not the crucial variable associated with educational achievement and satisfactory on-the-job performance. They stress the importance of a number of "personality" factors, one of which can be described in terms of one's relationship to authority at different levels of the work hierarchy.

Kohn (1967) distinguishes jobs at the lower level of the hierarchy, which he perceives as being characterized by external requirements, rules, regulations, and routine, from those at the higher levels, which he sees as requiring that employees internalize norms that are consistent with the goals of the organization. He suggests that workers at the lower levels are expected to accept the direction of external authority, while those at the higher levels are expected to show independence in their judgments and base their work behavior upon internalized values and motivation. In other words, it is presumed that employees in lower level jobs must be motivated and directed by structures *external* to themselves, while those at higher levels are presumed to be "self-directed" by *internal* motivations that correspond to organizational needs. Kohn's (1967) distinction is supported by a number of more recent theoretical and empirical studies (Gintis 1971, Bowles and Gintis 1976, Edwards 1976).

Looking at these traits in terms of schooling, one would expect to find that socialization for jobs in the lower portions of the work hierarchy would involve the use of *externally imposed* methods of motivating students to behave in ways that the teacher or school considers appropriate. Socialization for higher level roles, on the other hand, would involve teaching students to *internalize* and identify with the norms and requirements of the school so as to be "self-directing" within that context.

A third general dimension along which schools can be seen to prepare students for future work roles is self-image, that is, one's sense of personal capability and likely future role. Meyer (1970), in his review of the literature on anticipatory socialization (the tendency for people to become what society as a whole appears to expect of them), sug-

gests that schools may indeed create pupil self-images that correspond to expected future roles. He notes that the likelihood of an individual's acquiring the attributes of a given position in society is directly related to whether he or she is socially perceived as likely to acquire that position. The work of Sennett and Cobb (1972), who conducted in-depth interviews with American workers, also suggests a link between the experience of oneself in school and future work roles.

These three dimensions emerged and jelled during the process of data gathering and analysis. I will now describe briefly the research design—an ethnographic approach to the study of socialization for adult work roles in the classroom.

The Research Design

In order to study the effects of student social class background, or parental work role, on patterns of socialization for work roles within the classroom, two classrooms were selected for study, one in each of two schools located in neighborhoods which contrasted according to social class. Given the homogeneous character of urban and suburban neighborhoods in the contemporary United States, it was virtually impossible to find a single neighborhood containing within it substantial differences in social class of the residents. The study therefore took a form which is known in anthropology as a controlled comparison, in which an attempt is made to research more than one site, holding all variables as constant as possible except the one which is the independent variable under study (Nadel 1952; Nader 1964).

The typical research design in the field of social class and education has involved an implicit or explicit comparison between middle- or upper-middle-class white schools and lower-class minority schools (Herriott 1966; Conant 1961). While the educational problems of minorities have certainly merited this attention, this contrast tends to be unrepresentative of the social majority. The majority of people in the United States are neither wealthy nor poor. "Mainstream" differences are most likely to be noted within the "middle income" range. This study sought to compare the experiences of students in this middle range by selecting schools located in a lower-middle-class and an upper-middle-class community.

The study took two different but intimately related focuses. On was interaction *within* the classroom—in particular, teacher socialization behavior in the classroom. The other focus was *outside* the classroom, in the belief that, since the classroom is intimately embedded within a social context, knowledge of that social context will further understanding of interaction within the classroom. Spindler underlines the importance of interpreting the various levels of meaning involved in social interaction:

> The manifest content of any interaction set may be quite clear to the participants within it, but the latent, or implicit, content may be virtually undetected in a direct, conscious sense. It is the anthropologist's job to try to expose this implicit level in his or her interpretation

of behavior and its consequences. . . . The anthropologist records and analyzes the data in a continuous search for the underlying principles of organization, the undeclared meaning and functions of behavior in both verbal and non-verbal dimensions. [1963:8–9]

This interpretive process cannot be carried out effectively without an adequate understanding of the social and cultural context in which interaction takes place (Sindell 1969, Wax and Wax 1971, Leacock 1969).

Looking Outward: The Social Context of the Classroom

I will first describe the way in which the social context of the classroom was conceptualized. Classrooms can be thought of as embedded within a series of concentric circles representing aspects of the social and cultural environment in which interaction within the classroom takes place. Beginning from the outside, each circle can be thought of as influencing all those contained within it. Of course, there is also likely to be some degree of influence moving in the other direction, and inter-influence between the various levels. A sophisticated model of the situation would be covered with arrows going every which way. However, the strongest direction of influence is assumed to be from the outside in, or from macro structures to micro interactions. This is in accordance with the conception stated earlier that education is primarily a process of cultural transmission.

The research design involved a series of plans constructed to gather data on each of the various aspects of the sociocultural context represented by the ellipses in Figure 1. Obviously, it would not be possible to obtain in one study a full understanding of all the dynamics at work within each level and between all levels. However, some knowledge was considered to be better than none, and time was devoted to gathering data at each of the levels represented in the diagram. It is important to note here that the details of the diagram were not determined prior to the beginning of the study, but emerged as the study took place. What existed to begin with was a theoretical appreciation of the importance of the social context; the specific definitions of the social context emerged from the data during the course of the research.

Space does not allow a detailed description of the kind of data collected with respect to each ellipse in the diagram. I will rely on the data presented later in the chapter on the social context of the classroom to stand as indicative of the kinds of data gathered and the methods used at each level. Needless to say, the approach was one of in-depth participant observation, focused particularly around the three dimensions outlined earlier. It seems crucial, however, to describe a bit more fully the design and methodology employed in studying what took place within the two classrooms themselves.

Looking Inward: Interaction Within the Classroom

Two basic premises guided research within the classroom. One was that we wished to achieve a lengthy and intimate contact with the classroom while minimizing the degree to which our

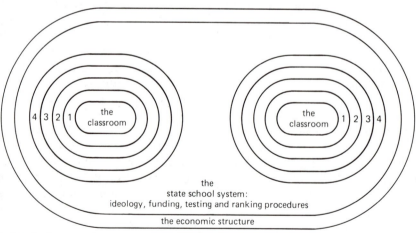

1 the school
2 the neighborhood: history, demographic makeup,
                      parents' relations with the school
3 the school district
4 the community: history, demographic makeup

Figure 1 Levels of the sociocultural context.

presence affected interactions among people there.[1] The other was that we wished to avoid as much as possible coming into the classroom with a predetermined idea of how teachers socialized children for work roles. We wished instead to become involved in a very open-ended observation of the teachers' own construction of the work process in the classroom, so that the socialization patterns we would eventually define would be as truly indigenous to the classroom as possible.

In line with the first premise, we planned on spending at least a three-month period in the classroom, during which we would become familiar with all the ins and outs of how the teacher constructed the process of daily life in the classroom. We did not become actively involved in taking responsibility within the classroom, preferring to retain an observer's role. The level of experience and confidence of the teacher seemed very important in enabling close contact with the observer while minimizing alteration of teacher behavior. Both of the teachers selected for the study were very experienced and appeared to have a great deal of confidence in their teaching ability. This seemed to make it possible for them to tolerate extended amounts of very close observation.

Designing Instruments for Observation

Operationalizing the concept of socialization for work roles within the classroom was obviously the key task of the study. Note again that this was done only in general ways before classroom observation began. Within the class-

room, a lengthy process was begun which involved paying strict attention to the details of classroom life while drawing upon the literature relating to social class and work roles to interpret these details and to construct patterns out of them, at the same time preserving the details of classroom interaction in themselves in order to have them available for continuing analysis. We expected our understanding of classroom interaction to grow fuller and fuller and probably to change over time. Having the data continuingly available in as "raw" a state as possible would enable us to go back over it with a fresh perspective as many times as we wished.

We began the first few days by simply writing down everything we noticed while we were in the classrooms. We worked together, alternating daily, one of us observing the teacher while the other observed the children. We put together a basic sense of the structure of the school day, work routines, and norms and values in the classroom, and then constructed working observation schedules which were used throughout the course of classroom observations. Each day observations were conducted that focused on one of the three categories: (1) the discipline and values taught through the teacher's control scheme; (2) the role of the student in the classroom, with special emphasis on the nature and amount of child participation and self-presentation; and (3) presentation of academic subject-matter.

At least 12 hours were devoted to intensive observation of behavior in each category in each of the two classrooms. We also conducted additional observations in one or another of the three categories, with primary focus on the teacher in the more teacher-centered classroom (Huntington) and on the children in the classroom where children were permitted to interact more freely (Smith). In addition, in order to ascertain whether behavior in the first-grade classrooms that we had selected was consistent with that found in other classrooms in the two schools, we visited the other first-grade classroom, as well as a third-grade and sixth-grade classroom in each school. In total, we devoted almost 56 hours to observations of Mrs. Newman's class and 17 hours to other classrooms at Huntington School, while observing Mrs. Jones' class and other classrooms at Smith School for 106 hours and 16 hours respectively. The observations were conducted over the last four months of the 1974–1975 school year.

Over time, we were able to construct satisfactory coding schemes for the types of behavior in which we were particularly interested. These will be explained shortly. Although in our initial observations we used a team approach in which we either carried out joint observation or exchanged observation sites, the data that were used for the classroom analysis were collected by one observer in each classroom. While the presence of observer bias cannot be ruled out, an analysis of parallel codings by the two observers for the same classroom for a full day's notes pointed to an acceptable level of inter-observer reliability (.91). In essence, our observations involved taking extensive verbatim notes on the various behaviors being studied, as well as making audio recordings of some classroom

activities. The notes were analyzed and converted to statistically manipulable data on the basis of the coding scheme that we had developed. During the course of the classroom observations, in which classrooms were being observed individually, the two observers met at least once a week to maintain close coordination of their efforts and to insure that the focus of observations was remaining congruent. (See Whiting's [1966] discussion of the importance of this process in a study involving fieldworkers in different sites.)

The working observation schedules were used throughout the course of classroom observations. They provided the raw material which was sifted through again and again throughout the process of analyzing and interpreting the data. Because of space limitations, we will describe this process only as it took place with the observation schedules recording teacher *control* of the work process in the classroom. It provides the most complex, and we think interesting, example of the process of analysis and interpretation. The coding scheme that we constructed represented an attempt to reduce a prodigious set of notes and recordings to a data set that was analyzable, while minimizing the loss of relevant information.

The hundreds of pages of observation schedules regarding control in the classroom were read over time and time again in order to identify recurring patterns of control. Frequently heard statements, recurring ways of structuring work situations, ways of rewarding and punishing, were noted and tabulated. This process produced a set of 83 basic categories of control-oriented teacher behavior which we felt summarized as fully as possible the modes of teacher behavior in this area in both classrooms. (See Appendix A.) It is very important to note that these categories only emerged after a long period of intense immersion in the classroom. It would have been impossible to produce them ahead of time. Their strength is that they are tailored precisely to reflect and capture socialization patterns *in these two classrooms*. They abstract from the mass of daily interactions, yet are still sensitively attuned to them.

One important aspect of the coding scheme is that all interactions were categorized in terms of a *strategy* and a *message*. *Strategy* can be viewed as the form of approach that the teacher uses to communicate, while *message* refers to the teacher's form of control (e.g., whether she gives reasons for her directives or simply issues them as commands). Messages were intended to capture the content of control, the generalized values taught in each classroom, particularly those relating to the dimension under study. This strategy/ message distinction blurs occasionally, but we found it to be a useful tool for conceptualizing and recording patterns of interaction in the classroom.

These 83 coding categories provided a very rich data base, accurate in its detailed reproduction of teacher socialization patterns but rendered unwieldy because of it. Consequently, after a careful analysis of patterns revealed by the coding scheme, the observations were reclassified into a streamlined external system which seemed relevant to this inquiry and could reasonably represent the more detailed information

which had been gathered. This reclassification was based on three contrasting pairs of variables:

- internal or external source of responsibility
- present or future orientation
- academic or behavioral application

Each interaction recorded on the initial observation sheets was coded according to the 83-category scheme, and was then recoded into the simplified reclassification scheme. A complete account of the manner in which the 83-category scheme was reorganized into the three simplified groups is in Appendix B.

An interaction was defined as a complete verbal transaction around a control-oriented event between a teacher and a child or between a teacher and a group of children. An interaction might contain one sentence or several. Each interaction, or transaction, could be coded by up to three categories; that is, it could include up to three strategies and three messages. More than three were never necessary. It was not difficult to judge the boundaries of disciplinary interactions, as they did not extend over long periods of time, or to judge what was and was not a control-oriented event.

Thus it was possible to compute a score for each child reflecting the number of interactions that child had with the teacher in the area of each of the coding categories and the three groups of recoded variables. This score reflected the percentage of total observed interactions between that child and the teacher that contained at least one occurrence of a given variable. Tests were run on these scores to determine whether a comparison of the average numbers of interactions of particular types between the two classrooms would yield statistically significant differences. These comparisons were based upon interactions involving 20 children at Huntington and 25 at Smith. The three midyear transferees at Smith were excluded from the data analysis. A total of 1,080 interactions were recorded between the teachers and these 45 children, 571 at Huntington and 509 at Smith. An arc sine transformation (Eisenhart 1947) was performed in order to normalize the distribution of the scores for purposes of statistical comparison. Analyses were based upon comparisons of the average number of interactions of particular types present in the two classrooms, the two sexes, ability groups, and ethnic groups.

The statistical results reported in this chapter are based upon a two-way analysis of variance of these scores, testing the relative effects of the independent variables by themselves (such as sex or classroom) as well as when other statistical effects are controlled (for example, sex and ability group taken together). The significance figures reported are derived from an analysis of variance which controls for sex, ability group, and ethnic group and makes an adjustment for the different numbers of children in each classroom.[2]

The coding scheme as finally fashioned was at a high level of abstraction from the original data. It therefore allowed the data to be manipulated relatively easily for the purpose of data analysis. At the same time, the original words of the teachers and the intermediate coding scheme remained available to allow for continuing clarification and reinterpretation.

The Sites Selected for Study

Several criteria were used in the selection of neighborhoods, schools, and classrooms appropriate for the study. As mentioned earlier, the research design called for choosing one school in a lower-middle-class neighborhood and another in an upper-middle-class neighborhood. In addition, I wished to select schools in which the principal and school district personnel were at least minimally receptive to the creation of the kinds of extensive personal contacts with school staff and parents called for by the research design. Given the delicate nature of many school-community relationships, this criterion was to prove fairly demanding. I also wished to find teachers who were respected, experienced, and well integrated into their respective schools and districts.

It was decided that the schools selected would be elementary schools and that the classrooms would be first-grade classrooms. The first-grade level was chosen in order to capture differences in the educational process at an early stage of formal education, thereby minimizing the influence of later factors which may affect both teachers' and students' expectations of relevant educational and occupational futures.

A major metropolitan area in California was selected as an appropriate locale in which to look for specific research sites. Neither the exact locations selected nor the schools and teachers themselves will be identified further, because of the schools' concerns about confidentiality.

The first step in the search for two appropriate classrooms involved an examination of 1970 Census data to determine appropriate lower-middle-class and upper-middle-class sites in the metropolitan area in question. This examination yielded a number of potential sites for each type of school and classroom, and permission was obtained from the appropriate school authorities to observe classrooms in 10 different schools. After a careful screening of 31 classrooms in these schools, the two schools that were used as the basis for this study were selected according to the criteria outlined previously. For the sake of preserving confidentiality, the lower-middle-class school will be referred to as Smith Elementary School, and the upper-middle-class school will be called Huntington Elementary School.

The principals at the two schools selected the particular teachers and classrooms in which they wished the observations to take place. The teachers they selected fit the criteria defined by the research design in many ways: both were a comfortable part of their respective worlds, both were highly regarded by colleagues, both had taught for more than 10 years, and both were willing to participate in the study. They will be referred to as Mrs. Jones (Smith Elementary School) and Mrs. Newman (Huntington Elementary School).

While a comparison between only two classrooms does not permit great generalizability, the richness of an in-depth ethnographic approach allows the potential of collecting a wealth of data at a high level of validity, an im-

portant concern in an exploratory study of this kind (Rist 1977). A summary of results of data gathered in this exploratory ethnographic study of socialization for work roles in the classroom will now be presented.

Ethnographic Results: Socialization for Work Roles in the Two Classrooms

Description of the Two Schools [3]

The two schools selected for the study are located in suburban communities of between 50,000 and 100,000 in population. Both communities lie near a major urban center in California. The communities are situated approximately nine miles apart in a county described in a local publication as a "rapidly growing and dynamic region . . . possessing tremendous assets in industry, educational facilities, geography and climate."

Smith Elementary School is located in a lower-middle-class area of Valley City, on a street lined with modest tract homes of the 1950s West Coast style. The following passage from a book about the American white majority describes at least the male inhabitants of Smith's neighborhoods well:

"He is the ordinary employee in the factory and in the office," says Robert C. Wood. Comprising half the nation's families, "he forms the bulk of the nation's working force. He makes five to ten thousand dollars a year; he has a wife and two children; owns a house in town—between the ghetto and the suburbs or perhaps in a *low cost subdivision on the urban fringe*; and he owes plenty in installment debts on his car and appliances. He finds his tax burden heavy, his neighborhood services poor. . . ." [Howe 1970:4] (italics added)

A school district socioeconomic profile of Smith's attendance area describes the neighborhood as a "stable blue collar area." A description of the neighborhood prepared by the school's Parents' Advisory Council speaks of a multicultural community with average to less-than-average incomes, some military families, and moderate transiency. The majority of the Smith community is Caucasian, with a sprinkling of Chicano, Filipino, and Samoan families.

A simple 15-minute drive separates Smith from Huntington, but the economic and social distance between the two neighborhoods is clearly evident. Huntington Elementary School serves a virtually all-white upper-middle-class neighborhood—Hillview. Instead of small tract houses showing signs of age, there are large, stately houses, architecturally individualized and surrounded by lush but immaculately groomed landscaping. A recent school district publication offers the observations of one four-year resident about the character of the community:

> In Hillview, everything works . . . And the Hillview resident works too. In the main, he's a professional or management person. . . .
> It's the Doctor Dentist Lawyer who divides his rare free time between his kids and the Tax Shelter Specialist. Mrs. Doctor Dentist Lawyer is very active in the PTA . . .
> If there's anything [Hillview] people do in larger measure than most communities, it's meet. Meet to plan meet-

ings. Meet to plan strategy to get their side heard at the Meeting. Meet to figure out how to avoid Meetings. Meet about school. . . . And if we can't Meet, we write the Editor. Thoughtful, impassioned letters . . .
> We don't seem overly concerned about our cars. They're relatively new. They work. That's enough. . . . Bikes we have in abundance. And we ride them. To work, with briefcase on the rear fender. To school in wheeled packs. To overcrowded tennis courts in our new whites. Using our generous bike lanes like conspicuous consumers.
> So here's what I see in Hillview: an intelligent, wealthy group of family-oriented individuals who want a happy, productive life for themselves and their children. They're active in seeking change for all society, but they are not driven to effect it. And they resist change that will ruffle their lives. Things are great as they are. . . .

Teacher estimates of parental occupation at the two schools (Table 1), submitted to the State of California as part of a state testing program, provide a reasonable approximation of the contrasts in occupational level between the two schools. Along with this difference in occupational level is a difference in level of education and, of course, income. Table 2 summarizes the contrast in years of education of parents of children in the two classrooms under study, as reported in parent interviews. Census figures for the two neighborhoods give contrasting incomes of approximately $9,850 at Smith and $14,550 at Huntington in 1970. Of course both these figures need to be adjusted upward to allow for inflation since 1970.

Characteristics of the schools reflect

TABLE 1   **Teachers' Estimate of Occupational Level of Parents**

Type of Occupation	Huntington	Smith
Professional	93%	4%
Semiprofessional, technical	3%	31%
Skilled and semiskilled	3%	56%
Unskilled	1%	7%
Unknown	——	1%

the contrast between the two neighborhoods. School spending for the 1973–1974 school year was approximately $840 per student in Smith's school district as compared to $1,350 in Huntington's. This difference in available resources translates into a series of other differences in the school environment. The median teacher salary in Huntington's district in 1973–1974 was approximately $16,200, as compared to $12,800 in Smith's district. The size of the two first-grade classrooms is indicative of average class sizes: about 28 pupils in the Smith classroom as compared to about 20 at Huntington.

Differences in demographic characteristics and economic resources are linked with differences in median achievement levels of pupils in the two schools. Smith second-grade pupils scored slightly below the 70th percentile on state reading tests in 1975, while Huntington second graders scored slightly below the 100th percentile.

While Smith's neighborhood is a bit below the state median in terms of its socioeconomic characteristics, its achievement scores are above the state median in the early grades. This may reflect the fact that the district's economic resources are also above the median, because of a high concentration of profitable industry as part of its tax base. The data on achievement scores should serve to remind the reader that the populations under comparison lie in different portions of the middle class.

The physical appearance of the two schools offers another element of contrast. Like the homes in the area, Smith School was built in the 1950s to absorb the increasing enrollments generated by the local tract developments that were providing postwar housing for workers. Smith School's spare and square concrete block architecture, few trees, and side lots filled with scrubby weeds all contribute to a less-than-inviting appearance. Huntington School, al-

TABLE 2   **Comparison of Parents' Level of Education**

All Parents	Advanced Degree	College Graduate	Some College	H.S. Graduate	Less than H.S. Graduate
Huntington (n = 37)	51%	24%	19%	6%	——
Smith (n = 38)	——	8%	18%	32%	42%

though considerably older than Smith, appears exceedingly well-groomed, with large expanses of windows reflecting the verdant growth of many trees and thick grass. The impression it offers is very much in tune with the affluence of the surrounding homes.

Mrs. Jones' First Grade

At Smith School, in-depth observations were carried out in Mrs. Jones' first-grade classroom. Though only in her thirties, Mrs. Jones had already taught for 10 years at the primary level, including five years in the first grade. She knew the neighborhood well, having grown up nearby and graduated from the local public high school. Other members of the school staff appeared to respect her highly as a teacher. As the principal commented:

> ... she is excellent without a doubt. ... She does interesting and different things in her classroom, and offers a lot of enrichment. ... She's a very professional person; she's constantly trying to improve herself as an educator. I think that people in the community think that she's a good teacher for their child to get.

It was clear that she took her job seriously and devoted a great deal of time and energy to devising interesting activities for her students.

A maximum of 28 students attended Mrs. Jones' class during the year, with five children leaving and five others entering between September and March, the month in which this study began. Four others left by June, reflecting the school's relatively high mobility rate. The ratio of boys to girls during most of the observations was 19 to 9, and was roughly the same as that in the other first-grade classroom at Smith.[4] Sixty-eight percent of the students were Caucasian, and the remaining 32 percent were Chicanos (21 percent), Filipinos (7 percent), and Samoans (4 percent). All of the children spoke English and came from homes in which English was spoken, although a few spoke Spanish as well.

During the school day, the Smith classroom was relatively freeform, comfortable, and, at times, frenetic. The children were often spread out all over the room, engaged in different kinds of activities, some academically oriented, some not. Frequent movement of children between activities was accompanied by a rather high level of noise within the classroom. The room had a lot of inviting, open territory with many interesting things for the children to do. It was organized to facilitate small group activities, with the children seated around four large tables rather than at separate desks. Although there were times for whole-class academic activities, children also worked under a system of "contracts" in which teacher and student made individual agreements as to which of several sets of exercises would be completed each week. Class time varied between group activities and individual ones in which students would utilize the several resource stations or learning centers around the room.

Despite the individualized nature of the work, Mrs. Jones did not always require that work be done individually. She sometimes suggested ways in which the children could cooperate, and joint activities were expressly encouraged at the learning centers. The children interacted almost constantly, circulating freely within the room, talking with each other and getting additional materials from supply cabinets kept open and within their reach. Classroom discipline was relatively loose, so that a child could easily switch from doing contracts to play without risking immediate correction from Mrs. Jones, who was likely to be occupied giving individual help to particular students. At such times, as well as at times when they had finished their work to the teacher's satisfaction, the children were free to play with each other. They often chose to play with one of the very popular rats who lived in a cage in the corner of the classroom, or to build elaborate tunnels across the floor with books that were shelved within easy reach.

Mrs. Newman's First Grade

If Mrs. Jones' classroom can be seen to represent the "open classroom" concept recently popular in the United States, Mrs. Newman's classroom brings to mind more traditional ideas about the educational process. Like most of the teachers at Huntington, Mrs. Newman was older and more experienced than Mrs. Jones and the other teachers at Smith. She had more than 20 years of classroom experience at the elementary school level, including eight at Huntington. While Mrs. Jones was still in the process of completing her requirements for a master's degree on a part-time basis at a nearby university, Mrs. Newman had long since obtained her master's degree from a far more prestigious institution.

Mrs. Newman had lived in the Huntington neighborhood even before joining the faculty, and her own children had attended Huntington. She was highly respected by parents and other members of the Huntington faculty. Parents whose older children had been in her classes requested her for their younger ones. The principal directed the observers to her classroom, saying, "She's one of the best."

Mrs. Newman's class was smaller than Mrs. Jones', with 10 boys and 10 girls for the greater part of the year. The basic overall stability of the neighborhood and the school was reflected by the fact that only one student transferred into or out of the class during the entire year. A great many of the children had attended kindergarten and even nursery school together. Other than two black males who were bused to Huntington from another neighborhood and one girl whose mother was from Central America, all of the children were Caucasian.

During the school day, the Huntington classroom was orderly, quiet, and productive. Desks were aligned in traditional rows and children worked by themselves, poring over assignments, moving quietly from their desks to resource materials that lined the room, only occasionally poking and playing with each other. Both Mrs. Newman's instruction and the organization of the classroom were structured so as to encourage independent cognitive work. Grouping of desks into clusters, as for art work or special projects, was quite rare.

It was a classroom in which everything had its place. During independent work times (comparable to contract times at Smith), some movement was allowed, but the style and scope of movement was clearly restricted. Resources circulated from child to child, children circulated from resource to resource, but both returned to their proper places. Children's activities were generally limited to various academic options.

Mrs. Newman allowed very little to interfere with her objective of promoting independent academic work, calling interaction between children "bothering your friends." She stated repeatedly that interaction would prevent children from finishing their assignments and producing high-quality work and that play should be saved for the playground. She made her priorities clear:

> I don't think anybody really has time to look at the frogs now. I know Debbie has work to do. She has a whole SRA kit to keep her busy.

> You can color when you're finished, but don't spend so much time on coloring. I found out some of my good people are just spending their time coloring.

Mrs. Newman indicated a strong sense of professional responsibility to prepare children for future schooling and she stressed reading as the key to success. She kept the classroom consistently orderly and productive toward this end, and both good study habits and high academic standards were emphasized.

How representative are these two teachers and classrooms? This is a very difficult question to answer. Obviously, a sample size of two classrooms does not provide a basis for conclusive generalizations. Demographic data about the neighborhoods make it clear that they are quite suitable for a comparison

of lower-middle-class and upper-middle-class communities. Differences in school resources and school mobility parallel this social class contrast. Tabulations resulting from 33 hours of observations in other classrooms in the two schools indicated that, while both Mrs. Jones and Mrs. Newman were unique individuals with a distinctive presence in the classroom, they were in line with other teachers in their schools in terms of the dimensions outlined earlier as relevant to the study.[5]

The amount of freedom given to the students, or the looseness of structure of the two classrooms, varied in a way which is contrary to what one would expect from a reading of the literature (Bowles and Gintis 1971, Binstock 1970). Typically, lower-class classrooms are described as having tighter discipline and control than upper-class classrooms. The results of the preliminary survey of 31 classrooms in the county conducted for this study convinced us that the two classrooms selected were not atypical in this respect. We observed no classrooms in Huntington-type neighborhoods which were structured as loosely as Mrs. Jones', although not all classrooms in Smith-type neighborhoods were structured equally loosely. The ambience in Mrs. Newman's classroom was quite similar to that in other upper-middle-class classrooms, even those specifically designated as "open" classrooms and taught by younger teachers. It is possible that the passage of time and the current popularity of the open classroom approach has changed the formal structure of many lower-middle-class classrooms. If so, this may have interesting ramifications in terms of changing patterns of socialization for work roles. On the other hand, these findings may indicate the relative superficiality of the changes involved in the move to an open classroom structure. If these classrooms are somewhat atypical in terms of organizational structure, it is possible that this study's findings may tend to understate typical differences with respect to the relationship to authority in the classroom. Differences could be expected to be even more pronounced in a situation in which the lower-middle-class school was more tightly structured than the upper-middle-class school.

Relationship to Authority: Internal Versus External Control in the Two Classrooms

It was suggested earlier that an important distinction among jobs is the type of relationship to authority established to motivate the employee and assure adequate performance. Jobs in the lower portion of the work hierarchy appear to be characterized by the assumption that employees must be motivated and guided by work arrangements and supervision *external* to themselves, while it is presumed that in jobs at the upper levels of the hierarchy employees will be motivated by *internalized* norms and values that correspond to the needs of the enterprise. This is not to say that employees at the upper levels of the hierarchy are free to direct themselves as they see fit; on the contrary, it seems more appropriate to describe them as being

by no means autonomous, self-actualizing and creatively self-directed. Rather,

they are probably super-socialized so as to internalize authority and act without direct and continuous supervision to implement goals and objectives relatively alienated from their own personal needs. [Bowles and Gintis 1976:145]

The ultimate source of authority is in both cases external, yet the motivational scheme which actualizes the authority is quite different.

Accordingly, we hypothesized that if children are socialized by the school for work roles that are relatively similar to those of their parents, students at Smith would be more likely to be exposed to teacher behavior emphasizing external controls and rules, while those at Huntington would experience more teacher behavior attempting to inculcate the internalization of norms.

This hypothesis was fully developed and tested through a process of general observation as well as through a more elaborate scheme of quantification, as described earlier. The distinction between internal and external control grew to be conceptualized as one embodying both teacher expectations and the nature of responsibilities given to the children. In general, an internal reaction was viewed as one in which the teacher treated the child as a self-directed person who was capable of handling a process in an independent way and of choosing the consequences of his or her activity. It is an interaction in which the teacher places on the child responsibility to shape his or her activity in a manner that promotes or relies upon internalized values, self-images, standards, or goals. By contrast, an external interaction is one in which the teacher emphasizes that the child is to follow certain standard rules, procedures, or directions to be set out by the teacher and made salient by his or her authority and direct power. In an internal interaction, the responsibility for compliance is placed on the child, while in an external interaction it is placed on the teacher.

External control proved to be the overriding control mechanism used by Mrs. Jones. In fact, the single most common strategy in evidence at Smith was the use of teacher commands. Mrs. Jones would simply order: "I want that done now" or "You have an assignment; sit down and get busy" or some similar command. The second most common strategy was the use of direct praise and blame, such as "That's good" or "No, that's not right," and so on, in which the teacher's opinion is a direct external sanction. Rule repetition was also common.

> You cannot get a rat out until you've finished your work.
> Come in right away when the recess bell rings.
> You have to get a pass to go to the office.
> You can't throw food in the cafeteria.
> No playing in the hall.
> No running in the room.
> We don't hit or kick.
> Use quiet voices.
> No fighting.

The use of commands or sanctions resting on the authority of the teacher and of rule repetition keeps the responsibility for control localized in an external source.

Not all of the control techniques used at Smith were external ones. Approximately 17 percent of teacher control strategies and 19 percent of teacher control messages at Smith were coded as internal. The way in which Mrs. Jones employed internal modes of control in the classroom was most revealing. She tended to employ an internal approach at times when she was trying to inculcate proper standards of general classroom behavior rather than when she was attempting to teach specifically academic skills. For instance, she consistently refused to act as an external authority when disputes arose among children, urging them to take responsibility for resolving their own differences.

> [to two children who came asking the teacher's judgment about who owned what] I don't know what happened. You two will have to decide that by yourselves. [internal]
>
> How would you feel if someone took your lunch? [internal]

And she urged the children to learn to use classroom resource materials without her help.

> [to a boy who came to her during art because he couldn't find the glue] You've been in this classroom since September and you still can't handle that? You can solve that problem yourself. [internal]

With respect to academic interactions, on the other hand, Mrs. Jones tended to employ an external approach to motivate her students.

> You have work to do and I want it done.
> I won't accept backwards numbers on your arithmetic paper.
> Here's a star for everybody who finished.
> Sit down and do that work; this is a work time.

About 9 percent of the academic interactions were coded as employing internal strategies, while about 10 percent involved internal messages.

In short, the overriding mode of control employed at Smith was external, and this was particularly strong in the area of academic interactions. On the whole, Mrs. Jones reinforced a pattern in which the impetus for action came not from the children themselves but from an external rule or authority figure who issued rules and regulations.

The pattern reinforced at Huntington was quite different. External modes of control were in evidence, but consistent emphasis was placed on the children's internalizing responsibility for academic work. If anything, Mrs. Newman's behavioral standards were stricter than those at Smith, but the central focus of almost all of her statements was on the academic implications of behavior. By pointing out the academic implications of behavior, Mrs. Newman offered reasons to the children, in effect engaging them in thinking in an internalized way about what they were doing.

> If you're talking to your neighbor, you're probably not looking at the clues and remembering what the answers are.

> Jim, maybe it's because you're wiggling in your chair that you counted more.

Children were held responsible for "using time wisely," which meant working quietly at their desks during the independent work period. They were expected to pace themselves and make choices not to interact with each other in order to complete daily assignments. These expectations were usually communicated in an internal fashion:

> Our fifteen minutes are up. Have you used them wisely?

> Tommy, talk to yourself quietly and tell yourself where you are and what's expected of you.

> [to a child who has not completed his work during the time allotted] Why do you do this to yourself?

There were strong external standards at Huntington, too. The children were clearly expected to follow the rules, most of them academic in their application—think for yourself, listen to directions, don't bother your friends. The teacher told them the reasons behind the rules and made them take the responsibility for the consequences of failure to follow them. Often, her corrections included both an external and an internal component:

> [Tommy was supposed to be listening to the story] No writing, Tommy. Play fair with yourself. Why is it so hard to follow directions, Tommy? You'll be a good football player, but no one will ask you to play. You really have to follow the rules. [both external and internal]

How is the control scheme at Huntington different from that at Smith? Both have their external rules and authority figures, but at Huntington there is an additional component to many of the teacher's statements. She expects the children to learn, and she expects them to internalize academic and behavioral standards. She throws the responsibility back to the children, constantly admonishing them to "play fair with yourself," "use good judgment," or "use your time wisely." She repeats that they know why the rules are there and that they will take the consequences of inferior work. She appeals to an internalized set of values, asking the children to think for themselves and decide what to do. The importance of the internal approach at Huntington is underlined by the quantitative analysis: 52 percent of the strategies at Huntington were coded as internal, along with 67 percent of the messages.

As noted earlier, Mrs. Newman was careful to employ an internal approach when dealing with academic interactions. She would find various ways to encourage the view that the child was engaged in a self-directed academic process.

> Will this misbehavior help you to become a better reader?

> That's being a real independent worker.

> Be fair to yourself, use your time wisely to help yourself become a better reader.

Of the academic interactions at Huntington, 38 percent were coded as involving internal strategies, while 59 percent were coded as involving internal messages. The comparable figures at Smith were 9 percent and 10 percent.

What is the significance of this rather striking contrast in the use of external and internal modes of motivation control in the classroom? There is one more piece of information which is useful in interpreting the above data. Children in the top half of the reading groups in both classrooms received significantly more internal messages than children in the bottom half of the reading groups in the two classrooms ($p = .005$). They also received significantly

more internal academic messages ($p = .046$). Thus, an internal approach, particularly with respect to academic interactions, is associated in both classrooms with children who are perceived to have the highest ability level and future potential. Ethnographic evidence from both classrooms revealed that the teachers associated reading group level with ability level; both considered reading to be the "name of the game" at the first-grade level. Comments like Mrs. Jones' when she first pointed out the top reading group to us saying, "This is the cream of the crop," are testimony to this association.

Generally speaking, the higher the perceived ability level of the child, the higher the occupational level the child is expected to attain in the future. An internal mode of control in the classroom can be seen as a method of socialization appropriate to higher levels of the stratified work place. It has been hypothesized that higher-level jobs are ones in which norms and objectives must be internalized for occupational success. Jobs at the upper levels of the hierarchy require a great deal of internalized direction such that action is self-motivated, yet consistent with the needs of the employer or with accepted professional standards. Supervision at this level tends to be rather remote, or, as in the case of self-employed professionals, nonexistent. One is expected to do the "right" thing without being told what to do, when to do it, or how to make a decision. This dynamic is evident as a lawyer plans a case, a physician makes a diagnosis, or a high-level manager makes a marketing decision. At times one may consult with other people for information or advice, but the relationship to authority is still quite different from that characterizing jobs at lower levels.

Jobs which the children at Smith are likely to attain appear to involve considerable supervision and more routinized work activities. Employees are expected to follow specific rules and procedures determined by the firm. To quote Carter and Carnoy:

> a ... worker [at this level of the work hierarchy] must come to work every day, be able to carry out the tasks within the assigned time, and accept task assignments without questioning them. Although ... [he, she] has responsibilities, these are responsibilities geared to a direct work objective. [1974:42]

The type of socialization taking place in a classroom such as Mrs. Jones', with its emphasis on rules and regulations and external sanctions, seems well suited to such an occupational future. In short, the differences in the way children at the two schools are socialized to relate to authority tend to parallel the differences in occupational level of the children's parents.

Skill Requirements: Self-Presentation Skills

As noted earlier, both the popular and the scholarly domain have recognized that work role is linked to particular styles of self-presentation. It appears that skills relevant to self-presentation are taught from the beginning of the school experience. The sharing session, or "show and tell," was one way in which these skills were taught in both classrooms. Time was set aside in which students presented themselves to others through telling about an item that they brought to school or an event that took place in their lives. In both schools, the sharing time was nominally run by a student leader or two who called on a fellow classmate with a hand waving in the air to come to the front, face the group, and tell what he or she had to share. The teacher might or might not comment, and other students might ask questions. Eventually the teacher would terminate the presentation and another volunteer would be selected.

At Smith, sharing took place only about once every three days at irregular times, often convened at the request of one of the students. The teacher appeared to think of sharing as a nice activity but not one so important that it needed to happen daily. Mrs. Jones' presence was relatively unobtrusive during sharing time; she seemed to think of the activity as the children's time. She approached it not as an explicit learning activity, but as a time for "kids to be kids," sharing their treasures with each other in whatever way they wished. Over the course of 102 sharing presentations during a six-week period, Mrs. Jones commented on the presentations only about half the time. When she did comment, the two most frequent responses consisted of asking a factual question which required a specific answer or making a positive closing remark like "That's nice." Only 8 percent of the time did she offer any procedural instructions about how to make presentations. If she did offer a procedural suggestion, it was usually a specific direction about what else to say. For example, someone got up to say that her family had just bought a new car, and Mrs. Jones prompted, "Tell us the color." A frequent procedural suggestion she would make to a child who was sharing a particular object was "Hold it up."

At Huntington, on the other hand, every day began with 10 minutes of sharing. It provided time for the children to settle down in preparation for the independent work period. But more importantly, it gave Mrs. Newman numerous opportunities to review academic materials through her follow-up questions and to give procedural suggestions to individual speakers about grammar and presentation. Almost 90 percent of the 87 presentations observed were followed by a response from Mrs. Newman, and in one-quarter of the cases the teacher interjected specific feedback about the process of speaking before a group.

> What nice sentences you made. You told us so many things. We know exactly when and where and what.
>
> I like the way Joanne shared yesterday. She called it a "poster"; she could describe it more than "this."
>
> I really like the way Matt spoke so nice and loud. Although I was looking in my desk and rattling papers, I could hear every word he had to say. When we have something that's important to say, then we should say it so people can hear it.

Mrs. Newman found many ways to draw the child and/or the class into further presentation or discussion based on what the child had originally said. More than 20 percent of the time she would tie the child's presentation to the subject matter of the previous day or use it as the basis for a discussion question for the class. Mrs. Jones did this approximately 3 percent of the

time. Another third of the time Mrs. Newman, while not extending the subject the child brought up, would sustain the discussion of it by asking an open-ended factual question which allowed the child to use language independently in formulating a response (Parsons 1971). When Mrs. Jones did sustain a child's presentation by asking a factual question, it was almost always phrased as a closed cue which called for restricted language use in response: a yes/no question, a naming or labeling response, or a question with a clearly defined answer.

The Smith children were being socialized to perform before a group in a relatively haphazard way, with very little attention placed on developing extended verbal skills of the kind appropriate to the upper levels of the occupational hierarchy. The children were receiving little opportunity to practice and gain verbal skills in performing in front of a group, in elaborating on an initial thought or statement, or in receiving feedback on how they presented themselves.

Data gathered from observation in another upper-middle-class elementary school in the county serve to underline the differential approaches to the activity of sharing and the relevance of these different approaches to the child's socialization. A volunteer parent-teacher committee in a first-grade classroom prepared a short statement explaining the sharing activity. The statement stressed explicitly the self-presentation skills which they were attempting to teach:

> Students are encouraged to share items of interest and experiences which they have had, and must plan to inform or

entertain the group rather than simply take up time or satisfy egos. . . . We provide on-the-spot guidance which hopefully helps the speaker and the audience to attain these goals.

While one may feel regret that a 6-year-old is subjected to these kinds of stereotyped performance expectations at such a tender and spontaneous age, it is undeniably suitable preparation for that smooth and carefully monitored interaction that characterizes the upper occupational echelons of the culture of the United States.

Images of the Child in the Classroom: Future Versus Present Orientation

The structure and content of classroom interaction inevitably sets up within it certain images of the child. It subtly defines the child's present being and mode of becoming, as well as constructing an image of who the child will become. These images are likely to filter into the child's consciousness in various ways and contribute, along with the actions they bring into being, to the socialization and development of the child. These images and related actions are likely to constitute a significant aspect of socialization for future work roles (Meyer 1970, Brookover 1975).

In a hierarchical and highly differentiated society, one might well expect the school to contribute to the development of differential images of self and related skills among children. If the society is to operate smoothly, the view of self that a child takes on must be realistically related to the child's likely future position. Everyone cannot have the same view of self, because everyone

cannot hold the same position in the occupational hierarchy; some must be prepared for the pressures and rewards of the presidency while others are prepared to persevere in the daily routines of the assembly line. Because work roles are different, effective socialization must lead people to feel at least minimally comfortable in and tolerant of their positions at different levels of the work hierarchy.

The two teachers consistently portrayed very different images of the child in the present and the future in the classrooms. They can be seen to be involved in socializing children to particular self- and role-orientation with respect to ways of handling the present and the future.

In general, the children at Huntington learned that they had positive futures ahead of them. In fact, they had already entered them:

> Good thinking. See, you're really thinking like a mathematician. [after a review of geometric shapes] You'll be a good scientist. [writing fantasy stories] You were artists—now you're authors.

The teacher continually reinforced a "you can do it" attitude.

> You just don't know how good you really are. Just keep trying, boys and girls.

> If you don't get it, that's perfectly all right, Jimmy. By Friday you'll get it without looking.

> I want you to take your time, Joanne. You were content to get words wrong before. Read to yourself and enjoy it. Say to yourself, "I'm a good reader, because this is a second-grade book."

The consequences of present activity were continually linked with the future. Students were regularly reminded that they needed to prepare for study at the major university near Hillview, or at other major universities around the country.

> It's real important to be a good listener. What you said wasn't wrong, but it didn't answer the question. This is important for taking tests, and you'll have them from now on, even if you get to Harvard.

Looking to the more immediate future, the pressures and glories of second grade were often brought to their minds:

> Eddie, this is gonna be expected of you next year. You have to listen and follow through.

> [after an independent work session in writing stories] You have worked great. [class subtracts to find that they have worked on their own for 35 minutes] You are ready for second grade, because first graders can only work 15 minutes.

It appears that students at Huntington were learning two different kinds of things with respect to the present and the future. They were learning that they could expect to end up at the upper levels of the occupational hierarchy. They were also learning to think of the future consequences of present actions, a sort of training which is crucial to being able to handle the kinds of choices and decisions with important future ramifications which characterize many managerial and professional roles. In contrast, work schedules and the organization of work tasks are fairly well prescribed at lower levels of the occupational hierarchy, and involve more set work routines.

The emphasis at Smith was almost totally on the present. The future con-

sequences of present activities were rarely mentioned. The teacher essentially tried to create a positive, present-oriented atmosphere, with a "let kids be kids" attitude prevailing. The children were allowed to play with each other for long periods in the classroom. The teacher encouraged parents to bring in family pets, and enjoyed watching the children spend time fondling them, rather than, for instance, using the animals as a pretext for a science lesson. Although the Huntington children had parties, too, the Smith children spent more time doing "fun" things like breaking piñatas and eating cake and ice cream at school.

They were expected to act like first graders, not like kindergarteners, but were not pushed to behave in the more mature ways that the future would demand of them. While the teacher at times reinforced the progress they had made in first grade, she rarely extrapolated it beyond the first grade. What references she did make to the second grade were negative ones:

> [when the class failed to bring a seed from home, as she had asked] We're not getting ready for second grade. This was homework.

> [after struggling with several children about writing their letters properly] In second grade they don't teach you printing. That's why you have to know it now.

> [when the class was not paying attention during math, in exasperation] We've got to get this before we get to second grade.

During the entire time of fieldwork, the only positive reference to second grade that I heard came from the second-grade teacher, who invited the first graders in one day to see how the second-grade seats felt, since they would be occupying them soon.

References to role models in the future were very infrequent, although the teacher would sometimes tell the children to correct their own work, saying, "Be your own teacher." The only reference to an educational future beyond the second grade was the following criticism issued during a music lesson:

> This is important. You can't play an instrument when you get to the upper grades if you can't read music. You need to know this stuff, and I'm really disappointed.

The nearby university whose existence was mentioned so often at Huntington was never discussed at Smith, nor was any other college or university. The constant reminder of a positive future and the importance of moving toward it through academic achievement that was so prevalent at Huntington simply did not exist at Smith. Future consequences of present activities were rarely pointed out. The Huntington teacher referred to future status and role almost eight times as often as the teacher at Smith. This difference was statistically significant after controlling for sex, ethnicity, and ability group factors. Thus, the overall emphasis on future roles and the consequences of present activities was far greater in the upper-middle-class first grade than in the lower-middle-class one. The most remarkable characteristic of Mrs. Jones' approach to the future of the children in her classroom was that she virtually ignored it. It seems plausible that this is the kind of experience that leads to what Jackall has called "personal drift," a phenomenon he observed among lower white collar workers in a large bank. He describes this as "an unsureness about future goals and a related uncertainty about one's own abilities." He continues:

> The absence of goals is especially critical. Younger people leaving high school often have no idea of what they want for their futures, at least regarding work. Schooling has provided no direction for them at all. [1976:33]

Mrs. Jones' classroom certainly provided no direction for the children at Smith. They seemed to experience the essence of being average: some successes, some failures, and no particular place to go.

The Sociocultural Context of the Classroom

The pattern of differences observed in the ways in which the two teachers socialized the children in their classrooms for adult work roles is, I believe, directly in conflict with the promise of equal opportunity offered by the educational system in the United States. At the tender age of six, these children have done practically nothing as individuals to account for the kind of differential treatment they are receiving, except to have been born by chance into one neighborhood and social class background or another. Interviews with the teachers themselves made it clear that they felt they were allowing and encouraging each child to develop and progress as far as each was able; they would have been shocked at any accusation of differential treatment based on social class. Why, given a social commitment to equal opportunity and a conscious effort on the part of the teachers to act on this commitment, do these profound and pervasive patterns of differential socialization exist?

This question leads us directly to an analysis of the sociocultural context of the classroom. Participant observation revealed a constellation of forces which tended to influence the classroom in such a way that, in general, characteristics of parental work role were transmitted to students. The extensive interviews, observations, and research conducted outside the walls of the classroom can barely be touched on here, but an attempt will be made to summarize some of the key findings and interpretations.

It became clear that the school staff, the district staff, and the state educational apparatus actually did have different expectations for children from upper-middle-class families than from lower-middle-class ones. The social class make-up of the neighborhood was a characteristic that was very much on the minds of educational personnel at all of these levels, and it was linked rather directly to their expectations of students.

The School Staff

Mrs. Jones did not have time to include many facts in the five-minute orientation that preceded the first day of observations at Smith, but she managed to emphasize the social class background of the children. She said, "The neighborhood, it's not a lower-class neighborhood; it's really more like lower middle class." I heard teachers describe the neighborhood as lower middle class over and over during the period of fieldwork. It was usually mentioned in

passing, but it was regularly included as salient background information.

A perception of the neighborhood as culturally deprived accompanied the categorization of lower middle class. The researchers were quite surprised to discover the extent to which the "culture of poverty" formulation, originally constructed to describe the lives of the urban poor in Puerto Rico (and heavily criticized even within this limited scope [Leacock 1970, Valentine 1968]), was being used to describe the lives of the average white American family. The version of the "culture of poverty" theory fashionable in educational circles today characterizes the homes of the poor and of ethnic minorities as empty, deprived, and characterized by semipathological patterns of functioning and inadequate care and education of children. The following quotes from interviews with teachers at Smith reveal the extent to which this formulation was being applied to the family life of the average American residing in Smith's attendance area:

I don't really feel that the parents, some of them, really realize what kind of a home life they are giving their kids, because they've got so many problems themselves that they can't solve. You get into a filtering-down thing, too, from the parent to the child.

I know kids that go home at three o'clock that are street kids until six. Or they go home to a babysitter, and the babysitter goes, "Sure, you know [do whatever you want]." ... There's families there that constantly give their kids money, "Go buy a popsicle or something." ... I think there's a lot of parents, I know there are parents because I've called on 'em and said, "Hey, we've got a problem with your kid." "Well, I can't come tonight, that's bowling," and the kid is the last thing on their minds. Kids just sort of happen.

The principal summarizes the prevailing attitude when he says that Smith "does not have the same home background as schools on the other [more affluent] side of town." Like proponents of the "culture of poverty" literature, the staff focused on the home rather than the school as the major cause of school failure or difficulty. And the perception of the homes led to a clear separation between the realm of the home and the realm of the school. During the year of fieldwork, events planned and sponsored by the school never involved visits by the class to parents' homes. Field trips were always trips *out* of the neighborhood. Implicitly, educational resources came to be defined as lying outside of the immediate community.

The characterization of the neighborhood as lower middle class fits remarkably well with Mrs. Jones' response when asked if she had any unusual children in her classroom.

> I have an awful lot of kids that are average, everyday children. I don't have any outstanding artists this year. ——— is a good actor. . . . There's a lot of children that have made an awful lot of growth, but I don't see that as being unusual. It's fun to sit back and see, is there anybody that's gonna be famous? I really think ——— is going to do something. [This was a child who was lowest academically in the class, but the teacher had praised his creative mechanical abilities.] I have an awful lot of everyday Joe Smiths.

The school staff at Huntington expressed very different views about parents and children in that neighborhood. While the words "average" and "deprived" come to mind at Smith, the words "gifted" and "fascinating" are in evidence at Huntington. The staff at Huntington repeatedly made reference to the income and power of the parents in the neighborhood, as if basking in the reflected glory. As the principal commented:

> The population, the community is fascinating. You have so many college-educated people who have such high expectations of their children and of school.

Just as at Smith, the Huntington staff seemed to generalize from the characteristics of the parents' achievements to a set of expectations for the children. Whereas this meant a relaxing of expectations at Smith, it meant a heightening of academic standards at Huntington. Mrs. Newman, when asked what the children in her class would go on to do, replied directly that they would be trained as professionals. The principal at Huntington takes a bow to the parents when he says:

> A lot of it is, of course, the way [the children] come to us. I mean ability, of course, heredity and a few other things.

Instead of posing a problem to the school, the home environment is seen to offer resources and educational possibilities at Huntington. School personnel set up opportunities to send the children out into the neighborhood for special programs like cookie baking, a trip to the local nature refuge, and watching tractors dig out a new swimming pool in one parent's backyard.

The differential expectations expressed for the children in the two classrooms appear to have strikingly different consequences in terms of the staff's reaction to individual learning problems on the part of individual children. Instead of viewing children as "average Joes" who will always have certain difficulties, the staff at Huntington marshaled substantial resources to solve problems. Experts were consulted and special attention was offered, and the staff intervened with a sureness based on having the resources to meet the need and having confidence in their own abilities and in that of the child to overcome the difficulty. One little girl who entered the Huntington class in the middle of the year could not read and often sat in tears at her desk. Mrs. Newman evaluated the problem, decided that she was certainly capable of reading, spent individual time with her each day, and arranged for a student from the nearby university to tutor her as well. By the end of the school year, the child was reading in class and happily taking additional books home. Children with reading problems in Mrs. Jones' class simply did not receive this kind of direct marshaling of forces to resolve problems.

In short, it seemed clear that the social class level of the neighborhood was a very salient characteristic in the minds of the staff at both schools. It generated general levels of expectations for children in each neighborhood which could be seen to influence the behavior of the teachers in the classroom. At Huntington, Mrs. Newman was helping future leaders on their way to academic and professional success, while at Smith, Mrs. Jones was coping with "an awful lot of average everyday Joe Smiths."

The District Staff

The attitude of the school district toward the parents and children at Smith was strikingly revealed in the course of a presumably routine contact between the researchers and the district for the purpose of gathering background information for the study. We wished to obtain the achievement test scores for both schools to learn their ranking with respect to each other and to the statewide population. We had gone to Huntington's district first, where raw scores, interpretive guides, and Xerox machines were made readily available to us, as they would have been to any concerned Hillview parent. The staff mentioned that such documents were public information and could not legally be withheld. To our surprise, when we went to Smith's district office, we were told that the schools' achievement test scores could not be given out. After moving through several levels of district personnel to the top in an effort to get this information (the research project had, after all, been approved by the school board), we were finally told what Smith's score had been, although scores for other schools in the district were withheld. We were told that the district had had too much trouble with Smith parents coming in and complaining that they had heard that test scores were higher in schools on the other side of town. A high-level district official said with considerable indignation that the parents simply did not understand that the scores were *a direct consequence of the average IQ and socioeco-*

nomic level of the neighborhood (italics added). Since the complaints about low achievement levels at the school were justified, the district would not release the information in an effort to minimize the complaints.

This incident reveals again a kind of ceiling placed on expectations for the children at Smith. While these limited expectations were expressed in other ways at the district level, space necessitates moving on to consider another level of the sociocultural context of the classroom—the state educational apparatus and its procedures and regulations.

The State Educational Apparatus

Observations at the two schools revealed that one other important expression of differential expectations for the children was the staff's reliance on an "objective" statistic produced by the State Department of Education's testing program. This was a measure of expected school performance on state achievement tests, known as the comparison score range. According to a small group of parents at Smith, the staff relied on this statistic to justify current levels of achievement at Smith and to downplay the chance of raising schoolwide achievement levels any further.

As part of its yearly testing program to monitor school performances, the State Department of Education executes a procedure in order to evaluate individual school test score performances on the basis of pupil characteristics. This procedure results in the computation of an expected test score

range for each district and for each school within the state, based on the following set of pupil characteristics: the children's score on an Entry Level Test, administered in October of first grade (used as a baseline measure of knowledge a child brings to school); a socioeconomic indicator computed from teachers' estimates of the occupational level of the children's parents; the percentage of bilingual pupils; and the percentage of pupil mobility. On the basis of these factors, a range is computed within which the school's achievement scores are expected to fall. A school receives an "A" for scoring above this range, a "W" for scoring within it, and a "B" for falling below it.

The precise score range varies depending on the grade level and on the subject matter of the achievement test, i.e., math, writing, and so on. However, Smith's predicted score range generally consisted of a range between the 30th and the 70th percentiles, whereas Huntington's predicted score range was between the 85th and 99th percentiles. Thus, an achievement score at the 60th percentile would be perfectly normal and to be expected at Smith, whereas it would be grossly under expectations at Huntington. It appears that the State Department of Education expects and will implicitly accept a vastly different level of performance from schools like Huntington than from schools like Smith. And most significant is the fact that all of the factors used to determine the level of expectations are factors operating outside the classroom walls. The implication is, unavoidably, that what is really important in terms of achievement is the characteristics a child brings from home rather than what takes place at school. As the state guide for interpretation of test scores explains:

> To compare a district with other districts without regard for the characteristics of the district is often meaningless and sometimes misleading. It is more useful to compare a district with similar districts in terms of social, financial, and educational problems and capabilities. [California State Testing Program 1974:23]

Despite language in official testing program documents warning against too narrow an application of the evaluations, there remains an explicit assertion that expected levels of performances are related to the backgrounds of the students:

> The ranks in the column for predicted score ranges represent the test score range in which each district could be "expected" to score based upon the pertinent characteristics of the pupils, the community, and the school district. [California State Testing Program 1974:25]

Moreover, the cautionary language found in the official reports rarely enters into the awareness of parents and school personnel, who generally receive only summaries of annual testing goals and outcomes. Insofar as these results are seen to establish distinctly lower expectations on the part of parents, teachers, and school officials for some children than for others, it is likely that they serve as a self-fulfilling prophecy in which poor performance is expected of students in schools with low ranges, while good performance is expected of students in high-range schools. The impact of such differential expectations has been documented in several studies (Rosenthal and Jacobsen 1968, Rist 1970, Leacock 1969), the results of which correspond well with the differential socialization hypothesis set forth here.

In fact, the comparison score range appeared to be used as an upper limit to expectations at Smith. (At Huntington, obviously, there was no upper limit, because the scores were already at the top.) A parent talked at length of being told by the Smith principal and another teacher that the school's achievement scores were near the top of the comparison score range for the school and could not be expected to be raised any further. According to the parent, this was used as a justification for setting school goals for academic achievement in the school's program proposal at currently existing levels, rather than raising them to a higher level.

As the teacher explained in an interview, the staff was simply thinking ahead to a potential state evaluation of the program, knowing that the school was liable to lose the funds if goals and objectives were set and not met. She said strongly that the fact that higher expectations did not appear on paper did not mean that they were nonexistent. The staff saw themselves as being cautious, putting down on paper what they were sure they could do.

Another parent pointed bitterly to the stated goals for achievement in the program proposal of an affluent school across town. In fact, the proposal of the school on the other side of town *was* filled with statements about discrepancies between actual performance and potential performance, in spite of the already high achievement of the children there. Reading levels were already above state established expectations, but still higher goals were set.

It is not difficult to imagine the mechanisms through which these differential responses on the part of the school staffs on opposite sides of town get set up. The theme of the self-fulling prophecy is repeated in yet another form. It is likely that, at the school across town, it *is* apparent to everyone that the children are very bright and have great capabilities. After all, look at their parents, their test scores, and so on: the culture has created massive evidence that this is true. At the very least, the culture of expectations has created demanding parents whose ambitious expectations are very difficult to dampen. And, by virtue of this certainty on the part of all involved, it becomes no major risk to commit oneself in writing to improved achievement. At Smith, on the other hand, the culturally created evidence is far less convincing. Mediocre IQ's, parents whose success in life has been average at best, evidence that similar children all over the state do no better—it seems quite sensible not to be too rash in committing oneself to perform the unlikely.

Thus the State Department of Education plays its part in setting the stage for educators and parents to differentiate their expectations according to the social class of the students' neighborhood.

Economic Structure and Organization of the Society as a Whole

At this point it is critical to return to the basic theoretical underpinnings of the study. From an anthropological perspective, schools are agents of cultural transmission involved in socializing a new generation to fit the needs of the culture. One overwhelming reality for which children must be prepared is the reality of the world of work. In many ways, the hallmark of the world of work in industrial and post-industrial society is the enormous degree of differentiation which characterizes the division of labor. The degree of differentiation is unprecedented in human history. In the United States, this differentiation of tasks is embedded in a hierarchical structure in which certain tasks are seen as infinitely more valuable, more important, and more demanding of talents than others (Davis and Moore 1945:48). Jobs at various levels of this hierarchy are characterized by very different levels of prestige. The social consensus about the levels of prestige of various occupations is remarkably strong, and has remained quite consistent over time. Members of the culture tend to rate the prestige levels of jobs similarly, regardless of their own position in the hierarchy. That is, doctors are rated high in prestige not only by doctors or others in similar occupations but by people at all occupational levels (Reiss 1961).

In spite of the fact that it is widely agreed that all occupational outcomes are not equal, children must be prepared to move into one niche or another. Children must be differentiated from each other at school in the same way that tasks are differentiated from each other in the world of work. The culture requires dropouts to fill the drop-out-level jobs, just as it requires M.D.'s and Ph.D.'s to fill the jobs at the top. Given this reality, it is logical to expect that one would find children being socialized very differently in the classroom. It would be cultural suicide to socialize all children to fully expect and prepare to become doctors, lawyers, scientists, or business executives, just as it would be to socialize all to become assembly-line workers.

The economic structure thus can be seen to account for the basic phenomenon of differential socialization, but why does differential socialization appear to take place along social class lines? It was clear from the data gathered for the study that the educational staff at the local, district, and state levels all approached their tasks with definite preconceptions at some level about the performance potential of the children in the two schools and the roles in which they were likely to end up. These preconceptions can be seen to develop through people's direct participation in everyday social and cultural life. Educational personnel have grown up absorbing the widespread cultural agreement about the value, worth, power, and ability of people at different occupational levels. They have experienced work role and social class stereotypes as acted out again and again in cartoons, on TV, and in books, magazines, and newspapers. They have been heavily exposed to the cultural world view that human ability is distributed in the form of a bell-shaped curve and that it is measurable using the social-class-biased instrument known as the IQ test. The examples could go on and on; it is clear that one's everyday experience in this culture leads one to cue immediately into a person's work role as an indicator of intelligence, worth, and power, and to behave in accordance

with this cueing. Having grown up with a massive cultural indoctrination in the face of a massive body of culturally created evidence, the educational personnel observed in this study behaved no differently than one could expect any cultural beings to behave in the situation.

Conclusions

The research findings, although exploratory in nature, have profound implications for educational policy in the United States. They call for a rethinking of our approach to educational reform and to the role of the school in promoting equal opportunity.

The research findings imply that without significant changes in social stratification by class background and its basis in the hierarchical structure of work, it is not likely that differential socialization on the basis of social class will be eliminated from schools. Until inequalities in the structure of work are changed, it is unrealistic to expect any teacher, however trained, to be completely free of the pervasive stereotyping fostered in everyday social experience that constantly recognizes and draws conclusions from work role and its associated social class status. It seems likely that equality and full human development can only be fostered by schools when adult social roles into which children move are changed to support and rely on these qualities as well. From this point of view, one cannot rely on the institution of the school to bring about substantial social reform or change, since what takes place in schools is likely to be *reflective of* social and cultural reality. The effort to bring about equal opportunity in education may be better served by turning energy and attention for reform away from the schools and toward the work place.

The research findings suggest that many popular educational reforms are likely simply to rearrange the appearance of classroom interaction, leaving the substance of what takes place in the classroom largely untouched. This is because the reforms are conceptualized and introduced with little understanding of the powerful cultural influences at work in the classroom. For instance, data from Smith Elementary School suggest that, while the formal structure of the classroom has probably changed substantially over the past 20 years so that the structure is now much less rigid and restrictive, the underlying messages communicated in spite of that structure remain strongly restrictive in many ways. While Mrs. Jones' classroom appears on the surface to be free-form, loose, and encouraging of internal direction on the part of the children, close and careful observation reveals that the substance of what is being transmitted is still strongly centered on authority and the presence of external sanctions. In the same vein, while the presence of equal funding for the two classrooms and schools would certainly help in promoting equal education, it would not address the problem of the pervasive cultural consciousness which notes and stereotypes according to social class. It would not change the "hidden curriculum" of the two classrooms or obliterate patterns of differential socialization.

In short, results from the study tend to document another kind of self-fulfilling prophecy in the classroom. A vast array of cultural clues cue the teacher as to the child's likely future position in the work hierarchy, and the teacher in turn behaves in such a way as to socialize the child for and encourage the child toward this position. Increases in spending are unlikely to eradicate this dynamic, as are changes in classroom organization such as the move to an open classroom. The measure most likely to be effective in removing this self-fulfilling prophecy is not a program to be instituted in the classroom, but one to be instituted in the wider society. This cultural restructuring could take many forms, but one central feature would necessarily be some sort of destratification of the work place, and a concomitant recognition of the importance and the particular kinds of complexity of all of the various kinds of work roles and of the value of the people who perform them.

There are smaller and more immediate steps which could be taken to minimize differential socialization in the classroom, although it is extremely important to keep the root of the problem and appropriate long term solutions firmly in mind. Educating educators and parents about the existence of differential patterns of work role socialization in the classroom and the cultural dynamics which account for them can hopefully introduce a certain amount of awareness which can begin to slow the operation of the self-fulfilling prophecy. Bringing real thoughtfulness about the nature of one's interaction with students into the classroom can be expected to promote the breaking down of stereotypes and the freeing of students' potential. Also, educational personnel and parents can certainly scrutinize educational practices for indications of varying levels of expectations for different kinds of students and work to eliminate these aspects of the educational scene. The comparison score range is one likely candidate for this kind of action.

In more theoretical terms, the significance of this study and of the ethnographic approach in general can be seen to be a continuing insistence that an understanding of social and cultural wholes is crucial for an understanding of what is taking place within the few hundred square feet that make up the classroom. The part cannot successfully be separated from the whole without violating fundamental aspects of its nature.

To understand the dynamics at work in the part and the whole, one must also come to grips with the fact that educational personnel are as thoroughly enculturated as all the rest of us. To assume that they act as neutral judges within the classroom is to adopt unquestioningly the culture's own view of itself, a practice which has proved rather unilluminating whenever it has been followed.

Action taken without these kinds of understandings of school and society has proved again and again to be unsuccessful in reaching the root of any problem and in coming up with lasting solutions.

APPENDIX A: FUNDAMENTAL UNITS OF TEACHER CONTROL BEHAVIOR

(The 83-Category Coding Scheme)

Teacher Control Strategies
1. Structuring of Work Situation
   1.1—During independent work time, provide enough work to fill the time completely, and check work if misbehavior occurs
   1.2—Emphasize wise use of time for work production, not social interaction
   1.3—Praise good behavior before the class enters a situation with high potential for behavior problems
   1.4—Express understanding that the previous activity was exciting, but that now it is time for work
   1.5—Express expectation that the child is capable in terms of academic skills of doing the assigned work

2, 3. Threaten for Academic/Behavioral Ends
   2.1, 3.1—Threaten to tell the parents about it during a conference
   2.2, 3.2—Threaten that the parents will repeat the child's neglect of responsibilities
   2.3, 3.3—Threaten with the teacher's responsibility to punish misbehavior
   2.4, 3.4—Threaten with fearful situations ("ghost story")
   2.5, 3.5—Threaten with academic failure (that the child won't be able to complete the assignment because of misbehavior)
   2,6, 3.6—Threaten with exclusion
   2.7, 3.7—Threaten with delay or denial of gratification

4, 5. Blame, Punishment for Academic Work/Behavior
   4.1, 5.1—Physical exclusion, either outside or inside the classroom
   4.2, 5.2—Shaming, sarcastic criticism as a negative model
   4.3, 5.3—Delay or denial of gratification
   4.4, 5.4—Blame on the basis of the teacher's personal reaction
   4.5, 5.5—Other individual criticism
   4.6, 5.6—Waiting
   4.7, 5.7—Ignore deviant behavior

6, 7. Praise, Reward for Academic Work/
Behavior
    6.1, 7.1—Personal praise as a positive
        model
    6.2, 7.2—Competitive praise as com-
        pared with a negative per-
        sonal model
    6.3, 7.3—Material reward
    6.4, 7.4—Promise of some sort of
        reward
    6.5, 7.5—Praise on the basis of the
        teacher's personal reaction
    6.6, 7.6—Other individual praise
8. Authority
    8.1—Command
    8.2—Explicit invocation of the
        teacher as an authority
    8.3—Explicit invocation of a rule
    8.4—Asking a question to invoke rule
        response
    8.5—Asking the reason for misbehav-
        ior, implying that there is none
    8.6—Repeating directions with the
        stated assumption that the child
        has not heard
    8.7—Command to follow directions
        (blame for disobedience)
9. Reason
    9.1—Reason explicitly stated

Teacher Control Messages
1. Individual Responsibility
    1.0—Ask the child to choose between
        compliance and exclusion
    1.1—Ask the child to play fair, not to
        cheat her/himself or others by
        misbehaving or by neglecting ac-
        ademic work
    1.2—The child is responsible for get-
        ting work done within a given
        time
    1.3—The child is responsible for ex-
        plicitly thinking about doing the
        right thing at the right time
    1.4—The child is responsible for
        doing his/her own work, think-
        ing for him/herself in doing it
    1.5—The child is responsible for solv-
        ing personal disputes

    1.6—The child is responsible for
        using materials properly, getting
        them ready, and putting them
        away
    1.7—Ask the child to remind him/
        herself of internalized values or
        self-image
    1.8—The child is responsible for be-
        having in a way that makes work
        possible (raising hand, paying
        attention, being in right place at
        right time, ready to start next ac-
        tivity, noise level)
    1.9—The child is responsible for be-
        having in such a way as to fur-
        ther the mastering of academic
        skills, with this goal explicitly
        stated
2. Others' Feelings
    2.1—The teacher stresses respect for
        feelings of other children as an
        important value in the
        classroom
    2.2—The teacher expresses under-
        standing of children's feelings in
        a sympathetic way
3. Achievement
    3.1—Compare the child with proper
        achievement of someone his/her
        age or grade
    3.2—Compare the child with proper
        achievement above grade level
    3.3—Compare the child with proper
        achievement below grade level
    3.4—Link achievement to self-image
        in the present
    3.5—Link achievement to self-image
        in the future
4. Child-Initiated Input
    4.1—Procedural ideas reinforced
    4.2—Procedural questions reinforced
    4.3—Child-initiated independent
        work reinforced
    4.4—Child-initiated ideas discouraged
5. Explicit Work Values
    5.1—Emphasis on hard work or
        trying hard
    5.2—Emphasis on independent work
        (self-image)

5.3—Work carefully because careful work is important

5.4—Work alone, don't bother other people

5.5—Enjoy reading

5.6—Work together, cooperate

5.7—Obey directions in carrying out work

6. Other

6.1—Reference to family or community standards

6.2—Get along, don't fight!

APPENDIX B:
RECODED STRATEGIES

Internal Behavior: 13, 35, 72, 84, 85 and 52, 55, 57, 71, 76, 91 if message is internal behavior

External Behavior: 14, 31, 32, 33, 34, 36, 37, 51, 53, 56, 73, 74, 75, 82, 83, 86, 87 and 52, 55, 71, 76, 81 if message is external behavior

Internal Academic: 12, 15, 62 and 42, 45, 61, 66, 91 if message is internal academic

External Academic: 11, 22, 27, 41, 43, 44, 46, 63, 64, 65 and 42, 45, 47, 61, 66, 81 if message is external academic

Internal: All codings for internal behavior strategies plus all codings for internal academic strategies

External: All codings for external behavior strategies plus all codings for external academic strategies

Behavior: All codings for internal behavior strategies plus all codings for external behavior strategies

Academic: All codings for internal academic strategies plus all codings for external academic strategies

Present: 11, 12, 13, 14, 15, 41, 42, 43, 44, 45, 46, 47, 51, 52, 53, 54, 55, 56, 57, 61, 62, 63, 65, 66, 71, 72, 73, 75, 76, 81, 82, 83, 84, 85, 86, 87 and 91 if message is present

Future: 22, 27, 31, 32, 33, 34, 35, 36, 37, 64, 74 and 91 if message is future

RECODED MESSAGES

Internal Behavior: 10, 15, 16, 21, 22 and 17, 31, 32, 33, 41, 42 if strategy is internal behavior

External Behavior: 18, 57, 72 and 44, 71 if strategy is external behavior

Internal Academic: 11, 13, 14, 19, 34, 35, 43, 51, 52, 53, 54, 55 and 17, 31, 32, 33, 41, 42 if strategy is internal academic

External Academic: 12, 44, 56, 57, 71 if strategy is external academic

Internal: All codings for internal academic messages plus all codings for internal behavior messages

External: All codings for external academic messages plus all codings for external behavior messages

Behavior: All codings for internal behavior messages plus all codings for external behavior messages

Academic: All codings for internal academic messages plus all codings for external academic messages

Present: 10, 12, 13, 14, 15, 16, 17, 18, 21, 22, 31, 33, 34, 41, 42, 43, 44, 51, 52, 53, 54, 55, 56, 57, 72 and 71 if strategy is present

Future: 11, 19, 32, 35 and 71 if strategy is future

Achievement: 31, 32, 33, 34, 35

Notes

[1] The actual fieldwork was carried out by two people, the author and Pia Moriarty. The presence of a second person made it possible for each fieldworker to concentrate on one school and one classroom, enabling more extensive study of each site.

[2] The inclusion of statistical results in this chapter does not represent an attempt at statistical "proof" of the hypothesis under study. The small sample size inevitably results in the violation of one of the assumptions underlying the analysis of variance procedure, and precludes the presentation of the results as proof. (See Hays [1973:529] and Wilcox [1978:162–163] for a more technical discussion of the problem.) However, the data do offer a rough estimate of the size of observed differences across a number of student groups in the two classrooms, and are introduced as one of many kinds of data supporting the hypothesis.

[3] In order to uphold promises of confidentiality to the two schools, certain minor details have been changed for the purposes of this description.

[4] I had hoped to find a classroom with a relatively even number of boys and girls, but such a classroom was not available at Smith.

[5] The relatively small number of observations conducted in other classrooms precluded any statistically meaningful analysis, but hand tabulations revealed similar patterns.

References

Becker, Gary. 1967. *Human Capital and the Personal Distribution of Income*. Ann Arbor: University of Michigan Press.

Binstock, Jeanne. 1970. *Survival in the American College Industry*. Ph.D. dissertation, Brandeis University.

Bowles, Samuel, and Herbert Gintis. 1976. *Schooling in Capitalist America*. New York: Basic Books, Inc.

Brookover, Wilbur B., and Edsel L. Erickson. 1975. *Sociology of Education*. Homewood, IL: The Dorsey Press.

Brophy, J. E., and T. L. Good. 1970. "Teachers' Communication of Differential Expectations for Children's Classroom Performance," *Journal of Educational Psychology*, 61:365–374.

California State Testing Program. 1974. *Profiles of School District Performance 1971–72*. Sacramento, CA.: California State Department of Education.

Carter, Michael A., and Martin Carnoy. 1974. *Theories of Labor Markets and Worker Productivity*. Discussion paper, Center for Economic Studies, Palo Alto, CA.

Conant, James B. 1961. *Slums and Suburbs*. New York: McGraw-Hill Book Company.

Davis, Kingsley, and Wilbert E. Moore. 1945. "Some Principles of Stratification," *American Sociological Review*, 10:242–249.

Edwards, Richard C. 1976. "Individual Traits and Organizational Incentives: What Makes a 'Good Worker'?" *Journal of Human Resources*, 11:51–68.

Eisenhart, Churchill. 1947. "Inverse Sine Transformation of Proportions." In Churchill Eisenhart, Millard W. Hastay, and W. Allen Wallis, eds., *Techniques of Statistical Analysis*. New York: McGraw-Hill Book Company.

Fischer, John, and Ann Fischer. 1963. "The New Englanders of Orchard Town, U.S.A." In Beatrice B. Whiting and John W. M. Whiting, eds., *Six Cultures: Studies of Child Rearing*. New York: John Wiley and Sons.

Gintis, Herbert. 1971. "Education, Technology and the Characteristics of Worker Productivity," *American Economic Review*, 61(2):266–279.

Goffman, Erving. 1959. *The Presentation of Self in Everyday Life*. Garden City, NY: Doubleday and Company.

Harvard Educational Review. 1968. Special issue on Equal Educational Opportunities, 38(1).

Hays, William L. 1973. *Statistics for the Social Sciences*, 2nd ed. New York: Holt, Rinehart and Winston.

Herriot, Robert, and Nancy St. John. 1966. *Social Class and the Urban School*. New York: John Wiley and Sons.

Howe, Louise Kapp, ed. 1970. *The White Majority: Between Poverty and Affluence*. New York: Random House, Inc.

Jackall, Robert. 1976. *Worker Characteristics and Productivity*. Occasional paper, Center for Economic Studies, Palo Alto, California.

Kohn, Melvin. 1967. *Class and Conformity: A Study in Values*. Homewood, IL: The Dorsey Press.

Leacock, Eleanor. 1969. *Teaching and Learning in City Schools*. New York: Basic Books Inc.

———, ed. 1970. *The Culture of Poverty: A Critique*. New York: Committee for Economic Development.

McMurrin, Sterling M. 1971. *The Conditions for Educational Equality*. New York: Committee for Economic Development.

Meyer, John W. 1970. "The Charter: Conditions of Diffuse Socialization in Schools." In W. R. Scott, ed., *Social Processes and Social Structures*. New York: Holt, Rinehart and Winston.

Mincer, Jacob. 1970. "The Distribution of Labor Incomes: A Survey," *Journal of Economic Literature* 7.

Nadel, S. F. 1952. "Witchcraft in Four African Societies: An Essay in Comparison," *American Anthropologist*, 54(1):18–29.

Nader, Laura. 1964. *Talea and Juquila: A Comparison of Zapotec Social Organization*. Berkeley, CA: University of California Press.

Parsons, Talcott. 1959. "The School Class as a Social System: Some of Its Functions in American Society," *Harvard Educational Review*, 29(4):297–318.

Parsons, Theodore W. 1971. *Guided Self-Analysis.* Berkeley, CA: Professional Development Systems.

Reiss, Albert J., et al. 1961. *Occupations and Social Studies.* New York: The Free Press.

Rist, Ray. 1977. "On the Relations Among Educational Research Paradigms: From Disdain to Detente," *Anthropology and Education Quarterly,* 8(2):42–49.

———.1970. "Student Social Class and Teacher Expectations: The Self-Fulfilling Prophecy in Ghetto Schools," *Harvard Educational Review*, 40(3):411–450.

Rosenthal, Robert, and Lenore Jacobson. 1968. *Pygmalian in the Classroom: Teacher Expectation and Pupils' Intellectual Development.* New York: Holt, Rinehart and Winston.

Sennett, Richard, and Jonathan Cobb. 1972. *The Hidden Injuries of Class.* New York: Alfred A. Knopf, Inc.

Sindell, Peter S. 1969. "Anthropological Approaches to the Study of Education," *Review of Educational Research*, 39:593–605.

Spindler, George D., ed. 1963. *Education and Culture.* New York: Holt, Rinehart and Winston.

Valentine, Charles A. 1968. *Culture and Poverty: Critique and Counter Proposals.* Chicago: University of Chicago Press.

Wax, Murray L., and Rosalie H. Wax. 1971. "Great Tradition, Little Tradition, and Formal Education." In Murray Wax, Stanley Diamond, and Fred Gearing, eds., *Anthropological Perspectives on Education.* New York: Basic Books, Inc.

Whiting, John W. M., et al. 1966. *Field Guide for a Study of Socialization.* New York: John Wiley and Sons.

Wilcox, Kathleen A. 1978. *Schooling and Socialization for Work Roles: A Structural Inquiry into Cultural Transmission in an Urban American Community.* Doctoral dissertation, Anthropology Department, Harvard University.

PART **IV**

Five Diverse Ethno- graphic Analyses

Editorial Commentary

This section contains the widest diversity of any in this book. Topics include the consequences of desegregation, ethnographic studies of children's spontaneous play, a bicultural-bilingual program in Spanish and English, the social organization of reading, and the historical study of a Kentucky school district. Diversity in topics is to be expected, for anthroethnography can be applied to the study of any phenomena anywhere. Each of the parts of this volume is topically diversified. The diversity of Part IV, and the diversity of anthroethnography, is expressed better in the variation in conceptual ordering and theoretical models used, or the lack of them.

The research methods used by the ethnographers in this section, and the assumptions behind them, express greater unity. None are microanalytic in the sense that the methods employed by Erickson and Mohatt or Gearing and Epstein are. Most current anthroethnography is not. The studies represented in this section are not lacking in detail, nor were they collected at a distance, through questionnaires. They are the result of continuous, long-term, up-close observation and ethnographic interviewing. They do not focus on highly specified variables or event chains in order to answer certain questions or test hypotheses that emerged out of stages one and two of the ethnographic inquiry discussed in the introduction to Part III. Finnan's study of play comes closest to being microethnographic, in that her focus is on a relatively narrow range of behaviors included in spontaneous play. Hanna's data are specific in detail, as are Warren's, but the scope of their inquiries is quite broad—a desegregated magnet school in one case and a bicultural-bilingual program in another. Both writers could move into a microanalytic phase from where they are, but it might not be directly relevant to their purposes.

Certain questions can only be answered by going to stage three, where microethnography is most likely to be done. It depends on what one wants to find out and in what depth one needs to know about it. The weakness in macroethnography is that it is not focused and limited enough to furnish data on the repetitive elements of behavior that make up the building units of larger patterns of behavior. Its strength lies in its breadth, its engagement with complex interactions in wide-ranging contexts.

Cultural transmission has been the most influential theoretical model in this volume. This model seemed most important when those few of us who were interested started formulating the purposes of educational anthropology some 30 years ago, and it has remained the dominant model. Most of the ethnographers represented in this volume appear to assume that cultural transmission is what they are studying. That we must study cultural transmission if we are to study education as a cultural process seems inescapable. However, in doing so we should remember that children at all ages place their own constructions on reality. Their behavior is not simply a childish translation of adult norms or patterns of behavior. It is a result of a complex interaction of child culture, adult culture, individual striving, and situational culture (the rules, expectations, and assumptions that emerge and stabilize in any continued social setting). Cultural transmission works, but for reasons we do not fully understand as yet. If we are to understand them better, we need, among a myriad of other things, to study the culture of children, including the constructions they place on the reality that we adults think we know and are trying to teach them.

Two papers in this section take some steps into the culture(s) of children—Christine Finnan's on spontaneous play and Judith Hanna's on "meddlin,'" a form of "harassment" in a desegregated "magnet" school. Both papers move into the culture of children with standard observational and eliciting techniques. As an anthroethnography of schooling develops further, it will be imperative to include careful attention to this dimension. The ethnographic tradition of emphasis on the view of the native, on emic cultural knowledge, makes the attention to children's culture possible, as well as imperative.

All of the papers in this section make useful contributions and raise issues, some explicitly stated and some not. Sylvia Hart, for example, attempts to apply a construct that is basic to a monumental amount of anthropological thinking and analysis—social organization. She translates the construct into the dimensions she sees as relevant to the organization of reading. In this attempt she is doing something quite different from what most of her anthropological colleagues have done in Parts II and III. With the exception of some sociolinguistic constructs, they have moved away from traditional anthropological concepts and vernacular toward many that would hardly be recognizable to a traditional anthropologist as anthropological. The emphases on small-group interaction, the hidden dimension as a form of tacit culture, socialization to work roles, use of speech markers maintaining group boundaries, etc., are as clearly interdisciplinary as they are anthropological, though the methods of study are ethnographic.

Hart tries to make the familiar strange in order to explain it. This is a reversal of what anthropologists usually do in their fieldwork and ethnographic reporting. They try to make the strange familiar. They study the Yanamamo, Mardudjara, Nandi, or

Ojibwa, and then try to tell us readers what these people are like, in a way that we will understand. In Louise Spindler's and my editing of the more than 100 volumes in our Case Studies series for introductory and intermediate anthropology courses, making the strange familiar has been the basic task.

The anthroethnography of schooling, as the first chapter in this volume indicated, has as one of its basic tasks making the familiar strange. We have to put our own schools into cross-cultural perspective in order for us, as anthroethnographers, to "see" them at all. What seems to the native (in this case the native of the U.S.A., including the ethnographer) to be universal, given, natural, and inevitable has to be understood as one of many human cultural solutions to universal problems of existence and as exotic as any of them. In any paper in this book there is an unstated assumption that this is a part of the task—that our own culture and its maintenance through education are to be understood as part of worldwide and time-spanning cultural variation.

Another issue that is derived most clearly from the chapters by Warren and Hanna, but to some extent from all the papers in this book, is that of ethnographic evaluation. We encountered this issue in the first sections of this book. No single topic has received more attention at recent C.A.E. (Council on Anthropology and Education) meetings. The term raises the hackles of many anthropologists, for the ethnographer in the field, in a field ethnographer's role, can never be an "evaluator." A friendly, nonthreatening relationship with those with whom one is working and from whom one is learning is essential. The "natives," whether medicine men or women, priests, headhunters, schoolteachers, or school children, are not going to reveal to a stranger, even a friendly stranger, anything that may be used against them.

The paradox is that *every* ethnography *is* a kind of evaluation. It is an analysis of how a social system or culture works—or doesn't work—as an adaptation to its setting. It brings to light matters that natives as a rule don't articulate. The hidden dimension is always present in sociocultural analysis. And yet, the ethnographer cannot do ethnography as an evaluator—the roles are too much in conflict to be carried into the field together—except in a limited sense and usually with only limited target groups within the system. The evaluation can be done after the fieldwork is completed. The functions of evaluation and ethnography can be separated, as are the roles of ethnographer and evaluator.

It would seem wise to deemphasize evaluation, insofar as we are concerned with doing ethnography, and aim instead for *understanding*. It is not a matter of how *well* a system or a program or a classroom works; it is a matter of how it *does* work. Evaluations may be derived from ethnographies, but evaluation cannot be the major purpose of ethnographic study. Ethnographic policy decisions should be based in part on ethnographic studies, because such studies can afford understanding at a level of sophistication and depth that other methods do not provide. An ethnographer, however, should never be made the tool of educational policy. To define the ethnographer as an evaluator is to define him or her as such a tool. Ethnographic study is not like the application of an experimental design or a questionnaire. It requires intimacy and depends on trust. We cannot "do our informants in" while doing ethnography. The basic position I am taking is that though evaluations and ethnographies are not necessarily in conflict, the ethnographer should not be asked to assume the role of evaluator in the field.

The position on ethnographic evaluation stated here and elsewhere in this volume will not be accepted by all anthroethnographers and probably not by a majority of nonanthropological ethnographers. The roles of evaluator and ethnographer will be refined as work goes on, but it seems desirable, at this point, to stress their separateness and the inherent conflicts between them. This will not be expedient, given the need for evaluative feedback in school administration and educational policy-making, but it seems crucial now in the formative stages of character definition for ethnography.

None of the chapters in this book were conducted as ethnographic evaluations. Even those by Hanna and Warren, though clearly on problems where evaluation is of critical importance, are written as descriptive ethnographic analyses of how a program worked, of how human beings as natives interacted in settings contrived by the nature of the educational program—"magnet" school or bicultural classroom. That both studies have implications for educational policy and can be interpreted in an evaluative framework is not to be gainsaid. It is the nature of ethnography that it produces useful understandings of how cultural systems work.

10

Judith Lynne Hanna

Public Social Policy and the Children's World: Implications of Ethnographic Research for Desegregated Schooling

Judith Lynne Hanna

The Author

Judith Lynne Hanna, a National Endowment for the Humanities fellow at the American Enterprise Institute for Public Policy Research and also affiliated with the University of Maryland, earned a Ph.D. in anthropology from Columbia University, an M.A. in political science from Michigan State University, and a General Secondary School Teaching Credential from the State of California. She has been on the teaching or research faculties of the University of Texas at Dallas; Fordham University, Lincoln Center Campus; American University; University of Ibadan; and Michigan State University. In addition, she has been a guest lecturer at more than 20 universities and colleges in the U.S. and Canada.

Personal family experience combined with professional work in the field of ecucation catalyzed Hanna's ethnography of a desegregated school. After training in the University of California at Los Angeles Graduate School of Education, she worked in schools in a variety of capacities: a teacher "on the firing line" in the Los Angeles and Lansing public schools and at the private Gill School in New Jersey; and a consultant for the New York City, Philadelphia, Englewood (New Jersey), and Westport (Connecticut) school systems. As a consultant, Hanna drew upon her African field research on urban areas, students and politics, and nonverbal communication to develop curricula for minority ethnic pride and academic achievement.

Her research studies, reported in numerous articles and books, include: *Urban Dynamics in Black Africa* (1971, revised edition 1981), *The Anthropology of Dance Ritual: Nigeria's Ubakala Nkwa di Iche Iche* (1976), *To Dance Is Human: A Theory of Nonverbal Communication* (1979), and contributions in *University Students and African Politics* (1975) and *Current Anthropology* (1979). She explains how she became involved with the study reported here:

"When my family and I moved to Dallas, Texas, my children enrolled in the local public school, which was reputed to be of the highest quality. The school had been recently desegregated and involved busing volunteer white children into a black community. After months of listening to my children talk about their daily school experiences, I realized that the children's reports differed significantly from what civil rights activists and researchers said about desegregated schools. I decided to search for an explanation of the discrepancies. Having studied interethnic relations and nonverbal communication, my initial hunch was that there were problems between blacks and whites in sending and receiving intended messages. Embarking on a study of the school, I soon realized the naivety and unfounded assumptions that I shared with other parents, educators, researchers, and private citizens committed to desegregation. *Like Me, Meddle Me: Life in a Desegregated School,* a fuller report of the study described in this book, reveals the realities—rather than the mythologies—of desegregation, and suggests ways to cope with the problems my research identified."

This Chapter

In this chapter Judith Hanna reports on her year-long study of a desegregated "magnet" elementary school that she calls "Pacesetter." She moves, in her analysis, from concerned parent of two children in the school to concerned researcher, probing beneath the surface of the relative calm and apparent success characterizing Pacesetter. She uses established methods of ethnography, starting with observation, participating in school affairs and activities, formulating interview questions on the basis of work *in situ,* and conducting interviews informally. She is true to the ethnographic concept that the views of the "natives" and their emic cultural knowledge are the object of study, but she interprets these data in her own framework, drawing from the interpretations of social scientists who have studied the consequences of desegregation.

She focuses on a process called "meddlin'" by the children who employ and express it. Meddlin' is an expression of aggression and takes many forms, some relatively subtle but most direct, disruptive, and destructive. The more openly aggressive forms of meddlin' occur most often in the interactions of black children and more often with other blacks than with whites. It is, however, a major source of tension and disengagement on the part of white children and white middle-class parents, as well as middle-class black parents. Of course, meddlin' behavior has functions. It is not purposeless. Hanna discusses the historical and motivational reasons for the behavior.

Hanna's analysis raises questions about desegregation policy that are not easily faced, much less answered. That segregation is unacceptable in a democratic society on ideological, moral, and practical grounds is not in question. What is in question is how to cope with the consequences of desegregation and how best desegregation may be accomplished. Ethnographic studies of desegregated schools, such as those carried out by Judith Hanna and those under the supervision of Murray Wax for the National Institute of Education, are steps in what might be called an ethnographic evaluation of desegregation. These studies are not "quick and dirty" forays into and out of context. They are months- or even years-long, intensive, participant-observer interview studies in depth. Ethnographic "evaluations" of this kind are potentially important contributions to the long-range formulation of workable as well as just educational policy.

The Beginning

"See what I mean? That hurt! And it would hurt you, too!" Aaron said to me. Aaron, a white boy who was a star goalie on a champion soccer team and generally a good athlete, had just run after the ball. A black boy also raced for it. Aaron reached the ball first. The other boy, taller and heavier, pushed him aside to grab it. Then the black youngster had kicked Aaron's buttocks so hard that he lurched painfully forward and blanched. I was observing playground social interaction that day. On other days I saw this particular black boy, as well as a few others, act the same way toward other children. Aaron had told me—more than once over a five-month period—that blacks did not play nicely; they were mean. I offered possible reasons for this kind of behavior and encouraged taking various perspectives on the problem. I pointed out that all children of whatever color sometimes misbehave. But Aaron's own everyday experiences in the classroom, moving from one setting to another, in the halls and lunchroom and on the playground, convinced him that blacks at Pacesetter School behaved differently.

Aaron's older brother had reported incidents of "honkies" versus "niggers" when he was in third grade. Shawn had never heard these epithets before attending Pacesetter and did not know their meanings. But he did know it was "whites" versus "blacks" and that there were gang leaders. Sometimes he said he belonged to the "white gang." I did not observe gang activity among the children in the fourth grade. However, I did stumble onto a third-grade interracial "rumble"—a fight involving two groups. If I had seen it on TV, I would have said, "That's not true to life; it's exaggerated!" Two black girls started arguing about something having to do with a jump rope game. Rachel, known to be hot-tempered, and Sheniqua, known not to take anything from anyone, began fighting. A circle of black girls formed around them. Some of the girls jumped up and down in sheer ecstasy. They cheered the combatants. Each contestant had an ally who entered the arena to hit her opponent. Two teachers broke up the fight, each hugging one of the contestants. Too busy to find the cause of a fight, they treated the symptoms.

Kids will be kids! We all know about Tom Sawyer, Huckleberry Finn, and the Little Rascals. Huizinga (1950) and Aldis (1975) report that aggressive play, with its contests between individuals or teams, is universal. Bullies, intimidation, fights, pranks, and defying authority exist in every school.

But how do children view their lives at school? How do they define the situation in which they find themselves? These perceptions affect their attitudes and behavior, which, in turn, have implications for school policy and socially stratified society. Children from white, civil rights activist families speaking like conservative "rednecks" about blacks after attending desegregated schools catalyzed my study of an urban desegregated magnet school with a court-mandated 50-50 black-white[1] ratio for each sex in each classroom. The school is located in a black community in a major metropolitan area in the Southwest. The desegregation plan explicitly specified a black neighborhood school. Many members of the black community had opposed busing their elementary school children. Their junior and senior high youngsters were being bused into white neighborhood schools, and they felt that whites should share the burden of busing. Black children who began their education at the school and then moved to residentially desegregated neighborhoods in the district were permitted to continue at the school. It was rumored that some blacks who lived outside the school neighborhood used addresses of friends inside the neighborhood so that their children could have access to the school. Under the court-mandated "magnet" plan, only whites may volunteer to be bused to the school. The attraction (thus the use of the label "magnet school") is the superior educational program of individualized in-struction for the gifted, the average, and the slow learner (thus the use of the name Pacesetter). Volunteer busing is also a means for individuals to show a commitment to educational equity through desegregation.

The purpose of my year-long study was to try to understand children's social relations and communication—what they said and what they did—in this elementary school. The research revealed "meddlin'" to be the key area of social dissonance. "If somebody just be messin' with you, just to try and aggravate you .... that's meddlin,'" a sixth-grade black girl explained.

My initial hypothesis was that black and white children did not understand each other's nonverbal communications. This turned out to be only partly true. They understood many of the messages. The problem was that they did not like them or the ways in which they were sent. In addition, social class appeared to intersect with color.[2] The few middle-class blacks in the school (e.g., those whose parents were educators or had college education) shared more social interaction styles with the middle-class whites than with the majority of blacks. Rarely did Pacesetter children identify middle-class children as those who caused difficulties. Illustrative of the middle-class orientation was the black PTA past-president and educator who reported that her 6-year-old child told her, "Mommy, I don't want to play with blacks, they don't play nice!" The mother explained that her son played with whites in their organized games; black children's activities such as sandlot baseball were too rough.

I will discuss the theory and method

that informed my field study of children's social relations in Pacesetter School, sketch key ethnographic findings, particularly in the area of "meddlin'," address some assumptions that guide the research (as well as the educational and civil rights enterprises), and then point out some of the immediate and projected consequences of these assumptions.

A Central Understanding

The child is not a passive receiver of intended or accidental instruction. Children have their own minds, sensory apparatus, and historical era. Children assess situations. Then they select strategies within their current repertoires for acting in light of the assessments as they see them, including their own capabilities. Current theoretical models portray the child as actively constructing social knowledge out of his or her conceptual abilities and limitations and unique experiences in the world (Shantz 1975). This study, generally drawing upon sociolinguistic cognitive and behavioral perceptives (cf. Hymes 1967, 1974), is concerned with Pacesetter children's communication and social relations within an ecological context—how they perceived their situations in the school and acted upon their perceptions.

Research Methods and Procedure

Being a casual parent-observer in Pacesetter School for five months during 1977 alerted me to certain problems

of multicultural communication that existed there. A survey of the literature on multicultural education indicated that these problems loomed larger elsewhere. During the summer I met with the school and district administrators to outline a study of these problems. The principal for instruction was enthusiastic, because she believed that insiders "get lulled into a false sense of security and complacency."

I used several data-collection procedures and analytic methods. Each has its limitations and strengths. By using more than one approach, the shortcomings of each may be compensated for to some extent. Some types of research methods are, for example, more liable to subjective bias than others. Observation was, however, my key method, for it led to others.

Observations were made in terms of who does what, when, with whom, and with what effect. Interactions were viewed in terms of "situational frames" (what happens in a particular instance), "action chains" (what happens sequentially over time), and history (prior situational frames and action chains). Naturalistic observations occurred somewhere in the midst of an ongoing "stream of behavior" that might have begun hours, days, weeks, months, or years earlier. One of the key fights observed had its inception in class dynamics in the previous grade. Students' verbal reports complemented observations and put them in perspective.

The results of preliminary observations and informal discussion in the multicultural school surprised me. I identified alliance (groups of children acting in unison), patron-client (a strong child protecting a weaker one in exchange for respect or favors), and gang (an antisocial group) behaviors that differed markedly from some school personnel and parent reports of student behavior and motivation. I expected such behavior among teenagers, not elementary school children. Adult denial of my observations led to the decision to conduct systematic interviews with the students. Perhaps some adults misinterpreted what occurred; alternatively, some were fully aware of what was going on and denied it.

On the basis of my observations I began developing the questions I would ask a representative group of students. What do children perceive as salient in their social milieu, and how do they cope?

Classroom questionnaires were not used, since children's reading comprehension varied considerably. Furthermore, children often copied each other's answers or talked about them. The open-ended interview questions were designed to bring to the surface the main ideas on children's minds, rather than imposing on them the researcher's preconceived categories or alternatives. Research instruments, such as a set of interview questions, formulated before preliminary research carry a construction of reality which may not capture the perceptions of the students.

The questions I asked (see Appendix) explored children's understanding of expressions of friendship and anger, social interactions among themselves and with teachers, likes and dislikes concerning the school and teachers, notions of appropriate behavior and how

to handle misbehavior, causes of fights, and fears. The questions were shown to the principals, the district administrator supervising the project, and special education teachers who work with slow learners, for suggestions concerning content and speech usage that children from different cultures would best understand. After pretesting the interview instrument with black and white boys and girls in grades 2, 4, and 6 (chosen to reflect different levels of cognitive and social development), I began interviewing 120 students in a random sample stratified on the bases of sex, race, and grade.

Because of parental or guardian refusal to permit their children to participate in "Project Understanding," as it was called, there were nine substitutions in the sample. Only one white parent did not want her timid second-grade daughter to participate. Substitutions were made for two second-grade black boys, a fourth-grade black boy and black girl, and three sixth-grade black girls and one black boy. Refusals on the part of blacks were related to antiwhite hostility that surfaced among the children and to expressed resentment that the school spent too much time testing and not enough time teaching. The antiwhite sentiment was based on a history, discussed later, of white harassment and control of blacks. Five of the black students whose parents refused permission to participate were reputed by teachers to be discipline problems and by their grade level peers to be tough kids.

Teachers informed me of the days and hours during which it would be most appropriate for me to talk with their students, so that they would not miss essential work. At the beginning of the approximately 15- to 20-minute interview, I told each child that I was writing a story about Pacesetter and wanted to know from the student's point of view what it was like to be a student at the school. I asked the child if he or she wished to share thoughts with me. No one refused. I was familiar to many of the children, as a visiting mother who had participated in numerous school activities. I usually interviewed students in a nonclassroom setting I called my "hidey hole," after a special place described in a children's story book. Located in the special resource room, my "conversation room" with its carpeted floors and walls was used for special record and video listening. It had the virtues of being generally available, unique, private, and quiet. The informality—I dressed informally, we had candy, and we sat whereever the child preferred (on the floor, cushions, or chairs)—was conducive to free expression. On an exceptionally nice day, we chatted outdoors.

Because I am an adult and white, some children might have been reserved in telling the story about life at Pacesetter.[3] Given apprehension over being evaluated, one would, if anything, expect the answers to be more in line with school norms and less focused on contrary behavior, in order to minimize risks of negative assessment. Thus, antischool norm behavior might be greater than reported.[4] On the other hand, most children easily have rapport with and confidence in a pleasant, attentive stranger who tries to provide no cues of disagreement. Most children appeared to enjoy the questions and to speak frankly. When I asked, "What did you think about these questions?" one child told me he thought they were "nosey!" Others thought they were "fun," "hard," "okay." Two children thought they were "weird." Only one youngster, a black sixth-grade boy, said they were "no good."

I taped the interviews, which later were transcribed and were checked by a person other than the transcriber. The quotations in this chapter are verbatim and reflect both local expressions and children's developing vocabulary. I explained to the children that I could not write as fast as they talked, and we'd spend more time than their teachers would like for them to be away from class if I tried. I assured respondents that their answers would be kept confidential, i.e., no child's name would be identified. At the end of the 16 questions, I asked each child if he or she thought there were questions I did not ask that would give me an idea of what it was like to be a student at Pacesetter. I asked the child whatever question was proposed. If a child wanted to hear himself or herself, I played back some of the recording.

Among children who knew each other, there was remarkable consistency in comments about specific youngsters. There were also some contradictions within a child's own answers to different questions. These appeared to reflect the student's perceptions of what school authorities believed was appropriate versus what actually occurred. If, on the day I interviewed a child, he or she had observed or participated in an incident relevant to one of the questions, it was usually described to me with great relish. Children's reports helped to focus further research observations. The children who were nominated relatively frequently by their peers as toughs and feared were observed especially. They are the individuals who create behavior problems and cause some black and white children to have negative feelings toward blacks in groups. Events which appeared likely to clarify an emerging understanding were given some observation time.

When a teacher was hired about a month into the school year to monitor what was first called a "discipline room" (and in September 1978 changed to an "alternative room"), I prepared a report form to be filled out for each student sent to her to work quietly, talk over difficulties, or develop a plan for improved schoolwork or social relations. The purpose of the report form was to try to identify what kinds of behaviors were proving difficult for teachers to handle in the classroom.

What was the effect of my presence at the school? The school was born in the limelight and continues to be watched. Consequently, children and teachers are used to being in the public eye. The school has a continual flow of visitors and student teachers. Parents are involved in an organized volunteer program to assist the instructional process.

My own children liked their mother's presence at their school. They correctly interpreted my interest as caring, and perhaps it made them feel more secure. They liked the attention from other children who were interviewed or who wanted to be. A number of the children thought it was "neat" that adults wanted to hear what they had to say: "The school must really care!"

Most of the teachers expressed great interest in what I was learning and in reading the report. Their openness mirrored the principals' hopes for an "outsider" perspective on what the educational enterprise was all about. Some teachers expressed anxiety to the administrators and other teachers about my ubiquitous presence. There had been parents with axes to grind who "monitored" the school. Perhaps a few teachers felt insecure about their ability to manage their own classrooms. Schafft, an anthropologist who studied a school in her home community, felt that some teachers feared sharing their children's affection with an outsider (1976). I became a sounding board for a few frustrated teachers and parents. Some teachers excused any problem and accepted difficulties as par for the course. Other teachers were less sanguine. Informal comments made in the hall or lunchrooms as we passed were often revealing.

Pacesetter School

Schools do not exist as isolated entities. They tend to reflect the values and experiences of the communities which feed them, in keeping with the American public education tradition. Pacesetter is located in a black community that was created in the 1950s as a result of white terrorism and fire bombing of black homes that were purchased or being built in formerly all-white residential areas. At the time there was a housing shortage. Through the efforts of a biracial group of civic leaders, a segregated housing project was undertaken within the city limits so that government regulatory services could be provided. At the opening ceremonies there were 50 homes, one-story frame dwellings with carport and graveled roof. Priority was given to families being displaced as a result of industrial development. Historically blacks were forced to live in segregated places and often were permitted some self-governance. Then, when whites realized the value of black areas for roads, airports, and white residences, or blacks became residentially too proximate, whites pushed the blacks out. Home bombings, school and water well destruction, and verbal intimidation encouraged black relocation.

The community had its own shopping center and school. Desegregation changed the black control of the school. A five-year U.S. Justice Department effort culminated in 1975. The judge accepted a plan for whites to be bused voluntarily to the community school, which is centrally located in the school district so that no student would have more than a 30-minute bus ride. By and large, members of the black community were not unemployed or from the inner-city ghetto, so that it was thought values would be similar enough to make the plan workable.[5] The goal was to attract whites through the compelling factor of educational excellence.

Desegregation at Pacesetter brought together black and white, neighborhood networks and unorganized volunteers who were strangers to each other and the black children, and working-class and middle-class youngsters. Most

of the black children had been together since preschool. They did not always readily accept strangers, even if they were black. For example, a girl who moved into the Pacesetter neighborhood said:

Sometimes they won't talk or play with you. When I first came here, it happened to me. Then after the second year was over it started getting, it was easier to get along because we had known each other for about a year then. Well, I am fully black, but it just seemed like I was from somewhere else that they treated me like that: like from outer space!

There is a disparity between the black and white family incomes, education, and occupations (Estes and Skipper 1976). The income and educational level of the whites are above the national average. Half earn in excess of $20,000 and are college graduates. Approximately two-thirds of the white fathers are in professional, managerial, or craftsmen occupations. In contrast, the average income in the Pacesetter community is about $9,000. One-third of the black fathers are laborers; another third are in professional, managerial, or craftsmen occupations. About 7 percent are unemployed; the others' occupations are unknown. The community has some college graduates. White mothers who work tend to be somewhat higher on the socioeconomic scale than their black counterparts. More whites (70 percent) live with their natural mother and father; more blacks (60 percent) live with a single parent or in a nonparent arrangement. Though originally the black community members owned their own homes, now many of them rent. Today middle-income blacks have more housing options than in the past.

From observations and students' reports, it is clear that children at Pacesetter generally have positive, pleasant experiences. Visitors notice a warm and friendly atmosphere. Most children appear to be having fun, and a bustling sense of activity pervades the school. The facility is contemporary, with clean, unlittered halls, and many windows for good lighting. The varied, eye-catching decor of the classrooms is at the discretion of the individual teachers. Children's work adorns many classrooms and hall walls. Some classrooms have learning centers. Work groups may sprawl out on the floor or spill into the halls, which have areas for special projects and individualized interest groups. There is much touching, embracing, and informality. There is also less peer pressure to conform to one style of dress and hair than in other schools, according to students with comparative experiences. Classroom groups usually move quietly and in an orderly line from one activity to another—e.g., from homeroom to reading, math, music, art, and physical education, and back to homeroom for social studies and science. Counselors and Spanish language teachers move their audiovisual equipment into and out of the homerooms they visit.

One senses the school philosophy: begin where you are and grow—"education for the total child." Most teachers are earnest, idealistic, and dedicated. The students, generally, like their teachers and view them as helpful and fair—"nice."

Since the school was formerly designed for grades K–12, the playground is spatially luxurious for an elementary school. For the upper grades there are a track, grass areas for two regulation-size ball fields, swings, and a merry-go-round. In the play area allocated to the lower grades, there are a blacktop with climbing, slide, and swing equipment and a grass ball field.

Having presented the catalyst for the study, its purpose of trying to understand children's social relations and communication in school, and the theory and method that informed the ethnography, I turn now to the key area of social dissonance.

Meddlin'

This chapter focuses on what the children call "meddlin,'" in what appears at one level of observation to be a nearly ideal situation. What occurs at Pacesetter, with its small classroom size and special teacher, counselor, and administrative and physical resources, occurs elsewhere in less ideal circumstances in much intensified form. Only by identifying a problem can we then explore solutions.

The discipline room referral records of a four-week period suggest who teachers believe disrupt the classrooms or have difficulties. Three-fourths were black, and three-fourths were boys. The most frequently reported types of misconduct were fighting or physically abusing another child (e.g., pushing, hitting, poking with a pencil), along with generally uncooperative behavior. In open-ended interviews with black, white, male, female, second, fourth, and sixth graders, the overriding differences that emerged between blacks and whites were the more positive value blacks placed upon fighting and their greater and more intense participation in meddlin'. Some parents and commentators outside the school claimed that white children engaged in meddlin' as much as black children but that the whites' styles were more subtle and therefore less visible to adults. A further claim is that some children misinterpret harmless meddlin' as threatening. These arguments may be true. Yet both black and white children said black children did more meddlin'. Children's reports and my observations suggest that although generally more physical, the black children's styles of aggravating others encompassed a broad range of behaviors. With the exception of three white second-grade boys, I did not observe white angry, impulsive meddlin' on the playground or in the classroom. From their several years of teaching and community work in Harlem, Silverstein and Krate (1975) describe the physical abuse and ridicule youngsters engage in "to an extent unheard of in most middle class communities" (ibid.:133). Willis (1977) found white working-class behavior to be similar. In his summary and integration of major findings of five studies of desegregated schools[6] that would be ranked among the better institutions in their respective areas, Wax (1980) reports that the level and kinds of aggression differ for black and white.

At Pacesetter, no white boy or girl whom I interviewed expressed a positive attitude toward fighting. When I asked, "If you could change one thing about Pacesetter, what would you change?" or "What don't you like about Pacesetter?" a common answer was "The fighting." Similarly, when asked, "What do you think is bad behavior in the classroom?" the most frequent answers were "Fighting" and "Meddlin' when the teacher goes out of the room." When asked, "What do you think is bad behavior on the playground?" most children replied, "Fighting!" Two white boys thought it was all right to fight if someone else started it. One black girl was positive; four thought it was fine in self-defense. Five black boys volunteered a positive judgment about fighting; seven, a qualified positive attitude. Of the whites 61 percent volunteered a negative attitude toward fighting, in contrast to 43 percent of the blacks. Girls were more negative toward fighting than boys. Sixth-grade boys and girls differed more than children in other grades, and sixth-grade black and white boys differed most. There is little evidence of negative attitudes among black boys. See Table 1 (Appendix).

When I asked children if they were afraid of anyone at school, they most often mentioned the names of black children or referred to blacks who engaged in meddlin'. Rarely was a white or middle-class black child mentioned. Among black and white children 52 (43 percent) said they feared black children. One black and two white second-grade boys (2 percent) were afraid of three white male classmates. See Table 2 (Appendix) for a breakdown by grade, sex, and race; 31 individual black boys, eight black girls, and three white boys were named, and 16 blacks as a group were mentioned as those who were feared.

Illustrative of children's perceptions are these comments:

> Most black kids act like they'll beat you up; a white person talks about it. [black girl] Fightin' is OK if you win and don't do it often. You can lose friends. [black girl] Fightin' toughens you for life. [black boy] Blacks try to hurt more in a fight; whites try to hurt less. [black boy]

I asked the last child, "Is it because they can't or because they don't want to?"

> They don't want to. Cause I seen a lot of people do it. When we be walkin' home, and there bes a fight, they [blacks] fight real bad, like somebody, they was staying by the apartments over there, and they had a person that had stabbed one person, and one of 'em had hit im.

"How old were they?"

> No, not that old, eleven. They did go to Pacesetter school before when I was about in third. [fourth-grade black boy]

A black girl said, "Whites are scared. They don't pick on each other." Blacks and whites share the notion that whites are weaker, afraid to "take on" blacks. A fourth-grade black boy said, "Whites fight less at school. They probably do it at home."

What are the *arenas* of meddlin'? A few children at Pacesetter said the classroom permits more opportunity for aggression against another child than the playground. In the classroom there is only one teacher to watch; on the playground there are several. Meddlin' also occurs in the hallways and especially the restrooms. Let us look at some illustrative incidents.

In a second-grade classroom early in the semester, the following physical action, recorded in my field notes, occurred in a 40-minute period that began with the teacher conducting a game in which someone has the name of an animal in mind and the other children try to guess what it is.

Two black boys in the back of the room jumped over chairs which they used as track horses. Keith jumped over the back of his chair to the seat and jumped up and down on it. Chris tried this feat, but was less agile. Otis also tried. Keith performed his skillful feat three times. The spelling lesson began. A white girl seated between Keith and Chris called out: "I want to move! Keith wants to cut my hair!" The spelling lesson continued. Keith jumped from his seat over the desk to the floor. He ate some of his lunch, walked about, went to the wall, and played with the clock. Chris walked about the room and played with some blocks. Keith and Chris then drummed on table tops. Turning his chair upside down, Keith sat on it. Spinning his chair around in a circle, he used the legs like a submachine gun. Chris hit Aaron, a white boy, who pushed a black girl. Keith hit Chris on the back twice. A black girl called out, "Dummy! dummy!" A black boy pulled a black girl's leg while she sat in her seat. Otis took his shoe off. A black girl was talking loudly. In response to the teacher's question, "Would you like to go out?" she got up from her seat and stood in the aisle, feet apart and knees bent. She brought her knees together and apart four times while crossing her hands together and apart in unison with the knees in a Charleston step. Then she sat down. Moments later she skipped to the door, opened it, picked up a book outside, and ran back to her seat. Then she got up on her seat and performed what in ballet is called an "arabesque." Standing on the ball of one foot, she lifted the other leg backward as high as she could, one arm held diagonally up and forward, the other diagonally down. From this position she lost her balance and fell to the floor. The teacher picked her up and carried her out of the classroom. A black boy seated in the front row hit a black girl, pushed and grabbed her; she screamed. Another child yelled, "Shut up y'all!" Michael was using a piece of paper as a musical instrument.

Most of the classroom disruptions were the result of a *few* black children countering school norms. If a teacher was not in firm control, they wandered about the classroom when they were supposed to be seated, clowned and joked, talked to their neighbors, and copied others' work when they were instructed to do their own. These children sometimes yelled or "chunked" books or pencils across the room. Walking to the pencil sharpener to repair a deliberately broken pencil, a child might tease or harass another person along the way. Blowing pins through straws at others was one fourth-grade game that got started. Another was breaking up crayons, wrapping the pieces tightly with silver foil, and shooting them with a rubber-band slingshot. Tripping a child going about his or her business also occupied classroom time. Pushing and shoving individuals into and out of the lines formed to move a class from one activity to another was common. Expressing sullen compliance, open contempt, or complete disinterest and talking back to the teacher or dancing insubordination (dancing a movement phrase at an inappropriate time and place) were yet other tactics that I observed.

In the sixth grade a very rare interracial fight broke out among former friends. The white girl, Gloria, commented:

> Well, we were outside and the word got around that Tracy [black] was mad at me, and so we walked in the gym, and she kicked me. So I kicked her back. And she kicked me, and it made me mad. So I kicked her real hard, and she fell down, and the other ones [black girls] started up on me and started hittin' me in the head. And she hit me in the back, and I ran to the bathroom. And so after that we fought. My face was all red, and so the next day I didn't go to school.

Apparently, from the stories each child in the fray told the principal and the counselors, a black boy eager for excitement in music class urged Marcia (black) to hit Gloria. She did. Marcia harbored smoldering resentment because Gloria and another girl had supposedly been talking about her since last year. Furthermore, Gloria got her into trouble the day before the fight. She told her, "Shut up, girl!" So Marcia hit Gloria "in the gum" (i.e., in the mouth), and Gloria told the teacher. The following day Tancy and another black girl said they were pretending to roll their eyes (a message in some black cultures that means "you make me sick"), when Gloria rolled her eyes at them. Tancy was upset that Gloria talked about her father: "I don't like nobody talking about my daddy, cause he's dead and my momma said, 'Don't let no one talk about him!'" All the black girls resented the fact that Jerry, an "all-American" black boy who had befriended Gloria, "took up for her."

Early in the semester sixth graders were standing in the lunch line. A black boy slapped the right cheek of a white boy standing next to him. Noticing me glance at what happened but do nothing, he continued his meddlin'. Teachers and aides did not notice. The boy hit the child's left cheek and then repeated the right-left smacking sequence twice more. The white boy, about four inches shorter, stood with his arms crossed. He said and did nothing.

Recess on the playground is a "free time" for children to do whatever they choose within the school rules for proper behavior. Action flows as some children go from one activity to another, from the swings to the merry-go-round to the ball field. At other times, the rhythm is staccato, as these examples suggest. One day two black fourth-grade boys were examining a white boy's hair and scalp. Frightened about this invasion of personal space, the victim kept saying, "You're hurting my head! Stop pulling my hair!"

A black fourth grader grabbed a white boy in a strangle hold and demanded, "Boy, you be my slave!" A sixth-grade white girl explained, "Blacks were slaves; they have it against you. You have to experience what it's like to be a student here."

Misunderstandings sometimes rouse racial sensitivity and erupt in fights.

All right, this guy was walkin' up to the teacher, and he was trying to ask a question. This other guy was a different race. He comes up and get his neck and jerks him 'cross the floor knocking, stompin' up the chair, jumpin', actin' like somethin' from the jungle. Talkin' back to the teacher and uh, then he gets abducted; he's taken away. You know, like Erny and John they're different races. John [black] did it to Erny [white]. Well, John

got the misunderstandin' point. What he should have done was wait till Erny got back and asked him what did he say to Ms. Wood, for Ms. Wood to look at John. But you know John, he really deserved what he got. John misunderstood what Erny said. Erny was askin' a question, but complainin' about how John was acting over there. And John got the wrong perspective and went right over there, didn't ask what he was saying, didn't, you know, take any time, just went in around his neck, just out of clear daylight. [sixth-grade black boy]

A white sixth grader said, "Blacks act like we're trespassing on their territory; they don't want us here."

Football is popular among the tough kids. Some black boys do not play; few whites do. As one white boy put it, "The blacks don't throw the ball to the whites." It is not just that the black boys practice a lot. They argue over rules and get into fights over them. Each black contestant has his group of friends. One youngster said, "If he meddles me, I get my friends, and he gets his friends." A circle delineates the fighting space; the whites stay on the outskirts of the mayhem.

Expressive forms are mostly exclusionary. Black pride, identity, boundaries, and neighborhood loyalty vis-à-vis the white establishment coalesce in the dances. Pacesetter black girls perform (Hanna 1979). On warm, sunny days black girls spontaneously organize dance cheers, ring plays, or line plays that combine stylized body movement and song. Using the spatial form of children's dances, probably of British origin and learned from white Americans, Afro-Americans merge the African style of loose, flexible torso, extending and flexing knees with an easy breathing quality, and pelvic swings and thrusts to create syncretistic dances. A leader sings a phrase that the group answers, or the leader merely coordinates the action. Movements accompany and accent the song text or illustrate it. Hand clapping or other body percussion punctuates the performance to create a syncopated rhythm with the song. The dances are to pass the time, assert comradery, have fun, and work through problems in a world the performers do not dominate. At Pacesetter the dances distinguish the in-group from the out-group. Occasionally black boys join in the dances.

When a white girl wished to join the black girls in one of the performances, a black girl stepped back, put her hands on her hips, looked the white girl up and down about the hips and feet, and with a disbelieving scowl said loudly for all to hear: "Show me you can dance!" Everyone looked at the white girl, who found it difficult to dance under the circumstances, got the exclusionary message, and withdrew to the sidelines. Another time a different white girl joined the "Check Me" ring play, in which the name of each participant in the circle is singled out in turn, going to the right. Her name is called by the girl standing to her left, and she identifies herself, sings a refrain, and then calls on the next girl. When it was the white girl's turn to be called, the black girl just passed her by and called the next black girl. Rejected, the white girl called out, "I can do it, too." No one paid attention. Some blacks who are not part of the in-group as long-time residents or cousins are similarly treated.

Dance themes reflect general atti-tudes (cf. Jones and Hawes 1972). One of the fourth-grade black girls said she made up the words to one of the songs: "Walking over people, I don't care, shampoo, shampoo." The dance reflects past or future white oppression of black people and possibly a reversal of power relations.[7] Girls form a line, arms about each others' waists, and move briskly about the play area. "Sock It" and "Power" are other favorites called "cheers." Children learned some of the ring games from their mothers, friends, and cousins. Not all white children appreciate the ring plays, nor are they defensive about being excluded. One said, "They always do that crap."

On a very hot day five fourth-grade classes were supposed to line up at the end of recess. Several nonacademically oriented black boys asserted themselves by refusing to take the burning sun and remaining on the shaded steps. The teacher kept the classes standing in the midday sun, expecting the punished innocent students to pressure the recalcitrants. However, no one was willing to tell the toughs what to do and risk a fight. Another day all the classes were punished by being kept standing in the rain while the recalcitrants stood under shelter lording it over the classes and teacher, whose hair frizzed in the precipitation.

Toilets are for toughs at Pacesetter and elsewhere (cf. Schafft 1976:64).

> Well, if the blacks see you use the restroom or the toilet, they start laughin' and stuff. And they say, "Ah, he's usin' the toilet" and all that stuff; and sometimes you got to run in there and use the restroom and get out 'fore they come in, 'cause they start takin' over the place. [sixth-grade white boy]

The restroom is an unpleasant area of teasing and harassment for the weaker children. Black and white children report verbal assaults, intimidating threats, being pushed into a urinal or pushed so that one's urine or feces misses the appropriate depository or having black bullies soil one's body or clothes with waste products. Such actions deter restroom use. After school many black and white children rush directly to their home toilets with physical discomfort and even soiled pants. The lack of toilet stall privacy doors in the boys' restroom makes some children feel self-conscious and vulnerable. Sometimes a child is "imprisoned" in the stall by several youngsters who block the exit to keep him from leaving. A sixth-grade white boy said, "When they try to jump over the door [walls] and their fingers overhang it, I chop their knuckles." Teachers and aides rarely enter the restrooms. Most are female, and the boys claim they get embarrassed by their presence. One sixth-grade white girl said, "Oh, this really gets me mad: some people grab on to the top of doors and look over at you." In mainstream American culture the toilet is regarded as a very "private space" where the individual has protective refuge from others. Thus an individual strongly feels a sense of being aggrieved when not left alone when on the "throne" (Remi Clignet, personal communication).

Incidents occur in the classroom, in the lunch line, on the playground, and in the restroom. Who are the primary targets? Although both blacks and whites are targets of meddlin', most fights in which someone gets hurt physically are intraracial, as is the case

among adult blacks, who direct most aggression against fellow blacks. Examples of interracial meddlin' incidents were described, because these affect desegregation.

A target of meddlin' may be an aggressor's equal. Most often children who are especially different from the aggressor are especially vulnerable to meddlin': for example, newcomers, children with physical handicaps, those who dress in an unusual way, academically successful youngsters who are poor athletes, children who appear to "put on airs" or brag, and those who are afraid to stand up to an aggressor (cf. Wax 1980:107–108).

What Are the Styles of Meddlin'?

Although there are one-on-one fights, as is the case when two equals challenge each other or a bully picks on an individual, among blacks who are kin or neighborhood friends alliance or gang behavior is common. Earlier I referred to the "rumble" that occurred on the playground. Standing in line to enter the school building, a black boy pinched the right buttock of the white boy standing in front of him. In response the child hit his antagonist with his elbow. Thereupon the aggressor's black friend, who was standing in front of the white child, hit him.

In addition to individual and group styles, there are verbal and nonverbal forms. Verbal aggression includes calling people insulting names or descriptive words denigrating the physical peculiarities or behavior traits of a child, parodying a child's name, talking about a black child's mother (a highly incendiary act because it is an abbreviation for "mother fucker"; indeed, teachers stopped children from talking about their own mothers' contribution to the school lest the black children misunderstand). A black, fat, and sensitive girl was the butt of "ol' fat chicken." Janey complained that in selecting leaders the children always "chose those skinny bones, not me." "Puttin' them down" is a style of meddlin' to make children "feel sorry that they ever came into this world; like saying, I got this and you don't; I got six model cars and you don't; laughing about someone's daddy being arrested." Sounds are as important as the verbal and visual sense that is communicated. Sidney makes farting noises during class. Talking about someone—rumor mongering and hearsay—to upset a person, lying to get someone in trouble; and threatening are other meddlin' styles. A second grader said to his teacher, "Wait, Ms. ———. I'll blow your head off if you don't!" One hears "Listen to me [give me] or I'll beat you up [knock out your gut] [kick you' hinney] Who's a nigger? Come oan nigger—you askin' for it, nigger. Pow!" Profanity is common. A second-grade white boy said he was afraid of other children:

> They say stupid words at me. "Shit" and all that stuff. When somebody starts pickin' on you and sayin' stupid words—and then a big fight comes.

Ostracism—not talking to a person—can be another aggressive mode at Pacesetter.

Styles of nonverbal aggression include body bluster (posing, moving, and arranging one's appearance in a menacing way to make oneself threatening or put someone down). Waiting to be dismissed for lunch, a black sixth-grade boy who lifts 100 pounds of iron flexes his muscle and shows it to the black boy sitting nearby. At a fourth-grade class picnic, a black boy boxes an imaginary adversary. A white fourth-grade boy reported an incident that occurred the morning of our conversation:

> He makes a fist and says, "I'm going to get you." He lifts me up by the shirt. K would not play. He's the nastiest. He told me to grab his shirt and say, "The law can't help you now." I did. He pulled his dick out.

Youngsters can "give the eye," roll the eyes, make the eyes small and beady, wrinkle the face, "frown up" with tense lips extended forward, the head and chin also thrust forward, "puff up," stick out the lip or jaw, and ball the fist. Girls send hostile body messages through pivoting away with tilted head or twitching nose or posing in a fixed stance with one hip extended and both hands placed on the hips. The shoulder shrug, swaggering walk, limp stance saying, "I'm not paying attention," and dancing where such behavior is inappropriate express defiance and insubordination. Part of body bluster includes arranging one's appearance, so some black boys let their hair grow in big Afros to increase their size and dominance in the peer pecking order. Another tack is to wear clothes that bare one's musculature. Individuals try to create impressions of themselves for others. A child acting tough, strong, and in charge is implicitly asking those around to believe in the image created before them.

Further styles of nonverbal aggression are abusing other's possessions, creating situations to get a child into trouble, and physical assaults—kicking, hitting, finger tweaking, blowing pins out of straws, "chunking" rocks, crickets, and other objects, pushing, and invading personal space in the restroom. There is a fascination with what is called booty, hinney, ass, or butt kicking or pinching. Another style of aggression is school vandalism, which includes throwing water bombs on the restroom walls or writing on them, wetting toilet paper and paper towels and throwing them on the windows, heaters, and fans to jam them; squirting soap on the floor, "using the bathroom all over the bathroom," and "making sissy on the floor and skiin' on it."

What Causes Meddlin'?

Children perceive the stimuli for meddlin' within six categories which are not mutually exclusive. Indeed, some youngsters, especially sixth graders, recognized multiple causes. Although children did not mention that there may be a different point for different groups of them at which teasing and play become meddlin', this is certainly a possibility.

1. Racism   When I asked what causes fights, a white sixth-grade girl replied:

> The color of the people. It's because, like they blame it on you sayin' it's your fault that they were slaves and sort of take that against you from back a long time ago. And *it's not my fault*, I didn't do it. I guess it's just the color. Sometimes the whites say something about black people. It just depends on if you're mad or not mad.

The student continued:

> There are some people who are sort of prejudiced. I think it's because the white girls went with the black boys. Well, sometimes the black girls got jealous and sometimes the white girls got jealous when the white girls started going with the black boys. Now there isn't anybody in the whole sixth grade who's going with a black boy who's white. I guess it's because they said that they took over, and so the black girls, you know, they all sort of pick somebody to go with. Well, it's not like that you're in love, but it means that you're taken and nobody else can have you.... Everybody's always fighting in this school. Some blacks don't like whites, and some whites don't like blacks. It's black versus whites. Like if they're listening to music, and the black says that's *white* music, that's when it starts off. I don't think it's white music. I just think it's music that that person likes. It doesn't matter if it's white music or black music. They fight with their fists and sometimes with names.

2. "Equality" Through Compensation and Alternative Achievement Systems   A black second-grade boy's comment on the situation that leads to aggression suggests saving face:

> I go away when somebody's mad. I don't go away when they say, "You crybaby!" I go back and fight 'em.

Most of the black children are two grade levels behind the national average in academic skills; public revelation of their inadequate schoolwork through oral recitation and the like leads them to try to gain recognition in other ways. Meddlin' may allow a child to be in control and achieve self-validation by performing to approving, assertive peers.

This recognition becomes the standard of competence in a kind of defensive structuring (Siegel 1970). According to Silverstein and Krate (1975), black ghetto low-income children appear self-reliant at an early age. They become adapted to surviving without adult security or instrumental aid. Because it is common for ghetto parents to be unpredictable in being able to help their children materially and psychologically, the children develop a mistrust of adults. Building defenses against tenderness, dependency, and disappointment, they turn to the peer group for dependency needs. The peer group supports many behaviors that run counter to the objectives and expectations of the school; it serves as a locus for peers to meet and participate in joint activities.

Neighborhood peer groups often see the school ecology as hostile. By belittling formal schooling and its ethic, they deny the authorities power to confer negative evaluations that affect an individual's self-image.[8]

The whites, as a group, are dominant in the intellectual performance arena. The blacks often compensate and assert themselves in physical arenas. Several children commented that the tough bullies can get what they want with their muscles, so they do not have to study to get rewards. Alternative achievement systems operate at Pacesetter. A sixth-grade boy expressed a commonly held view of academic achievement among blacks: "Fags [homosexuals] book it!" Boys generally exhibit traits of aggressiveness and independence which the school does not reward, although society does. Ray Warner (quoted in Raspberry 1979), a program coordinator with the Federal Office of Education,

believes that "because the behavior demanded by schools is more 'feminine' than 'masculine,' enthusiasm for schools tends to be defined as feminine—particularly among groups that place high value on 'masculinity.'" When I asked how the neatest, smartest, most admirable child acted, a sixth-grade black girl said, "They don't have no high goals and a lot of learning—but they nice and everything." Another black girl told me, "See, sometimes you fight 'cause you have to fight every once in awhile—'cause you not really puttin' on a good impression on yourself, you know [if you don't]."

Some blacks gang up and push for a fight. A white sixth-grade boy said, "If a bully makes fun of you and you do it back, they [onlookers] say 'beat him up!'" A black sixth grader said that when age mates fight no one breaks it up. The person who tries is likely to get into a fight. "Kids like to talk about it." The "group" eggs on a trouble-maker— it comments, laughs, and crowds around. A white girl whose friends are black said:

> Well, sometimes when you really get mad you hit 'em back and tell them you're not chicken of 'em, so they wouldn't think that you wouldn't fight back and take up for yourself.

3. Peer Hierarchy Rank   Many black children desire to test their strength in comparison with other youngsters and establish the highest possible position in a peer hierarchy. "What causes fights?" I asked.

> Somebody showin' off. Somebody trying to pick a fight and then it gets even worse after one little thing happens. And then ones will crowd around. And the

fight gets bigger and bigger and bigger. And they are staying there hittin' and sluggin'. [white sixth-grade boy]

Another white child commented:

I think the neighborhood children do it more. . . . I guess their parents, maybe, are rougher on 'em or whatever. . . . I guess they've been in fights before a lots. I think it's their parents, the way they see their point of view: you have to be tough to live.

When a child challenged another to fight, a youngster explained, "They're just trying to prove who's tougher.

4. Getting a Friend Before a friendship can be established, many black children first create an understanding of who ranks higher. A white fourth-grade boy finally figured it out: "They pick on you to make you recognize them. Some kids—okay, I'm talking about different races now—they go up and hit you. Hey man, this stuff and all this." "Yeah, they just hit you," a sixth-grade black girl reported. Her classmate put it this way: "In sixth grade now, it seems black kids want to beat up white kids when they want to be friends with them."

"Why do they pick fights if they want to make friends?" I asked. "So you can try to fuss at them, try to get along, so you can get closer to them," replied an older student.

5. Uncontrolled Anger Black and white children both recognized that black children at Pacesetter had poor control of anger. A black girl said, "Volunteers [whites], yeah, they . . . just patient or something." A black boy remarked, "Lot of people in sixth grade

lose their temper," referring to his black peers. A white fourth-grade girl reported the following:

Sometimes I say something that makes them [blacks] mad—they are mad already at something, and I say something and I laugh, not at them. I'm just laughing—they come over and hit me. And I try to explain to them I was not laughing at them, that I was laughing at something else. They won't listen. They just come over there and hit me and then go back to their seats.

I observed a second-grade black girl do exactly what she told me she does when she is angry:

I go beat 'em up. If they hurt me, I beat em up. I start to almost cry, but then I go beat up the person and tell the teacher. If she don't do nothin' about it, I go beat 'em up. If someone meddle my friend I go and tell 'em, "If you pick on my friend one more time, I'm gonna kick your hinny"; and if they do that I sneak up behind 'em and my foot come up there and then they start beatin' up me and I start beatin' on them, and then we go to the office. I keep goin' till I get a whuppin'. If I get a whuppin', I don't do it anymore if it hurts.

A black second-grade boy complained:

When they get mad at you and you do somethin' wrong to 'em, they get mad and start fighting. I didn't do nothin' to 'em today, and he just said he was gonna beat me up after school. Ryan just said that. He just said, "I oughta tear your name tag off and beat you up after school."

6. Sexual Competition "Girls! Fighting over girls. It starts in kindergarten," reported a black sixth-grade male. A black second grader reported: "A white

and black boy was fighting. The black boy had a girl friend and the white boy was messin' with his girl." Earlier I mentioned another incident in connection with racism: fighting because of interracial heterosexual friendship. One of the black teacher aides at Pacesetter reflected black female student sentiment. She said "One thing I can't stand is black men going with white women." Compared to other groups, low-income black adults are more open about heterosexual relations. Consequently, many black youngsters engage in similar anticipatory socialization.

What Are the Responses to Meddlin'?

Children use tactics that draw upon their strengths, what Schofield (1978) calls "strong suit" tactics, and socialization. Middle-class children are usually taught to work through difficulties verbally as part of the mainstream litigious culture, and many have no experience in fighting. At Pacesetter they tend to respond to meddlin' with passive "safe" strategies of taking it, complying with demands, or disengaging oneself with the mediation of a teacher or protection of "patron" or one's ability to divert an aggressor with humor, negotiation, or withdrawal. Physically weaker children or those taught not to fight often have protectors whom they go to if someone meddles them, and the "patron" takes up for the youngster. For example, black children repeatedly pushed Tommy, a star goalie on his neighborhood team, off the lunchtime soccer field. He refused to go to school. His mother asked, "Who is the toughest kid in your class?" Tommy answered,

"Kenneth." "Does he push you off?" "No ... oh, Patrick and Kenneth are friends and when someone bugs Patrick, Patrick tells Kenneth and he takes up for him." Tommy went to school, became friends with Kenneth, and played soccer at lunch.

Some white and more black children respond to meddlin' in a reciprocal matter, tit for tat. Indeed, if a child perceives the possibility of attack, the effective strategy is believed to be to strike first.

> If someone meddles me, I slug 'um. This kid, he took a branch [from a tree on the playground], and he started choking around my neck. I just swung my arms behind my back and slapped him inside his face, and before he could recover, I just gave him a bloody nose.

Possible Sources of Aggression

Thus far I have sketched meddlin' arenas, targets, styles, and responses. A comment on two apparent wellsprings of black aggression is warranted. Cultural and social dynamics create the context within which Pacesetter black children express individual needs. In *Why Blacks Kill Blacks*, the black psychiatrist Poussaint (1972) presents a historical perspective in which he argues that black violence is self-hatred—for repressed rage at being docile and self-effacing in order to survive. Although black children have not been discriminated against as older members of their families have been, they pick up attitudes from home and media reports. Comer and Poussaint (1975:12) explain, "Racism forces blacks to fight for the respect that whites take for granted." (Cf. Silberman 1978.) Another black psychiatrist, Harrison-Ross (1973), found some black parents now satisfy their antiwhite hostility through encouraging their children not to "let any of those whites push you around."

Blacks have been socialized to aggression through experience in slavery, the South, and Texas. Lunsgaarde's (1977) cultural analysis of Houston homicide patterns is revealing in this regard. Emphasis on the importance of the body in strong action has roots in ontogenetic development for all children—the body being the first instrument of power—and especially for blacks in slave auctions, where the body indicated the individual's capability for work. Continued work opportunities requiring physical prowess and a black cultural pattern of expressive performance and role validation, such as acting out (Gay and Abrahams 1973, Kochman 1971), sustain the body emphasis. Lower-class children, including the majority of blacks at Pacesetter, often experience inconsistent harsh, physical discipline and ridicule, and this socialization encourages similar kinds of behavior (Gans 1962). If one has few material possessions and little power in the adult world, as is the case with oppressed minorities, many working-class people, and children, the body and its use are especially important (cf. O'Neill 1975, Willis 1975, 1977).

Related to the black children's bodily self-assertion is the widespread expectation for black physical communication. A sixth-grade black girl said, "Everyone thinks that a black person is a blade" ["a fightin' tough"]. In a rare interracial fight at Pacesetter, a white boy beat a black boy. Children expressed disbelief. Their school talk sustained the image of blacks as fighters. Not only is there a greater emphasis on physical prowess and its manifestation in fighting among the neighborhood than volunteer children, but some youngsters may emit signals suggesting they fight. Consequently, some blacks "pick up the gauntlet" in a self-fulfilling prophecy.

Meddlin', of course, has contingencies. A child who is aggressive among classmates may behave differently when alone with parents, teachers, or unknown children. There are four general constraints: an authoritative adult presence, the ending of an activity during which meddlin' occurs, fear of painful retaliation, and knowledge that authority figures will learn of aggression and penalize it.

What Are the Consequences of Meddlin'?

The aggressors' rewards are gaining attention; improving self-concept, esteem, and position in the peer hierarchy; getting one's way (material or immaterial gain); reducing tension built up from classroom anxiety or anger; and having the thrill of exploring alternatives—being dominant rather than subordinate in society.

Aldis, an ethologist who studied play aggression (1975), argues that thrill-seeking in play has the advantage of acquiring skills for emergencies. The predators, and victims who learn to handle the aggression (deflecting it or retaliating), develop inner strength, control, adaptability, and sensitivity to multiple communication channels. Part of handling aggression is assertiveness. This trait is associated with black educational achievement and such middle-class characteristics as knowing where to find jobs. Fighting causes pain. Children learn how to avoid threats and to use brokers to mediate between themselves and adversaries.

There are, of course, negative consequences of aggression. When meddlin' is pervasive, the work of formal schooling takes second place to the foremost challenges of bullies, bullied, protected, and funny people—the hidden curriculum.[9]

Too much or too dramatic aggression gets an individual into trouble with the authorities. Fighters are sent to the principal's office. When blacks' parents are called in, the child usually gets "whupped." "They beat the shit out of them" when they have to lose wages, a parent noted. Suspension or being sent to a special school are possibilities.

The Pacesetter school children's perception of more black than white aggression leads some blacks and whites to have negative attitudes toward blacks. Of course, these are further shaped and supported by prejudices in American society. "Dumb, physical, mean, and unpredictable" are common categorizations deriving from perceived black aggression. Some blacks, especially those from middle-class backgrounds who share white middle-class cultural values, feel embarrassed by being identified with the group "black." The courts mandate class assignments by color, not class. Children generalize to an entire group. They become resentful when black aggressors cause the entire class to be punished for the misbehavior of a few—the assumption that pressure brings misbehavers into line is fallacious when the children's social rule is

to fight whom you challenge. Some black children escape disciplinary measures because teachers fear their authority will only be publicly shattered. They also fear confrontation with black parents.

Friend or foe? The ambivalence is a pervading source of anxiety and occasional discomfort for blacks and whites.

> Hey man, com' on. All of a sudden they play. It's just like magic. A kid might have sort of a frowny smile. I'll run. Sometimes it means "I'm going to get you." Sometimes it means, "I want to play with you." [white fourth-grade boy]

Verbal and nonverbal taunting and teasing caused a new white girl who was a tomboy at her former school to fear blacks at Pacesetter. She was popular among the blacks, according to the teacher, but she did not perceive their approach as friendly. When she cried, they "zeroed in." Although she had adjusted to blacks, she socialized with whites. Making friends is difficult for newcomers anywhere. Cultural differences compound the problem:

> Sometimes they act mean; they sorta hit you and sometimes they're nice.

"How do you know whether they are being mean or being friendly?" I asked.

> Sometimes the teachers said that, and sometimes I sort of wonder. Some people say they might be friendly, the word might get around. [white sixth grade girl]

Meddlin' contributes to segregation in desegregation. Voluntary seating patterns observed over the school year revealed that blacks were with blacks, and whites with whites. Only occasionally was there a person of a different color in a group.

A few whites behave in an integrated fashion at Pacesetter, but they express wariness when a black friend gets mad and rallies a black gang. In response to the question, "Are you afraid of anyone at school?" a white girl said:

> At times. Sometimes if there's gangs. Tina's tall and Gogo, she is bigger than I am, and they just, they're the biggest at school, so you're kind of afraid of 'em, and when there's a gang of black kids against whites and the whites against blacks, I think the blacks can stand lot more if they're in a fight—'cause I've been in that situation two or three times. [white sixth-grade girl]

In addition to the negative consequences of aggression for children—aggressors being punished, antiblack attitudes, and segregation persisting at lunch tables, in dance, in the restroom, and on the football field—there are also negative consequences of children's meddlin' for adults. Middle-class Anglo and black teachers are humans too. They often experience culture shock when they are the target of children's physical and verbal abuse or they are deprecated for their efforts to be sympathetic. Baffled and hurt, some emotionally withdraw or find jobs elsewhere. Dr. Alfred Bloch, Los Angeles psychiatrist, says that as a group teachers are "generally obsessional, passive, idealistic, dedicated people who are unable to understand or cope with the violence directed toward them" (1978). They suffer anxiety symptoms similar to the combat fatigue suffered by soldiers. At least one teacher left Pacesetter during the school year for health reasons, and there is a high turnover of teachers for a variety of interrelated reasons.

During my study and after its completion, Pacesetter School has, however, been experiencing growth and development. The parents and staff members who became aware of the problems that were identified by the study have been taking steps to ameliorate them. Many youngsters have matured under the collaborative efforts of school, family, and neighborhood. Change *is* possible!

Significance in the National Context

The United States courts mandate school desegregation in order to open the blocked access to socioeconomic and psychological opportunities for blacks. Bringing blacks and whites together is supposed to provide equal educational opportunity. However, in forcing school desegregation with prescribed racial ratios, the courts are creating new dilemmas which could perpetuate some of the very ills American policy makers wish to remedy.

Equal, formal educational opportunity is not sufficient for individuals to achieve the skills necessary for socioeconomic success in adult pursuits carried on within the law. Positive social relations and shared communicative patterns are also critical. The kind and amount of meddlin' are new and dramatic for many white and black children, and for some they negatively affect academic achievement and perhaps later socioeconomic advancement. The unpleasant encounters may have far-reaching and powerful implications if they are not dealt with. The process of identifying a problem and exploring its ramifications is critical to effective social policy.

This study is an evaluation of the implementation of government policy as well as several assumptions that sometimes guide the research enterprise, parents, teachers, and civil rights advocates. Let us examine four major assumptions.

(1) As data-gathering and data-processing instruments, fieldworkers may assume that if they study a public school in their own society they generally share the participants' language and thus have access to what is going on. However, there are important considerations that may be overlooked: the greater primacy of *play* and *nonverbal* modes of social interaction among children and the researcher's *nonpunitive* role.

(1a) What is overlooked as trivial play or "horsing around" in the classroom or informal areas of the school covers a great deal of children's social life ordinarily hidden from adult eyes. Children receive experiential lessons from each other—the "meddlin'" curricula may subvert formal education.

(1b) Because researchers usually overspecialize in the vocal and auditory channels of communication, they lose access to what occurs nonverbally among children whose senses of sight, touch, movement, smell, and space are especially active. While adults tend to regard the body as a platform for the head, children tend to regard the body as more of an instrument of action, including aggression. People who speak

the same verbal language often make the unwarranted assumption that they share other communication systems as well. Illustrative are the faulty-communication attempts to develop friendships. Middle-class children perceive black working-class children's fighting initiative as a message that friendship is precluded. White children take a black child's invasion of personal space to brush their hair, which is meant to say "Hi" or "I'm curious,"[10] as an aggressive act.

(1c) Anthropologists debate the insider-outsider advantages and disadvantages of access to data collection and analysis of individual and group behavior. Although Williams and Morland (1976) found no differences between responses given to black and white interviewers, there is an assumption that a researcher should be of the same color, culture, group, or status in order to gain maximum understanding. In addition to the insider-outsider considerations, yet another factor of importance in my field research was my nonpunitive role. I was somewhat of an outsider-insider participant-observer as a helping parent of two boys attending the school and an author writing a story about Pacesetter. However, children learned what was primary to them—I was a nonpunishing person. Children misbehaved before my eyes and spoke about their misbehavior in ways they did not before school authorities (cf. Wax 1980:20).

To summarize my discussion of the first assumption, my study disclosed that if someone works with children in his or her own society, a shared verbal language is insufficient to understand what is occurring. Being aware of the serious business of children's play, the saliency of body language, and the need to prove oneself as nonpunitive are also necessary.

(2) Let us turn to the second assumption—that children reflect home values, that their school experiences are similar to the researcher's own, and that teachers are the dispensers of knowledge at school. When I asked parents, school personnel, or researchers a question, they often replied, "I remember when I was in ——grade." Obviously, there is some continuity across generations. However, not only do children rely heavily on multichanneled communication which adults forget, but children's experiences today are enmeshed in a different milieu of increased lack of discipline in school and society. Furthermore, there is an important interface of childhood experience—peer interactions in a new era of black assertiveness without adult historical perspective create generational differences. Peer social survival often takes precedence over academic task performance in the dual agenda of schooling. This is especially the case in a setting with large numbers of black working-class children who are sensitive to race relations. At Pacesetter, lower-income children who are generally two grade levels behind national average in academic skills confront middle-class children who are generally two grade levels above average. Problems occur through the interplay among school demands, black working-class peer pressure against trying hard to succeed academically (they say "that's for fags"), and the nonacademically oriented individual's creation and validation of self-identity and dignity

through meddlin' and otherwise gaining peer attention in an alternative reward system. The resulting fear, anxiety, and psychosomatic illness among both white and black children perpetuate negative images and impede processes of equal educational opportunity that lead to adult socioeconomic success in activities within the law in a white-dominated society.

Many children who had had black friends in their former schools began speaking negatively about "black" children when they attended this court-ordered desegregated school in which race and class intersect. Such statements as "They get me in trouble," "I don't like Pacesetter," "I'm sick, I can't go to school," "It was so noisy in class I got a headache and spent two hours in the nurse's office today" were common, as were reports of black children's misdeeds. Many parents tend to dismiss such comments. Usually the white adult's interactions with blacks have been with middle-class individuals who share their values and behavior or with maids who follow instructions. Many black parents who grew up in an era of self-effacing shuffling before whites had attended strict schools. Now some black adults satisfy their antiwhite hostility through their children, telling them not to let any white people push them around. Although most parents at Pacesetter shared the same educational goals for their children, the neighborhood low-income children's peer dynamics worked against these children's academic success. Some scholars (e.g., Ogbu 1974, Silverstein and Krate 1975) place such dynamics within the structural context of adult employment opportunities and the consequent role models and socialization patterns within the children's family and neighborhood. Other researchers criticize school actions. Forced to live out parents' and society's idealistic visions and assumptions of experiential continuity across generations, children in their own worlds of new experiences cannot help but lose trust in naive adult pronouncements.

(3) Turning to the third commonly held proposition, desegregation is assumed to be working[11] if there are no media reports of violence, schools allocate special resources to assist the process of desegregation and promote multiculturalism, and desegregation is begun with young children.

(3a) Although children's social relations often appear harmonious, children have rarely been asked what it is like to be a student in a desegregated school where race and class intersect. Rarely have children been observed to see to what extent their reports correlate with what actually occurs. Pacesetter children perceive meddlin' as salient and unpleasant.

(3b) Desegregation is assumed to be served if a school staff has training in multicultural education and the school celebrates cultural pluralism. However, multicultural training programs at Pacesetter as elsewhere have neglected children's social worlds. Consider the classroom management technique of punishing an entire class for the misbehavior of a few so that peer pressure will bring these few into line. It usually works among a homogeneous middle-class group. The technique does not work when black working-class children's rules require that a child who tells a tough youngster what to do

should fight the tough to make him or her do it. In preparation for a litigious society, the school requires verbal negotiation of conflict; training programs often overlook the fact that survival in some children's worlds requires physically striking out first.

Multicultural education is related to the view that life is relativistic, and celebrates bilingualism and ethnic identity. This perspective often does not consider that the *unmodified* public existence of an autonomous minority culture, especially if manifestations such as meddlin' violate notions of appropriateness in dominant American culture, may serve as a barrier for the minority to opportunities controlled by the majority. The issue of assimilation versus cultural pluralism, perhaps falsely drawn, centers on communication styles, human relations, incentive motivation, and teaching and curriculum. Cultural pluralists sometimes view the school in terms of a clash or black or other minority versus Anglo culture. They confound some of the traits required for a Western industrial, technological, capitalist system and those which are adequate for rural, preindustrial, or low-level technological development or an unemployment-welfare orientation. Certain economic systems require specific values and skills, wherever they operate and whatever the color of their participants. Thus the need may be to provide all individuals with the opportunity for *choice:* teaching the skills that allow a person access to socioeconomic mobility, with the possibility of *code-switching* (being able to operate in one or another at will). Therefore, desegregation's provision of resource equalization should include not only material physical plant, teaching and enrichment, and recognition and respect for the achievements and selected cultural patterns of different groups but also access to mainstream communicative modes, codes, and processes—explicit knowledge of what the middle-class knows implicitly.

Schools must also provide arenas for individuals to achieve self-dignity in academic subjects. Schools have built-in pressures of comparison, embarrassment, anxiety, and self-doubt that lead some youngsters to behave in ways which are not conducive to succeeding academically and to developing harmonious interracial relationships or friendships. By disrupting the classroom routines and academic performances, children communicate through humor or aggression that they do not recognize the evaluative processes of the school. They define both the situation and their own performance in it as matters to be taken lightly and inappropriate for judging their serious worth or capabilities.

Civil rights advocates in multicultural education often claim that tracking, streaming, or ability grouping within a school is a deliberate subterfuge for segregation in desegregation, a maneuver to maintain the status quo. Yet they overlook the rights of individuals to human dignity. Consider this case of sixth-grade black male nonreaders. In a group of four, one member would not participate. Ridiculed by the other three more advanced nonreaders, who called him "dummy," the youngster "clammed up." The perceptive special education teacher worked individually with the boy. He learned to read. In the system of positive reinforcement,

he asked to have more individualized reading instruction as his reward. Ability grouping for specific subjects and separation from peer pressure may be essential if a child is to have equal opportunity. However, ability grouping must be coupled with continual evaluation and procedures for moving children to appropriate groups so that a child does not become locked in.

(3c) Beginning desegregation in the early school grades is assumed to promote positive race relations. It is thought that children are color blind, and if they are left alone interracial harmony will occur naturally; they will resolve interracial problems on their own. However, social contact and social distance theories (Pettigrew 1971) are confused. Even preschoolers notice the color and physiognomy of individuals and may generalize an experience with one person of a group to all of its members.

Young children may not be able to cope with diverse cultural styles. In the first evaluation of Pacesetter conducted by Estes and Skipper (1976), white students in grades one to three declined in self-concept concerning their intellectual status, popularity, and happiness. For blacks, there was an increase from pretest to posttest on popularity and total self-concept scores.

The decline of white self-concept may lie in the fact that students in this age group are relatively rigid about what is correct behavior. They lack tolerance for alternative norms and empathy. Older children acquire these qualities and can rationalize deviations from their own norms. The white children at Pacesetter encounter black children who have a wider normative range of acceptable behavior among peers. The exposure to behavior the white youngsters think wrong may challenge their self-concepts. The fact that some second graders had more negative attitudes toward blacks than their older siblings at Pacesetter suggests a developmental pattern.

The increase of black self-concept scores concerning popularity and happiness may be due to the fact that the black children and their families had anticipated interracial problems which did not occur. Historically, blacks often experienced harassment by whites; when Pacesetter was created as a desegregated school, black children feared going into a situation where they thought they might be disliked and subject to embarrassment. Black self-concept concerning intellectual status, however, did not increase, perhaps because of the black/white comparisons.

Interracial friendship involves more than social contact, at any age. Previously established friendships on the bases of similar interests and neighborhood networks often preclude openness to voluntarily making friends. "The stigma attached to those few who venture out and seek friendships among members of other groups is often so strong that many are discouraged at the outset," reports Wax (1980:114–115, 120) in his summary of five desegregated schools. Without social intervention that occasionally brings children with similar interests together in structured small cooperative team tasks where each person has equal status, segregation in desegregation is likely to persist.

Underestimating the complexity and subtlety of social knowledge a child

needs to interact successfully among multicultural peers, some adults say "kids pick up" the "common sense" principles of social performance. Some do so, in the same way others learn to read without formal instruction. However, self-starters need work on the subtleties of language arts and social relations respectively. Children who are picked on, for example, may need instruction in patron-client relationships in order to get along. In sum, the third assumption that desegregation is working if the media report no violence, multicultural training occurs, and desegregation is begun with young children overlooks children's perceptions of meddlin', the variety of children's rules for social behavior, working-class neighborhood network peer pressure, and the developmental ability to tolerate norms that differ from one's own.

(4) The fourth assumption: although we recognize that the family, church, and other institutions no longer fulfill their traditional roles, Americans still assume the school will be a panacea for social problems. By mandating desegregation plans without providing direction for considering unintended consequences in the development of a unique social experiment designed to meet constitutional law, the courts have unwittingly set in motion forces that are counterproductive of providing equal educational opportunity. One of the key unintended consequences is that children and teachers are thrust into abusive physical or psychological environments which are the result of historical patterns, the influences of children upon each other, and adult naivety. The injured dignity of those weak of mind or muscle and those with soiled pants

or headaches speaks to unintended consequences and unfulfilled expectations. So far the evidence of desegregation's leading to black academic achievement and improved social relations is equivocal.

Because there is a taboo—unspoken behavioral norms preventing reference to differences that involve color—in civil rights circles, critical problems are ignored. Some parents say that racial difficulties exist in real life beyond the school, so children in desegregated schools are learning about reality. The unintended consequence is the absence of problem-solving[12] and the perpetuation of the status quo. Discussing "racial" problems often leads to emotional charges of subverting civil rights. However, more subversive and certainly more harmful is ignoring experiential realities as children perceive them and observers document them.

A critical unintended consequence of ignoring desegregation problems appears to be a drift toward a more socioeconomically stratified society, as those who can afford it send their children to private schools rather than have them attend desegregated schools. This exodus could erode the local tax base and state legislative allocations for public education. Historically, whites put their children in private schools to avoid desegregation. Now numerous middle-class blacks are taking their children out of public schools (Hechinger 1979) or engaging in "anticipatory nonentrance," acting to avoid a desegregated school (Wegmann 1977). Wax (1980) describes situations of schools losing many white students, changing curricula away from "academics," and facing

budgetary difficulties. An elite private school population reflects a clear pool of resources for professional and managerial positions, whereas the public schools provide a lower-level pool. The gap between the two groups could widen, for the opportunities for the working class to learn the hidden curriculum of the middle class and for talented individuals to be trained for high socioeconomic positions would decrease.

Sociologist James S. Coleman, whose massive study in the mid-1960s was used to support school desegregation, now says it is a "mistaken belief that black students learn better in desegregated classrooms. Desegregation has turned out to be much more complicated than any of us ever realized" (quoted in Feinberg 1978). Four pairs of contrastive threads weave through the story of my fieldwork. Black and white, working class and middle class, neighborhood friendship networks and strangers, and children and adults. Evaluation—the process of identifying problems and exploring their ramifications—is critical to solving social problems.

Since schools are part of the local, state, and national contexts, they are limited in what they can do. For example, the positive motivation of working-class students toward academic achievement and school norms is affected by their potential employment opportunities; nonschool structures significantly impact upon the school.[13] However, within their arena of authority, schools confront a chief source of difficulty in the adult failure to recognize the distinctness of the child's social world and their unwitting roles in it. Schools may unintentionally act in ways that stimulate and legitimize negative behaviors rather than intervene to promote the goals they desire.

Conclusion

In sum, the data from my study challenge assumptions that may guide the research and educational enterprises. (1) Besides sharing a verbal language with children, those trying to understand schooling must consider seriously children's play, body language, and tests of adult trustworthiness. (2) In addition to assuming generational continuity, it is necessary to recognize the contingencies of a new era of youth and black assertiveness in which children are enmeshed. (3) Successful desegregation requires more than a public record of nonviolence, multicultural education training as it has so far been provided, and interracial mixing in the early grades. Awareness of children's perceptions and experiences can lead to the development of mediating intervention strategies to deal with meddlin' and black working-class peer pressure against a member's serious academic efforts. (4) Schools can only solve society's problems when other powerful institutions work in tandem toward equity goals. Anthropologists are committed to taking the native's view in evaluating social policy for the natives. In schools, children's perceptions and experiences of what it is like to be a student may present a reality that mocks adult ideals and the policies meant to realize them.

APPENDIX: PROJECT UNDERSTANDING: INTERVIEW SCHEDULE I

Begin with, "I am writing a story about P. I am interested in students' views and I have some questions to ask you."

O. How long have you been at P?

A. What do you like best about P?

B. If you could change one thing, what would you change? (What don't you like about P?)

1. How can you tell if a child (kid) wants to be your friend?
   (What does the child *do?*
   How does the child *look?*
   What do *you do?*)
   a. Do all kids act the same way if they want to be friends?
   b. How do they act differently?
   c. How do you make friends?

2. How can you tell if a child is mad?
   (What does the child *do?*
   How does the child *look?*)
   a. Do all kids act the same way when they are mad?
   b. How do they act differently?
   c. How do you act when a child gets mad?
   d. How do you act when you get mad?

3. If a child is bothering you (bugging, messing with, meddlin' you), how do you let the child know you want her or him to stop?
   a. Do you act the same at home? (If not, how?)
   b. Do you act the same at school? In class, the hall, toilet, on the playground?

4. a. When a child picks on (bugs, messes with, meddles) your friend, what do you do?
   b. How do you know a child is picking on (bugging, messing with, meddlin') your friend?

5. What do you do to put a child down (tease, get the best of someone)?

6. a. What is your idea of a nice (favorite) teacher? (How does the teacher act, look?)
   b. What is your idea of a mean teacher? (How does the teacher act, look?)

7. If a child misbehaves, what do *you* think a teacher should do?
   a. If they do the same wrong thing, should boys be treated differently from girls? (If so, how?)
   b. If they do the same wrong thing, should neighborhood (black) children be treated differently from volunteer (white) children? (If so, how?)

8. a. The school has rules, but what do you think is bad behavior in the classroom?
   b. What do you think is bad behavior on the playground? in the hall? toilet?
   c. What do you think is bad behavior at home?

9. Think of the toughest (strongest) child in your grade: (a) What does the child do? (b) Is the child a bully? (c) What is a bully?

10. Think of the neatest, smartest, most admirable child in your grade: How does the child act?

11. Think of the dumbest child in your grade: How does the child act?

12. Think of the child who does the best school work: How does the child act?

13. Are you afraid of anyone at school? (If so, why?)

14. What do you think causes fights? (When, where, what, why and how?)

C. What did you think of these questions?
D. Do they give me an idea of what it's like to be a student at P?
E. What other questions would you ask to find out what it's like to be a student at P?

Ask the child the question(s) suggested.

TABLE 1   **Children Who Volunteered a Negative Opinion Toward Fighting**

Grade			Race		Sex	
Grade (n = 40)	Number	Percent	Black (n = 60)	White (n = 60)	Boys (n = 60)	Girls (n = 60)
2	19	47%	26 (43%)	37 (61%)	23 (38%)	40 (66%)
4	20	50%				
6	24	60%				

		2	4	6		
Black	Boy	30%	30%	10%	Sample n = 120	
	Girl	60%	60%	70%	Cell n = 10	
White	Boy	40%	40%	80%		
	Girl	60%	70%	80%		

TABLE 2   **Unequivocal Fear of Some Children at School**

		Grade 2		Grade 4		Grade 6		
Black	Boy	B	0	B	2	B	0	Sample = 120
		wb	1	wb	0	wb	0	Sample per grade/sex/race category = 10
		bb	0	bb	2	bb	1	Percent = % within category who are
		bg	0	bg	0	bg	0	fearful
		10% afraid		40% afraid		10% afraid		
	Girl	B	0	B	2	B	3	*Feared*
		wb	0	wb	0	wb	0	B = blacks as a group
		bb	3	bb	2	bb	1	wb = white boy
		bg	0	bg	1	bg	1	bb = black boy
		30% afraid		50% afraid		50% afraid		bg = black girl
								(a child may fear more than one of the above)
White	Boy	B	1	B	3	B	0	*Fearful*
		wb	2	wb	0	wb	0	Grade (n = 40)
		bb	3	bb	7	bb	3	2nd 33%
		bg	0	bg	1	bg	1	4th 60%
						everyone	1	6th 47%
		60% afraid		100% afraid		40% afraid		
	Girl	B	0	B	1	B	4	
		wb	0	wb	0	wb	0	
		bb	3	bb	3	bb	3	
		bg	2	bg	2	bg	2	
		30% afraid		50% afraid		90% afraid		

Notes

I wish to thank William John Hanna, George W. Noblit, Remi Clignet, Stephen Elkin, Clarence Stone, Robert Wegmann, and George Spindler for helpful criticisms on earlier drafts of this chapter. I appreciate Robert Rockwell's invitation to prepare a paper for his symposium on "Anthropology as American Culture" at the Annual Meeting of the Society for Applied Anthropology, March 1979. The latter part of this chapter draws upon that paper, "Some Unintended Consequences of Desegregation: Adult Naivety About Kids' Social Worlds." Conversations with Harold Childs, Ernest Gotts, James Griffin, Ronald Henderson, Pat Magruder, Judy Nassif, Phyllis Owen, and Allen Sullivan helped me grapple with some of the issues that came to the fore in this study. The support of the University of Maryland Department of Family and Community Development and Institute for Urban Studies and of the National Endowment for the Humanities Fellowship at the American Enterprise Institute for Public Policy Research in preparing this chapter is gratefully acknowledged.

[1] Because the court mandated racial ratios, and many adults and children designate individuals and groups by "black" and "white," I use these terms. Recognizing that color classifications are in many ways insidious misnomers, the school used the terms "neighborhood" for black and "volunteer" for white. Some individuals did not know the meanings of these words.

[2] If one takes a comparative perspective, which is important, one finds that the values, styles, and behaviors common among the black school children also occur in working-class white neighborhood schools, as Sennett and Cobb (1973) illustrate in their study of a school in Boston, Willis (1977) demonstrates in research in the United Kingdom, and Cosnow (1979) reports on the basis of his work among white children in Parkersburg, West Virginia. The National Institute of Education team that studied six desegregated schools noticed that many of the difficulties they identified were associated with class (Cassell 1978:9).

[3] However, Williams and Morland (1976) in their summary of studies of children's perceptions of race and color found no difference between responses given to black and white interviewers.

[4] Although a student might try to aggress by shocking, it does not seem likely, given the nature of the interview situation and the number of children who reported "contrary" behavior, much of which I also observed.

[5] Although four out of every five Americans put themselves in the middle class, the economist Robert Heilbroner suggests the middle class is located entirely above the median income level of $16,000; its income range is from $18,000 to $40,000

(McGrath 1978). For blacks the median income is $9,252 (Roberts 1978).

⁶ During 1978, the following National Institute of Education contracted reports were submitted: *The Emerging Order: An Ethnography of a Southern Desegregated School* (Bradford: Grandin Elementary School), by Dorothy C. Clement, Margaret Eisenhart, and Joe R. Harding, with Michael Livesay; *Stratification and Resegregation: The Case of Crossover High School* (Memphis, Tennessee), by Thomas W. Collins and George W. Noblit; *A Field Study of Culture Contact in an Urban High School* (New York City: Sheridan High School), by Francis A. J. Ianni, Mercer Sullivan, Margaret Orr, Samuel Henry, and John Mavors: *Hard Walls—Soft Walls: The Social Ecology of an Urban Desegregated High School* (Pawnee: Pawnee West High School), by Jacqueline Scherer and Edward J. Slawski, Jr.; *Social Process and Peer Relations in a "Nearly Integrated" Middle School* (Waterford: Wexler Middle School), by Janet Ward Schofield with H. Andrew Sagar.

⁷ The white children have the "outsider" status in Pacesetter that blacks have had in broader arenas of life. What the national context offers in prestige for the whites, the local context offers in power for the blacks. For children in this desegregated setting, the present takes center stage. Perhaps the school situation is similar to the animal trickster tales of the slave folk culture that afforded their creators psychic relief, a sense of mastery, and a vision of a possible future. Corsaro (1979) points out that even nursery school children have clear conceptions of honor, prestige, and status as power.

⁸ Self-concept and self-esteem are assumed to be significant forces in determining human action. In his appraisal of these forces, Coopersmith found that "in general, the consequences of low self-esteem and uncertain self-concept, i.e., underachievement and poor motivation, are more predictable than are notable attainment at the higher levels of esteem" (1975:151). He raises the possibility that the self-image and self-esteem of blacks in their minority status have maintained separate and often conflicting pictures of who they are and how they can attain self respect (ibid.:160). In preponderantly black communities they can avoid the demeaning and invidious effects of white prejudice and rejection. Black children were found not to value themselves less when they performed poorly in school, because of the support of other children and adults who reject the school judgments of academic performance as a valid judgment of their worth. See also Powell (1973) and Rosenberg and Simmons (1973) on minority children who have developed positive concepts of themselves, sometimes more positive than the majority students have of themselves.

⁹ LeCompte (1978), among others, speaks of the special func-

tion of schooling which prepares youngsters for the work world through an implicit curriculum stressing authority, time, work, and order. I use the term more broadly to include children's styles of social relations.

[10] White children's hair has a fascination for black children. They like to see "the fluff fly" as one black child put it.

[11] The criteria for successful desegregation vary. Maintaining a numerical racial balance may satisfy the courts. A boost in academic achievement may satisfy the educational agencies. Quality, orderly education may be the criteria of success for local communities. Willie (1978) said the goal of desegregation is the "control, understanding and patience" children acquire in integrated settings and the understanding of the functions of the court in a democratic society in promoting justice and equity.

[12] In *Like Me, Meddle Me: Life in a Desegregated School* (1981), I conclude by directing attention to policy needs for parents, teachers, counselors, administrators, boards of education, the business community, and state and federal governments by drawing upon techniques some Pacesetter teachers, students, and parents found to be effective, as well as those evaluated in the educational and psychological literature, to suggest some prescriptive strategies for improving desegregated schooling.

[13] See Ogbu 1974. Herbers (1979) reports that the unemployment picture for minority youths, particularly blacks, is about what it was for the entire nation in the depths of the Great Depression. Flint (1979) reports the jobless rate for nonwhite youths at 35.3 percent. Dallas, at the time of my study, was better off than many other cities, especially in the Northeast. Below is a 1976 breakdown (U.S. Bureau of Labor Statistics):

	Dallas-Ft. Worth	*New York City*
overall unemployment	4.6 %	10.4 %
black and other minority	7.1	12.6
white teen	15.2	22.1
black and other teen	27.0	47.0

In 1975 about 7 percent of the Pacesetter black children's fathers were unemployed. The relationship between academic performance, school policy, and employment is suggested by the Wingate School experience. Hentoff (1979) reported that a principal transformed a chaotic high school by individualizing programs, stressing reading in all subjects, discouraging teachers from treating students as losers, providing realistic vocational training, *and* providing after school and summer jobs through a nearly one-million-dollar federally funded Cooperative Education Program.

References

Aldis, Owen. 1975. *Play Fighting.* New York: Academic Press, Inc.

Bloch, Alfred M. 1978. "Combat Neurosis in Inner City Schools," *The American Journal of Psychiatry,* 135(10):1189–1192.

Cassell, Joan, 1978. *A Fieldwork Manual for Studying Desegregated Schools.* Washington, D.C.: National Institute of Education.

Chance, Michael R. A., and Ray R. Larsen, eds. 1976. *The Social Structure of Attention.* New York: John Wiley and Sons.

Comer, James P., and Alvin F. Poussaint. 1975. *Black Child Care.* New York: Simon and Schuster.

Coopersmith, Stanley. 1975. "Self-concept, Race and Education." In Gajendra K. Verma and Christopher Bagley, eds., *Race and Education Across Cultures* London: William Heinemann, Ltd., 145–167.

Corsaro, William A. 1979. "Young Children's Conception of Status and Role," *Sociology of Education,* 52(1):46–58.

Cosnow, Jeffrey E. 1979. *Cultural Adaptation Among Lower Class Children.* Paper presented at the Annual Meeting of the Society for Applied Anthropology, March.

Estes, Robert, and Kent Skipper. 1976. *Comprehensive Evaluation of the Pacesetter Program.* Unpublished Richardson (Texas) Independent School District contracted report.

Feinberg, Lawrence. 1978. "Coleman Now Discounts Advantages of School Desegregation," *Washington Post,* September 18, A1,5.

Flint, Jerry. 1979. "Jobless Rate of Blacks Still Rising Despite a 25 Year Federal Effort," *New York Times,* March 13, A1, B6.

Gans, Herbert J. 1962. *The Urban Villagers.* New York: The Free Press.

Gay, Geneva, and Roger D. Abrahams. 1973. "Does the Pot Melt, Boil, or Brew? Black Children and White Assessment Procedures," *Journal of School Psychology,* 2(4):330–340.

Hanna, Judith Lynne. 1979. *Identity, Defiance, and "Race" Relations: Children's Spontaneous Dance in Urban Education.* Paper presented at the Annual Meeting of the American Anthropological Association. Revision under publication review.

———. 1981. *Like Me, Meddle Me: Life in a Desegregated School* (under publication review).

Harrison-Ross, Phyllis, and Barbara Wyden. 1973. *The Black Child.* Berkeley: Medallion Books.

Hechinger, Fred M. 1979. "About Education: 'Frills' in Schools Are Often Basic," *New York Times,* January 23, C5.

Hentoff, Nat. 1979. "The Principal Principle," *Village Voice*, January 15, 64–65.

Herbers, John. 1979. "Changes in Society Holding Black Youth in Jobless Web," *New York Times*, March 11, 1, 44.

Huizinga, Johan. 1950. *Homo Ludens: A Study of the Play Element in Culture*. Boston: Beacon Press.

Hymes, Dell. 1967. "The Anthropology of Communication." In Frank E. Dance, ed., *Human Communication Theory*. New York: Holt, Rinehart, and Winston, 1–39.

————. 1974. *Foundations in Sociolinguistics: An Ethnographic Approach*. Philadelphia: University of Pennsylvania Press.

Jones, Bessie, and Bess Lomax Hawes. 1972. *Step It Down*. New York: Harper & Row.

Kochman, Thomas. 1971. "Cross-cultural Communication: Contrasting Perspectives, Conflicting Sensibilities," *Florida FL Reporter*, 9:3–17.

LeCompte, Margaret. 1978. "Learning to Work: The Hidden Curriculum of the Classroom," *Anthropology and Education*, 9(1):22–37.

Lundsgaarde, Henry P. 1977. *Murder in Space City: A Cultural Analysis of Houston Homicide Patterns*. New York: Oxford University Press.

McGrath, Peter. 1978. "The Middle Class Is Mad as Hell," *The Washingtonian*, 14(1):150–154.

Ogbu, John U. 1974. *The Next Generation: An Ethnography of Education in an Urban Neighborhood*. New York: Academic Press.

O'Neill, John. 1975. "Gay Technology and the Body Politic." In Jonathan Benthall and Ted Polhemus, eds., *The Body as a Medium of Expression*. New York: E. P. Dutton & Co., Inc., 291–302.

Pettigrew, Thomas F. 1971. *Racially Separate or Together?* New York: McGraw-Hill Book Company.

Poussaint, Alvin F. 1972. *Why Blacks Kill Blacks*. New York: Emerson Hall Publications, Inc.

Powell, Gloria Johnson. 1973. "Self-Concept in White and Black Children." In Charles V. Willie, et al., eds., *Racism and Mental Health*. Pittsburgh: University of Pittsburgh Press, 229–318.

Raspberry, William. 1979. "Boys: Endangered Species?" *Washington Post*, March 19, A23.

Roberts, Steve V. 1978. "Black Progress and Poverty Are Underlined by Statistics," *New York Times*, February 28.

Rosenberg, Morris, and Roberta G. Simmons. 1972. *Black and White Self-Esteem: The Urban School Child*. Washington: The American Sociological Association.

Schafft, Gretchen Engle. 1976. *The Unexpected Minority: White Children in an Urban School and Neighborhood.* Ph.D. dissertation, Catholic University.

Schofield, Janet W. 1978. "School Desegregation and Intergroup Relations." In D. Bar-Tal and L. Saxe, eds., *The Social Psychology of Education: Theory and Research.* New York: John Wiley and Sons, 329–363.

Sennett, Richard, and Jonathan Cobb. 1973. *The Hidden Injuries of Class.* New York: Alfred A. Knopf, Inc.

Shantz, Carolyn Uhlinger. 1975. "The Development of Social Cognition." In E. Mavis Hetherington, ed., *Review of Child Development Research.* Chicago: University of Chicago Press, 257–323.

Siegel, Bernard J. 1970. "Defensive Structuring and Environmental Stress," *American Journal of Sociology*, 76(1):11–32.

Silberman, Charles E. 1978. *Criminal Violence, Criminal Justice.* New York: Random House, Inc.

Silverstein, Barry, and Ronald Krate. 1975. *Children of the Dark Ghetto: A Developmental Psychology.* New York: Praeger Publishers, Inc.

U.S. Bureau of Labor Statistics. 1976. "Unemployment Declined in Metropolitan Areas and Central Cities in 1976—But Black Workers Made Few Gains," *News.* USDL #77-867.

Wax, Murray L., principal ed. 1980. *Desegregated Schools: An Intimate Portrait Based on Five Ethnographic Studies.* New Brunswick, NJ: Transaction Books.

Wegmann, Robert G. 1977. "Desegregation and Resegregation: A Review of the Research on White Flight from Urban Areas." In Daniel U. Levine and Robert J. Havighurst, eds., *The Future of Big-City Schools.* Berkeley, CA: McCutchan Publishing Corp., 11–54.

Williams, John E., and J. Kenneth Morland. 1976. *Race, Color, and the Young Child.* Chapel Hill: The University of North Carolina Press.

Willie, Charles Vert. 1978. *The Sociology of Urban Education.* Lexington, MA: Lexington Books.

Willis, Paul E. 1975. "The Expressive Style of a Motor-Bike Culture." In Jonathan Benthall and Ted Polhemus, eds., *The Body as a Medium of Expression.* New York: E. P. Dutton, 233–252.

———. 1977. *Learning to Labour: How Working Class Kids Get Working Class Jobs.* Farnborough, England: Saxon House.

11

Christine Robinson Finnan

The Ethnography of Children's Spontaneous Play

Christine Robinson Finnan

The Author

Christine Robinson Finnan received the Ph.D. degree in education and anthropology at Stanford University and is an educational anthropologist on the staff of SRI International, a nonprofit research organization in Menlo Park, California. She first became interested in educational anthropology through her work on children's folklore and play. She began studying children's spontaneous play while working on a master's degree in anthropology (folklore) at the University of Texas, Austin. Her interest in the role of play in child development took her to the School of Education at Stanford for her further graduate work. At Stanford, she turned her studies of play toward issues of cultural adaptation of Vietnamese refugee children.

Also while at Stanford, she was exposed to an array of other educational issues and became interested in applications of anthropological theory and method to them. She began increasingly to focus her investigations on issues beyond the scope of children's play. Her doctoral dissertation, "The Development of Occupational Identity Among Vietnamese Refugees," which exemplifies her interest in the area of education and work, describes a further ethnographic study.

An example of the work Finnan has been doing at SRI International is an evaluation of the Teacher Corps, a federally funded teacher training program. The evaluation combines modified ethnographic methods with more traditional evaluation methods. This study has triggered interest in adapting ethnographic methods to policy-relevant research.

This Chapter

In this chapter Christine Finnan does an ethnographic analysis of spontaneous play, such as self-structured chase games. These activities transcend the normal boundaries of appropriate behavior for children, because they are defined by the frame "play." The players are thus freed from society's rules for as long as the frame is maintained. As Finnan points out, these phenomena cannot be studied with survey instruments, tests, or even formal interviews. Observation must be on-the-spot, and of relatively long duration. This chapter is therefore a particularly apt demonstration of the utility of anthroethnography. Fortunately, Finnan furnishes us with detailed information about types of games and their sequences of behavior. This enables us to understand both the play and the methodology of data elicitation and collection. It becomes clear that though the kinds of play engaged in, such as chase games, are spontaneous, they are not without tacit rules.

Finnan's observations also bring to our attention the fact of sex differences in spontaneous play. She describes elements distinguishing the play of boys from that of girls. She also shows how the boundaries and role ascriptions in spontaneous play are flexible and ambiguous enough to permit girls to experiment with forms of aggression and disorder which are not typical of their ordinary play roles. Finnan takes the analysis further in her discussion of the relationship between play and mature sex roles and raises some interesting points concerning the changing role of women in American society.

To conclude her discussion of spontaneous play Finnan compares the play of Vietnamese refugee children with that of American children. The Vietnamese children play rule-governed games. They are not yet sure what social rules they would violate in spontaneous play—a necessary precondition to engaging in it. Again, there is a sex difference in play that may make a difference in the adjustment of the two sexes in American culture.

Finnan's analysis in this chapter is also useful to us as we attempt to find the range of methodologies that we can call ethnographic. While not microethnographic in the sense that Erickson and Mohatt's was in their study of the Ontario Indian school, her work is not entirely "macroethnographic" either. She makes fine-grained observations of relationships in small groups, and places her observations in the larger contexts of sex roles and play theory.

Though an ethnographic study of spontaneous play may not seem at first glance to have implications for educational policy, Finnan pursues this subject briefly at the end of her paper. It would seem useful for any elementary school administrator who has the problem of how to govern recess periods to know something of the ethnography of spontaneous play.

Introduction

One girl made a mock lunge at another girl. The second girl ran a few feet and stopped, taunting the chaser to try to catch her. The chaser responded with another lunge, and the other player again ran only a few feet. This continued for several minutes; the girls moved away from the school building. Suddenly the chasee ran several yards to hide behind a woman and child standing near the edge of the playground. The players ducked and circled around the woman, laughing as they played. They eventually worked their way back to the building, darting and teasing. Finally, the chasee sat down near a group of girls and refused to continue playing. [Third grade, 3/19/74]

A quick glance at any school playground in the United States shows the prevalence of this kind of spontaneous play. It is brief, seemingly chaotic, often rough, and little understood by adults. A closer look, though, shows that it has a structure which gives children[1] freedom rather than imposing rules. These chase games are unlike formal games, such as Tag, because there are no pre-established rules and roles. In fact, rules from the nonplay world are often overturned and mocked. Rules are replaced by signals that announce that anything goes because "This is play."

Insights into children's behavior and development can be drawn from observations of spontaneous play. This kind of play flourishes away from adult influence, expectations, and approval. Children participate for their own enjoyment, not for adult sanction. Spontaneous play reflects behavioral patterns of the children's nonplay world. Insights drawn from analysis of spontaneous play are applicable to problems children have outside of the play framework.

Observations of spontaneous play lead one to ask why groups of children participate differently in spontaneous play when there are no rules or roles to adopt. I will focus on two examples of how play preferences and style differ in spontaneous play. First, I will explore sex differences in play style. In a study of white American children's play, I found that girls' and boys' styles of play

differ. Boys' play is aggressive and girls' play is halting and teasing. Boys are proud of their role on the playground, while girls are dissatisfied with their role unless they can involve boys. I suggest that these differences reflect children's general attitudes toward future sex roles.

In my second example, I will show that children must possess a degree of cultural knowledge to enjoy spontaneous play. This work is based on observations of Vietnamese refugee children's play on American playgrounds. I found that they generally play highly structured, rule-governed games rather than participating in free-flowing spontaneous play. I hypothesize that they are using play to learn the rules of the playground and society, while their American peers choose spontaneous play because they know these rules so well they enjoy breaking them.

What Is Spontaneous Play?

Spontaneous play is activity created for the moment, without the rules and roles that dominate more formal games. Self-structured chase games[2] are perpetuated through their own adaptive structure rather than through preestablished rules. Spontaneous play involves the basic elements of more highly structured activities—chase-elude, attack-defend, and capture-rescue (Sutton-Smith 1972)—but there are no restrictions on the when, where, how, and whom of these activities.

There has been little research on children's spontaneous play, in part because most research methodologies are not suited to studying anything so seemingly chaotic. Surveys, interviews, and short-term observations uncover activities that are named and replicable. Most of the research on children's play has either (1) directed children into adult specified activities, (2) elicited game preference by asking for the names of games, or (3) compiled collections of games (Avedon 1971, Herron and Sutton-Smith 1971, I. and P. Opie 1969). Activities that do not have rules, roles, purpose, and a result are lumped into a category "pastimes" (Avedon 1971: 422).

Structures of Behavior

One must look for structures more fundamental to activity than formalized rules and roles to understand children's spontaneous play. These patterns and structures emerge only after extensive observation. They cannot be assumed *a priori* and cannot be elicited through surveys, tests, interviews, or brief observations.

Gregory Bateson's translation of behavior as communication stimulated interest in underlying structures of behavior. Bateson introduced the idea that activities are "framed" or set off from each other through signals. In play, we transcend normal boundaries of appropriate behavior because we frame behavior as play. Through signals, we say, "It is OK for us to scream, hit, wrestle, and pinch because we are playing." Framing gives a minimal structure to activity. Players are freed from society's rules and its emphasis on order as long as the frame is maintained. When the frame is broken, however, the players no longer read a message "This is play," but ask the question

"Is this play?" Play cannot continue if this question remains (Bateson 1972).

Why has so little attention been focused on the process of signaling boundaries between play and nonplay behavior? In part it is because the signals are so much a part of play that they disappear into its structure.

All players can read and send signals that set play behavior off from nonplay behavior. However, signals are rarely verbalized in a player's description of play and even less often in adult research on play. Signaling is "just one of those things we do" in play. It is something all players do, but they do not think about why, or what it means. This creates a dilemma; researchers cannot ignore what players cannot pay attention to. Players cannot play if they analyze their own actions, and researchers cannot analyze behavior if they do not understand what the players take for granted. The solution to this dilemma lies in the researcher's orientation and methodology. Both must be geared to discovering patterns of behavior central to the activity. Anthropological ethnography is well suited to this task because of its emphasis on structural interaction. The following is a description of how I used anthropological ethnography to study children's spontaneous play.

Methodology

This chapter is based on data gathered in two separate research projects. The first study was conducted in conjunction with a children's folklore project undertaken by the Southwest Education Development Laboratory in Austin, Texas. This laboratory contacted several local folklorists to record children's natural playground activity. Each of the researchers chose a group of children or a kind of activity to observe. I chose the play of white girls. Observation took place from January to May 1974.

The second project focused on the role of play in the social adaptation of culturally different children, in this case Vietnamese refugee children. At the time of the study (October 1976 to April 1977) the Vietnamese children had been in the United States for a little over one year. I chose four schools differing in their racial composition and their treatment of students with limited English. There were 22 Vietnamese children enrolled in the four schools: 12 in the fourth to sixth grades.[3]

My observations in both studies were nondirective. I tried to stand on the periphery of activity and made no attempt to influence the play. I talked to children when they came up to me, but I never drew children out of their play to interview them. I was looking primarily for the signals children used to set the frame "This is play" and to record what occurred within the frame. I tried to record as much detail as possible on movements, vocalization, and players' flow into and out of games. In both studies, I relied primarily on note-taking to record play behavior; however, I also used a tape recorder in the first study. Before entering the playgrounds, I would make note of weather conditions, time, date, and anything that might affect the children's play (holidays, changes in school schedule, etc.).

I arrived at the playground before the children were let out for recess, so that I could watch play groups form. In the first project I did not focus on specific children, but on kinds of play. In the second project, however, my focus was on specific children.

I developed an informal code for participants and movements. I used an abbreviation of their names if I knew them; otherwise, I relied on their most obvious physical characteristics, such as race, size, hair color, and sex. Notes such as "blo. b." or "fat w.g." are sufficient to bring back an image of a blond boy or a fat white girl. I also made note of the time, in at least five-minute intervals. When I used a tape recorder along with notes, I wrote down verbalizations as well as behavior, so that my notes and the tape would coincide.

The most important part of note-taking is immediate transcription. I tried to transcribe my notes into full, typed field notes as soon as I returned from the playground. Otherwise, scribbled notes lose their meaning and unrecorded activity is forgotten.

Although I used a tape recorder in the first project, I did not in the second. I felt it would be more distractive than useful, since my focus was on a specific group of children. I did not want to shun other children, but I was more interested in watching Vietnamese children than in talking to others. From my experience in the first study, I did not want to draw attention to myself through the tape recorder, and I found that I was able to write down most of the verbalization I could hear. I suggest that before using a tape recorder in recording playground behavior, researchers should be sure it warrants the distraction it creates. Often, when one is not directly involved in the activity, there is enough time to record behavior and verbalization through notes. Also, it is often difficult to make sense of the layers of talk picked up by a tape recorder, and important speech can be lost in a garble of screams and shouts.

The Continuum of Chase Games

All chase games share several basic features. They depend on communication of the message "This is play," as all spontaneous play does, and they are based on the elements chase and elude. Chase games, however, are not all simple dashes across a playground. They differ according to the sex of the participants, the ratio of chasers to chasees, type of flight, purpose of the game, provocation, and use of space.

The following outlines the continuum of chase games from simple spurts across a field to complex fantasy-based interactions. This illustrates what occurs within the frame "This is play" and how seemingly chaotic activity shares a common structure with other self-structured chase games.[4]

TYPE A

1. Number of participants	Two
2. Sex of the pair	Same sex or girl/boy
3. Ratio of chasers to chasees	1:1
4. Type of flight	A long spurt
5. Purpose of the game	The purpose is to capture the chasee or for the chasee to outdistance the chaser.
6. Provocation	1. The chasee attacks the chaser and retreats. 2. The chasee takes a possession from the chaser. 3. The chaser or chasee gives a verbal or nonverbal signal of aggression.
7. Use of space and territory	The chase is usually into space that is not occupied by other children. The territory covered in the chase is rather large. In some cases the chasee can flee to a safety area.
8. Fate of the captured chasee	*Boy/boy*—the chaser pins the chasee to the ground. *Boy/girl*—sometimes she is pinned to the ground, but usually only for a few seconds. *Girl/boy*—she holds the boy as long as possible, but often needs help from a friend or a prop (jumprope) to hold him.

Girl/girl—the chaser holds the chasee for a few seconds.

Example   Three second-grade girls showed a fieldworker how to perform a hand clap game. When they finished, they stood up and played with a wad of paper, trying to push it into each other's clothes and hands. Barbara[5] tried to push it up Cathy's sleeve, but Cathy ran away. Cathy ran toward a building across the field, but was captured before reaching it. Barbara held her for a few seconds before Cathy ran back to where they had been playing. Barbara did not follow Cathy again, and walked away in another direction. [Second grade, 3/8/74]

TYPE B

1. Number of participants	Two if girl/boy; 2, 3, or 4 if same sex
2. Sex of the group	Girl/boy or same sex
3. Ratio of chasers to chasees	1:1, 2:1, 3:1
4. Type of flight	Short, evasive movements
5. Purpose of the game	The chasee tries to evade the chaser. If the chaser is not a skillful runner, the chasee will taunt him/her, usually nonverbally. For girls, the main purpose is to tease each other. For boys, the chase seems to be secondary to wrestling.
6. Provocation	The provocation is similar to that in Type A, but usually the chaser and chasee share the desire to participate in this game.
7. Use of space and territory	The chase usually takes place in a space that is occupied by other people or playground equipment. They are used to shield the chasee from the chaser. Since there is little distance between the chaser and the chasee, the chasee does not have a safety area.
8. Fate of the captured chasee	*Boy/boy*—the object of the game is to wrestle on the ground. The chasee is almost always knocked down by the chaser; roles are often reversed when the game resumes. *Boy/girl*—she is sometimes knocked down, but they do not wrestle. Usually, the boy playfully hits the girl, or grabs her for a few moments. *Girl/boy*—this situation is rare, but when it occurs the chaser slaps or grabs at the boy but rarely captures him.

Girl/girl—the chaser generally only pokes at the chasee or grabs her by the arm or around the shoulders.

Example Three second-grade boys were engaged in a wrestling-type chase game. They were playing in an area occupied by a group of kindergarten children. The chaser would catch the chasee from the back, and usually tried to knock him down by pushing his knees forward. When the chasee fell, he was immediately pinned to the ground. Soon the victim was up and another boy was captured and knocked to the ground. The three boys switched roles throughout the games and never tried to escape from the chaser. They seemed to enjoy the capture more than the chase. [Second grade, 2/15/74]

TYPE C

1. Number of participants — Three to six

2. Sex of the group — Girl/boy

3. Ratio of chasers to chasees — 3:1, 4:1, 5:1, 2:2, 3:2, 4:2

4. Type of flight — The flight flows between long spurts and short evasive movements. The short movements are most common.

5. Purpose of the game — The purpose is to inflict some kind of punishment on the chasee. It is important for the chasers to establish their superiority over the chasee.

6. Provocation — These games are often offshoots of Type A or B, with the same provocation. However, the chasers often initiate the game without provocation from the chasee.

7. Use of space and territory — These games are played in both open and occupied space. There are rarely safety areas.

8. Fate of the captured chasee — The chasee is almost always punished when captured. He/she is either detained by the chasers or knocked down, hit with a ball, robbed of clothing (shoes, coat), etc.

Example It was a hot afternoon, and the children clustered in the shade. Two girls ran out from the shade of the second-grade building, chasing after a blonde boy. He got about halfway to the bar that separates the school from the street when the girls caught up with him. They encircled him with their arms and hauled him back to the shady area. They held him for several minutes as he squirmed and pulled and finally escaped. By this time, some other girls joined their friends, and when the original two chasers brought him back again, the whole group pinned him to a tree and hit at him. A few minutes later, I saw the boy running after one of the girls, and he soon captured her. [Second grade, 3/19/74]

TYPE D

1. Number of participants	Five or more
2. Sex of the group	Either all male or all female
3. Ratio of chasers to chasees	*Boys*—more chasers than chasees. *Girls*—more chasees than chasers
4. Type of flight	*Boys*—these games involve long runs; they are actually similar to very simple ball games. *Girls*—the flight is short, on the whole, and is often terminated when the chasee darts into a safety area.
5. Purpose of the game	*Boys*—they usually use some equipment, such as a ball, and the object is to catch the person who has control of the ball. The chaser/chasee roles are more fluid than in kickball, and there are no pre-established rules. *Girls*—the game often incorporates role playing along with chasing.
6. Provocation	Provocation is not especially important in these games because no players have to be coerced to play.
7. Use of space and territory	*Boys*—the boys cover the entire playing field and have no safety area. *Girls*—the girls' games are played primarily in a mandatory safety area, and a semi-safe territory.
8. Fate of the captured chasee	*Boys*—he becomes a chaser. He may be knocked down in the process of the capture, but that is secondary to the chaser's wish to become the chasee. *Girls*—often nothing happens. The girls may take on a similar role to the chaser (witch or vampire). Sometimes a chasee is captured and held hostage or punished by the chaser.

Example—Girls' games Several boys briefly joined a girls' chase but soon lost interest, leaving a group of 8–10 girls under their shelter (a piece of play equipment resembling a lean-to). This shelter served as a safety zone when witches or monsters attacked. Karen assumed the role of witch and, with a friend, captured another girl, pinning her to a tree. She announced, "She's still tied 'til the wicked witches come." Karen then yelled to a girl across the playground, "All right, Connie, Witchie-poo, get her." Connie left her game and became a witch. A small girl tapped one witch and the prisoner on the shoulder, saying "I'm a fairy, bing." Karen sloughed this off saying, "Oh, that's what you think." With Connie as wicked witch, Karen and her friend became protectors of the other players. Karen yelled, "My children, my children, come here!" They took the girls under the shelter. Connie announced, "I'll get you, you little rats!" Karen: "No, you won't; no, you won't." The game became rather chaotic as girls enacted scenes from the film *The Wizard of Oz* (shown on television that week). Brief chases between two and three girls ensued. Several boys invaded the safety zone, but by this time the play group had splintered into many small disconnected groups. [Third grade, 2/28/74]

Example—Boys' game   A large group of boys ran past me in a pack. They were pursuing one boy who had control of a kickball. He was grabbed by several boys after being caught, but was not knocked down. Another boy captured the ball, and the chase resumed with the pack chasing the boy with the ball. [Third grade, 3/12/74]

TYPE E

1. Number of participants	Five or more
2. Sex of the group	Girl/boy
3. Ratio of chasers to chasees	The chasees outnumber the chasers.
4. Type of flight	The game includes both short spurts and long runs.
5. Purpose of the game	One purpose is for the girls to be chased by the boys. Another purpose is to gather a large group of players to act out a group fantasy.
6. Provocation	The girls tease and taunt the boys until they join the game. Boys may also be attracted to the role they can play in the game (monster, vampire).
7. Use of space and territory	Most activity revolves around the safety zone (a piece of play equipment). Eventually boys ignore the sanctity of the safety zone and the children cover more territory.

8. Fate of the captured chasee

The chasee can either return to the shelter, be held hostage, or be transformed into a monster or a vampire. This often involves a ritualized imitation of bloodsucking.

Example A chase began when Tony chased Karen, Vickie, and two other girls into the lean-to shelter. The girls screamed, "Can't come into our house" to the nearby boys. Karen and another girl ran in and out of the house, taunting the boys by chanting, "Na, na, ne, boo, boo." The girls began to play house in the shelter. Tony knocked on the door, and said, "Hey, I need some dinner for me and my pal here." One girl pestered Tony about his pal's name, until he replied, "His name is Jesus." Another girl began shooting at the boys with an imaginary shotgun. Tony said, "You put that down. That's what, what makes me mean, people who shoot guns all the time." Tony affected a "monster stance" and stormed through the shelter, sending the girls screaming into the open field. Soon, about 20 children were playing. Eventually all of the girls were caught by monsters or vampires and they too became threatening creatures. The game moved away from the now abandoned safety zone. The game became chaotic, with many small groups chasing and capturing each other. One girl insisted she was a ghost, but when other players challenged her power as a ghost, she left the game in tears. The chasing became more aggressive as the boys experimented with their monster or vampire roles. Eventually, most of the girls wandered away from the game, leaving it to the boys. [Third grade, 3/29/74]

TYPE F

These are rule-governed chasing games, such as Touch or Tag. I did not record any of these games during my first project, but they also fit into the chase game continuum. For example, the game of Touch is outlined below (Opie, 1969:62).

1. Number of participants

Generally more than four

2. Sex of the group

Same sex or girl/boy

3. Ratio of chasers to chasees

Chasees outnumber the chasers

4. Type of flight

The flight is long unless the chaser is an unskillful runner or the chasee is very confident.

5. Purpose of the game

To chase and evade and to become or remain a chasee

6. Provocation

Desire to play a simple rule-governed game

7. Use of space and territory

Games usually take place in open space. Some versions have a safety area built into the rules.

8. Fate of the captured chasee

The preceding outline shows both the similarities and the differences of these self-structured chase games. All games are set off as play. They revolve around the basic elements of chase and elude, and they become more complex as the number of players increases, as boys and girls play together, and as new elements, such as fantasy roles, are added. Despite the complexity of some activities, children do not rely on rules to hold the games together. What holds the games together is the maintenance of the frame "This is play."

The play frame gives players freedom to act as they please, as well as freedom to remove responsibility for their actions, especially aggressive acts. Within the play frame, a player can "cremate" a friend without fear of punishment or a sense of guilt. In the context of the self-structured chase games, a player can become intensely involved in the play until eventually the play frame breaks. He or she then asks, "Is this play?" and is frightened by the consequences of a negative answer. The following occurred during the Type E game described earlier. Vickie's play frame broke and she retreated to the teacher and to the comfort of the rule-governed world:

> VICKIE I'm already a vampire. I'm a vampire already, Gilbert.
> OTHER I'm not . . . growl!
> VICKIE I'm a dying soul.
> GILBERT You what?
> VICKIE Tony, Tony, I'm a ghost! I'm a ghost! (Earlier in the game, Vickie was Tony's "helper.")
> GILBERT He's a vampire.

He/she becomes the new chaser until someone is captured or until everyone is captured.

> GILBERT You're invisible so you can go through anything. (Vickie now clings to my waist.)
> GILBERT We can see you. (He chases her around me.)
> VICKIE Quit it!
> GILBERT You can't see a ghost.
> VICKIE No, Gilbert! (She begins to whine.) Why don't you (?) Teacher!
> OTHER Growl.
> VICKIE Leave me alone!
> BOYS He's already a vampire.
> VICKIE Tony, Tony, I'm a ghost.
> TONY A vampire could kill a ghost. (Vickie becomes very upset and leaves in tears.) [Third grade, 3/28/74]

Differences in Children's Participation in Spontaneous Play

The intent of the previous discussion was to show how a structure emerges from seemingly chaotic activity. Once the basic elements of an activity are known, differences in children's involvement in the activities become obvious. The following sections will show first, how there are sex-typed differences in children's spontaneous play, and second, that cultural knowledge is required for these games.

Sex-Typed Differences

Three boys raced toward me, with two girls in close pursuit. The boys stopped, wheeled around, and lunged at the girls. The girls fled in mock terror to the other end of the playground. They huddled together, giggling, anticipating the boys' possible retaliation. Meanwhile, another boy explained, "This school is weird. Usually the boys chase the girls, but here, the girls chase the boys." [Sixth grade, Redwood City, CA, 2/19/77]

Contrary to this boy's opinion, there is nothing unusual about his school. In fact, it is more common for girls to chase boys than the reverse. The continuum of chase games points to numerous examples of differences in boys' and girls' style of play and play preferences. Several examples of girls coercing reluctant boys to join their games were also given. This may seem like a sign of changing sex roles on the playground, but closer observation reveals that girls still act out traditional feminine roles in their play.

Male and female roles are clearly marked in many traditional rule-governed games (Sutton-Smith and Rosenburg 1960, 1961; Sutton-Smith, Rosenburg, and Morgan 1963). The labels "boys' game" or "girls' game" follow many activities through generations of players. For example, marbles is a boy's game; jacks, a girls' game. Boys' games are traditionally aggressive and competitive; girls' games are passive and accommodating. Boys and girls play differently, even when they participate in the same game.

Distinct boys' and girls' chase styles exist, even in the simplest self-structured chase game. Basically, boys' chase style is aggressive and physical and girls' style is passive and teasing. A simple chase between girls will be quite different from one between boys, and when boys and girls play together, they combine the most powerful elements of their respective styles. The disorder and chaos created in large girl/boy self-structured chase games gives girls a rare opportunity to transcend the restraints traditionally inhibiting them in their play.

Boys' self-structured chase games require a great expenditure of physical energy. They are a test of boys' physical strength and consist of competition in running, wrestling, and tackling. Two boys' games were used as examples under Type B and Type D. These examples illustrate the importance of physical strength in boys' self-structured chase games. The emphasis in small games is on the capture; in the large games, it is on the chase. In the small games, the players create a mock fight in which they attempt to "cremate" each other. The large games resemble kickball, but the self-structured games have no preestablished rules or winners.

Four elements characterize the boys' self-structured chase games. First, aggression is a key component. The boys claim to kill, cremate, and destroy each other. A nonaggressive participant has no place in these games. Second, there is a great deal of physical contact. Bodies are pressed together during the capture. The players separate only during the chase. Third, boys enjoy freedom of movement in their chase games. No safety zones are established, so the chaser is always free to pursue his victim. Fourth, no roles are permanent. The roles of chaser and chasee are constantly fluctuating. No player has the power to dictate the flow of the game, i.e., one boy cannot tell another to keep a role permanently.

These elements of boys' chase games stand in contrast to the girls' style of play. The girls have a teasing, halting style of chasing. Physical strength is not a key element. In small games (those involving two or three players), the chasee teases the chaser; prolonged running chases are not found. In large games, girls assume fantasy roles such as witch, fairy, and slave. A dominant player establishes the roles and sets the flow of the game, in contrast to the free flow of boys' chase games. Girls' small-scale chase games find the players keeping their respective roles throughout the game (i.e., the chaser and chasee never exchange roles), while in large-scale games roles are exchanged after a chasee is captured by the chaser. In contrast to large-scale boys' games, however, role changes in large-scale girls' games are relatively structured, with changes permitted only after capture. Examples of girls' games appear on the first page and as an example of Type D games.

Girls' self-structured chase games are characterized by five basic elements. First, all chases are short and halting. The object is to tease, not to overpower the opponent. There is little or no wrestling. Second, roles are often permanent. In the small games, one girl remains the chaser and the other the chasee. In the large games, there is more flexibility, but witches are usually permanent and the victims only change roles when captured. Permanent roles are often maintained because one girl directs the movement of the game. Third, a safety zone must be respected. The safety zone can be a person, or a stationary object. The fourth and fifth elements are most frequently found in the large games. They are the use of fantasy roles and the underlying desire of the players to eventually involve boys as participants. The aggressive fantasy

roles serve to attract boys who are otherwise disinterested in girls' games.

Behavioral differences found in boys' and girls' chase games are similar to differences observed in their nonplay behavior (Mussen, Conger, and Kagan 1969; Whiting and Edwards 1973; Maccoby and Jacklin 1975; Barry, Bacon, and Child 1957; D'Andrade 1966). According to cross-cultural studies, boys tend to be more aggressive than girls, while girls are more nurturant and supportive than boys (Whiting and Edwards 1973; Maccoby and Jacklin 1975; Barry, Bacon, and Child 1957). Children's attitudes toward their play reflect their sex role satisfaction. Studies of American children's attitudes toward feminine and masculine roles outside of play show that boys are happier with their sex role than are girls (Maccoby 1966; Stein, Pohly, and Mueller 1971; Rabban 1950; Brown 1957; Smith 1939; Gardner 1947).

On the playground, boys are proud of their games and their status. They express no desire to include girls in their play or to play girls' games. During an aggressive all-boy game, a third-grade boy offered his opinion:

I We're trying to figure out how you play your games. We want to teach other kids the games you're playing.
BOY I don't think the girls would like this one.
I Why not?
BOY Because we get cremated.
I They'll get what? [I didn't understand him at first.]
BOY They'll get cremated. That's the whole idea of the game, is getting killed. [Third grade, 3/1/74]

Girls, on the other hand, are discontented with their role on the playground and are envious of boys' play.

Three third-grade girls express both a longing to play traditional girls' games and an attraction to boys' play:

I Why are they chasing the boys? [referring to several other girls]

KAREN Because the girls like to chase the boys.

I Do you have to play with the boys?

PAM No, they [other girls] like to.

I Oh, they like to?

PAM And they don't like to play jumping rope, so there's hardly any girls to play jumping rope.

[skip one minute]

PAM They [the boys] play too rough. They knock you down on purpose and get all dirty and all muddy and all that.

I Yeah, what kind of games do you play when you play with the boys?

KAREN Boys catch the girls, um, whatever.

GINA Yeah, boys chase the girls or the girls chase the boys, or the boys knock down the girls or the girls knock down the boys.

I Sounds pretty good. Do the girls chase the boys more than the boys chase the girls or [interruption]

GIRL The girls chase the boys more than the boys chase the girls.

I Really? Why?

GIRL Because, I don't know [interruption]

PAM Because they don't want to chase us, and we want to play a game, and so we chase them and hit them, and knock them down.

KAREN And then whenever we [interruption]

PAM And they they get mad and start chasing us. [Third grade, 3/1/74]

These second- and third-grade girls resemble other 9-year-old girls described by Rosenberg, Sutton-Smith, and Morgan (1963) in another study on play. The girls they studied exhibited ambivalent play preferences. The re-searchers noticed that the girls were attracted to immature games such as jump rope and hopscotch and also to mature games such as basketball and soccer. The 9-year-old boys described by Rosenburg, Sutton-Smith, and Morgan were only interested in mature games. The researchers credit boys' clear play preferences to the traditional involvement of men in sports and the ambivalence of girls to the absence of a similar tradition of women's participation in adult competitive sports (1963).

Why are some girls this age so interested in involving boys in their play? One reason may lie in the impact of boys on girls' games. When boys and girls play together in self-structured chase games, the games take on aspects of both boys' and girls' games, but most importantly, they lose the order and conformity characteristic of girls' play. Most girls quickly accept the absence of rules and lack of organization. There is little protest from girls when boys ignore their safety zone, even though it is rarely violated in the all-girl games. No rules exist once chasers have driven all the players out of the safety zone. At this point, girls can no longer cling to the safety of a home and conformity to rules. All players, both boys and girls, must use aggression to protect themselves, since they are no longer protected by rules. On the other hand, girls as well as boys can assert themselves forcefully, since no rules restrain them.

Rather than assuming this aggressive, seemingly chaotic play is nonproductive, one can see it as the response of children preparing for a changing society. Games of disorder address the dialetic between the order created in society and the disorder associated with the environment and with new societal demands. These games do not equip children to be mommys or daddys or doctors and nurses, but help children cope with change and uncertainty in a nonstatic society. Games of disorder are found in diverse societies, but are more prevalent in complex societies and are played more frequently today than in the past (Sutton-Smith 1977, Sutton-Smith and Rosenburg 1961).

Involvement in the girl/boy self-structured chase games is a rare opportunity for girls to play aggressively with disorder. Girls are adept at fantasy play but rarely permit disorder to override order. Even in children's storytelling, girls tell stories of deprivation (disorder) followed by reward (order), while boys reverse the order in their stories, leaving the characters in a state of disorder (May 1966). The fantasy play in girl/boy self-structured chase games, however, is pure disorder; players must leave the game to find order. It is significant that girls initiate the play in these games despite their preoccupation with order.

There are three possible reasons why girls initiate these particular games of disorder. First, boys and girls generally adopt sex-typed play styles. The girls' style is relatively restrictive; girls are encouraged to "be nice" even when they play. Their play is often closely connected with nonplay situations, such as playing house or playing school. Janet Lever found that white American girls play indoors with fewer playmates in less competitive activities lasting a shorter time than boys. She concludes that play patterns perpetuate traditional sex-role divisions by preparing boys for occupational interactions and girls for familial interactions

(1976). Reports of play in other cultures usually mention gender segregation in play groups and the role of play in sex-role acquisition. Boys are generally more free to play, because they are away from adult supervision, while girls assume household duties at an early age (Mead 1928, 1930; Deng 1972; Schwartzman and Barbera 1976). Girls' conventional play permits little room for impulsive or aggressive behavior. Only in the self-structured games are American girls free to abandon these restrictions and act as they please. They find the disorder in the girl/boy self-structured chase games unusual and compelling.

Second, girls are in limbo in their play choice. By the age of 8 or 9, they are no longer satisfied with immature games, such as jump rope, but are not preparing for mature sports, as are boys at this age. Boys are also in a transition period, but are offered an alternative to their earlier play styles. The girls' play world is disjointed, with little promise for a satisfying future play role.

Third, girls are not satisfied with the traditional feminine sex role, and they are presented with few alternatives to it. In a sense, their image of themselves as women is in disorder. They want respect and status, but there are few models to emulate.

The sex roles ascribed to boys and girls above may seem outdated in light of the changing role of women. It would be too speculative at this point to draw strong connections between changes in the status of women and the play of third-grade girls. Girls' play will change as the status of women changes. Playground activities will reflect the increasing interest in women's professional sports. Girls' participation in organized sports such as Little League will affect their status on the playground. These changes will be superficial, though, unless children also learn different sex role behavior. Boys are, at present, encouraged to play aggressively and competitively, while girls are encouraged to be accommodating and thoughtful in their play. Boys and girls must learn to be both accommodating and competitive to function successfully as adults. Children are now using self-structured chase games to experiment with disorder and the challenges of a changing society. If the role of women in the adult society continues to change dramatically, girls must necessarily utilize self-structured play to develop the skills relevant to a new status.

Cultural Knowledge and Self-Structured Play [6]

It should already be clear that spontaneous play serves a positive role in children's development. However, not all children choose to participate in spontaneous play. Observations of Vietnamese refugee children's play showed that these 9- to 12-year-olds have more restricted play preferences than their American peers. Vietnamese children tend to choose highly structured games, even though their American peers often choose spontaneous play.

I found two patterns in the play of Vietnamese children. First, Vietnamese boys have very different patterns of play involvement than Vietnamese girls. All Vietnamese boys play actively, while few girls participate in play activities. Second, Vietnamese children play

rule-governed games almost exclusively. They rarely participate in the spontaneous, free-flowing play created by their peers.

It was no surprise that Vietnamese girls and boys adopted different play patterns; however, the differences were more marked than I expected. I attribute the girls' lack of participation to the lack of fit between their play in Vietnam and games played by their American peers. When asked what they played in Vietnam, most girls said badminton and jump rope. Neither game is played by fourth- to sixth-graders at the four American schools. Most of the girls alternate between talking to friends and joining rather aggressive games during their recess periods. Vietnamese girls have few minimally verbal play options.

All Vietnamese boys play during recess, but they limit their play participation to rule-governed games. When Vietnamese girls play, they also play rule-governed games. Free-flowing, spontaneous play exists on all of the playgrounds, but the Vietnamese children choose rule-governed games instead. Since they are free to choose their play activity, there must be a reason why they prefer rule-governed games to spontaneous play. It seems that the security of rule-governed games is attractive to Vietnamese children. Vietnamese children choose play forms with well-defined boundaries and well-defined roles. They rely on the game's structure to clarify and define their position in relation to the other players. It is not clear if they are retreating from the confusion of learning a new culture into the safety of rules, or if they are pulled to a structure they can work within. According to Caillois, all game players try to eliminate confusion: "The confused and intricate laws of ordinary life are replaced in this fixed space and for this given time by precise, arbitrary, unexceptionable rules that must be accepted as such and that govern the correct playing of the game" (Caillois 1961:7).

The children who are fairly sure of their status on the playground and understand the social rules create novel play situations by transcending and overturning social rules. In contrast, children unfamiliar with American culture find rule-governed games novel because they learn new social rules. D. E. Berlyne writes that we are most responsive to an intermediate degree of novelty. We are indifferent to situations that are either too remote or too familiar (1960:21). Different criteria for novelty influence the play patterns of Vietnamese children and their American peers. A novel situation for an immigrant child may seem boring to an American child because it is too familiar, while a novel situation for an American child may be too foreign for an immigrant child.

Previous discussions of spontaneous play have not recognized the importance of a shared cultural base. New social structures and interactions intrigue those who are so secure in their culture they can think about changing it. If children do not fully understand the social structure and rules spontaneous play turns against, play boundaries and signaling will not be strong enough to hold children in spontaneous play. Vietnamese children avoid spontaneous play with American peers because they

are still trying to establish boundaries and understand social relations in their everyday world. They engage in play forms that strengthen social relations and clarify social rules rather than participating in play that breaks down the social structure they are trying to build.

Children do not participate wholeheartedly in spontaneous play unless they are sure of the social rules they violate. Vietnamese children will gain this security by first mastering rule-governed games. I do not mean they must become good athletes; rather, they must understand the rules along with what lies beneath the rules. A parallel development of rule manipulation occurs in children's riddling.

Children go through three stages in learning to riddle. They begin with learning the structure and linguistic rules and end with transcending and distorting the rules. First, children learn the linguistic code, in this case, the question/answer sequence. They enjoy asking riddles such as "What two letters do Indians live in? T.P." Once the code is learned, they play with and distort the linguistic sequence by demanding answers that do not follow as clearly from the question, for example, "What is black and white and red all over? A bloody zebra." Children eventually subordinate the linguistic code to their interpersonal relations and substitute victimization as the proper response to the question. They ask a question such as "Do you want a Hawaiian punch?" and follow it by punching the child in the face (McDowell 1974).

The development of riddling skills is analogous to the development of play skills. Rules of proper speech or play behavior are learned in the first stage. At this time, children enjoy mastering rules they will use in daily life. Learning rules loses its novelty once children are proficient in them. Children then begin testing the sensation of rule distortion. Players are not bound by the rules, because they are playing, either physically or linguistically. Eventually, the riddles or games trascend the limits of their codes. Communication in both cases goes beyond verbalization or patterned interaction into what Bateson calls "metacommunication" or communication about communication (Bateson 1972:191).

Vietnamese children are essentially in the first stage, learning the linguistic and social codes. Vietnamese girls are at a disadvantage because they are avoiding both spontaneous play and rule-governed games. They are like the child who never tells a riddle. They stand back and observe the social interactions of play, but they do not learn what it is like to participate in the play. The girls learn the social rules, just as the nonriddler learns the question/answer sequence, but they do not learn how to play with the codes. In contrast, Vietnamese boys are learning social rules through play and may eventually know them well enough to play with them. These data suggest that Vietnamese boys will gain a deeper understanding of American culture than will Vietnamese girls, because of their participation in play.

Vietnamese boys are learning American cultural roles through the informal channel of play. They will learn to play with the rules and adapt to changes in American society if they go beyond rule-governed games. Vietnamese girls, in contrast, are learning social rules through the more formal channel of school and adults. They may be less prepared for change than Vietnamese boys, because school and adults do not give children an opportunity to play with the rules they have learned.

Significance

Most educational research focuses on aspects of schooling that adults hope to improve. To improve a situation, one must manipulate it. Researchers interested in children's play are torn between a desire to influence play and the realization that children's play should remain their own domain. The kind of play described in this chapter does not lend itself to adult intervention, but is a rich source for insights into child development and social interaction. I discourage any attempts to tap spontaneous play for improving classroom learning, but I offer the following to support my belief that spontaneous play is an important expression and outlet for children.

Spontaneous Play Offers a Positive Learning Environment

On playgrounds where violence is a problem, it is difficult to see spontaneous play as anything but potentially destructive behavior. However, if adults learn to read the signals for "This is play," the distinction between playful interactions and real fighting is evident. Children often resent adult interference into what they know is play, but what looks like a fight to the untrained observer. Adults often see spontaneous play as potentially dangerous, but from my observations it is no more dangerous than formal games.

Spontaneous play should not be discouraged among children of any age. It is not childish regression to an earlier stage of development, but a level of play that demands knowledge of both rule-governed play and societal rules. Children involved in spontaneous play are like clowns in ice-skating shows. They know how to play or skate so well they can play with the structure of the activity. Children respond to pressures from the nonplay world in their spontaneous play. They know how to follow rules, but they also know that the rules constantly change. Spontaneous play gives them an opportunity to disregard rules.

Children's Involvement in Spontaneous Play Reflects Sex-Role Acquisition

Historical and cross-cultural accounts of children's play usually mention differences in the play patterns of girls and boys (Sutton-Smith 1961, Schwartzman and Barbera 1976). Generally, boys' play is preparation for competitive, aggressive roles in society, while girls' play is geared to nurturant, accommodating roles. Girls' involvement in spontaneous play exemplifies an attempt to break from traditional play patterns. Unfortunately, few ethnographies and cross-cultural studies of play describe children's spontaneous play (Schwartzman 1976), so it is impossible to show comparable sex-specific behavior in other cultures. However, I speculate that many of the

patterns described above do not characterize black American girls' play. Black girls proudly perpetuate many traditional games, such as hand claps and ring play (Jones and Hawes 1972) and do not seek boys' involvement in their play (Brady 1975). Black girls' opinion of their future sex-role may be more positive than that of their white counterparts.

Observations of children's spontaneous play will give us a clue to changes in deep-rooted sex-role differences. David Lancy's study of culture change among the Kpelle shows that changes in play were among the first reflectors of culture change (1976). Changes in play preference may also reflect changes in sex roles. Other influences on both sex roles and play behavior are adults' efforts to expand athletic opportunities for women through increased exposure of women's sports on television and the availability of Title IX funds. Girls will have both role models and financial encouragement to pursue more competitive sports. These efforts will succeed only if girls' early play behavior changes. I see their interest in more aggressive self-structured chase games as an indicator of such change.

Spontaneous Play Demands a Degree of Cultural Knowledge Some Children Do Not Possess

Adults cannot assume that all children are capable of enjoying the same activities. Often the games that seem the easiest to join, such as spontaneous play, are not suited to the needs or desires of culturally different children. Culturally different children need to learn the rules of play and society before they can enjoy breaking them. This may also be true in the classroom. Culturally different students may excel in clearly structured environments but flounder in loosely structured classes. Rule violations are probably due to ignorance rather than to a desire to test the teacher.

The Normal Flow of Children's Play Must Remain Unaltered for Relevant Research

Ethnography is well suited to this task because it is both unobtrusive and non-directive. Ethnographers try to blend into the background and watch children play as they normally play rather than recording what they say, what they play, or what they will play if asked. Anthropological ethnography is especially useful because anthropologists are trained to draw their assumptions from the data, rather than coming to the site with *a priori* assumptions about the nature of children's play. Through cross-cultural experiences, anthropologists realize that one must not look for what should be there, but should try to understand what is there.

Notes

[1] Children referred to in this paper are between the ages of 7 and 12.

[2] I use "game" because the children call their play "games." The activities, however, do not conform to a formal definition of games (Avedon 1971).

[3] In the first study, permission to conduct research at the school was obtained by SEDL. In the second, I obtained permission from the school principals.

[4] Data are drawn from the first study in Austin, Texas.

[5] Names have been changed.

[6] An account of this research also appears in *Play: Anthropological Perspectives*, edited by Michael Salter (Cornwall, NY: Leisure Press, 1978).

References

Avedon, Elliot. 1971. "The Structural Element of Games." In Elliot Avedon and Brian Sutton-Smith, eds., *The Study of Games*. New York: John Wiley and Sons.

Barry, Herbert, III, Margaret K. Bacon, and Irvin L. Child. 1957. "A Cross-Cultural Survey of Some Sex Differences in Socialization," *Journal of Abnormal and Social Psychology*, 55:327–332.

Bateson, Gregory. 1972. "A Theory of Play and Fantasy." In *Steps to an Ecology of Mind*. New York: Ballantine Books.

Berlyne, D. E. 1960. *Conflict, Arousal and Curiosity*. New York: McGraw-Hill Book Company.

Brady, Margaret K. 1975. "This Little Lady's Gonna Boogaloo: Elements of Socialization in the Play of Black Girls." In *Black Girls at Play: Folkloristic Perspectives on Child Development*. Austin, TX: Southwest Education Development Laboratory.

Brown, D. G. 1957. "Masculinity and Femininity Development in Children," *Journal on Consulting Psychology*, 21:197–202.

Caillois, Roger. 1961. *Men Play and Games*. New York: Free Press of Glencoe.

D'Andrade, Roy G. 1966. *Sex Differences and Cultural Institutions: The Development of Sex Differences*. E. E. Maccoby, ed. Stanford: Stanford University Press, 174–204.

Deng, Francis. 1972. *The Dinka of the Sudan*. New York: Holt, Rinehart and Winston.

Gardner, L. P. 1947. "An Analysis of Children's Attitudes Towards Fathers," *Journal of Genetic Psychology*, 70:3–28.

Herron, R. E., and Brian Sutton-Smith, eds. 1971. *Child's Play*. New York: John Wiley and Sons.

Jones, Bessie, and Bess Lomax Hawes. 1972. *Step It Down*. New York: Harper & Row.

Lancy, David. 1976. "The Play Behavior of Kpelle Children During Rapid Cultural Change." In D. Lancy and B. A. Tindall, eds., *Problems and Prospects in the Study of Play*. New York: Leisure Press.

Lever, Janet. 1976. "Sex Differences in the Games Children Play." In *Social Problems*, 32(4) (April) 478–487.

Maccoby, Eleanor E. 1966. *The Development of Sex Differences*. Stanford. Stanford University Press.

———, and Carol N. Jacklin. 1975. *The Psychology of Sex Differences*. Stanford: Stanford University Press.

McDowell, John. 1974. "Interrogative Routines in Mexican-American Children's Folklore." *Working Papers in Sociolinguistics* 20.

May, Robert. 1966. "Sex Differences in Fantasy Patterns," *Journal of Projective Techniques*, 30(6):464–469.

Mead, Margaret. 1928. *Coming of Age in Samoa*. New York: William Morrow & Co., Inc.

———. 1930. *Growing Up in New Guinea*. New York: William Morrow & Co., Inc.

Mussen, Paul, John Conger, and Jerome Kagan. 1969. *Child Development and Personality*. New York: Harper & Row.

Opie, Iona, and Peter Opie. 1969. *Children's Games of Street and Playground*. Oxford, England: Clarendon Press.

Rabban, M. 1950. "Sex Role Identification in Young Children in Two Diverse Social Groups," *Genetic Psychology Monographs*, 42:81–158.

Rosenburg, B. G., Brian Sutton-Smith, and E. F. Morgan. 1963. "Development of Sex Differences in Play Choice," *Child Development*, 34:119–126.

Schwartzman, Helen. 1976. "The Anthropological Study of Children's Play," *Annual Review of Anthropology*, 5:289–328.

———, and L. Barbera. 1976. "Children's Play in Africa and South America: A Review of the Ethnographic Literature." In D. Lancy and B. A. Tindau, eds., *Problems and Prospects in the Study of Play*. New York: Leisure Press.

Smith, S. 1939. "Age and Sex Differences in Children's Opinion Concerning Sex Differences," *Journal of Genetic Psychology*, 54:17–25.

Stein, Aletha, Sheila Pohly, and Edward Mueller. 1971. "The Influence of Masculine, Feminine and Neutral Tasks on Children's Achievement Behavior; Expectances of Success and Attainment Values," *Child Development*, 42(1):195–207.

Sutton-Smith, Brian. 1972. "A Syntax for Play and Games." In R. E. Herron and B. Sutton-Smith, eds., *Child's Play*. New York: John Wiley and Sons.

————. 1977. "Games of Order and Disorder." In *The Dialectics of Play*. Schorndorf: Verlag Karl Hofmann.

————. 1961. "Sixty Years of Historical Change in the Game Preferences of American Children," *Journal of American Folklore*, 74:17–46.

————, and E. P. Morgan. 1963. "The Development of Sex Differences in Play Choice During Preadolescence," *Child Development*, 34:119–126.

————, and B. G. Rosenburg. 1960. "A Revised Conception of Masculine-Feminine Differences in Play Activities," *Journal of Genetic Psychology*, 96:165–170.

Whiting, Beatrice B., and Carolyn P. Edwards. 1973. "A Cross-Cultural Analysis of Sex Differences in the Behavior of Children Aged 3–11," *Journal of Social Psychology*, 91:171–188.

12

Richard L. Warren

Schooling, Biculturalism, and Ethnic Identity: A Case Study

Richard L. Warren

The Author

Richard Warren is professor of anthropology and education at the University of Kentucky, where his main appointment is in the Department of Social and Philosophical Studies in Education. He has published widely on schooling in our society and in Germany. He says of himself:

"I began graduate study at Stanford University after two years in the Education Division of the Office of Military Government for Bavaria, 10 years as a high school history teacher, and a memorable encounter with anthropology at a National Science Foundation Summer Institute. I hoped I could put together a workable synthesis of education, anthropology, and history. But the interest in studies of American character and reinterpretations of American history soon became tangential to the field of anthropology and education.

"My first field study, of a rural German village and school, done as a Ph.D. dissertation with George Spindler as adviser, established a direction for subsequent research—studies of elementary schools in different cultural settings, with emphasis on the teaching experience. In the organization of these studies there has been a considered attempt at replication, with the goal of isolating cultural variables from common schooling characteristics. The research was carried out while I was employed first at Stanford's Center for Research and Development in Teaching and later at the University of Kentucky. A central point of view in my research is that schooling and teaching are intricate phenomena made more complex by our disposition to render them in overly simple terms."

This Chapter

In this chapter Richard Warren describes a bicultural, bilingual program in an elementary school in southern California, close to the Mexican border.

There is no area of educational management and development more indicative of the basic problem areas in our society and of the attempts to accommodate to them. Cultural pluralism is now recognized as a fact of American life, ironically at a time when it may be disappearing in its manifestations of ethnic cultural differences in depth. Bicultural programs such as that described by Warren are a belated attempt to recognize the validity and significance of cultural and linguistic differences in U.S. society. Warren describes the program in sufficient ethnographic detail that one can draw one's own conclusions. One significant inference is that the basic messages concerning punctuality, achievement, orderliness, and the individual as a unit of social behavior are communicated through both sides of the bicultural program. The cultural differences may be less impressive than the cultural commonalities.

The importance of the bicultural program is not in the different competencies inculcated and developed in children but in the recognition of the worth of a cultural heritage other than that of Anglo North America. In the long run this may, paradoxically, enhance functional assimilation, since it removes significant static from the messages communicated in our cultural matrix to the culturally "different"—though this is not the declared goal of bicultural programs.

Introduction

Current and emerging programs in bilingual-bicultural education represent a significant development in the evolution of the public school. They are in one sense the ultimate test of whether schools can become meaningfully responsive to cultural heterogeneity and can foster a bicultural experience and identity. Such programs—and related research—attend to second-language acquisition, differential learning styles, bilingual assessment, and school-family interaction. There is a growing body of research on these topics, but a dearth of ethnographic material.[1] This chapter reports research on a bilingual-bicultural program in an elementary school with a high proportion of Mexican-American children. The focus is on the role of schooling processes in structuring, reinforcing, *or* muting a bicultural experience.

Setting

Campbell Elementary School[2] is one of nine elementary schools in Westland, a coastal community of 45,000 located in a metropolitan area close to the California-Mexico border. The community's history has been shaped by economic developments to the north and cultural and linguistic ties to the south. The city was incorporated in 1887 under the leadership of John Campbell, a northern California entrepreneur who purchased a 26,000-acre cattle ranch and planned to develop an industrial port city. For lack of a major railroad connection his plans failed, and Westland evolved slowly from a rural to a suburban community. Only in the past three decades has it become the city Campbell originally envisioned; there are now over 50 manufacturing plants and a thriving marine terminal. The city is an excellent labor market for skilled and semiskilled workers and has become for this socioeconomic group an attractive residential area because of low-rental housing. For these same reasons, over the years Westland has attracted a large number of Mexicans, part of the continuous in-migration that characterizes the border area. Among communities in the metropolitan area, according to a 1975 head of household census, Westland has the highest percentage of Hispanic people. Its culturally diverse population is reflected in the school district's 1977 report on racial and ethnic distribution of enrollment, as the following figures indicate: Hispanic (47.05 percent), White (30.78 percent), Black (7.30 percent), Asian or Pacific Isle (14.61 percent), and American Indian or Alaskan (0.21 percent).

When Campbell School was built in 1941 (and named for the city's founder), the site was still close to the center of the city. In the postwar years the population expanded to the east. The attendance area is now in the westernmost part of the city, adjacent to an industrial complex and the port facility and divided by a major north/south highway. To residents the neighborhood is still "Old Town Westland," a title confirmed by scattered "O.T.W." graffiti. The school's high proportion of Hispanic pupils (86.7 percent) confirms that it serves a Mexican American neighborhood.

Site Selection and Entrée

Campbell was chosen as the site because its bilingual program had been in operation for eight years. I wanted a school that had progressed beyond the initiation stage in program development. This would enable me to obtain data on characteristics and problems persisting over a period of time and on adaptations the school was making to judicial and legislative mandates.[3] I assumed at the outset that a district with nine elementary schools serving a heterogeneous population including a large number of Hispanics would have such schools. As it turned out, Campbell was the only school that met the criterion. Seven of the remaining eight schools were to begin bilingual programs the year of my study; the eighth had had a program for only two years.

The initiation of fieldwork in January, 1978, was preceded by three extended visits to Westland over a year's time—to discuss the proposal with district administrators, to obtain their permission to conduct the research, to determine which school would be the preferable site, and to present the proposal to the school faculty for review and approval. During these visits a parallel sequence of site selection procedures was carried out in a Mexican border community. In total design the research included a secondary line of inquiry to obtain data on the schooling experience Mexican children brought with them when they crossed the border with their families and eventually enrolled in Westland schools.[4] During my residence in the Westland area I observed in one of the Mexican community elementary schools at least once each week, while I spent the rest of the time at Campbell or at district-level activities relating to the Campbell program.

The letter of approval from the Westland School District affirmed support for research studies which "have implications for improving the instructional program of the district." The matter of relevance to school and district needs also came up in discussions with school board officials, teachers, and parents. One can argue that ethnography contains its own justification, as a scientific document which enlightens us on both diversity and commonality in human behavior. But the test of relevance appears to be endemic to educational research. It is an issue made more pressing through the intense and continuing critique of the schools' failure to provide equal educational opportunity. Hence the social-political context of educational ethnography creates a client relationship between ethnographer and subjects, even in the absence of a formal contractual agreement.

This relationship is made more complex by an evaluative dimension in educational research. To some degree all ethnographies are evaluative. As the ethnographer fits discrete pieces into patterns and systems, there emerge profiles of multiple realities—those of single individuals and groups—and ultimately that orderliness which the ethnographer finds in the system. Things are found to be not always as they seem or are believed or asserted to be—a basic tenet of the character structure of anthropology (Spindler 1963:5–14). However, for those being studied the findings become a form of evaluation. It is the "irreducible conflict" between researcher and subject (Becker 1964: 272–276) and an almost inevitable phenomenon of school ethnographies in our own culture.[5] The value system of public education levies an unrealizable schedule of expectations on schools. Consequently there is always a measure of failure or shortcoming of some proportion, and ethnographies of schooling inevitably to some degree expose this failure.

The Bilingual Program— History and Structure

The Campbell program predates by five years the 1974 Supreme Court decision, Lau vs. Nichols, which ruled that a school district's failure to provide non-English-speaking students with a program to deal with their language needs is in violation of Title VI of the Civil Rights Act. The decision was followed by the Lau Remedies, a set of guidelines developed by the Office of Civil Rights to assist districts that were out of compliance and those that wished to file a plan voluntarily. The remedies require adherence to the following conditions:

1. Schools must develop a systematic approach to determine those students who are linguistically different;
2. Schools must systematically and validly ascertain the language characteristics of their clients;
3. Schools must assess the achievement levels of their clients;
4. Schools must develop and implement a comprehensive instructional program that matches those identified needs.

The bilingual program at Campbell began as part of an interdistrict project involving three elementary districts and one high school district, and was funded by the U.S. Office of Education under Title VII (Bilingual Education) of the Elementary and Secondary Education Act. Each school was assigned a different grade level(s) at which to initiate a bilingual program. It fell to Campbell to start with grades 2 and 3. The problems associated with beginning in the middle grades were such that the following year the school shifted program development activities to kindergarten and first grade. Each year thereafter a grade was added until Campbell had its first six-year graduates in 1976.

Political shifts in district governance also affected the progress of bilingual education. In the early 1970s Mexican Americans achieved a majority on the school board. The incumbent superintendent's contract was terminated, and his deputy was promoted with the clear mandate to support and expand bilingual education. A Mexican American was employed as new deputy superintendent. In 1976 Fred Whitman, also a Mexican American, was promoted from fourth-grade teacher at Campbell to principal. The board chose him over non Spanish speaking Anglos who had more seniority in the system. It was felt his bilingual facility and ethnic background were essential to the successful development of the program and increased involvement of the predominantly Mexican American parental constituency in the life of the school.

The Campbell program began as a program open to all children in the district, in order to effect a better balance in the school's ethnic distribution and to try to maintain a 50–50 ratio of English-dominant and Spanish-dominant students in each classroom (stipulated by the guidelines of Title VII,

Bilingual Education Act). Open enrollment dropped the Hispanic population at Campbell only 5 percent, from 85 percent in 1971 to 80 percent in 1974, when approximately 100 children were bused in from other attendance areas. The ethnic imbalance did not change markedly, because many of the children bused in were themselves Hispanic. In 1974 the ethnic imbalance increased again as a second school began a bilingual program and children returned to that attendance area.

The judicial mandate and implementing guidelines do not prescribe a specific type of bilingual program model. The Westland School District adopted at Campbell a *language maintenance* model—as opposed to a *transitional* model, where a gradual shift is made from bilingual to English-only instruction, or an *immersion* model, in which all instruction is in English. In this maintenance model 80 percent of the instruction in the first grade is in the dominant language; 20 percent in the second language. By the fourth grade, instruction is divided equally between the two languages. Team teaching (as opposed to self-contained classrooms) is the mode at Campbell; each grade level (excepting the sixth) has both a Spanish component section taught by a bilingual teacher and an English component section taught by a teacher for whom bilingual competence is optional. The sixth grade is divided into two self-contained classes. One is an integral part of the bilingual program and is taught by a bilingual teacher. The second is an English-only combined 4/5/6 class created to serve transfer students with no bilingual background and students whose par-

FIRST GRADE

Time	Activity	Grouping
9:00–9:15	Opening exercises	Homeroom
9:15–10:00	Reading	Dominant language component
10:00–10:15	Recess	Primary grades
10:15–10:45	Language Arts	Dominant language component
10:45–11:15	Language Arts	Second language component
11:15–11:25	Preparation for lunch	Homeroom
11:25–12:00	Lunch	All grades
12:10–12:25	Post-lunch activities	Homeroom
12:25–1:00	Mathematics	Dominant language component
1:00–1:25	Social studies, etc.	Dominant language component
1:25–1:40	Recess	Primary grades
1:40–2:10	Music, etc.	Homeroom

FOURTH GRADE

Time	Activity	Grouping
8:30–8:50	Opening exercises, music, math	Homeroom
8:50–10:00	Reading	Dominant language component
10:00–10:15	Recess	Intermediate grades
10:15–11:20	Reading	Second language component
11:20–11:30	Preparation for lunch	Homeroom
11:30–12:10	Lunch	All grades
12:10–1:00	Language arts	Dominant/second language components (switch every two weeks)
1:00–1:30	Physical Education	Homeroom
1:30–2:10	Mathematics	Homeroom

ents do not want them in a bilingual program, their right under state law.

The accompanying schedules represent the daily activities of both components in the first and fourth grades. Pupils change classrooms and teachers whenever the "second language component" is designated. In the first grade, for example, between 10:45 and 11:15 Ms. Seda's Spanish component section exchanges classrooms with Ms. Langer's English component section and each section receives second language instruction in language arts. The increase in second language instruc-

tional time in the fourth-grade schedule is reflected in the reading and language arts time assigned to the "second language component."

In the class schedules, *Homeroom* is designated as a distinct grouping because it is the organizational device used to meet the state law requirement that no more than two-thirds of a bilingual class shall be limited-English-speaking pupils. Table 1 shows the language dominance proportions in the first-grade homerooms of Ms. Seda and Ms. Langer. In the early grades, homeroom activities are typically *social* (sto-

TABLE 1 **Language Dominance Proportions in the First-Grade Homerooms**

Pupils	Teachers	
	Seda	*Langer*
Spanish component	two-thirds	one-third
English component	one-third	two-thirds

rytelling, sharing weekend experiences), *ceremonial* (pledge to the flag), and *administrative* (taking roll, making announcements) in function. By the fourth grade, as the class schedule indicates, the homeroom grouping is also used for formal instruction. Table 2 indicates by group the change in the percentage of instructional time from the first to the fourth grade.

The district's stated goal is to develop literate bilingual-bicultural students who can function in two languages in the milieus of two cultures. Westland has developed a complex system of classifying and assessing a student's *bilingual* profile. But *bicultural* "literacy" remains a diffuse and difficult objective. Gibson critiques the application of biculturalism theory to educational practice:

First, in actual practice it runs the danger of equating culture with a language or ethnic group, for example, Chicanos,

Chicano culture. . . . Second, it tends to overemphasize ethnic identity, running the risk of preventing students from choosing to emphasize other identities. Third, it tends to see bilingual-bicultural education as a panacea for all social and educational ills. . . . And, finally, a fourth weakness with the bicultural education approach . . . is that it tends to equate education with formal school instruction and to presume that the school is responsible or should take responsibility for the child's "socialization in two or more cultures." [Gibson, 1976:14]

In reference to a theoretical perspective on the individual experience within two convergent cultural systems, the term *bicultural* (or its variations *biculturation, biculturalism, biculturality*) has been used infrequently, mainly in studies of socialization (Polgar 1960), acculturation (Bruner 1956, McFee 1968), acculturation and self-concept (Arias 1976), and ethnic identity and acculturation (Clark, Kaufmann, and

TABLE 2 **Percentage of Instructional Time by Groups in First and Fourth Grades**

	First Grade	Fourth Grade
Dominant language component	57%	32%
Second language component	13%	31%
Homeroom	30%	37%

Pierce 1976). The research by Clark, Kaufmann, and Pierce on three generations of Mexican Americans and Japanese Americans is especially pertinent to this study. The authors describe six ways in which the three generations define themselves in relation to their "bicultural life situations." They report that the most significant factor in the six different "styles of bicultural life" is individual choice in the presentation of the self as more Anglicized or more "ethnic" (1976:236).

We may legitimately think of Campbell as a bicultural life situation. To be sure, ethnic proportions are heavily skewed toward Hispanic children. Eighty-seven percent, or 355 pupils, are of Spanish origin. Ten percent (41) are Anglo, 1 percent (4) are Filipino, and slightly over 1 percent (5) are black. But we shall see that traditional Anglo values are strongly reflected in schooling processes and in the socializing goals of the teachers. As a school Campbell is infinitely more complex than a "life situation." It is viewed here both as an academic organization with internally generated social norms, role expectations, and patterned behavior and as an instrument of cultural transmission and socialization for the parental constituency, the community, and the state.

I turn now to an examination of schooling processes and the bicultural experience. I will draw primarily on data from classroom observations and from parent and teacher interviews. I will seek to answer the following questions: How sensitive or impervious to cultural differences are schooling processes? Does the dominant Mexican American pupil presence in the classroom affect in observable ways classroom practices or teacher behavior and teacher values?

Parents and faculty play important roles as socialization agents and models of bilingual-bicultural adaptation. I will, therefore, preface the examination of schooling processes with parent and teacher data relating to ethnic identity and attitudes toward the bilingual-bicultural program.

Parents and Teachers: Background and Attitudes

When parents register their children at Campbell, they are asked to provide the school with information about ethnic identity and language dominance. The process for determining the latter begins with a Home Language Survey. Racial/ethnic proportions among Campbell pupils are derived from parental responses to the following checklist about the "racial or ethnic background" of their children:

_____ Black (Black, Negro, Afro-American, African descent)
_____ Asian (Asian American, Japanese, Chinese or Korean)
_____ Spanish origin (Chicano, Mexican, Mexican American, Spanish descent)
_____ Filipino (Filipino American, Filipino descent)
_____ White (White, Anglo, Pakistani, Indo-European)
_____ Decline to answer

Most Campbell parents checked the "Spanish origin" category.[6] They have close ties to Mexico. Typically all but one member of the immediate family—husband, wife, and both sets of parents—were born in Mexico. Slightly more husbands than wives were born in the United States. Almost half of the families maintain continuing contacts with Mexico through weekly or bimonthly trips across the border to shop or visit relatives.

Approximately 20 percent of Campbell parents classify themselves as Mexican and another 20 percent as Mexican American; 50 percent state they do not care whether they are referred to as Mexican or Mexican Americans.[7] Dissatisfaction with the term Chicano is frequently expressed, as in these four examples:

It is not a nice word; it's used for lower-class Mexicans.

Sounds kind of vulgar.

I don't feel insulted if I am called Chicana, but I prefer Mexican and want my children to be referred to as Mexican American.

If I were called Chicana I would use the experience to judge the person who used the term on me. It is a name used for us in these times. Mexican American is used by those who are not too political-minded.

In general, when Mexican American parents talk about the ethnic identity of their children they relate it to language learning and bilingual competence. As one parent said:

The bilingual program is valuable because you learn about your own heritage and you can't learn about your culture without knowing the language.

Anglo parents value bilingual competence as a tool for adapting to cultural diversity. In the words of one of them:

You should know the language of the people you live in the midst of.

Most Campbell parents (including Anglos, blacks, and Filipinos) express strong support for the bilingual program.[8] The school's standing has improved dramatically over the past 10 years. When the program was initiated in 1968, the school building was in a state of deterioration, playground facilities were poor, and parents felt the school's location in a Mexican American neighborhood would prevent any change in the school's fortunes. Now, 10 years later, the building has been renovated, the playground greatly improved, and an adjacent mini-park developed, and the school itself has a statewide reputation for the quality of its program. Also, parents perceive their children as having an experience in the school much different from their own. The point is most vividly illustrated in this interview with a bilingual Mexican American parent:

Q What was it like to go to school at Campbell when there was no bilingual program?

A We weren't allowed to speak Spanish and were often punished if we did. It got to be embarrassing to be Mexican American.

Q What is your feeling about the program today?

A *La salvación para los latinos.*

The value this parent places on Campbell's bilingual program has its genesis in his schooling experience as a member of an ethnic minority in an Anglo-dominated society. The expectations he *now* has for schooling at Campbell reflect his judgment about what kind of education is functional in a world in which biculturalism is still a continuing reality.

Parental attitudes about the program are presumably affected also by the quality of interpersonal relations among faculty, staff, and parents. Parents characterize the school as very friendly, a judgment which is informed by the increasingly significant role they play in the life of the school. Under the leadership of Martha Cuñeo, the school's community aide, there is an active classroom volunteer program. Of more importance, parents are involved in recommending and evaluating changes and improvements in the school's academic and extracurricular program. Campbell has three parent advisory committees—for compensatory education, bilingual education, and preschool programs. A report on the membership, plans, and accomplishments of these committees is mandated by the California State Department of Education. The committees and committee officers meet monthly in combined session, along with the Parent Teachers Association. It is in this setting that the quality of parental involvement is shaped. In their review role, committee members become knowledgeable in a great number of school-centered topics about which they are asked to make a judgment. The monthly meetings do not seem restrained by any preconceived notion of committee boundaries. Parents ask if new basketball nets can be installed; whether noon supervisors check the bathrooms; how the weekly in-service teacher meetings are going; what is being done about articulation problems between elementary and junior high schools; what better system can be developed for preschool sign-up; and what is the real role of parent advisory groups.

The Campbell faculty, which parents find to be friendly, is composed of relatively young individuals (average age in the early 30s) with diverse social and ethnic backgrounds. There are 14 teachers, excluding the preschool and learning disability classes—13 females and one male. Gene Stinson jokes about what an invaluable "token" he is—male, black, raised in a Mexican American barrio, bilingual. Among the 13 female teachers, seven are Mexican American and bilingual. Three of them were born in Mexico and attended Mexican schools in the early grades. One of the six female Anglo teachers is also bilingual. The first-grade English component teacher, Betty Langer, began teaching at Campbell in 1963, five years before the bilingual program was begun. The other teachers have joined the faculty since 1968. When the bilingual program was initiated, retirement and voluntary transfer eliminated opposition within the faculty. Those joining the faculty since 1968 were attracted to the program and were employed because they could work effectively within it. The teachers believe in the value of a language-maintenance program but differ about organizational aspects—for example, the best use of oral language-development aides, the amount of time Spanish-dominant children spend in English instruction, the necessity for English-only classes.

In addition to the teachers, there are other important adults in the school who present differing models of bilingual-bicultural adaptation. Fred Whitman, the principal, Martha Cuñeo, the community aide, and Norma Sevilla, the school secretary, are Mexican American and bilingual. All instructional aides in the Spanish component classes are Mexican American and to varying degrees bilingual.[9] Two of the instructional aides in the English component classes are also Mexican American, and one of them is bilingual. One instructional aide is Filipino. The rest are Anglo. The two reading specialists and the part-time speech therapist are Anglo. The part-time school psychologist is Mexican American and bilingual. The full-time librarian and the part-time nurse are Filipino. Their aides are Mexican American and bilingual. The oral language development aides are Mexican American and again to varying degrees bilingual. The head custodian is Filipino. His assistant is Anglo. The head of the cafeteria staff is Mexican American. Her co-workers are Anglo. The noon supervisors are Mexican American. The preschool and learning disability teachers are Anglo. Their aides, with one exception, are Mexican American.

When children enter Campbell classrooms, they encounter teachers who make few distinctions between the social and cultural characteristics of Mexican American and Anglo pupils. The following six statements respond to the question "What ethnic differences do you find among Campbell pupils?"

As to ethnic differences, well, the Mexican child is more dependent, more sensitive. With the Anglo child you can say "Do this" or "Do that" and he will. With the Mexican child you have to be there to help. I don't see any other differences, but I think because I have a Mexican background I use gestures and body movements that children with a Mexican background understand better than Anglo children. When it comes to talking to them about their ethnic identity, I sometimes try to help them if I know

their background, but I don't want to put something in their head. If children are Mexican American I let them find out their own identity.

I think there are ethnic differences, but I'm not sure how to pinpoint them. The children do seem different from previous schools I've taught at where there were mainly Anglo children. They seem to get along better, to resolve conflicts better. Maybe it is because of close family ties, so that when there are conflicts on the playground older brothers take care of younger brothers or sisters and intervene to protect them and end a conflict.

Maybe there do not seem to be ethnic differences among Campbell children because of the high percentage of Mexican Americans. Still, it is my experience that Mexicans show more affection. It is a touching culture and Anglos have more of a hands-off culture. Then, too, a child with a Mexican background seldom looks an adult in the eye.

Sometimes Anglo children exhibit more individuality in doing and choosing assignments when I give them the opportunity. Then to threaten a Mexican child with reporting his behavior to a parent is much more serious than it would be for an Anglo child. As to a child's sense of ethnic identity, well, I told them I was Mexican American because I was born in America but have a Mexican background. But kids, even if they are born here, don't accept that version of themselves. I was trying to show them that Mexicans are those who live in Mexico. You have to live there, not just be born there, to consider yourself a Mexicano. A few children in my class say they are Chicanos, but I think they get that from their bigger brothers.

Mexican Americans are more cooperative and respectful. Otherwise I don't see any differences.

When I taught an English component class and the Spanish component group would come in during the day, I thought there was a difference, that is, the Spanish component children were more quiet. Now I'm not as certain. Maybe it is because I'm now teaching a Spanish component class and I see more variation within this group than across the two groups. There is a difference; I just can't verbalize it. I don't know that I behave any differently toward one ethnic group than another. Perhpas my teaching is more affected by achievement level than ethnicity.

The ethnic differences teachers identify are characteristics of social behavior. Mexican American pupils are more "polite," "respectful," "quiet," "affectionate," and "cooperative." These are traits which parents value. In response to the question "What personal traits do you want most of all for your children to develop?" Spanish-speaking parents replied: "*respecto*," "*buena conducta*," "*serio*," "*educado*," "*disciplinado*." English-speaking parents responded with: "respect for elders," "respect for others' rights, privileges, and property," "good behavior," "being a good student," "honest." These are traits which teachers also value and which, incidentally, enable them to proceed more efficiently with the management of classroom life.

Instructional Processes

The bilingual-bicultural model at Campbell emphasizes developmental placement and individualized instruction. The latter is implemented through the use of curriculum management sys-

tems. These are essentially systems of terminal objectives (lengthy lists) and criterion-referenced tests to be used with each student, primarily in the areas of reading and math. The demand these systems place on teachers' time is formidable. Their widespread use determines to a great extent the kinds of socializing experiences pupils are, in fact, having. In brief, curriculum management systems are, like state and federal mandates, a kind of intervention in the life of the school—and quite literally an intervention between teacher and pupil. Teachers observe rightly that these systems free them for more individualized instruction. At the same time, the systems (by definition and in operation) provide not only the content of learning experience but also the structure and sequence of behaviors required to reach a learning goal. In the process they foster the formation and maintenance of small groups of pupils who function as a part of the system but who also evolve adaptations to it. A practical consequence for pupils is the opportunity to learn how to manage a group-oriented academic enviroment.

To explicate curriculum system organization and process I will use observational data on two classrooms, a first/second-grade-combined Spanish component class and a fifth-grade English component class. Over a week of observations were made in the Spanish component class.[10] The description which follows also draws on a sequence of 35mm slides covering every major activity in the class during a day, and on protocols from an interview which focused on the teacher's perceptions of the content and context of each slide. Figure 1 is a schematic diagram of the

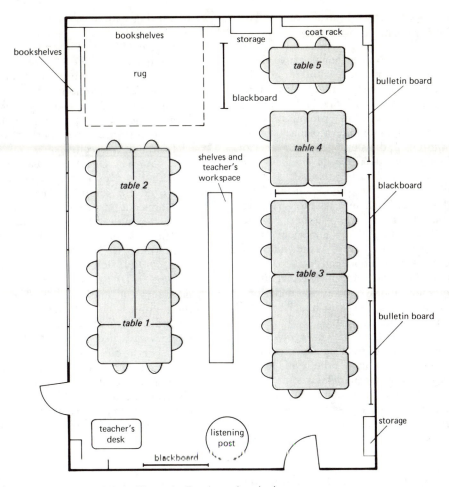

Figure 1 First/second-grade classroom.

classroom, in which tables are numbered to designate group work areas referred to in the notes. The teacher is Olivia Flores, who is in her second year of teaching. She earned her bachelor's degree in Spanish and her teaching credential from a California university and is presently working on a bilingual/bicultural teaching credential. She was born in Mexico and at age 10 came to the United States with her family. Her instructional aide, Gloria Rendon, was also born in Mexico. Ms. Rendon is a part-time student at a local community college and aspires to become a teacher.

School begins at 9:00 A.M. for first graders. When the bell rings, the children line up in two rows at the edge of the playground near the classroom. When they are quiet Ms. Flores signals them to go in. They hang up their jackets and sweaters and gather on the rug in the far corner of the room.

9:00–9:15 Homeroom (two-thirds Spanish component and one-third English component pupils). Most mornings the aide is in charge of opening homeroom activities—announcements, taking roll, obtaining information from children, and listening to accounts of their weekend *(Vamos a compatir que hacían al fin de la semana).* Ms. Rendon asks a girl to start *(¿Quieres decir algo?).* The girl talks about a visit to a relative. Other hands go up. Another girl describes (in English) an automobile accident her family was in. At the end of the account Ms. Rendon translates for Spanish component children. The girl adds a comment and a boy sitting on the outside of the rug turns to his friend and translates into Spanish.

9:15–10:00 Spanish Component. Ms. Flores dismisses the English component children, who cross the hall to the English component classroom. Their Spanish component counterparts enter and sit down at assigned tables, in groups organized on the basis of reading levels. This period is for handwriting, vocabulary, spelling, and special topics in social studies. Ms. Flores is sitting on the rug, using flash cards with three pupils who are the slowest group. Before she starts she makes sure the groups at tables 1 and 2 are started with writing exercises. Those groups are middle to above average in reading. Ms. Rendon is working at table 3 with the second-grade reading group, the fastest group, to which the more advanced first graders are also assigned. She writes the following words on the board: *cielo, ciudad, violín, piano, viaje, peine, reina, seis diamente, murcielago.* She talks about their meaning and tells the pupils to use the words in sentences.

The Oral Language Development aide is working with a slow-to-average reading group at table 4.

9:30 Ms. Flores sends the slow group back to table 5 to draw and she moves to tables 1 and 2 to check their progress. Ms. Rendon finishes working with second graders at table 3, gives them an assignment, and moves to a work area to prepare materials for the next lesson.

9:40 The O.L.D. aide has finished with the group at table 4 and departed for another classroom. Ms. Flores and Ms. Rendon are now preparing materials for the next hour. The children are at work on various exercises.

10:00–10:15 Recess

10:15–11:00 Spanish Component. This period is for mathematics. There are three groups. The fast students, mostly second graders, are at table 3. Two first graders are also in this group. They come over to the table to get the assignment and then return to their "reading level" seats at tables 1 and 2. The other children at tables 1 and 2 are at the medium achievement level in mathematics. The slowest math group sits at tables 4 and 5 and the pupils move back and forth between the tables and the rug as Ms. Flores works with them in small groups or on an individual basis. Three children from this group are working on a numbers puzzle. The fast math students are working with the aide on clock time practice.

10:40 The teacher is now at tables 1 and 2 with the medium group, working on sets of five.

11:00–11:45 Spanish Component. All groups are working on reading. The aide is with the fast group at table 3. They are using a second-grade reader and doing exercises. Ms. Flores starts the groups at tables 1 and 2 on exercises and moves to the rug to work with the slowest children, again using flash cards. The O.L.D.

aide has come back to the classroom to work for 20 minutes with a slow group of pupils.

11:40–11:45 Homeroom. Homeroom classes are formed again as an exchange takes place between the two rooms. Tables are straightened and cleaned up, lunch tickets are handed out, and the children are taken to the cafeteria.

11:45–12:20 Lunch

12:20–12:25 Homeroom. The children come in from the playground. Ms. Flores instructs them on the activities for the rest of the day, and the Spanish component children go to the other classroom.

12:25–1:25 English Component. The English component class gathers on the rug with the teacher, who shows them a picture book on hygiene. She talks in Spanish about each picture. There is much laughter, especially at the last picture, which shows a little boy and a little girl in a tub. When she finishes the book she divides them up into two groups. The aide works at table 3 with children who are already beginning to read in Spanish. Ms. Flores works at tables 1 and 2 with 15 children who are not ready to read in Spanish. She uses the Peabody kit and other materials. They look at pictures and she talks with them about the pictures in Spanish, now and then translating to help them with the lesson.

12:45 The teacher goes to the board and writes *A mi me gusteria ser* . . . and tells them in English and Spanish they are to draw a picture of someone they want to be when they grow up. Then they are to tell the teacher in Spanish what they have drawn. The aide continues to work with the faster group at table 3.

1:05 Ms. Flores calls the children to the rug. She has them come up one at a time, stand by her, hold up the drawing, and talk about it. In most cases she has to tell the child what the Spanish word is for the occupation the child has drawn. They have drawn pictures of a nurse *(enfermera)*, painter *(artista)*, teacher *(maestra)*, and gardener *(jardinero)*.

1:25–1:40 Recess

1:40–2:10 Homeroom. The children listen to records, sing, practice dances, finish drawings, copy messages to their parents, and prepare to go home.

Ms. Flores believes dependency is a basic trait of Mexican American children. She thinks teachers need to instill independence if the children are not to be at a disadvantage throughout school.[11] She describes how she does this:

I tell them at the very beginning of the year one of the most important lessons they can learn is how to become independent. I work on that over and over, because the Mexican family is very dependent on each other. Mexican children have a more difficult time learning the skills and attitudes necessary to proceed more independently. It takes a lot of discipline. I am very strict. They know when I assign something they are to sit down and do it. I tell them, "If you do the work I'll come to you after working with the other groups. All groups need help but there are only two people." If they make noise or are disruptive I cut down on the time I work with them or I keep them in at recess or deny them physical education time or, in more severe cases, assign them detention after school. Basically, I tell them not to waste time, but to make good use of their time because the clock is always running.

Learning to work independently in a small group is required for successful adaptation to curriculum systems. Now and then pupils engage in cooperative behavior—give spelling tests, hear each other read, answer questions, correct mistakes. Most of the time they proceed independently through each phase of the system—from one exercise to another, from one unit to another, from one color code to another. Their progress is evaluated by the teacher, who then assigns the next learning increment to be undertaken. But the isolating influence of a curriculum system is muted by the dynamics of small groups, and this effect is enhanced by the absence of continuous direct adult supervision.

Pupil attributes which Ms. Flores seeks to develop in her class of predominantly Mexican American children reflect traditional Anglo values: independence, productivity, time-orientation. She believes such values (and those teaching processes and required pupil behavior which follow from them) are functional to academic progress—as functional for Mexican American children as for the small number of Anglo children she sees every day during homeroom periods. We shall see that the fifth-grade English component teacher, Ms. Blakey, shares this point of view. Through observations of her class I will examine in more detail organizational and instructional aspects of curriculum systems.

Gwen Blakey has had five years of teaching experience but is in her first year at Campbell. There are 22 pupils in the English component, 17 of whom are classified (by their parents) as of "Spanish origin," in most cases because both parents were born in Mexico. Four of these 17 pupils were themselves born in Mexico and are completely bilingual.

For two other pupils English was once a second language but is now their dominant language. When Ms. Blakey starts the school day—with Homeroom—there are 29 pupils (13 from her English component group and 16 from the Spanish component group) and the ethnic mix is more complex. She has a class which includes nine pupils who were born in Mexico, five of whom attended school in Mexico in the early grades. She also has six NES/LES pupils (non-English speaking/limited English speaking) from the Spanish component group, who, since neither she nor her instructional aide is bilingual, must depend on bilingual peers to translate instructional messages when needed.

The classroom has the same kind of furniture and spatial arrangement as Ms. Lopez' class—tables grouped together, partitions to isolate the sight and sound of special instructional groups, library and curriculum system material, and files. The day begins at 8:30. I will describe only the morning classes of one day.

8:30–9:00 Homeroom. The usual activity is handwriting practice. Today the class is going to write a letter to a United States Senator.

8:35 Ms. Blakey calls the class to order and describes the format of the letter and the kind of information appropriate.

8:38 B. [Ms. Blakey] hands out cards with basic information about the format and possible subjects of the letters and then answers questions about the assignment.

8:43 B. moves about the room helping individual pupils with their letters. Mrs. Prescott, the aide, does the same.

8:47 Two sixth graders enter the room and deliver a message to B. She writes on the board information about a school dance scheduled for the next Friday afternoon and then reads the announcement to the class.

8:50 B. and P. [Prescott] continue helping with the letters.

9:00–10:00 Spanish Component

9:00 The bell rings and B. says, "If you haven't finished, we will work on the letter later today. Everything off your desks."

9:02 English component pupils in B.'s homeroom leave for instruction in Spanish, and Spanish component pupils from Gene Stinson's homeroom (Mr. Stinson is Ms. Blakey's team teacher) come in from across the hall for a reading and spelling lesson in English.

9:03 Sylvia Gomez, an O.L.D. aide, comes in to work with the slowest pupils on English oral language development. She talks with them at a table behind a portable partition in one corner of the room.

9:05 "Pearl Divers!" the teacher calls out, and a group with readers in hand come to B.'s table.

In addition to Ms. Gomez' ESL group there are four other groups (from three to five pupils in each group) spread out at different tables. The pupils move to an assigned table and group as soon as they enter the room and without prompting from the teacher. Each group begins work in one of four different curriculum or instructional systems and in the course of a period complete a unit of work in that system. They begin (and frequently complete) a unit of work in a second system. The four systems in use are: graded readers in a reading series; a "multilevel reading laboratory" consisting of sets of color-coded reading selections and tests; an individualized spelling program with color-coded word lists and a log to fill in with the completion of each list; a reading skills series consisting of sets of booklets covering topics such as "working with sounds," "following directions," and "getting the main idea." Associated with these systems, to varying degrees depending on the structure of the system and the predilections of teachers, are pedagogical devices such as pretests, post-tests, peer tutoring, and an almost unending flow of ditto sheets.

During this first period Ms. Blakey works for most of the hour with the reading series. She calls each group in turn to a table near her desk and hears them read. The aide works with one of the other groups for a short period of time and then moves to still another group to check their progress. At intervals teacher and aide pause to talk to each other or to obtain and distribute additional curriculum materials.

10:00–10:15 Recess. B. has playground duty this week. When the bell rings, tables are cleaned, and the room is quiet, she signals dismissal and accompanies her class to the upper playground reserved for the older pupils.

10:15–11:00 English Component. Reading and language arts. Organizational and instructional processes are the same as in the previous period except there are six groups instead of five.

11:00–11:35 Social Studies. English and Spanish components alternate each week. An elaborated version of a topic is presented in the primary language; a simplified, summarizing version in the second language.

11:00 B. is setting up a film on California missions. There is a knock at the door and a father of one of the boys enters. He says he wants to know something about math, about how proportions and ratios are done, so that he can help his son know when he is wrong. B. works with the father for 10 minutes. The pupils remain quiet but do little work. When the father leaves, B. turns to the son and says, "Now your father can help you when you get that kind of problem wrong." The boy says nothing but continues to look at the baseball glove he has in his hand.

11:15 B. begins describing the film. The room is noisy. She keeps talking and then pauses and starts asking them questions about what she has just said. The room becomes quieter and she begins the film.

11:38 The film ends. B. comments about life in the missions and then tells them to get ready to switch back to homeroom.

11:40–11:45 Homeroom. Announcements and preparations for lunch. When the bell rings she takes them to the cafeteria line and then goes to the faculty room for her lunch.

The afternoon period begins at 12:25 with math. Art and science are at 1:10 and physical education at 1:50. The

school day ends at 2:15. The Homeroom grouping is used for all afternoon periods.

Excluding recess, the lunch period, and physical education, there are approximately 4 hours and 5 minutes of instructional time in the school day. On the basis of an analysis of my observational notes for the entire day, instructional time was distributed as shown in Table 3. During the remaining 16 percent (approximately 40 minutes) of class time, Ms. Blakey was mainly involved in class management activities, e.g., making announcements, disciplining the class, supervising a change in class periods, organizing class activities. In comparing the nature and sequence of classroom activities reported here with observations made on other days in Ms. Blakey's class and in other classrooms, I find the use of the various instructional modes indicated above to be representative of classroom life in general at Campbell. There are, to be sure, variations in Ms. Blakey's class as well as those of the other teachers. Generally, however, across all classes the group and individual instruction modes predominate, and those values of inde-

TABLE 3   **Distribution of Instructional Time**

Mode	Time	Percentage
Class instruction: The attention of the entire class is required for purposes of instruction; the teacher (or a film) is soliciting pupil involvement	29 min.	12
Group instruction: The teacher is working with a small group (3–6 students)	1 hr. 18 min.	32
Individual instruction: The teacher is working with a single student, at her desk or at the student's place of work	<u>1 hr. 39 min.</u>	<u>40</u>
	3 hrs. 26 min.	84

pendence, productivity, and time-orientation which Ms. Flores deemed to be essential to academic success in her first/second-grade class are operative in other classes as well.

Within these instructional modes, social as well as academic transactions are a continuing part of the daily life of classrooms—at the tables, at bookshelves where system units and records are kept in boxes, at the sink where students clean up after art work or wash off plastic sheets used to write answers to workbook exercises. While the data I have are inconclusive, there is some evidence that such transactions increase through the grades as pupils become more practiced in the mechanics of curriculum systems. In the upper grades there is more movement in classrooms, more social interaction within and across groups, more temporary deviations from assignments underway, more language switching in informal exchange. Presumably these social settings are useful to pupils as they work out personal adaptations to the bilingual-bicultural program.

The consequences these modes have for individual students may be further explicated through observational notes on the classroom experience of a single student. At my request, Gene Stinson chose a "typical" boy from his fifth-grade Spanish component class and obtained permission for me to accompany him throughout the school day.[12] Gilberto Estrada is 11 years of age, and of medium height and weight for his age. He has light skin, dark hair, pleasant angular features, and a stocky frame. With his parents, an older brother, and two younger sisters, he lives in a small frame house three blocks from school.

His father is a cannery worker; his mother manages the household and is active as a classroom volunteer at the school. Mr. Estrada was born in Mexico, Mrs. Estrada, in California. The two boys were born in California, the girls, in Mexico. The movement of the family back and forth across the border over the years was due to changing job opportunities and extended family relationships. Gilberto was three when the family moved to Mexico and five when they returned to California. He says that in Mexico he forgot his English and that after several years in California he forgot his Spanish. Now he feels he is bilingual, but stronger in English. He speaks English at home but generally speaks Spanish with his friends at school, because most of them are not so bilingual as he is. Mr. Stinson rates Gilberto as bilingual but not yet biliterate and thinks he is stronger in Spanish than in English.

The day begins with Homeroom. I will describe only the first two periods.

8:20 G. [Gilberto] arrives at school, goes to the upper playground, puts down his books, and greets a classmate, and the two join in an impromptu kickball game.

8:30 The bell rings. The game continues until S. [Gene Stinson] appears and calls them to line up at the door. G. stops, retrieves his books, and moves into the line. He leans against the student in front of him, an expression of mock fatigue on his face.

8:32 S. tells them to go in. G. straightens up and moves forward into the building, down the hall, and into the classroom.

8:34 G. sits down at a table near the back of the room, takes books and papers out of the storage drawer under the table, stacks them next to books he has brought, rearranges the collection, and puts most of it back. He keeps out his language arts book and a piece of writing paper.

8:35 S. says, "May I have your attention. We'll start today with handwriting. Take out your books and do p. 17 and p. 34. Sit up, use good posture, and [he turns to one boy] don't clinch the pencil so tightly. Relax and you can write better." G. turns to a boy sitting at the table with him and asks, *"Qué páginas dijo?"* His classmate tells him and G. turns to page 17 and begins copying sentences from the exercise.

8:40 G. writes slowly. He completes four sentences, looks up and gazes around the room, and taps his pencil on his teeth. Then he returns to copying sentences.

8:45 G. is still writing. S. is returning paragraphs on "America, Land of Opportunity" which the class wrote the previous day. He says, "Some of you wrote good papers." He puts G.'s paper down on the table. The grade is C. G. picks it up, looks at it, turns to his tablemate and, pointing to the grade at the bottom of the sheet, says, *"Vea!"*

8:47 G. starts copying sentences again. S. breaks in, "When you finish the exercise you can do homework if you haven't finished that assignment ... *Cuando terminan el ejercicio pueden hacer la tarea, si no la completaran."* G. writes one more sentence, sets the paper aside, puts the book in drawer, and takes out his math text and homework paper. He is doing two- and three-digit multiplication exercises. He has six problems completed on his homework paper and, turning to the text, finds the seventh, copies it down, and starts to work.

8:53 G. has completed three problems and is working on a fourth. He continues to work slowly; now and then he looks up and around the room to see what others are doing; he watches the teacher help a boy at a nearby table.

8:55 G. has stopped in the middle of a problem. S. comes by and asks what's wrong. G. shrugs his shoulders and S. proceeds to work the problem and explain it to G.

9:00 The bell rings. The Spanish component class is scheduled to go to Ms. Blakey's room for instruction in English. G. continues to work on the math problems. S. says "O.K." G. puts away the math, gets out a reader, stands up, and says to a classmate "Jorge, are you going to play keep-away *otra vez?"* Jorge answers, *"Sí."* G. leaves the room, goes across the hall into Ms. Blakey's room, and sits down at a table with Jorge.

9:06 G. and Jorge start talking about a Walk-a-Thon they might sign up for. B. tells class to get into reading groups. The boys stop talking. B. says they can read silently or to each other. G. and Jorge find the story in the reader and begin alternately reading sentences to each other.

9:17 G. and Jorge are still reading to each other. They have not interrupted their work in the past 10 minutes. They work to the persistent but low-key sound of classmates reading to each other or to the teacher—or talking. It is a sound punctuated at irregular intervals by Ms. Blakey's call for another reading group.

9:29 G. and Jorge finish the story. G. stretches, and looks around the room, and then he and Jorge begin idly thumbing through the reader, pausing to look at the pictures.

9:32 G. looks up, lets the page slip from his hand, gazes around the room, says *"Pues . . . ,"* gets up, and goes over to the reading skills series kit on a desk near the door. He takes out his folder. In it he has written what his assignment would be for today. The aide has already removed from the folder the previous assignment he completed. He takes a green booklet with a story, "A Hero of the Air," returns to his seat, and begins reading.

9:39 He finishes the story and begins to answer the questions on a work sheet.

9:41 G. gets up and goes to the pencil sharpener on the wall near the teacher's desk and a bulletin board. Begins looking at class pictures that are tacked on the board. Jorge comes up to look too.

9:43 They return to their table and continue working on the story questions.

9:49 B. says, "May I have Silver Twist?" G. and Jorge put away the booklets, pick up their readers, and go to the teacher's table. They are joined by two girls who are in the same reading group but who sit at a separate table. As they mill around the table G. starts arranging where everyone is to sit: *"Sienta te alli e yo, aqui."*

9:52 They are settled and B. says, "Listen as I read the questions to you and I will tell you how and where to find the answer." She has written questions on the board about the story they are to read. She takes one question and shows them where the answer is in the text. Then she says, "Any questions? Who needs paper?" She hands out paper and the two girls and Jorge return to their tables. G. remains to copy the questions and then returns to his table.

9:57 G. begins reading the story.

9:59 G. finishes the story and starts on the first question. He glances at Jorge and points to where the answer to the first question can be found.

10:00 The bell rings. G. gets up and the students return to Mr. Stinson's room.

Ms. Blakey says that "to make the system work you have to keep after them from the first day—to teach them to work on their own. I'm not in the business of saying to children, 'Now take out your books.'" So Gilberto (like his Mexican American and Anglo classmates) has to learn to "work on his own," while he is in Ms. Blakey's room as well as Mr. Stinson's, whether English is the language of communication or Spanish and without regard to his ethnic background and identity or the bilingual/bicultural program.

Extra-Classroom Activities and Biculturalism

Although Campbelll has a multiethnic/multiracial pupil population, the program emphasis has been bicultural. The effect has been a rich infusion of Mexican-oriented tradition into the life of the school and significantly more participation by the predominantly Mexican American parental constituency. In recent years the principal's concern has been that the school's program would disproportionately reflect Mexican culture. He has sought to make sure that Anglo and Mexican traditions are fairly represented in the school's program of celebrations, folk dances, and dramatic presentations. In assemblies this year the school celebrated Halloween, multiethnic American leaders, Thanksgiving, Christmas, *Día de la Bandera* (Mexican Flag Day), *Día del Niño* (Children's Day), *Cinco de Mayo* (Battle of Puebla, May 5, 1862), and Flag Day. There were other celebrations. Parents gave a dinner (at 3:00 P.M.) in honor of the teachers (*Día del Maestro).* When the state superintendent of instruction paid a morning visit to the school and the district superintendent requested that a coffee hour be arranged, six long tables were loaded with Mexican dishes, salads, and desserts.

There are celebrations which have no ethnic or national identification but which are anchored in the normative system of the school. Each month a citizenship awards assembly is held. Certificates are given to those students nominated by their teacher in each class. The assembly is held on the playground. Pupils bring out chairs and arrange rows in a semicircle. A podium with a public address system is set up, and the principal begins with introductory remarks about the importance of the awards.[13]

> Today we are going to recognize the students who have been good citizens for the months of April and May. It's a very important ceremony and assembly for us and it should be for you too.
>
> *Hoy vamos a reconocer los alumnos quien sidos buenos ciudadanos para los meses de abril y mayo. Esto es una asamblea que es muy importante para todos, para los maestros, para los ayudantes y el director y los alumnos también.*

> I want you to listen again to all the various reasons that the teachers present and express, when they come to the microphone, about how you can be a good citizen. And although this is our last month for recognizing good citizens, many of you will be here again next year and I want you to work hard toward receiving one of these awards for next year, if, in fact, you didn't receive one this year.
>
> *Otra vez espero todos los alumnos que escuchen las varias razones que expresan los maestros. Una persona pueda ser buen ciudadano en varias maneras y varias modos y es importante que todos escuchemos estas razones. Aunque esta es la última asamblea para este año de buen*

comportamiento, muchos de ustedes van a estar aquí el año entrante y yo espero que ustedes trabajan muy industrioso para recibir este certificado de buen comportamiento en al año entrante si no fue posible recibir uno en este año.

Spanish component teachers, like the principal, translate as they present awards—and, like their English component colleagues, base their awards on achievement values which facilitate academic success and social values which enhance interpersonal relations in classroom life. They reward students for working hard, helping others, making unusual progress, being sensitive to the needs of others, completing work on time, and assuming responsibilities without being asked.

The principal and the bilingual teachers display the bilingual competence—using two languages to manage their work and social environment—which Campbell parents (almost without exception) want first of all from the bilingual program.[14] Parents are not content with the traditional assimilative-oriented admonition that their children have to learn English to "make it" in the Anglo-dominated society. They believe the bilingual job market offers far more opportunity for employment and upward mobility—and they observe critically and carefully the qualifications of those among them who move into positions as bilingual instructional aides.

Conclusions

In the introductory section two interrelated questions were posed as a focus for the organization, presentation, and analysis of data. One question concerned the relationship of cultural differences to schooling processes; the second concerned the effects of ethnic/cultural characteristics of pupils on classroom practice and teacher behavior. These questions have been answered primarily through a description and analysis of curriculum systems and extra-classroom activities.

Curriculum systems have been presented as prototypical instructional processes and have been found to be culturally "Anglo" in their socializing effects—oriented toward individualistic achievement values—and (whether presented in English or in Spanish) eliciting from pupils common patterns of adaptive behavior. Certainly the attributes of these systems are not characteristic of all classroom and school activities. Through social studies units, literature, drama, song, and festivities, ethnic heritage is studied, reinforced, and celebrated. Nevertheless, curriculum systems represent a powerful influence on the life of Campbell classrooms and on the values and teaching practices teachers believe to be fundamental to success. Although the systems serve the objective of individualized instruction, they impose on classroom life a required structure and sequence of teacher and pupil behavior.

To understand the role of curriculum systems and extra-classroom activities in structuring, reinforcing, or muting a bicultural experience, it is important to view them within the context of the language-maintenance bilingual education model used at Campbell. Unlike major alternative program models (*transitional* or *immersion*), the maintenance model assumes the continuing importance of bilingual competence to the present and developing needs of Campbell pupils. At every grade, pupils can express these needs in that language which provides them the most meaning. Hence the constant availability to pupils of their mother tongue affords them a more open relationship with teachers and more freedom in their evolving adaptation to a bicultural environment. Of more importance, the maintenance model affirms the equal worth of ethnic backgrounds and the inseparability of language and culture.

Notes

[1] A recent and comprehensive survey and analysis of research and developments in bilingual education is a set of five volumes issued by the Center for Applied Linguistics (1977). In Volume One, Fishman (1977) has an excellent review chapter on the social science perspective, Mehan (1977) discusses ethnographic approaches to the study of classrooms, and Nieves-Squires (1977) presents a point of view about the uses of *functionalism* and *acculturation* in relating anthropology to bilingual education. In the volume on linguistics, Paulston (1977) includes in her discussion questions which relate to ethnographic research on bilingual education. See also the National Dissemination and Assessment Center (1978) and Cornejo (1974) for additional surveys.

[2] Pseudonyms are used for the school, the community, and individuals.

[3] See Irizarry (1977) for a report on state and federal legislation.

[4] Research findings on the Mexican school will be described in a later publication.

[5] Wolcott (1975) discusses the issues ethnographers face in formal evaluation research.

[6] Among the small number of parents who checked the "white" category are several who were born and raised in Mexico and whose children are Spanish dominant. In terms of the research by Clark, Kaufmann, and Pierce (1976) these parents choose to present themselves as more Anglicized than "ethnic."

[7] For purposes of in-depth interviews, a 10 percent stratified random sample of families was drawn—weighted to include larger numbers of parents of first- and sixth-grade pupils—in order to be able to obtain more data on attitudes relating to school entry and exit. Data on parental attitudes about ethnic identity and the bilingual program come from these interviews, from other interviews with officers of parental advisory committees and with the school faculty and staff, and from the results of a bilingual program evaluation questionnaire sent out to parents by the school.

[8] Six of approximately 250 families stipulated that their children were not to be in the program. They wanted them to receive instruction only in English. Four of these families were Mexican American; two were Anglo. Neither the interviews nor the responses (Spanish or English) to the evaluation questionnaire produced evidence of major opposition to the program. Approximately 10 percent of parents expressed some dissatisfaction, mainly with the academic progress of their children.

[9] They are not all equally fluent in English.

[10] The equivalent of three to four days of observations was

carried out—as a minimum—in each of the 14 classrooms. Observations in several classrooms extended over a week. Instructional processes in six classrooms were also filmed. The author has produced a 30-minute 16mm documentary film of the bilingual program.

[11] Ramirez and Castañeda (1974) outline a system of teaching procedures and curriculum materials to be used with "field dependent" Mexican American children. Figueroa and Gallegos (1978), using a behavioral rating scale, obtained ratings from 39 Spanish bilingual teachers on 263 children from four ethnic groups (Latino, Mexican, U.S.-born Spanish surnamed, and Anglo). Their findings include the following:

> Mexican children are perceived by their predominantly Hispanic bilingual-education teachers as being more shy, less sociable, less communicative, less assertive, less bright, less competitive, less sure, and less pressured to achieve than most of the other groups and especially less than the Anglo group.... The only positive trait ascribed to Mexican children is that of being well mannered. [1978:295]

The authors argue for the need to eliminate the social distance which, their data indicate, exists between teachers and Mexican pupils.

[12] I sat at a table nar Gilberto, with writing materials in hand as classes were accustomed to seeing me. There were several instances when my proximity appeared to be intrusive for Gilberto; at those times I moved away to a position that I felt would not be associated with him. The afternoon before these observations, I talked with Gilberto about my interest in learning more about what a day in school was like for him.

[13] The remarks which follow are taken from a verbatim transcript of the assembly presentations.

[14] Now called bilingual/multicultural—with the issuance of a new curriculum handbook in the fall of 1978. The apparent demise of "bicultural" as a secondary descriptor of a bilingual program is a function of complex interacting factors—programmatic, conceptual, political.

References

Arias, M. B. 1976. *A Bicultural Approach to the Issue of Self-Concept Assessment.* Unpublished dissertation. Stanford University.

Becker, Howard S. 1964. "Problems in the Publication of Field Studies." In Arthur J. Vidich, J. Bensman and M. R. Stein, eds., *Reflections on Community Studies.* New York: Harper & Row.

Bruner, E. M. 1956. "Primary Group Experience and the Processes of Acculturation," *American Anthropologist,* 58:605–623.

Center for Applied Linguistics. 1977. *Bilingual Education: Current Perspectives.* (Volume 1: Social Science; Volume 2: Linguistics; Volume 3: Law; Volume 4: Education; Volume 5: Synthesis.) Arlington, Virginia.

Clark, M., S. Kaufman, and R. C. Pierce. 1976. "Explorations of Acculturation: Toward a Model of Ethnic Identity," *Human Organization,* 35:231–238.

Cornejo, Ricardo J. 1974. *A Synthesis of Theories and Research on the Effects of Teaching in First and Second Languages: Implications for Bilingual Education.* Austin, Texas: National Educational Laboratory Publishers, Inc.

Figueroa, R. A., and E. A. Gallegos. 1978. "Ethnic Differences in School Behavior," *Sociology of Education,* 51:289–298.

Fishman, Joshua A. 1977. "The Social Science Perspective," in *Bilingual Education: Current Perspectives,* Volume 1: Social Science. Arlington, Virginia: Center for Applied Linguistics.

Gibson, M. 1976. "Approaches to Multicultural Education in the United States: Some Concepts and Assumptions," *Anthropology and Education Quarterly,* 7:7–18.

Irizarry, Ruddie A. 1977. *Bilingual Education: State and Federal Legislative Mandate.* Los Angeles: National Dissemination and Assessment Center.

McFee, M. 1968. "The 150% Man, A Product of Blackfoot Acculturation," *American Anthropologist,* 70:1096–1103.

Mehan, Hugh. 1977. "Ethnography," in *Bilingual Education: Current Perspectives,* Volume 1: Social Science. Arlington, Virginia: Center for Applied Linguistics.

National Dissemination and Assessment Center. 1978. *Bilingual/Bicultural Education: Titles and Abstracts of Doctoral Dissertations.* Los Angeles.

Nieves-Squires, Sarah. 1977. "Anthropology," in *Bilingual Education: Current Perspectives,* Volume 1: Social Science. Arlington, Virginia: Center for Applied Linguistics.

Paulston, Christina B. 1977. "Research," in *Bilingual Education: Current Perspectives,* Volume 2, Linguistics. Arlington, Virginia: Center for Applied Linguistics.

Polgar, S. 1960. "Biculturation of Mesquakie Teenage Boys," *American Anthropologist,* 62:217–235.

Ramirez, M., III, and A. Castañeda. 1974. *Cultural Democracy, Bicognitive Development, and Education.* New York: Academic Press.

Spindler, George D. 1963. "The Character Structure of Anthropology." In George D. Spindler, ed., *Education and Culture:*

Anthropological Approaches. New York: Holt, Rinehart and Winston.

Wolcott, Harry F. 1975. "Fieldwork in Schools: Where the Tradition of Deferred Judgment Meets a Subculture Obsessed with Evaluation," *Council on Anthropology and Education Quarterly,* 6:17–20.

13

Sylvia Hart

Analyzing the Social Organization for Reading in One Elementary School

Sylvia Hart

The Author

Sylvia Hart studied anthropology at the University of Oregon in Eugene and received the doctorate after studying social organization at "Emerald," the school encountered in the following article.

After embarking on her cross-cultural studies by spending a year in Zürich, Switzerland, as an American Field Service exchange student, she earned an undergraduate degree for coursework at the University of California at Santa Cruz and the University of Wisconsin–Milwaukee. At first she focused on psychology and anthropology, but, becoming tired of being the recipient in classroom situations, she tried her hand at educating others. In the process of earning a teaching credential she assisted teachers in a variety of elementary schools in Milwaukee, including an urban "ghetto" school and an Indian Community School (set up by and for urban Native Americans).

In the future she would like to investigate two topics she considers essential, neglected, and well-suited to methods and theories of educational anthropology: morality and aesthetics implicit in education processes. While preparing to meet this challenge, she is currently researching formal education in a nonschool setting. Believing that we may be overloaded with studies of learning and teaching in schools, she hopes that by looking outside schools we can illuminate education processes and apply this knowledge in schools. The formal education she is looking into is the explicit instruction in methods of housekeeping and child-rearing that is popular among adult women in Portland, Oregon.

Hart is part of the new wave of "patchwork professors" who put careers together by "collecting" courses across a metropolitan area: she teaches anthropology at Portland State University, Marylhurst Education Center, and Lewis and Clark College. Her interest in Latin America, increased by time spent in Mexico and Cuba, has made Peoples and Cultures of Latin America one of her favorite courses to teach. Her home is in Portland, where, she says, her nonprofessional concerns are "pets, house, and spouse."

This Chapter

In her study of the social organization of reading at "Emerald" School, Sylvia Hart did something often advocated by ethnographers but rarely implemented. She was actively engaged as a helper at Emerald, tutoring students floundering in reading. She also substituted for student tutors at times. These activities enabled discussions with teachers "in the crucial context of trying to teach students" to be more realistic and meaningful than would other-

wise have been the case. Hart did not know that "social organization was the framework supporting not one, but many, 'readings.'" Perhaps she benefited from not knowing what it was that
she was looking for, because circumstances and processes heuristic
to the situation rather than her own preformed ideas "revealed a
vital facet of reading reality—social organization."

For Hart, social organization is "best seen as a map of social
space in which classes may be located by their positions on four
dimensions—grade, ability level, subject, and schedule." Hart describes how the intersection of these dimensions organizes reading
activity in Emerald School. She attempts a comparative stance
with a brief comparison to the age grades of the Nandi and to "subjects" in medieval European schools where scholars divided the
content of education into oral recitation, arts, and theology. This
comparative posture is only partially effective, but it calls attention
to the fact that alternative forms of social organization are possible
and that what she calls a social organization of reading is an artifact, created partly out of rational self-conscious design and partly
through evolution and the accumulation of tradition.

Introduction

As a self-proclaimed "helper" to students and teachers in Reading[1] classes
in one U.S. public elementary school, I
came to realize the importance of social
organization for the topic which I intended to research—Reading. By "social organization" I mean the patterns
of students' movements and membership in forming classes to study this
subject. Although educators and social
scientists often emphasize Reading and
address issues of group size and characteristics, they do not usually consider
the social organizational aspect to be a
foundation on which Reading education rests. I wish to show that Reading

social organization as one facet of
Reading behavior has consequences for
other facets (e.g., course content and individuals' intellectual activity) in the
way that anthropologists have shown
that social organization (e.g., matrili-
neal clans) pertains to many facets of
life, including ideology and personality.
By analyzing the criteria of class formation and considering the qualities of
Reading classes I attended throughout
the school, I learned that the key dimensions of school social organization
intersect to form classes with people
and pursuits which vary in accordance
with these dimensions. Understanding
the links between social organization
and other aspects of education—signif-

icantly, individual involvement and the means and ends of instruction—may be one way to improve education. At the very least, such understanding is essential for identifying the education practices with which we are concerned.

Before considering this construct of social organization, let us "visit" the school and "observe" two Reading sessions for the sake of familiarity with two Reading "realities" which fit with many others into that construct. The two descriptions illustrate the efforts students put into Reading, suggesting that reading is crucial in the school. The passages also exemplify the diversity among Reading situations in the school, thus prefiguring my conclusion that class variations with which we are familiar (and often consider in terms of pedagogical philosophy) are patterned along the lines of social organization.

Emerald School: Two Reading Sessions

Emerald School is on the outskirts of a small Western city situated amidst a green valley, a mountain range, and coastal hills near the Pacific Ocean. Because of this location, many Emerald parents work in the lumber and rail industries (mostly at nonprofessional jobs) and sport out-of-doors orientations. The school is influenced by the presence of a state university in the city and a school district with teacher-student ratio, teacher salaries, and dollar expenditure per student higher than the national averages.

As anthropological researcher and helper during the fall semester of 1977, I participated in a variety of school events, including classes for many subjects, recess and lunch periods on the playground and indoors, and faculty meetings and lunch sessions. I visited most Reading classes at least once and many Reading classes repeatedly. As tutor to individual students or assistant to teachers working with their classes, I had a regular role in some Reading classes; in others I was an irregular observer, helping anyone who called on me spontaneously.

First Graders Take Reading Tests

Teachers administered Reading tests to all students in the first week of school (increasing its excitement). During this week a special schedule reigned; other activities replaced Reading until students had been assigned ability-levels. For the student the tests "stood out": he or she left the homeroom class, confronted an adult (a teacher, teacher-aide, or me, the researcher), and responded to printed items. The child and the adult were alone in a small room designated "the Reading room." Reading materials were stacked around them. No sounds from the adjacent classroom could be heard. Nothing moved except the adult's finger pointing to letters (unless the child was squirming). Aside from the voices of the adult and child, there were no sounds except that of the adult's pencil recording the child's mistakes.

The child to be tested came into the room, was greeted by the adult who stood at the open door, asked the child his or her name, and told the child her own. After the student and tester made small talk on topics chosen by the tester and the student had been directed to a chair next to the tester, he or she was confronted with a sheet displaying many symbols.

The child followed the tester's finger as it pointed to each symbol for a few seconds. He or she tried to tell the tester the sound each symbol "makes" and to answer other questions the tester asked, e.g., "What is this letter?", "Do you know the *name* of the letter?", and "Now can you tell what *sound* it makes?" The child appeared to try very hard to answer correctly. After some incorrect answers the child heard "Not quite" (school euphemism for "That's wrong") or "No, that one sounds like this. . . ."

The child proceeded at the pace determined by the pointing finger. But the finger was not terribly rigid; it stopped when the tester answered a question, like the inquiry, apparently out of genuine interest, "Now what *is* that one? I can *almost* remember it." The finger also paused while the child heard encouragement and established eye contact with the tester. Encouraging phrases were, "You can't remember *everything* over the summer, can you?" and "You're doing just fine." Sometimes the child asked why the tester made a mark after a certain response, indicating that he or she had figured out that the pencil recorded important facts (mistakes).

The total procedure lasted 10 or 15 minutes. If the student had responded successfully to many items, the tester pulled out another (more difficult) sheet.

Fifth Graders Work-and-Play in Reading

In a session for low-ability-level fifth graders the aim was to read passages and do lessons involving "dissection" of reading into the mental processes it may involve.

The students and teacher sat on a rug and pillows in a corner of the room. A girl complained that she could not remember the story they had read the day before. The teacher responded by leading a discussion on its content, and students recalled the tale by answering her questions. The next task was more formal. The teacher read questions about the story from the teachers' edition of the text. After each question students wrote answers, working individually. The idea was to make sure each answer was a complete sentence, not a phrase beginning "Because . . ." They reviewed the written answers: the teacher reread a question, called on a student to read his or her own answer, and sometimes called on a second person to correct the answer. Each remark was an exchange between the teacher and one student.

With little risk of exaggeration, the atmosphere of the session can be likened to a parlor-game situation. The students sprawled on the rug, constrained only by the necessity of managing equipment and communicating with the teacher. The tasks were like games or puzzles with correct answers; students could keep and compare scores, but did not pay much attention to them in this session. The pace was lively. Work was punctuated by the teacher humorously chiding students who were not responding as she desired and by students kidding with her and sharing reactions to the work with each other. "Players" appeared engrossed— intellectually in the "games" and socially in the interaction.

The two passages above give a "flavor" of Reading life at Emerald which includes the differences of separate settings and the apparent attention participants gave to the settings. In this article I present my construct of the social organization and its consequences for characteristics of classes (defined as groups assigned to study together at certain times and places with certain teachers) and academic traits of individuals. First, however, I explain my own activities at Emerald. This way, the reader can understand how school experience "caught me up" in social organization as the students asked teachers about it and learned how to operate in it and teachers planned and discussed it.

The Ethnographer as Helper

In order to understand my data and interpretation of social organization for Reading, we must look at the way in which I participated and observed in the school. During my first days at Emerald I consulted teachers and sometimes students in order to establish routines for helping in Reading classes. Here I describe three such routines (not my total helping activities).

Helping Students Embark on Reading

The first routine occurred because the Reading specialist scheduled me to help her as she taught a first-grade Reading class. For about nine weeks I helped her daily for a 50-minute class session. She did not noticeably alter her own activities because of my presence, but my labor increased the number of individuals who received help and were tested for progress. I never substituted for her in direct instruction to the class (but I did read stories to the class once). My effect on instruction was probably only to amplify the aspects she considered significant (and suitable for me to lead).

At first I had misgivings about distorting the "natural" course by helping, but about two weeks after I stopped helping in this class these misgivings diminished when a teacher-aide joined to perform my former duties. The Reading specialist and I put "stars" on more work sheets than the Reading specialist would have been able to put on alone; the cost of altered events was far less than the benefit of greater understanding. Although I influenced the events observed by participating, my involvement deepened my insight.

In this class there were six to nine students (the number fluctuated). Through my regular participation and well-defined duties I got to know their personalities in Reading class and in other situations. The extent to which some of us knew each other is shown by such cases as a girl who often whispered to me how amazed she was at being able to read, another who yelled across the playground to me that she would show cocoons in Reading (thus breaking the rule against "bringing things to class" and posing an ethical dilemma for a researcher who likes children and cocoons), and a boy who complained to me that he couldn't practice his word list outside school because of the pressures of the Prince Pepper Nursery School he attended after school and cousins who distracted him at home. These and other intimacies arose because our work together provided conditions for becoming friends.

Tutoring a Student Floundering in Reading

In a second routine I tutored Bill. The Reading specialist had only two adult volunteers and therefore assigned tutors only to students she judged desperate for help and eager to respond. Bill was such a student. Bill and I worked together daily for 15 weeks. We changed time, length of session, technique, and mood, following a rocky course which did seem to improve his ability to read. Working with Bill enabled me to learn about the challenge a "nonreading" 12-year-old confronts, the techniques advocated for teaching him, his interpersonal relations in the classroom, various persons' priorities regarding sessions he should miss in order to see me, library resources, and countless other matters precious to my own understanding.

Monitoring Students Steered by Students

In a third helping routine I had less impact on behavior, relative to the class and tutorial sessions mentioned above. I attended a daily session for "problem readers" two days a week for about six weeks. One teacher taught the "lowest ability" Readers from third and fourth grades. She administered a highly structured program with "individual-

ized" materials and student-tutors from the fifth and sixth grades for each "problem" student. She used my assistance to help oversee practicing, recording results, and equipment dispersal. I explained procedures to student-tutors more than I talked to the early-grade Readers. When a student-tutor was absent, I substituted. On days I was not there, students probably had fewer questions answered and received less praise for increased scores. I learned about a Reading class which was radically different from others at Emerald and significant for "poor" Readers. I learned also about the lives of such children. One boy, for instance, was proud to demonstrate how to store record charts: he had been in the same remedial program the previous school year too.

Helping Rapport

My role as helper enhanced rapport. For instance, since I frequently stopped by one classroom to pick up a tutee, teacher and students often greeted me and gave me an excuse to stay. One time when I tried to enter, they asked me to pretend I was opening my front door to a student canvassing for energy conservation. On a similar errand I became a director of "commercials" students were rehearsing.

Sometimes when I sat on the sidelines in order to observe classes, students made use of me, carefully and directly (the way a student respectfully picks up a large dictionary and lugs it to her seat). A student would say, "Who are you?" and upon hearing any answer would ask me to come to her seat to answer a question. Or, without such an identifying probe, a student would bring a minute scratch paper and ask me to spell a word by writing it out.

In regard to my relationships with teachers, the helping role allowed me to discuss Reading with them in the crucial context of trying to teach students. Perhaps my helping role showed them that although my primary aim was to "gather" data, I also wanted to contribute to the school and enjoyed being with students. Teachers inquired several times, however, whether I had enough data, revealing their attention to my purpose at Emerald.

The above accounts of rapport could leave a false impression that I was eminent on students' and teachers' horizons. Actually, to the students, I think I was one of many vaguely identified adults (teachers, specialists, aides, volunteers, parents, visitors, and researchers from the nearby university) who sometimes surfaced in classrooms. As did the students, teachers had many matters other than me on their minds. Their lack of concern over me probably increased the "naturalness" of the data.

Helping Insight

Although Reading was my major interest as I started out at Emerald, I had not been "clued in" that social organization was the framework supporting not one, but many, "Readings." Therefore I was not in a position to follow Agatha Christie's legendary detective Hercule Poirot's style of searching the scene of the crime only when I knew "exactly what I'm looking for." Neither could I follow the advice of William Whyte's informant who told him not to ask too many questions: "You can just hang around and you'll learn the answers in the long run without ever having to ask the questions" (Whyte 1943).

Since I was actively engaged as helper at Emerald, I benefited from *not* "knowing exactly what I was looking for," because circumstances, rather than my preformed ideas, revealed a vital facet of Reading reality—social organization. As helper I also benefited from *not* "just hanging around . . . without ever having to ask the questions," because circumstances revealed which questions I should ask. The attempt to participate in Reading situations and my theoretical interests in academic content *both* required me to ask questions about "locating" classes and students in the social framework.

In addition to revealing the importance of social organizations, helping lent substance to my analysis. I empathized with teachers and students because I shared their tasks and had a small stake in the results of teaching and learning. I became familiar with teacher "techniques" and student "strategies."

Helping also led me to emphasize active student participation. Social organization is not merely a pattern laid upon students from above, but one they enact with their minds and bodies.[2] Students talk about and use information on social organization in order to know their "places" as they attend classes, work, and interact. Somewhat like social scientists, they abstract the ways people relate to each other. Thus, in a neat but unplanned twist, the students were performing reflexive research on the same topic I was researching. We all needed the same information in order to figure out how to get to the correct room at the correct time, why we were in that particular class (because, for instance, its students were older or smarter or from a certain homeroom class), what behavior was expected from that class, and how to accept or alter one's position in it.

Consequentially for my findings, helping was fun. *Observing classes* can be dull and lead to the false conclusion that *classes themselves* are dull to students. Mentally engaged with the participants, I could be more objective about dullness. "Gathering" data is mainly a "talking" activity; it was refreshing to give a small amount of time and effort to Readers. In short, helping helped me to actualize the first term in "participant observation" (difficult for researchers in schools because they cannot always participate as teachers or students). Now let us consider some "products" of this participation—the construct of social organization which emerged.

The Dimensions of Social Organization

The school setting, its diverse Reading classes, and my adaptation of the participant observation approach were linked together in Emerald's social organization. After reading the complex schedule, called the "back-to-back schedule," and learning how it worked day by day, I abstracted the principles behind class formation.

The social organization is best seen as a map of social space in which classes may be "located" by their "positions" on four dimensions—grade,

ability-level, subject, and schedule (see Table 1). Each class has a set of four coordinates on these dimensions which identify it. An example is a class of grade "1," ability-level "lowest," subject "Reading," and period in the schedule "early morning." In Table 1 most classes are represented in the upper left corner, because their memberships are determined by grade and subject as depicted. The comparatively large empty area of the table reveals the alternative ways classes could be formed on the basis of the same dimensions. For instance, a class could be formed without an assigned subject or grade, in which case it would be represented in the lower right corner of the table. Thus the table reveals how Emerald's four dimensions of social organization could be used to form classes different from the actual classes. Reading classes, by definition, have a clearly circumscribed subject; they also have a precise time in the schedule (see Table 2). In grades one, two, and three, Reading classes do not consist of students from only one homeroom class; in grades four, five, and six, they do.

In this section I show how each dimension is defined and used as a criterion of class formation at Emerald and present a contrasting case in which the use of that dimension differs from its use at Emerald. For the dimension *grade*, we may relativize our view by looking at grades in an African society. Similarly, for the dimension *ability-level*, we look outside Emerald School to the use of ability-levels measured in terms of Intelligence Quotient. For the dimension *subject*, we look at subjects in medieval European schools. Finally, for the dimension *schedule* we look at a common schedule in U.S. elementary schools which I call a "traditional arrangement." Such alternative uses suggest: (1) that dimensions are socially defined, and (2) that the *way* they are defined affects social organization and content of education.

Grade

At Emerald the number of school years a student has successfully completed determines her or his grade. Normally a child entering first grade is six years old (or will be before January). He or she passes to a later grade each year.[3] For the dimension *grade,* material highlighting the social definition is from another culture. All societies differentiate people according to age grade, usually in very general terms. Members expect basic role dispositions and specific behaviors from members of each grade. For instance, they have ideas about actual and proper behaviors of "old men" and "young men." But societies differ in emphasis on age grade—it may involve indistinct divisions or clear bases for group membership and role allocation (Eisenstadt 1956:21–55). The age set system of the Nandi, a tribe in Kenya, is a good example because it shows how such a system can be intricate and significant to the whole society.

The Nandi age set system consists of seven ages, each lasting about 15 years. A group of men born within 15 years of one another belong to one age set and advance through each age together. As a category of similar individuals, they face the obligations and privileges that correspond to each stage of develop-

ment. Thus an age set supplies the society's fighting men at one age, the society's elders at the succeeding age, and so forth. The seven ages are cyclical, so that there is always a group of boys in the first age; they will be about 105 years old if they live through all the ages.

Nandi age grades are different from Emerald's in at least two major ways. First, they span the individual's entire life. (If we looked at the individual's elementary school life as one "life" spanned by age grades, they would be similar to the Nandi age grades in this respect.) Secondly, Nandi age grades provide role specialization in terms of interaction among grades; each Nandi grade serves a unique function for the whole society. All Emerald grades serve the same function for the total school; each grade does not have a particular area of expertise as in the Nandi system.

Within each grade at Emerald are two or three subgroups—homeroom classes. Faculty devise lists of members for each homeroom class, apparently with the intention of having homerooms composed of many kinds of students. Each grade member is in one and only one homeroom class, and all members of one homeroom class belong to one grade. Homeroom membership normally lasts as long as grade membership—one year. Homeroom classes are half or a third the size of classes which would result if grades were not subgrouped. Students in homeroom classes spend more time and do more varied activities together than do any other groups in the school. Their small size may be a factor con-

TABLE 1 Intersection of Dimensions to Form Classes for Academic Subjects

Dimensions (of Subject and Schedule)		Dimensions (of Personal Attributes)							
		Grade determines members				*Grade does not determine members*			
		Homeroom class determines members		*Homeroom class does not determine members*		*Homeroom class determines members*		*Homeroom class does not determine members*	
		Ability-level determines members	*Ability-level does not determine members*	*Ability-level determines members*	*Ability-level does not determine members*	*Ability-level determines members*	*Ability-level does not determine members*	*Ability-level determines members*	*Ability-level does not determine members*
Subject is clearly circumscribed	*Back-to-back schedule sets time*	Reading classes in grades 4, 5, 6[a]		Reading classes in grades 1, 2, 3[a]	Back-to-back subject classes[b]				
	Back-to-back schedule influences time		Some Math classes[c]	Some Math classes					
	Back-to-back schedule does not influence time								

		Homeroom classes[d]				
	Back-to-back schedule sets time					
Subject is less clearly circumscribed	*Back-to-back schedule influences time*					
	Back-to-back schedule does not influence time					
	Back-to-back schedule sets time					
Subject is not circumscribed	*Back-to-back schedule influences time*					
	Back-to-back schedule does not influence time					

[a] *Two grades* are specified for **Reading** classes in grades 3 and 4. Reading classes in grade 4 are only partially determined by *homeroom class.*

[b] Ability-level in *Reading* determines back-to-back subject classes.

[c] These Math classes usually have ability-level subgroups.

[d] The exception is grade 4, in which students of generally *low ability* form one homeroom class (E.L.P.).

421

TABLE 2 **Intersection of Dimensions to Form Reading Classes**

Dimensions (of Subject and Schedule)		**Dimensions (of Personal Attributes)**	
		Grade determines members	
		Ability-level determines members	
		Homeroom class determines members	*Homeroom class* does *not* determine members
Subject is clearly circumscribed	*Back-to-back schedule sets* time	Reading classes in grades 4, 5, 6[a]	Reading classes in grades 1, 2, 3[a]

[a]*Two grades* are specified for Reading classes in grades 3 and 4. Reading classes in grade 4 are only partly determined by *homeroom class.*
Explanation: Rows and columns represent the four dimensions of social organization. The two large squares on the intersections of rows and columns represent Reading classes at Emerald. Thus the table shows intersections of dimensions—grade, homeroom class (a subgroup of grade), ability-level, subject, and back-to-back schedule—to form Reading classes. Referring to dimensions on the horizontal axis, we see that all Reading classes are determined by grade and ability-level but not all are determined by homeroom class. Referring to the vertical axis, we see that for all Reading classes subject is clearly circumscribed and the back-to-back schedule sets the time. The table may be seen as a two-dimensional portrayal of a four-dimensional "space" in which each Reading class has its own "location" according to whether it is of specified dimensions.

tributing to a warm, family-like atmosphere in homeroom classes at Emerald.

Ability-Level

Ability-levels are categories of students believed to be of similar ability in a particular subject. Teachers assign individuals to ability-levels as they assign them to classes. Ability-level assignments are not made in isolation from other factors, but are influenced by numbers and sizes of classes. Students influence ability-level assignments by achievement.

In order to emphasize the social nature of ability-level, I compare it to another method of categorizing ability—I.Q. In establishing I.Q. scores, people use a behavior (answering test items correctly) to indicate "intelligence."

Scores representing individual differences (in number of correct answers) are equated with different levels of intelligence.

I.Q. and Emerald's ability-levels resemble each other in that both are methods of categorizing people with reference to behavior indicating mental processes. I.Q. score assignment, however, does not reflect the broad awareness of students and situations that makes ability-level determination so complex. Emerald's faculty often talk about ability in ways suggesting that they are sensitive to subtle differences among students and believe their categorizations of ability are necessary only for convenience. Because they recognize the impossibility of perfectly demarcating ability differences, they use diverse criteria and flexibly change decisions based on them.

Subject

Teachers do not completely determine subjects. Tradition, the school district's written curriculum goals, the school's schedule, and students influence subjects. These factors and others interact in their effects on subjects, but are described separately below.

Education tradition, including current U.S. trends, influences circumscription of subjects, e.g., Spelling, Music, Mathematics. In many sessions at Emerald, however, students' activities are hard to classify in terms of traditional subjects. *Curriculum goals*[4] established in Emerald's school district require teachers to teach particular skills and concepts by the end of particular grades. In order to fulfill the goals, teachers refer to the subjects in which the goals are embedded. *The school's schedule* "crystallizes" these influences by coordinating subjects with periods and therefore may be seen as partly determining subjects. *Students*, in responding to the subjects taught, influence teachers' circumscription of them. They reveal which activities and subjects benefit, please, or disrupt them; teachers react to this information as they define subjects.

In order to emphasize that subjects don't "exist out there" but that people define them, let us consider possible alternative subjects. The first logical possibility is that, as "slices" of reality, *subjects can be "sliced" in different ways*. At Emerald students might study all arts as one subject, instead of separating Music, the Visual and Performing Arts, and other arts as they often do. A second possibility is that *subjects can be added and deleted*. Potential subjects not studied at Emerald include foreign languages, Embroidery, Occult Sciences, Auto-Mechanics, and the Cuban Revolution. A third possibility is that *subjects can be emphasized differently*. All academic content might "revolve around" one subject: social science could involve Reading, Mathematics, Music, and Physical Education.

By way of comparison, medieval European schools employed one scheme for defining subjects which illuminates our own. Medieval scholars divided the content of education into oral recitation, arts, and theology. Schools in the Middle Ages did not differentiate subjects according to difficulty and assign them to people according to their ages, abilities, or aims. "The older students were distinguished from the new not in the subjects they studied—they were the same—but by the number of times they had repeated them" (Ariés 1962:150). Emerald is similar in that students in all grades have the same subjects. (The total school experience of a U.S. student is different from the medieval schools in that students have different subjects in junior high and elementary schools, etc.)

Schedule

The back-to-back schedule is Emerald's scheme for coordinating groups and times and purposes. Teachers plan it as they delineate subjects, emphasize Reading, and employ teachers of back-to-back subjects. These subjects are Guidance, Health, Library, Music, Physical Education, and Science. The students of each grade have Physical

Education and a second back-to-back subject four days a week all year. The second back-to-back subject changes about every eight weeks, so that each student has each subject for at least one eight-week period during the year.

The schedule provides times four days a week for each student to have Reading, two back-to-back subjects, and homeroom class subjects. It assigns times for Reading and back-to-back subjects by grade. A student has Reading when half the members of his or her grade have it, while the other half have two back-to-back subjects. Thus Tracy had Physical Education and Music with other students from all first grade homeroom classes early in the morning. While she and about half of all first graders had these back-to-back subjects, the other half had Reading. Next, Tracy had Reading with six to twelve students[5] from all first grade homeroom classes. All the others who had back-to-back subjects when she did were also in Reading classes at this time. The half of the first grade who were in Reading first were now in the back-to-back subjects.

Schedules structure education in schools, and the back-to-back schedule's impact on education at Emerald is illuminated by comparing it with another common way of organizing students for Reading. In a traditional U.S. arrangement[6] each grade is divided into several homeroom classes with one teacher each (as at Emerald). The homeroom classes subdivide into about three Reading groups based on ability-level. (This subdivision is different from cross-homeroom subdivision at Emerald.) Each group meets with the homeroom class teacher while the other groups remain in the room. The other groups have Reading tasks to perform individually. The teacher directly instructs one group at a time and "keeps an eye on" the other students (cf. McDermott 1977a). The homeroom class schedule for studying various subjects and ability-level designations is not as interdependent with subjects and ability-level designations of other homeroom classes as in the Emerald case.[7]

In contrast to Emerald's schedule, the traditional arrangement does not prescribe precise times for subjects or involve cross-homeroom class Reading groups or cross-grade groups.[8] Times for Reading *may* be long, regular, and adjusted to ability in the traditional alternative, just as they are with Emerald's back-to-back schedule, but the traditional alternative neither precisely schedules Reading with these characteristics nor other subjects (at Emerald, the back-to-back subjects) in order to accommodate Reading. The back-to-back schedule not only arranges Reading times but also interlocks them with other subjects and classes.

The major difference between the back-to-back schedule and the traditional alternative is that, with the former, students who are not taking Reading from a teacher are present in the room where a group and the teacher are doing Reading together. Other factors, e.g., numbers of teacher-aides and subgroups, complicate classroom situations and modify distinctions between the two alternatives. The traditional alternative illuminates Emerald's schedule as just one of many possibilities.

Intersection of Dimensions to Form Classes With Certain Characteristics

Just as the dimensions of space intersect and we can use them to locate points, so Emerald's dimensions of social "space"—grade ability-level, subject, and schedule—intersect in ways which help us "locate" classes. Thus we can locate a class in terms of all dimensions which are criteria of its formation. An example is a Reading class of specified grade, ability-level, subject (Reading), and period in the schedule.[9] I show here how several characteristics of Reading classes—their aims, atmospheres, and tasks—vary according to the class' location along the dimensions. Since the dimensions are related to the kinds of classes which form, it may be possible to affect education by altering the dimensions of social organization. Factors of classroom settings other than the dimensions of social organization influence class characteristics; such factors include teacher personality and student interaction. Even with these powerful personal factors at work, however, the general characteristics of a specific class at Emerald can be identified if one knows the class's grade, ability-level, subject, and period in the schedule.

Two final tables suggest how the dimensions of social organization are associated with other classroom variables. Table 3 presents associations between the four dimensions which determine classes and other social organizational aspects of these classes. We see that as a dimension varies, such variables as size, range of ability-level, and teacher attention change. This table merely indicates one direction in which we might look to see how the dimensions of social organization are tied to certain kinds of classes. At Emerald the dimensions are used in such a way that a class' characteristics along one dimension have important associations with other social factors. For instance, a class of low ability-level is more apt to have an earlier meeting time, smaller membership (in grades 1 through 3), and a unique instruction program including extra helpers than is a class of high ability-level.

The dimension schedule (called the back-to-back schedule) is also associated with Reading class characteristics, as listed in the bottom section of Table 3.

Again suggesting how the dimensions of social organization are associated with other classroom variables, Table 4 presents associations among the four dimensions which determine classes and aspects of Reading assignments. The table illustrates that as dimensions vary, academic concerns vary too. Some of the variations in academic concerns are relevant to our most cherished assumptions about Reading. For instance, the changes in Reading aims, atmosphere, and tasks which occur as grade becomes later are the same as those which occur as ability-level becomes higher. Students in earlier grades and students in lower-ability-levels confront small language units, simple assignments, and business-like atmospheres. Those in later grades and those in higher ability-levels confront larger units, more complex assignments, and more informal atmo-

TABLE 3 **Associations Between Each Dimension and Other Aspects of Social Organization**

Dimensions	Aspects of Social Organization Which Change as Each Dimension Changes	
Grade[a]	*Earlier grades have:* Less homeroom class recognition Small range of ability-level distinction within classes Few ability-level subgroups	*Later grades have:* More homeroom class recognition Great range of ability-level distinction within classes Ability-level subgroups
Homeroom class	Homeroom classes within each grade have similar social organization for Reading. Differences among homeroom classes occur only when they are due to *grade* differences, as delineated above.	
Ability-level	*Lower ability-levels have:* Earlier time Smaller class in the early grades More unique classes and special arrangements	*Higher ability-levels have:* Later time Larger class in later grades Fewer unique classes and special arrangements
Subject	Reading as one subject is a major factor, if not the major factor, behind the entire social organization of Reading and the total academic program.	
Back-to-back subjects	*The back-to-back schedule arranges:* Small Reading classes Full teacher attention Separation of students of different ability-levels Uniting of students of different homeroom classes	Multiple class membership Different teachers for different subjects Several teachers familiar with each student's reading

[a]Grades also differ in the period they have for Reading (which of the three segments with each academic day), but this difference is not associated with whether a grade is early or late.

spheres. Most students advance through all the grades, but according to Emerald's teachers, few students in low ability-levels advance to higher ability-levels. The students who never read well continue with "cut up" words and sentences, repetitive assignments, and formal classes; they may experience more boredom and less freedom than do their more "able" schoolmates. The dimensions *grade* and *ability-level* are very different from one another, yet variation in each is associated with similar Reading variations.

Another crucial example from Table 4 may be less familiar than the one above (which serves an aim of educational anthropology by presenting "old" facts in fresh perspective). The dimension *subject* does not vary: all students are assigned to classes for studying the subject Reading and have the same goal of acquiring or practicing literacy skills. Conceivably, as students change in age, interest, or ability, they could take more or less (or no) Reading, or define it differently (e.g., Reading Newspapers).

Having identified the dimensions of social organization for Reading and shown how they intersect to form classes with characteristics associated

TABLE 4   **Associations Between Each Dimension and Reading Culture**

	Aspects of Reading Assignments		
Dimensions	*Overall aim*	*Materials and tasks*	*Atmosphere*
Grade	Earlier grades concentrate on smaller language units than do later grades	As grade increases: *books* and *workbooks* are more complex, *seating* more flexible, *silent reading* more common, *individualized programs* more common, *drill* and *charts* less common	Earlier grades are more businesslike and unified (around common tasks) and stress more independent work than do later grades
Homeroom class			Many variables differ with homeroom class
Ability-level	Lower ability-levels focus on Reading as a skill and look at language fragments, whereas, to a slight extent, higher ability-levels focus on language as a means of expression	Lower ability-levels have less difficult material. *Extremely* low ability-levels have more structured programs, more fragmented tasks, lower interest-value than do higher ability-levels	*Extremely* low ability-levels have more regular pace, more restriction to Reading business, more frequent rewards than do higher ability-levels
Subject	The fact that Reading is *one* subject influences culture through: Emphasis on literacy as a skill Lack of emphasis on content The importance of Reading		
Back-to-back schedule	The back-to-back schedule influences culture by stressing: The regularity of Reading The importance of Reading		

Explanation: Differences along the dimensions of social organization (the dimensions determining Reading classes—grade, homeroom class, ability-level, subject, and back-to-back schedule) correspond to differences in the culture of Reading classes. A class determined by a dimension has certain cultural characteristics associated with the "value" the class has for that dimension. For example, Reading classes, all determined by the dimension ability-level, differ in atmosphere according to ability-level: extremely low ability-level classes have more regular pace, etc., than do higher ability-levels.

with the dimensions, I now look at the same dimensions in relation to individual students' characteristics pertaining to academic concerns of Reading. In uniting and dividing groups of students according to certain criteria, the dimensions do not take into account other criteria. Considering the general educational purposes of Reading classes, it seems imperative to consider whether the dimensions unite or divide groups on the basis of students' intellectual tendencies. I say "imperative" for two reasons: the individual and his/her mental activity are primary foci of education, and we may want to recognize and stimulate intellectual qualities by choosing certain ones as criteria of group formation.

The Academic Features of Individuals

Having traced some relationships between social organization and other characteristics of classes, I now identify individual distinctions which stand out in Reading (especially the assignments of "official business" of Reading). These distinctions are individual ability, style, taste in Reading situations, and taste in Reading substance. The social organization involves students in recognizing or ignoring these distinctions.

Every person has an infinite number of "features" (including facial, personality, and other features). Some features go unnamed or unnoticed, while others are objects of thought, word, and deed. At Emerald I observed four features relating to individual Reading work: ability, style, taste in situation,

and taste in substance (hereafter abbreviated: ability, style, situation, and substance). We can see each student as having a Reading profile with his/her unique expression of the four features, or traits of orientation toward Reading. These academic features are familiar ones; my point is that they are vital concerns to students, prominent in conversations and behavior as they do Reading.

Social organization results in classes which unite or separate students with similar expressions of each feature. A dimension of social organization "recognizes" a feature if students are separated into different classes according to their different characteristics for that feature. A dimension "obscures" a feature if students are united or divided in classes regardless of their characteristics for that feature.[10] First I show how each feature is crucial in classes. Then I indicate whether the social organization recognizes individual differences in these crucial features.

Ability

"Ability" refers to a student's speed, accuracy, and comprehension in Reading work, whether stemming from innate aptitudes, ingrained habits, or momentary inclinations. At almost any moment in a session such variations are obvious, complex, and important. I now illustrate the powerful reality of ability differences by describing students performing with various sorts of success.

The goal for one first-grade, low-ability-level class was to learn how to read. On any given day, although all students had the same tasks, each was at his/her own stage approaching this goal. In drill the teacher asked the class to pronounce a syllable in unison (e.g., "am," "er") and to make rhymes by adding consonants as she "supplied" them (e.g., "Sam," "her"). The chorus of correct rhymers included individuals who did not rhyme correctly when called on alone, suggesting that some voices led the others. A common approach was to call out a stream of syllables that rhyme, in hopes that one would be correct, i.e., start with the consonant the teacher provided. Thus some students had learned how to rhyme, but not how to rhyme correctly. The class practiced this routine regularly for weeks before many students could do it correctly; several weeks after that some students still could not do it.

Progress charts recorded certain abilities which two tutees expressed. The charts indicated that Ted always read *lists* of sounds poorly, but Bill read them with increasing ease. After each boy chose books to read, we tried to use the charts to record progress reading *passages*. Ted read fairly well if he could start some new piece every day and if he was in a cooperative mood, whereas Bill, tackling more difficult books and sticking with them, steadily improved. The charts did not reveal the complexity of Ted's and Bill's many ability characteristics.

A "news program" illustrated the relationship between ability in Reading and ability in other activities. The fifth/sixth-grade homeroom class wrote, performed, videotaped, and played the program. Several students announced news "on the air," some reading clearly and others barely able to read. Al-though all had accomplished four or five years of Reading, some did not have the ability to read competently as a news anchorperson.

Style

Individual characteristics of style in attitude and means of accomplishing (or not accomplishing) tasks are as numerous and complex as students' personalities. Reading style includes goals, attention, and patterns of behavior. The case of one third-grade girl illustrates a distinctive goal. Louise interacted with other students less than most students did, yet told the teacher and me details of her progress in a game-assignment. She achieved "landmarks" on a mythical voyage by reading certain numbers and types of books. No one else in the class mentioned this "voyage" or spoke to me at such length as this girl did. Her idiosyncratic use of the "voyage" goal was a style which pervaded her schoolwork.

In contrast to the unusual goal above, another student's goal *in the classroom* was to let his comrades know that he was "keeping up" with them. Bill, a tutee mentioned above, told me that he was ashamed to "get behind" classmates in his regular classroom assignments, as he did if he attended tutorial sessions with me. "Getting behind" in Reading class bothered Bill because he and other boys compared their speed and accuracy in completing workbook assignments. Since he was not present to do them, he "lost," regardless of whether the teacher required him to do them. Not being able to win in a competition he could not enter, he apparently avoided many Reading tasks even when he *was* in the class and *could* work on them. He spent Reading time talking, flirting, and aggravating the teacher. His goal to "win" was tempered by his no-win situation and became a goal to "not lose because I didn't try."

Bill's goal in tutorial sessions was not only to learn to read for junior high school, but also to "beat the clock" (so that the chart revealed progress) and to enjoy the social studies books he chose. His separate styles in classroom and tutorial sessions both expressed his overall aim to succeed and show others his success.

In considering style further, let us compare attention and behavior patterns of three Readers in the lowest-ability-level, third/fourth-grade class. The focal points for this class were 60-second trials during which each student read to a later-grade tutor. The aim was to read as quickly and with as few errors as possible. From the intense concentration, staccato rhythms of pronunciation, and tense bodies, it was apparent that most students aspired to that aim, but with different behavioral manifestations.

Alice, with her tidy, bowl-shaped hair-do, sat straight in her chair and pronounced each syllable with painful slowness. She waited for the tutor to count and record the results, and carefully practiced for the next trial in the same stiff stance. Kevin, running his fingers through tousled hair, hunched over his book and shouted each syllable, tapping his foot and bobbing his head with each utterance. By the end of the timed trial he was physically frenzied. Sometimes the teacher (who walked around the room monitoring the stopwatch, tutors, and tutees) put her hands firmly on his shoulders, to all appearances restraining him from propelling his head into the book. During practice time Kevin ran around the room or leaned over the back of his chair and intensely watched others work, unless a teacher or tutor urged him to work. Linda appeared to work "for" her tutor. She was so fond of her tutor that she brought her mother to look at the tutor. Linda always worked during the 60-second timings (as all did), but she only worked during practice times if her favorite tutor was present. (Another characteristic of Linda's approach was that she cried frequently when she felt she was failing.)

Individuals "weave" styles from patterns of purpose, attention, and other behavior. The same Reading tasks do not elicit similar Reading behavior from all students.

Situation

"Situation" refers to a student's tendency (actual choice) and taste (desired choice) in settings—time, place, and companions—for Reading work. Individuals choose situations in which they like to do, or actually do, Reading work. Within the limits set by teachers, rooms, and assignments, students increase variety in situation by choosing whether and how to comply with assignments.

One first grader, Bob, expressed characteristics for situation by "reading" independently. In most Reading situations he worked erratically, but in this self-created situation he read eagerly and successfully: he regularly finished writing his workbook exercises before the others did, pulled another workbook from unused materials, took a seat away from the others, and tried to read. In its current work the class was learning to recognize isolated letters, not letters forming words or sentences as in the workbook Bob chose. Bob recognized letters and read some words, looking up proudly after each one. The teacher praised Bob and suggested that I listen to him. With help he was even more successful. Most words demanded discussion, segmentation, and repeated attempts before he could read them correctly. When he saw words he had just read, he had to repeat this analysis, but he was reading words, something none of the other students could do.

Substance

Students display tastes in literature: *genre*, topic, appearance (e.g., kind of binding, difficulty). Ted and Bill, whom I tutored individually, each talked about their preferences, "experimented" with various topics, and read better from material they chose than from "standardized" programs. Ted chose books on fantasy and animal behavior; Bill chose books on social studies.

Bob (who had his own mind about most matters) aggressively requested that the teacher read stories but later sought to be excused from such readings. Once he remained at the table to work on written exercises after the other students had moved to a row of chairs to hear the tale. But by the middle of the story he had scooted toward the group and was peering from behind

the teacher, trying to see the pictures. Apparently Bob was torn between liking stories and wanting to work on his written exercises. Often students' strongest preferences combined their tastes for situation and substance. Thus most fifth graders in the class with the parlor-game atmosphere preferred "doing workbooks" and "playing password" (the game-like activities) to reading from texts.

The foregoing descriptions establish the wide variation in academic profiles which students express in Reading at Emerald. Since Reading experience for each person is "filtered" by means of social organization in such a way that some individuals encounter certain Reading realities and some encounter other Reading realities, it is important to ask about the relationship between the dimensions of social organization and the academic traits of individuals. Is the effect of a given dimension to bring together or to segregate "like-minded" Readers? With such information in hand we might investigate the possibilities of new groupings based on selected academic qualities as alternatives for social organization in our schools.

Academic Features of Students and Dimensions of Social Organization

The dimensions of social organization discussed in previous sections—grade, ability-level, subject, and schedule—are socially relevant aspects of school reality which are the bases for arranging children into classes. There are other criteria which could be, but are not, used to arrange classes. Among such criteria are the sex, ethnic background, and intellectual aspirations of students. In this section on academic features of individuals we have looked at one crucial aspect of school reality which is not used as a criterion of class formation: individual students' personality traits which pertain to their academic concerns. Each person has his or her own intellectual interests and approaches in the study of Reading. Students may develop or express these characteristics, which I discuss in terms of ability, style, taste in situation, and taste in substance, as they do Reading activities. But these academic features are not the object of explicit classification for sorting students into classes of individuals with similar or different academic characteristics.

In general, academic characteristics of individuals are not the basis of Reading class formation, since the dimensions of social organization (grade, ability-level, subject, and schedule) are used to form classes which cut across academic distinctions among individuals. For example, Reading classes formed by grade are neither the purposeful "mixing" of students with similar academic interests nor the purposeful separation of students with contrasting academic interests. The grade dimension of social organization can be said to "obscure" academic differences.

Emerald's dimensions of social organization obscure all the academic features discussed above. Grade and homeroom class, ability-level, subject, and schedule as criteria of class formation do not take into account individual variation in style, taste in situation, or taste in substance. A student with

given traits for those three features is in Reading class with others who have a variety of characteristics for those features. There are two exceptions in which dimensions do not obscure individual academic traits: ability-level and back-to-back schedule recognize ability, to some extent.

With regard to ability, a student with given characteristics is in class with others who have similar abilities, insofar as two dimensions—ability-level and back-to-back schedule—determine class membership. Since the other dimensions—grade and subject—do not lead to classes based on ability, a student who has certain ability characteristics takes Reading only with students of similar ability from his or her own grade (and not with students of similar ability from other grades). Thus certain dimensions recognize ability and others obscure it. Ability recognition is also limited because ability-level and back-to-back schedule recognize other factors (size and number of teachers) along with ability and because assessment of "ability" to do Reading tests and work probably is imperfect.

Since the actual dimensions of social organization—grade, ability-level, subject, and schedule—do not recognize the academic features I found to be important in Reading, except for ability, students' understanding and enactment of the social organization do not need to take these features into account. Students are the "actors" in social organization, for it is their movements which we abstract when we apply the term. Students implicitly understand and even ask questions about social organization. In knowing what to do and what others do, they relate thought and deed to the dimensions on which social organization is based. Insofar as social organization does not involve recognition of significant academic traits (e.g., style and tastes), it does not encourage the students to recognize these traits.[11] As students operate in the social organization, they know about and observe characteristics of ability more than any other individual traits. Conversely, in considering ability, students may notice that it is "organized."

Implications for Ethnography and Education

Researchers of reading often emphasize behaviors that support inferences about two sorts of mental activity: (1) cognitive processes of decoding symbols for sound and meaning (Flesch 1955; Goodman and Fleming 1969; Kleederman 1975; Smith 1973) and (2) emotions (often in terms of motivation, expectations, self-concept, and other attitudes) and their interplay with academic achievement (Carlton and Moore 1968; Purkey 1970; Rosenthal and Jacobson 1968). In their concentration on how students think and feel they may neglect the ways students join and leave classes, which are the contexts of mental activity.

Another research emphasis is the "cause" of failure to learn. Many people point to influences operating on the child before entering school and suggest that these are the likely cause of the child's failure to learn reading in school. When not finding the cause of failure in the children themselves and their experiences before entering school, researchers seek them in the current classroom situation. They have discovered important factors in the stream of behavior there, but they still have not investigated thoroughly the way that stream is patterned in accordance with social organization of the schools.

It is true that many teacher education textbooks on reading instruction have one chapter about organizing groups for Reading among many chapters on materials, instruction techniques, and interpersonal relations (Dallmann et al. 1974; Ruddell 1974; Smith and John 1976). Descriptions of various arrangements in U.S. schools and their advantages and disadvantages for teachers include the Joplin Plan, the Cambridge Plan, and the ungraded plan. Such plans are outlined in terms of the roles of ability (degrees of ability often being associated with certain grades), age, and grade in determining membership in Reading groups. Text authors, however, usually do not relate these organization plans to the kinds of schools or students, media of presentation, instruction techniques, time and space allocation, or academic interests of students which the plans enhance. Although future teachers reading these texts learn that social organization is pertinent, they do not study its relationships to other aspects of Reading reality.

Certain anthropologists have studied structures of education settings, but have not focused on the school as a population which is subdivided into classes. R. P. McDermott (1974, 1977a, 1977b) relates diverse student preparations for schoolwork and pressures on teachers to the ways Reading is organized. He discusses this classroom environment not as an amorphous influence on learning, but as a *structure* for interaction among people and their use of time, space, and materials which influence learning. Whereas McDermott shows how social organization within the *classroom* is a foundation for specific interactions leading to failure, I show how social organization in one elementary *school* is a foundation determining what kinds of people, aims, and tasks come together in classrooms within a school.

Frederick O. Gearing (1975) attends to the patterns of social interaction inherent in all education events. In terms of his concept of education as patterned constraints on the display of information, people have certain attributes which "qualify" them to receive certain kinds of information and not other kinds. An initial step in analyzing education in these terms might be to analyze a school's classes in terms of members' personal attributes and information, including content of Reading assignments and messages about comportment.

Aside from being the focal topic of research, social organization may be preliminary information for orienting data on other topics in education. The construct of dimensions of social space may allow us to precisely "locate" people and activities we are analyzing, thus identifying *the* education to which our analysis pertains. The construct might also benefit community studies of education by providing a structural framework for isolating factors in a school situation which could be related to parallel factors in community social organization.

In addition to being the "flesh" (main topic) or the "skeleton" (facts which identify the data) for ethnographic study, the social framework for education is an essential topic for addressing practical issues of education. Since social organization helps to mold education realities, it may be possible to achieve desired realities by manipulating it. Understanding the systematic interrelations of social organization, Reading assignments, and individual academic features might allow us to design Reading class social organization with clear expectations as to its pedagogical value. For a simple example, if we want to encourage students to read books they enjoy, we might use student choice in literature as a criterion of class formation. Thus we might bolster verbal encouragement with the firm underpinning of groups based on reading tastes. Or we might undercut "ability" recognition by using elements of style as a criterion of class assignment. We might consider grouping children according to "how hard they try" (surely no more difficult to assess than "ability" and certainly not covariant with "ability"). In addition, we could carefully examine the many aspects of Reading classes, including their size, number of teachers and aides, and kinds of assignments, which we may have linked to the dimensions of social organization, intentionally or unintentionally. Thus we may change the tendency to create small or otherwise special classes for certain grades or ability-levels. Or we may ignore subject as a basis of class formation for certain groups, times, and places. The criteria we use and the way we use them structure the sorts of groups we end up with. We can consciously choose the structures as a major means of guiding the children in their studies.

New social organization for students might result in more effective teaching and learning. Cole, Gay, Glick, and Sharp (1971) suggest that people may differ more in the *conditions* in which they can perform a mental task than in their abstract abilities to perform the task. Extended to Reading situations, this suggests that we might alter social organization to promote conditions which encourage reading success, rather than trying to improve performance under the same social organization. Insofar as the *circumstances* conducive to learning are our focus, the social organization of schools is central.

In conclusion, ethnographers of schools study events which occur in a social framework. The broad purpose of an approach to Reading analysis via social organization for Reading classes is to jolt us into seeing the obvious facts about who does what with whom and realizing their impact on the "educations" which occur in the variety of settings, including types of classes, which comprise a school. One of anthropologists' main topics of inquiry among traditional preliterate peoples has been their patterns of group membership and activities. I found the same topic to be essential among elementary school "preliterates."

Notes

[1] "Reading" is capitalized when referring to the formal subject which classes form to study. The activity "reading" is significant in many other settings in the school.

[2] Raymond Firth (1961) influenced this conception of social organization.

[3] I refer to primary grades—1, 2, and 3—as "early" and upper elementary grades—4, 5, and 6—as "late" to avoid confusion with "upper" and "lower" ability-levels.

[4] A panel of educators and laypersons wrote these goals.

[5] In the first grade, Reading classes for lower ability-levels have about six members, those for higher ability-level members about twelve.

[6] One variation of this basic plan is described by Bond and Wagner (1966) as an "instructional pattern."

[7] Such classes are sometimes called "self-contained classrooms."

[8] At Emerald, third- and fourth-grade Reading classes are grouped across the two grades so that members of each grade are together in Reading.

[9] Some classes are not specified precisely for each dimension: homeroom classes, for instance, have imprecise subject specifications.

[10] The purpose is not to prove that distinctions of the features are *cause* or *effect* of the dimensions of social organization. Rather, the relationships between individual Reading characteristics and dimensions of social organization show which categories of people, in terms of academic matters, are united and which are divided in classes.

[11] The claim here is only that in enacting the *social organization*—joining classes and trying to understand the criteria of class formation—students do not need to recognize academic differences. I do not address the question of whether the "mixture" of students in classes regardless of their academic traits leads them to be more or less aware of these traits *as they do Reading work*. Whether such "mixture" leads to increased or decreased awareness of academic traits, *the social organization is instrumental in arranging the conditions for such awareness* and merits study in light of that question.

References

Ariés, Phillippe. 1962. *Centuries of Childhood: A Social History's Family Life*. New York: Random House.

Bond, Guy L., and Eva Bond Wagner. 1966. *Teaching the Child to Read.* New York: The Macmillan Company.

Carlton, Lessie, and Robert H. Moore. 1968. *Reading, Self-Directive Dramatization, and Self-Concept.* Columbus, OH: C. E. Merrill.

Cole, Michael, John Gay, J. A. Glick, and D. W. Sharp. 1971. *The Cultural Context of Learning and Thinking: An Exploration in Experimental Anthropology.* New York: Basic Books.

Dallmann, Martha, Roger L. Rouch, Lynette Y. C. Char, and John J. DeBoer. 1974. *The Teaching of Reading.* New York: Holt, Rinehart and Winston.

Eisenstadt, S. N. 1956. *Essays on Comparative Institutions.* New York: John Wiley and Sons.

Firth, Raymond. 1961. *Elements of Social Organization.* Boston: Beacon Press.

Flesch, Rudolf. 1955. *Why Johnny Can't Read.* New York: Harper & Row.

Gearing, Frederick O. 1973. "Why Indians?" In A. J. Ianni Francis and Edward Storey, eds., *Cultural Relevance and Educational Issues.* Boston: Little, Brown and Co.

———. 1975. "Structures of Censorship, Usually Inadvertant: Studies in a Cultural Theory of Education," *Council on Anthropology and Education Quarterly*, 6:2.

Goodman, Kenneth S., ed. 1968. *The Psycholinguistic Nature of the Reading Process.* Detroit: Wayne State University Press.

———, and James T. Fleming, eds. 1969. *Psycholinguistics and the Teaching of Reading.* Newark, DE: International Reading Association.

Kleederman, Frances F. 1975. "Linguistics and Reading," *Reading World*, 15:1.

McDermott, R. P. 1974. "Achieving School Failure." In *Education and Cultural Process.* New York: Holt, Rinehart and Winston.

———, with Jeffry Aron. 1977a. *Pirandello in the Classroom: On the Possibility of Educational Opportunity in American Culture.* Paper presented to a Conference on Issues Relating to the Future of Special Education. Minneapolis: University of Minnesota, Apr. 27, 1977.

———. 1977b. "Social Relations as Contexts for Learning in School," *Harvard Educational Review*, 47:2.

Purkey, William W. 1970. *Self-Concept and School Achievement.* Englewood Cliffs, NJ: Prentice-Hall, Inc.

Rosenthal, Robert, and Lenore Jacobson. 1968. *Pygmalion in the Classroom: Teacher Expectation and Pupils' Intellectual Development.* New York: Holt, Rinehart and Winston.

Ruddell, Robert B. 1974. *Reading-Language Instruction: Innovative Practices.* Englewood Cliffs, NJ: Prentice-Hall, Inc.

Smith, Frank. 1973. *Psycholinguistics and Reading.* New York: Holt, Rinehart and Winston.

Smith, Richard J., and Dale D. John. 1976. *Teaching Children to Read.* Reading, MA: Addison-Wesley Publishing Co., Inc.

Whyte, William F. 1943. *Street Corner Society.* Chicago: University of Illinois Press.

14

Walter Precourt

Ethnohistorical Analysis of an Appalachian Settlement School

Walter Precourt and his "Key informant," who started Mountain Creek Community School in the 1930s

The Author

Walter Precourt is assistant professor of anthropology at the University of Kentucky. He says of himself:

"My interest in Appalachia developed when I attended the University of Cincinnati (1968–1970). There has been considerable migration of Appalachians into Cincinnati and surrounding areas. The result is that a complex set of attitudes emerged among local residents of Cincinnati toward Appalachians. Generally, Appalachians were categorized as a 'low-class' population. Terms such as 'Briar' and 'Sam' (Southern Appalachian Migrant) were frequently used in a derogatory sense to refer to them. The experience of living in Cincinnati, combined with my anthropological background and initial research on Appalachia, made me realize that many of the numerous problems and stereotypes associated with Appalachians were the result of an almost total lack of understanding on the part of non-Appalachians of Appalachian culture and the historical factors that had influenced Appalachians.

"In a master's thesis entitled 'Poverty in Appalachia: A Cultural-Historical Analysis,' I traced Appalachian culture history and delineated the cultural forces associated with poverty in Appalachia. My approach, however, did not use a definition of poverty that emphasized access to economic resources and consumption patterns. Instead, I was concerned with the phenomenon of poverty as an ideological manifestation of contrasting lifestyles, values, and standards of behavior. After graduating from the University of Cincinnati in 1970, I entered the Ph.D. program at the State University of New York at Buffalo and participated in the Project in Ethnography and Education. My fieldwork plan combined my interest in Appalachia as an ethnographic area with an interest in research on American education. I conducted research at an eastern Kentucky settlement school. Since the date of the initial ethnographic research in 1973 and 1974, I have been in continuous contact with the community and have gathered additional data on the school. In 1975, I was appointed to the school's board of directors. In conjunction with the applied anthropology program, University of Kentucky, I am presently developing plans for ethnic heritage programs and environmental education programs at Appalachian settlement schools."

This Chapter

This study of an Appalachian settlement school is very different in approach from any other represented in this volume. It reconstructs, largely through the memory of a living informant, the changing relationships between a community and its school over time. The relationship is not a simple one, and goes beyond the all-too-frequent concept of the community as a strictly local, self-contained entity. Rather, the school is seen as relating to a complex interweaving of local and regional patterns.

This chapter is tantalizing in its brevity and in the kinds of understandings that in its brevity it suggests but cannot pursue. It serves as a reminder that relationships and adaptations occur over time and that the shape of any particular situation at any given time is a product of these relationships. We are so caught up in immediate reality and its synchronic relationships that this elemental fact is often overlooked. Anthropology had to rediscover history in its recovery from the excesses of structural functionalism. The diachronic orientation will be represented more frequently in the total range of approaches in educational anthropology as time goes on. There are indeed compelling synchronic problems to pursue and they dominate our efforts for the present. But these efforts are time-flat. Phenomena are studied as though there were no past. And yet every school and its community has a past. It would be well to include it within the framework of holism which is held to be one of the special features of anthropological ethnography.

Introduction

Ethnographic studies on education tend to be synchronic in orientation. The historical context, while implicit in many studies, is seldom dealt with systematically. Long-range historical trends are frequently ignored or treated only tangentially. Ethnographers obviously must observe specific events and discover how educational phenomena manifest in the stream of behavior. Ethnographers must not, however, lose sight of the fact that the unfolding of educationally relevant behavior is embedded in a broader historical complex of cultural patterns and processes.

The historical side of the ethnographic coin is the subject of this chapter, which examines education from an ethnohistorical perspective.

The chapter focuses on the educational patterns of a small Appalachian settlement school in eastern Kentucky, which will be referred to as Mountain Creek Community School. This school is analyzed in light of educational developments in Kentucky since 1792, when Kentucky became a state.

In the first part of the chapter the main historical trends in education for the entire state of Kentucky are outlined, with emphasis on the Appalachian counties of eastern Kentucky.

The development of the settlement school is considered in light of these educational trends.

Throughout, an attempt is made to demonstrate the historical relationship between the settlement school and state educational policies, on the one hand, and local Appalachian cultural patterns, on the other. The aim of this paper is to demonstrate how these relationships are manifested in the educational patterns of a specific school in a complex interweaving of local and regional patterns with policies, regulations, and trends of the state.

The ethnohistorical material presented on the settlement school was gathered during ethnographic field work conducted in 1973–1974 and 1978. This research focused on the relationship between the school and the community.

The development of the school is closely associated with the work of the present school director, who organized the school in 1933 and has coordinated school affairs since that date. The ethnohistorical material on the school is based upon interviews with the school director, supplemented by school records and relevant archival materials.

Kentucky Educational History

When Kentucky became a state in 1792, provision was made for a system of public secondary education. The goal was to establish a county academy in each county of the state, endowed with state lands. By 1830, about 65 of these academies were established. This system, however, was very difficult to administer, because of the state's geographical characteristics and communications system. Futhermore, most of these academies were financially unstable, and in some cases counties sold the land designated for academies to private businesses. By 1850, the state relinquished control and supervision of most academies to local authorities marking the end of the state's first attempt to establish a system of public education. Throughout the mid-1800s private schools owned and controlled by religious denominations, by stock companies, and by private individuals replaced most of the academies (Ligon 1942, McVey 1949).

In 1838, an education bill was passed that was designed to develop a system of primary education. This law mandated the county courts to divide each county into school districts, and to initiate a system of local taxation for education. At first, eastern Kentucky counties were slow in adopting the provisions of the bill. For instance, in 1841, only two counties in eastern Kentucky had adopted the bill's provisions, in contrast to central and western Kentucky, where it was adopted by 18 counties. It was not until the late 1800s that the district school became an established part of the educational system of eastern Kentucky (Ligon 1942:77–90).

In the 1890s the district schools of the Kentucky mountains were in session for five months, from August 1 till Christmas. The number of pupils at a school ranged from 50 to 100, of all ages from 6 to 20. All were in charge of one school teacher. School started in August, but it was soon interrupted for a week, because the instructor had to leave to attend the Teacher's Institute at the county seat. In October the older boys and girls were withdrawn from school for two weeks to help get in the harvest.

Preparation for teaching consisted of the course of instruction at the district school and a few months' training at the so-called normal school of the county seat.

The school building was a log cabin, equipped with desks or benches manufactured locally. The unplaned planks of the inside of the walls were stained a dark color for a space of 12 feet and used as a blackboard (Semple 1901).

Other than the academies, the first public high schools were established about 1855 in Kentucky's larger cities. Until after 1908, however, there were very few high schools in eastern Kentucky. In 1879 only one of the 36 eastern Kentucky counties established by that time had public secondary education. By 1908, the number of counties with secondary education was three. In comparison, 30 of the 54 counties in central and western Kentucky had public secondary education (Clark 1924:39–45).

The passage of the county administration law in 1908 profoundly influenced the subsequent development of education in eastern Kentucky. This act abolished the local district as the unit of school administration and established the county as the administrative unit. The act also made it compulsory upon the county board of education to establish one or more county high schools in rural counties (Ligon 1942:142).

The passage of this act was followed by the Whirlwind Campaigns of 1908 and 1909. The first campaign continued for nine days. In these campaigns, the provisions of the new education law and other matters of interest in education were explained to the people by the newspapers of the state and by a group of 29 speakers, who traveled to every county in the state. It is estimated that nearly 60,000 people heard these addresses. As a result of the new school law and the Whirlwind Campaigns, the number of county secondary schools in Kentucky increased rapidly. By 1912 only 18 of Kentucky's 90 counties did not have public secondary education. However, 14 of the 18 counties that did not have secondary education were located in eastern Kentucky (Clark 1924:48; Ligon 1942:143–144).

The educational directives established by the law of 1908 were strongly supported by most of the county superintendents of eastern Kentucky. For instance, the superintendent of Knott county schools remarked, "Under the new law we have thirteen new school houses. The new school law is an excellent law—the ideal is reached." The Perry county superintendent remarked, "Since the new school law, there has been an educational awakening among the people. The character of the schools is much better." These comments were solicited by John Crabbe, the superintendent of public instruction of Kentucky about a year after the law had been passed (Hamlett 1914:216–219).

Although at the county level there was considerable support for establishing county secondary schools, there were relatively few county schools actually established in eastern Kentucky. Even when schools were established, they usually were available to only a small percentage of the children in a county. The education tax base was usually not sufficient to compensate for the problems created by geographical conditions, which made school construction and student transportation difficult. Furthermore, the county-based system was resisted by many inhabitants accustomed to the district system of school administration. These individuals believed in freedom of action in local affairs and resisted relinquishing their control of schools to a county educational board. For instance, local variations in subsistence farming patterns could be compensated for much more easily if the local producers could arrange the school schedule so that it would complement the cycle of planting, harvesting, and processing plants. The introduction of county-controlled secondary schools would restrict decision-making at the community level.

The Settlement School

The settlement school that developed between the 1880s and 1935 in Appalachia was responsive to both state educational policies and Appalachian cultural patterns. Most of these schools were financed by religious organizations, private agencies, and private donations. They usually were not dependent upon public funds and the local tax base. In addition, many of these schools incorporated into their curriculum and organizational structure aspects of the local culture (Stokely 1977, Moses 1976, Hardy 1972, Campbell 1969).

Vance (1932:254–255) comments on the general characteristics of the settlement school as it existed throughout the Southern Appalachian Region and indicates the significance of this type of school for local Appalachian culture.

One hundred forty-nine mountain schools are maintained in eight southern states by denominational and independent agencies. Through the girls many of them attempt to teach a science and an art of homemaking. Through the boys they teach an agriculture that will reach back into mountain coves and homesteads. In Georgia the Berry Schools have achieved national recognition. At Brass Town, North Carolina, Mrs. John C. Campbell has founded an institution patterned after the Danish folk schools. At Pine Mountain, Kentucky, the school has succeeded in merging itself with the life of the community. At Raeburn, in North Georgia, a school has worked out a family plan of training. The institution moves the family to the school farm and educates their children while the adults are operating the farm under direction. The knowledge of agriculture thus gained is afterwards put into practice on the home farm.

It is estimated that in eastern Kentucky there were up to 80 settlement schools in the 1920s. The number has gradually diminished, and about 10 schools now remain.

To illustrate the process of interaction and integration of the settlement school within the local cultural context I will focus on the development of Mountain Creek Community School. In 1974, Mountain Creek Community School had an enrollment of 186 students, grades 1–12. The community of Mountain Creek has a population of about 800 persons. The enrollment of this school is equivalent to most of the settlement schools that developed and many of the public schools that existed before 1950. Since 1950, the enrollment of individual public schools has grown substantially and is greater than the enrollment of settlement schools. Thus, Mountain Creek Community School is one of the smallest in Kentucky and among the few remaining settlement schools in the state (Kentucky Department of Education 1937, Butler 1963). Local residents of Mountain Creek helped the school director in establishing the school. They helped construct the school's first building, a log structure designed to house a variety of school-related activities. They contributed food, land, materials, and labor to the school and participated in school organizational activities and decision-making processes. Many of the first teachers who came from outside the community boarded in the homes of community residents.

At the beginning of 1933, the school consisted of a grade school with two one-room classes, and it was organized according to the district system of administration. The one-room school structure has an obvious and distinctive administrative characteristic: the one-room class is essentially an autonomous unit in terms of school administration. Except for the basic statewide curriculum requirements, there is no overriding administrative structure that directs the affairs of a one-room teacher. It is usually unnecessary to integrate the activities of one class with those of another. In this social context, the one-room structure represented a microcosm of the local community, since the decision-making process in the one-room class paralleled that of the autonomous kinship groupings, which maintained decision-making authority in virtually all areas of community life. Indeed, members of the local community identified with the grade school, and resisted subsequent changes in the school structure.

The addition of new high school grades during 1933 meant that a local administrative structure that transcended the single class was needed. It was not simply a matter, however, of imposing or adding such an organizational unit. The one-room ideology was very strong; it was deeply ingrained within the daily activities of each classroom as well as in the attitudes of the community residents. A formal administrative structure was not simply "added"; it gradually evolved over the years, and not until the early 1960s did it become fully established.

The development of the school administration approximating that of the county secondary schools was not a matter exclusively internal to the school; it was closely related to the school's relationship to the community. Many community members resisted the high school. Some persons regarded the mere existence of a high school as an imposition on the freedom of the students and parents. If a full-blown formal administrative structure had been instituted in 1933, this would have aggravated the situation. Thus, during the first several years, the high school was characterized as a "system of one-room schools."

It is instructive to examine the development of the administrative structure in terms of the school director's position in the school affairs. When the school director established the high school, it was her intent to minimize her role as administrator or director.

She regarded herself as an organizer rather than an administrator. For the first several years, the school director taught full-time; thus it was possible to identify herself in the school context as a teacher, not an administrator. When it did come to administrative responsibilities, she was "first among equals" in relation to the other teachers; she did not occupy a distinct administrative role.

In this respect, the principle of informal leadership in the school paralleled very closely the leadership structure of the wider community. It is evident that the school director structured her administrative position so that it would not conflict with certain organizational principles of the existing school structure and local community.

There is another significant dimension to the change in the overall system of the school. When the high school was first introduced, it remained an entity very distinct from the grade school. Since a grade school education was regarded as an end in itself, not as preparation for high school, the grade school was considered a separate school system. This attitude was reinforced by the idea of many community members that the high school represented an imposition by the wider urban society.

Between 1940 and 1960 there was a gradual integration of the high school and grade school. They became regarded as a single school system. This system became more demanding of a single centralized administrative structure. Various changes in administration occurred in the late 1940s and early 1950s. As these changes occurred, the school director assumed the role of "principal-teacher," though the role of principal gradually became dominant. By the 1960s, the formal administrative position of school principal had fully developed, although many characteristics of the more informally organized administrative structure were maintained and still persist.

The development of this school clearly reflects a general pattern of change whereby different principles of school organization were integrated into a single system. One set of principles corresponds to the traditional district system of education and indigenous culture, while the other corresponds to the county-based administrative system and the bureaucracy of the county and state. These contrasting principles are represented not only in the overall system of school administration but also in an indigenous classification of educational activity that emerged in the course of the school's development. The classification entails a distinction between "formal" and "informal" education. This distinction has nothing to do with whether an activity occurs within or outside of the school. That is, "formal" does not refer to school-related education, or "informal" to education that occurs outside of the school. "Informal" refers to education in which the rules governing educational activities and processes are generated from *within* the immediate context. "Formal" education is governed by the rules imposed from *outside* the immediate context. The immediate context is the particular setting where educational activity occurs, e.g., a classroom, playground, or teacher's meeting.

The formal/informal distinction can

apply to any educational activity, whether related to curriculum, class organization, regulations, or social relationships. Thus, a specific activity is not intrinsically formal or informal; the salient defining characteristics entail how the activity is generated, organized, and integrated with other activities and with the overall structure of the school.

School activities that entailed social patterns similar to those indigenous to the local community gradually became categorized as informal; those that reflected the county administration structure and state bureaucracy became categorized as formal. For instance, a nature study program introduced locally (i.e., it was not a state curriculum requirement) was regarded as a type of informal education. The main criterion for identifying it as informal was that it was a local invention. These categories were identified by the school director and were recognized by school teachers, students, and other members of the community.

In order to convey the importance of the principle of informal education to the organization of school activities and patterns of school behavior, let us consider its influence on student behavior. Here the informal principle is manifested in a pattern by which children were given considerable responsibility in school affairs. This pattern reflects the traditional role of children in mountain families transferred into the school context. At home, children, from a very early age, were given substantial work responsibilities. Siblings were held responsible for one another and younger children were often almost totally under the care of an older brother or

sister. An older child would often take younger preschool siblings to school. Children also contributed substantially to daily subsistence activities. They often worked side by side with their parents in the fields. Children frequently officiated at funerals, a task considered to entail a good deal of responsibility.

The classroom behaviors described here to illustrate the principle of informal education represent those that occurred in the classes of the school director in the 1940s. According to the school director, responsibility for organizing classroom activities, as well as the actual teaching of classes, was often assumed by students. The school director recalls that she would sometimes leave the classroom for days at a time, leaving the entire responsibility of conducting the class to one or more students. The students not only assumed teaching responsibilities, but also had their own system of self-government; that is, they would formulate rules and, in some cases, carry out disciplinary procedures. Another important student input into the operation of the classroom was their participation in selecting textbooks and in determining what materials should be included in the curriculum. Student participation in teaching activities is described by the school director in the following interview:

> In organizing the school there are many times when I would have to be away. If I had to go to Frankfort, I could count on a better part of a week, because it would take me that long to get there and do whatever I had to do and come back. So there were times when I could be entirely out of the valley for a week

at a time. And the students themselves took over the classes. I'd say, here's all my material and you have your material. By that time I had all kinds of books for them. They had excellent directions, which I gave them; teacher directions, which I put in the hands of the students. Well, it was a learning experience for me, so why not a learning experience for them, and they could use it. The students would carry on the work of their own education. They were self-directed.

QUESTION   How was this organized?

Well, we had the objective that we wanted. We had so much work that needed to be covered in order to make a year's work, and get a year's credit for high school work. And so we had all the materials there.

QUESTION   When students would take over their classes, would one student assume the role of teacher?

It would be more like an open discussion. Sometimes, now, like in the case of Ellis Simpson, one student would take over. Ellis Simpson just devoured history and it came easier to him; he just had a natural bent for history, so really I would put him in charge of the class. I'd put him in charge of the history class and then I of course would get the tests and that kind of thing, but he would conduct the class. But mostly it was open discussion, like a round table type of thing. But whoever knew the problem or the situation took over the lead—everybody was the leader. That is true about the mountain people, too, that in their frame of existence they can all be leaders or they can all be followers, to a certain extent. You may have noticed that in your dealings. Well, my experience was that they all could take leadership and they weren't backward in their discussions; they had ideas, they presented them. They were free and easy; there was a lot of amusement in the class, ban-

tering—friendliness, *not formal.* Of course, the *formal classes* came later. I don't suppose you'd find that openness exactly now in the classroom.

QUESTION   What year did formal classes come in?

They came in gradually, as I relinquished more and more to the teachers who had been trained in *formal education.*

Informal educational activities were also very prevalent in what was known as "chapel." Chapel consisted of a daily gathering of the entire school. It was usually held in the morning before classes started and lasted from 30 minutes to one hour. During chapel, a variety of activities occurred, namely, singing, prayer, storytelling, socializing, "playacting," and town hall meetings. Chapel was set up so that the entire school participated (grades 1–12 and all of the teachers). Furthermore, there was no established segregation of students by grade or sex; the students were free to mingle with each other and could speak to any of the teachers.

The entire structure of the chapel reflected the informal education principle, though informal educational activity is most clearly evident in the "town hall sessions." During these sessions, problems regarding any subject that pertained directly or indirectly to the school could be discussed openly by any student, regardless of grade. The teachers also actively participated in these meetings. During the town hall meetings, decision as to school policy and discipline would be made, and any grievances of students toward teachers or vice versa would be discussed and solutions would be worked out. There was no structuring of the proceedings of these meetings by the teachers; the meetings proceeded mainly according to the interests of the students.

Informal education, while most prevalent during the 1940s, is still present in the 1970s. It is present in the classroom, and also can be found in playground behaviors. During recess periods, students from the entire grade school (grades 1–8) participate together in the same playground area. There is no attempt to separate students by grade or sex, nor do teachers organize specific playground activities. The students are free to organize the playground activities themselves and choose from among the available activities. Teachers generally observe playground behaviors from the porch of the school building.

The school's integration with local culture is also evident in kinship involvement in the school. While the importance of kinship as a mechanism of social and political organization and control has declined over the last 50 years, kinship still has significant influence. Some nuclear families are almost autonomous with respect to kinship affiliation, but a good proportion are integrated within a larger kinship network. For instance, in one family both husband and wife have numerous kinfolk in the community, and their various kinship relationships make up a significant part of the sphere of social interaction of family members. This same family is closely involved with the community settlement school. Various members of their kinship group participate in the school as teachers, students, and staff. The result of this kinship involvement in the school is that there is

almost a continuous flow of information back and forth between the school and the wider community. What is going on in the school is *known* in the community. What is going on in the community is *known* in the school. As a result, the school is sensitive and responsive to the wants and needs of the local people. For instance, when an attempt was made to introduce into the school a musical band that was modeled after bands in urban schools, the students and parents did not show interest. Instead, they wanted square and folk dancing, which are indigenous to the community. The school adopted these dances as part of both physical education and music curriculum, and did not attempt to impose a band.

There are other situations where the local community comes first in school affairs vis-à-vis the demands of agencies located outside the community.

Discussion

The development of the school administration structure, the occurrence of the informal/formal classificatory distinction, and kinship involvement in school affairs demonstrate an historical process whereby the interaction of state and local aspects of education and culture evolved into distinctive patterns of educational administration, school organization, and student behavior.

The patterns of school/community involvement and integration of the school within the local cultural setting address some general problems faced by educators and social scientists dealing with the community context of schooling. In most community settings there is a perpetual "split" between the school and community. Schensul and Scheinfeld (1974) describe the results of a Chicago-based Research and Development program conducted in a Puerto Rican school and black school. This report outlines various kinds of school-community relationships.

The *Limited Engagement Model* places great restrictions on interaction and transmission of information between school and community. It assumes that what happens in the school and what happens in the wider community are two very different domains and there is little or no overlap between them. Most schools in America fall into this category.

The *Service Approach* goes a step further toward a school-community relationship by focusing more attention on the home environment. This approach attempts to resolve problems by providing services, references, assistance, and efforts at reeducating the family so that it will be able to offer a better, more stimulating environment to the child. Although this approach increases community involvement in school affairs, it tends to emphasize converting families to whatever social and educational standards the educational institutions happen to be upholding.

The *Community Development Approach* recognizes the importance of directing efforts both toward the school and toward the community. It argues for the redistribution of knowledge, power, and resources of each so that school and community can engage in a partnership of equals, a true dialogue.

It is difficult to place the school/community relationships of Mountain Creek into one of these categories. The

community development model perhaps comes closest, but it does not convey the extent to which the community is involved in school affairs. In fact, the dichotomy of school and community is in some respects a misnomer, because underlying social patterns of kinship and networks of informal interaction constitute an interactional structure that transcends "school/community" boundaries.

Local patterns of social organization and decision-making were incorporated in the school and given expression in categorization of formal and informal education. Today, members of the community feel that the school is the core of the community; if the school goes, the community goes. In a sense, the school's roots are in the community.

When comparing Mountain Creek Community School to schools in larger communities, we may question what patterns of school/community relationship are most effective for serving community needs and for implementing the explicit goals of education. At Mountain Creek it appears that a close school/community involvement has a positive effect on various aspects of education. Community involvement in school affairs increased the responsiveness by the school to the wants and needs of the local people, and also served the needs of the community by providing an interactional and organizational center for community activities.

Another way to determine the effectiveness of a school is by measuring high school and college attendance rates. Rates of high school graduation have been substantially higher in Mountain Creek than in other parts of the Appalachian region in which Mountain Creek is located. This was determined by comparing the high school dropout rate among students attending the Mountain Creek school to the region's average (Walls and Stephenson 1972). There has also consistently been a high college attendance rate among Mountain Creek school graduates— much higher than for the region as a whole. In fact, during the 1940s and early 1950s nearly 100 percent of high school graduates attended college. It would be inappropriate to say that close school/community involvement was the main *causal* factor in bringing about these high attendance rates, but it is clear that such a school/community relationship is not *incompatible* with high academic achievement, and may provide a supportive environment for such attainment.

Each school develops its own tradition and pattern of community relationships! The ethnohistorical approach used in this analysis demonstrates that the histories of particular schools offer insight into educational processes that may not be obtainable from studies using instrumented measures of large samples of schools, broad-scale historical studies, or synchronic studies. This is not meant to undermine the value and relevance of these studies, but certain patterns that develop in schools are difficult to ascertain by any method other than ethnohistory.

Settlement schools and similar educational institutions represent a phase of American education that may be coming to an end or undergoing substantial modification. Ethnohistorical studies can help us discover aspects of this form of schooling applicable to America's educational future.

References

Butler, Wendell. 1963. *History of Education in Kentucky: 1939–1964.* Educational Bulletin, Kentucky Department of Education, Vol. 31, No. 11.

Campbell, John C. 1969. *The Southern Highlander and His Homeland.* Lexington: University of Kentucky Press.

Clark, Clarence. 1924. *A History of the Development of the High Schools of Kentucky.* Master's thesis, Department of Education, University of Chicago.

Hamlett, Barksdale. 1914. *History of Education in Kentucky.* Bulletin of Kentucky Department of Education, Vol. 7, No. 4.

Hardy, Amy J. 1972. "Settlement Institutions in Appalachia," *Appalachia,* 5(6):24–42.

Kentucky Department of Education. 1937. *A Study of Local School Units in Kentucky.* Frankfort: State Department of Education.

Ligon, Moses E. 1942. *History of Public Education in Kentucky.* Bulletin of The Bureau of School Service, University of Kentucky, Vol. 14, No. 4.

McVey, Frank L. 1949. *The Gates Open Slowly: A History of Education in Kentucky.* Lexington: University of Kentucky Press.

Moses, Allan. 1976. "Settlement Schools." In Bruce Ergood and Bruce E. Kuhre, eds., *Appalachia: Social Context Past and Present.* Dubuque, IA: Kendall Hunt Publishing Company, 226–244.

Schensul, Jean J., and Daniel R. Scheinfeld. 1974. *New Approaches to School-Community Dialogue.* A Report Submitted to the H.E.W. Office of Education.

Semple, Ellen C. 1901. *The Anglo-Saxons of the Kentucky Mountains.* Bulletin of the American Geographic Society 42: 561–594.

Stokely, Jim. 1977. *To Make a Life: Settlement Institutions of Appalachia.* Berea, KY: Settlement Institutions of Appalachia, Inc.

Vance, Rupert B. 1932. *Human Geography of the South.* Chapel Hill: University of North Carolina Press.

Walls, David, and John Stephenson, eds. 1972. *Appalachia in the Sixties.* Lexington: University of Kentucky Press.

PART V

Methods and Issues: A Review

Editorial Commentary

Reviews are hard to write. There are two opposing strains that every reviewer must somehow reconcile. One is to summarize and cite; the other is to interpret and forecast. In this review of the current ethnography of education, Kathleen Wilcox strikes a happy balance between the two. Her interpretations concerning change and innovation in educational practice are particularly pertinent to the context in which ethnography is relevant to education. The ultimate real-life purpose of studies of schools, classrooms, administration, curriculum, bicultural programs, and so forth, is to help make it possible to change things for the better. The resistance to change in educational institutions is monumental, not simply because educators are conservative or especially impotent but because schools are transmitters of culture and exist within a community context. They recruit for and help maintain the status quo. Besides giving us an insight into the complexities and compelling issues of ethnography as applied to the study of schooling, Wilcox calls our attention to this crucial problem area of change and persistence.

15

Kathleen Wilcox

Ethnography as a Methodology and Its Application to the Study of Schooling: A Review

The Author

Kathleen Wilcox has been a member of the faculty of the Department of Human Development at California State University, Hayward. She also spent a year as a Visiting Scholar at the Center for Educational Research at Stanford University. The biographical note preceding her Chapter 9 in this book and that chapter itself give further information about her work.

The project of which this review is a product was supported by the Institute for Research on Educational Finance and Governance at Stanford for the purpose of reviewing current and recent anthropological ethnographies of schooling.

Introduction

The methodology of ethnography has been developed and utilized within the discipline of anthropology. As a methodology, it involves far more than a set of easily described and readily adopted data-gathering techniques. Its conceptual underpinnings and mode of use reflect heavily the characteristics of the discipline within which it was conceived and developed. Ethnography is not synonymous with participant observation, fieldwork, or qualitative research. A thorough understanding of ethnography requires an understanding of the discipline of anthropology as well.

Ethnography has been variously defined as anthropologists have tried to construct a research tool, capture its essence, and develop it over time: Malinowski 1922, Kluckhohn 1940, Herskovits 1954, Powdermaker 1966, Berreman 1968, Cohen 1970, Freilich 1970, R. Wax 1971, Spindler 1971, Geertz 1973, Pelto and Pelto 1973, 1978, Hymes 1974, Spradley 1979, 1980. Recently, a number of anthropologists and others have attempted to outline and define the characteristics of an ethnographic approach to studying education: Burnett 1968, Erickson 1973, Lutz and Ramsey 1974, Rist 1975, Wolcott 1975a, Burns 1976, Smith and Pohland 1976, Overholt and Stallings 1976, Sanday 1976, Erickson 1977, Herriott 1977, Rist 1977, Wilson 1977, Salomone 1979, Spindler: General Intro.: this volume, Knapp 1981, Ogbu 1981. Wolcott's (1975b) annotated bibliography on method, entitled *Ethnographic Approaches to Research in Education*, is a useful sourcebook for those who wish to read in this area in depth, as is the *Fieldwork Manual for Studying Desegregated Schools* written by Joan Cassell (1978) for the National Institute of Education.

The Science of Cultural Description

Wolcott's (1975a) definition of ethnography as the science of cultural description captures a theme which is basic to all of these accounts. Ethnography is first and foremost a *descriptive* endeavor in which the researcher attempts accurately to describe and interpret the nature of social discourse among a group of people. Geertz (1973) discusses the task of description with great sensitivity. He suggests that the ethnographer is aiming at "thick description," in which a wink can be distinguished from a twitch, or a parody of a wink from a wink itself, and contrasts thick description with thin description, in which a wink may be described as the rapid contraction of an eyelid. The thinner the description, the more it is stripped of multilayered social meaning. Geertz's conception of ethnography is shared by many, in that what is to be described is seen as including both meaning and behavior (Gearing 1973b, Spindler 1974b). One must be in a position both to observe behavior in its natural setting and to elicit from the people observed the structures of meaning which inform and texture behavior. As Spindler summarizes it in this volume, the practice of ethnography enables one to discover the cultural knowledge possessed by people as natives (members of groups or communities), as well as the ways in which this cultural knowledge is used in social interaction.

While ethnography has traditionally been thought of as the description of the culture of a whole community, it has been and is equally applicable to the description of social discourse among any group of people among whom social relations are regulated by custom. Classrooms and schools are both well suited to ethnographic inquiry, although the difference in scope and setting requires certain adaptations (Erickson 1973).

The Inquiry Process

One's goal as an ethnographer is to focus on a setting and, in Wolcott's words, to discover what is going on there. One is engaged in a thoroughgoing process of inquiry, aided by certain fundamental anthropological precepts. First, one is attempting to set aside one's own preconceptions or stereotypes about what is going on and to explore the setting as it is viewed and constructed by its participants. Second, one is attempting to make the familiar strange, to notice that which is taken for granted either by the researcher or by the participants, to assume that that which seems commonplace is nonetheless extraordinary and to question why it exists or takes place as it does, or why something else does not (Erickson 1973, Spindler and Spindler, this volume). Third, one is assuming that, to understand why things take place as they do, one must look at the relationship between the setting and its context—for instance, between the classroom and the school as a whole, the community, the community of the teacher, the economy, and so on. A judgment of relevant context must always be made, and the character of this context must be explored to the extent that resources allow. Fourth, one is utilizing one's knowledge of existing social theory to guide and inform one's observations.

Direct experience in other cultures,

or at least extensive familiarity with the cross-cultural literature, is extremely helpful in establishing the first two characteristics of the ethnographic mind-set. A familiarity with anthropological and other social scientific thought is essential in regard to the last two. Without this kind of background, it is very difficult to analyze or assess fully the significance of what one has seen. While it is possible to engage in participant observation without this kind of background, one may be overly constrained by cultural biases and blinders, may fail to see significance in what has been observed, or may focus too much on individuals apart from social context to do good ethnography.

One of the initial tasks in doing ethnography is deciding what to focus on. It becomes immediately apparent to the thoughtful observer that one cannot describe *everything*. Even the early ethnographies, which attempted to be extremely comprehensive in their descriptions of the ways of life of people in whole communities, concentrated out of design and necessity on certain types of belief and behavior. As ethnography has developed as a research tool, the scope of focus has become increasingly narrow. Throughout the history of ethnography, however, the ethnographer has had to make decisions about the focus on inquiry. The conceptual framework of anthropology has from the beginning guided ethnographers in making these kinds of decisions (Malinowski 1922). There are many schools of anthropological thought, and researchers have begun their tasks with widely varying topics of interest and theoretical approaches. However, each competent researcher has begun with some sort of scheme,

based on knowledge of previous anthropological and other social scientific work, which enables the researcher to select among phenomena for observation and to assign significance to phenomena uncovered in the process of the research.

One begins fieldwork not with a tabula rasa but with a foreshadowed problem in mind. However, the problem is of necessity general in scope. Because one is attempting to understand a system in its own terms, according to its own criteria of meaningfulness, one cannot predict in advance which aspects of the system will have significance or the kind of significance they will have. Because one assumes as an ethnographer that particular parts of the system can be understood only in the context of the working of the whole, one cannot predict in advance precisely where one should focus. It is crucial to begin the research without specifically predetermined categories of observation, questionnaires, precise hypotheses, and so on. This can be considered a fifth characteristic of ethnographic research. Ready made instruments and overly precise formulations of the problem are seen to close off prematurely the process of discovery of that which is significant in the setting. An essential part of the research task is discovering what is significant, what makes sense to count (Erickson 1977), what is important to observe. One is continuously involved in a process of inquiry.

The inquiry process is carried out through a series of acts performed by the ethnographer: maintaining and developing one's relationship to the people one is with to ensure the flow of data; employing a variety of research techniques to collect a wide range of data; remaining in the field long enough to ensure that one has been able to observe events often enough to note regularities and irregularities and interpret them with confidence; and so on. Throughout all of this, the researcher is constantly drawing on relevant bodies of theory and knowledge to move the research process forward, to assess the significance of what s/he has seen and heard, to develop specific hypotheses and categories of observation, and continually to refocus and refine the process of study. The interested reader will find much in the chapters of this volume to expand these statements and may also turn to Erickson (1973, 1977), Hansen (1979), Lutz and Ramsey (1974), Ogbu (1974a), Overholt and Stallings (1976), Rist (1975, 1977) and Smith and Pohland (1976) for further discussion of various aspects of the research process.

Methods of Data-Gathering and Analysis

Ethnographers of schooling have employed a tremendous variety of methods and techniques to gather data. I will discuss some of the most prominent ones in this section of the paper. Although I cite examples from the ethnographic literature to illustrate the use of particular methods and techniques, the works cited are illustrative rather than exhaustive. The interested reader may consult the series of Case Studies in Education and Culture (particularly Wolcott 1967 and 1973, Singleton 1967, King 1967, and Warren 1967) for a broad sampling of the use of many different methods and techniques.

The variation in types of data gath-

ered and techniques employed may bewilder nonethnographers (Mulhauser 1975), since it makes it difficult to define what an ethnography will or should look like, and thus to judge its quality. Traditionally, from the ethnographer's point of view, the gathering of many different kinds of data has been seen to increase the validity and reliability of the study, and the uniqueness of each setting and each area of study has been thought to require a tailor-made set of methods and techniques.

However, Pelto and Pelto (1973) note a general trend in all areas of anthropology toward increasing quantification and operationalization, increasing attention to structured interviewing of samples rather than key informants, and increasing observation of significant behavioral settings. Brim and Spain (1974) recommend such procedures in their monograph on methodology in anthropology. The ethnography of schooling bears witness to this trend, although there is a rather solid resistance to the takeover of a "hard sciences" approach.

The observation process in school ethnography has been characterized by the recording of extensive descriptive detail about the "imponderabilia of actual life and everyday behavior" (Malinowski 1922:22). Observers have attempted to capture in concrete detail the conduct of everyday life in classrooms and schools, often recording in longhand detailed running descriptions of interaction within the setting (LeCompte 1978, Burnett 1968, Varenne 1976). In some cases, ethnographers have developed and employed more structured observation instruments (Wilcox 1978 and this volume, Talbert

1970, Leacock 1969). School ethnographers have employed audiotape (Borman 1978, Spindler 1974c), cameras (Collier 1973, Spindler 1974c), and film or videotape (Erickson 1976, McDermott and Gospodinoff 1977, Florio and Schultz 1978, Byers and Byers 1972, Spindler and Spindler, this volume) to increase the precision of their observational efforts. However, these mechanical recording devices are not viewed as a substitute for the direct and active presence of the ethnographer on site. The inquiry process requires the immediate presence of the ethnographer, as a person constantly absorbs a wider variety of data than any mechanical device can record.

Ethnographers also use interviews and questionnaires as data-gathering techniques. Interviews vary from completely informal encounters to highly structured sessions, although the questions asked are almost always quite open-ended. Ethnographers have employed questionnaires for gathering sociometric and other kinds of data to perhaps a greater extent than might be imagined (Burnett 1969, Lacey 1976, Ogbu 1974b, Peshkin 1978, Rist 1978, Singleton 1968). Of course, questionnaires are never seen as the primary data-gathering technique.

Occasionally ethnographers will design instruments other than interview schedules to elicit data. Spindler's (1973, 1974c) development of the Instrumental Activities Inventory is an example of the role instruments of this kind can play in ethnographic work. Spindler (1974a) has also used more standard instruments such as TATs and Rorschachs in ethnographic research within the framework of clinical anthropology. Others have generated data in other ways, for instance by asking children to keep diaries recording their daily experience in and out of school (Peshkin 1978).

In addition to generating their own data, ethnographers have assiduously collected already existing sources of data. These have included school documents (Ogbu 1974b), cumulative school records (Sanday 1976), student essays or other student products (Warren 1974), textbooks and other curriculum materials (Spindler 1973, 1974c), and almost any other conceivable bit of material which might prove relevant to the topic under study. Since one is continuously attempting to explore the nature of the relationship between the setting and its context, a broad range of materials may prove to be of value.

Similarly, the ethnographer often chooses to spend time in a rather wide variety of settings within and surrounding the school. While observation within the classroom is often of the nonparticipant observation variety, the ethnographer frequently moves into the role of participant observer as s/he has coffee in the faculty lounge, hangs around the playground, goes to PTA meetings, and so on.

Approaches to the analysis of data depend, of course, on the types of data gathered and the conceptual framework employed. The extent of quantification of data varies widely depending on the study, from none at all to the use of statistical techniques of varying degrees of complexity. The "key incident" approach has been employed frequently in the analysis of classroom data (Erickson 1977, Burnett 1969, Dumont and Wax 1969, Peshkin 1978, Rist

1978, Rosenfeld 1971). It involves the analysis of qualitative data in which incidents or events have been recorded in extensive descriptive detail. Analysis of the data leads the researcher to focus on certain incidents as key incidents, or concrete instances of the working of abstract principles of social organization. As Erickson (1977:61) summarizes, "This involves pulling out from field notes a key incident, linking it to other incidents, phenomena, and theoretical constructs, and writing it up so others can see the generic in the particular, the universal in the concrete, the relation between part and whole." Erickson notes that the key incident approach may involve massive leaps of inference over many different kinds of data from different sources, including field notes, documents, elicited texts, demographic information, unstructured interviews, and so on.

Another approach to data analysis relies upon the quantification of qualitative data. The two approaches are in no sense mutually exclusive and may easily be incorporated in the same study. Qualitative data may be quantified by coding from longhand descriptive accounts or audio and video records of interaction (Wilcox 1978, this volume, Borman 1978, Erickson 1976, LeCompte 1978). Rist's (1970) and Leacock's (1969) work provides examples of the effective use of very simple tabulations of types of teacher-student interaction. Others have begun to use more complicated statistical techniques (Wilcox 1978, Erickson 1976, Spindler 1974c, Spindler and Spindler, this volume). As Erickson (1977) states, the statistical techniques that seem most appropriate for the analysis of

qualitatively derived data are relatively simple—the chi-square, the Mann-Whitney two-tailed test in the analysis of "categorical" data, and the two- and three-way analysis of variance.

At the end of the inquiry process, including the gathering and analysis of data, the ethnographer traditionally produces an extensive written report. The report is written in a descriptive style, conveying to the reader the fine detail of social discourse which enabled the ethnographer to see and interpret patterns of social life. Extensive quotes and lengthy descriptions of settings and interactions are often included to present as full a picture of the setting as possible and to provide validating evidence in support of the ethnographer's interpretation of data.

This, in brief, is the research strategy referred to as ethnography. It is a naturalistic, observational, descriptive, contextual, open-ended, and in-depth approach to doing research. Within these bounds, a variety of instruments and data-gathering tools may be employed. The goal of ethnography is to combine the view of an insider with that of an outsider to describe a social setting. The resulting description is expected to be deeper and fuller than that of the ordinary outsider, and broader and less culture-bound than that of the ordinary insider.

An Ethnographic View of Schools in Continuity and in Change

Ethnographers have turned their attention toward the process of teaching and learning in a wide variety of situations and with a wide variety of research concerns. They have looked at teaching and learning in urban schools, in rural schools, and in situations where schools are not part of the cultural milieu. They have observed the teaching and learning process as it takes place across the entire life span in both formal and informal situations. They have studied students, teachers, parents, and school administrators; individuals, groups, classrooms, schools, families, neighborhoods, school districts, and communities.

It is impossible, given the scope of this paper, to review the entire field of educational ethnography. My comments are confined to work which is, in my opinion, most directly relevant to policy-making in the United States, and I offer examples rather than exhaustive chronicles of work to date. Since the denial of equal educational opportunity to diverse sectors of the population is probably the key problem in contemporary education, this paper focuses particularly on ethnographic work of direct relevance to this issue. There are several excellent bibliographies and annotated bibliographies available to the reader who wishes further exploration of the literature (Rosenstiel 1977; Roberts and Akinsanya 1976a; Burnett 1974; Wax, Diamond, and Gearing 1971), as well as other summary or critical reviews (Ogbu 1981, Hansen 1979, Comitas and Dolgin 1978, Gearing 1973a, Sindell 1969). While most of the studies reviewed here are clearly ethnographic, I have at times mentioned some which have not been conducted strictly as ethnographies but which have nonetheless produced interesting

qualitative observations of life in schools.

Two major categories encompass much of the ethnographic work done to date: the exploration of the school as an instrument of cultural transmission, and the exploration of cultural conflict in the classroom. These general categories include many different strains of research based on a variety of analytic frameworks (Hansen 1979, Ogbu 1981).

Schooling as Cultural Transmission

Ethnographers have most frequently framed their view of schools around the concept of cultural transmission. In this view, the school acts primarily as an agent of the culture, transmitting a complex set of attitudes, values, behavior, and expectations which will enable a new generation to maintain the culture as an ongoing phenomenon (Spindler 1955, 1963a; Kimball 1974). This kind of analysis falls within the structural-functional tradition in social scientific thought. Ethnographers have often utilized their contextual knowledge of the culture as a whole to illuminate their investigation of what is being transmitted in schools.

The conceptualization of schooling as cultural transmission runs in direct opposition to the conception of schools shared by many scholars, educational administrators, teachers, and members of the public, in which schools are regarded as instruments of reform and of change. The dominant view of schooling within the culture is that of an institution existing to improve society, not to reproduce it more or less as is. Much of the ethnographic work serves to challenge this familiar way of thinking about schools.

Schools have been seen to reproduce or to transmit culture from one generation to the next in a variety of ways. The common indigenous conception of what is transmitted in schools is curriculum content—a body of academic skills which it is generally agreed the schools should transmit. Ethnographers have focused instead on what has been referred to as the "hidden curriculum," or that which is taught implicitly rather than explicitly. This focus has involved a view and an explanation of educational personnel as active cultural beings, suffused with the orientations of the culture, rather than as neutral dispensers of information about reading, writing, and arithmetic.

The transmission of that which is implicit in the culture can be thought of as including a set of skills, different from those taught in the formal curriculum, of values, of motivational strategies and goals, of self-images, of relationships to peers and authorities, and so on. A working formal theory of education as cultural transmission has not yet been fully developed. While initial steps have been taken (Gearing 1973b, Spindler 1974b, Dobbert 1975), there is as yet no unifying theory or model which guides research. The body of research investigating the process of cultural transmission is therefore quite diverse.

A large group of studies have been oriented around general structural-functional theory, analyzing what goes on in classrooms as reflective of the wider society. Ethnographers have been particularly interested in exploring how the nature of the wider society constrains the educational process.

A number of studies have noted and explored in various ways the influence of the wider economic structure on schooling. Eddy (1978) offers a general historical overview of changes in organizational models of schooling in the United States and links the change in organizational models to changes in the mode of economic organization. Cohen (1973) suggests a similar link, focusing more specifically on changes within the last 20 years. Eddy notes the movement to the modern corporate model, remarking upon parallels in terms of physical layout, deployment of personnel, management systems, type of work flow, and so on. She describes the values and perceptions which underlie the industrial-business approach to education and the anthropological knowledge which challenges the educational soundness of this approach.

A number of ethnographic studies flesh out the ways in which schools can be seen to prepare students for life in a capitalist industrial economy. Parallels between the structure of schooling and the uniformity and regimentation of industry have been noted and developed by a number of observers (Lynd and Lynd 1929, Jackson 1968, LeCompte 1978, Cusick 1973, Wilcox 1978). These observers and others (Henry 1963) have also likened the structure of power and authority in the classroom to that characteristic of industry. Another testimony to the influence of the wider economic structure on the classroom is the observation of the presence of constant evaluation of student performance and of the competitive ethic (Jackson 1968, Henry 1963). The authority structure, competition, routine, regimentation, time orientation, batch processing, and relative alienation from the learning task that have characterized U.S. classrooms have all been compared with similar characteristics of workplaces.

The individualistic orientation of schooling in American society can also be related to the economic structure. Although Varenne (1976) does not make this connection explicit, his analysis illustrates the transmission of an individualistic orientation in school. He describes his observation of a high school sociology class in which, despite the conscious intention of the teacher, the cultural orientation toward the individual as the fundamental unit of society was transmitted in such a way that the "sociology" had a fundamentally psychological quality.

The significance of these classroom characteristics is more fully appreciated when one realizes that processes of teaching and learning are substantially different in small-scale nonindustrial societies (Mead 1943, Fortes 1938).

In addition to teaching common sets of values, orientations, and motivational structures, schools in capitalist industrial societies have been observed to teach students their likely future position in the work hierarchy. In terms of extracurricular activities, the school social organization, with its clubs and elites, has long been observed to mirror the stratified social life of the community (Hollingshead 1949). Stratification by social class and ethnic background is endemic to the economic system, and ethnographers have noted the impact of class and racial stratification inside the classroom as well as out. Lowered expectations and the teaching of skills and attitudes appropriate to the lower

levels of work hierarchies have been observed in classrooms populated with students from minority and lower-middle-class and lower-class backgrounds, while high expectations and skills and attitudes appropriate to the upper levels of the hierarchy have been observed to be transmitted in classrooms populated by students from Caucasian and/or upper-middle-class backgrounds (Leacock 1969, Wilcox this volume, Rosenfeld 1971, Spindler 1963a and 1974a, Sennett and Cobb 1972). Thus, it appears that schools are engaged in differential education and socialization based on student social class and ethnic background. This perception is in direct opposition to the common cultural perception that schools are agents of equal opportunity, teaching children from all backgrounds what they need to be successful, if only the children will learn what is taught. It is also in opposition to the conclusions of prominent social scientists (Coleman 1966, 1971, Jencks 1972) that schools have little effect on student futures.

Lacey (1976) and Sennett and Cobb (1972) have explored the impact of differential student success in the highly evaluative and stratified world of the school on students themselves and on relationships among students. They offer insight into the turning away of certain groups of students from the norms and values of the school, and the polarization which develops between those students who identify with the world of the school and those who grow into opposition to it. Henry (1963) notes the economic usefulness of developing large groups of students who see themselves as failures and move without substantial complaint into low-level positions in industry and bureaucratic work structures.

This does not begin to exhaust the list of ways in which schools have been observed to transmit the structures and orientations of the wider society. However, the works cited serve as examples of the ways in which ethnographers have attempted to penetrate essential aspects of the wider culture and to explore the classroom as an arena in which these essential aspects are revealed. While the ethnographies to date have offered important insights into the ways in which schools may reproduce a stratified society, a comprehensive understanding of the variables involved has not yet been achieved. There is no precise understanding of the types of linkages which may exist between schooling and other social institutions. Wilcox's (1978 and this volume) attempt to explore the linkages between socialization to work in the classroom and characteristics of adult work roles is a useful example of the kind of work that needs to be done.

Schools as Arenas of Cultural Conflict

Another major conceptualization revealed in the ethnography of schooling is that of cultural relativity. Efforts to understand and to document the integrity of minority cultures have been frequent. Classrooms have been explored as arenas of cultural conflict in which mutual misunderstandings produce learning difficulties. Learning difficulties are not attributed to some sort of incapacity on the part of the child from a minority culture. Topics addressed have included language and cognition

as well as conflicts in cultural values, interactional norms, styles of learning, and so on.

Language and the ethnography of language use has been an important topic of research in recent years (Cazden, John, and Hymes 1972; Hymes 1971; Leacock 1971; Aarons, Gordon, and Steward 1969). One strand of research has suggested that the vernacular speech of every social group is based on similarly complex structures and exhibits a similar integrity of patterns (Labov 1969, 1972). It is social stereotype rather than objective fact that labels some languages, dialects, or linguistic styles as superior or inferior. Hymes (1972:xxxiii, xxxiv) summarizes the practical implications of negative stereotyping of children's language or linguistic styles, evident from classroom ethnography:

> If one rejects a child's speech, one probably communicates rejection to the child. In rejecting what one wishes to change (or to which one wishes to add), one probably is throwing away the chance of change. In accepting what one wishes to change (or to which one wishes to add) for what it is to the child, one probably is maximizing one's opportunity for change. . . . It was and will seem reasonable to many for the stigmatized individual to make the adaptation. When we see the great limitations of this approach, what might be considered its large-scale failure, we may find it reasonable to insist on adaptation as well on the part of those who stigmatize.

He continues:

> Attitudes are fundamental, but good will obviously is not enough. The best of teachers can unconsciously convey rejection to a black child while favoring a

white, simply through differences in accustomed cues for gaining and giving attention. . . . Hence the need for ethnography of the classroom.

It is the ethnography of *communication* in the classroom, not simply a study of children's grammar or even verbal behavior, which can illuminate areas of mutual misunderstanding and frustration and the accompanying cessation of learning (McDermott 1974, Dumont and Wax 1969). Ethnographers have begun to use film or videotape to capture as much as possible of the communicative interchange for detailed analysis: direction of glances, body positions, speech rhythm, and so on (Byers and Byers 1972, Erickson 1976, McDermott and Gospodinoff 1977). Considerable attention has been devoted to the ethnography of *participation structures* in the classroom, or of the cultural organization of rights and obligations in face-to-face social interaction (Philips 1972, Erickson and Mohatt, this volume, Au 1979). This kind of microethnographic inquiry exhibits substantial promise in enabling functional communication to occur in situations where the modes of generating and interpreting language and associated communicative behavior differ between teachers and children.

Ethnographers have also begun to explore the relationship between culture and cognition as it may affect the success of children from minority cultures in the classroom. Just as the process of communication has proved to be totally saturated with culture, so has the process of teaching, learning, and measuring the acquisition of academic skills. Although much work remains to

be done, major findings to date indicate that different cultural milieus impart different kinds of cognitive skills and conceptual styles (Cohen 1969; Cole, Gay, Glick, and Sharp 1971; Cole and Scribner 1974). As with language, the ability to demonstrate a particular skill depends on context (lack of performance in any given setting cannot be taken to indicate lack of competence). Also, the acquisition of particular skills depends not so much on individual characteristics as on the types of skills demanded by the environment. The tasks and activities one engages in shape the kinds of skills that are developed. Difficulties arise for children when schools recognize or incorporate a very restricted set of skills and conceptual styles which does not include those that the children have come to learn and employ. The underlying implication is that there is more than one legitimate method of knowing and of learning and more than one body of significant skills. Attention is directed toward life outside the classroom, where a rich body of skills is constantly being taught and learned. This body of research suggests that efforts must be made to transfer skills learned and used in one environment to another.

Conflicts in values between one culture and another have also been noted (Cazden and John 1971, Henry 1963). Children may have to attempt to function in an alien environment that requires behavior which is in striking contradiction to that which they have been taught to value.

The fundamental issue here has been outlined by Burnett (1970) in her discussion of the culture of reference of the school. She suggests that the school, as an organization which is a part of a larger whole, has a culture of reference: the culture of the dominant segment of the community of which it is a part. The culture of reference, following Goodenough (1963), provides the standards for deciding what is, for deciding what can be, and for deciding what to do, or operational procedures for dealing with people and things. Political and economic factors tend to ensure that teachers are in tune with the culture of reference. Difficulties arise when the reference culture is different from the culture of the students. Not only is the organization and curriculum of the school inappropriate, but teachers as cultural beings who have emerged from the culture of reference are likely to be incapable even of communicating to students, much less of responding flexibly to their needs. Jacob and Sanday (1976) hypothesize a series of undesirable effects upon children, resulting from a situation of cultural conflict in the classroom.

Working from this kind of analysis, ethnographers have begun to attempt to measure the differences between school cultures and home cultures as a step toward creating a common public culture of the classroom (Jacob and Sanday 1976, Burnett 1969, Sanday 1976). Kileff's (1975) article provides a hopeful example from another culture of what can happen in a classroom when the teacher is able to act as a mediator and cultural broker between the worlds of the schools and the home. Lightfoot (1978) emphasizes again and again the vital importance of incorporating the culture of the home into the culture of the school, while Rist (1972) makes specific suggestions about how

to do this in classrooms populated by substantial numbers of black children. Research emerging from the Kamehameha Early Education Program in Hawaii indicates the potential positive impact on minority children's school achievement when teaching methods can be made more consistent with the ways children learn in their own environment (Jordan et al. 1977, Au and Jordan 1981). While there are constraints on our ability to bring the culture of the home and the culture of the school into closer alignment, in terms of both our technical know-how and the political realities surrounding the classroom, this kind of effort seems much more likely to lead to fruitful results than do efforts based on the "culture of poverty"/difference-as-deficit formulation so rampant in educational circles today.

A Micro-Level View of Schools and Change

Promoting effective change requires not only a thorough understanding of the status quo in classrooms and in schools but also a theory of change and a method of investigating the change process. Ethnographers have, directly or indirectly, provided glimpses or extended views of the process of change in schools, and have often worked with, or in some cases contributed to, a general theory of change with regard to the institution of the school and to cultural transmission in general. This part of the paper discusses the contribution made by ethnographies of schooling to our knowledge of the change process as it takes place at the micro level, within the classroom and the school or school district. This discussion is followed by a consideration of the schools and change at the macro level, in which the role of the school as a change agent within the society as a whole is examined.

I turn first to a discussion of what the ethnography of schooling indicates about the process of change as it takes place within the classroom. The classroom has been, theoretically at least, the scene of a series of significant educational reforms. Given the traditional focus on the teacher-student dyad and on the formal curriculum, educational reform or change efforts have traditionally been aimed at the classroom. A series of reforms with regard to methods of instruction and classroom organization have been introduced in recent years: team teaching, diagnostic testing and individualized instruction, the use of teaching machines, the open classroom, mastery learning, and many more. In assessing the impact of these reforms, several important questions arise. Are changes actually introduced in the day-to-day operating procedure of the classroom? How different in degree or kind is classroom interaction as a result of the supposed introduction of the reform? Are the consequences of the reform as intended, or do unintended consequences, desirable or undesirable, arise? If so, of what sort?

The ethnographic work tends to suggest that it is very difficult to introduce significant change into the classroom setting. While a reform may nominally be instituted, strong continuities with past arrangements can be observed, although the ways in which the continuities are expressed may change somewhat. A sensitive and open-ended approach is required in order to perceive the new form in which the old dynamics are reemerging. Some of the available ethnographic evidence on this point has to do with classroom organization, in particular with the organizational form of the "open classroom." The apparent change in classroom organization may not be associated with substantial change in other aspects of classroom interactional dynamics.

None of the studies mentioned below were carried out with the specific intent of assessing or evaluating changes in classroom organization. They all can be thought of as "basic research," and all appear to have begun with a rather general focus. One of the distinctions of basic ethnographic research is that its broad scope makes it likely that data will be gathered about a substantial number of issues going beyond the specific focus of the research.

One relevant study is Borman's (1978) analysis of the dynamics of social control in two urban kindergarten classrooms, one an open classroom in an open school patterned after the British infant school and the other a classroom with a traditional program in a traditional school. Results of the investigation revealed that, contrary to what one might expect, the teacher in the open classroom was more frequently observed using regulative or control strategies with the children than the teacher in the traditional classroom. One result of the organization was that the teacher was more frequently in the children's midst, and as a result was apparently monitoring activities more closely than was the case in the presumably tighter, more controlled traditional classroom. Also, there was no observed difference in the type of control employed by the teachers in the two classrooms, when control was coded in terms of Bernstein's (1971) categorization of open and closed or elaborated and restricted systems of control. Both teachers used closed systems of control or restricted language to enforce control. Borman did observe more conjoint (teacher-child) regulation in the open classroom, although it was clear throughout that the teacher retained greater social power. In short, the "open" classroom was not as open as one might expect it to be, and in some ways it embodied teacher control to a greater extent than the traditional classroom.

LeCompte's (1978) work also points to the existence of strong continuities between classrooms which appear superficially to be organized quite differently. LeCompte studied four fourth-grade classrooms in depth, with teaching styles ranging from rigidly structured and teacher centered to open, individualized, and unconventional. She found that in spite of considerable variations in teaching style, it was possible to identify a universal and uniform "management core" of teacher behavior which consumed at least 50 percent of noninstructional talking in each classroom. The management core involved statements of authority, orderliness, and task and time orientation which appeared to arise inevitably out of the structure and content of the school, that is, as managerial demands that teachers must make to get children to perform tasks mandated by the institution in the crowded classroom setting. Even supposedly unconventional open classrooms were dominated by a very traditional management core.

Wilcox's (1978) survey of 32 classrooms supports a view of open classrooms as much more highly regulated by teachers than one would expect, while her in-depth study of two first-grade classrooms provides additional evidence that open classrooms may have closed systems of control. She stresses the overriding influence of student and teacher social class on classroom control systems, as opposed to the formal organizational structure of the classroom. The superficially more "open" classroom of the two she studied, replete with learning centers, individualized contracts with students, and so on, was actually far more laden with authoritarian teacher control mechanisms. It was also the classroom which drew from a lower-middle-class neighborhood, as opposed to the upper-middle-class environment of the other first-grade classroom. Wilcox's work suggests that the social class background of the neighborhood, and the accompanying social class background of the teacher, exert a powerful influence on the teacher's selection of control strategies, one which is more powerful in important respects than the formal organizational structure of the classroom.

Studies of this kind raise a number of issues with regard to schooling and change. First and foremost is a glimpse of the complexity of the problem of change and of the assessment of change. When is it possible to say that a real change in program has taken place? How is one to assess fully the nature of the change? The number of variables which must be observed to assess the nature of the change is likely to be far greater than may be anticipated by the visionary or the planner of change.

It is likely to be difficult to predict in advance which variables will be relevant to this assessment and which will not. The nature of the change, including all of its anticipated and unanticipated consequences, must be fully understood in order to evaluate its educational significance. What is it that children are learning in this new situation? Are they learning to make educational choices in an "open classroom" if at the same time they are more closely monitored by the teacher than in the traditional structure? To what extent are they learning to make choices if they are at the same time being controlled and regulated in a quite closed and authoritarian manner? These kinds of questions are difficult to answer, but an avoidance of them is an abdication of the responsibility to ensure that "change" is in fact change, rather than a warmed-over rehash of familiar patterns. Given the American infatuation with educational reform, and the assembly line manner in which reforms are processed through American classrooms, it becomes crucial to investigate their actual significance in the daily lives of children in classrooms.

Ethnographers have begun to examine directly the introduction of other educational reforms, including multicultural education (Rosen 1977, *Anthropology and Education Quarterly* Special Issue 1976) and desegregation. Although the work on multicultural education has developed important data about factors affecting the degree of success of multicultural education programs, my remarks here concentrate on the issue of desegregation, since it has received more sustained ethnographic attention.

The desegregation of American schools is a reform which has received a tremendous amount of attention from both educational professionals and the public at large. As a cornerstone of educational policy in the U.S., it is a prime example of a reform which demands intense in-depth investigation of its impact on the day-to-day reality of classroom life. Rist's (1978) ethnographic study of a school undergoing integration is an example of the kind of contribution that ethnographers can make to looking at schools in change.

Rist's study examines a situation of token integration in which a small number of black students are bused into a predominantly white upper-middle-class elementary school in Portland, Oregon. The classroom observations of Rist and a graduate assistant point to a major dynamic thwarting the intent of integration: black children in classrooms quickly become effectively re-segregated because of the disparity in levels of academic achievement between black and white children. The tremendous value placed on high academic achievement by the dominant white upper-middle-class culture meant that the black students were immediately relegated to positions of low worth within the classroom, and remained there throughout the year of fieldwork. Rist analyzes the dynamics in school and society which placed and kept them there, which are discussed hereafter. His observations suggest strongly that until the nature of the classroom experience is changed, we cannot pretend that schools have been meaningfully desegregated. As Hanna's chapter in this volume demonstrates, integration cannot be brought about at the drop of a hat by busing students from one school to another. It is clear that we need to keep observing in depth to understand the nature of the change which has been brought about and to redirect, refine, and refocus our change efforts.

Ethnographers have also looked outside the walls of the classroom to the process of change as it is instituted in schools and school districts, and to the relationship between in-classroom events and those taking place in the vicinity of the classroom. The investigation of the desegregation process at the level of the school as a whole has emphasized the relative superficiality of the changes that have taken place. For example, Eddy's (1975) study of a newly desegregated junior high school, although executed in a very brief period of time, manages to illustrate clearly the persistence of patterns of interaction which support the traditional subordinate relationship of blacks to whites. The school Eddy studied was changed from a traditional junior high school (grades 7–8) staffed and attended by blacks to an integrated middle school (grades 6–7). She writes:

> The transformation of the [Booker T.] Washington [junior high] school into the Longview Middle School represented a claiming of the school by the whites of Royal Palm. The assignment of a white principal to the school was the first in a sequence of symbolic acts which communicated to all that the school was no longer one in which blacks would play major roles.... The building of the fence around the school to shut it off from the black community, the change of the school entrance so that it no longer faced the black community, and the renaming of the school were additional symbolic acts which reaffirmed the dominant status of whites within the school. [1975:170]

Clement's (1978) overview of a series of papers offering ethnographic perspectives on desegregated schools concludes that, while different ethnographies offer somewhat different views of the results of desegregation and attest to the complexities of the situation, they reveal that informal segregation is frequently evident, with black students involved in less prestigious learning experiences and activities.

The impact of administrative behavior on the change process has also been observed. Attention to the administrative component of schools seems very useful in redirecting the inordinate amount of attention focused on teachers and children to a more holistic view of the various actors involved in the processes of change. Rist (1978) investigated the part played by administrators at all levels of the Portland school system in planning and implementing desegregation within the city's schools. He describes the evolution of the tokenist approach to integration and the political pressures involved, and links this approach to the difficult nature of the minority children's experience in the classroom. He investigates the common-sense notions of integration guiding the action of district and school administrators, and describes the philosophy of racial assimilation and its ultimate impact on the children: rendering them invisible and therefore leaving them without the assistance and support they needed to escape positions of low worth within the structure of the school. He outlines a dynamic in which the taken-for-granted assimilationist conceptual substructure of school administrators, which remained totally unquestioned throughout the desegregation effort, defeated the program before it ever got off the ground. Rist notes the inability of the principal to help teachers learn to address the academic difficulties of the new students and the inability of the district office to help the principal in this task. People in leadership positions, blinded by their insistence that everyone be treated equally, were unable to assist the implementation of the program and to perceive and address the particular needs of minority students. Teachers were provided with an ineffective in-service program which appeared to them to level accusations of racism and failed to provide means of developing new teaching styles or historical information about black people. No effort was made to develop a coherent multicultural curriculum. He concludes that an understanding of the managerial and administrative context of the classroom appears to be highly relevant to understanding and interpreting classroom events.

Other ethnographers have included some sort of description and analysis of administrative behavior in their studies of schools. Anthropologists have traditionally focused "down" rather than "up," so that there is much more ethnographic material available on classrooms than on administrators and educational decision-makers. Still, the work that has been done points to the value of this kind of investigation. An understanding of the process of governance as it actually takes place in concrete situations, and of the values, assumptions, and beliefs which guide it, is essential to an understanding of the process of change. Wolcott's (1973) account of "the man in the principal's office" is an example of an attempt to define and articulate the culture of school

leadership and governance on the most local level. Gallaher (1973) and Spindler (1963b) provide further analyses. Of particular relevance to the investigation of change are accounts of administrative attempts to introduce change in schools. Wolcott's (1977) examination of administrative attempts to introduce a program supposed to ensure greater teacher accountability in one particular school district provides an account of the rise and fall of a reform effort, as well as an interesting interpretation of the culture of teachers and administrators in relation to the change process.

Rist (1978) and Smith and Pohland (1974) discuss ways in which educational decision-makers anticipate or respond to surrounding political pressures, with apparently negative educational consequences for children in classrooms. Rist points to, among other things, the negative consequences for minority children of selecting a tokenist approach to integration. Smith and Pohland describe the local political pressures which led decision-makers to disperse scarce educational resources (computers to assist math instruction) widely across disparate terrain, thus increasing maintenance problems and decreasing the ability of teachers and students to make use of the resources.

The interface between parents and school staff and administrators has also been investigated by school ethnographers. Lightfoot (1978), Wilcox (1978), Ogbu (1974b), and Rist (1978) have all described varying facets of the relationship of parents to schools and the response of staff and administrators to parents. The relationship between parents and schools may be an important one with respect to continuity and change in schooling, as parents are potentially capable of calling for either continuity or change and of attempting to influence in a variety of ways what takes place within the school. Lightfoot reviews and critiques the literature on parents and the parent-school relationship, describing the portrayal of this relationship as distorted, oversimplified, and stereotyped. In her view, the transactional process between families and schools has not really been described from the points of view of all participants; the literature is preoccupied with a view of the relationship emerging from a description and analysis of the perspectives and behaviors of only the more powerful mainstream group. Groups of parents, particularly poor and/or minority parents, are seen as reluctant, uncooperative consumers merely responding to the power of the school, or as uncaring, ignorant, or culturally deprived. The ethnographic data generated so far challenges all of these stereotypes and begins to provide information necessary for understanding, as opposed to judging or condemning, the stance of parents, whatever it may be.

Lightfoot presents, and Wilcox's data supports, a view of parents as systematically excluded from life inside schools, with the extent of their participation reflecting, among other things, their social class, race, and ethnicity. Teachers and administrators apparently tend to fear the intrusion of parents into the domain of the school, anticipating interference, criticism, and hostility. They tend to welcome only directly supportive parents and parent groups. The social power and status of certain groups of parents make it easier for them to penetrate the walls of the school, whether invited or not, and to make their concerns heard. Since the needs of lower-class and minority parents and their children tend to be less well served by the school, and require more substantial change, this dynamic works doubly to retard change: the criticism which may point to the need for change is discouraged across the board, and it is particularly discouraged from those with the greatest need for change.

The exclusion of parents from schools also tends to keep parents relatively uninformed about what is taking place within the school. This too can retard needed change, as Rist (1978) points out. Minority parents in the school he observed tended to be unaware of the stratified position in which their children were placed in the newly integrated classrooms, and thus were rendered ineffective as a force for change.

The relationship between school principals and parents has been described at some length by Fuchs (1966) and by Rist (1978), among others. Both of these studies include descriptions of public conflict over statements made or positions taken by principals with respect to minority children. Studies of incidents of this type are valuable in illuminating issues in school-community relations.

In short, ethnographic data on administrators often portrays people in these positions providing little real leadership and generally avoiding substantial change. Of course, given the holistic perspective and attention to context that is part of any good ethnography, administrative behavior must be viewed in terms of the surrounding structural realities which are likely to account for

it. Moving up another level, ethnographers have also turned attention to this broader context in which teachers and administrators effect and respond to change.

A Macro-Level View of the School and Change

Much of the apparent ineffectiveness of educational leadership and policy-making can ultimately be traced to the constraints placed on the institution of the school and on the perspectives of decision-makers and educational actors by the culture as a whole. There has been a fundamental lack of understanding of the role of the school in the culture, and a vulnerability to the mystification of the role of the school which is promulgated by the culture. Cultures are well known for the ways in which they mystify the reality of their own workings. Anthropologists have learned to elicit the cultural knowledge of members of the culture as important data, yet not to take explanations of the working of things at face value. Social scientists studying schools, and educational decision-makers and actors drawing on social scientific studies and on their own common-sense knowledge, have remained to a large extent taken in by the mystifications of the culture.

As summarized earlier in this paper, many ethnographers have investigated schools as instruments of cultural transmission. The results of their investigations suggest a view of the school as reproducing in many respects the status quo of the culture, with its hierarchical stratification of people according to their membership in particular ethnic, social class, or sexual groups. It also suggests the functional necessity of this result for the maintenance of the culture—that this recurring hierarchical stratification by group membership is not an accident but a functional necessity for the maintenance of existing economic and political structures.

The work of Ogbu (1978b, 1974b) and Wilcox (1978) is relevant here, although Ogbu employs an ecological rather than a structural-functional framework and a more dynamic view of the stratification process. Ogbu's studies have striking implications for educational policy-making. Insights gained from his ethnographic work in schools and communities in the United States, his status as a Nigerian-born outsider, and a thoroughly cross-cultural perspective have led him to stand educational thought on its head, as it were, and propose connections which are precisely opposite to those suggested by the indigenous cultural view. In *Minority Education and Caste: The American System in Cross-Cultural Perspective* (1978b), he reviews and critiques the standard current explanations of differences in school performance of black and white children: theories of cultural deprivation, culture conflict, institutional deficiency, heredity, and lack of equal educational opportunity. He suggests that none of these theories really points to the ultimate cause of black school failure, although the theory of institutional deficiency, which maintains that the failure of black children in schools can be attributed to the fact that schools are organized to promote success among white middle-class children and failure among black children, comes closest. He points out that this theory does not really explain why schools are organized like this, and then proceeds to do so himself. He focuses on the instrumental role of education in the culture, pointing out that its value has always been seen primarily as that of a ticket to adult success, in terms of a prestigious job and monetary reward. Drawing on Berreman's (1967) and Bohannan's (1963) work, he distinguishes between castelike and noncastelike minorities in the United States, according to the extent to which status is ascribed at birth, group membership is endogamous, and the denigrated group is excluded from major portions of the social structure, although required to perform important social and economic functions for the society. He classifies blacks, along with other nonimmigrant minorities in the U.S.—American Indians, Mexican-Americans, and Puerto Ricans—as caste-like minorities and emphasizes the rigid nature of the stratification system with respect to these groups, particularly in terms of what he calls the job ceiling, or the restricted nature of occupational opportunities available after finishing school. He documents the existence of the job ceiling for blacks in the United States and the relationship of changes in occupational advancement to the job ceiling rather than to educational attainments. He then argues that black school performance can be seen primarily as an adaptation to the job ceiling. The ascribed nature of black status and the existence of the job ceiling are readily perceived by blacks, and this inevitably saps motivation to do well in school. Also, following the Whitings' (1963, 1975) model of the socialization and the ac-

quisition of cognitive skills, he suggests that adults learn themselves and socialize in children skills, attitudes, and motivation appropriate to their ascribed social, occupational, and political roles. Both parents and school do this.

For the purposes of fundamental change, then, what must take place is not further tinkering with classroom instruction, but the elimination of caste barriers and associated social, economic, and political stratification in the society as a whole. What is required is the establishment of a new social order. Ogbu (1978b:358–360) summarizes:

> So long as caste remains the principle of social organization, no efforts to use the schools to equalize the social and occupational status of different minority and majority castes can succeed because the social system demands that both desirable and undesirable social and occupational positions be filled on an ascriptive basis. The schools therefore continue to prepare a disproportionate number of lower-caste groups for their traditional menial positions, although they may not do this consciously.... To change this situation—to eliminate black academic retardation—requires, first a total destruction of the caste system—that is, the creation of a new social order in which blacks do not occupy a subordinate position vis-à-vis whites. If we destroy the caste system, both schools and blacks will begin to manifest changes compatible with the new social order, and academic retardation will disappear. Under the new social order, schools have no choice but to change their policies and practices and train blacks as effectively as they train whites because the new society will demand the same degree of competence from both. Destroying the caste system will have

important consequences for blacks' response to schooling.... Blacks will respond to their new opportunities by persevering in their schoolwork and by developing behavior patterns compatible with high academic achievement.

Other school ethnographers have also suggested that attention must be turned away from the school itself in order to achieve a lasting solution to contemporary educational dilemmas. Wilcox (1978) makes a case similar to Ogbu's with respect to the successful education of lower-middle-class white children. Her data indicate that the distinction between caste and class status may be overdrawn. She documents the ways in which lower-middle-class children are socialized in schools in skills and attitudes appropriate to lower-middle-class work roles, while upper-middle-class children are socialized appropriately for upper-middle-class work roles, and suggests that this dynamic is not likely to change until stratification by class is eradicated.

Spindler's (1974c) work throws additional light on the role of the school in society. His data suggest that the school, when it does express values in opposition to dominant economic trends in situations of culture changes, has only limited influence on children's instrumental choice-making activity. That is, children evidence an idealized identification with traditional values taught in the school, yet make practical choices affecting adult roles and lifestyles on the basis of modern urban values, whether or not those values are taught in school. It appears that in conditions of rapid social change when socialization in schools has not kept

pace with larger economic realities, these economic realities are dominant nonetheless.

Conclusion

As we have seen, ethnographers have investigated schools and classrooms from the perspectives of both stability and change. They have focused on interactional dynamics in schools and classrooms: on relationships between school staff and parents; on the role of educational administrators; and on ways in which the assumptions, values, and structures of the culture as a whole are expressed in the arena of schooling. They have illuminated the role of the school in perpetuating social stratification on the basis of class and ethnicity and have explored a number of dynamics which limit equal opportunity. Ethnographers have conducted this research according to principles of inquiry emerging from the discipline of anthropology.

What can be said, in sum, about the ways in which the ethnography of schooling has contributed to our understanding of the educational process in an industrial society such as the United States? Of primary importance, in my opinion, has been the challenge that ethnography has posed to the traditional formulation of educational problems. This challenge arises from the use of particular conceptual frameworks and a particular style of investigation. The cross-cultural conflict, the orientation to context, the open-ended scope of research, the attempt at detailed empirical description, and the fine-grained nature of analysis together challenge the dominant technocratic approach to education (Eddy 1978, Wolcott 1977) in fundamental ways. The ethnography of schools reveals again and again the complexity of the educational process and the need to move beyond the pretest-posttest approach to the solution of educational problems.

Although the ethnography of schooling has made a substantial contribution toward the demystification of the educational process, its contribution to date has been limited by the level of development of the methodology and the analytic frameworks which have guided its use. There remain a number of areas in which theory and practice are underdeveloped, to the detriment of progress in both scholarly and applied work. I will briefly mention two of these areas.

First, the historical origin of ethnography has led ethnographers to focus primarily at the level of face-to-face interaction, and has left them less equipped to investigate or to analytically handle social processes beyond the local level. To the extent that life in schools is affected by structures and processes at the level of the large-scale social aggregate, ethnographic analysis may be unacceptably naive and unsophisticated (Erickson 1979b). The inevitable tension between scope and specificity in research is usually resolved in the direction of specificity, so that a small portion of the social universe is described in the absence of a thoroughgoing understanding of macro-level social processes (note that I am using the terms "scope" and "specificity" differently than does Erickson 1979b). This naiveté may lead to an overdependence on the cultural conflict model and a failure to pursue an understanding of micro-macro linkage in the realm of education (Ogbu 1981).

Second, when ethnographers have incorporated models of large-scale social processes into their analysis, these models have almost always been static rather than dynamic. An ecological framework (Ogbu 1978a, Hansen 1979) may prove to be much more useful than the traditional structural-functional framework in that it recognizes the dynamic nature of social process and interpersonal interaction.

Ethnography is nonetheless an extremely useful tool which allows us to explore in minute and concrete detail the highly complex series of phenomena which operate in and around the classroom. It is only through our ability to construct a detailed picture of the full range of dynamics at work that we have any hope of intervening effectively toward the resolution of persisting educational problems.

Note

I am particularly grateful to Henry Levin and George Spindler for their support of this project. I would also like to thank Frederick Erickson, Christine Finnan, Judith Hanna, John Ogbu, Hervé Varenne, and Harry Wolcott for their thoughtful comments on the longer manuscript from which this paper was derived.

References

Aarons, Alfred C., Barbara Y. Gordon, William A. Stewart. 1969. "Linguistic-Cultural Differences and American Education," Special Anthropology Issue *Florida Reporter*, 7(1).

Au, Kathryn Hu-pei. 1979. *Participation Structures in a Reading Lesson with Hawaiian Children: Analysis of a Culturally Appropriate Instructional Event.* Paper, Kamehameha Early Education Project.

Au, Kathryn H., and Catherine Jordan. 1981. "Teaching Reading to Hawaiian Children: Finding a Culturally Appropriate Solution." In Henry T. Trueba, Grace P. Guthrie, and Kathryn H. Au, eds., *Culture in the Bilingual Classroom*. Rowley, MA: Newbury House.

Bernstein, Basil. 1971. *Class, Codes and Control, Volume 1: Theoretical Studies Towards a Sociology of Language.* London: Routledge and Kegan Paul.

Berreman, Gerald D. 1967. "Structure and Function of Caste System." In G. DeVos and W. Hiroshi, eds., *Japan's Invisible Race*. Berkeley: University of California Press.

————. 1968. "Ethnography: Method and Product." In J. A. Clifton, ed., *Introduction to Cultural Anthropology*. Boston: Houghton Mifflin Company.

Bohannan, Paul. 1963. *Social Anthropology*. New York: Holt, Rinehart and Winston.

————. 1973. "Field Anthropologists and Classroom Teachers." In Francis A. J. Ianni, and E. Storey, eds., *Cultural Relevance and Educational Issues: Readings in Anthropology and Education*. Boston: Little, Brown & Co.

Borman, Kathryn. 1978. "Social Control and Schooling: Power and Process in Two Kindergarten Settings," *Anthropology and Education Quarterly*, 9(1):38–53.

Brim, John, and David Spain. 1974. *Research Design in Anthropology: Paradigms and Pragmatics in Testing Hypotheses*. New York: Holt, Rinehart and Winston.

Burnett, Jacquetta Hill. 1968. *Event Description and Analysis in the Micro-ethnography of Urban Classrooms*. Paper presented at the Annual Meetings of the American Anthropology Association. Reprinted in J. Roberts and S. Akinsanya, eds., *Educational Patterns and Cultural Configurations.* New York: David McKay, 1976.

———. 1969. "Ceremony, Rites, and Economy in the Student System of an American High School," *Human Organization,* 28(1):1–10.

———. 1970. "Culture of the School: A Construct for Research and Explanation," *Council on Anthropology and Education Newsletter,* 1(1):4–13.

———. 1974. "On the Analog Between Culture Acquisition and Ethnographic Method," *Council on Anthropology and Education Quarterly,* 5(1).

Burns, Allan F. 1976. "On the Ethnographic Process in Anthropology and Education," *Anthropology and Education Quarterly,* 7(3):25–33.

Byers, Paul, and Happie Byers. 1972. "Nonverbal Communication and the Education of Children." In C. B. Cazden, V. P. John, and D. Hymes, eds., *Functions of Language in the Classroom.* New York: Teachers College Press.

Cassell, Joan. 1978. *A Fieldwork Manual for Studying Desegregated Schools.* Washington, DC: National Institute of Education.

Cazden, Courtney B., and Vera P. John. 1971. "Learning in American Indian Children." In M. L. Wax, S. Diamond, and F. O. Gearing, eds., *Anthropological Perspectives on Education.* New York: Basic Books, Inc.

Cazden, Courtney B., Vera P. John, and Dell Hymes, eds. 1972 (reissued 1985). *Functions of Language in the Classroom.* Prospect Heights, IL: Waveland Press, Inc.

Clement, Dorothy C. 1978. "Ethnographic Perspectives on Desegregated Schools," *Anthropology Education Quarterly,* 9(4):245–247.

Cohen, Ronald. 1970. "Generalizations in Ethnography." In R. Navoll and R. Cohen, eds., *A Handbook of Methods in Cultural Anthropology.* Garden City, NY: Natural History Press.

Cohen, Rosalie A. 1969. "Conceptual Styles, Culture Conflict, and Nonverbal Tests of Intelligence," *American Anthropologist,* 71:828–856.

———. 1973. "School Reorganization and Learning: An Approach to Assessing the Direction of Social Change." In Solon T. Kimball, and Jacquetta Hill-Burnett eds., *Learning and Culture.* Seattle: University of Washington Press.

Cole, Michael, Johy Gay, J. A. Glick, and D. W. Sharp. 1971. *The Cultural Context of Learning and Thinking.* New York: Basic Books, Inc.

Cole, Michael, and Sylvia Scribner. 1974. *Culture and Thought: A Psychological Introduction.* New York: John Wiley and Sons.

Coleman, James S., et al. 1966. *Equality of Educational Opportunity*. Washington: U. S. Government Printing Office.

Coleman, James S. 1971. "Increasing Educational Opportunity: Research Problems and Results." In McMurrin and Sterling, eds., *The Conditions for Educational Equality*. New York: Committee for Economic Development.

Collier, John. 1973. *Alaskan Eskimo Education*. New York: Holt, Rinehart and Winston.

Comitas, Lambros, and Janet Dolgin. 1978. "On Anthropology and Education: Retrospect and Prospect," *Anthropology and Education Quarterly*, 9(3):164–180.

Cusick, Phillip. 1973. *Inside High School: The Student's World*. New York: Holt, Rinehart and Winston.

Dobbert, Marion L. 1975. "Another Route to a General Theory of Cultural Transmission: a Systems Model," *Council on Anthropology and Education Quarterly*, 6(2).

Dumont, Robert V., Jr., and Murray L. Wax. 1969. "Cherokee School Society and the Intercultural Classroom," *Human Organization*, 28(3):217–226.

Eddy, Elizabeth M. 1975. "Educational Innovation and Desegregation: A Case Study of Symbolic Realignment," *Human Organization*, 34(2):163–172.

———. 1978. "The Reorganization of Schooling: An Anthropological Challenge." In E. M. Eddy and W. L. Partridge, eds., *Applied Anthropology in America*. New York: Columbia University Press.

Erickson, Frederick. 1973. "What Makes School Ethnography 'Ethnographic'?" *Council on Anthropology and Education Newsletter*, (2):10–19.

———. 1975. "One Function of Proxemic Shifts in Face-to-Face Interaction." In A. Kendon, R. Harris, and M. Ritchie Key, eds., *Organization of Behavior in Face-to-Face Interactions*. The Hague: Mouton and Company.

———. 1976. "Gatekeeping Encounters: A Social Selection Process." In P. Sanday, ed., *Anthropology and the Public Interest*. New York: Academic Press.

———. 1977. "Some Approaches to Inquiry in School-Community Ethnography," *CAE Newsletter*, 8(2):58–69.

———. 1979a. "Mere Ethnography: Some Problems in Its Use in Educational Practice," *Anthropology and Education Quarterly*, 10(3):182–188.

———. 1979b. *Patterns of Sophistication and Naivety in Anthropology: Some Distinctive Features of Anthropological Approaches to the Study of Education*. Paper presented at the Annual Meeting of the American Educational Research Association, San Francisco.

———, and Gerald Mohatt. 1982. "Cultural Organization of Participation Structures in Two Classrooms of Indian Students."

In George Spindler, ed., *Doing the Ethnography of Schooling.* New York: Holt, Rinehart and Winston.

Florio, Susan, and Jeffrey Schultz. 1978. *Social Competence at Home and at School.* Paper presented at the annual meetings of the American Anthropological Association, Los Angeles.

Fortes, Myer. 1938. "Social and Psychological Aspects of Education in Taleland," *Supplement to Africa,* 11(4). Reprinted in J. Middleton, ed., *From Child to Adult: Studies in the Anthropology of Education.* Garden City, NY: Natural History Press, 1970.

Freilich, Morris, ed. 1970. *Marginal Natives: Anthropologists at Work.* New York: Harper & Row.

Fuchs, Estelle. 1966. *Pickets at the Gates.* New York: The Free Press.

Gallaher, Art, Jr. 1973. "Directed Change in Formal Organizations: The School System." In Francis A. J. Ianni and E. Storey, eds., *Cultural Relevance and Educational Issues: Readings in Anthropology and Education.* Boston: Little, Brown & Company.

Gearing, Frederick O. 1973a. "Anthropology and Education." In J. Honigmann, ed., *Handbook of Social and Cultural Anthropology.* Chicago: Rand McNally.

———. 1973b. "Where We Are and Where We Might Go: Steps Toward a General Theory of Cultural Transmission," *Council on Anthropology and Education Quarterly,* 4(1):1–10.

———, et al. 1975. "Structures of Censorship, Usually Inadvertent: Studies in a Cultural Theory of Education," *Council on Anthropology and Education Quarterly,* 6(2).

Geertz, Clifford. 1973. "Thick Description: Toward an Interpretive Theory of Culture." In C. Geertz, ed., *The Interpretation of Cultures: Selected Essays by Clifford Geertz.* New York: Basic Books, Inc.

Goodenough, Ward. 1963. *Cooperation and Change: An Anthropological Approach to Community Development.* New York: Russell Sage Foundation.

Hansen, Judith Friedman. 1979. *Sociocultural Perspectives on Human Learning: An Introduction to Educational Anthropology.* Englewood Cliffs, NJ: Prentice-Hall, Inc.

Henry, Jules. 1963. *Culture Against Man.* New York: Random House, Inc.

Herriott, Robert E. 1977. "Ethnographic Case Studies in Federally Funded Multidisciplinary Policy Research: Some Design and Implementation Issues," *Anthropology and Education Quarterly,* 8(2):106–115.

Herskovits, Melville J. 1954. "Some Problems in Ethnography." In Robert F. Spencer, ed., *Method and Perspective in Anthropology.* Minneapolis: University of Minnesota Press.

Hollingshead, August B. 1949. *Elmtown's Youth: The Impact of Social Classes on Adolescents.* New York: John Wiley and Sons.

Hymes, Dell. 1971. "On Linguistic Theory, Communicative Competence, and the Education of Disadvantaged Children." In M. L. Wax, S. Diamond, and F. O. Gearing, eds., *Anthropological Perspectives on Education.* New York: Basic Books, Inc.

———. 1972. "Introduction." In C. B. Cazden, V. P. John, and D. Hymes, eds., *Functions of Language in the Classroom.* New York: Teachers College Press.

———. 1974. "The Use of Anthropology: Critical, Political, and Personal." In D. Hymes, ed., *Reinventing Anthropology.* New York: Random House, Inc.

Jackson, Phillip. 1968. *Life in Classrooms.* New York: Holt, Rinehart and Winston.

Jacob, Evelyn, and Peggy Reeves Sanday. 1976. "Dropping Out: A Strategy for Coping with Cultural Pluralism." In P. R. Sanday, ed., *Anthropology and the Public Interest.* New York: Academic Press.

Jencks, Christopher., et al. 1972. *Inequality: A Reassessment of the Effect of Family and Schooling in America.* New York: Harper & Row.

Jordan, Catherine, et al. 1977. *A Multidisciplinary Approach to Research in Education: The Kamehameha Early Education Program.* Paper delivered to the annual meetings of the American Anthropological Association, Houston.

Kileff, Clive. 1975. "The Rebirth of a Grandfather's Spirit: Shumba's Two Worlds," *Human Organization,* 34(2):129–138.

Kimball, Solon T. 1974. *Culture and the Educative Process.* New York: Teachers College Press.

King, A. Richard. 1967. *The School at Mopass: A Problem of Identity.* New York: Holt, Rinehart and Winston.

Kluckhohn, Florence R. 1940. "The Participant Observer Technique in Small Communities," *American Journal of Sociology,* 46:331–343.

Knapp, Michael S. 1981. "Ethnography in Evaluation Research: The Experimental Schools Program Studies and Some Recent Alternatives." In C. P. Richardt and T. D. Cook, eds., *Qualitative and Quantitative Methods in Evaluation Research.* Beverly Hills, CA: Sage Publications.

Labov, William. 1969. "The Logic of Non-Standard English." In J. E. Alatis, ed., *Linguistics and the Teaching of Standard English.* Washington: Georgetown University Press.

———. 1972. "Statement and Resolution on Language and Intelligence," *LSA Bulletin,* 52:19–22.

Lacey, Colin. 1976. "Intragroup Competitive Pressures and the Selection of Social Strategies: Neglected Paradigms in the Study of Adolescent Socialization." In C. J. Calhoun and Francis A. J. Ianni, eds., *The Anthropological Study of Education.* The Hague: Mouton and Company.

Leacock, Eleanor B. 1969. *Teaching and Learning in City Schools.* New York: Basic Books, Inc.

———. 1971. *The Culture of Poverty: A Critique.* New York: Simon and Schuster.

LeCompte, Margaret. 1978. "Learning to Work: The Hidden Curriculum of the Classroom," *Anthropological Education Quarterly,* 9(1):22–37.

Lightfoot, Sarah Lawrence. 1978. *Worlds Apart: Relationships Between Families and Schools.* New York: Basic Books, Inc.

Lutz, Frank W., and Margaret A. Ramsey. 1974. "The Use of Anthropological Field Methods in Education," *Educational Researcher,* 3(10):5–9.

Lynd, Robert S., and Helen M. Lynd. 1929. *Middletown: A Study in Modern American Culture.* New York: Harcourt, Brace, and World., Inc.

Malinowski, Bronislaw. 1922 (reissued 1984). *Argonauts of the Western Pacific.* Prospect Heights, IL: Waveland Press, Inc.

McDermott, R. P. 1974. "Achieving School Failure: An Anthropological Approach to Illiteracy and Social Stratification." In G. Spindler, ed., *Education and Cultural Process: Toward an Anthropology of Education.* New York: Holt, Rinehart and Winston.

———, and Kenneth Gospodinoff. 1977. *Social Contexts for Ethnic Borders and School Failure.* Paper presented to the First International Conference on Nonverbal Behavior, Ontario, Canada.

Mead, Margaret. 1943. "Our Educational Emphasis in Primitive Perspective," *American Journal of Sociology,* 48:633–639.

Mulhauser, Frederick. 1975. "Ethnography and Policy-Making: The Case of Education," *Human Organization,* 34(3):311–314.

Ogbu, John. 1974a. "Learning in Burgerside: An Ethnography of Education." In George M. Foster and Robert V. Kemper, eds., *Anthropologists in Cities.* Boston: Little, Brown, & Company.

———. 1974b. *The Next Generation: An Ethnography of Education in an Urban Neighborhood.* New York: Academic Press.

———. 1978a. *An Ecological Approach to the Study of School Effectiveness.* Paper presented for National Institute of Education Conference on School Organization and Effects, San Diego.

———. 1978b. *Minority Education and Caste: The American System in Cross-Cultural Perspective.* New York: Academic Press.

————. 1981. "Anthropological Ethnography in Education: Some Methodological Issues, Limitations, and Potentials." In Hendrik Gideonse, et al., eds., *Values Imposed by the Social Sciences*. National Society for the Study of Education.

Overholt, George E., and William M. Stallings. 1976. "Ethnographic and Experimental Hypotheses in Educational Research," *Educational Researcher*, 5(8):12–14.

Pelto, Pertti J., and Gretel H. Pelto. 1973. "Ethnography: The Fieldwork Enterprise." In J. J. Honigmann, ed., *Handbook of Social and Cultural Anthropology*. Chicago: Rand McNally.

————. 1978. *Anthropological Research: The Structure of Inquiry*. Cambridge, England: Cambridge University Press.

Peshkin, Alan. 1978. *Growing Up American: Schooling and the Survival of Community*. Chicago: University of Chicago Press.

Philips, Susan U. 1972. "Participant Structure and Communicative Competence: Warm Springs Children in Community and Classrooms." In Courtney Cazden, Vera John, and Dell Hymes, eds., *Functions of Language in the Classroom*. New York: Teachers College Press.

Powdermaker, Hortense. 1966. *Stranger and Friend: The Way of an Anthropologist*. New York: W. W. Norton.

Rist, Ray C. 1970. "Student Social Class and Teacher Expectations: The Self-fulfilling Prophecy in Ghetto Schools," *Harvard Educational Review*, 40:411–450.

————. 1972a. "Black English for Black Schools: A Call for Educational Congruity." In Rist, ed., *Restructuring American Education*. New York: E. P. Dutton.

————. 1972b. "Introduction." In Rist, ed., *Restructuring American Education*. New York: E. P. Dutton.

————. 1975. "Ethnographic Techniques and the Study of an Urban School," *Urban Education*, 10(1):86–108.

————. 1977. "On the Relations Among Educational Research Paradigms: From Disdain to Détente," *Anthropology and Education Quarterly*, 9(2):42–49.

————. 1978. *The Invisible Children: School Integration in American Society*. Cambridge, MA: Harvard University Press.

Roberts, Joan I., and Sherrie K. Akinsanya, eds. 1976a. *Educational Patterns and Cultural Configurations*. New York: David McKay Co.

————. 1976b. *Schooling in the Cultural Context: Anthropological Studies of Education*. New York: David McKay Co.

Rosen, David M. 1977. "Multi-Cultural Education: An Anthropological Perspective," *Anthropology and Education Quarterly*, 8(4):221–226.

Rosenfeld, Gerry. 1971 (reissued 1983). *"Shut Those Thick Lips!"* Prospect Heights, IL: Waveland Press, Inc.

Rosenstiel, Annette. 1977. *Education and Anthropology: An Annotated Bibliography*. New York: Garland Publishing Co.

Salamone, Frank A. 1979. "Epistemological Implications of Fieldwork and Their Consequences," *American Anthropologist,* 81(1):46–60.

Sanday, Peggy Reeves. 1976. "Emerging Methodological Developments for Research Design, Data Collection, and Data Analysis in Anthropology and Education." In C. J. Calhoun and Francis A. J. Ianni, eds., *The Anthropological Study of Education.* The Hague: Mouton and Company.

Sennett, Richard, and Jonathan Cobb. 1972. *The Hidden Injuries of Class.* New York: Alfred A. Knopf, Inc.

Sindell, Peter S. 1969. "Anthropological Approaches to the Study of Education," *Review of Education Research,* 39:593–605.

Singleton, John. 1967. *Nichu: A Japanese School.* New York: Holt, Rinehart and Winston.

———. 1968. *The Ethnography of a Japanese School: Anthropological Field Technique and Models in the Study of a Complex Organization.* Paper presented at the annual meeting of the American Anthropological Association. Reprinted in J. Roberts and S. Akinsanya, eds., *Educational Patterns and Cultural Configurations: The Anthropology of Education.* New York: David McKay Co., Inc., 1976.

Smith, Louis M., and Paul A. Pohland. 1974. "Education, Technology, and the Rural Highlands." In American Educational Research Association Monograph Series on Curriculum Evaluation. *Four Evaluation Examples: Anthropological, Economic, Narrative, and Portrayal.* Volume 7. Chicago: Rand McNally.

———. 1976. "Grounded Theory and Educational Ethnography: A Methodological Analysis and Critique." In J. Roberts and S. Akinsanya, eds., *Educational Patterns and Cultural Configurations: The Anthropology of Education.* New York: David McKay Co., Inc.

Spindler, George D., ed. 1955. *Anthropology and Education.* Stanford, CA: Stanford University Press.

———. 1963a. "The Transmission of American Culture." In G. D. Spindler, ed., *Education and Culture: Anthropological Approaches.* New York: Holt, Rinehart and Winston.

———. 1963b. "The Role of the School Administrator." In G. D. Spindler, ed., ibid.

———, ed. 1970 (reissued 1986). *Being an Anthropologist: Fieldwork in Eleven Cultures.* Prospect Heights, IL: Waveland Press.

——— 1973. "Schooling and the Young People." In G. Spindler, ed., *Burgbach: Urbanization and Identity in a German Village.* New York: Holt, Rinehart and Winston.

———. 1987. "Beth Anne: A Case of Culturally Defined Adjustment and Teacher Perception." In G. Spindler, ed., *Education and Cultural Process: Anthropological Approaches,* 2/e. Prospect Heights, IL: Waveland Press, Inc.

————. 1974b. "From Omnibus to Linkages: Cultural Transmission Models," *Council on Anthropology and Education Quarterly*, 5(1).

————. 1974c. "Schooling in Schönhausen: A Study of Cultural Transmission and Instrumental Adaptation in an Urbanizing German Village." In G. Spindler, ed., op. cit.

————. 1974d. "Transcultural Sensitization." In G. Spindler, ed., op. cit.

————, and Louise Spindler. 1982 (reissued 1988). "Roger Harker and Schönhausen: From the Familiar to the Strange and Back Again." In G. Spindler, ed., *Doing the Ethnography of Schooling*. Prospect Heights, IL: Waveland Press, Inc.

Spradley, James. 1979. *The Ethnographic Interview*. New York: Holt, Rinehart and Winston.

————. 1980. *Participant Observation*. New York: Holt, Rinehart and Winston.

Talbert, Carol. 1970. "Interaction and Adaptation in Two Negro Kindergartens," *Human Organization*, 29(2):103–113.

Varenne, Hervé. 1976. "American Culture and the School: A Case Study." In C. J. Calhoun and Francis A. J. Ianni, eds., *The Anthropological Study of Education*. The Hague: Mouton and Company.

Warren, Richard L. 1967. *Education in Rebhausen: A German Village*. New York: Holt, Rinehart and Winston.

————. 1974. "The School and Its Community Context: The Methodology of a Field Study." In G. D. Spindler, ed., *Education and Cultural Process: Toward an Anthropology of Education*. New York: Holt, Rinehart and Winston.

Wax, Murray, S. Diamond, and F. Gearing, eds. 1971. *Anthropological Perspectives on Education*. New York: Basic Books, Inc.

Wax, Rosalie H. 1971. *Doing Fieldwork: Warnings and Advice*. Chicago: University of Chicago Press.

Whiting, Beatrice B., ed., 1963. *Six Cultures: Studies of Child-rearing*. New York: John Wiley and Sons.

Whiting, Beatrice B., and John Whiting. 1975. *Children of Six Cultures: A Psycho Analysis*. Cambridge, MA: Harvard University Press.

Wilcox, Kathleen A. 1978. *Schooling and Socialization for Work Roles: A Structural Inquiry into Cultural Transmission in an Urban American Community*. Doctoral dissertation, Anthropology Department, Harvard University.

————. 1982. "Differential Socialization in the Classroom: Implications for Equal Opportunity." In G. Spindler, ed., *Doing the Ethnography of Schooling*. New York: Holt, Rinehart and Winston.

Wilson, Stephen. 1977. "The Use of Ethnographic Techniques in Educational Research," *Review of Educational Research*, 47(1):245–265 (Winter).

Wolcott, Harry F. 1967 (reissued 1984). *A Kwakiutl Village and School.* Prospect Heights, IL: Waveland Press, Inc.

————. 1973 (reissued 1984). *The Man in the Principal's Office: An Ethnography.* Prospect Heights, IL: Waveland Press, Inc.

————. 1975a. "Criteria for an Ethnographic Approach to Research in Schools," *Human Organization,* 34(2):111–127.

————. 1975b. *Ethnographic Approaches to Research in Education: A Bibliography on Method.* Anthropology Curriculum Project Publication No. 75-1. Athens: University of Georgia.

————. 1977. *Teachers vs. Technocrats: An Educational Innovation in Anthropological Perspective.* Eugene, OR: Center for Educational Policy and Management.

George Spindler

CONCLUDING REMARKS

What I find different about ethnographic methodology isn't so much the methods or techniques of research—other fields use observation, sociometrics, autobiographies, interviews, and so forth. The real difference is the point of view. Just to think of teachers, students, and parents as natives in cultural systems makes it necessary to approach them, their behavior, and what they have to say in a way that is quite different from the ways we have learned previously.

—Graduate student in ethnographic training seminar

Each chapter in this book presents information and interprets it in a conceptual framework. Certain relationships deemed significant have been discussed in editorial commentaries and in Wilcox's review. The questions at both levels listed in the General Introduction have been addressed and tentative answers have been produced. No answers to these kinds of problems can be final. They will change with time and with new information interpreted within different conceptual frameworks. Nor are the questions themselves eternal. They change with changes in society, ideology, and the circumstances of inquiry.

This volume has, as promised in the Introduction, taken a series of steps in the direction of applying anthroethnographic methods to the study and analysis of basic educational processes. As we proceed with our studies, methods and theoretical models will become more refined; we must not, however, let this refinement diminish the present scope, variety, and vigor of this dynamic field of inquiry.

The world view that is implicit in the ethnographic enterprise as a whole, and as practiced by anthropologists, is also important. Educators, and others, have sometimes applied the techniques and methods of anthroethnography without fully understanding this world view. Without this understanding, the methods, isolated from their roots in meaning, are shallow and may produce misleading results.

Features of the Ethnographic World View

This ethnographic world view emphasizes the importance of the native, the actor in the scene, as informant — literally as instructor. Too often social scientists have assumed (though usually unintentionally) a superior stance in relation to their "subjects." In ethnography, people are not subjects; they are experts on what the ethnographer wants to find out about and accordingly are treated with great respect and always in good faith. A trust relationship must be built between researcher and informant that cannot be violated by insensitivity or misuse of information.

The ethnographic world view also emphasizes that natives do not, in fact cannot, realize the full implications of their own cultural knowledge and social behavior. Their knowledge is necessarily partial and often ambiguous. Explicit, verbalizable cultural knowledge is never complete, even when the lapses of any one informant are corrected or filled in by the knowledge of other informants. There are always tacit, nonverbalized understandings or unforeseen consequences of behavior — consequences that are not anticipated by the cultural knowledge of the actors. There is always a hidden or at least obscured curriculum, an implicit convention, a latent function, an unanticipated consequence, a hidden or covert dimension of understanding, motivation, and patterns for and of behavior. Such elements must be uncovered, inferred, and interpreted if the analysis is to be at all complete — and if it is to tell natives what they do not already know and inform others beyond the level of common sense. There is always the danger that the hidden dimension will be a fabrication of the ethnographer's mind. This possibility must be controlled by observation of both the consistency of behaviors and cultural explanations for relevant situations, as working hypotheses are cast up in the course of fieldwork. And there is always some danger that the ethnographer will begin to assume a superior stance, as he or she realizes that there are limitations on the knowledge of any native. This can be corrected by the realization that the native, the informant, the actor, is the ultimate source of all data upon which any and all inferences must be based. The untranslated knowledge and behavior of the native constitute the only surely valid data to which the ethnographer has access.

The ethnographic world view also holds that all behaviors occur in contexts, and that not only do contexts continuously change but people change with contexts. So we do not assume that a child in school is behaviorally the same child at home or on the street, though there will always be continuity, if only in the form of role behavior reversals or compensations. We are committed to the study of behavior in contexts and of cultural knowledge held by natives as relevant to contexts. We chase contexts as far as time and resources permit, but we acknowledge the importance of the single context as an object of intensive study.

The ethnographic world view assumes that any classroom, any school, any group or community is a variant adaptation within a regional, national, and world-wide variation in culture and social organization. The culture we study at any time is one of many. This assumption calls for a perspective that makes the familiar strange, that exoticizes behavior and meanings that are all too familiar because they are our own. The ethnographic world view places high value on being "thrice born," as the noted Brahmin anthropologist Srnivas phrased it in a lecture delivered at the University of Chicago (Turner 1978). One is born into one's own culture and enculturated within it. As an anthropologist studying outside one's own culture, one is "born again"—one must learn a new culture and learn to "think like a native" (albeit imperfectly). Making the strange familiar, or familiarizing the exotic, is done both in the field and in one's interpretation, in the form of lectures and writings. Upon our return to our own native land, we are born for the third time as we refamiliarize ourselves with what has now become exotic but was once familiar. This process, so violent at times that it, like the experience of a foreign culture, is termed "culture shock," gives us a perspective that can never be laid aside. We see our own culture with new eyes. It is present in some form in the writings by those ethnographers who have been "thrice born." It is one of the dimensions of the anthroethnographic world view that may be lost as ethnography is done, even according to anthropological directives, by workers who, however excellent in other ways, have not had cross-cultural experience in depth. There are ways, however, of incorporating analogues to this experience in the training of ethnographers, and this can be touched upon a little later.

Lastly, the ethnographic world view assumes that the function of schooling is to transmit the culture(s). The school transmits what *is*, not what *should* be. Even when innovations are attempted and educators are dedicated to change, if these innovations and intentions stray too far from the center of the culture and social system they will be defused and vitiated in the process of transmission and cultural acquisition. This is not to say that teachers, like other transmitters of culture, have no choices. There is much in the culture of the United States that is not transmitted in the classrooms. And teachers can choose positively as well as negatively. The choices, however, are from our culture, or are translated into our cultural idiom in the transmission. Nor is it my intention to say that there are no possibilities for improvement. Various forms of intervention can raise the consciousness of teachers and administrators about what they are doing and why they are doing it. Every chapter in this book points to specific areas where consciousness-raising, if well handled, could have positive results. Teachers can change their style of questioning, interaction, engagement, reproval, approval, attention, and reinforcement. Administrators can learn which conditions in the school are conducive to communication and which block it. They can reinforce and reward, to some extent, those behaviors among teachers that are conducive to implementing agreed-upon goals of equalizing opportunity, reducing tensions, absorbing differences, recognizing ethnic pride, teaching cultural as well as technical competence, and so forth. The studies reported in this volume point out and clarify specific areas where changes in policy, classroom management, and assumptions about teaching and learning can be effective. They also demonstrate that the school cannot be held responsible for society. Rather, they demonstrate that society is responsible for the school.

Ethnographic Training

Statements about an ethnographic world view or the operational attributes of a good ethnography are of little use unless the results of their application and the procedures of their application can be diffused beyond the small coterie of aficionados in anthropology and education. Books like this one are a starting point, but it remains to be seen how influential it and others like it become in professional educational circles. Resistance to the methodologies advocated and demonstrated in this volume may be expected to be substantial, particularly because, though lip service may be given to "ethnography," the results of disciplined ethnography may never have much effect on what happens in classrooms or even be read by many educational practitioners or their instructors in teacher-training institutions.

Beyond the dissemination of the results of ethnographic studies through publication and teaching, we should consider ethnographic training not only for doctoral candidates in various divisions of professional education but also for classroom teachers and school administrators, counselors, supervisory personnel, and so forth, as a significant means of dissemination. This is more easily said than done. Though many educators are willing and able to learn ethnographic methods and apply them, most anthropologists, understandably, want to teach anthropology. They often do not move far enough into the situation of their educationist learners to realize that many anthropological concerns are in-house, in-group concerns. Much of what we regard as important in graduate training in anthropology is not relevant to the training of teachers and other educationist personnel or even doctoral candidates in education who want to learn to do ethnography and make relevant interpretations and applications of its results. Nevertheless, it will be imperative for educators to get some training in the conceptual structures of anthropological thinking because they cannot learn how to do anthroethnography without some anthropology. Naturally, some courses and professors are more relevant than others, and educators seeking selective anthropological exposure must have good advice (which is not always easy to find).

There are ways of teaching the principles of ethnographic research methodology effectively to nonanthropologists who have only a modest understanding of anthropological thinking. Many contributors to this volume have recently engaged in ethnographic training seminars or programs for graduate students in advanced professional education programs. There will be more of these efforts in the near future, given the strong demand in schools of education for such training. Some of our colleagues have taught ethnographic methods to classroom teachers and other practitioners. And many of the students in both categories have had little or no formal anthropological training—not a desirable state of affairs, but a fact of life. I will discuss briefly Louise Spindler's and my own experience in such training. From what we have seen of colleagues' syllabi for such training seminars and from what little has been published on the topic, we judge that our purposes and procedures are, though novel at points, not so wildly variant that this discussion will be irrelevant to an emerging corpus of training practices.

In our experience in ethnographic training seminars we have held at the University of Wisconsin (Madison) and at Stanford, as well as for a school district in the Bay Area (California), we find that we have two most important problems to solve: (1) how to communicate understandings of theory dealing mainly with cultural processes while we train participants in the techniques of doing ethnography in schools; (2) how to preserve and enhance the perspective, usually gained only by cross-cultural experience in depth, that we (and others) have termed "making the familiar strange." The problem in the first instance is that we must teach culture theory and ethnographic practice simultaneously to people who, though usually mature graduate students or practitioners, know little about either. The problem in the second instance is that through vicarious experience we must condense the crucial results of what would ordinarily take from one to three years into a few weeks. We do not claim that we are entirely successful in the attempt to solve either of these problems.

Our attempt to solve both problems depends heavily upon an inductive method of instruction that does not allow the instructor(s) to resort to linear, authority-to-neophyte forms of communication, except at crucial points when the understandings and skills wanted are beginning to coalesce through experience. And what is that experience? We try to bring the field experience into the seminar room with films, videotapes, slides, and audiotapes. But we do not use these materials simply to inform the students about various cultures. We use them as behavior that must be observed first, then inquired about using informants. We play the role of informants. Participants observe, formulate inquiries, apply them, and then go back to observing, only to return to inquiry once again. Most of the materials used are from our own fieldwork, so we know the cultures and their contexts thoroughly. For purposes of reference, we have termed this procedure the "Ethnographic Inquiry Reinforcement Procedure." Though the procedure sounds simple enough, it is not. A rather subtle and complex communication takes place that leads to both theory and practice. The "cultural knowledge" of the "native" unfolds, but never in an orderly way. Some questions that are too blunt or probing are turned aside or simply not answered. Participants become very involved. Their emotions are aroused, frustrations mount, questions are reformulated, and the complex serendipity of observation and inquiry, of theory and practice, is demonstrated again and again. At certain points in the process, when students seem already to have arrived, in various approximations, at where we want them to go in their understandings and skills, we do engage, though succinctly, in linear exposition. We tell them what they already know by then, but in a more orderly and focused way.

There are, to be sure, many other aspects of our ethnographic training procedures. For instance, each participant does several mini-studies in the field. Any event or context is a possible field site. Students have done mini-ethnographies of standing in line to get into the restroom during intermission at a film, role-taking at a disco, smoking in an early-teen peer group, making deposits to bank accounts, a fashion show, and of course classrooms, counseling, play-yards, and other school-related situations. Various interview techniques are demonstrated and practiced. Making maps of classrooms and movement within them, taking notes and annotating and storing them in ways that preserve access to them, taking still and moving pictures and using them for inquiry and observation after the fieldwork is finished, constructing "instruments" out of the field experience, and so forth, are all taught through demonstration and practice. Students also read widely from a highly selected bibliography which includes both classic nonschool site works by seasoned anthropologists (and others) and pieces by ethnographers of schooling. Concept and theory are stressed more than how-to-do-it in these assigned readings, and these matters are regularly discussed in the seminar as students raise questions stimulated by their reading.

It has seemed possible, in our experience so far, to condense theory, practice, and cross-cultural experience (even though it is vicarious) into a relatively short time-span for neophytes. The effectiveness of the effort must be measured by the research done by former participants who have incorporated ethnographic methods into their doctoral or other studies. It is too soon to make a judgment. Though student enthusiasm for ethnography and for the training seminars is high, this enthusiasm may or may not produce good research. We would feel more certain of the results if the participants uniformly had more background in anthropology.

Judging from comments by colleagues who have had experience with ethnographic training, they also found it essential to move away from linear, lecture-type, telling-how-to-do-it styles of teaching. Many have incorporated some form of direct experience in observation and elicitation into their seminars. Literature that demystifies ethnographic procedures is beginning to appear—for example, James Spradley's two volumes, one on the ethnographic interview and the other on participant observation (1979, 1980) and Joan Cassell's useful manual on ethnographic research, prepared for the National Institute of Education (1978). These publications have been influential in the development of our approach in our seminars. It will be important, as more directive how-to-do-it literature appears, to avoid reducing ethnographic procedures to cookbook predictability. The most slavishly followed procedures are likely to result in mediocre research results. Productive ethnography will always require flexibility, sensitivity, an ability to defer judgment and tolerate ambiguity, and a desire to innovate.

With some exceptions, the purpose of ethnographic training for educators is not to produce professional ethnographers. For doctoral candidates in our seminars, ethnography is one technique they can incorporate in their research designs for certain purposes that are not served as well or at all by experimental or correlational procedures. For the classroom teacher, the purpose in acquiring ethnographic training may be to acquire a point of view and modest competencies that can be applied in the classroom, particularly the multiethnic one. It can be a sensitization experience. This experience teaches that the native view of reality is important and that each child has cultural knowledge that is significant and that influences educational outcomes. Ethnography leads one to an essentially clinical and objective rather than personalized view of the educational process and of the interactions that make it happen. Ethnography calls attention to the complexities of everyday life, but also shows how they may be understood. It makes people better observers and more realistic interpreters of social interaction and communication. The world view of the ethnographic culture may become a significant influence on education in our society. The results of ethnography carried out as the operational attributes of a good anthroethnography are defined may become an important influence on educational practice and policy-making. This volume, it is hoped, will make a contribution in both of these dimensions.

References

Cassell, Joan. 1978. *A Fieldwork Manual for Studying Desegregated Schools.* Washington: National Institute of Education.

Spradley, James. 1979. *The Ethnographic Interview.* New York: Holt, Rinehart and Winston.

———. 1980. *Participant Observation.* New York: Holt, Rinehart and Winston.

Turner, Victor. 1978. Foreword, in Barbara Myerhoff, *Number Our Days.* New York: Simon and Schuster (a Touchstone Book).

Name Index

Subject Index